Avizandum Statutes on

Scots Family Law
2021–2022

A Practitioner's Handbook

Avizandum Statutes on

Scots Family Law
2021–2022

A Practitioner's Handbook

Editor
Jane Mair LLM, PhD
Professor of Private Law, University of Glasgow

EDINBURGH
University Press

Edinburgh University Press is one of the leading university presses in the UK. We publish academic books and journals in our selected subject areas across the humanities and social sciences, combining cutting-edge scholarship with high editorial and production values to produce academic works of lasting importance. For more information visit our website: edinburghuniversitypress.com

First published 2022

© Edinburgh University Press, 2022

Edinburgh University Press Ltd
The Tun – Holyrood Road
12(2f) Jackson's Entry
Edinburgh EH8 8PJ

Typeset in 9/10 pt, Palatino
by Cheshire Typesetting Ltd, Cuddington, Cheshire, and
printed and bound in Great Britain by Clays

A CIP record for this book is available from the British Library

ISBN 978 1 4744 9908 8 (paperback)
ISBN 978 1 4744 9921 7 (webready PDF)
ISBN 978 1 4744 9922 4 (epub)

Public sector information is licensed under the Open Government Licence 3.0
(http://www.nationalarchives.gov.uk/doc/open-government-licence/version/3)

PUBLISHER'S NOTE

This volume was intended primarily as a resource for undergraduate students of child and family law, and the provisions which are included reflect the content of undergraduate courses. It has come to our attention, however, that family law practitioners are also finding the volume a useful resource, and we have therefore taken the decision to produce this *Practitioner's Handbook* to better meet the requirements of practitioners.

The most significant difference from the student version is the inclusion of the principal Rules of Court – the Child Care and Maintenance Rules 1997, the Sheriff Court Adoption Rules 2009 and the Children's Hearings Rules 2013 – applying to court actions involving children. The Rules are reproduced as currently in force. For the provisions applying to applications lodged before the dates specified here, reference should be made to the website of Scottish Courts at https://www.scotcourts.gov.uk/rules-and-practice/rules-of-court/sheriff-court---civil-procedure-rules. We have not included the forms contained in, respectively, the Schedule to the Child Care and Maintenance Rules and the Appendix to the Adoption Rules, for which reference should be made to the website of Scottish Courts.

Other new material includes relevant provisions of the Matrimonial Proceedings (Children) Act 1958 and of the Family Law Act 1986.

Both the Scottish Government and the Scottish Law Commission have been engaged in law reform projects related to child and family law. Two recent statutes – the Civil Partnership (Scotland) Act 2020 and the Children (Scotland) Act 2020 – are included in full in this volume. Amendments made by these Acts which are in force have been incorporated into the principal legislation. Consequential amendments arising from Brexit have also been included. While EU membership did not have direct effect on the substance of Scots family law, it did affect questions of jurisdiction and cross-border enforceability of judgments which have been amended by a series of regulations.

As with the student edition, statutory instruments are not included. When there is a need to refer to them, statutory instruments are readily available electronically.

All provisions appear in amended form and have been updated to 30 November 2021. Material which was not included in the legislation as originally enacted has been identified by the use of square brackets.

We welcome feedback from users of the volume. Any comments on either the content or the format of the materials should be addressed to the publisher.

Edinburgh University Press
December 2021

CHRONOLOGICAL LIST OF CONTENTS

ALPHABETICAL LIST OF CONTENTS

PART I

STATUTES

MATRIMONIAL PROCEEDINGS (CHILDREN) ACT 1958
(1958, c 40)

11 Reports as to arrangements for future care and upbringing of children

(1) [Where the court is considering any question relating to the care and upbringing of a child, it may], without prejudice to its power to appoint any other person [, not being an officer of the local authority for the purpose, appoint an appropriate local authority] to investigate and report to the court on all the circumstances of the child and on the proposed arrangements for the care and upbringing of the child.

[(1A) In this section 'local authority' has the same meaning as in the Social Work (Scotland) Act 1968.]

[. . .]

(4) If on consideration of a report furnished in pursuance of subsection (1) of this section the court, either *ex proprio motu* or on the application of any person concerned, thinks it expedient to do so, it may require the person who furnished the report to appear and to be examined on oath regarding any matter dealt with in the report, and such person may be examined or cross-examined accordingly.

(5) Any expenses incurred in connection with the preparation of a report by a [local authority or other person appointed] under this section shall form part of the expenses of the action and be defrayed by such party to the action as the court may direct, and the court may certify the amount of the expenses so incurred.

[. . .]

15 Interpretation of Part II

In this Part of this Act, the expression 'the court' means the Court of Session or the sheriff, the expression 'child' means a child under sixteen years of age [. . .].

[16 Expenses

There shall be paid out of moneys provided by Parliament any increase attributable to this Act in the sums payable out of moneys so provided—

    (a) under section forty-seven of the Children Act, 1948, or

    (b) under Part I of the Local Government Act, 1948, or the Local Government (Financial Provisions) (Scotland) Act 1954, as amended by the Valuation and Rating (Scotland) Act, 1956.]

17 Application of enactments regulating the enforcement of maintenance orders

Any order for maintenance or other payments made by virtue of this Act or any corresponding enactment of the Parliament of Northern Ireland shall be included among the orders to which section sixteen of the Maintenance Orders Act, 1950, applies (which section specifies the maintenance orders which are enforceable under Part II of that Act) [. . .]

18 Short title, extent and commencement

(1) This Act may be cited as the Matrimonial Proceedings (Children) Act, 1958.

(2) Any reference in this Act to any enactment shall be construed as a reference to that enactment as amended or extended by any other Act, including this Act.

(3) This Act (except so far as it affects Part II of the Maintenance Orders Act, 1950) shall not extend to Northern Ireland.

REGISTRATION OF BIRTHS, DEATHS AND MARRIAGES (SCOTLAND) ACT 1965
(1965, c 49)

PART II
REGISTRATION OF BIRTHS

13   Particulars of births to be registered

[(1)   The prescribed particulars of the birth of every child born in Scotland shall be registered in accordance with this Part of this Act and for that purpose each district registrar for each registration district shall keep—

   (a)   a register of births, and

   (b)   a register of still-births.]

   [. . .]

(4)   Where a child is born (whether within or out of Scotland) in a ship, aircraft or land vehicle in the course of a journey, and that child is brought by such ship, aircraft or land vehicle to any place in Scotland, the birth shall, unless the Registrar General [of Births, Deaths and Marriages for Scotland] otherwise directs, be deemed for the purposes of this section to have occurred at that place.

14   Duty to give information of particulars of birth

(1)   Subject to the subsequent provisions of this Part of this Act, in the case of every birth it shall be the duty of—

   (a)   the [child's father or mother (whether or not they have attained the age of sixteen years)], or

   (b)   in the case of the death or inability of the father and mother, each other person who under the next following subsection is qualified to give information concerning the birth,

within twenty-one days from the date of the birth, [to give to the district registrar for a registration district information of the prescribed particulars concerning the birth]:

Provided that the giving of that information [. . .] by the father or the mother or by any one of those persons shall constitute a discharge of any duty imposed by this subsection on any other person.

   [(1A)   For the purposes of subsection (1) above, a person shall give information of the prescribed particulars concerning a birth to the district registrar for a registration district by—

   (a)   attending personally at the registration office for that district and—

      (i)   giving to the registrar information of the particulars required to be registered concerning the birth, and

      (ii)   attesting, in the prescribed manner, the prescribed form (in this Part, the 'birth registration form') concerning the birth in the presence of the registrar, or

   (b)   submitting to the registrar by a prescribed means a birth registration form concerning the birth which has been completed by the person and attested by him in the prescribed manner.]

(2)   The following persons, in addition to the father and mother, shall be qualified to give information concerning the birth of a child, that is to say—

   (a)   any relative of either parent of the child, being a relative who has knowledge of the birth;

   (b)   the occupier of the premises in which the child was, to the knowledge of that occupier, born;

   (c)   any person present at the birth;

   (d)   any person having charge of the child.

(3) Nothing in this [. . .] section shall authorise the registration of the particulars of any birth in two or more registers, or more than once in any one register.

(4) If it appears to the Registrar General that the particulars of the birth of any child have been registered in two or more registers, or more than once in any one register, he may give directions for the cancellation of all those registrations except such one of them as may be specified in the directions.

[(4A) In the case of a child who has a parent by virtue of section 42 of the Human Fertilisation and Embryology Act 2008, the references in subsections (1) and (2) to the father of the child are to be read as references to the woman who is a parent by virtue of that section.]

[(5) In this section, any reference to the father or parent of the child shall not include a reference to a father who is not married to [or in a civil partnership with] the mother and has not been married to [or in a civil partnership with] her since the child's conception.]

18 Births of children born out of wedlock

[(1) Subject to section 18ZA of this Act no person who is not married to [or in a civil partnership with] the mother of a child and has not been married to [or in a civil partnership with] her since the child's conception shall be required, as father of the child, to give information concerning the birth of the child and, save as provided in section 20 of this Act, the [district registrar for the registration district] shall not enter in the [birth registration form concerning the birth] the name and surname of any such person as father of the child except—

   (a) at the joint request of the mother and the person acknowledging himself to be the father of the child (in which case that person shall [attest, in the prescribed manner, the birth registration form] together with the mother); or

   (b) at the request of the mother—

      (i) on the production of—

        (aa) a declaration in the prescribed form made by the mother stating that that person is the father of the child; and

        (bb) a statutory declaration made by that person acknowledging himself to be the father of the child; or

      (ii) on production of a decree by a competent court finding or declaring that person to be the father of the child; or

   (c) at the request of that person on production of—

      (i) a declaration in the prescribed form by that person acknowledging himself to be the father of the child; and

      (ii) a statutory declaration made by the mother stating that that person is the father of the child.]

[(1A) Where a person acknowledging himself to be the father of a child makes a request to the [district registrar for the registration district] in accordance with paragraph (c) of subsection (1) of this section, he shall be treated as a qualified informant concerning the birth of the child for the purposes of this Act; and the giving of information concerning the birth of the child by that person and the [attesting of the birth registration form concerning the birth] by him in the presence of the registrar shall act as a discharge of any duty of any other qualified informant under section 14 of this Act.]

(2) In any case where the name and surname of the father of a [. . .] child has not been entered in the [birth registration form concerning the birth], the Registrar General may record that name and surname by causing an appropriate entry to be made in the Register of Corrections Etc—

   (a) if a decree of paternity has been granted by a competent court; or

   (b) if there is produced to him [a declaration and a statutory declaration such as are mentioned in paragraph (b) or (c) of subsection 1 of this section]; or

   (c) if, where the mother is dead [or cannot be found or is incapable of making a request under subsection (1)(b) of this section, or a declaration under subsection (1)(b)(i)(aa) of this section, or a statutory declaration under subsection (1)(c)(ii) of this section] he is ordered so to do by the sheriff upon application made to the sheriff [. . .] by the person acknowledging himself to be the father of the child.

Where a decree of paternity has been granted by any court the clerk of court shall, where no appeal has been made against such decree, on the expiration of the time within which such an appeal may be made, or where an appeal has been made against such a decree, on the conclusion of any appellate proceedings, notify the import of such decree in the prescribed form to the Registrar General.

[(3)   A person under the age of sixteen years has legal capacity—

(a)   to make a request, declaration or statutory declaration under subsection (1) or (2)(b) above if, in the opinion of the registrar; or

(b)   to make an application under subsection (2)(c) above if, in the opinion of the sheriff,

that person understands the nature of the request or, as the case may be, of the declaration, statutory declaration or application; and without prejudice to the generality of this subsection a person twelve years of age or more shall be presumed to be of sufficient age and maturity to have such understanding.]

[18ZA   Registration of father or second female parent by virtue of certain provisions of the Human Fertilisation and Embryology Act 2008

(1)   The registrar shall not enter in the register—

(a)   as the father of a child the name of a man who is to be treated for that purpose as the father of the child by virtue of section 39(1) or 40(1) or (2) of the Human Fertilisation and Embryology Act 2008 (circumstances in which man to be treated as father of child for purpose of registration of birth where fertility treatment undertaken after his death); or

(b)   as a parent of the child, the name of a woman who is to be treated for that purpose as a parent of the child by virtue of section 46(1) or (2) of that Act (circumstances in which woman to be treated as parent of child for purposes of registration of birth where fertility treatment undertaken after her death),

unless the condition in subsection (2) below is satisfied.

(2)   The condition in this subsection is satisfied if—

(a)   the mother requests the registrar to make such an entry in the register and produces the relevant documents; or

(b)   in the case of the death or inability of the mother, the relevant documents are produced by some other person who is a qualified informant.

(3)   In this section 'the relevant documents' means—

(a)   the consent in writing and election mentioned in section 39(1), 40(1) or (2) or 46(1) or (2) (as the case requires) of the Human Fertilisation and Embryology Act 2008;

(b)   a certificate of a registered medical practitioner as to the medical facts concerned; and

(c)   such other documentary evidence (if any) as the registrar considers appropriate.]

[18A   Decrees of parentage and non-parentage

(1)   Where a decree of parentage or non-parentage has been granted by any court the clerk of court shall—

(a)   where no appeal has been made against such decree, on the expiration of the time within which such an appeal may be made, or

(b)   where an appeal has been made against such a decree, on the conclusion of any appellate proceedings,

notify the import of such decree in the prescribed form to the Registrar General.

(2)   Where it appears to the Registrar General that the import of a decree notified to him under subsection (1) above does not correspond with the entry in the

register of births in respect of any person to whom the decree relates he shall cause an appropriate entry to be made in the Register of Corrections Etc.]

[18B   Births of children where second female parent by virtue of section 43 of the Human Fertilisation and Embryology Act 2008

(1)   No woman shall as a parent of a child by virtue of section 43 of the Human Fertilisation and Embryology Act 2008 ('the woman concerned') be required, as a parent of the child, to give information concerning the birth of the child and, save as provided in section 20 of this Act, the district registrar for the registration district shall not enter in the birth registration form concerning the birth the name and surname of any woman as a parent of the child by virtue of section 43 of that Act of 2008 except—

(a)   at the joint request of the mother and the woman concerned (in which case the woman concerned shall attest, in the prescribed manner, the birth registration form together with the mother); or

(b)   at the request of the mother on production of—

(i)   a declaration in the prescribed form made by the mother stating that the woman concerned is a parent of the child by virtue of section 43 of the Human Fertilisation and Embryology Act 2008; and

(ii)   a statutory declaration made by the woman concerned acknowledging herself to be a parent of the child by virtue of section 43 of that Act; or

(c)   at the request of the mother on production of a decree by a competent court finding or declaring the woman concerned to be a parent of the child by virtue of section 43 of that Act; or

(d)   at the request of the woman concerned on production of—

(i)   a declaration in the prescribed form made by the woman concerned acknowledging herself to be a parent of the child by virtue of section 43 of that Act; and

(ii)   a statutory declaration made by the mother stating that the woman concerned is a parent of the child by virtue of section 43 of that Act.

(2)   Where a person acknowledging herself to be a parent of the child by virtue of section 43 of the Human Fertilisation and Embryology Act 2008 makes a request to the district registrar for the registration district in accordance with paragraph (d) of subsection (1) of this section, she shall be treated as a qualified informant concerning the birth of the child for the purposes of this Act; and the giving of information concerning the birth of the child by that person and the attesting of the birth registration form concerning the birth by her in the presence of the registrar shall act as a discharge of any duty of any other qualified informant under section 14 of this Act.

(3)   In any case where the name and surname of a woman who is a parent of a child by virtue of section 43 of the Human Fertilisation and Embryology Act 2008 has not been entered in the birth registration form concerning the birth, the Registrar General may record that name and surname by causing an appropriate entry to be made in the Register of Corrections Etc—

(a)   if there is produced to him a declaration and a statutory declaration such as are mentioned in paragraph (b) or (d) of subsection (1) of this section; or

(b)   if, where the mother is dead or cannot be found or is incapable of making a request under subsection (1)(b) or (c) of this section, or a declaration under subsection (1)(b)(i) or a statutory declaration under subsection (1)(d)(ii) of this section, the Registrar General is ordered so to do by the sheriff upon application made to the sheriff by the person acknowledging herself to be a parent of the child by virtue of section 43 of the Human Fertilisation and Embryology Act 2008.]

[. . .]

20   Re-registration in certain cases

(1)   In the case of any person, if—

(a)   the entry relating to him in the register of births is affected by any matter contained in the Register of Corrections Etc respecting his status [parentage or non-parentage], or

(b)   the entry relating to him in the register of births has been so made as to imply that he was found exposed, or

(c)   the entry relating to him in the register of births [has been so made as to imply that his parents were not then married to [or in a civil partnership with] one another and his parents have subsequently married [or entered into a civil partnership with] one another and subject to subsection (1B) below] [; or

(d)   the entry relating to the child in the register of births has been made so as to imply that the person, other than the mother, recorded as a parent of the child is so by virtue of section 43 of the Human Fertilisation and Embryology Act 2008 and the mother and that person have subsequently become parties to a civil partnership with each other and subject to subsection (1B) below,]

the [birth may, where subsection (1A) below applies, be re-registered], and any such re-registration shall be effected in such manner as may be prescribed:

[(1A)   This subsection applies—

(a)   where the Registrar-General authorises the re-registration, and

(b)   in such other cases or classes of case as may be prescribed.

(1B)   A birth may not be re-registered] in pursuance of paragraph (c) [or (d)] [. . .], in a case where the paternity [or parentage] of the person has not been entered in the register of births or in the Register of Corrections Etc in accordance with section 18 [or 18B] of this Act, or any corresponding enactment in force before the commencement of this Act, save with the sanction of the sheriff granted upon the application—

(i)   of both parents of the person jointly, or

(ii)   where one of the parents is dead, of the surviving parent, or

(iii)   where both parents are dead, of or on behalf of the person,

after such intimation as the sheriff may direct, and after due inquiry, and a hearing of any party having interest who may appear to oppose such application.

(2)   In this section any reference to the register of births includes a reference to any register of births kept under any enactment in force at any time before the commencement of this Act.

[. . .]

43   Recording of baptismal name or change of name or surname

(1)   The following provisions of this section, except subsection 6(b), shall apply only to persons whose births are registered in Scotland, and, without prejudice to the provisions of section 24 of the Adoption Act 1958 relating to the giving or taking of a new name, to persons in respect of whom there is an entry in the Adopted Children Register maintained by the Registrar General under section 22 of that Act.

(2)   In this section 'change' in relation to a name or surname includes any change by way of substitution, addition, omission, spelling or hyphenation.

(3)   Where, within twelve months from the date of the birth of any child, the name by which it was registered is changed or, if it was registered without a name, a name is given to the child, the Registrar General [. . .], shall [, where within two years from the date of the birth of the child, an application in the prescribed form is made to the Registrar General in respect of that matter by the qualified applicant,] cause an entry containing the name mentioned in the [application] to be made in the Register of Corrections Etc, and only one such entry may be made under this subsection in respect of any one child. [. . .]

(4)   Where an application in the prescribed form is made to the Registrar General by the qualified applicant in respect of the change of name or surname of a child under sixteen years of age the Registrar General may record that change of

name or surname by causing an appropriate entry to be made in the Register of Corrections Etc.

[. . .]

Only one change of name and one change of surname in respect of any one child may be recorded under this subsection, but no change of name shall be recorded under this subsection in the case of a child in respect of whom a change of name has been recorded by virtue of the last foregoing subsection.

(5) Where an application in the prescribed form is made to the Registrar General in respect of a change of name or surname, in the case of a person over sixteen years of age [. . .] by that person, the Registrar General may record that change of name or surname by causing an appropriate entry to be made in the Register of Corrections Etc.

[. . .]

Only one change of name and three changes of surname in respect of any one person may be recorded under this subsection, and a period of five years must elapse after one change of surname is recorded before another such change may be recorded.

(6) Notwithstanding the foregoing provisions of this section, where an application is made to the Registrar General in respect of a change of name or surname—

(a) in the case of a child under sixteen years of age, by the [qualified applicant] of that child, in the case of a person over sixteen years of age [. . .] by that person, and there is produced to the Registrar General—

(i) a decree or certificate of change of name or surname pronounced or, as the case may be, granted by or on behalf of the Lyon King of Arms, or

(ii) a certified copy of a will, settlement, or deed of trust containing a condition that the person concerned shall take a name or surname different from that in which his birth was registered, together with evidence to the satisfaction of the Registrar General that the name or surname has thereafter been so changed, or

(b) in the case of a male person who has married in Scotland and who has changed his name or surname following his marriage, by that person, and there is produced to the Registrar General a decree or certificate as described in the foregoing paragraph,

the Registrar General may record that change of name or surname by causing an appropriate entry to be made in the Register of Corrections Etc.

(7) Where an application is made to the Registrar General in respect of the recording of an alternative name, being the English equivalent of a non-English name, in the case of a child under sixteen years of age, by the [qualified applicant] of that child, in the case of a person over sixteen years of age [. . .] by that person the Registrar General may record that name as an alternative name by causing an appropriate entry to be made in the Register of Corrections Etc.

(8) On making an application under any of the provisions of this section the applicant shall pay such fees as may be prescribed.

(9) Nothing in this section shall affect any rule of law as respects change of name or surname, and in particular, without prejudice to that generality, the validity as evidence of change of name or surname of a decree or certificate pronounced or, as the case may be, granted by or on behalf of the Lyon King of Arms.

[(9A) In this section 'qualified applicant' means—

(a) where only one parent has parental responsibilities in relation to the child, that parent;

(b) where both parents have such responsibilities in relation to the child, both parents; and

(c) where neither parent has such responsibilities, any other person who has such responsibilities.

(9B) A person may be a qualified applicant for the purposes of this section whether or not he has attained the age of sixteen years].

ABORTION ACT 1967
(1967, c 87)

1 Medical termination of pregnancy

(1)   Subject to the provisions of this section, a person shall not be guilty of an offence under the law relating to abortion when a pregnancy is terminated by a registered medical practitioner if two registered medical practitioners are of the opinion, formed in good faith—

[(a)   that the pregnancy has not exceeded its twenty-fourth week and that the continuance of the pregnancy would involve risk, greater than if the pregnancy were terminated, of injury to the physical or mental health of the pregnant woman or any existing children of her family; or

(b)   that the termination is necessary to prevent grave permanent injury to the physical or mental health of the pregnant woman; or

(c)   that the continuance of the pregnancy would involve risk to the life of the pregnant woman, greater than if the pregnancy were terminated; or

(d)   that there is a substantial risk that if the child were born it would suffer from such physical or mental abnormalities as to be seriously handicapped.]

(2)   In determining whether the continuance of a pregnancy would involve such risk of injury to health as is mentioned in paragraph (a) [or (b)] of subsection (1) of this section, account may be taken of the pregnant woman's actual or reasonably foreseeable environment.

(3)   Except as provided by subsection (4) of this section, any treatment for the termination of pregnancy must be carried out in a hospital vested in [. . .] the Secretary of State [. . .] for the purposes of [his functions under the National Health Service Act 2006 or the National Health Service (Scotland) Act 1978 or in a hospital vested in a [. . .] National Health Service Trust [or an NHS foundation trust] or in a place approved for the purposes of this section by the Secretary of State.]

[(3A)   The power under subsection (3) of this section to approve a place includes power, in relation to treatment consisting primarily in the use of such medicines as may be specified in the approval and carried out in such manner as may be so specified, to approve a class of places.]

(4)   Subsection (3) of this section, and so much of subsection (1) as relates to the opinion of two registered medical practitioners, shall not apply to the termination of a pregnancy by a registered medical practitioner in a case where he is of the opinion, formed in good faith, that the termination is immediately necessary to save the life or to prevent grave permanent injury to the physical or mental health of the pregnant woman.

SOCIAL WORK (SCOTLAND) ACT 1968
(1968, s 49)

PART I
ADMINISTRATION

Central Authority

5 Powers of the Secretary of State

[(1)   Local authorities shall perform their functions under this Act [, Part 2 of the Children (Scotland) Act 1995, the Social Care (Self-directed Support) (Scotland) Act 2013 (asp 1) [Part 6 (in so far as it applies to looked after children) and Parts 12 and 13 of the Children and Young People (Scotland) Act 2014 (asp 8)]] [, Parts 5, 6, 9 to 11, 13 to 16, and 18 of the Children's Hearings (Scotland) Act 2011 (asp 1)] [and the Carers (Scotland) Act 2016] under the general guidance of the Secretary of State.

[(1A) Without prejudice to subsection (1) above, the Secretary of State may issue directions to local authorities, either individually or collectively, as to the manner in which they are to exercise any of their functions under this Act or any of the enactments mentioned in [subsection (1B) below] and a local authority shall comply with any direction made under this subsection.]

[(1B) The enactments referred to in subsection (1A) above are—

(a)   this Act as read with sections 1 and 2(1) of the Chronically Sick and Disabled Persons Act 1970 and the Disabled Persons (Services, Consultation and Representation) Act 1986;

(b)   Part IV of the Children and Young Persons (Scotland) Act 1937;

(c)   section 22(2) to (5A), (7) and (8), section 26(2) to (4) and sections 43, 45, 47 and 48 of the National Assistance Act 1948;

(d)   the Disabled Persons (Employment) Act 1958;

(e)   sections 10 to 12 of the Matrimonial Proceedings (Children) Act 1958, and sections 11 and 12 of the Guardianship Act 1973;

(f)   [section 51 of the Criminal Procedure (Scotland) Act 1995;]

(g)   the Children Act 1975;

(h)   the Adoption Act 1976;

[. . .]

(j)   sections 21 to 23 of the Health and Social Services and Social Security Adjudications Act 1983;

(k)   [the Mental Health (Care and Treatment) (Scotland) Act 2003];

(l)   the Foster Children (Scotland) Act 1984;

(m)   sections 38(6) and 235 of the Housing (Scotland) Act 1987;

(n)   the Access to Personal Files Act 1987; [. . .] and

[. . .]

(p)   Part II of the Children (Scotland) Act 1995;

[(q)   the Adoption and Children (Scotland) Act 2007 (asp 4).]]

[(r)   the Social Care (Self-directed Support) (Scotland) Act 2013 (asp 1);]

[(s)   Parts 5, 6, 9 to 11, 13 to 16, and 18 of the Children's Hearings (Scotland) Act 2011(asp 1);]

[(t)   Part 6 (in so far as it applies to looked after children) and Parts 12 and 13 of the Children and Young People (Scotland) Act 2014 (asp 8);]

[(u)   the Carers (Scotland) Act 2016.]

[(1C)   In subsections (1) and (1B) of this section, the references to looked after children are to be construed in accordance with section 17(6) of the Children (Scotland) Act 1995.]

[(2)   The Secretary of State may make regulations in relation to—

(a)   the performance of the functions assigned to local authorities by this Act;

(b)   the activities of voluntary organisations in so far as those activities are concerned with the like purposes;

[(c)   the performance of the functions of local authorities under any of the enactments mentioned in paragraphs (b), (d), (e), (g), (h), (i), (l), (o), [(p) and [, (q) and (s)]] of subsection (1B) above.

[. . .]

(3)   Without prejudice to the generality of subsection (2) above, regulations under this section may make such provision as is mentioned in subsection (4) of this section as regards—

(a)   the boarding out of persons other than children by local authorities and voluntary organisations, whether under any enactment or otherwise; and

(b)   the placing of children under paragraph (a), or the making of arrangements in respect of children under paragraph (c), of section 26(1) of the Children (Scotland) Act 1995, by local authorities.

(4)   The provision referred to in subsection (3) of this section is—

(a)   for the recording—

(i)   by local authorities and voluntary organisations, of information relating to those with whom persons are so boarded out, or who are willing to have persons so boarded out with them; and

(ii) by local authorities, of information relating to those with whom children are so placed or with whom such arrangements are made or who are willing to have children so placed with them or to enter into such arrangements,

(b) for securing that—

(i) persons are not so boarded out in any household unless it is for the time being approved by such local authority or voluntary organisation as may be prescribed by the regulations; and

(ii) children are not so placed or, in accordance with such arrangements, provided with accommodation, in any household unless it is for the time being approved by the local authority placing the child or as the case may be making the arrangements;

(c) for securing that, where possible, the person with whom a child is so placed or with whom such arrangements are made is either of the same religious persuasion as the child or gives an undertaking that the child shall be brought up in that persuasion;

(d) for securing—

(i) that a person who is, and the place in which he is, so boarded out by a local authority or voluntary organisation is supervised and inspected by that authority or organisation; and

(ii) that a child who is, and the place in which he is, so placed or, in accordance with such arrangements, provided with accommodation, by a local authority is supervised and inspected by that authority,

and that he shall be removed from the place in question if his welfare appears to require it.

(5) In subsections (3) and (4) of this section, 'child' [means a person who is under the age of 18].]

[. . .]

[6A Inquiries

(1) Without prejudice to section 6B(1) of this Act, the Secretary of State may cause an inquiry to be held into—

(a) the functions of a local authority under this Act or any of the enactments mentioned in section 5(1B) of this Act;

(b) the functions of an adoption society, within the meaning of [section 119(1) of the Adoption and Children (Scotland) Act 2007 (asp 4)];

[. . .]

(d) the detention of a child under—

(i) section 57 of the Children and Young Persons (Scotland) Act 1937; or

(ii) section 44 or 208 of the Criminal Procedure (Scotland) Act 1995;

(e) the functions of the Principal Reporter under [the Children's Hearings (Scotland) Act 2011] or any other enactment [; or

(f) the functions conferred on the National Convener of Children's Hearings Scotland by virtue of the Children's Hearings (Scotland) Act 2011 (asp 1).]

(2) The Secretary of State may, before an inquiry is commenced, direct that it shall be held in private, but where no such direction has been given the person holding the inquiry may if he thinks fit hold it or any part of it in private.

(3) Subsections (2) to (8) of section 210 of the Local Government (Scotland) Act 1973 (powers in relation to local inquiries) shall apply in relation to an inquiry under this section as they apply in relation to a local inquiry under that section.]

[6B Local authority inquiries into matters affecting children

(1) Without prejudice to section 6A(1) of this Act, a local authority may cause an

inquiry to be held into their functions under this Act, or any of the enactments mentioned in section 5(1B) of this Act, in so far as those functions relate to children.

[(1A)   Where a function mentioned in subsection (1) is delegated by a local authority to a person in pursuance of an integration scheme prepared under section 1 or 2 of the Public Bodies (Joint Working) (Scotland) Act 2014, this section applies to that person as it applies to a local authority (but subject to the modification in subsection 1B).

(1B)   The modification is that the reference in subsection (3) to an officer of the local authority must be construed as if it were a reference to a member of staff of the person to whom the function is delegated.]

(2)   The local authority may, before an inquiry under this section is commenced, direct that it be held in private; but where no such direction is given, the person holding the inquiry may if he thinks fit hold it, or any part of it, in private.

(3)   Subsections (2) to (6) of section 210 of the Local Government (Scotland) Act 1973 (powers in relation to local inquiries) shall apply in relation to an inquiry under this section as they apply in relation to a local inquiry under that section, so however that, for the purposes of the application, any reference in those subsections to a Minister shall be construed as a reference to the local authority and any reference to an officer of his Department as a reference to an officer of that authority.

(4)   The expenses incurred by a local authority in relation to an inquiry under this section (including such reasonable sum as the authority may determine for the services of any of their officers engaged in the inquiry) shall, unless the authority are of the opinion that those expenses should be defrayed in whole or in part by them, be paid by such party to the inquiry as they may direct; and the authority may certify the amount of the expenses so incurred.

(5)   Any sum certified under subsection (4) above and to be defrayed in accordance with a direction under that subsection shall be a debt due by the party directed and shall be recoverable accordingly.

(6)   The local authority may make an award as to the expenses of the parties at the inquiry and as to the parties by whom such expenses shall be paid.]

PART II
PROMOTION OF SOCIAL WELFARE BY LOCAL AUTHORITIES

General

12   General social welfare services of local authorities

(1)   It shall be the duty of every local authority to promote social welfare by making available advice, guidance and assistance on such a scale as may be appropriate for their area, and in that behalf to make arrangements and to provide or secure the provision of such facilities (including the provision or arranging for the provision of residential and other establishments) as they may consider suitable and adequate, and such assistance may, [subject to subsections (3) to (5) of this section, be given in kind or in cash on, or in respect of, any relevant person.

(2)   A person is a relevant person for the purposes of this section if, not being less than eighteen years of age, he is] in need requiring assistance in kind or, in exceptional circumstances constituting an emergency, in cash, where the giving of assistance in either form would avoid the local authority being caused greater expense in the giving of assistance in another form, or where probable aggravation of the person's need would cause greater expense to the local authority on a later occasion.

[(2A)   A person to whom section 115 of the Immigration and Asylum Act 1999 (exclusion from benefits) applies is not to receive assistance under subsection (1) of this section (whether by way of residential accommodation or otherwise) if his need for assistance has arisen solely—

(a)   because he is destitute; or

(b)   because of the physical effects, or anticipated physical effects, of his being destitute.

(2B)   Subsections (3) and (5) to (8) of section 95 of the Immigration and Asylum Act 1999, and paragraph 2 of Schedule 8 to that Act, apply for the purposes of subsection (2A) as they apply for the purposes of that section, but for the references in subsections (5) and (7) of that section and in that paragraph to the Secretary of State substitute references to a local authority.]

(3)   Before giving assistance to, or in respect of, a person in cash under subsection (1) of this section a local authority shall have regard to his eligibility for receiving assistance from any other statutory body and, if he is so eligible, to the availability to him of that assistance in his time of need.

[(3A)   In determining, for the purposes of this section, whether to make available assistance by providing, or securing the provision of, residential accommodation to a person, a local authority shall disregard so much of the person's resources—

(a)   as may be prescribed; or

(b)   as is determined by them in such a way as may be prescribed, and any order made by virtue of this subsection may make different provision for different cases and for different persons.

(3B)   An order made by virtue of paragraph (a) of subsection (3A) of this section may prescribe circumstances in which assistance such as is mentioned in that subsection is to be made available disregarding entirely a person's resources.

(3C)   In subsections (3A) and (3B) of this section, references to a person's resources are to resources within the meaning of the order prescribing the amount, or as the case may be the way, in question.

(3D)   A statutory instrument made in exercise of the power conferred by paragraph (a) or (b) of subsection (3A) of this section shall be subject to annulment in pursuance of a resolution of the Scottish Parliament.]

(4)   Assistance given in kind or in cash to, or in respect of, persons under this section may be given unconditionally or subject to such conditions as to the repayment of the assistance, or of its value, whether in whole or in part, as the local authority may consider reasonable having regard to the means of the person receiving the assistance and to the eligibility of the person for assistance from any other statutory body.

(5)   Nothing in the provisions of this section shall affect the performance by a local authority of their functions under any other enactment.

[(6)   For the purposes of subsection (2) of this section 'person in need' includes a person who is in need of care and attention arising out of drug or alcohol dependency or release from prison or other form of detention.]

[12A   Duty of local authority to assess needs

(1)   Subject to the provisions of this section, where it appears to a local authority that any person for whom they are under a duty or have a power to provide, or to secure the provision of, community care services may be in need of any such services, the authority—

(a)   shall make an assessment of the needs of that person for those services; and

[(b)   shall then decide, having regard to the results of that assessment, and taking account—

[(i) if an adult carer provides, or intends to provide, care for that person, of the care provided by that carer,

(ia) if a young carer provides, or intends to provide, care for that person, of the care provided by that carer,]

(ii)   in so far as it is reasonable and practicable to do so, [. . .] of the views of the person whose needs are being assessed [. . .] (provided that [. . .] there is a wish, or as the case may be a capacity, to express a view), whether the needs of the person being assessed call for the provision of any such services.]

[(1A) In subsection (1)(b)(i) and (ia), the reference to the care provided by a carer means—

(a) in the case of an adult carer who has an adult carer support plan, the information about that care set out in that plan,

(b) in the case of a young carer who has a young carer statement, the information about that care set out in that statement.

(1B) In—

(a) assessing the needs of a person for services under subsection (1)(a),

(b) deciding under subsection (1)(b) whether those needs call for the provision of any services, and

(c) deciding how any such services are to be provided,

a local authority must take account of the views of the carer, in so far as it is reasonable and practicable to do so.]

(2) Before deciding, under subsection (1)(b) of this section, that the needs of any person call for the provision of nursing care, a local authority shall consult a medical practitioner.

(3) If, while they are carrying out their duty under subsection (1) of this section, it appears to a local authority that there may be a need for the provision to any person to whom that subsection applies—

(a) of any services under the National Health Service (Scotland) Act 1978 by the Health Board—

(i) in whose area he is ordinarily resident; or

(ii) in whose area the services to be supplied by the local authority are, or are likely to, be provided; or

(b) of any services which fall within the functions of a housing authority (within the meaning of section 130 (housing) of the Local Government (Scotland) Act 1973) which is not the local authority carrying out the assessment,

the local authority shall so notify that Health Board or housing authority, and shall request information from them as to what services are likely to be made available to that person by that Health Board or housing authority; and, thereafter, in carrying out their said duty, the local authority shall take into account any information received by them in response to that request.

(4) Where a local authority are making an assessment under this section and it appears to them that the person concerned is a disabled person, they shall—

(a) proceed to make such a decision as to the services he requires as is mentioned in section 4 of the Disabled Persons (Services, Consultation and Representation) Act 1986 without his requesting them to do so under that section; and

(b) inform him that they will be doing so and of his rights under that Act.

(5) Nothing in this section shall prevent a local authority from providing or arranging for the provision of community care services for any person without carrying out a prior assessment of his needs in accordance with the preceding provisions of this section if, in the opinion of the authority, the condition of that person is such that he requires those services as a matter of urgency.

(6) If, by virtue of subsection (5) of this section, community care services have been provided for any person as a matter of urgency, then, as soon as practicable thereafter, an assessment of his needs shall be made in accordance with the preceding provisions of this section.

(7) This section is without prejudice to section 3 of the said Act of 1986.

(8) In this section—

['adult carer' and 'adult carer support plan' have the meanings given by the Carers (Scotland) Act 2016,]

['community care services' means services, other than services for children, which a local authority is under a duty or has a power to provide, or to secure the provision of, under—

(a)   Part 2 of this Act; or

(b)   any of the following provisions of the Mental Health (Care and Treatment) (Scotland) Act 2003—

(i)   section 25 (care and support services etc);

(ii)   section 26 (services designed to promote well-being and social development);

(iii)   section 27 (assistance with travel);]

'disabled person' has the same meaning as in the said Act of 1986; and

'medical practitioner' means a fully registered person within the meaning of section 55 (interpretation) of the Medical Act 1983.]

['person' means a natural person;]

['young carer' and 'young carer statement' have the meanings given by the Carers (Scotland) Act 2016.]

[12AZA   Assessments under section 12A: assistance

(1)   Subsection (4) applies where—

(a)   a local authority is required by section 12A(1)(a) to carry out an assessment of the needs of a person (the 'supported person') for community care services,

(b)   it appears to the authority that the supported person falls within subsection (2), and

(c)   the conditions in subsection (3) are satisfied.

(2)   A supported person falls within this subsection if—

(a)   because of mental disorder, the supported person would benefit from receiving assistance from another person in relation to the carrying out of the assessment,

(b)   because of difficulties in communicating due to physical disability, the supported person would benefit from receiving assistance from another person to communicate in relation to the carrying out of the assessment.

(3)   The conditions are—

(a)   there is no guardian, continuing attorney or welfare attorney with powers as respects the provision of assistance in relation to the carrying out of the assessment, and

(b)   an intervention order has not been granted as respects the provision of assistance in relation to the carrying out of the assessment.

(4)   The authority must take reasonable steps—

(a)   to identify persons who are able to assist the supported person, and

(b)   if the supported person agrees, to involve them in assisting the supported person in relation to the carrying out of the assessment or, as the case may be, communicating in relation to the carrying out of the assessment.

(5)   In this section—

'the 2000 Act' means the Adults with Incapacity (Scotland) Act 2000 (asp 4),

'continuing attorney'—

(a)   means a continuing attorney within the meaning of section 15 of the 2000 Act, and

(b)   includes a person granted, under a contract, grant or appointment governed by the law of any country, powers (however expressed) relating to the granter's property or financial affairs and having continuing effect despite the granter's incapacity,

'guardian'—

(a)   means a guardian appointed under the 2000 Act, and

(b)   includes a guardian (however called) appointed under the law of any country to, or entitled under the law of any country to act for, an adult during the adult's incapacity, if the guardianship is recognised under the law of Scotland,

'intervention order' is to be construed in accordance with section 53 of the 2000 Act,

'mental disorder' has the meaning given by section 328 of the Mental Health (Care and Treatment) (Scotland) Act 2003 (asp 13),
'welfare attorney'—
    (a)   means a welfare attorney within the meaning of section 16 of the 2000 Act, and
    (b)   includes a person granted, under a contract, grant or appointment governed by the law of any country, powers (however expressed) relating to the granter's personal welfare and having effect during the granter's incapacity.]

[13ZA Provision of services to incapable adults

(1) Where—
    (a)   a local authority have decided under section 12A of this Act that an adult's needs call for the provision of a community care service; and
    (b)   it appears to the local authority that the adult is incapable in relation to decisions about the service,
the local authority may take any steps which they consider would help the adult to benefit from the service.

(2) Without prejudice to the generality of subsection (1) above, steps that may be taken by the local authority include moving the adult to residential accommodation provided in pursuance of this Part.

(3) The principles set out in subsections (2) to (4) of section 1 of the 2000 Act apply in relation to any steps taken under subsection (1) above as they apply to interventions in the affairs of an adult under or in pursuance of that Act.

(4) Subsection (1) does not authorise a local authority to take steps if they are aware that—
    (a)   there is a guardian or welfare attorney with powers relating to the proposed steps;
    (b)   an intervention order has been granted relating to the proposed steps; or
    (c)   an application has been made (but not yet determined) for an intervention order or guardianship order under Part 6 of the 2000 Act relating to the proposed steps.

(5) In this section—
    (a)   'the 2000 Act' means the Adults with Incapacity (Scotland) Act 2000 (asp 4);
    (b)   'adult' has the meaning given in section 1(6) of the 2000 Act;
    (c)   'community care service' has the meaning given in section 5A of this Act;
    (d)   'incapable' has the meaning given in section 1(6) of the 2000 Act;
    (e)   'intervention order' is to be construed in accordance with section 53 of the 2000 Act;
    (f)   the reference to a guardian includes a reference to—
        (i)   a guardian appointed under the 2000 Act; and
        (ii)   a guardian (however called) appointed under the law of any country to, or entitled under the law of any country to act for, an adult during his incapacity, if the guardianship is recognised by the law of Scotland;
    (g)   the reference to a welfare attorney includes a reference to—
        (i)   a welfare attorney within the meaning of section 16 of the 2000 Act; and
        (ii)   a person granted, under a contract, grant or appointment governed by the law of any country, powers (however expressed) relating to the granter's personal welfare and having effect during the granter's incapacity.]

Residential accommodation with nursing

[13A Residential accommodation with nursing

(1) Without prejudice to section 12 of this Act, a local authority shall—
    [(a) provide and maintain, or

(b)   make such arrangements as they consider appropriate and adequate for the provision of]
suitable residential accommodation where nursing is provided for persons who appear to them to be in need of such accommodation by reason of infirmity, age, illness or mental disorder, dependency on drugs or alcohol or being substantially handicapped by any deformity or disability.

[(2)   [A]rrangements made by virtue of subsection (1) above shall be made with a voluntary or other organisation or other person, being an organisation or person providing—

(a)   an independent health care service which is a private psychiatric hospital; or

(b)   a care home service.]

[(2A)   In subsection (2)(a) above, 'independent health care service' and 'private psychiatric hospital' have the same meanings as in section 10F of the National Health Service (Scotland) Act 1978 (c 29).]

[(2B)   In subsection (2)(b) above, 'care home service' has the same meaning as in paragraph 2 of schedule 12 to the Public Services Reform (Scotland) Act 2010 (asp 8).]

(3)   The provisions of section 6 of this Act apply in relation to premises where accommodation is provided for the purposes of this section as they apply in relation to establishments provided for the purposes of this Act.

[(4)   No arrangements under subsection (1) above may be given effect to in relation to a person to whom section 115 of the Immigration and Asylum Act 1999 (exclusion from benefits) applies solely—

(a)   because he is destitute; or

(b)   because of the physical effects, or anticipated physical effects, of his being destitute.

(5)   Subsections (3) and (5) to (8) of section 95 of the Immigration and Asylum Act 1999, and paragraph 2 of Schedule 8 to that Act, apply for the purposes of subsection (4) above as they apply for the purposes of that section, but for the references in subsections (5) and (7) of that section and in that paragraph to the Secretary of State substitute references to a local authority.]

Provision of care and after-care

[13B   Provision of care and after-care

(1)   Subject to subsection (2) below, a local authority may, with the approval of the Secretary of State, and shall, if and to the extent that the Secretary of State so directs, make arrangements for the purpose of the prevention of illness, the care of persons suffering from illness, and the after-care of such persons.

(2)   The arrangements which may be made under subsection (1) above do not include arrangements in respect of medical, dental or nursing care, or health visiting.

[(3)   No arrangements under subsection (1) above may be given effect to in relation to a person to whom section 115 of the Immigration and Asylum Act 1999 (exclusion from benefits) applies solely—

(a)   because he is destitute; or

(b)   because of the physical effects, or anticipated physical effects, of his being destitute.

(4)   Subsections (3) and (5) to (8) of section 95 of the Immigration and Asylum Act 1999, and paragraph 2 of Schedule 8 to that Act, apply for the purposes of subsection (3) above as they apply for the purposes of that section, but for the references in subsections (5) and (7) of that section and in that paragraph to the Secretary of State substitute references to a local authority.]]

PART IV
RESIDENTIAL AND OTHER ESTABLISHMENTS
Provision of residential and other establishments

59 Provision of residential and other establishments by local authorities, and maximum period for repayment of sums borrowed for such provision

(1) [Without prejudice to their duties under sections 12 and 13A of this Act it] shall be the duty of a local authority to provide and maintain such residential and other establishments as may be required for their functions under this Act [, Part 2 of the Children (Scotland) Act 1995 or the Children's Hearings (Scotland) Act 2011] or arrange for the provision of such establishments.

(2) For the purpose of discharging their duty under the foregoing subsection a local authority may—

    (a) themselves provide such establishments as aforesaid; or

    (b) join with another local authority in providing those establishments; or

    (c) secure the provision of such establishments by voluntary organisations or other persons including other local authorities.

(3) The maximum period for the repayment of sums borrowed by a local authority for the purposes of this section shall be such period not exceeding sixty years as may be sanctioned by the Secretary of State; and accordingly in Schedule 6 to the Local Government (Scotland) Act 1947, at the end, there shall be added the following entry, that is to say—

Section 59 of the Social Work (Scotland) Act 1968.	Such period not exceeding sixty years as may be sanctioned by the Secretary of State.

PART VI
CONTRIBUTIONS IN RESPECT OF CHILDREN IN CARE ETC

78 Duty to make contributions in respect of children in care etc

(1) Where a child [is being looked after by a local authority] or a compulsory supervision order to which this Part of this Act applies has been made in respect of him, contributions in respect of the child (hereinafter in this Part of this Act referred to as the 'maintainable child') shall be payable—

    (a) while the maintainable child is under sixteen years of age, by [any natural person who has parental responsibilities (within the meaning of section 1(3) of the Children (Scotland) Act 1995)] in relation to him;

    (b) if he is over sixteen years of age [. . .] by the maintainable child himself.

[(2) This Part of this Act applies to any compulsory supervision order which requires the child concerned to reside in a place or places other than his own home.]

[(2A) No contributions shall be payable under subsection 1(a) of this section by a contributor during a period when he is in receipt of [universal credit under Part 1 of the Welfare Reform Act 2012, income support, an income-based jobseeker's allowance (payable under the Jobseekers Act 1995), an income-related allowance under Part I of the Welfare Reform Act 2007 (employment and support allowance) or family credit.]

(3) In this Part of this Act 'contributor' means a person liable to make contributions by virtue of subsection (1) of this section in respect of a maintainable child.

[78A Recovery of contributions

(1) Section 87 of this Act (charges for services and accommodation) shall not apply to the provision of services (including accommodation) under this Act in respect of maintainable children, and the provisions of this section shall apply thereto.

(2) A local authority providing such services may recover from a contributor a

contribution (if any) of such amount as is reasonable and, subject to that, may recover—

(a)   a standard contribution determined by them in respect of maintainable children who are [looked after by them]; or

(b)   such other contribution as they consider reasonable in the circumstances.]

79   Recipients of contributions

(1)   Subject to the provisions of the following subsection, contributions payable under the last foregoing section shall be payable to the local authority within whose area the contributor is residing, and shall, in the case of contributions paid in respect of a maintainable child [looked after by] a local authority, other than the authority to whom the contributions are payable as aforesaid, be paid over by the last-mentioned authority to that other authority, but subject to such deductions in respect of services rendered by the local authority to whom the contributions were payable as may be agreed between the authorities concerned or as, in default of agreement, may be determined by the Secretary of State.

(2)   Where a contributor is for the time being residing in England or Wales or Northern Ireland contributions payable by him under the last foregoing section shall be payable to the local authority [looking after the child].

80   Enforcement of duty to make contributions

(1)   Where a child becomes a maintainable child by virtue of being [looked after by a local authority] any court of summary jurisdiction, having jurisdiction in the place where the contributor is for the time being residing, may, on the application of the local authority, at any time make an order on any contributor, hereinafter in this Act referred to as a contribution order, for weekly contributions in respect of the child of such amount as the court thinks proper.

[. . .]

(4)   Subject to the following provisions of this section, a contribution order in respect of a maintainable child shall remain in force [throughout the period during which he is looked after by a local authority].

(5)   No contribution shall be payable, by virtue of a contribution order by a contributor who, [being a natural person, has parental responsibilities (within the meaning of section 1(3) of the Children (Scotland) Act 1995) in relation to the maintainable child], in respect of any period after the maintainable child becomes sixteen.

(6)   A contribution order may be revoked or varied by any court of summary jurisdiction having jurisdiction in the place where the contributor is for the time being residing and shall be enforceable in like manner as a decree for aliment.

(7)   Where a contributor resides in England or Wales or Northern Ireland this section shall have effect as if for any reference to a court of summary jurisdiction having jurisdiction in a place where the contributor is for the time being residing there were substituted a reference to a court of summary jurisdiction having jurisdiction in any place within the area of the local authority [looking after] the child.

81   Provisions as to decrees for aliment

(1)   [. . .]

(2)   Where [. . .] a decree for aliment [of a maintainable child] is in force, on the application of the local authority concerned, any court of summary jurisdiction having jurisdiction in the place where the [person liable under the decree] is for the time being residing may, at any time, order the payments under the decree [. . .] to be paid to the local authority who are from time to time entitled under either of the last two foregoing sections to receive contributions in respect of the child.

(3)   Where [. . .] an order made under this section in respect to a decree for

aliment is in force any sums received under the decree for aliment shall be applied in like manner as if they were contributions received under a contribution order.

(4)(a)   In this section the local authority concerned means the local authority which may make application for a contribution order in respect of a child under the last foregoing section;

(b)   where the [person liable to pay aliment for a child under a decree] is resident in England or Wales or Northern Ireland, subsection (2) of this section shall have effect as if for the reference to a court of summary jurisdiction having jurisdiction in the place where [that person] is for the time being residing, there were substituted a reference to a court of summary jurisdiction having jurisdiction in any place within the area of the local authority concerned.

82   Recovery of arrears of contributions

(1)   Where, by virtue of an order or decree made under either of the last two foregoing sections, any sum is payable to a local authority, the local authority in whose area the person liable under the order or decree is for the time being residing, or, as the case may be, the local authority [looking after] the child to whom the order or decree relates, shall be entitled to receive and give a discharge for, and, if necessary, enforce payment of, any arrears accrued due under the order or decree, notwithstanding that those arrears may have accrued at a time when he was not resident in that area or, as the case may be, when the authority were not entitled to sums payable under the order or decree.

(2)   In any proceedings under either of the last two foregoing sections, a certificate purporting to be signed by the clerk to a local authority for the time being entitled to receive contributions, or by some other officer of the authority duly authorised in that behalf, and stating that any sum due to the authority under an order or decree is overdue and unpaid, shall be sufficient evidence of the facts stated therein.

83   Variation of trusts

(1)   Where a child is by virtue of a compulsory supervision order removed from the care of any person and that person is entitled under any trust to receive any sum of money in respect of the maintenance of the child, on the application of the local authority concerned any court of summary jurisdiction, having jurisdiction in the place where that person is for the time being residing, may at any time order the whole or any part of the sums so payable under the trust to be paid to the local authority, to be applied by the authority for the benefit of the child in such manner as, having regard to the terms of the trust, the court may direct.

(2)   Where the person in whose care a child has been residing is for the time being residing in England or Wales or Northern Ireland the foregoing subsection shall have effect as if for the reference to a court having jurisdiction in the place where that person is residing there were substituted a reference to a court of summary jurisdiction having jurisdiction in any place within the area of the local authority [looking after] the child.

[83A   References in this Part of this Act to child being looked after

In this Part of this Act, references to a child being looked after by a local authority shall be construed in accordance with section 17(6) of the Children (Scotland) Act 1995.]

DOMICILE AND MATRIMONIAL PROCEEDINGS ACT 1973
(1973, c 45)

PART I
DOMICILE

Husband and wife

1   Abolition of wife's dependent domicile

(1)   Subject to subsection (2) below, the domicile of a married woman as at any time after the coming into force of this section shall, instead of being the same as her husband's by virtue only of marriage, be ascertained by reference to the same factors as in the case of any other individual capable of having an independent domicile.

(2)   Where immediately before this section came into force a woman was married and then had her husband's domicile by dependence, she is to be treated as retaining that domicile (as a domicile of choice, if it is not also her domicile of origin) unless and until it is changed by acquisition or revival of another domicile either on or after the coming into force of this section.

(3)   This section extends to England and Wales, Scotland and Northern Ireland.

[. . .]

PART III
JURISDICTION IN CONSISTORIAL CAUSES (SCOTLAND)

7   Jurisdiction of Court of Session

(1)   Subsections [(2A) to (10)] below shall have effect, subject to section 12(6) of this Act, with respect to the jurisdiction of the Court of Session to entertain—

(a)   an action for divorce, separation, declarator of nullity of marriage, declarator of marriage; [or

(aa)   an action for declarator of recognition, or non-recognition, of a relevant foreign decree.]

[. . .]

[(2A)   The Court shall have jurisdiction to entertain an action for divorce or separation if (and only if) [either of the parties to the marriage]—

[(a)   is domiciled in Scotland on the date when the action is begun, or

(b)   was habitually resident in Scotland throughout the period of one year ending with that date.]

(3)   The Court shall have jurisdiction to entertain an action for declarator of marriage . . . if (and only if) either of the parties to the marriage—

(a)   is domiciled in Scotland on the date when the action is begun; or

(b)   was habitually resident in Scotland throughout the period of one year ending with that date; or

(c)   died before that date and either—

(i)   was at death domiciled in Scotland, or

(ii)   had been habitually resident in Scotland throughout the period of one year ending with the date of death.

[(3A)   The Court shall have jurisdiction to entertain an action for declarator of nullity of marriage or for declarator of recognition, or non-recognition, of a relevant foreign decree if (and only if) [either of the parties to the marriage]—

[. . .]

[(a)   is domiciled in Scotland on the date when the action is begun,

(b)   was habitually resident in Scotland throughout the period of one year ending with that date, or

(c)   died before that date and either—

(i)   was at death domiciled in Scotland; or

(ii)   had been habitually resident in Scotland throughout the period of one year ending with the date of death.]

[. . .]

(5)   The Court shall, at any time when proceedings are pending in respect of which it has jurisdiction by virtue of subsection (2) [(2A), (3) or (3A)] above (or of this subsection), also have jurisdiction to entertain other proceedings, in respect of the same marriage, for divorce, separation or declarator of marriage [or] declarator of nullity of marriage [. . .] notwithstanding that jurisdiction would not be exercisable [under any of those subsections].

[. . .]

(6)   Nothing in this section affects the rules governing the jurisdiction of the Court of Session to entertain, in an action for divorce, an application for payment by a co-defender of damages or expenses.

(7)   The foregoing provisions of this section are without prejudice to any rule of law whereby the Court of Session has jurisdiction in certain circumstances to entertain actions for separation as a matter of necessity and urgency.

(8)   No action for divorce in respect of a marriage shall be entertained by the Court of Session by virtue of [this section] while proceedings for divorce or nullity of marriage, begun before the commencement of this Act, are pending (in respect of the same marriage) in England and Wales, Northern Ireland, the Channel Islands or the Isle of Man; and provision may be made by rules of court as to when, for the purposes of this subsection, proceedings are to be treated as begun or pending in any of those places.

[(9)   In this section, 'relevant foreign decree' means a decree of divorce, nullity or separation granted outwith [the United Kingdom, the Channel Islands and the Isle of Man.]

(10)   References in subsection (3A) to a marriage shall, in the case of an action for declarator of recognition, or non-recognition, of a relevant foreign decree, be construed as references to the marriage to which the relevant foreign decree relates.]

8   Jurisdiction of sheriff court in respect of actions for separation

(1)   Subsections (2) to [(6)] below shall have effect, subject to section 12(6) of this Act, with respect to the jurisdiction of the sheriff court to entertain—

[(za)   an action for declarator of marriage;]

[(a)]   an action for separation [or divorce.]; [. . .]

[(b)   an action for declarator of recognition, or non-recognition, of a relevant foreign decree] [; and

(c)   an action for declarator of nullity of marriage.]

(2)   The court shall have jurisdiction to entertain an action for separation [or divorce . . .] if (and only if)—

[(a)   either of the parties to the marriage—

(i)   is domiciled in Scotland on the date when the action is begun, or

(ii)   was habitually resident in Scotland throughout the period of one year ending with that date, and]

(b)   either party to the marriage—

(i)   was resident in the sheriffdom for a period of forty days ending with that date, or

(ii)   had been resident in the sheriffdom for a period of not less than forty days ending not more than forty days before the said date, and has no known residence in Scotland at that date.

[(2ZA)   The court has jurisdiction to entertain an action for declarator of marriage if (and only if)—

(a)   either party to the marriage—

(i)   was resident in the sheriffdom for a period of 40 days ending with the date on which the action is begun, or

(ii)   had been resident in the sheriffdom for a period of not less than 40 days ending not more than 40 days before that date, and has no known residence in Scotland on that date, and

(b) any of the following requirements is met in relation to either of the parties to the marriage—

    (i) the party is domiciled in Scotland on the date on which the action is begun,

    (ii) the party was habitually resident in Scotland throughout the period of one year ending with that date, or

    (iii) the party died before that date and either—

        (A) was at death domiciled in Scotland, or

        (B) had been habitually resident in Scotland throughout the period of one year ending with the date of death.]

[(2A) The court shall have jurisdiction to entertain an action for declarator of nullity of marriage [or for declarator of recognition, or non-recognition, of a relevant foreign decree] if (and only if)—

(a) either party to the marriage—

    (i) was resident in the sheriffdom for a period of forty days ending with the date when the action is begun; or

    (ii) had been resident in the sheriffdom for a period of not less than forty days ending not more than forty days before that date and has no known residence in Scotland at that date; and

[(b) either party to the marriage—

    (i) is domiciled in Scotland on the date when the action is begun,

    (ii) was habitually resident in Scotland throughout the period of one year ending with that date, or

    (iii) died before that date and either—

        (A) was at death domiciled in Scotland, or

        (B) had been habitually resident in Scotland throughout the period of one year ending with the date of death.]

[. . .]

(3) In respect of any marriage, the court shall have jurisdiction to entertain an action for separation [or divorce] [or declarator of [marriage or of] nullity of marriage] (notwithstanding that jurisdiction would not be exercisable under subsection (2) [, (2ZA)] [or (2A)] above) if it is begun at a time when an original action is pending in respect of the marriage; and for this purpose 'original action' means an action in respect of which the court has jurisdiction by virtue of subsection (2) [, (2ZA)] [(2A) or] this subsection.

(4) The foregoing provisions of this section are without prejudice to any jurisdiction of a sheriff court to entertain an action of separation [or divorce] [or declarator of [marriage or of] nullity of marriage] remitted to it in pursuance of any enactment or rule of court [. . .].

[(5) In this section, 'relevant foreign decree' has the meaning given by section 7(9).

(6) References in subsection (2) to a marriage shall, in the case of an action for declarator of recognition, or non-recognition, of a relevant foreign decree, be construed as references to the marriage to which the relevant foreign decree relates.]

[8A   Same sex marriages

(1) Sections 7 and 8 do not apply in relation to marriages between persons of the same sex.

(2) Schedule 1B (jurisdiction in relation to same sex marriages (Scotland)) has effect.]

10   Ancillary and collateral orders

(1) [Where after the commencement of this Act, an application is competently

made to the Court of Session or to a sheriff court for the making, or the variation or recall, of an order which is ancillary or collateral to] an action for any of the following remedies, namely, divorce, separation, declarator of marriage and declarator of nullity of marriage (whether the application is made in the same proceedings or in other proceedings and whether it is made before or after the pronouncement of a final decree in the action), then, if the court has or, as the case may be, had by virtue of this Act or of any enactment or rule of law in force before the commencement of this Act jurisdiction to entertain the action, it shall have jurisdiction to entertain the application [. . .] whether or not it would have jurisdiction to do so apart from this subsection.

[(1A) For the purposes of subsection (1) above, references to an application for the making, or the variation or recall, of an order are references to the making, or the variation or recall, of an order relating to children, aliment, financial provision on divorce, judicial separation, nullity of marriage or expenses.]

[. . .]

(2) It is hereby declared that where—

(a) the Court of Session has jurisdiction by virtue of this section to entertain an application for the variation or recall as respects any person of an order made by it, and

(b) the order is one to which section 8 (variation and recall by the sheriff of certain orders made by the Court of Session) of the Law Reform (Miscellaneous Provisions) (Scotland) Act 1966 applies,

then, for the purposes of any application under the said section 8 for the variation or recall of the order in so far as it relates to that person, the sheriff, as defined in that section, has jurisdiction as respects that person to exercise the power conferred on him by that section.

11 Sisting of certain actions

[(1)] The provisions of Schedule 3 to this Act shall have effect with respect to the sisting of actions for any of the following remedies, namely, divorce, separation, declarator of marriage or declarator of nullity of marriage, and with respect to the other matters mentioned in that Schedule; but nothing in that Schedule—

(a) requires or authorises a sist of an action which is pending when this Act comes into force; or

(b) prejudices any power to sist an action which is exercisable by any court apart from the Schedule.

[. . .]

12 Supplementary

(1) In relation to any action for any of the following three remedies, namely, declarator of marriage, declarator of nullity of marriage, and declarator of freedom and putting to silence, references in this Part of this Act to the marriage shall be construed as including references to the alleged, or, as the case may be, the purported, marriage.

(2) References in this Part of this Act to an action for a particular remedy shall be construed, in relation to a case where the remedy is sought along with other remedies in one action, as references to so much of the proceedings in the action as relates to the particular remedy.

(3) References in this Part of this Act to the remedy of separation shall be construed, in relation to an action in a sheriff court, as references to the remedy of separation and aliment.

(4) For the purposes of this Act the period during which an action in the Court of Session or a sheriff court is pending shall be regarded as including any period while the taking of an appeal is competent and the period while any proceedings on appeal are pending; and in this subsection references to an appeal include references to a reclaiming motion.

(5) In this Part of this Act—

(a) any reference to an enactment shall, unless the contrary intention appears, be construed as a reference to that enactment as amended or extended, and as including a reference thereto as applied, by or under any other enactment (including this Act);

[. . .]

(6) Nothing in this Part of this Act affects any court's jurisdiction to entertain any proceedings begun before the commencement of this Act.

(7) Subject to subsection (6) above, the enactments described in Schedule 4 to this Act shall have effect subject to the amendments therein specified, being amendments consequential on the provisions of this Part of this Act.

DIVORCE (SCOTLAND) ACT 1976
(1976, c 39)

Divorce

1 [Grounds of divorce]

(1) In an action for divorce the court may grant decree of divorce if, but only if, it is established in accordance with the following provisions of this Act that—

[(a)] the marriage has broken down irretrievably [, or

(b) [subject to subsection (3B)] an interim gender recognition certificate under the Gender Recognition Act 2004 has, after the date of the marriage, been issued to either party to the marriage.]

References in this Act (other than in sections 5(1) and 13 of this Act) to an action for divorce are to be construed as references to such an action brought after the commencement of this Act.

(2) The irretrievable breakdown of a marriage shall, subject to the following provisions of this Act, be taken to be established in an action for divorce if—

(a) since the date of the marriage the defender has committed adultery; or

(b) since the date of the marriage the defender has at any time behaved (whether or not as a result of mental abnormality and whether such behaviour has been active or passive) in such a way that the pursuer cannot reasonably be expected to cohabit with the defender; or

[. . .]

(d) there has been no cohabitation between the parties at any time during a continuous period of [one year] after the date of the marriage and immediately preceding the bringing of the action and the defender consents to the granting of decree of divorce; or

(e) there has been no cohabitation between the parties at any time during a continuous period of [two] years after the date of the marriage and immediately preceding the bringing of the action.

(3) The irretrievable breakdown of a marriage shall not be taken to be established in an action for divorce by reason of subsection (2)(a) of this section if the adultery mentioned in the said subsection (2)(a) has been connived at in such a way as to raise the defence of *lenocinium* or has been condoned by the pursuer's cohabitation with the defender in the knowledge or belief that the defender has committed the adultery.

[(3A) For the avoidance of doubt, in relation to marriage between persons of the same sex, adultery has the same meaning as it has in relation to marriage between persons of different sexes.

(3B) Subsection (1)(b)—

(a) does not apply where, under the Gender Recognition Act 2004, the Gender Recognition Panel issue a full gender recognition certificate to the person to whom the interim gender recognition certificate was issued, but

(b) continues to apply despite a full gender recognition certificate being issued to that person by the sheriff under section 4E of that Act.]

(4)   Provision shall be made by act of sederunt—

(a)   for the purpose of ensuring that, where in an action for divorce to which subsection (2)(d) of this section relates the defender consents to the granting of decree, he has been given such information as will enable him to understand—

(i)   the consequences to him of his consenting as aforesaid; and

(ii)   the steps which he must take to indicate his consent; and

(b)   prescribing the manner in which the defender in such an action shall indicate his consent, and any withdrawal of such consent, to the granting of decree;

and where the defender has indicated (and not withdrawn) his consent in the prescribed manner, such indication shall be sufficient evidence of such consent.

[. . .]

(6)   In an action for divorce the standard of proof required to establish the ground of the action shall be on balance of probability.

2   Encouragement of reconciliation

(1)   At any time before granting decree [under paragraph (a) of section 1(1)], if it appears to the court that there is a reasonable prospect of a reconciliation between the parties, it shall continue, or further continue, the action for such period as it thinks proper to enable attempts to be made to effect such a reconciliation; and if during any such continuation the parties cohabit with one another, no account shall be taken of such cohabitation for the purposes of that action.

(2)   Adultery shall not be held to have been condoned within the meaning of section 1(3) of this Act by reason only of the fact that after the commission of the adultery the pursuer has continued or resumed cohabitation with the defender, provided that the pursuer has not cohabited with the defender at any time after the end of the period of three months from the date on which such cohabitation as is referred to in the said section 1(3) was continued or resumed as aforesaid.

[. . .]

(4)   In considering whether any period mentioned in paragraph [. . .], (d), or (e) of section 1(2) of this Act has been continuous no account shall be taken of any period or periods not exceeding six months in all during which the parties cohabited with one another; but no such period or periods during which the parties cohabited with one another shall count as part of the period of non-cohabitation required by any of those paragraphs.

3   Action for divorce following on decree of separation

(1)   The court may grant decree in an action for divorce notwithstanding that decree of separation has previously been granted to the pursuer on the same, or substantially the same, facts as those averred in support of the action for divorce; and in any such action (other than an action for divorce by reason of section 1(2)(a) of this Act) the court may treat an extract decree of separation lodged in process as sufficient proof of the facts upon which such decree was granted.

(2)   Nothing in this section shall entitle the court to grant decree of divorce without receiving evidence from the pursuer.

[3A   Postponement of decree of divorce where religious impediment to remarry exists

(1)   Notwithstanding that irretrievable breakdown of a marriage has been established in an action for divorce, the court may—

(a)   on the application of a party ('the applicant'); and

(b)   if satisfied—

(i)   that subsection (2) applies; and

(ii)   that it is just and reasonable to do so,

postpone the grant of decree in the action until it is satisfied that the other party has complied with subsection (3).

(2)   This subsection applies where—

(a)   the applicant is prevented from entering into a religious marriage by virtue of a requirement of the religion of that marriage; and

(b)   the other party can act so as to remove, or enable or contribute to the removal of, the impediment which prevents that marriage.

(3)   A party complies with this subsection by acting in the way described in subsection (2)(b).

(4)   The court may, whether or not on the application of a party and notwithstanding that subsection (2) applies, recall a postponement under subsection (1).

(5)   The court may, before recalling a postponement under subsection (1), order the other party to produce a certificate from a relevant religious body confirming that the other party has acted in the way described in subsection (2)(b).

(6)   For the purposes of subsection (5), a religious body is 'relevant' if the applicant considers the body competent to provide the confirmation referred to in that subsection.

(7)   In this section—

'religious marriage' means a marriage solemnised by a marriage celebrant of a prescribed religious body, and 'religion of that marriage' shall be construed accordingly;

'prescribed' means prescribed by regulations made by the Scottish Ministers.

(8)   Any reference in this section to a marriage celebrant of a prescribed religious body is a reference to—

(a)   a minister, clergyman, pastor or priest of such a body;

(b)   a person who has, on the nomination of such a body, been registered under section 9 of the Marriage (Scotland) Act 1977 as empowered to solemnise marriages; or

(c)   any person who is recognised by such a body as entitled to solemnise marriages on its behalf.

(9)   Regulations under subsection (7) shall be made by statutory instrument; and any such instrument shall be subject to annulment in pursuance of a resolution of the Scottish Parliament.]

Actions for separation

4   Actions for separation

(1)   Sections 1, 2 and 11 of this Act shall apply to an action for separation or separation and aliment brought after the commencement of this Act and decree in such action as those sections apply to an action for divorce and decree therein subject to—

(a)   the modification that any reference to irretrievable breakdown of a marriage shall be construed as a reference to grounds justifying decree of separation of the parties to a marriage; and

(b)   all other necessary modifications.

(2)   In an action for separation or separation and aliment brought after the commencement of this Act, decree of separation shall not be pronounced except in accordance with the provisions of this section.

[. . .]

Supplemental

[. . .]

10   Right of husband to cite paramour as a co-defender and to sue for damages abolished

(1)   After the commencement of this Act the following rights of a husband shall be abolished, that is to say—

(a)   the right to cite a paramour of his wife as a co-defender in an action for divorce, and

(b)   the right to claim or to obtain damages (including solatium) from a paramour by way of reparation.

(2)   Nothing in the provisions of the foregoing subsection shall preclude the court from awarding the expenses of the action for or against the paramour or alleged paramour in accordance with the practice of the court.

[. . .]

11   Curator *ad litem* to be appointed in certain cases

Provision shall be made by act of sederunt for the purpose of securing that, where in an action for divorce the defender is suffering from mental illness, the court shall appoint a curator *ad litem* to the defender.

12   Amendments, repeals and transitional provisions

[. . .]

(3)   Subject to the following provisions of this section and without prejudice to the operation of section 38 of the Interpretation Act 1889 (effect of repeals), nothing in this section shall affect any proceedings brought, anything done, or the operation of any order made, under any enactment repealed by this section; nor shall anything in this Act be taken to revive any rule of law superseded by any enactment repealed by this section.

(4)   Anything which, prior to the commencement of this Act, could have been done under section 2 of the Divorce (Scotland) Act 1938 or section 26 or 27 of the Succession (Scotland) Act 1964 may, after the commencement of this Act, be done under the corresponding provision of section 5 or 6 of this Act.

(5)   An order under section 2 of the Divorce (Scotland) Act 1938 for the payment of an annual or periodical allowance to or for the behoof of a child of the marriage may, after the commencement of this Act, be varied or recalled by a subsequent order under subsection (2) of that section as if that section had not been repealed by this Act.

(6)   Subsection (5) of section 5 of this Act shall apply in relation to an order for the payment of an annual or periodical allowance under section 2 of the Divorce (Scotland) Act 1938 or of a periodical allowance under section 26 of the Succession (Scotland) Act 1964 as it applies in relation to an order for the payment of a periodical allowance under the said section 5.

13   Interpretation

(1)   In this Act, unless the context otherwise requires—

'action for divorce' has the meaning assigned to it by section 1(1) of this Act;

'the court' means in relation to an action [. . .] the Court of Session or the sheriff [court] as the case may require.

(2)   For the purposes of this Act, the parties to a marriage shall be held to cohabit with one another only when they are in fact living together as man and wife; and 'cohabitation' shall be construed accordingly.

(3)   References in this Act to any enactment are references to that enactment as amended, and include references thereto as applied, by any other enactment, including, except where the context otherwise requires, this Act.

14   Citation, commencement and extent

(1)   This Act may be cited as the Divorce (Scotland) Act 1976.

(2)   This Act except section 8 shall come into operation on 1st January 1977.

(3)   So much of section 12 of, and Schedule 1 to, this Act as affects the operation of section 16 of the Maintenance Orders Act 1950 shall extend to England and Wales and to Northern Ireland as well as Scotland, but save as aforesaid this Act shall extend to Scotland only.

MARRIAGE (SCOTLAND) ACT 1977
(1977, c 15)

Minimum age for marriage

1 Minimum age for marriage

(1)   No person domiciled in Scotland may marry before he attains the age of 16.

(2)   A marriage solemnised in Scotland between persons either of whom is under the age of 16 shall be void.

Forbidden degrees

2 Marriage of related persons

[(1)   Subject to subsection (1A), a marriage between persons who are related to each other in a forbidden degree is void if solemnised—

(a)   in Scotland; or

(b)   at a time when either party is domiciled in Scotland.

(1ZA)   For the purposes of subsection (1), a person is related to another person in a forbidden degree if related to that person in a degree specified in Schedule 1.]

[(1A)]   [A person who is related to another person in a degree specified in paragraph 2 of Schedule 1 (relationships by affinity) is not related to that person in a forbidden degree] if—

(a)   both parties have attained the age of 21 at the time of the marriage; and

(b)   the younger party has not at any time before attaining the age of 18 lived in the same household as the other party and been treated by the other party as a child of his family.

[. . .]

[(1C)   For the purposes of paragraph 2 of Schedule 1, 'spouse' means—

(a)   in the case of a marriage between persons of different sexes, a wife in relation to her husband or a husband in relation to his wife; and

(b)   in the case of a marriage between persons of the same sex, one of the parties to the marriage in relation to the other.]

(2)   For the purposes of this section a degree of relationship exists—

(a)   in the case of a degree specified in paragraph 1 of Schedule 1 to this Act, whether it is of the full blood or the half blood.

[. . .]

(3)   Where a person is related to another person in a degree not specified in Schedule 1 to this Act that degree of relationship shall not, in Scots law, bar a valid marriage between them; but this subsection is without prejudice to—

(a)   the effect which a degree of relationship not so specified may have under the provisions of a system of law other than Scots law in a case where such provisions apply as the law of the place of celebration of a marriage or as the law of a person's domicile; or

(b)   any rule of law that a marriage may not be contracted between persons either of whom is married to a third person.

[(4)   References in this section and in Schedule 1 to this Act to relationships and degrees of relationship shall be construed in accordance with section 1(1) of the Law Reform (Parent and Child) (Scotland) Act 1986.

(5)   Where the parties to an intended marriage are related in a degree specified in paragraph 2 of Schedule 1 to this Act, either party may (whether or not an objection to the marriage has been submitted in accordance with section 5(1) of this Act) apply to the Court of Session for a declarator that the conditions specified in paragraphs (a) and (b) of subsection (1A) above are fulfilled in relation to the intended marriage.]

[(6)   Subsection (1A) [. . .] above and paragraph 2 [. . .] of Schedule 1 to this Act have effect subject to the following modifications in the case of a party to a marriage whose gender has become the acquired gender under the Gender Recognition Act 2004 ('the relevant person').

(7) Any reference in [subsection (1C)(a) as it applies to paragraph 2 of Schedule 1] to a [. . .] wife or [. . .] husband of the relevant person includes (respectively) any [. . .] husband or [. . .] wife of the relevant person.]

[(7A) This section and Schedule 1 to this Act have effect as if any reference in paragraphs 1 and 2 of that Schedule to a [parent] within any of the degrees of relationship specified [. . .] included a woman who is a parent of a child by virtue of section 42 or 43 of the Human Fertilisation and Embryology Act 2008 (c 22).]
[. . .]

Preliminaries to regular marriage

3 Notice of intention to marry

(1) Subject to subsections (2) to (4) below, each of the parties to a marriage intended to be solemnised in Scotland shall submit to the district registrar a notice, in the prescribed form, of intention to marry (in this Act referred to as a 'marriage notice') [and] the prescribed fee, his birth certificate and—

(a) if he has previously been married and the marriage has been dissolved, a copy of the decree of divorce, dissolution or annulment;

[(aa) if he has previously been in civil partnership and the civil partnership has been dissolved, a copy of the decree of dissolution or annulment;]

[(b) if the person has previously been married and the marriage ended on the death of the other party to that marriage, the death certificate of that other party;

(ba) if the person has previously been in a civil partnership which ended on the death of the other party to the civil partnership, the death certificate of that other party;

(bb) if the person is in a qualifying civil partnership within the meaning of [section 5(6)(i)(A)] with the other party to the intended marriage, an extract from the entry in the civil partnership register relating to the civil partnership;]

[(bc) if the person is in a qualifying civil partnership within the meaning of section 5(6)(a)(i)(B) or (b) with the other party to the intended marriage—

(i) information equivalent to an extract from an entry in the civil partnership register; and

(ii) such documentary evidence in support of that information, as the district registrar may require;]

(c) in any case where a certificate is required under subsection (5) below, that certificate;

[(d) where he is related to the other party in a degree specified in paragraph 2 of Schedule 1 to this Act, a declaration in the prescribed form stating—

(i) the degree of relationship; and

(ii) that the younger party has not at any time before attaining the age of 18 lived in the same household as the other party and been treated by the other party as a child of his family.]

(2) If a party is unable to submit his birth certificate or any document referred to in paragraph (a) [, (aa), (b), (ba), (bb) or (bc)] of subsection (1) above, he may in lieu thereof make a declaration stating that for reasons specified in that declaration it is impracticable for him to submit that certificate or document; and he shall provide the district registrar with such—

(a) information in respect of the matters to which such certificate or document would have related; and

(b) documentary evidence in support of that information, as the district registrar may require.

(3) If any document submitted under subsection (1) above is written in a language other than English, the party submitting it shall [, unless subsection (3ZA) applies,] [also submit] a translation of it in English certified by the translator as a correct translation.

[(3ZA)   This subsection applies where—

(a)   the document submitted is accompanied by a multilingual standard form issued by an authority in a Member State of the European Union in accordance with Regulation (EU) 2016/1191 of the European Parliament and of the Council; and

(b)   the district registrar considers that the information included in the multilingual standard form is sufficient for processing the document.]

[(3A)   A person submitting a notice under subsection (1) above shall make and attest in the prescribed manner the necessary declaration (the form for which shall be included in any form prescribed for the notice).

(3B)   The necessary declaration is a declaration that the person submitting the notice believes that the parties to the marriage are eligible to be married to each other.]

(4)   Where a party to a marriage intended to be solemnised in Scotland is residing in another part of the United Kingdom, he may submit to the district registrar a valid certificate for marriage (in this Act referred to as an 'approved certificate') issued in that other part: and where that party so submits an approved certificate, he need not, unless the Registrar General so directs, comply with the other provisions of this section.

[(4A)   A district registrar to whom a notice under subsection (1) is submitted may require the person submitting the notice to provide the district registrar with specified nationality evidence relating to each of the parties to the marriage.

(4B)   A requirement under subsection (4A) may be imposed at any time—

(a)   on or after the submitting of the notice under subsection (1); but

(b)   before the district registrar completes the Marriage Schedule.

(4C)   In subsection (4A), 'specified nationality evidence' means such evidence of that person's nationality as may be specified in guidance issued by the Registrar General.]

(5)   A party to a marriage intended to be solemnised in Scotland who is not domiciled in any part of the United Kingdom is required, if practicable, to submit under subsection (1)(c) above a certificate, issued by a competent authority in the state in which the party is domiciled, to the effect that he is not known to be subject to any legal incapacity (in terms of the law of that state) which would prevent his marrying:

Provided that such a party—

(i)   may, where under the law of the state in which he is domiciled his personal law is that of another foreign state, submit in lieu of the said certificate a like certificate issued by a competent authority in that other state;

(ii)   need not submit a certificate under paragraph (c) of subsection (1) above—

(a)   if he has been resident in the United Kingdom for a period of 2 or more years immediately before the date on which he submits a marriage notice under that subsection in respect of the said marriage; or

[(b)   if no such certificate has been issued only by reason of the fact that the validity of a divorce or annulment granted by a court of civil jurisdiction in Scotland or entitled to recognition in Scotland under section 44 or 45 of the Family Law Act 1986 is not recognised in the state in which the certificate would otherwise have been issued.] [;

(c)   if no such certificate has been issued only by reason of the fact that the parties to the intended marriage are of the same sex [; or

(d)   if no such certificate has been issued only by reason of the fact that the law of the state in which the party is domiciled prevents the parties to a qualifying civil partnership within the meaning of section 5(6) from marrying.]

[(6)   In this section, 'the district registrar' means—

(a)   where the marriage is to be solemnised in a registration district, the district registrar for that district;

(b)   where the marriage is to be solemnised in Scottish waters—

(i)   in the case where the marriage is to be solemnised by an approved celebrant, the district registrar for any registration district;

(ii)   in the case where the marriage is to be solemnised by an authorised registrar, the district registrar for the registration district of the proposed authorised registrar.]

[3A   Additional information if party not relevant national

(1)   This section applies to a marriage notice submitted to a district registrar in accordance with section 3 if one, or each, of the parties to the proposed marriage is not a relevant national.

(2)   But this section does not apply if the parties are in a qualifying civil partnership (within the meaning of section 5(6)(1)) with each other.

(3)   For each party to the proposed marriage who is not a relevant national, the notice shall be accompanied by whichever of statements A, B or C is applicable to that person.

(4)   Statement A is a statement that the person has the appropriate immigration status.

(5)   Statement B is a statement that the person holds a relevant visa in respect of the proposed marriage.

(6)   Statement C is a statement that the person neither—

(a)   has the appropriate immigration status, nor

(b)   holds a relevant visa in respect of the proposed marriage.

(7)   If the notice is accompanied by the statement referred to in the first column of an entry in this table, the notice shall also be accompanied by the information and photographs referred to in the second column of that entry (insofar as that entry is applicable to the parties to the proposed marriage)—

If the notice is accompanied by this statement . . .	. . . the notice shall also be accompanied by . . .
Statement A (in respect of one or both of the parties to the proposed marriage	For each party in respect of whom statement A is made, details of the particular immigration status which that party has
Statement B (in respect of one or both of the parties to the proposed marriage)	1. For each party, a specified photograph of that party 2. For each party in respect of whom statement B is made, details of the relevant visa which that party has
Statement C (in respect of one or both of the parties to the proposed marriage)	1. For each party, a specified photograph of that party 2. For each party, the usual address of that party 3. For each party who has previously used any name or names other than the person's name stated in the marriage notice, a statement of the other name or names 4. For each party who currently uses, or has previously used, an alias or aliases, a statement of the alias or aliases

(8) If the notice is accompanied by more than one of statements A, B and C, subsection (7) shall be complied with in relation to each of those statements; but where the notice is accompanied by statements B and C, subsection (7) does not require the notice to be accompanied by more than one specified photograph of each party.

(9) If the notice is accompanied by statement C for a party to the proposed marriage—

(a) the notice may also be accompanied by a statement ('statement D') of that person's immigration position in the United Kingdom;

(b) if the notice is accompanied by statement D for a party to the proposed marriage, the person may provide the district registrar with details of his immigration position in the United Kingdom; and

(c) if any such details are provided, the district registrar shall record them.

(10) In this section and section 3B—

(a) a reference—

(i) to a person having the appropriate immigration status, or

(ii) to a person holding a relevant visa,

is to be construed in accordance with section 49 of the 2014 Act;

(b) a reference to the particular immigration status which a person has is a reference to the immigration status set out in any of paragraphs (a) to (c) of section 49(2) of that Act which the person has;

(c) a reference to a person's immigration position in the United Kingdom includes a reference to the person's not being entitled to be in the United Kingdom.

(11) In this section 'specified photograph' means a photograph that is in accordance with regulations made by the Secretary of State under section 54(2) of, and paragraph 3 of Schedule 5 to, the 2014 Act (and for this purpose 'photograph' includes other kinds of images).]

[3B Additional evidence if party not relevant national

(1) If a marriage notice to which section 3A(1) applies ('the notice') is accompanied by statement A (referred to in section 3A(4)) and accordingly is also accompanied by details of the particular immigration status which a party to the proposed marriage has, the notice shall also be accompanied by specified evidence of that status.

(2) If the notice is accompanied by statement B (referred to in section 3A(5)), the notice shall also be accompanied by specified evidence of the holding of the relevant visa by the party to the proposed marriage.

(3) If, in accordance with section 3A(7), the notice is accompanied by the usual address of a party to the proposed marriage, the notice shall also be accompanied by specified evidence that it is that party's usual address.

(4) If the notice is accompanied by statement D (referred to in section 3A(9)), the notice may also be accompanied by evidence of the person's immigration position in the United Kingdom.

(5) If subsection (1) or (2) applies to the notice, and the notice is not accompanied by the specified evidence required by that subsection, the notice shall be accompanied by—

(a) photographs and addresses of the kinds referred to in paragraphs 1 and 2 in the relevant entry in section 3A(7);

(b) as respects the usual address of each party that is provided in accordance with paragraph (a), specified evidence that the address provided is that party's usual address; and

(c) names and aliases of the kinds referred to in paragraphs 3 and 4 in the relevant entry in section 3A(7) (insofar as those paragraphs are applicable to the parties to the proposed marriage).

(6) In this section—

'relevant entry in section 3A(7)' means the second column of the last entry in the table in section 3A(7);

'specified evidence' means evidence that is in accordance with regulations made by the Secretary of State under section 54(2) of, and paragraph 3 of Schedule 5 to, the 2014 Act.]

[3C Declaration to accompany information and evidence

Where the marriage notice is accompanied by—

    (a)   information provided in accordance with section 3A, and

    (b)   information and evidence provided in accordance with section 3B,

that information and evidence shall also be accompanied by a declaration in writing and signed by the party who makes it that the party believes all of the information and evidence accompanying the notice to be true.]

[3D Rejection of false information or evidence

(1)   A district registrar may reject—

    (a)   any evidence relating to a party's nationality provided in accordance with section 3(4A)(2),

    (b)   any information or photograph provided under section 3A or 3B, or

    (c)   any evidence provided under section 3B,

if (in particular) the district registrar has reasonable grounds for suspecting that the information, photograph or evidence is false.

(2)   If the district registrar rejects any information, photograph or evidence, the district registrar may proceed under this Act as if the rejected information, photograph or evidence had not been provided.

(3)   This section does not limit the powers of district registrars to reject anything provided under any other enactment.

(4)   In this section 'enactment' includes an enactment comprised in, or an instrument made under, an Act of the Scottish Parliament.]

[3E Marriage notice: treated as not given

(1)   Where any of the requirements mentioned in subsection (2) is applicable but not complied with by either or both parties to the proposed marriage, the parties are to be taken not to have submitted a marriage notice under section 3.

(2)   The requirements are—

    (a)   a requirement imposed by or under any of the following provisions of this Act—

        (i)   section 3(4A);

        (ii)   section 3A(3) to (8);

        (iii)   section 3B(3);

        (iv)   section 3B(5);

    (b)   the requirement imposed by section 21(2) of the Asylum and Immigration (Treatment of Claimants, etc) Act 2004.]

[3F Referral of proposed marriage to Secretary of State

(1)   On every occasion when a marriage notice is submitted under section 3, a district registrar shall decide whether or not each of the parties to the proposed marriage is an exempt person.

(2)   But this section does not apply if the parties are in a qualifying civil partnership (within the meaning of section 5(6)) with each other.

(3)   In making a decision under subsection (1) about a party to a proposed marriage, a district registrar may rely on any advice given in relation to that decision by the Secretary of State.

(4)   In a case where—

    (a)   section 3A applies to the marriage notice, and

    (b)   specified evidence required by section 3B(1) or (2) in relation to a party to the proposed marriage is not produced in accordance with that section, the district registrar shall decide that that party to the proposed marriage is not an exempt person.

(5)   If the district registrar decides that either of the parties is not an exempt person, or that both of the parties are not exempt persons, the district registrar shall—

(a)   refer the proposed marriage to the Secretary of State;

(b)   notify the parties to the proposed marriage that the proposed marriage must be referred to the Secretary of State;

(c)   give the parties to the proposed marriage prescribed information about—

(i)   the effects of the referral;

(ii)   the requirement under regulations to notify the Secretary of State of changes of address.

(6)   The district registrar shall act in accordance with regulations when complying with the duty in subsection (5)(a) to refer a proposed marriage to the Secretary of State.

(7)   If the district registrar refers the proposed marriage to the Secretary of State, this Act has effect in relation to the proposed marriage subject to the modifications in Schedule 1A.

(8)   In this section—

(a)   a reference to a person being an exempt person has the same meaning as in section 49 of the 2014 Act;

(b)   'prescribed information' means information prescribed in regulations;

(c)   'regulations' means regulations made by the Secretary of State under section 54(2) of, and Schedule 5 to, the 2014 Act.]

4   Marriage notice book and list of intended marriages

(1)   On receipt of a marriage notice or an approved certificate in respect of a party to an intended marriage, the district registrar shall forthwith enter such particulars, extracted from such notice or certificate, as may be prescribed, together with the date of receipt by him of such notice or certificate, in a book (in this Act referred to as 'the marriage notice book') supplied to him for that purpose by the Registrar General.

[(2)   The district registrar shall maintain a list of the intended marriages in respect of which he has received a marriage notice or an approved certificate (the 'district list').

(2A)   Subject to subsection (2B) below, the district list shall be displayed in a conspicuous place at the registration office.

(2B)   If the registration office comprises more than one set of premises, it shall be sufficient for the purpose of subsection (2A) above if the district registrar displays the list in a conspicuous place at the principal premises only.

(2C)   The district registrar shall, as soon as practicable after he has received a marriage notice or an approved certificate in relation to an intended marriage—

(a)   make an entry in the district list containing the relevant particulars of the marriage; and

(b)   provide (in such form and by such means as the Registrar General thinks fit) the relevant particulars of the marriage to the Registrar General.

(2D)   The Registrar General shall maintain a list of proposed marriages in Scotland (the 'Scottish list').

(2E)   The Registrar General shall make the Scottish list available for public inspection (at such locations, by such means and in such forms as the Registrar General thinks fit).

(2F)   The Registrar General shall, as soon as practicable after the relevant particulars of a marriage are provided to him under subsection (2C)(b) above, make an entry in the Scottish list containing those particulars.

(2G)   An entry in a district list or the Scottish list shall remain in that list until the proposed date of the marriage to which it relates has elapsed.]

(3)   Any person claiming that he may have reason to submit an objection to an intended marriage, or to the issue of a certificate under section 7 of this Act to a party to such marriage, may, free of charge and at any time when the registration office is open for public business, inspect any entry relating to the marriage in the marriage notice book.

[(4)   For the purpose of this section, the relevant particulars of a marriage are such particulars, extracted from the marriage notice book, as may be prescribed.

(5)   In this section and sections 5 and 6 of this Act, 'the district registrar' means—

(a)   where the marriage is to be solemnised in a registration district, the district registrar for that district;

(b)   where the marriage is to be solemnised in Scottish waters—

(i)   in the case where the marriage is to be solemnised by an approved celebrant, the district registrar to whom the marriage notices or approved certificates in respect of the marriage were submitted;

(ii)   in the case where the marriage is to be solemnised by an authorised registrar, the district registrar for the registration district of the proposed authorised registrar.]

[(6)   This section is subject to section 3E.]

5   Objections to marriage

(1)   Any person may at any time before the solemnisation of a marriage in Scotland submit an objection in writing thereto to the district registrar:

Provided that where the objection is on the ground mentioned in subsection (4)(d) below, it shall [not be treated as submitted until there has also been produced to the registrar] a supporting certificate [attested in the prescribed manner] by a registered medical practitioner.

[(1A)   For the purpose of subsection (1) above, an objection which is submitted to the registrar by electronic means is to be treated as in writing if it is received in a form which is legible and capable of being used for subsequent reference.]

(2)   Where the district registrar receives an objection in accordance with subsection (1) above he shall—

(a)   in any case where he is satisfied that the objection relates to no more than a misdescription or inaccuracy in the marriage notice or approved certificate, notify the parties to the marriage of the nature of the objection and make such enquiries into the matter mentioned in it as he thinks fit; and thereafter he shall, subject to the approval of the Registrar General, make any necessary correction to any document relating to the marriage;

(b)   in any other case—

(i)   forthwith notify the Registrar General of the objection;

(ii)   pending consideration of the objection by the Registrar General, suspend the completion or issue of the Marriage Schedule in respect of the marriage;

(iii)   where, in the case of a marriage to be solemnised by an approved celebrant, the Marriage Schedule has already been issued to the parties, if possible notify that celebrant of the objection and advise him not to solemnise the marriage pending the said consideration.

(3)   [Subject to subsection (3A) below,] if the Registrar General is satisfied, on consideration of an objection of which he has received notification under subsection (2)(b)(i) above, that—

(a)   there is a legal impediment to the marriage, he shall direct the district registrar to take all reasonable steps to ensure that the marriage does not take place and shall notify, or direct the district registrar to notify, the parties to the intended marriage accordingly;

(b)   there is no legal impediment to the marriage, he shall inform the district registrar to that effect.

[(3A)   Where—

(a)   an objection of which the Registrar General has received notification under subsection (2)(b)(i) above is on the ground that—

(i)   the parties are related in a degree specified in paragraph 2 of Schedule 1 to this Act; and

(ii)   the conditions specified in paragraphs (a) and (b) of section 2(1A) of this Act are not satisfied; and

(b)   an extract decree of declarator that those conditions are satisfied, granted on an application under section 2(5) of this Act, is produced to the Registrar General,

the Registrar General shall inform the district registrar that there is no legal impediment to the marriage on that ground.

(4)   For the purposes of [this section] and section 6 of this Act, there is a legal impediment to a marriage where—

(a)   that marriage would be void by virtue of section 2(1) of this Act;

(b)   one of the parties is, or both are, already married [or in civil partnership [other than a qualifying civil partnership with each other]];

(c)   one or both of the parties will be under the age of 16 on the date of solemnisation of the intended marriage;

(d)   one or both of the parties is or are incapable of understanding the nature of a marriage ceremony or of consenting to marriage;

[. . .]

(f)   one or both of the parties is, or are, not domiciled in Scotland and, on a ground other [than—

(i)   one mentioned in paragraphs (a) to (d) above; or

(ii)   the ground that the parties are of the same sex,]

a marriage in Scotland between the parties would be void *ab initio* according to the law of the domicile of the party or parties as the case may be.

(5)   A person who has submitted an objection in accordance with subsection (1) above may at any time withdraw it:

Provided that the Registrar General shall be entitled to have regard to that objection notwithstanding such withdrawal.

[(6)   For the purposes of subsection (4)(b) a 'qualifying civil partnership' is—

(a)   a civil partnership which—

(i)   was registered in—

(A)   Scotland, or

(B)   England and Wales or Northern Ireland; and

(ii)   has not been dissolved, annulled or ended by death; or

(b)   a civil partnership which is treated under Chapter 2 of Part 5 of the Civil Partnership Act 2004 as having formed by virtue of an overseas relationship being registered and has not been dissolved, annulled or ended by death.]

(7)   A civil partnership which was registered outside the United Kingdom under an Order in Council made under Chapter 1 of Part 5 of the Civil Partnership Act 2004 is to be treated for the purposes of [subsection (6)(a)(i)(A)] as having been registered in Scotland if—

(a)   the parties to the civil partnership elected Scotland as the relevant part of the United Kingdom under the Order; and

(b)   details of the civil partnership have been sent to the Registrar General of Births, Deaths and Marriages for Scotland.]

[(8)   A civil partnership which was registered outside the United Kingdom under an Order in Council made under Chapter 1 of Part 5 of the Civil Partnership Act 2004 is to be treated for the purposes of subsection (6)(a)(i)(B) as having been registered in England and Wales or, as the case may be, Northern Ireland if—

(a)   the parties to the civil partnership elected England and Wales or, as the case may be, Northern Ireland as the relevant part of the United Kingdom under the Order; and

(b)   details of the civil partnership have been sent to the Registrar General for England and Wales or, as the case may be, the Registrar General in Northern Ireland.]

6   The Marriage Schedule

(1)   Where the district registrar has received a marriage notice or approved certificate in respect of each of the parties to a marriage intended to be solemnised in Scotland and is satisfied that there is no legal impediment to the marriage or, as the case may be, is informed by the Registrar General under section 5(3)(b) [or (3A)] of this Act that there is no such legal impediment, he shall, subject to subsection (2) below, complete a Marriage Schedule in the prescribed form.

[(1A)   Regulations under subsection (1) prescribing the form of the Marriage Schedule may make different provision for different cases or circumstances.]

(2)   If a period of more than 3 months has elapsed since the date of receipt (as entered by the district registrar in the marriage notice book) of a marriage notice or an approved certificate in respect of a party to the marriage, the Registrar General may direct that the district registrar shall not complete the Marriage Schedule unless that party submits a new marriage notice or approved certificate to the district registrar.

(3)   Subject to subsection (4) below, in the case of a marriage to be solemnised by an approved celebrant, the Marriage Schedule completed in accordance with subsection (1) above shall be issued by the district registrar at the registration office to one or both of the parties to the intended marriage.

(4)   The district registrar shall not issue a Marriage Schedule under subsection (3) above—

(a)   within [28 days] of the date of receipt (as entered by him in the marriage notice book) of a marriage notice in respect of the marriage to which the Marriage Schedule relates, except where—

(i)   he has received a written request from one or both of the parties for the issue of the Marriage Schedule on a specified date within the said [28 days] stating the reason for the request; and

(ii)   he has been authorised to issue the Marriage Schedule on that specified date by the Registrar General;

(b)   on a date earlier than 7 days before the date of the intended marriage unless he has been authorised to issue the Marriage Schedule on that earlier date by the Registrar General.

[(4ZA)   Unless subsection (4ZB) applies, if a proposed marriage is referred to the Secretary of State under section 3F(10) ('the referred marriage') the Registrar General may not authorise the district registrar to issue the Marriage Schedule on the date mentioned in subsection (4)(a)(ii) without the consent of the Secretary of State.

(4ZB)   This subsection applies if the request made under subsection (4)(a)(i) is made because a party to the referred marriage is gravely ill and not expected to recover.]

[(4A)   For the purpose of subsection (4)(a)(i) above, a request which is made by electronic means is to be treated as being written if it is received in a form which is legible and capable of being used for subsequent reference.]

(5)   Subject to subsections (6) and (7) below and section [23A] of this Act, a [religious or belief marriage] may be solemnised only on the date and at the place specified in the Marriage Schedule.

(6)   Subject to subsection (7) below, if, for any reason, the marriage cannot be solemnised on the date or at the place so specified and a new date or place is fixed for the marriage, the district registrar shall—

(a)   issue another Marriage Schedule under subsection (3) above, in lieu of that already issued, specifying that new date or place; or

(b)   substitute, or direct the approved celebrant to substitute, that new date or place in the Marriage Schedule already issued.

(7)   Subsection (6) above shall not apply in a case where the new date fixed for the marriage is more than 3 months after the date for the marriage as specified in the Marriage Schedule already issued or where the new place so fixed is in a different registration district, [is in Scottish waters instead of a registration district or is in a registration district instead of Scottish waters,] but in such a case the Registrar General may, according to the circumstances, direct—

(a)   the district registrar [. . .] to proceed as in paragraph (a) or (b) (whichever the Registrar General considers the more appropriate) of subsection (6) above; or

(b)   each party to the marriage to submit to the said district registrar a new marriage notice or approved certificate.

[(8)   This section has effect subject to section 6A.]

[6A   Marriage notice: false information or evidence

(1)   A district registrar may refuse to complete a Marriage Schedule under section 6 in a case where—

(a)   a marriage notice has been submitted under section 3(1), and

(b)   the district registrar has reasonable grounds for suspecting that a relevant decision was made incorrectly because of the provision of false information or evidence in or accompanying that notice.

(2)   If the district registrar refuses to complete a Marriage Schedule under subsection (1), the parties to the proposed marriage are to be taken not to have submitted a marriage notice under section 3; but that does not prevent criminal proceedings from being brought against either party, or any other person, in relation to the submission of notice.

(3)   This section is without prejudice to any other powers of district registrars to refuse to complete a Marriage Schedule.

(4)   In this section—

'evidence' includes a photograph or other image;

'exempt person' has the same meaning as in section 3F;

'relevant decision' means a decision of a district registrar that a party to the proposed marriage is an exempt person.]

7   Marriage outside Scotland where a party resides in Scotland

(1)   Where a person residing in Scotland is a party to a marriage intended to be solemnised in—

(a)   England or Wales with a party residing in England or Wales and desires; or

(b)   any country, territory or place outside Great Britain, and, for the purpose of complying with the law in force in that country, territory or place, is required to obtain from a competent authority in Scotland,

a certificate in respect of his legal capacity to marry, he may submit, in the form and with the fee and documents specified in [section 3(1)(a), [(aa),] (b) [, (ba), (bb)] and (d)] of this Act, notice of intention to marry to the district registrar for the district in which he resides (the said registrar being in this section referred to as the 'appropriate registrar') as if it were intended that the marriage should be solemnised in that district, and sections 3(2) [, (3) [, (3ZA)] and (4A) to (4C)] and 4 of this Act shall apply accordingly.

(2)   The appropriate registrar shall, if satisfied (after consultation, if the appropriate registrar considers it necessary, with the Registrar General) that a person who has by virtue of subsection (1) above submitted a marriage notice to him is not subject to any legal incapacity (in terms of Scots law) which would prevent his

marrying, issue to that person a certificate in the prescribed form that he is not known to be subject to any such incapacity:

Provided that the certificate shall not be issued earlier than [28 days] after the date of receipt (as entered by the appropriate registrar in the marriage notice book) of the marriage notice.

(3) Any person may, at any time before a certificate is issued under subsection (2) above, submit to the appropriate registrar an objection in writing to such issue; and the objection shall be taken into account by the appropriate registrar in deciding whether, in respect of the person to whom the certificate would be issued, he is satisfied as mentioned in the said subsection (2).

[(4) For the purpose of subsection (3) above, an objection which is submitted by electronic means is to be treated as in writing if it is received in a form which is legible and capable of being used for subsequent reference.]

Persons who may solemnise marriage

8 Persons who may solemnise marriage

(1) [Subject to section 23A of this Act,] a marriage [between persons of different sexes] may be solemnised by and only by—

(a)   a person who is—

(i)   a minister [or deacon] of the Church of Scotland; or

(ii)   a minister, clergyman, pastor, [priest or other celebrant of a religious or belief body] prescribed by regulations made by the Secretary of State, or who, not being one of the foregoing, is recognised by a [religious or belief body] so prescribed as entitled to solemnise [marriage between persons of different sexes] on its behalf; or

(iii)   registered under section 9 of this Act [to solemnise marriage between persons of different sexes]; or

(iv)   temporarily authorised under section 12 of this Act [to solemnise marriage between persons of different sexes]; or

(b)   a person who is a district registrar or assistant registrar appointed under section 17 of this Act.

[(1A)   The Scottish Ministers may prescribe a religious or belief body under subsection (1)(a)(ii) only if—

(a)   the body requests them to do so; and

(b)   the Scottish Ministers are satisfied that the body meets the qualifying requirements.

[(1AA)   For the avoidance of doubt, nothing in subsection (1)(a)—

(a)   imposes a duty on any person who is an approved celebrant in relation to marriage between persons of different sexes to solemnise a marriage between civil partners in a qualifying civil partnership (within the meaning of section 5(6)),

(b)   imposes a duty on any person to apply for temporary authorisation under section 12 to solemnise such a marriage.]

(1B)   Subject to section 23A, a marriage between persons of the same sex may be solemnised by and only by—

(a)   a person who is—

(i)   a minister, clergyman, pastor, priest or other celebrant of a religious or belief body prescribed by regulations made by the Scottish Ministers, or who, not being one of the foregoing, is recognised by a religious or belief body so prescribed as entitled to solemnise marriage between persons of the same sex on its behalf;

(ii)   registered under section 9 to solemnise marriage between persons of the same sex; or

(iii)   temporarily authorised under section 12 to solemnise marriage between persons of the same sex; or

(b)   a person who is a district registrar or assistant registrar appointed under section 17.

(1C)   The Scottish Ministers may prescribe a religious or belief body under subsection (1B)(a)(i) only if—

(a)   the body requests them to do so; and

(b)   the Scottish Ministers are satisfied that the body meets the qualifying requirements.

(1D)   For the avoidance of doubt, nothing in subsection (1B)(a) or (1C)(a)—

(a)   imposes a duty on any religious or belief body to make a request referred to in subsection (1C)(a);

(b)   imposes a duty on any such body to nominate under section 9 any of its members to be registered as empowered to solemnise marriages between persons of the same sex;

(c)   imposes a duty on any person to apply for temporary authorisation under section 12 to solemnise marriages between persons of the same sex;

(d)   imposes a duty on any person who is an approved celebrant in relation to marriages between persons of the same sex to solemnise such marriages.

(1E)   In subsections (1A)(b) and (1C)(b), the 'qualifying requirements' are such requirements as may be set out in regulations made by the Scottish Ministers.

(1F)   Regulations under subsection (1E)—

(a)   may make different provision for different cases or circumstances;

(b)   may include transitional and saving provision.

(1G)   Regulations under subsection (1)(a)(ii), (1B)(a)(i) or (1E) are subject to the negative procedure.]

(2)   In this Act—

(a)   any such person as is mentioned in subsection (1)(a) [or (1B)(a)] above is referred to as an 'approved celebrant', and a marriage solemnised by an approved celebrant is referred to as a ['religious or belief marriage'];

(b)   any such person as is mentioned in subsection (1)(b) [or (1B)(b)] above is referred to as an 'authorised registrar', and a marriage solemnised by an authorised registrar is referred to as a 'civil marriage'.

[Religious or belief marriages]

9   Registration of nominated persons as celebrants

(1)   A [religious or belief body], not being—

(a)   the Church of Scotland; or

(b)   prescribed by virtue of section 8(1)(a)(ii) of this Act,

may nominate to the Registrar General any of its members who it desires should be registered under this section as empowered to solemnise marriages [between persons of different sexes]:

[. . .]

[(1A)   A religious or belief body, not being prescribed by virtue of section 8(1B)(a)(i), may nominate to the Registrar General any of its members who it desires should be registered under this section as empowered to solemnise marriages between persons of the same sex.]

(2)   The Registrar General shall reject a nomination made under subsection (1) [or (1A)] above if in his opinion—

(a)   the nominating body is not a [religious or belief body]; or

(b)   the marriage ceremony used by that body is not of an appropriate form; or

(c)   the nominee is not a fit and proper person to solemnise a marriage; or

(d)   there are already registered under this section sufficient members of the same [. . .] body as the nominee to meet the needs of that body [in relation to solemnising marriages between persons of different sexes or, as the case may be, marriages between persons of the same sex] [; or

(e)   the nominating body does not meet the qualifying requirements.]

[(2A)   In subsection (2)(e), the 'qualifying requirements' are such requirements as may be set out in regulations made by the Scottish Ministers.

(2B)   Regulations under subsection (2A)—

(a)   may make different provision for different cases or circumstances;

(b)   may include transitional and saving provision.

(2C)   Regulations under subsection (2A) are subject to the negative procedure.]

(3)   For the purposes of subsection (2)(b) above, a marriage ceremony [for marriage between persons of different sexes] is of an appropriate form if it includes, and is in no way inconsistent with—

(a)   a declaration by the parties, in the presence of each other, the celebrant and two [witnesses—

(i)   that they accept each other as husband and wife;

(ii)   that they accept each other in marriage; or

(iii)   either or both of sub-paragraphs (i) and (ii);] and

(b)   a declaration by the celebrant, after the declaration mentioned in paragraph (a) of this [subsection—

(i)   that the parties are then husband and wife;

(ii)   that the parties are then married; or

(iii)   either or both of sub-paragraphs (i) and (ii),]

and the Registrar General may, before deciding whether to accept or reject a nomination, require the nominating body to produce to him in writing the form of words used at its marriage ceremonies [for marriage between persons of different sexes].

[(3A)   For the purposes of subsection (2)(b) above, a marriage ceremony for marriage between persons of the same sex is of an appropriate form if it includes, and is in no way inconsistent with—

(a)   a declaration by the parties, in the presence of each other, the celebrant and two witnesses, that they accept each other in marriage;

(b)   a declaration by the celebrant, after the declaration mentioned in paragraph (a), that the parties are then married,

and the Registrar General may, before deciding whether to accept or reject a nomination, require the nominating body to produce in writing the form of words used at its marriage ceremonies for marriage between persons of the same sex.]

(4)   Where the Registrar General accepts a nomination made to him under subsection (1) [or (1A)] above, he—

(a)   shall determine the period during which the nominee shall be empowered to solemnise marriages, being a period of not more than 3 years; and

(b)   may determine that the nominee shall be empowered to solemnise marriages only in such area [or place] as the Registrar General may specify,

and may make his acceptance subject to such other conditions as he thinks fit:

Provided that nothing in paragraph (a) above shall preclude the Registrar General from accepting a further nomination of that nominee, in accordance with this section, to take effect at any time after the end of the period determined by the Registrar General under the said paragraph (a).

(5)   The Registrar General shall—

(a)   where he accepts a nomination made to him under subsection (1) [or (1A)] above—

(i)   so inform the nominee and the nominating body, specifying the period during which the acceptance shall have effect and any condition to which the acceptance is subject;

(ii)   enter the name of the nominee, the nominating body and such other particulars as he deems appropriate in a register which he shall establish and maintain and which shall be made available for public inspection at all reasonable times without charge;

(b)   where he rejects the nomination, by notice in writing inform the nominating body of the reasons for that rejection.

[(5ZA)   The register mentioned in subsection (5)(a)(ii) is to be in two parts—

(a)   the first part containing the details mentioned in subsection (5)(a)(ii) in relation to persons nominated by religious or belief bodies to solemnise marriages between persons of different sexes; and

(b)   the second part containing those details in relation to persons nominated by religious or belief bodies to solemnise marriages between persons of the same sex.]

[(5A)   For the purpose of subsection (5)(b) above, notice which is given by electronic means is to be treated as in writing if it is received in a form which is legible and capable of being used for subsequent reference.]

(6)   The nominating body may, if aggrieved by a rejection under this section, within 28 days of receiving notice of that rejection, appeal to the Secretary of State, and on any such appeal the Secretary of State may direct the Registrar General to accept the nomination or may confirm its rejection and shall inform the nominating body of his direction or confirmation, as the case may be, and the reason for it; and such direction or confirmation shall be final:

Provided that if a reason given for a confirmation of the rejection of a nomination is that the nominating body is not a [religious or belief body], that body may, within 42 days of receiving notice of the confirmation, appeal against the confirmation to the Court of Session and seek the determination of that court as to whether the body is a [religious or belief body]; and if—

(a)   the court determine that the nominating body is a [religious or belief body]; and

(b)   the said reason was the only reason given for the confirmation,

that determination shall be given effect to by the Registrar General as if it were a direction under this subsection to accept the nomination.

10   Removal of celebrant's name from registers

(1)   Subject to the provisions of this section, the Registrar General may remove the name of a person registered under section 9 of this Act from the register on the ground that—

(a)   that person has requested that his name should be so removed; or

(b)   the body which nominated that person under section 9(1) [or (1A)] of this Act no longer desires that he should be so registered; or

(c)   the marriage ceremony used by the said body is no longer of an appropriate form within the meaning of section 9(3) [or (3A)] of this Act; or

(d)   that person—

(i)   has, while registered as an approved celebrant, been convicted of an offence under this Act; or

(ii)   has, for the purpose of profit or gain, been carrying on a business of solemnising marriages; or

(iii)   is not a fit and proper person to solemnise marriages; or

(iv)   for any other reason, should not be so registered.

[(1A)   In relation to any ground mentioned in subsection (1)(a) to (c), references in this section to removal from and restoration to the register include removal from and restoration to the appropriate part of the register.]

(2)   The Registrar General shall not remove the name of a person from the register on any ground mentioned in subsection (1)(d) above unless he has given to that person at least 21 days notice in writing of his intention to do so.

[(2A)   For the purpose of subsection (2) above, notice which is given by electronic means is to be treated as in writing if it is received in a form which is legible and capable of being used for subsequent reference.]

(3) The Registrar General shall—

(a) in the notice given under subsection (2) above, specify the ground of removal and call upon the said person to show cause, within the period specified in the notice, why his name should not be removed from the register; and

(b) consider any representations made to him within the said period by that person.

(4) Where a person's name has been removed from the register on any of the grounds mentioned in paragraphs (c) and (d) of subsection (1) above, that person or the body which nominated him under section 9(1) [or (1A)] of this Act may, if aggrieved by the removal, within 28 days of receiving notice of the removal appeal to the Secretary of State, and on any such appeal the Secretary of State may give such direction as he thinks proper to the Registrar General as to the removal from, or restoration to, the register of that name; and such direction shall be final.

(5) Where a person has received a notice in pursuance of subsection (2) above, he shall not solemnise a marriage unless and until his name is restored to the register or, as the case may be, the Registrar General has decided not to remove his name from the register.

11 Alterations to register maintained under s 9

A body registered in pursuance of section 9(5)(a)(ii) of this Act shall notify the Registrar General of any of the following events (if practicable, within 21 days of its occurrence)—

(a) any change in the name or the address of the body or any amalgamation with any other [religious or belief body], giving the name and address of any approved celebrant who is a member of the body so registered;

(b) the death of an approved celebrant who is a member of the body so registered;

(c) any change of name, address or designation of an approved celebrant who is a member of the body so registered;

(d) the cessation of an approved celebrant who is a member of the body so registered from exercising the functions of an approved celebrant, giving his name and address;

and the Registrar General shall, on receipt of any such notification, make whatever alteration to the register maintained by him under section 9 of this Act as he considers necessary or desirable.

12 Temporary authorisation of celebrants

[(1)] The Registrar General may, in accordance with such terms and conditions as may be specified in the authorisation, grant to any [member of a religious or belief body] a temporary written authorisation to solemnise—

(a) a marriage or marriages specified in the authorisation, or

(b) marriages during such period as shall be specified in the authorisation:

[. . .]

[(1A) The Registrar General may grant an authorisation to a person under subsection (1) only if satisfied that the religious or belief body of which the person is a member meets the qualifying requirements.

(1B) An authorisation under subsection (1)(b) may be granted in relation to—

(a) only marriages between persons of different sexes;

(b) only marriages between persons of the same sex; or

(c) both.

(1C) The Registrar General may grant an authorisation to a person under subsection (1)(b) to solemnise marriages between persons of the same sex only if the religious or belief body of which the person is a member—

(a) is prescribed by virtue of section 8(1B)(a)(i); or

(b) has nominated members (whether or not including that person) under section 9(1A) to solemnise marriages between persons of the same sex.

(1D) In subsection (1A), the 'qualifying requirements' are such requirements as may be set out in regulations made by the Scottish Ministers.

(1E) Regulations under subsection (1D)—

(a) may make different provision for different cases or circumstances;

(b) may include transitional and saving provision.

(1F) Regulations under subsection (1D) are subject to the negative procedure.]

[(2) For the purposes of subsection (1) above, an authorisation which is issued by electronic means is to be treated as written if it is received in a form which is legible and capable of being used for subsequent reference.]

13 Preliminaries to solemnisation of [marriages by approved celebrants]

(1) A marriage shall not be solemnised by an approved celebrant unless—

(a) the parties produce to him before the marriage ceremony a Marriage Schedule, in respect of the marriage, issued in accordance with this Act;

(b) both parties to the marriage are present; and

(c) two persons professing to be 16 years of age or over are present as witnesses.

[. . .]

14 Form of ceremony to be used by approved celebrant

An approved celebrant who is a person specified—

(a) in section 8(1)(a)(i) or (ii) [or (1B)(a)(i)] of this Act shall not solemnise a marriage except in accordance with a form of ceremony recognised by the [religious or belief body] to which he belongs as sufficient for the solemnisation of marriages;

(b) in section 8(1)(a)(iii) or (iv) [or (1B)(a)(ii) or (iii)] of this Act shall not solemnise a marriage except in accordance with a form of ceremony which includes and is in no way inconsistent with the declarations specified in section 9(3) [or (3A)] of this Act.

15 Registration of [religious or belief marriages]

(1) Immediately after the solemnisation of the marriage the Marriage Schedule shall be signed by the parties contracting the marriage, by both witnesses present thereat and by the approved celebrant.

(2) The parties to the marriage shall, within 3 days thereafter, deliver the Marriage Schedule, or send it by post or arrange that it is delivered, to the district registrar.

(3) As soon as possible after receipt of the Marriage Schedule, the district registrar shall cause the particulars as set forth in that Schedule to be entered in the register of marriages kept by him; and subject to subsection (4) below, he shall not register a [religious or belief marriage] unless and until he receives a duly signed Marriage Schedule in respect of that marriage.

(4) Where the Registrar General is satisfied that a marriage has been properly solemnised and that the Marriage Schedule in respect of the marriage has been duly signed but has been lost or destroyed, he may direct the district registrar to complete an exact copy of the original Marriage Schedule and, so far as practicable, to arrange for its signature by those persons who signed the original Schedule; and as soon as possible thereafter, the district registrar shall cause the particulars as set forth in that copy to be entered in the register of marriages kept by him.

[(5) In this section and section 16 of this Act, 'the district registrar' means—

(a) where the marriage has been solemnised in a registration district, the district registrar for that district;

(b) where the marriage has been solemnised in Scottish waters, the district registrar who issued the Marriage Schedule in respect of the marriage.]

16 Registrar's power to require delivery of Marriage Schedule

(1) Where after the expiration of 21 days from the date of marriage as entered in the Marriage Schedule that Schedule has not been delivered to the district regis-

trar, he may serve a notice in the prescribed form on either of the parties to the marriage requiring that party within 8 days from the date of service of the notice to deliver the said Schedule, or send it by post, to the district registrar.

(2) If any party on whom a notice has been served in pursuance of subsection (1) above fails to comply with the notice, the district registrar may serve on that party a second notice in the prescribed form requiring that party to attend personally at the registration office of the district registrar, within 8 days from the date of service of the second notice, for the purpose of delivering the Marriage Schedule to the district registrar to enable him to register the marriage.

Civil marriages

17 Appointment of authorised registrars

For the purpose of affording reasonable facilities for the solemnisation of civil marriages throughout Scotland, the Registrar General—

(a) shall appoint such number of district registrars as he thinks necessary; and

(b) may, in respect of any district for which he has appointed a district registrar under paragraph (a) above, appoint one or more assistant registrars, as persons who may solemnise marriages:

[. . .]

18 Places at which civil marriages may be solemnised

(1) Subject to the provisions of this section, an authorised registrar shall solemnise a civil marriage—

[(a)] in his registration office;

[(aa) at an appropriate place in the registration district of the authorised registrar; or

(ab) with the approval of the Registrar General, at—

(i) the registration office of another authorised registrar;

(ii) an appropriate place in the registration district of another authorised registrar; or

(iii) an appropriate place in Scottish waters.]

[. . .]

[(1A) In this section—

'appropriate place' means a place which—

(a) the parties to the intended marriage and the local registration authority agree is to be the place of solemnisation; and

(b) is not religious premises;

'local registration authority' means—

(a) the local registration authority for the registration district which includes the place; or

(b) where the place is in Scottish waters, the local registration authority for the authorised registrar's registration district;

'religious premises' means premises which—

(a) are used solely or mainly for religious purposes; or

(b) have been so used and have not subsequently been used solely or mainly for other purposes.]

[. . .]

19 Marriage ceremony and registration of marriage

(1) An authorised registrar shall not solemnise a marriage within [28 days] of the date of receipt (as entered in the marriage notice book) of a marriage notice in respect of that marriage, unless—

(a) he has received a written request from one or both of the parties to solemnise the marriage on a specified earlier date stating the reason for the request, and

(b)   he has been authorised to solemnise the marriage on that earlier date by the Registrar General.

[(1ZA)   Unless subsection (1ZB) applies, if a proposed marriage is referred to the Secretary of State under section 3F ('the referred marriage') the Registrar General may not authorise an authorised registrar to solemnise the referred marriage on the date mentioned in subsection (1)(b) without the consent of the Secretary of State.

(1ZB)   This subsection applies if the request made under subsection (1)(a) is made because a party to the referred marriage is gravely ill and not expected to recover.]

[(1A)   For the purpose of subsection (1) above, a request which is made by electronic means is to be treated as written if it is received in a form which is legible and capable of being used for subsequent reference.]

(2)   A marriage shall not be solemnised by an authorised registrar unless—

(a)   he has available to him at the time of the ceremony a Marriage Schedule, in respect of the marriage, completed in accordance with this Act and the prescribed fee for the marriage has been paid;

(b)   both parties to the marriage are present; and

(c)   two persons professing to be 16 years of age or over are present as witnesses.

(3)   Immediately after the solemnisation of the marriage the Marriage Schedule shall be signed by the parties contracting the marriage, by both witnesses present thereat and by the authorised registrar who solemnised it.

(4)   As soon as possible after the Marriage Schedule has been signed in accordance with subsection (3) above—

[(a)   in a case where the marriage has been solemnised by the authorised registrar—

(i)   in his registration office;

[(ii)   at an appropriate place (within the meaning given by section 18) in the registration district of the authorised registrar; or]

[. . .]

(iv)   [at an appropriate place (within the meaning given by section 18)] in Scottish waters,

that authorised registrar;

(b)   in a case where the marriage has been solemnised by the authorised registrar—

(i)   in the registration office of another authorised registrar; or

(ii)   at an [appropriate place (within the meaning given by section 18)] in the district of another authorised registrar,

that other authorised registrar,]

shall cause the particulars as set forth in that Schedule to be entered in the register of marriages kept by him.

[. . .]

20   Second marriage ceremony

(1)   Where two persons have gone through a marriage ceremony with each other outside the United Kingdom, whether before or after the commencement of this Act, but they are not, or are unable to prove that they are, validly married to each other in Scots law, an authorised registrar, on an application made to him by those persons, may, subject to the approval of the Registrar General and to subsection (2) below, solemnise their marriage as if they had not already gone through a marriage ceremony with each other.

(2)   Sections 3 to 6 and 18 and 19 of this Act shall apply for the purpose of solemnising a marriage under this section except that—

(a)   there shall be submitted to the authorised registrar a statutory declaration by both parties—

(i) stating that they have previously gone through a marriage ceremony with each other; and

(ii) specifying the date and place at which, and the circumstances in which, they went through that ceremony;

(b) section 5(4)(b) of this Act shall not apply in respect of the parties already being married to each other;

(c) the Marriage Schedule shall contain such modifications as the Registrar General may direct to indicate that the parties have previously gone through a marriage ceremony with each other; and

(d) after the Marriage Schedule has been signed in accordance with section 19(3) of this Act, the authorised registrar shall make an endorsement on it in the following terms—

'The ceremony of marriage between the parties mentioned in this Schedule was performed in pursuance of section 20 of the Marriage (Scotland) Act 1977, following a statutory declaration by them that they had gone through a ceremony of marriage with each other on the   day of   , at

Dated the   day of   ,

(Signature of authorised registrar)'.

[Void marriages

20A Grounds on which marriage void

(1) Where subsection (2) or (3) applies in relation to a marriage solemnised in Scotland, the marriage shall be void.

(2) This subsection applies if at the time of the marriage ceremony a party to the marriage who was capable of consenting to the marriage purported to give consent but did so by reason only of duress or error.

(3) This subsection applies if at the time of the marriage ceremony a party to the marriage was incapable of—

(a) understanding the nature of marriage; and

(b) consenting to the marriage.

(4) If a party to a marriage purported to give consent to the marriage other than by reason only of duress or error, the marriage shall not be void by reason only of that party's having tacitly withheld consent to the marriage at the time when it was solemnised.

(5) In this section 'error' means—

(a) error as to the nature of the ceremony; or

(b) a mistaken belief held by a person ('A') that the other party at the ceremony with whom A purported to enter into a marriage was the person whom A had agreed to marry.]

Irregular marriages

21 Registration of irregular marriages

Where decree of declarator establishing—

(a) a marriage by cohabitation with habit and repute; or

(b) a marriage contracted before 1st July 1940 by declaration *de praesenti* or by promise *subsequente copula*,

has been granted in the Court of Session, the principal clerk of Session shall forthwith cause the decree, the names, designations and addresses of the parties, and the date, as determined by the Court, on which the marriage was constituted to be intimated to the Registrar General, and on receipt of such intimation the Registrar General shall cause the marriage to be registered.

General

22 Interpreters at marriage ceremony

(1)   Where the person by whom a marriage is to be solemnised under this Act considers that it is necessary or desirable, he may use the services of an interpreter (not being a party or a witness to the marriage) at the marriage ceremony.

(2)   The interpreter shall—

(a)   before the marriage ceremony, sign a written statement that he under-stands, and is able to converse in, any language in respect of which he is to act as interpreter at that ceremony; and

(b)   immediately after the marriage ceremony, furnish the person solemn-ising the marriage with a certificate written in English and signed by the inter-preter that he has faithfully acted as interpreter at that ceremony.

(3)   Any fee for the services of the interpreter shall be paid by the parties to the marriage.

23 Cancellation of entry in register of marriages

If a marriage in respect of which an entry has been made in a register of marriages is found or declared to be void, the Registrar General shall direct the cancellation of the entry.

[23A Validity of registered marriage

(1)   Subject to sections 1 and 2 of, and without prejudice to section 24(1) of, this Act, where the particulars of any marriage at the ceremony in respect of which both parties were present are entered in a register of marriages by or at the behest of an appropriate registrar, the validity of that marriage shall not be questioned, in any legal proceedings whatsoever, on the ground of failure to comply with a requirement or restriction imposed by, under or by virtue of this Act.

(2)   In subsection (1) above, 'appropriate registrar' means

(a)   in the case of a civil marriage, an authorised registrar; and

(b)   in any other case, a district registrar.]

24 Offences

[(A1)   A person ('A') commits an offence if A purports to enter into a marriage with another person ('B') knowing that either or both—

(a)   A is already married to or in a civil partnership with a person other than B, or

(b)   B is already married to or in a civil partnership with a person other than A.

(A2)   A person who commits an offence under subsection (A1) is liable—

(a)   on conviction on indictment, to imprisonment for a term not exceeding 2 years or to a fine (or both),

(b)   on summary conviction, to imprisonment for a term not exceeding 12 months or to a fine not exceeding the statutory maximum (or both).]

(1)   Any person who—

(a)   falsifies or forges any Marriage Schedule, certificate or declaration issued or made, or purporting to be issued, or made, under this Act;

(b)   knowingly uses, or gives or sends to any person as genuine, any false or forged Marriage Schedule, certificate, declaration or other document issued or made, or purporting to be issued or made, or required, under this Act;

(c)   being an approved celebrant, solemnises a marriage without a Marriage Schedule in respect of the marriage, issued in accordance with this Act, being available to him at the time of the marriage ceremony;

(d)   not being an approved celebrant or an authorised registrar, conducts a marriage ceremony in such a way as to lead the parties to the marriage to believe that he is solemnising a valid marriage;

(e)   being an approved celebrant or an authorised registrar, solemnises a marriage without both parties to the marriage being present, shall be guilty of an offence and shall be liable—

    (i) on conviction on indictment, to a fine or to imprisonment for a term not exceeding 2 years or to both;

    (ii) on summary conviction, to a fine not exceeding [the statutory maximum] or to imprisonment for a term not exceeding 3 months or to both [; or

    (f) being an authorised registrar, solemnises a marriage in a place otherwise than in accordance with section 18(1) of this Act.]

(2) Any person who—

    (a) solemnises a marriage in an area [or place] in which by virtue of section 9(4)(b) of this Act he is not permitted to solemnise a marriage;

    (b) solemnises a marriage in contravention of section 10(5) of this Act;

    (c) being a person temporarily authorised under section [12 of this Act—

      (i) if authorised under subsection (1)(a) of that section, solemnises a marriage not specified in the authorisation;

      (ii) if authorised under subsection (1)(b) of that section, solemnises a marriage outwith the period specified in the authorisation;

      (iii) in either case, solemnises a marriage otherwise than in accordance with such terms and conditions as may be specified in the authorisation;]

    (d) solemnises a marriage in contravention of section 14 of this Act; or

    (e) being a party to a marriage, fails to comply with a notice served under section 16(2) of this Act,

shall be guilty of an offence and shall be liable on summary conviction to a fine not exceeding £100.

(3) Summary proceedings for an offence under this Act or, in relation to information supplied under or for the purposes of this Act, section 53(1)(a) of the Registration of Births, Deaths and Marriages (Scotland) Act 1965, may be commenced at any time within the period of 3 months from the date on which evidence sufficient in the opinion of the Lord Advocate to justify the proceedings comes to his knowledge or within the period of 12 months from the commission of the offence, whichever period last expires; and subsection (3) of [section 136 of the Criminal Procedure (Scotland) Act 1995] (date of commencement of summary proceedings) shall have effect for the purposes of this section as it has effect for the purposes of that section.

[24A   Form, and manner of attestation, of documents

(1) Regulations prescribing the form of a document may, unless the document requires to be signed, make provision for the document to be electronic rather than paper-based.

(2) Regulations prescribing the manner in which a document requires to be attested may make different provision for different cases or circumstances.]

25   Regulations

(1) Any power to make regulations conferred by this Act shall be exercisable by statutory instrument and no such regulations shall be made by the Registrar General except with the approval of the Secretary of State.

(2) Any statutory instrument containing regulations which prescribe fees for the purposes of this Act shall be subject to annulment in pursuance of a resolution of either House of Parliament.

(3) The Statutory Instruments Act 1946 shall apply to a statutory instrument containing regulations made for the purposes of this Act by the Registrar General as if the regulations had been made by a Minister of the Crown.

26   Interpretation

(1) Except where the context otherwise requires and subject to [subsections (2) and (2A)] below, expressions used in this Act and in the Registration of Births, Deaths, and Marriages (Scotland) Act 1965 have the same meanings in this Act as in that Act.

(2)   In this Act, except where the context otherwise requires—

['2014 Act' means the Immigration Act 2014;]

'annulment' includes any decree or declarator of nullity of marriage, however expressed;

'approved celebrant' has the meaning assigned to it by section 8(2)(a) of this Act;

'authorised registrar' has the meaning assigned to it by section 8(2)(b) of this Act;

['marriage' means marriage between persons of different sexes and marriage between persons of the same sex;]

[. . .]

'name' includes surname;

'prescribed' means prescribed by regulations made by the Registrar General;

['religious or belief body' means an organised group of people—

    (a)   which meets regularly for religious worship; or

    (b)   the principal object (or one of the principal objects) of which is to uphold or promote philosophical beliefs and which meets regularly for that purpose;]

['religious or belief marriage' has the meaning given by section 8(2)(a);]

['relevant national' means—

    (a)   a British citizen,

    (b)   a national of an EEA State [. . .] or

    (c)   a national of Switzerland;

['Scottish waters' means the area comprising such of the internal waters and territorial sea of the United Kingdom as are within Scotland ('Scotland' having the meaning given by section 126(1) and (2) of the Scotland Act 1998 (c 46)), other than any area which is part of a registration district;

'vessel' includes any—

    (a)   vehicle; or

    (b)   other structure.

(2A)   For the purposes of this Act—

    (a)   the seaward boundary of a registration district which extends into the sea shall, subject to paragraph (b) below, be the low water mark of the ordinary spring tide;

    (b)   a vessel which is below the low water mark of the ordinary spring tide is to be regarded as [a place within a registration district if the vessel] is—

        (i)   positioned adjacent to land which is within the district;

        (ii)   affixed to the land for the purpose of maintaining its position; and

        (iii)   so positioned for the purpose of enabling access to and from the land;

    (c)   a jetty or similar structure which is partly above the low water mark of the ordinary spring tide and partly below that mark is to be regarded as being wholly above that mark.]

(3)   Except where the context otherwise requires, any reference in this Act to any other enactment shall be construed as a reference to that enactment as amended by or under any other enactment, including this Act.

27   Transitional and saving provisions

(1)   Where, before the commencement of this Act—

    (a)   proclamation of banns or publication of notice has been applied for by one or both of the parties to; or

    (b)   a licence has been granted by a sheriff in respect of,

an intended marriage in accordance with an enactment repealed by this Act, then the marriage shall proceed in accordance with the enactments repealed by this Act as if they had not been so repealed:

Provided that this subsection shall cease to have effect in respect of the marriage if—

    (i)   a certificate of proclamation of banns or publication of notice issued in respect of the said application; or

    (ii)   the said licence,

ceases to be valid in accordance with any enactment so repealed.

(2)　Any form used, and any requirement as to the particulars to be entered in any form used, for the purposes of any enactment repealed by this Act shall continue in force as though prescribed under this Act until other forms or particulars are so prescribed.

(3)　Nothing in this Act shall affect the validity of any marriage solemnised or contracted before 1st January 1978.

(4)　Nothing in the foregoing provisions of this section shall be taken as prejudicing the operation of section 38 of the Interpretation Act 1889 (which relates to the effect of repeals).

29　Short title, commencement and extent

(1)　This Act may be cited as the Marriage (Scotland) Act 1977.

(2)　This Act, except this section, shall come into force on 1st January 1978.

(3)　This Act, except this section and, in so far as relating to the Marriage with Foreigners Act 1906, the Marriage Act 1939, the Marriage Act 1949 and the Marriage (Scotland) Act 1956, section 28, shall extend to Scotland only.

SCHEDULES

[SCHEDULE 1
DEGREES OF RELATIONSHIP

(introduced by section 2)

1　Relationships by consanguinity

Parent	Aunt or uncle
Child	Niece or nephew
Grandparent	Great-grandparent
Grandchild	Great-grandchild
Sibling	

2　Relationships by affinity referred to in section 2(1A)

Child of former spouse	Former spouse of grandparent
Child of former civil partner	Former civil partner of grandparent
Former spouse of parent	Grandchild of former spouse
Former civil partner of parent	Grandchild of former civil partner

3　Relationships by adoption

Adoptive parent or former adoptive parent
Adopted child or former adopted child.]

[SCHEDULE 1A
MODIFICATIONS IF PROPOSED MARRIAGE REFERRED UNDER SECTION 3F

Introduction

1.—(1)　These are the modifications subject to which this Act has effect if the district registrar refers a proposed marriage to the Secretary of State.

(2)　In this Schedule 'referred marriage' means the proposed marriage referred to the Secretary of State.

No Marriage Schedule to be completed until decision about investigation etc

2.—(1)   The duty under section 6(1) to complete a Marriage Schedule in respect of the referred marriage does not apply unless and until one of the following events occurs.

(2)   Event 1 occurs if—

(a)   the Secretary of State gives the district registrar the section 48 notice, and

(b)   that notice is of a decision not to investigate whether the referred marriage is a sham.

(3)   Event 2 occurs if—

(a)   the relevant statutory period ends, and

(b)   the Secretary of State has not given the district registrar the section 48 notice.

(4)   Event 3 occurs if—

(a)   the Secretary of State gives the district registrar the section 48 notice,

(b)   that notice is of a decision to investigate whether the referred marriage is a sham,

(c)   the Secretary of State gives the district registrar the section 50 notice, and

(d)   that notice is of a decision that both of the parties to the referred marriage have complied with the investigation.

(5)   Event 4 occurs if—

(a)   the 70 day period ends, and

(b)   the Secretary of State has not given the district registrar the section 50 notice.

(6)   Event 5 occurs if the Secretary of State gives the district registrar notice that the duty under section 6(1) is applicable.

(7)   The Secretary of State may give a notice for that purpose only if—

(a)   the Secretary of State has given the district registrar the section 48 notice,

(b)   that notice is of a decision to investigate whether the referred marriage is a sham,

(c)   the Secretary of State has given the district registrar the section 50 notice, and

(d)   that notice is of a decision that one or both of the parties to the referred marriage have not complied with the investigation.

(8)   This paragraph applies in addition to any other requirements applicable to the completion of the Marriage Schedule.

(9)   This paragraph is subject to paragraph 4.

(10)   In this paragraph—

'70 day period' has the same meaning as in section 50(11) of the 2014 Act;

'relevant statutory period' has the same meaning as in section 62 of the 2014 Act;

'section 48 notice' means notice under section 48(8C) of the 2014 Act;

'section 50 notice' means notice under section 50(7) of the 2014 Act.

Marriage to be investigated: extension of 28 day period to 70 days

3.—(1)   The modifications in this paragraph have effect if the Secretary of State gives the district registrar notice under section 48(8C) of the 2014 Act of a decision to investigate whether the referred marriage is a sham.

(2)   Section 6(4)(a) has effect as if—

(a)   for the words from '28 days' to 'relates' there were substituted 'the relevant 70 day period', and

(b)   in sub-paragraph (i), for '28 days' there were substituted 'relevant 70 day period'.

(3) Section 19(1) has effect as if for the words from '28 days' to 'that marriage' there were substituted 'the relevant 70 day period'.

(4) In sections 6(4)(a) and 19 (as modified by this paragraph) 'relevant 70 day period' means the period—

(a) beginning the day after receipt of the marriage notice (as entered by the district registrar in the marriage notice book), and

(b) ending at the end of the period of 70 days beginning with that day.

(5) This paragraph is subject to paragraph 4.

Effect of reducing statutory period

4.—(1) Where—

(a) either—

(i) a district registrar is authorised to issue a Marriage Schedule under section 6(4)(a) (including as modified under paragraph 3), or

(ii) an authorised registrar is authorised to solemnise a marriage under section 19(1)(b) (including as modified under paragraph 3), and

(b) the authorisation mentioned in sub-paragraph (i) or, as the case may be, (ii) of paragraph (a) is given at a time when the duty under section 6(1) to complete a Marriage Schedule in respect of the referred marriage has not arisen in accordance with paragraph 2,

the duty under section 6(1) to complete the Marriage Schedule arises on the giving of the authorisation, subject to any other requirements applicable to the completion of the Schedule being met.

(2) But the requirements of paragraph 2 are not applicable in such a case.

(3) The Secretary of State is not prevented from deciding to conduct, conducting, or continuing, an investigation if a Marriage Schedule is completed or, as the case may be, issued or the marriage solemnised, as mentioned in sub-paragraph (1).

(4) But in such a case, nothing in the 2014 Act requires the Secretary of State to decide whether to conduct, or to continue, an investigation.

(5) In this paragraph 'investigation' means an investigation, conducted following a decision by the Secretary of State under section 48 of the 2014 Act, whether a proposed marriage is a sham.]

ADOPTION (SCOTLAND) ACT 1978
(1978, c 28)

PART IV
STATUS OF ADOPTED CHILDREN

38 Meaning of 'adoption order' in Part IV

(1) In this Part 'adoption order' means—

(a) an adoption order within the meaning of section 65(1);

(b) an adoption order under the Children Act 1975, the Adoption Act 1958, the Adoption Act 1950 or any enactment repealed by the Adoption Act 1950;

(c) an order effecting an adoption made in England, Wales, Northern Ireland, the Isle of Man or any of the Channel Islands;

[(cc) a Convention adoption;]

(d) an 'overseas adoption' within the meaning of section 65(2); or

(e) any other adoption recognised by the law of Scotland; and cognate expressions shall be construed accordingly.

(2) The definition of adoption order includes, where the context admits, an

adoption order which took effect before the commencement of the Children Act 1975.

39   Status conferred by adoption

   [(1)   A child who is the subject of an adoption order shall be treated in law—

      (a)   where the adopters are a married couple, as if—

         (i)   he had been born as a [. . .] child of the marriage (whether or not he was in fact born after the marriage was constituted); and

         (ii)   [subject to subsection (2A)] he were not the child of any person other than the adopters;

      (b)   where the adoption order is made by virtue of section 15(1)(aa) as if—

         (i)   he had been born as a [. . .] child of the marriage between the adopter and the natural parent to whom the adopter is married (whether or not he was in fact born after the marriage was constituted); and

         (ii)   [subject to subsection (2A)] he were not the child of any person other than the adopter and that natural parent; and

      (c)   in any other case, as if—

         (i)   he had been born as a [. . .] child of the adopter; and

         (ii)   [subject to subsection (2A)] he were not the child of any person other than the adopter.]

   (2)   Where [a] child has been adopted by one of his natural parents as sole adoptive parent and the adopter thereafter marries the other natural parent, subsection (1) shall not affect any enactment or rule of law whereby, by virtue of the marriage, the child is rendered the [. . .] child of both natural parents.

   [(2A)   Where, in the case of a child adopted under a Convention adoption, the Court of Session is satisfied, on an application under this subsection—

      (a)   that under the law of the country in which the adoption was effected the adoption is not a full adoption;

      (b)   that the consents referred to in Article 4(c) and (d) of the Convention have not been given for a full adoption, or that the United Kingdom is not the receiving State (within the meaning of Article 2 of the Convention); and

      (c)   that it would be more favourable to the child for a direction to be given under this subsection,

the Court may direct that sub-paragraph (ii) of, as the case may be, paragraph (a), (b) or (c) of subsection (1) shall not apply, or shall not apply to such extent as may be specified in the direction: and in this subsection 'full adoption' means an adoption by virtue of which the child falls to be treated in law as if he were not the child of any person other than the adopters or adopter.]

   (3)   This section has effect—

      (a)   in the case of an adoption before 1st January 1976, from that date, and

      (b)   in the case of any other adoption, from the date of the adoption.

   (4)   Subject to the provisions of this Part, this section—

      (a)   applies for the construction of enactments or instruments passed or made before or after the commencement of this Act so far as the context admits; and

      (b)   does not affect things done or events occurring before the adoption or, where the adoption took place before 1st January 1976, before that date.

   (5)   This section has effect subject to the provisions of section 44.

[. . .]

41   Miscellaneous enactments

   (1)   Section 39 does not apply in determining the forbidden degrees of consanguinity and affinity in respect of the law relating to marriage [, to the eligibility of persons to register as civil partners of each other] or in respect of the crime of incest, except that, on the making of an adoption order, the adopter and the child shall be deemed, for all time coming, to be within the said forbidden degrees in

respect of the law relating to marriage and incest [, to such eligibility and to incest].

(2) [S]ection 39 does not apply for the purposes of any provision of—

(a) [the British Nationality Act 1981],

(b) the Immigration Act 1971,

(c) any instrument having effect under an enactment within paragraph (a) or (b), or

(d) any other law for the time being in force which determines [British citizenship, British Overseas Territories citizenship, the status of a British National (Overseas) or British Overseas citizenship].

42 Pensions

Section 39(1) does not affect entitlement to a pension which is payable to or for the benefit of a child and is in payment at the time of his adoption.

43 Insurance

Where a child is adopted whose natural parent has effected an insurance with a friendly society or a collecting society or an industrial insurance company for the payment on the death of the child of money for funeral expenses, the rights and liabilities under the policy shall by virtue of the adoption be transferred to the adoptive parents who shall for the purposes of the enactments relating to such societies and companies be treated as the person who took out the policy.

44 Effect of s 39 on succession and *inter vivos* deed

Section 39 (status conferred by adoption) does not affect the existing law relating to adopted persons in respect of—

(a) the succession to a deceased person (whether testate or intestate), and

(b) the disposal of property by virtue of any *inter vivos* deed.

MATRIMONIAL HOMES (FAMILY PROTECTION) (SCOTLAND) ACT 1981
(1981, c 59)

Protection of occupancy rights of one spouse against the other

1 Right of spouse without title to occupy matrimonial home

(1) Where, apart from the provisions of this Act, one spouse is entitled, or permitted by a third party, to occupy a matrimonial home (an 'entitled spouse') and the other spouse is not so entitled or permitted (a 'non-entitled spouse'), the non-entitled spouse shall, subject to the provisions of this Act, have the following rights—

(a) if in occupation, a right [. . .] to [continue to occupy] the matrimonial home [. . .];

(b) if not in occupation, a right to enter into and occupy the matrimonial home.

[(1A) The rights conferred by subsection (1) above to continue to occupy or, as the case may be, to enter and occupy the matrimonial home include, without prejudice to their generality, the right to do so together with any child of the family.]

(2) In subsection (1) above, an 'entitled spouse' includes a spouse who is entitled, or permitted by a third party, to occupy a matrimonial home along with an individual who is not the other spouse only if that individual has waived his or her right of occupation in favour of the spouse so entitled or permitted.

(3) If the entitled spouse refuses to allow the non-entitled spouse to exercise the right conferred by subsection (1)(b) above, the non-entitled spouse may exercise that right only with the leave of the court under section 3(3) or (4) of this Act.

(4)   In this Act, the rights mentioned in paragraphs (a) and (b) of subsection (1) above are referred to as occupancy rights.

(5)   A non-entitled spouse may renounce in writing his or her occupancy rights only—

    (a)   in a particular matrimonial home; or

    (b)   in a particular property which it is intended by the spouses will become a matrimonial home.

(6)   A renunciation under subsection (5) above shall have effect only if at the time of making the renunciation, the non-entitled spouse has sworn or affirmed before a notary public that it was made freely and without coercion of any kind.

[In this subsection, 'notary public' includes any person duly authorised by the law of the country (other than Scotland) in which the swearing or affirmation takes place to administer oaths or receive affirmations in that other country.]

[(7)   Subject to subsection (5), if—

    (a)   there has been no cohabitation between an entitled spouse and a non-entitled spouse during a continuous period of two years; and

    (b)   during that period the non-entitled spouse has not occupied the matrimonial home,

the non-entitled spouse shall, on the expiry of that period, cease to have occupancy rights in the matrimonial home.

(8)   A non-entitled spouse who has ceased to have occupancy rights by virtue of subsection (7) may not apply to the court for an order under section 3(1).]

2   Subsidiary and consequential rights

(1)   For the purpose of securing the occupancy rights of a non-entitled spouse, that spouse shall, in relation to a matrimonial home, be entitled without the consent of the entitled spouse—

    (a)   to make any payment due by the entitled spouse in respect of rent, rates, secured loan instalments, interest or other outgoings (not being outgoings on repairs or improvements);

    (b)   to perform any other obligation incumbent on the entitled spouse (not being an obligation in respect of non-essential repairs or improvements);

    (c)   to enforce performance of an obligation by a third party which that third party has undertaken to the entitled spouse to the extent that the entitled spouse may enforce such performance;

    (d)   to carry out such essential repairs as the entitled spouse may carry out;

    (e)   to carry out such non-essential repairs or improvements as may be authorised by an order of the court, being such repairs or improvements as the entitled spouse may carry out and which the court considers to be appropriate for the reasonable enjoyment of the occupancy rights;

    (f)   to take such other steps, for the purpose of protecting the occupancy rights of the non-entitled spouse, as the entitled spouse may take to protect the occupancy rights of the entitled spouse.

(2)   Any payment made under subsection (1)(a) above or any obligation performed under subsection (1)(b) above shall have effect in relation to the rights of a third party as if the payment were made or the obligation were performed by the entitled spouse; and the performance of an obligation which has been enforced under subsection (1)(c) above shall have effect as if it had been enforced by the entitled spouse.

(3)   Where there is an entitled and a non-entitled spouse, the court, on the application of either of them, may, having regard in particular to the respective financial circumstances of the spouses, make an order apportioning expenditure incurred or to be incurred by either spouse—

    (a)   without the consent of the other spouse, on any of the items mentioned in paragraphs (a) and (d) of subsection (1) above;

(b)   with the consent of the other spouse, on anything relating to a matrimonial home.

(4)   Where both spouses are entitled, or permitted by a third party, to occupy a matrimonial home—

(a)   either spouse shall be entitled, without the consent of the other spouse, to carry out such non-essential repairs or improvements as may be authorised by an order of the court, being such repairs or improvements as the court considers to be appropriate for the reasonable enjoyment of the occupancy rights;

(b)   the court, on the application of either spouse, may, having regard in particular to the respective financial circumstances of the spouses, make an order apportioning expenditure incurred or to be incurred by either spouse, with or without the consent of the other spouse, on anything relating to the matrimonial home.

(5)   Where one spouse owns or hires, or is acquiring under a hire-purchase or conditional sale agreement, furniture and plenishings in a matrimonial home—

(a)   the other spouse may, without the consent of the first mentioned spouse—

(i)   make any payment due by the first mentioned spouse which is necessary, or take any other step which the first mentioned spouse is entitled to take to secure the possession or use of any such furniture and plenishings (and any such payment shall have effect in relation to the rights of a third party as if it were made by the first mentioned spouse); or

(ii)   carry out such essential repairs to the furniture and plenishings as the first mentioned spouse is entitled to carry out;

(b)   the court, on the application of either spouse, may, having regard in particular to the respective financial circumstances of the spouses, make an order apportioning expenditure incurred or to be incurred by either spouse—

(i)   without the consent of the other spouse, in making payments under a hire, hire-purchase or conditional sale agreement, or in paying interest charges in respect of the furniture and plenishings, or in carrying out essential repairs to the furniture and plenishings; or

(ii)   with the consent of the other spouse, on anything relating to the furniture and plenishings.

(6)   An order under subsection (3), (4)(b) or (5)(b) above may require one spouse to make a payment to the other spouse in implementation of the apportionment.

(7)   Any application under subsection (3), (4)(b) or (5)(b) above shall be made within five years of the date on which any payment in respect of such incurred expenditure was made.

(8)   Where—

(a)   the entitled spouse is a tenant of a matrimonial home; and

(b)   possession thereof is necessary in order to continue the tenancy; and

(c)   the entitled spouse abandons such possession,

the tenancy shall be continued by such possession by the non-entitled spouse.

(9)   In this section 'improvements' includes alterations and enlargement.

3   Regulation by court of rights of occupancy of matrimonial home

(1)   [Subject to section 1(7) of this Act,] where there is an entitled and a non-entitled spouse, or where both spouses are entitled, or permitted by a third party, to occupy a matrimonial home, either spouse may apply to the court for an order—

(a)   declaring the occupancy rights of the applicant spouse;

(b)   enforcing the occupancy rights of the applicant spouse;

(c)   restricting the occupancy rights of the non-applicant spouse;

  (d) regulating the exercise by either spouse of his or her occupancy rights;

  (e) protecting the occupancy rights of the applicant spouse in relation to the other spouse.

  (2) Where one spouse owns or hires, or is acquiring under a hire-purchase or conditional sale agreement, furniture and plenishings in a matrimonial home, the other spouse, if he or she has occupancy rights in that home, may apply to the court for an order granting to the applicant the possession or use in the matrimonial home of any such furniture and plenishings; but, subject to section 2 of this Act, an order under this subsection shall not prejudice the rights of any third party in relation to the non-performance of any obligation under such hire-purchase or conditional sale agreement.

  (3) The court shall grant an application under subsection (1)(a) above if it appears to the court that the application relates to a matrimonial home; and, on an application under any of paragraphs (b) to (e) of subsection (1) or under subsection (2) above, the court may make such order relating to the application as appears to it to be just and reasonable having regard to all the circumstances of the case including—

  (a) the conduct of the spouses in relation to each other and otherwise;

  (b) the respective needs and financial resources of the spouses;

  (c) the needs of any child of the family;

  (d) the extent (if any) to which—

   (i) the matrimonial home; and

   (ii) in relation only to an order under subsection (2) above, any item of furniture and plenishings referred to in that subsection,

is used in connection with a trade, business or profession of either spouse; and

  (e) whether the entitled spouse offers or has offered to make available to the non-entitled spouse any suitable alternative accommodation.

  (4) Pending the making of an order under subsection (3) above, the court, on the application of either spouse, may make such interim order as it may consider necessary or expedient in relation to—

  (a) the residence of either spouse in the home to which the application relates;

  (b) the personal effects of either spouse or of any child of the family; or

  (c) the furniture and plenishings:

Provided that an interim order may be made only if the non-applicant spouse has been afforded an opportunity of being heard by or represented before the court.

  (5) The court shall not make an order under subsection (3) or (4) above if it appears that the effect of the order would be to exclude the non-applicant spouse from the matrimonial home.

  (6) If the court makes an order under subsection (3) or (4) above which requires the delivery to one spouse of anything which has been left in or removed from the matrimonial home, it may also grant a warrant authorising a messenger-at-arms or sheriff officer to enter the matrimonial home or other premises occupied by the other spouse and to search for and take possession of the thing required to be delivered, if need be by opening shut and lockfast places, and to deliver the thing in accordance with the said order:

Provided that a warrant granted under this subsection shall be executed only after expiry of the period of a charge, being such period as the court shall specify in the order for delivery.

  (7) Where it appears to the court—

  (a) on the application of a non-entitled spouse, that that spouse has suffered a loss of occupancy rights or that the quality of the non-entitled spouse's occupation of a matrimonial home has been impaired; or

  (b) on the application of a spouse who has been given the possession or use of furniture and plenishings by virtue of an order under subsection (3) above, that the applicant has suffered a loss of such possession or use or that the quality of the applicant's possession or use of the furniture and plenishings has been impaired,

in consequence of any act or default on the part of the other spouse which was intended to result in such loss or impairment, it may order that other spouse to pay to the applicant such compensation as the court in the circumstances considers just and reasonable in respect of that loss or impairment.

(8)   A spouse may renounce in writing the right to apply under subsection (2) above for the possession or use of any item of furniture and plenishings.

4   Exclusion orders

(1)   Where there is an entitled and a non-entitled spouse, or where both spouses are entitled, or permitted by a third party, to occupy a matrimonial home, either spouse [whether or not that spouse is in occupation at the time of the application] may apply to the court for an order (in this Act referred to as 'an exclusion order') suspending the occupancy rights of the other spouse ('the non-applicant spouse') in a matrimonial home.

(2)   Subject to subsection (3) below, the court shall make an exclusion order if it appears to the court that the making of the order is necessary for the protection of the applicant or any child of the family from any conduct or threatened or reasonably apprehended conduct of the non-applicant spouse which is or would be injurious to the physical or mental health of the applicant or child.

(3)   The court shall not make an exclusion order if it appears to the court that the making of the order would be unjustified or unreasonable—

(a)   having regard to all the circumstances of the case including the matters specified in paragraphs (a) to (e) of section 3(3) of this Act; and

(b)   where the matrimonial home—

(i)   is or is part of an agricultural holding within the meaning of section 1 of the [Agricultural Holdings (Scotland) Act 1991]; or

(ii)   is let, or is a home in respect of which possession is given, to the non-applicant spouse or to both spouses by an employer as an incident of employment,

subject to a requirement that the non-applicant spouse or, as the case may be, both spouses must reside in the matrimonial home, having regard to that requirement and the likely consequences of the exclusion of the non-applicant spouse from the matrimonial home.

(4)   In making an exclusion order the court shall, on the application of the applicant spouse,—

(a)   grant a warrant for the summary ejection of the non-applicant spouse from the matrimonial home;

(b)   grant an interdict prohibiting the non-applicant spouse from entering the matrimonial home without the express permission of the applicant;

(c)   grant an interdict prohibiting the removal by the non-applicant spouse, except with the written consent of the applicant or by a further order of the court, of any furniture and plenishings in the matrimonial home;

unless, in relation to paragraph (a) or (c) above, the non-applicant spouse satisfies the court that it is unnecessary for it to grant such a remedy.

(5)   In making an exclusion order the court may—

(a)   grant an interdict prohibiting the non-applicant spouse from entering or remaining in a specified area in the vicinity of the matrimonial home;

(b)   where the warrant for the summary ejection of the non-applicant spouse has been granted in his or her absence, give directions as to the preservation of the non-applicant spouse's goods and effects which remain in the matrimonial home;

(c)   on the application of either spouse, make the exclusion order or the warrant or interdict mentioned in paragraph (a), (b) or (c) of subsection (4) above or paragraph (a) of this subsection subject to such terms and conditions as the court may prescribe;

(d)   on application as aforesaid, make such other order as it may consider necessary for the proper enforcement of an order made under subsection (4) above or paragraph (a), (b) or (c) of this subsection.

(6)   Pending the making of an exclusion order, the court may, on the application of the applicant spouse, make an interim order suspending the occupancy rights of the non-applicant spouse in the matrimonial home to which the application for the exclusion order relates; and subsections (4) and (5) above shall apply to such interim order as they apply to an exclusion order:

Provided that an interim order may be made only if the non-applicant spouse has been afforded an opportunity of being heard by or represented before the court.

(7)   Without prejudice to subsections (1) and (6) above, where both spouses are entitled, or permitted by a third party, to occupy a matrimonial home, it shall be incompetent for one spouse to bring an action of ejection from the matrimonial home against the other spouse.

5   Duration of orders under ss 3 and 4

(1)   The court may, on the application of either spouse, vary or recall any order made by it under section 3 or 4 of this Act, but, subject to subsection (2) below, any such order shall, unless previously so varied or recalled, cease to have effect—

(a)   on the termination of the marriage; or

(b)   subject to section 6(1) of this Act, where there is an entitled and a non-entitled spouse, on the entitled spouse ceasing to be an entitled spouse in respect of the matrimonial home to which the order relates; or

(c)   where both spouses are entitled, or permitted by a third party, to occupy the matrimonial home, on both spouses ceasing to be so entitled or permitted.

(2)   Without prejudice to the generality of subsection (1) above, an order under section 3(3) or (4) of this Act which grants the possession or use of furniture and plenishings shall cease to have effect if the furniture and plenishings cease to be permitted by a third party to be retained in the matrimonial home.

Occupancy rights in relation to dealings with third parties

6   Continued exercise of occupancy rights after dealing

(1)   Subject to subsection (3) below—

(a)   the continued exercise of the rights conferred on a non-entitled spouse by the provisions of this Act in respect of a matrimonial home shall not be prejudiced by reason only of any dealing of the entitled spouse relating to that home; and

(b)   a third party shall not by reason only of such a dealing be entitled to occupy that matrimonial home or any part of it.

[(1A)   The occupancy rights of a non-entitled spouse in relation to a matrimonial home shall not be exercisable in relation to the home where, following a dealing of the entitled spouse relating to the home—

(a)   a person acquires the home, or an interest in it, in good faith and for value from a person other than the person who is or, as the case may be, was the entitled spouse; or

(b)   a person derives title to the home from a person who acquired title as mentioned in paragraph (a).]

(2)   In this section and section 7 of this Act—

'dealing' includes the grant of a heritable security and the creation of a trust but does not include a conveyance under section 80 of the Lands Clauses Consolidation (Scotland) Act 1845;

'entitled spouse' does not include a spouse who, apart from the provisions of this Act,—

(a)   is permitted by a third party to occupy a matrimonial home; or

(b)   is entitled to occupy a matrimonial home along with an individual who is not the other spouse, whether or not that individual has waived his or her right of occupation in favour of the spouse so entitled;

and 'non-entitled spouse' shall be construed accordingly.

(3)   This section shall not apply in any case where—

(a)   the non-entitled spouse in writing either—

(i)   consents or has consented to the dealing, and any consent shall be in such form as the Secretary of State may, by regulations made by statutory instrument, prescribe; or

(ii)   renounces or has renounced his or her occupancy rights in relation to the matrimonial home or property to which the dealing relates;

(b)   the court has made an order under section 7 of this Act dispensing with the consent of the non-entitled spouse to the dealing;

(c)   the dealing occurred, or implements, a binding obligation entered into by the entitled spouse before his or her marriage to the non-entitled spouse;

(d)   the dealing occurred, or implements, a binding obligation entered into before the commencement of this Act; . . .

(e)   the dealing comprises [a transfer for value to] a third party who has acted in good faith if, [. . .] there is produced to the third party by the [transferor—

(i)   a written declaration signed by the transferor, or a person acting on behalf of the transferor under a power of attorney or as a guardian (within the meaning of the Adults with Incapacity (Scotland) Act 2000 (asp 4)), that the subjects of the transfer are not, or were not at the time of the dealing, a matrimonial home in relation to which a spouse of the transferor has or had occupancy rights; or

(ii)   a renunciation of occupancy rights or consent to the dealing which bears to have been properly made or given by the non-entitled spouse or a person acting on behalf of the non-entitled spouse under a power of attorney or as a guardian (within the meaning of the Adults with Incapacity (Scotland) Act 2000 (asp 4))]; or

(f)   the entitled spouse has permanently ceased to be entitled to occupy the matrimonial home, and at any time thereafter a continuous period of [2] years has elapsed, during which the non-entitled spouse has not occupied the matrimonial home.]

7   Dispensation by court with spouse's consent to dealing

(1)   [Subject to subsections (1A) to (1D) below the] court may, on the application of an entitled spouse or any other person having an interest, make an order dispensing with the consent of a non-entitled spouse to a dealing which has taken place or a proposed dealing, if—

(a)   such consent is unreasonably withheld;

(b)   such consent cannot be given by reason of physical or mental disability;

(c)   the non-entitled spouse cannot be found after reasonable steps have been taken to trace him or her; or

(d)   the non-entitled spouse is [under legal disability by reason of nonage].

[(1A)   Subsection (1B) applies if, in relation to a proposed sale—

(a)   negotiations with a third party have not begun; or

(b)   negotiations have begun but a price has not been agreed.

(1B)   An order under subsection (1) dispensing with consent may be made only if—

(a)　the price agreed for the sale is no less than such amount as the court specifies in the order; and

(b)　the contract for the sale is concluded before the expiry of such period as may be so specified.

(1C)　Subsection (1D) applies if the proposed dealing is the grant of a heritable security.

(1D)　An order under subsection (1) dispensing with consent may be made only if—

(a)　the heritable security is granted for a loan of no more than such amount as the court specifies in the order; and

(b)　the security is executed before the expiry of such period as may be so specified.]

(2)　For the purposes of subsection (1)(a) above, a non-entitled spouse shall have unreasonably withheld consent to a dealing which has taken place or a proposed dealing, where it appears to the court—

(a)　that the non-entitled spouse has led the entitled spouse to believe that he or she would consent to the dealing and that the non-entitled spouse would not be prejudiced by any change in the circumstances of the case since such apparent consent was given; or

(b)　that the entitled spouse has, having taken all reasonable steps to do so, been unable to obtain an answer to a request for consent.

(3)　The court, in considering whether to make an order under subsection (1) above, shall have regard to all the circumstances of the case including the matters specified in paragraphs (a) to (e) of section 3(3) of this Act.

[(3A)　If the court refuses an application for an order under subsection (1), it may make an order requiring a non-entitled spouse who is or becomes the occupier of the matrimonial home—

(a)　to make such payments to the owner of the home in respect of that spouse's occupation of it as may be specified in the order;

(b)　to comply with such other conditions relating to that spouse's occupation of the matrimonial home as may be so specified.]

(4)　Where—

(a)　an application is made for an order under this section; and

(b)　an action is or has been raised by a non-entitled spouse to enforce occupancy rights,

the action shall be sisted until the conclusion of the proceedings on the application.

[. . .]

8　Interests of heritable creditors

(1)　The rights of a third party with an interest in the matrimonial home as a creditor under a secured loan in relation to the non-performance of any obligation under the loan shall not be prejudiced by reason only of the occupancy rights of the non-entitled spouse; but where a non-entitled spouse has or obtains occupation of a matrimonial home and—

(a)　the entitled spouse is not in occupation; and

(b)　there is a third party with such an interest in the matrimonial home,

the court may, on the application of the third party, make an order requiring the non-entitled spouse to make any payment due by the entitled spouse in respect of the loan.

(2)　This section shall not apply [to secured loans in respect of which the security was granted prior to the commencement of section 13 of the Law Reform (Miscellaneous Provisions) (Scotland) Act 1985] unless the third party in granting the secured loan acted in good faith and . . . there was produced to the third party by the entitled spouse—

(a)　[a written declaration signed] by the entitled spouse declaring that there is no non-entitled spouse; or

(b) a renunciation of occupancy rights or consent to the taking of the loan which bears to have been properly made or given by the non-entitled spouse.

[(2A) This section shall not apply to secured loans in respect of which the security was granted after the commencement of section 13 of the Law Reform (Miscellaneous Provisions) (Scotland) Act 1985 unless the third party in granting the secured loan acted in good faith and [. . .] there was produced to the third party by the grantor—

(a) [a written declaration signed] by the grantor declaring that the security subjects are not or were not at the time of the granting of the security a matrimonial home in relation to which a spouse of the grantor has or had occupancy rights; or

(b) a renunciation of occupancy rights or consent to the granting of the security which bears to have been properly made or given by the non-entitled spouse.

(2B) for the purposes of subsections (2) and (2A) above, the time of granting a security, in the case of a heritable security, is the date of delivery of the deed creating the security.]

9 Provisions where both spouses have title

(1) Subject to subsection (2) below, where, apart from the provisions of this Act, both spouses are entitled to occupy a matrimonial home—

(a) the rights in that home of one spouse shall not be prejudiced by reason only of any dealing of the other spouse; and

(b) a third party shall not by reason only of such a dealing be entitled to occupy that matrimonial home or any part of it.

(2) The definition of 'dealing' in section 6(2) of this Act and sections 6(3) and 7 of this Act shall apply for the purposes of subsection (1) above as they apply for the purposes of section 6(1) of this Act subject to the following modifications—

(a) any reference to the entitled spouse and to the non-entitled spouse shall be construed as a reference to a spouse who has entered into or, as the case may be, proposes to enter into a dealing and to the other spouse respectively; and

(b) in paragraph (b) of section 7(4) the reference to occupancy rights shall be construed as a reference to any rights in the matrimonial home.

[Reckoning of non-cohabitation periods in sections 1 and 6]

[9A Effect of court action under section 3, 4 or 5 on reckoning of periods in sections 1 and 6

(1) Subsection (2) applies where an application is made under section 3(1), 4(1) or 5(1) of this Act.

(2) In calculating the period of two years mentioned in section 1(7)(a) or 6(3)(f) of this Act, no account shall be taken of the period mentioned in subsection (3) below.

(3) The period is the period beginning with the date on which the application is made and—

(a) in the case of an application under section 3(1) or 4(1) of this Act, ending on the date on which—

(i) an order under section 3(3) or, as the case may be, 4(2) of this Act is made;

(ii) the application is otherwise finally determined or abandoned;

(b) in the case of an application under section 5(1) of this Act, ending on the date on which—

(i) the order under section 3(3) or, as the case may be, 4(2) is varied or recalled; or

(ii) the application is otherwise finally determined or abandoned.]

[. . .]

11 Poinding

Where [an attachment] has been executed of furniture and plenishings of which the debtor's spouse has the possession or use by virtue of an order under section 3(3) or (4) of this Act, the sheriff, on the application of that spouse within 40 days of the date of execution of [the attachment], may—

(a)   declare that [the attachment] is null; or

(b)   make such order as he thinks appropriate to protect such possession or use by that spouse,

if he is satisfied that the purpose of the diligence was wholly or mainly to prevent such possession or use.

12 Adjudication

(1)   Where a matrimonial home of which there is an entitled spouse and a non-entitled spouse is adjudged, the Court of Session, on the application of the non-entitled spouse within 40 days of the date of the decree of adjudication, may—

(a)   order the reduction of the decree; or

(b)   make such order as it thinks appropriate to protect the occupancy rights of the non-entitled spouse,

if it is satisfied that the purpose of the diligence was wholly or mainly to defeat the occupancy rights of the non-entitled spouse.

(2)   In this section, 'entitled spouse' and 'non-entitled spouse' have the same meanings respectively as in section 6(2) of this Act.

Transfer of tenancy

13 Transfer of tenancy

(1)   The court may, on the application of a non-entitled spouse, make an order transferring the tenancy of a matrimonial home to that spouse and providing, subject to subsection (11) below, for the payment by the non-entitled spouse to the entitled spouse of such compensation as seems just and reasonable in all the circumstances of the case.

[(2)   In an action—

(a)   for divorce, the Court of Session or a sheriff;

(b)   for nullity of marriage, the Court of Session,

may, on granting decree or within such period as the court may specify on granting decree, make an order granting an application under subsection (1) above.]

(3)   In determining whether to grant an application under subsection (1) above, the court shall have regard to all the circumstances of the case including the matters specified in paragraphs (a) to (e) of section 3(3) of this Act and the suitability of the applicant to become the tenant and the applicant's capacity to perform the obligations under the lease of the matrimonial home.

(4)   The non-entitled spouse shall serve a copy of an application under subsection (1) above on the landlord and, before making an order under subsection (1) above, the court shall give the landlord an opportunity of being heard by it.

(5)   On the making of an order granting an application under subsection (1) above, the tenancy shall vest in the non-entitled spouse without intimation to the landlord, subject to all the liabilities under the lease (other than any arrears of rent for the period before the making of the order, which shall remain the liability of the original entitled spouse).

(6)   The clerk of court shall notify the landlord of the making of an order granting an application under subsection (1) above.

(7)   It shall not be competent for a non-entitled spouse to apply for an order under subsection (1) above where the matrimonial home—

(a)   is let to the entitled spouse by his or her employer as an incident of employment, and the lease is subject to a requirement that the entitled spouse must reside therein;

(b)   [is on or pertains to land comprised in an agricultural lease];

(c)   is on or pertains to a croft or the subject of a cottar or the holding of a landholder or a statutory small tenant;

(d)   is let on a long lease;

(e)   is part of the tenancy land of a tenant-at-will.

(8)   In subsection (7) above—

['agricultural lease' means a lease constituting a 1991 Act tenancy within the meaning of the Agricultural Holdings (Scotland) Act 2003 (asp 11) or a lease constituting a limited duration tenancy [, a short limited duration tenancy, a modern limited duration tenancy or a repairing tenancy] (within the meaning of that Act);]

'cottar' has the same meaning as in section 28(4) of the [Crofters (Scotland) Act 1993];

'croft' has the same meaning as in the [Crofters (Scotland) Act 1993];

'holding', in relation to a landholder and a statutory small tenant, 'landholder' and 'statutory small tenant' have the same meanings respectively as in sections 2(1), 2(2) and 32(1) of the Small Landholders (Scotland) Act 1911;

'long lease' has the same meaning as in section [9(2) of the Land Registration etc (Scotland) Act 2012];

'tenant-at-will' has the same meaning as in section 20(8) of the Land Registration (Scotland) Act 1979.

(9)   Where both spouses are joint or common tenants of a matrimonial home, the court may, on the application of one of the spouses, make an order vesting the tenancy in that spouse solely and providing, subject to subsection (11) below, for the payment by the applicant to the other spouse of such compensation as seems just and reasonable in the circumstances of the case.

(10)   Subsections (2) to (8) above shall apply for the purposes of an order under subsection (9) above as they apply for the purposes of an order under subsection (1) above subject to the following modifications—

(a)   in subsection (3) for the word 'tenant' there shall substituted the words 'sole tenant';

(b)   in subsection (4) for the words 'non-entitled' there should be substituted the word 'applicant';

(c)   in subsection (5) for the words 'non-entitled' and 'liability of the original entitled spouse' there shall substituted respectively the words 'applicant' and 'joint and several liability of both spouses';

(d)   in subsection (7)—

(i)   for the words 'a non-entitled' there shall substituted the words 'an applicant';

(ii)   for paragraph (a) there shall be substituted the following paragraph—

'(a) is let to both spouses by their employer as an incident of employment, and the lease is subject to a requirement that both spouses must reside there;';

(iii) paragraphs (c) and (e) shall be omitted.

[. . .]

Matrimonial interdicts

14 Interdict competent where spouses live together

(1)   It shall not be incompetent for the court to entertain an application by a spouse for a matrimonial interdict by reason only that the spouses are living together as man and wife.

(2)   In this section [. . .] of this Act—

'matrimonial interdict' means an interdict including an interim interdict which—

(a)   restrains or prohibits any conduct of one spouse towards the other spouse or a child of the family, or [(b)   subject to subsection (3), prohibits a spouse from entering or remaining in—

      (i)   a matrimonial home;

      (ii)   any other residence occupied by the applicant spouse;

      (iii)   any place of work of the applicant spouse;

      (iv)   any school attended by a child in the permanent or temporary care of the applicant spouse.]

[(3)   Subsection (4) applies if in relation to a matrimonial home the non-applicant spouse—

      (a)   is an entitled spouse; or

      (b)   has occupancy rights.

(4)   Except where subsection (5) applies, the court may not grant a matrimonial interdict prohibiting the non-applicant spouse from entering or remaining in the matrimonial home.

(5)   This subsection applies if—

      (a)   the interdict is ancillary to an exclusion order; or

      (b)   by virtue of section 1(3), the court refuses leave to exercise occupancy rights.

(6)   In this section [. . .], 'applicant spouse' means the spouse who has applied for the interdict; and 'non-applicant spouse' shall be construed accordingly.]

[. . .]

Cohabiting couples

18   Occupancy rights of cohabiting couples

(1)   If a man and a woman are living with each other as if they were man and wife [or two persons of the same sex are living together as if they were civil partners] ('[in either case] a cohabiting couple') in a house which, apart from the provisions of this section—

      (a)   one of them (an 'entitled partner') is entitled, or permitted by a third party, to occupy; and

      (b)   the other (a 'non-entitled partner') is not so entitled or permitted to occupy,

the court may, on the application of the non-entitled partner, if it appears that the [entitled partner and the non-entitled partner] are a cohabiting couple in that house, grant occupancy rights therein to the applicant for such period, not exceeding [6] months, as the court may specify:

Provided that the court may extend the said period for a further period or periods, no such period exceeding 6 months.

(2)   In determining whether for the purpose of subsection (1) above [two persons] are a cohabiting couple the court shall have regard to all the circumstances of the case including—

      (a)   the time for which it appears they have been living together; and

      (b)   whether there [is any child—

          (i)   of whom they are the parents; or

          (ii)   who they have treated as a child of theirs.].

(3)   While an order granting an application under subsection (1) above or an extension of such an order is in force, or where both partners of a cohabiting couple are entitled, or permitted by a third party, to occupy the house where they are cohabiting, the following provisions of this Act shall subject to any necessary modifications—

      (a)   apply to the cohabiting couple as they apply to parties to a marriage; and

      (b)   have effect in relation to any child residing with the cohabiting couple as they have effect in relation to a child of the family,

      section 2;

      section 3, except subsection (1)(a);

section 4;

in section 5(1), the words from the beginning to 'Act' where it first occurs;

[section 13]; and

section 22,

and any reference in these provisions to a matrimonial home shall be construed as a reference to a house.

(4)   Any order under section 3 or 4 of this Act as applied to a cohabiting couple by subsection (3) above shall have effect—

(a)   if one of them is a non-entitled partner, for such a period, not exceeding the period or periods which from time to time may be specified in any order under subsection (1) above for which occupancy rights have been granted under that subsection, as may be specified in the order;

(b)   if they are both entitled, or permitted by a third party, to occupy the house, until a further order of the court.

(5)   Nothing in this section shall prejudice the rights of any third party having an interest in the house referred to in subsection (1) above.

(6)   In this section—

'house' includes a caravan, houseboat or other structure in which the couple are cohabiting and any garden or other ground or building attached to, and usually occupied with, or otherwise required for the amenity or convenience of, the house, caravan, houseboat or other structure;

'occupancy rights' means the following rights of a non-entitled partner—

(a)   if in occupation, a right to [continue to occupy] the house [and, without prejudice to the generality of these rights, includes the right to continue to occupy or, as the case may be, to enter and occupy the house together with any child residing with the cohabiting couple];

(b)   if not in occupation, a right to enter into and occupy the house;

'entitled partner' includes a partner who is entitled, or permitted by a third party, to occupy the house along with an individual who is not the other partner only if that individual has waived his or her right of occupation in favour of the partner so entitled or permitted.

[Domestic interdicts]

[18A   Meaning of 'domestic interdict'

(1)   In section 18B, 'domestic interdict' means—

(a)   an interdict granted on the application of a person ('A') who is (or was) living with another person ('B') as if they were husband and wife against B for any of the purposes mentioned in subsection (2); or

(b)   an interdict granted on the application of a person ('C') who is (or was) living with another person ('D') as if they were civil partners against D for any of the purposes mentioned in subsection (2).

(2)   Those purposes are—

(a)   restraining or prohibiting such conduct of the defender towards—

(i)   the pursuer; or

(ii)   any child in the permanent or temporary care of the pursuer,

as the court may specify;

(b)   prohibiting the defender from entering or remaining in—

(i)   a family home occupied by the pursuer and the defender;

(ii)   any other residence occupied by the pursuer;

(iii)   any place of work of the pursuer;

(iv)   any school attended by a child in the permanent or temporary care of the pursuer.

(3)   In this section and in section 18B—

'family home' means, subject to subsection (4), any house, caravan, houseboat or other structure which has been provided or has been made available by the pursuer or the defender (or both of them) as (or has become) a family residence for them and includes any garden or other ground or building usually occupied with, or otherwise required for the amenity or convenience of, the house, caravan, houseboat or other structure; but does not include a residence provided or made available by any person for the pursuer or, as the case may be, the defender to reside in (whether or not with any child of the pursuer and the defender) separately from the defender or, as the case may be, the pursuer; and

'interdict' includes interim interdict.

(4) If the tenancy of a family home is transferred from a pursuer to a defender (or, as the case may be, from a defender to a pursuer) by agreement or under any enactment, the home shall, on such transfer, cease to be a family home.

(5) In subsection (3), 'child of the pursuer and the defender' includes any child or grandchild of the pursuer or the defender, and any person who has been brought up or treated by the pursuer or the defender as if the person were a child of the pursuer or, as the case may be, the defender, whatever the age of such a child, grandchild or person.]

[18B   Domestic interdicts: further provision

(1)   Subsection (2) applies if the defender—

(a)   is entitled to occupy a family home;

(b)   is permitted by a third party to occupy it; or

(c)   has, by virtue of section 18(1), occupancy rights in it.

(2)   Except where subsection (3) applies, the court may not grant a domestic interdict prohibiting the defender from entering or remaining in the family home.

(3)   This subsection applies if—

(a)   the interdict is ancillary to an exclusion order; or

(b)   an order under section 18(1) granting or extending occupancy rights is recalled.]

Miscellaneous and general

19   Rights of occupancy in relation to division and sale

Where a spouse brings an action for the division and sale of a matrimonial home which the spouses own in common, the court, after having regard to all the circumstances of the case including—

(a)   the matters specified in paragraphs (a) to (d) of section 3(3) of this Act; and

(b)   whether the spouse bringing the action offers or has offered to make available to the other spouse any suitable alternative accommodation,

may refuse to grant decree in that action or may postpone the granting of decree for such period as it may consider reasonable in the circumstances or may grant decree subject to such conditions as it may prescribe.

[. . .]

22   Interpretation

[(1)]   In this Act—

'caravan' means a caravan which is mobile or affixed to the land;

'child of the family' includes any child or grandchild of either spouse, and any person who has been brought up or [treated] by either spouse as if he or she were a child of that spouse, whatever the age of such a child, grandchild or person may be;

'the court' means the Court of Session or the sheriff;

'furniture and plenishings' means any article situated in a matrimonial home which—

(a)   is owned or hired by either spouse or is being acquired by either spouse under a hire-purchase agreement or conditional sale agreement; and

(b)   is reasonably necessary to enable the home to be used as a family residence,

but does not include any vehicle, caravan or houseboat, or such other structure as is mentioned in the definition of 'matrimonial home';

'matrimonial home' means [subject to subsection (2)] any house, caravan, houseboat or other structure which has been provided or has been made available by one or both of the spouses as, or has become, a family residence and includes any garden or other ground or building [. . .] usually occupied with, or otherwise required for the amenity or convenience of, the house, caravan, houseboat or other structure [but does not include a residence provided or made available by [a person for one] spouse to reside in, whether with any child of the family or not, separately from the other spouse];

'occupancy rights' has, subject to section 18(6) of this Act, the meaning assigned by section 1(4) of this Act;

'the sheriff' includes the sheriff having jurisdiction in the district where the matrimonial home is situated;

'tenant' includes sub-tenant and a statutory tenant as defined in section 3 of the Rent (Scotland) Act [1984 and a statutory assured tenant as defined in section 16(1) of the Housing (Scotland) Act 1988] and 'tenancy' shall be construed accordingly;

'entitled spouse' and 'non-entitled spouse', subject to sections 6(2) and 12(2) of this Act, have the meanings respectively assigned to them by section 1 of this Act.

(2)   If—

(a)   the tenancy of a matrimonial home is transferred from one spouse to the other by agreement or under any enactment; and

(b)   following the transfer, the spouse to whom the tenancy was transferred occupies the home but the other spouse does not,

the home shall, on such transfer, cease to be a matrimonial home.

23   Short title, commencement and extent

(1)   This Act may be cited as the Matrimonial Homes (Family Protection) (Scotland) Act 1981.

(2)   This Act (except this section) shall come into operation on such day as the Secretary of State may by order made by statutory instrument appoint, and different days may be so appointed for different provisions and for different purposes.

(3)   This Act extends to Scotland only.

ADMINISTRATION OF JUSTICE ACT 1982
(1982, c 53)

PART II
DAMAGES FOR PERSONAL INJURIES ETC—SCOTLAND

7   Damages in respect of services

Where a person (in this Part of this Act referred to as 'the injured person')—

(a)   has sustained personal injuries, or

(b)   has died in consequence of personal injuries sustained,

as a result of an act or omission of another person giving rise to liability in any person (in this Part of this Act referred to as 'the responsible person') to pay damages, the responsible person shall also be liable to pay damages in accordance with the provisions of sections 8 and 9 of this Act.

8   Services rendered to injured person

(1)   Where necessary services have been rendered to the injured person by a relative in consequence of the injuries in question, then, unless the relative has expressly agreed in the knowledge that an action for damages has been raised or is in contemplation that no payment should be made in respect of those services, the responsible person shall be liable to pay to the injured person by way of damages

such sum as represents reasonable remuneration for those services and repayment of reasonable expenses incurred in connection therewith.

[(2)   The injured person shall be under an obligation to account to the relative for any damages recovered from the responsible person under subsection (1) above.

(3)   Where, at the date of an award of damages in favour of the injured person, it is likely that necessary services will, after that date, be rendered to him by a relative in consequence of the injuries in question, then, unless the relative has expressly agreed that no payment shall be made in respect of those services, the responsible person shall be liable to pay to the injured person by way of damages such sum as represents—

(a)   reasonable remuneration for those services; and

(b)   reasonable expenses which are likely to be incurred in connection therewith.

(4)   The relative shall have no direct right of action in delict against the responsible person in respect of any services or expenses referred to in this section.]

9   Services to injured person's relative

(1)   The responsible person shall be liable to pay to the injured person a reasonable sum by way of damages in respect of the inability of the injured person to render the personal services referred to in subsection (3) below.

[(1A)   In assessing the amount of damages payable by virtue of subsection (1) above to an injured person whose date of death is expected to be earlier than had the injuries not been sustained, the court is to assume that the person will live until the date when death would have been expected had the injuries not been sustained.]

[. . .]

(3)   The personal services referred to in subsection (1) [. . .] above are personal services—

(a)   which were or might have been expected to have been rendered by the injured person before the occurrence of the act or omission giving rise to liability,

(b)   of a kind which, when rendered by a person other than a relative, would ordinarily be obtainable on payment, and

(c)   which the injured person but for the injuries in question might have been expected to render gratuitously to a relative.

(4)   Subject to [section 6(1) of the Damages (Scotland) Act 2011 (relative's loss of personal services)], the relative shall have no direct right of action in delict against the responsible person in respect of the personal services mentioned in subsection (3) above.

10   Assessment of damages for personal injuries

Subject to any agreement to the contrary, in assessing the amount of damages payable to the injured person in respect of personal injuries there shall not be taken into account so as to reduce that amount—

(a)   any contractual pension or benefit (including any payment by a friendly society or trade union);

(b)   any pension or retirement benefit payable from public funds other than any pension or benefit to which section 2(1) of the Law Reform (Personal Injuries) Act 1948 applies;

(c)   any benefit payable from public funds, in respect of any period after the date of the award of damages, designed to secure to the injured person or any relative of his a minimum level of subsistence;

(d)   any redundancy payment under the [Employment Rights Act 1996], or any payment made in circumstances corresponding to those in which a right to a redundancy payment would have accrued if [section 135] of that Act had applied;

(e)   any payment made to the injured person or to any relative of his by the injured person's employer following upon the injuries in question where the recipient is under an obligation to reimburse the employer in the event of damages being recovered in respect of those injuries;

(f)　subject to paragraph (iv) below, any payment of a benevolent character made to the injured person or to any relative of his by any person following upon the injuries in question;

but there shall be taken into account—

(i)　any remuneration or earnings from employment;

(ii)　any [contribution-based jobseeker's allowance (payable under the Job-seekers' Act 1995);]

(iii)　any benefit referred to in paragraph (c) above payable in respect of any period prior to the date of the award of damages;

(iv)　any payment of a benevolent character made to the injured person or to any relative of his by the responsible person following on the injuries in question, where such a payment is made directly and not through a trust or other fund from which the injured person or his relatives have benefited or may benefit.

13　Supplementary

(1)　In this Part of this Act, unless the context otherwise requires—
'personal injuries' [means—

(a)　any disease, and

(b)　any impairment of a person's physical or mental condition;]
'relative', in relation to the injured person, means—

(a)　the spouse or divorced spouse;

[(aa) the civil partner or former civil partner;]

(b)　any person, not being the spouse of the injured person, who was, at the time of the act or omission giving rise to liability in the responsible person, living with the injured person as husband or wife;

[(ba)　any person, not being the civil partner of the injured person, who was, at the time of the act or omission giving rise to liability in the responsible person, living with the injured person as the civil partner of the injured person;]

(c)　any ascendant or descendant;

(d)　any brother, sister, uncle or aunt; or any issue of any such person;

(e)　any person accepted by the injured person as a child of his family.
In deducing any relationship for the purposes of the foregoing definition—

(a)　any relationship by affinity shall be treated as a relationship by con-sanguinity; any relationship of the half blood shall be treated as a relationship of the whole blood; and the stepchild of any person shall be treated as his child; and

(b)　[section 1(1) of the Law Reform (Parent and Child) (Scotland) Act 1986 shall apply; and any reference (however expressed) in this Act to a relative shall be construed accordingly].

(2)　Any reference in this Part of this Act to a payment, benefit or pension shall be construed as a reference to any such payment, benefit or pension whether in cash or in kind.

(3)　This Part of this Act binds the Crown.

LAW REFORM (HUSBAND AND WIFE) (SCOTLAND) ACT 1984
(1984, c 15)

Abolition of actions of breach of promise of marriage, adherence and enticement

1　Promise of marriage not an enforceable obligation

(1)　No promise of marriage or agreement between two persons to marry one another shall have effect under the law of Scotland to create any rights or obligations; and no action for breach of any such promise or agreement may be brought in any court in Scotland, whatever the law applicable to the promise or agreement.

(2) This section shall have effect in relation to any promise made or agreement entered into before it comes into force, but shall not affect any action commenced before it comes into force.

2 Actions of adherence and enticement abolished

(1) No spouse shall be entitled to apply for a decree from any court in Scotland ordaining the other spouse to adhere.

(2) No person shall be liable in delict to any person by reason only of having induced the spouse of that person to leave or remain apart from that person.

(3) This section shall not affect any action commenced before this Act comes into force.

Abolition of miscellaneous rules relating to husband and wife

3 Curatory after marriage

(1) No married person shall, by reason only of minority, be subject to the curatory of his parent or of any person appointed by his parent.

[. . .]

(3) Section 2 of the Married Women's Property (Scotland) Act 1920 (husband to be curator to his wife during her minority) is repealed.

4 Abolition of husband's right to choose matrimonial home

Any rule of law entitling the husband, as between husband and wife, to determine where the matrimonial home is to be, shall cease to have effect.

5 Abolition of certain rules relating to antenuptial marriage contracts

(1) In relation to an antenuptial contract of marriage entered into after this Act comes into force—

(a) any rule of law enabling a woman to create an alimentary right in her own favour in respect of any property provided by her shall cease to have effect;

(b) any rule of law whereby the marriage is onerous consideration for any provision of the contract, shall cease to have effect.

(2) Nothing in paragraph (b) of subsection (1) above shall affect the operation of any enactment relating to gifts in consideration of marriage.

6 Abolition of husband's remaining liability for wife's debts incurred before marriage

(1) A husband shall not be liable, by reason only of being her husband, for any debts incurred by his wife before marriage.

(2) Subsection (1) above shall have effect in relation to any such debts, whether incurred before or after this Act comes into force.

(3) Section 4 of the Married Women's Property (Scotland) Act 1877 (liability of husband for wife's antenuptial debts limited to amount of property received through her) is repealed.

7 Abolition of *praepositura*

(1) For the purpose of determining a husband's liability for any obligation incurred by his wife after this Act comes into force, a married woman shall not be presumed as a matter of law to have been placed by her husband in charge of his domestic affairs, and any rule of law to the contrary shall cease to have effect.

(2) No warrant of inhibition or inhibition in whatever form may be granted at the instance of a husband for the purpose of cancelling his wife's authority to incur any obligation on his behalf.

(3) No such inhibition granted before the date this Act comes into force shall be registered on or after that date, and any such inhibition registered before that date shall be treated as discharged on that date.

CHILD ABDUCTION ACT 1984
(1984, c 37)

6 Offence in Scotland of parent, etc taking or sending child out of United Kingdom

(1) Subject to subsections (4) and (5) below, a person connected with a child under the age of sixteen years commits an offence if he takes or sends the child out of the United Kingdom—

(a) without the appropriate consent if there is in respect of the child—

(i) an order of a court in the United Kingdom awarding custody of the child to any person [or naming any person as the person with whom the child is to live; or]

(ii) an order of a court in England, Wales or Northern Ireland making the child a ward of court;

(b) if there is in respect of the child an order of a court in the United Kingdom prohibiting the removal of the child from the United Kingdom or any part of it.

(2) A person is connected with a child for the purposes of this section if—

(a) he is a parent or guardian of the child; or

(b) there is in force an order of a court in the United Kingdom awarding custody of the child to him [or naming him as the person with whom the child is to live] (whether solely or jointly with any other person); or

(c) in the case of [a child whose parents are not and have never been married to one another], there are reasonable grounds for believing that he is the father of the child.

(3) In this section, the 'appropriate consent' means—

(a) in relation to a child to whom subsection (1)(a)(i) above applies—

(i) the consent of each person

(a) who is a parent or guardian of the child; or

(b) to whom custody of the child has been awarded [or who is named as the person with whom the child is to live (whether the award is made, or the person so named is named] solely or jointly with any other person) by an order of a court in the United Kingdom; or

(ii) the leave of that court;

(b) in relation to a child to whom subsection (1)(a)(ii) above applies, the leave of the court which made the child a ward of court;

Provided that, in relation to a child to whom more than one order referred to in subsection (1)(a) above applies, the appropriate consent may be that of any court which has granted an order as referred to in the said subsection (1)(a); and where one of these orders is an order referred to in the said subsection (1)(a)(ii) no other person as referred to in paragraph (a)(i) above shall be entitled to give the appropriate consent.

(4) In relation to a child to whom subsection (1)(a)(i) above applies, a person does not commit an offence by doing anything without the appropriate consent if—

(a) he does it in the belief that each person referred to in subsection (3)(a)(i) above—

(i) has consented; or

(ii) would consent if he was aware of all the relevant circumstances; or

(b)   he has taken all reasonable steps to communicate with such other person but has been unable to communicate with him.

(5)   In proceedings against any person for an offence under this section it shall be a defence for that person to show that at the time of the alleged offence he had no reason to believe that there was in existence an order referred to in subsection (1) above.

(6)   For the purposes of this section—

(a)   a person shall be regarded as taking a child if he causes or induces the child to accompany him or any other person, or causes the child to be taken; and

(b)   a person shall be regarded as sending a child if he causes the child to be sent.

(7)   In this section 'guardian' means a person appointed by deed or will or by order of a court of competent jurisdiction to be the guardian of a child.

MATRIMONIAL AND FAMILY PROCEEDINGS ACT 1984
(1984, c 42)

PART IV
FINANCIAL PROVISION IN SCOTLAND AFTER OVERSEAS DIVORCE ETC

28   Circumstances in which a Scottish court may entertain application for financial provision

(1)   Where parties to a marriage have been divorced in an overseas country, then, subject to [subsection (3A)] below, if the jurisdictional requirements and the conditions set out in subsections (2) and (3) below respectively are satisfied, the court may entertain an application by one of the parties for an order for financial provision.

(2)   The jurisdictional requirements mentioned in subsection (1) above are that—

(a)   the applicant was domiciled or habitually resident in Scotland on the date when the application was made; and

(b)   the other party to the marriage—

(i)   was domiciled or habitually resident in Scotland on the date when the application was made; or

(ii)   was domiciled or habitually resident in Scotland when the parties last lived together as husband and wife; or

(iii)   on the date when the application was made, was an owner or tenant of, or had a beneficial interest in, property in Scotland which had at some time been a matrimonial home of the parties; and

(c)   where the court is the sheriff court, either—

(i)   one of the parties was, on the date when the application was made, habitually resident in the sheriffdom; or

(ii)   paragraph (b)(iii) above is satisfied in respect of property wholly or partially within the sheriffdom.

(3)   The conditions mentioned in subsection (1) above are that—

(a)   the divorce falls to be recognised in Scotland;

(b)   the other party to the marriage initiated the proceedings for divorce;

(c)   the application was made within five years after the date when the divorce took effect;

(d)   a court in Scotland would have had jurisdiction to entertain an action for divorce between the parties if such an action had been brought in Scotland immediately before the foreign divorce took effect;

(e)   the marriage had a substantial connection with Scotland; and

(f)   both parties are living at the time of the application.

[(3A)   If an application or part of an application relates to a matter [in relation to which Article 18 of the 2007 Hague Convention applies, the court may not entertain the application or that part of it except where permitted by Article 18].]

[. . .]

[(5) 'The 2007 Hague Convention' means the Convention on the International Recovery of Child Support and Other Forms of Family Maintenance concluded on 23 November 2007 at The Hague.]

29 Disposal of application in Scotland

(1) Subject to subsections (2) to (5) below, Scots law shall apply, with any necessary modifications, in relation to an application under section 28 above as it would apply if the application were being made in an action for divorce in Scotland.

(2) In disposing of an application entertained by it under the said section 28, the court shall exercise its powers so as to place the parties, in so far as it is reasonable and practicable to do so, in the financial position in which they would have been if the application had been disposed of, in an action for divorce in Scotland, on the date on which the foreign divorce took effect.

(3) In determining what is reasonable and practicable for the purposes of subsection (2) above, the court shall have regard in particular to—

(a) the parties' resources, present and foreseeable at the date of disposal of the application;

(b) any order made by a foreign court in or in connection with the divorce proceedings for the making of financial provision in whatever form, or the transfer of property, by one of the parties to the other; and

(c) subsection (5) below.

(4) Except where subsection (5) below applies, the court may make an order for an interim award of a periodical allowance where—

(a) it appears from the applicant's averments that in the disposal of the application an order for financial provision is likely to be made; and

(b) the court considers that such an interim award is necessary to avoid hardship to the applicant.

(5) Where but for section 28(2)(b)(iii) above the court would not have jurisdiction to entertain the application, the court may make an order—

(a) relating to the former matrimonial home or its furniture and plenishings; or

(b) that the other party to the marriage shall pay to the applicant a capital sum not exceeding the value of that other party's interest in the former matrimonial home and its furniture and plenishings,

but shall not be entitled to make any other order for financial provision.

[29A Application of Part IV to annulled marriages

This Part of this Act shall apply to an annulment, of whatever nature, of a purported marriage, as it applies to a divorce, and references to marriage and divorce shall be construed accordingly.]

30 Interpretation of Part IV

(1) In the foregoing provisions of this Part of this Act unless the context otherwise requires—

'the court' means the Court of Session or the sheriff court;

'furniture and plenishings' has the meaning assigned by section 22 of the Matrimonial Homes (Family Protection) (Scotland) Act 1981;

'matrimonial home' has the meaning assigned by the said section 22;

'order for financial provision' means any one or more of the orders specified in [section 8(1) of the Family Law (Scotland) Act 1985] (financial provision) or an order under section 13 of the Matrimonial Homes (Family Protection) (Scotland) Act 1981 (transfer of tenancy of matrimonial home);

'overseas country' means a country or territory outside the British Islands; and

'tenant' has the meaning assigned by the said section 22.

(2)   Any reference in the foregoing provisions of this Part of this Act to a party to a marriage shall include a reference to a party to a marriage which has been terminated.

FAMILY LAW (SCOTLAND) ACT 1985
(1985, c 37)

Aliment

1   Obligation of aliment

(1)   From the commencement of this Act, an obligation of aliment shall be owed by, and only by—

(a)   a husband to his wife;

(b)   a wife to her husband;

[(bb) a partner in a civil partnership to the other partner,]

(c)   a father or mother to his or her child;

(d)   a person to a child (other than a child who has been boarded out with him by a local or other public authority or a voluntary organisation) who has been accepted by him as a child of his family.

(2)   For the purposes of this Act, an obligation of aliment is an obligation to provide such support as is reasonable in the circumstances, having regard to the matters to which a court is required or entitled to have regard under section 4 of this Act in determining the amount of aliment to award in an action for aliment.

(3)   Any obligation of aliment arising under a decree or by operation of law and subsisting immediately before the commencement of this Act shall, except insofar as consistent with this section, cease to have effect as from the commencement of this Act.

(4)   Nothing in this section shall affect any arrears due under a decree at the date of termination or cessation of an obligation of aliment, nor any rule of law by which a person who is owed an obligation of aliment may claim aliment from the executor of a deceased person or from any person enriched by the succession to the estate of a deceased person.

(5)   In subsection (1) above—

'child' means a person—

(a)   under the age of 18 years; or

(b)   over that age and under the age of 25 years who is reasonably and appropriately undergoing instruction at an educational establishment, or training for employment or for a trade, profession or vocation;

'husband' and 'wife' include the parties to a valid polygamous marriage.

2   Actions for aliment

(1)   A claim for aliment only (whether or not expenses are also sought) may be made, against any person owing an obligation of aliment, in the Court of Session or the sheriff court.

(2)   Unless the court considers it inappropriate in any particular case, a claim for aliment may also be made, against any person owing an obligation of aliment, in proceedings—

(a)   for divorce, separation, declarator of marriage or declarator of nullity of marriage;

[(aa)   for dissolution of a civil partnership, separation of civil partners or declarator of nullity of a civil partnership,]

(b)   relating to orders for financial provision;

[(c) concerning parental responsibilities or parental rights (within the meaning of sections 1(3) and 2(4) respectively of the Children (Scotland) Act 1995) or guardianship in relation to children;]

(d) concerning parentage or legitimacy;

(e) of any other kind, where the court considers it appropriate to include a claim for aliment.

(3) In this Act 'action for aliment' means a claim for aliment in proceedings referred to in subsection (1) or (2) above.

(4) An action for aliment may be brought—

(a) by a person (including a child) to whom the obligation of aliment is owed;

(b) by the curator bonis of an incapax;

(c) on behalf of a child under the age of 18 years, by—

(i) the [parent or guardian] of the child;

[. . .]

[(iii) a person with whom the child lives or who is seeking a residence order (within the meaning of section 11(2)(c) of the Children (Scotland) Act 1995) in respect of the child.]

(5) A woman (whether married or not) may bring an action for aliment on behalf of her unborn child as if the child had been born, but no such action shall be heard or disposed of prior to the birth of the child.

(6) It shall be competent to bring an action for aliment, notwithstanding that the person for or on behalf of whom aliment is being claimed is living in the same household as the defender.

(7) It shall be a defence to an action for aliment brought by virtue of subsection (6) above that the defender is fulfilling the obligation of aliment, and intends to continue doing so.

(8) It shall be a defence to an action for aliment by or on behalf of a person other than a child under the age of 16 years that the defender is making an offer, which it is reasonable to expect the person concerned to accept, to receive that person into his household and to fulfil the obligation of aliment.

(9) For the purposes of subsection (8) above, in considering whether it is reasonable to expect a person to accept an offer, the court shall have regard among other things to any conduct, decree or other circumstances which appear to the court to be relevant: but the fact that a husband and wife [or the partners in a civil partnership] have agreed to live apart shall not of itself be regarded as making it unreasonable to expect a person to accept such an offer.

(10) A person bringing an action for aliment under subsection (4)(c) above may give a good receipt for aliment paid under the decree in the action.

3 Powers of court in action for aliment

(1) The court may, if it thinks fit, grant decree in an action for aliment, and in granting such decree shall have power—

(a) to order the making of periodical payments, whether for a definite or an indefinite period or until the happening of a specified event;

(b) to order the making of alimentary payments of an occasional or special nature, including payments in respect of inlying, funeral or educational expenses;

(c) to backdate an award of aliment under this Act—

(i) to the date of the bringing of the action or to such later date as the court thinks fit; or

(ii) on special cause shown, to a date prior to the bringing of the action;

(d) to award less than the amount claimed even if the claim is undisputed.

(2) Nothing in subsection (1) above shall empower the court to substitute a lump sum for a periodical payment.

4 Amount of aliment

(1) In determining the amount of aliment to award in an action for aliment, the court shall, subject to subsection (3) below, have regard—

(a)   to the needs and resources of the parties;

(b)   to the earning capacities of the parties;

(c)   generally to all the circumstances of the case.

(2)   Where two or more parties owe an obligation of aliment to another person, there shall be no order of liability, but the court, in deciding how much, if any, aliment to award against any of those persons, shall have regard, among the other circumstances of the case, to the obligation of aliment owed by any other person.

(3)   In having regard under subsection (1)(c) above generally to all the circumstances of the case, the court—

(a)   may, if it thinks fit, take account of any support, financial or otherwise, given by the defender to any person whom he maintains as a dependant in his household, whether or not the defender owes an obligation of aliment to that person; and

(b)   shall not take account of any conduct of a party unless it would be manifestly inequitable to leave it out of account.

[(4)   Where a court makes an award of aliment in an action brought by or on behalf of a child under the age of 16 years, it may include in that award such provision as it considers to be in all the circumstances reasonable in respect of the expenses incurred wholly or partly by the person having care of the child for the purpose of caring for the child.]

5   Variation or recall of decree of aliment

(1)   A decree granted in an action for aliment brought before or after the commencement of this Act may, on an application by or on behalf of either party to the action, be varied or recalled by an order of the court if since the date of the decree there has been a material change of circumstances.

[(1A)   Without prejudice to the generality of subsection (1) above, the making of a [maintenance calculation] with respect to a child for whom the decree of aliment was granted is a material change of circumstances for the purposes of that subsection.]

(2)   The provisions of this Act shall apply to applications and orders under subsection (1) above as they apply to actions for aliment and decrees in such actions, subject to any necessary modifications.

(3)   On an application under subsection (1) above, the court may, pending determination of the application, make such interim order as it thinks fit.

(4)   Where the court backdates an order under subsection (1) above, the court may order any sums paid under the decree to be repaid.

6   Interim aliment

(1)   A claim for interim aliment shall be competent—

(a)   in an action for aliment, by the [person] who claims aliment against the other [person];

(b)   in an action for divorce, separation, declarator of marriage or declarator of nullity of marriage, by either party against the other party,

[(c)   in an action for dissolution of a civil partnership, separation of civil partners or declarator of nullity of a civil partnership, by either partner against the other partner,]

on behalf of the claimant and any person on whose behalf he is entitled to act under section 2(4) of this Act.

(2)   Where a claim under subsection (1) above has been made, then, whether or not the claim is disputed, the court may award by way of interim aliment the sum claimed or any lesser sum or may refuse to make such an award.

(3)   An award under subsection (2) above shall consist of an award of periodical payments payable only until the date of the disposal of the action in which the award was made or such earlier date as the court may specify.

(4) An award under [this section] may be varied or recalled by an order of the court; and the provisions of this section shall apply to an award so varied and the claim therefor as they applied to the original award and the claim therefor.

7 Agreements on aliment

(1) Any provision in an agreement which purports to exclude future liability for aliment or to restrict any right to bring an action for aliment shall have no effect unless the provision was fair and reasonable in all the circumstances of the agreement at the time it was entered into.

(2) Where a person who owes an obligation of aliment to another person has entered into an agreement to pay aliment to or for the benefit of the other person, on a material change of circumstances application may be made to the court by or on behalf of either person for variation of the amount payable under the agreement or for termination of the agreement.

[(2ZA) On an application under subsection (2) above, the court may—

(a) pending determination of the application, make such interim order as it thinks fit;

(b) make an order backdating a variation of the amount payable under the agreement to—

(i) the date of the application or such later date as the court thinks fit; or

(ii) on special cause shown, a date prior to the date of the application.

(2ZB) Where the court makes an order under subsection (2ZA)(b) above, it may order any sums paid under the agreement to be repaid on such terms (including terms relating to repayment by instalments) as the court thinks fit.

(2ZC) Nothing in subsection (2ZA) shall empower the court to substitute a lump sum for a periodical payment.]

[(2A) Without prejudice to the generality of subsection (2) above, the making of a [maintenance calculation] with respect to a child to whom or for whose benefit aliment is payable under such an agreement is a material change of circumstances for the purposes of that subsection.]

(3) Subsections (8) and (9) of section 2 of this Act (which afford a defence to an action for aliment in certain circumstances) shall apply to an action to enforce such an agreement as is referred to in subsection (2) above as they apply to an action for aliment.

(4) In [this section] 'the court' means the court which would have jurisdiction and competence to entertain an action for aliment between the parties to the agreement to which the application under that subsection relates.

(5) In this section 'agreement' means an agreement entered into before or after the commencement of this Act and includes a unilateral voluntary obligation.

Financial provision on divorce, etc

8 Orders for financial provision

(1) In an action for divorce, either party to the marriage [and in an action for dissolution of a civil partnership, either partner] may apply to the court for one or more of the following orders—

(a) an order for the payment of a capital sum [. . .] to him by the other party to the [action];

[(aa) an order for the transfer of property to him by the other party to the [action];]

(b) an order for the making of a periodical allowance to him by the other party to the [action];

[(baa) a pension sharing order;

(bab) a pension compensation sharing order;

(ba) an order under section 12A(2) or (3) of this Act;

(bb) an order under section 12B(2);]

(c)   an incidental order within the meaning of section 14(2) of this Act.

(2)   Subject to sections 12 to 15 of this Act, where an application has been made under subsection (1) above, the court shall make such order, if any, as is—

(a)   justified by the principles set out in section 9 of this Act; and

(b)   reasonable having regard to the resources of the parties.

(3)   An order under subsection (2) above is in this Act referred to as an 'order for financial provision'.

[(4)   The court shall not, in the same proceedings, make both a pension sharing order and an order under section 12A(2) or (3) of this Act in relation to the same pension arrangement.

[. . .]

(5)   Where, as regards a pension arrangement, the parties to a marriage [or the partners in a civil partnership] have in effect a qualifying agreement which contains a term relating to pension sharing, the court shall not—

(a)   make an order under section 12A(2) or (3) of this Act; or

(b)   make a pension sharing order,

relating to the arrangement unless it also sets aside the agreement or term under section 16(1)(b) of this Act.

(6)   The court shall not make a pension sharing order in relation to the rights of a person under a pension arrangement if there is in force an order under section 12A(2) or (3) of this Act which relates to benefits or future benefits to which he is entitled under the pension arrangement.

(7)   In subsection (5) above—

(a)   'term relating to pension sharing' shall be construed in accordance with section 16(2A) of this Act; and

(b)   'qualifying agreement' has the same meaning as in section 28(3) of the Welfare Reform and Pensions Act 1999.]

[(8)   The court shall not, in the same proceedings, make both a pension compensation sharing order and an order under section 12B(2) in relation to the same PPF compensation.

(9)   The court shall not make a pension compensation sharing order in relation to rights to PPF compensation that—

(a)   derive from rights under a pension scheme which is subject to an order made under section 12A(2) or (3) in relation to the marriage or (as the case may be) civil partnership or a previous one between the same persons,

(b)   derive from rights under a pension scheme which were at any time the subject of a pension sharing order in relation to the marriage or (as the case may be) civil partnership or a previous one between the same persons,

(c)   are or have been the subject of a pension compensation sharing order in relation to the marriage or (as the case may be) civil partnership or a previous one between the same persons, or

(d)   are the subject of an order made under section 12B(2) in relation to the marriage or (as the case may be) civil partnership or a previous one between the same persons.

(10)   Where, as regards PPF compensation, the parties to a marriage or the partners in a civil partnership have in effect a qualifying agreement which contains a term relating to pension compensation sharing, the court shall not—

(a)   make an order under section 12B(2); or

(b)   make a pension compensation sharing order,

relating to the compensation unless it also sets aside the agreement or term under section 16(1)(b) of this Act.

(11)   For the purposes of subsection (10)—

(a)   the expression 'term relating to pension compensation sharing' is to be construed by reference to section 16(2AA) of this Act; and

(b)   a qualifying agreement is one to which section 110(1) of the Pensions Act 2008 relates.]

[8A Pension sharing orders: apportionment of charges
If a pension sharing order relates to rights under a pension arrangement, the court may include in the order provision about the apportionment between the parties of any charge under section 41 of the Welfare Reform and Pensions Act 1999 (charges in respect of pension sharing costs) or under corresponding Northern Ireland legislation.]

[8B Pension compensation sharing orders: apportionment of charges
The court may include in a pension compensation sharing order provision about apportionment between the parties of any charge under section 117 of the Pensions Act 2008 or under corresponding Northern Ireland legislation.]

9 Principles to be applied
(1) The principles which the court shall apply in deciding what order for financial provision, if any, to make are that—
(a) the net value of the matrimonial property should be shared fairly between the parties to the marriage [or as the case may be the net value of the partnership property should be so shared between the partners in the civil partnership];
(b) fair account should be taken of any economic advantage derived by either [person] from contributions by the other, and of any economic disadvantage suffered by either [person] in the interests of the other [person] or of the family;
(c) any economic burden of caring should be shared fairly between the [persons]—
[(i)] after divorce, for a child of the marriage under the age of 16 years;
[(ii) after dissolution of the civil partnership, for a child [of the civil partnership] under that age [. . .];
(d) a [person] who has been dependent to a substantial degree on the financial support of the other [person] should be awarded such financial provision as is reasonable to enable him to adjust, over a period of not more than three years from—
[(i)] the date of the decree of divorce, to the loss of that support on divorce;
[(ii) the date of the decree of dissolution of the civil partnership, to the loss of that support on dissolution,]
(e) a [person] who at the time of the divorce [or of the dissolution of the civil partnership] seems likely to suffer serious financial hardship as a result of the divorce [or dissolution] should be awarded such financial provision as is reasonable to relieve him of hardship over a reasonable period.
(2) In subsection (1)(b) above and section 11(2) of this Act—
'economic advantage' means advantage gained whether before or during the marriage [or civil partnership] and includes gains in capital, in income and in earning capacity, and 'economic disadvantage' shall be construed accordingly;
'contributions' means contributions made whether before or during the marriage [or civil partnership]; and includes indirect and non-financial contributions and, in particular, any such contribution made by looking after the family home or caring for the family.

10 Sharing of value of matrimonial property [or partnership property]
(1) In applying the principle set out in section 9(1)(a) of this Act, the net value of the matrimonial property [or partnership property] shall be taken to be shared fairly between the [persons] when it is shared equally or in such other proportions as are justified by special circumstances.
(2) [Subject to subsection (3A) below,] the net value of the [. . .] property shall be the value of the property at the relevant date after deduction of any debts incurred by [one or both of the parties to the marriage or as the case may be of the partners]—

(a)   before the marriage so far as they relate to the matrimonial property [or before the registration of the partnership so far as they relate to the partnership property], and

(b)   during the marriage [or partnership],

which are outstanding at that date.

(3)   In this section 'the relevant date' means whichever is the earlier of—

(a)   subject to subsection (7) below, the date on which the [persons] ceased to cohabit;

(b)   the date of service of the summons in the action for divorce [or for dissolution of the civil partnership].

[(3A)   In its application to property transferred by virtue of an order under section 8(1)(aa) of this Act this section shall have effect as if—

(a)   in subsection (2) above, for 'relevant date' there were substituted 'appropriate valuation date';

(b)   after that subsection there were inserted—

'(2A)   Subject to subsection (2B), in this section the "appropriate valuation date" means—

(a)   where the parties to the marriage or, as the case may be, the partners agree on a date, that date;

(b)   where there is no such agreement, the date of the making of the order under section 8(1)(aa).

(2B)   If the court considers that, because of the exceptional circumstances of the case, subsection (2A)(b) should not apply, the appropriate valuation date shall be such other date (being a date as near as may be to the date referred to in subsection (2A)(b)) as the court may determine.'; and

(c)   subsection (3) did not apply.]

(4)   Subject to [subsections (5) and (5A)] below, in this section and in section 11 of this Act 'the matrimonial property' means all the property belonging to the parties or either of them at the relevant date which was acquired by them or him (otherwise than by way of gift or succession from a third party)—

(a)   before the marriage for use by them as a family home or as furniture or plenishings for such home; or

(b)   during the marriage but before the relevant date.

[(4A)   Subject to [subsections (5) and (5A)] below, in this section and in section 11 of this Act 'the partnership property' means all the property belonging to the partners or either of them at the relevant date which was acquired by them or by one of them (otherwise than by way of gift or succession from a third party)—

(a)   before the registration of the partnership for use by them as a family home or as furniture or plenishings for such a home, or

(b)   during the partnership but before the relevant date.]

(5)   The proportion of any rights or interests of either [person]—

[(a)]   under a life policy [. . .] or similar arrangement [; and

(b)   in any benefits under a pension arrangement which either [person] has or may have (including such benefits payable in respect of the death of either [person]),

[. . .]

which is] referable to the period to which subsection (4)(b) [or (4A)(b)] above refers shall be taken to form part of the matrimonial property [or partnership property].

[(5A)   Where either person is entitled to [PPF compensation], the proportion of the compensation which is referable to the period to which subsection (4)(b) or (4A)(b) above refers shall be taken to form part of the matrimonial property or partnership property.]

(6)   In subsection (1) above 'special circumstances', without prejudice to the generality of the words, may include—

(a) the terms of any agreement between the [persons] on the ownership or division of any of the matrimonial property [or partnership property];

(b) the source of the funds or assets used to acquire any of the matrimonial property [or partnership property] where those funds or assets were not derived from the income or efforts of the [persons] during the marriage [or partnership];

(c) any destruction, dissipation or alienation of property by either [person];

(d) the nature of the [family] property [or partnership property], the use made of it (including use for business purposes or as a [family] home) and the extent to which it is reasonable to expect it to be realised or divided or used as security;

(e) the actual or prospective liability for any expenses of valuation or transfer of property in connection with the divorce [or the dissolution of the civil partnership].

(7) For the purposes of subsection (3) above no account shall be taken of any cessation of cohabitation where the [persons] thereafter resumed cohabitation, except where the [persons] ceased to cohabit for a continuous period of 90 days or more before resuming cohabitation for a period or periods of less than 90 days in all.

[(8) The Secretary of State may by regulations make provision about calculation and verification in relation to the valuation for the purposes of this Act of benefits under a pension arrangement or relevant state scheme rights.]

[(8A) Regulations under subsection (8) above may include—

(a) provision for calculation or verification in accordance with guidance from time to time prepared by a prescribed person; and

(b) provision by reference to regulations under section 30 or 49(4) of the Welfare Reform and Pensions Act 1999.]

[(8B) The Scottish Ministers may by regulations make provision for the purposes of this Act about—

(a) calculation and verification of PPF compensation;

(b) apportionment of PPF compensation.

(8C) Regulations under subsection (8B) may include provision—

(a) for calculation of verification in a manner approved by a prescribed person,

(b) by reference to regulations under section 112 of the Pensions Act 2008.]

(9) Regulations under subsection (8) [or (8B)] above [may make different provision for different purposes and] shall be made by statutory instrument which shall be subject to annulment in pursuance of a resolution of either House of Parliament.

11 Factors to be taken into account

(1) In applying the principles set out in section 9 of this Act, the following provisions of this section shall have effect.

(2) For the purposes of section 9(1)(b) of this Act, the court shall have regard to the extent to which—

(a) the economic advantages or disadvantages sustained by either [person] have been balanced by the economic advantages or disadvantages sustained by the other [person], and

(b) any resulting imbalance has been or will be corrected by a sharing of the value of the matrimonial property [or the partnership property] or otherwise.

(3) For the purposes of section 9(1)(c) of this Act, the court shall have regard to—

(a) any decree or arrangement for aliment for the child;

(b) any expenditure or loss of earning capacity caused by the need to care for the child;

(c)   the need to provide suitable accommodation for the child;

(d)   the age and health of the child;

(e)   the educational, financial and other circumstances of the child;

(f)   the availability and cost of suitable child-care facilities or services;

(g)   the needs and resources of the [persons]; and

(h)   all the other circumstances of the case.

(4)   For the purposes of section 9(1)(d) of this Act, the court shall have regard to—

(a)   the age, health and earning capacity of the [person] who is claiming the financial provision;

(b)   the duration and extent of the dependence of that [person prior to divorce or to the dissolution of the civil partnership];

(c)   any intention of that [person] to undertake a course of education or training;

(d)   the needs and resources of the [persons]; and

(e)   all the other circumstances of the case.

(5)   For the purposes of section 9(1)(e) of this Act, the court shall have regard to—

(a)   the age, health and earning capacity of the [person] who is claiming the financial provision;

(b)   the duration of the marriage [or of the civil partnership];

(c)   the standard of living of the [persons] during the marriage [or civil partnership];

(d)   the needs and resources of the [persons]; and

(e)   all the other circumstances of the case.

(6)   In having regard under subsections (3) to (5) above to all the other circumstances of the case, the court may, if it thinks fit, take account of any support, financial or otherwise, given by the [person] who is to make the financial provision to any person whom he maintains as a dependant in his household whether or not he owes an obligation of aliment to that person.

(7)   In applying the principles set out in section 9 of this Act, the court shall not take account of the conduct of either party [to the marriage or as the case may be of either partner] unless—

(a)   the conduct has adversely affected the financial resources which are relevant to the decision of the court on a claim for financial provision; or

(b)   in relation to section 9(1)(d) or (e), it would be manifestly inequitable to leave the conduct out of account.

12   Orders for payment of capital sum or transfer of property

(1)   An order under section 8(2) of this Act for payment of a capital sum or transfer of property may be made—

(a)   on granting decree of divorce [or of dissolution of a civil partnership]; or

(b)   within such period as the court on granting [the decree] may specify.

(2)   The court, on making an order referred to in subsection (1) above, may stipulate that it shall come into effect at a specified future date.

(3)   The court, on making an order under section 8(2) of this Act for payment of a capital sum, may order that the capital sum shall be payable by instalments.

(4)   Where an order referred to in subsection (1) above has been made, the court may, on an application by—

[(a)]   either party to the marriage;

[(b)   either partner,]

on a material change of circumstances, vary the date or method of payment of the capital sum or the date of transfer of property.

[12A   Orders for payment of capital sum: pensions lump sums

(1)   This section applies where the court makes an order under section 8(2) of

this Act for payment of a capital sum (a 'capital sum order') by a party to the marriage [or a partner in a civil partnership ('the liable person')] in circumstances where—

(a)   the matrimonial property [or the partnership property] within the meaning of section 10 of this Act includes any rights or interests in benefits under a pension [arrangement] which the liable [person] has or may have (whether such benefits are payable to him or in respect of his death); and

(b)   those benefits include a lump sum payable to him or in respect of his death.

(2)   Where the benefits referred to in subsection (1) above include a lump sum payable to the liable [person] the court, on making the capital sum order, may make an order requiring the [person responsible for the pension arrangement] in question to pay the whole or part of that sum, when it becomes due, to the other party to the marriage [or as the case may be to the other partner ('the other person')].

(3)   Where the benefits referred to in subsection (1) above include a lump sum payable in respect of the death of the liable [person], the court, on making the capital sum order, may make an order—

(a)   if the [person responsible for the pension arrangement in question has] power to determine the person to whom the sum, or any part of it, is to be paid, requiring them to pay the whole or part of that sum, when it becomes due, to the other [person];

(b)   if the liable [person] has power to nominate the person to whom the sum, or any part of it, is to be paid, requiring the liable [person] to nominate the other [person] in respect of the whole or part of that sum;

(c)   in any other case, requiring the [person responsible for the pension arrangement] in question to pay the whole or part of that sum, when it becomes due, to the other [person] instead of to the person to whom, apart from the order, it would be paid.

(4)   Any payment by the [person responsible for the pension agreement] under an order under subsection (2) or (3) above—

(a)   shall discharge so much of the [liability of the person responsible for the pension arrangement] to or in respect of the liable [person] as corresponds to the amount of the payment; and

(b)   shall be treated for all purposes as a payment made by the liable [person] in or towards the discharge of his liability under the capital sum order.

(5)   Where the liability of the liable [person] under the capital sum order has been discharged in whole or in part, other than by a payment by the [person responsible for the pension arrangement] under an order under subsection (2) or (3) above, the court may, on an application by any person having an interest, recall any order under either of those subsections or vary the amount specified in such an order, as appears to the court appropriate in the circumstances.

(6)   Where—

(a)   an order under subsection (2) or (3) above imposes any requirement on the [person responsible for a pension arrangement] ('the first [arrangement]') and the liable [person] acquires transfer credits under another [arrangement] ('the new [arrangement]') which are derived (directly or indirectly) from a transfer from the first [arrangement] of all his accrued rights under that [arrangement]; and

(b)   [the person responsible for the new arrangement has] been given notice in accordance with regulations under subsection (8) below,

the order shall have effect as if it had been made instead in respect of the [person responsible for the new arrangement]; and in this subsection 'transfer credits' has the same meaning as in the Pension Schemes Act 1993.

(7)   Without prejudice to subsection (6) above, any court may, on an application by any person having an interest, vary an order under subsection (2) or (3) above

by substituting for [the person responsible for the pension arrangement] specified in the order [person responsible for any other pension arrangement] under which any lump sum referred to in subsection (1) above is payable to the liable [person] or in respect of his death.

[(7ZA) Subsection (7ZB) applies where a right under an occupational pension scheme to payment of a lump sum in respect of death would, but for the provisions of Chapter 3 of Part 2 of the Pensions Act 2004 (c 35), arise during an assessment period (within the meaning of section 132 of that Act).

(7ZB) An order under subsection (3) shall not take effect until the assessment period comes to an end for a reason other than the giving of a transfer notice under section 160 of that Act.

(7ZC) [For] the purpose only of giving effect to subsection (7), the court may deal with an order under subsection (2) so that it—

(a) is addressed to the Board of the Pension Protection Fund instead of the person responsible for a pension arrangement; and

(b) takes effect in respect of an entitlement to compensation payable under Chapter 3 of Part 2 of the Pensions Act 2004 or the Northern Ireland provision, instead of rights in relation to any lump sum referred to in subsection (1) which is payable to the liable party.

(7A) Where—

(a) the court makes an order under subsection (3); and

(b) after the making of the order the Board gives the trustees or managers of the scheme a notice under section 160 of the Pensions Act 2004 ('the 2004 Act'), or the Northern Ireland provision, in relation to the scheme,

the order shall, on the giving of such notice, be recalled.

(7B) Subsection (7C) applies where—

(a) the court makes an order under subsection (2) imposing requirements on the trustees or managers of an occupational pension scheme; and

(b) after the making of the order the Board gives the trustees or managers of the scheme a notice under section 160 of the 2004 Act, or the Northern Ireland provision, in relation to the scheme.

(7C) The order shall have effect from the time when the notice is given—

(a) as if—

(i) references to the trustees or managers of the scheme were references to the Board; and

(ii) references to any lump sum to which the person with benefits under a pension arrangement is or might become entitled under the scheme were references to the amount of any compensation payable under that Chapter of the 2004 Act, or the Northern Ireland provision, to which that person is or might become entitled in respect of the lump sum; and

(b) subject to such other modifications as may be prescribed by regulations by the Scottish Ministers.]

(8) The Secretary of State may by regulations—

(a) require notices to be given in respect of changes of circumstances relevant to orders under subsection (2) or (3) above.

[. . .]

(9) Regulations under [subsections (7C)(b) and] (8) above shall be made by statutory instrument which shall be subject to annulment in pursuance of a resolution of either House of Parliament.

[(10) The definition of 'benefits under a pension scheme' in section 27 of this Act does not apply to this section.

(11) In subsections [(7ZC)] to (7C) 'the Northern Ireland provision', in relation to a provision of the 2004 Act, means any provision in force in Northern Ireland corresponding to the provision of that Act.]

[12B   Order for payment of capital sum: pension compensation

(1)   This section applies where the court makes an order under section 8(2) for payment of a capital sum (a 'capital sum order') by a party to a marriage or a partner in a civil partnership ('the liable person') in circumstances where the matrimonial or (as the case may be) partnership property within the meaning of section 10 includes any rights to PPF compensation.

(2)   On making the capital sum order, the court may make an additional order requiring the Board of the Pension Protection Fund, if at any time any payment in respect of PPF compensation becomes due to the liable person, to pay the whole or part of that payment to the other party or (as the case may be) other partner ('the other person').

(3)   Any such payment by the Board of the Pension Protection Fund—

(a)   shall discharge so much of its liability to the liable person as corresponds to the amount of the payment, and

(b)   shall be treated for all purposes as a payment made by the liable person in or towards the discharge of the person's liability under the capital sum order.

(4)   Where the liability of the liable person under the capital sum order has been discharged in whole or in part, other than by a payment by the Board of the Pension Protection Fund, the court may, on an application by any person having an interest, recall the order or vary the amount specified in such an order as appears to the court appropriate in the circumstances.

(5)   The court may not make an additional order under subsection (2) in relation to rights to PPF compensation that—

(a)   derive from rights under a pension scheme which is subject to an order made under section 12A(2) or (3) in relation to the marriage or (as the case may be) civil partnership or a previous one between the same persons,

(b)   derive from rights under a pension scheme which were at any time the subject of a pension sharing order in relation to the marriage or (as the case may be) civil partnership or a previous one between the same persons,

(c)   are or have been the subject of a pension compensation sharing order in relation to the marriage or (as the case may be) civil partnership or a previous one between the same persons, or

(d)   are the subject of an order made under subsection (2) in relation to the marriage or (as the case may be) civil partnership or a previous one between the same persons.]

13   Orders for periodical allowance

(1)   An order under section 8(2) of this Act for a periodical allowance may be made—

(a)   on granting decree of divorce [or of dissolution of a civil partnership];

(b)   within such period as the court on granting [the decree] may specify; or

(c)   after [such decree] where—

(i)   no such order has been made previously;

(ii)   application for the order has been made after the date of decree; and

(iii)   since the date of decree there has been a change of circumstances.

(2)   The court shall not make an order for a periodical allowance under section 8(2) of this Act unless—

(a)   the order is justified by a principle set out in paragraph (c), (d) or (e) of section 9(1) of this Act; and

(b)   it is satisfied that an order for payment of a capital sum or for transfer of property [or a pension sharing order or pension compensation sharing order] under that section would be inappropriate or insufficient to satisfy the requirements of the said section 8(2).

(3)   An order under section 8(2) of this Act for a periodical allowance may be for a definite or an indefinite period or until the happening of a specified event.

(4)   Where an order for a periodical allowance has been made under section 8(2) of this Act, and since the date of the order there has been a material change of circumstances, the court shall, on an application by or on behalf of either party to the marriage or his executor [, or as the case may be either partner or his executor], have power by subsequent order—

(a)   to vary or recall the order for a periodical allowance;

(b)   to backdate such variation or recall to the date of the application therefor or, on cause shown, to an earlier date;

(c)   to convert the order into an order for payment of a capital sum or for a transfer of property.

[(4A)   Without prejudice to the generality of subsection (4) above, the making of a maintenance [calculation] with respect to a child who has his home with a person to whom the periodical allowance is made (being a child to whom the person making the allowance has an obligation of aliment) is a material change of circumstances for the purposes of that subsection.]

(5)   The provisions of this Act shall apply to applications and orders under subsection (4) above as they apply to applications for periodical allowance and orders on such applications.

(6)   Where the court backdates an order under subsection (4)(b) above, the court may order any sums paid by way of periodical allowance to be repaid.

(7)   An order for a periodical allowance made under section 8(2) of this Act—

(a)   shall, if subsisting at the death of the [person] making the payment, continue to operate against that [person's] estate, but without prejudice to the making of an order under subsection (4) above;

[(b)   shall cease to have effect on the person receiving payment—

(i)   marrying,

(ii)   entering into a civil partnership,

(iii)   dying,]

except in relation to any arrears due under it.

14   Incidental orders

(1)   Subject to subsection (3) below, an incidental order may be made under section 8(2) of this Act before, on or after the granting or refusal of decree of divorce [or of dissolution of a civil partnership].

(2)   In this Act, 'an incidental order' means one or more of the following orders—

(a)   an order for the sale of property;

(b)   an order for the valuation of property;

(c)   an order determining any dispute between the parties to the marriage [or as the case may be the partners] as to their respective property rights by means of a declarator thereof or otherwise;

(d)   an order regulating the occupation of—

[(i)]   the matrimonial home; or

[(ii)   the family home of the partnership,]

or the use of furniture and plenishings therein or excluding either [person] from such occupation;

(e)   an order regulating liability, as between the [persons], for outgoings in respect of—

[(i)]   the matrimonial home; or

(ii)   the family home of the partnership,]

or furniture or plenishings therein;

(f)   an order that security shall be given for any financial provision;

(g)   an order that payments shall be made or property transferred to any curator bonis or trustee or other person for the benefit of the [person] by whom or on whose behalf application has been made under section 8(1) of this Act for an incidental order;

(h) an order setting aside or varying any term in an antenuptial or post-nuptial marriage settlement [or in any corresponding settlement in respect of the civil partnership];

(j) an order as to the date from which any interest on any amount awarded shall run;

[(ja) in relation to a deed relating to moveable property, an order dispensing with the execution of the deed by the grantor and directing the sheriff clerk to execute the deed;]

(k) any ancillary order which is expedient to give effect to the principles set out in section 9 of this Act or to any order made under section 8(2) of this Act.

(3) An incidental order referred to in subsection (2)(d) or (e) above may be made only on or after the granting of [the decree].

(4) An incidental order may be varied or recalled by subsequent order on cause shown.

(5) So long as an incidental order granting a party to a marriage the right to occupy a matrimonial home or the right to use furniture and plenishings therein remains in force then—

(a) section 2(1), (2), (5)(a) and (9) of the Matrimonial Homes (Family Protection) (Scotland) Act 1981 (which confer certain general powers of management on a spouse in relation to a matrimonial home), and

(b) subject to section 15(3) of this Act, section 12 of the said Act of 1981 and section [114 of the Bankruptcy (Scotland) Act 2016] (which protect the occupancy rights of a spouse against arrangements intended to defeat them),

shall, except to the extent that the order otherwise provides, apply in relation to the order—

(i) as if that party were a non-entitled spouse and the other party were an entitled spouse within the meaning of section 1(1) or 6(2) of the said Act of 1981 as the case may require;

(ii) as if the right to occupy a matrimonial home under that order were 'occupancy rights' with the meaning of the said Act of 1981; and

(iii) with any other necessary modifications; and

subject to section 15(3) of this Act, section 11 of the said Act of 1981 (protection of spouse in relation to furniture and plenishings) shall apply in relation to the order as if that party were a spouse within the meaning of the said section 11 and the order were an order under section 3(3) or (4) of the said Act of 1981.

[(5A) So long as an incidental order granting a partner in a civil partnership the right to occupy a family home or the right to use furnishings and plenishings therein remains in force then—

(a) section 102(1), (2), (5)(a) and (9) of the Civil Partnership Act 2004, and

(b) subject to section 15(3) of this Act, section 111 of that Act,

shall, except to the extent that the order otherwise provides, apply in relation to the order in accordance with subsection (5B).

(5B) Those provisions apply—

(a) as if that partner were a non-entitled partner and the other partner were an entitled partner within the meaning of section 101 or 106(2) of that Act as the case may require,

(b) as if the right to occupy a family home under that order were a right specified in paragraph (a) or (b) of section 101(1) of that Act, and

(c) with any other necessary modification.]

(6) In subsection (2)(h) above, 'settlement' includes a settlement by way of a policy of assurance to which section 2 of the Married Women's Policies of Assurance (Scotland) Act 1880 relates.

(7) Notwithstanding subsection (1) above, the Court of Session may by Act of Sederunt make rules restricting the categories of incidental order which may be made under section 8(2) of this Act before the granting of decree of divorce.

15 Rights of third parties

(1) The court shall not make an order under section 8(2) of this Act for the transfer of property if the consent of a third party which is necessary under any obligation, enactment or rule of law has not been obtained.

(2) The court shall not make an order under section 8(2) of this Act for the transfer of property subject to security without the consent of the creditor unless he has been given an opportunity of being heard by the court.

(3) Neither an incidental order, nor any rights conferred by such an order, shall prejudice any rights of any third party insofar as those rights existed immediately before the making of the order.

16 Agreements on financial provision

(1) Where the parties to a marriage [or the partners in a civil partnership] have entered into an agreement as to financial provision to be made on divorce [or on dissolution of the civil partnership], the court may make an order setting aside or varying—

(a) any term of the agreement relating to a periodical allowance where the agreement expressly provides for the subsequent setting aside or variation by the court of that term; or

(b) the agreement or any term of it where the agreement was not fair and reasonable at the time it was entered into.

(2) The court may make an order—

(a) under subsection (1)(a) above at any time after granting decree of divorce; and

[(b) under subsection (1)(b) above, if the agreement [contains neither a term relating to pension sharing nor a term relating to pension compensation sharing], on granting decree of divorce [or of dissolution of the civil partnership] or within such time as the court may specify, on granting decree of divorce [or of dissolution of the civil partnership]; or

(c) under subsection (1)(b) above, if the agreement contains a term relating to pension sharing [or pension compensation sharing]—

(i) where the order sets aside the agreement or sets aside or varies the term relating to pension sharing [or (as the case may be) the term relating to pension compensation sharing], on granting decree of divorce; and

(ii) where the order sets aside or varies any other term of the agreement, on granting decree of divorce or within such time thereafter as the court may specify on granting decree of divorce.]

[(2A) In subsection (2) above, a term relating to pension sharing is a term corresponding to provision which may be made in a pension sharing order and satisfying the requirements set out in section 28(1)(f) or 48(1)(f) of the Welfare Reform and Pensions Act 1999.

[(2AA) For the purpose of subsection (2), a term relating to pension compensation sharing is a term corresponding to provision which may be made in a pension compensation sharing order and satisfying the requirements set out in section 109(g) of the Pensions Act 2008.]

(2B) Subsection (2C) applies where—

(a) the parties to a marriage or the partners in a civil partnership have entered into an agreement as to financial provision to be made on divorce or on dissolution of the civil partnership; and

(b) the agreement includes provision in respect of a person's rights or interests or benefits under an occupational pension scheme.

(2C) The Board of the Pension Protection Fund's subsequently assuming responsibility for the occupational pension scheme in accordance with Chapter 3 of Part 2 of the Pension Act 2004 or any provision in force in Northern Ireland corresponding to that Chapter shall not affect—

(a) the power of the court under subsection (1)(b) to make an order setting aside or varying the agreement or any term of it;

(b) on an appeal, the powers of the appeal court in relation to the order.]

(3) Without prejudice to subsections (1) and (2) above, where the parties to a marriage [or the partners in a civil partnership] have entered into an agreement as to financial provision to be made on divorce [or on dissolution of the civil partnership] and—

(a) the estate of the [person] by whom any periodical allowance is payable under the agreement has, since the date when the agreement was entered into, been sequestrated, the award of sequestration has not been recalled and the [person] has not been discharged;

(b) an analogous remedy within the meaning of section [17(7) of the Bankruptcy (Scotland) Act 2016] has, since that date, come into force and remains in force in respect of that [person's] estate;

(c) that [person's] estate is being administered by a trustee acting under a voluntary trust deed granted since that date by the [person] for the benefit of his creditors generally or is subject to an analogous arrangement [; or

(d) by virtue of the making of a maintenance calculation, child support maintenance has become payable by either party to the agreement with respect to a child to whom or for whose benefit periodical allowance is paid under that agreement,]

the court may, on or at any time after granting decree of divorce [or of dissolution of the civil partnership], make an order setting aside or varying any term of the agreement relating to the periodical allowance.

(4) Any term of an agreement purporting to exclude the right to apply for an order under subsection (1)(b) or (3) above shall be void.

(5) In this section, 'agreement' means an agreement entered into before or after the commencement of this Act.

17 Financial provision on declarator of nullity of marriage

(1) Subject to the following provisions of this section, the provisions of this Act shall apply to actions for declarator of nullity of marriage [or of a civil partnership] as they apply to actions for divorce [or for dissolution of a civil partnership]; and in this Act, unless the context otherwise requires, 'action for divorce' includes an action for declarator of nullity of marriage [and 'action for dissolution of a civil partnership' includes an action for declarator of nullity of a civil partnership] and, in relation to such an action, 'decree' [, 'divorce' and dissolution of a civil partnership] shall be construed accordingly.

(2) In an action for declarator of nullity of marriage [or of nullity of a civil partnership], it shall be competent for either party to claim interim aliment under section 6(1) of this Act notwithstanding that he denies the existence of the marriage [or civil partnership].

(3) Any rule of law by virtue of which either party to an action for declarator of nullity of marriage may require restitution of property upon the granting of such declarator shall cease to have effect.

Supplemental

18 Orders relating to avoidance transactions

(1) Where a claim has been made (whether before or after the commencement of this Act), being—

(a) an action for aliment,

(b) a claim for an order for financial provision, or

(c) an application for variation or recall of a decree in such an action or of an order for financial provision,

the [person] making the claim may, not later than one year from the date of the disposal of the claim, apply to the court for an order—

(i) setting aside or varying any transfer of, or transaction involving, property effected by the other [person] not more than 5 years before the date of the making of the claim; or

(ii) interdicting the other [person] from effecting any such transfer or transaction.

(2)   Subject to subsection (3) below, on an application under subsection (1) above for an order the court may, if it is satisfied that the transfer or transaction had the effect of, or is likely to have the effect of, defeating in whole or in part any claim referred to in subsection (1) above, make the order applied for or such other order as it thinks fit.

(3)   An order under subsection (2) above shall not prejudice any rights of a third party in or to the property where that third party—

(a)   has in good faith acquired the property or any of it or any rights in relation to it for value; or

(b)   derives title to such property or rights from any person who has done so.

(4)   Where the court makes an order under subsection (2) above, it may include in the order such terms and conditions as it thinks fit and may make any ancillary order which it considers expedient to ensure that the order is effective.

[. . .]

20   Provision of details of resources
In an action—

(a)   for aliment;

(b)   which includes a claim for an order for financial provision; or

(c)   which includes a claim for interim aliment,

the court may order either party to provide details of his resources or those relating to a child or incapax on whose behalf he is acting.

21   Award of aliment or custody where divorce or separation refused
A court which refuses a decree of divorce [, separation or dissolution of a civil partnership] shall not, by virtue of such refusal, be prevented from making an order for aliment [. . .] or an incidental order determining any dispute between the [persons] as to their respective property rights.

22   Expenses of action
The expenses incurred by a [person] in pursuing or defending—

(a)   an action for aliment brought [—

(i)] by either party to the marriage or

[(ii) by either party in a civil partnership,]

on his own behalf against the other party;

(b)   an action for divorce, separation [(whether of the parties to a marriage or the civil partners in a civil partnership)], declarator of marriage or declarator of nullity of marriage;

[(bb)   an action for dissolution of a civil partnership, declarator that a civil partnership exists or declarator of nullity of a civil partnership,]

(c)   an application made after the commencement of this Act for variation or recall of a decree of aliment or an order for financial provision in an action brought before or after the commencement of this Act,

shall not be regarded as necessaries for which the other party to the marriage [or the other partner in a civil partnership] is liable.

Matrimonial property, etc

24   Marriage not to affect property rights or legal capacity
(1)   Subject to the provisions of any enactment (including this Act), marriage [or civil partnership] shall not of itself affect—

(a) the respective rights of the parties to the marriage [or as the case may be the partners in a civil partnership] in relation to their property;

(b) the legal capacity of [those parties or partners].

(2) Nothing in subsection (1) above affects the law of succession.

25 Presumption of equal shares in household goods

(1) If any question arises (whether during or after a marriage [or civil partnership]) as to the respective rights of ownership of the parties to a marriage [or the partners in a civil partnership] in any household goods obtained in prospect of or during the marriage [or civil partnership] other than by gift or succession from a third party, it shall be presumed, unless the contrary is proved, that each has a right to an equal share in the goods in question.

(2) For the purposes of subsection (1) above, the contrary shall not be treated as proved by reason only that while [—

(a)] the parties were married;

[(b) the partners were in a civil partnership],

and living together the goods in question were purchased from a third party by either party alone or by both in unequal shares.

(3) In this section 'household goods' means any goods (including decorative or ornamental goods) kept or used at any time during the marriage [or civil partnership in any family] home for the joint domestic purposes of the parties to the marriage [or the partners], other than—

(a) money or securities;

(b) any motor car, caravan or other road vehicle;

(c) any domestic animal.

26 Presumption of equal shares in money and property derived from housekeeping allowance

If any question arises (whether during or after a marriage [or civil partnership]) as to the right of a party to a marriage [or as the case may be of a partner in a civil partnership] to money derived from any allowance made by either party [or partner] for their joint household expenses or for similar purposes, or to any property acquired out of such money, the money or property shall, in the absence of any agreement between them to the contrary, be treated as belonging to each party [or partner] in equal shares.

General

27 Interpretation

(1) In this Act, unless the context otherwise requires—

'action' means an action brought after the commencement of this Act;

'action for aliment' has the meaning assigned to it by section 2(3) of this Act;

'aliment' does not include aliment pendente lite or interim aliment under section 6 of this Act;

['benefits under a pension arrangement' includes any benefits by way of pension, including relevant state scheme rights, whether under a pension arrangement or note;]

'caravan' means a caravan which is mobile or affixed to the land;

'child' includes [a child whether or not his parents have ever been married to [or in a civil partnership with] one another], and any reference to the child of a marriage [or the child of a civil partnership] (whether or not subsisting) includes a child (other than a child who has been boarded out with the parties, or one of them, by a local or other public authority or a voluntary organisation) who has been accepted by the parties as a child of the family;

['child support maintenance' has the meaning assigned to it by section 3(6) of the Child Support Act 1991;]

['civil partnership', in relation to an action for declarator of nullity of a civil partnership, means purported civil partnership;]

'the court' means the Court of Session or the sheriff, as the case may require;

'decree' in an action for aliment includes an order of the court awarding aliment;

'family' includes a one-parent family [. . .];

'incidental order' has the meaning assigned to it by section 14(2) of this Act;

['maintenance calculation' has the meaning assigned to it by section 54 of the Child Support Act 1991;]

'marriage', in relation to an action for declarator of nullity of marriage, means purported marriage;

'matrimonial home' has the meaning assigned to it by section 22 of the Matrimonial Homes (Family Protection) (Scotland) Act 1981 [as amended by section 13(10) of the Law Reform (Miscellaneous Provisions) (Scotland) Act 1985];

'needs' means present and foreseeable needs;

'obligation of aliment' shall be construed in accordance with section 1(2) of this Act;

'order for financial provision' means an order under section 8(2) of this Act and, in sections 18(1) and 22(c) of this Act, also includes an order under section 5(2) of the Divorce (Scotland) Act 1976;

['partner', in relation to a civil partnership, includes a person who [was] a partner in a civil partnership which has been terminated and an ostensible partner in a civil partnership which has been annulled;]

'party to a marriage' and 'party to the marriage' include a party to a marriage which has been terminated or annulled;

['pension arrangement' means—

(a)   any occupational pension scheme within the meaning of the Pension Schemes Act 1993;

(b)   a personal pension scheme within the meaning of that Act;

(c)   a retirement annuity contract;

(d)   an annuity or insurance policy purchased or transferred for the purpose of giving effect to rights under an occupational pension scheme or a personal pension scheme;

(e)   an annuity purchased or entered into for the purpose of discharging liability in respect of a pension credit under section 29(1)(b) of the Welfare Reform and Pensions Act 1999 or under corresponding Northern Ireland legislation;]

['pension compensation sharing order' is an order which—

(a)   provides that one party's shareable rights to PPF compensation that derive from rights under a specified compensation scheme (that is, specified in the order) are to be subject to pension compensation sharing for the benefit of the other party, and

(b)   specifies the percentage value or amount to be transferred;]

['pension sharing order' is an order which—

(a)   provides that one party's—

(i)   shareable rights under a specified pension arrangement, or

(ii)   shareable state scheme rights,

be subject to pension sharing for the benefit of the other party, and

(b)   specifies the percentage value, or the amount, to be transferred;]

['person responsible for a pension arrangement' means—

(a)   in the case of an occupational pension scheme or a personal pension scheme, the trustees or managers of the scheme;

(b)   in the case of a retirement annuity contract or an annuity falling within paragraph (d) or (e) of the definition of 'pension arrangement' above, the provider of their annuity;

(c)   in the case of an insurance policy falling within paragraph (d) of the definition of that expression, the insurer;]

'property' in sections 8, 12, 13 and 15 of this Act does not include a tenancy transferable under section 13 of the Matrimonial Homes (Family Protection) (Scotland) Act 1981;

['relevant state scheme rights' means—

[(za) shareable new state scheme rights, within the meaning given by section 47(3) of the Welfare Reform and Pensions Act 1999 or corresponding Northern Ireland legislation;]

(a)   entitlement, or prospective entitlement, to a Category A retirement pension by virtue of section 44(3)(b) of the Social Security Contributions and Benefits Act 1992 or under corresponding Northern Ireland legislation; and

(b)   entitlement, or prospective entitlement, to a pension under section 55A [or 55AA] of the Social Security Contributions and Benefits Act 1992 (shared additional pension) or under corresponding Northern Ireland legislation;]

'resources' means present and foreseeable resources;

['retirement annuity contract' means a contract or scheme approved under Chapter III of Part XIV of the Income and Corporation Taxes Act 1988;]

['trustees or managers' in relation to an occupational pension scheme or a personal pension scheme means—

(a)   in the case of a scheme established under a trust, the trustees of the scheme; and

(b)   in any other case, the managers of the scheme;]

'voluntary organisation' means a body, other than a local or other public authority, the activities of which are not carried on for profit.

[(1A)   In subsection (1), in the definition of 'pension sharing order'—

(a)   the reference to shareable rights under a pension arrangement is to rights in relation to which pension sharing is available under Chapter I of Part IV of the Welfare Reform and Pensions Act 1999, or under corresponding Northern Ireland legislation, and

(b)   the reference to shareable state scheme rights is to rights in relation to which pension sharing is available under Chapter II of Part IV of the Welfare Reform and Pensions Act 1999, or under corresponding Northern Ireland legislation.]

[(1B)   In subsection (1), in the definition of 'pension compensation sharing order', the reference to shareable rights to PPF compensation is to rights in relation to which pension compensation sharing is available under Chapter 1 of Part 3 of the Pensions Act 2008 or under corresponding Northern Ireland legislation.

(1C)   In this Act—

'PPF compensation' means compensation payable under the pension compensation provisions,

'the pension compensation provisions' means—

(a)   Chapter 3 of Part 2 of the Pensions Act 2004 and any regulations or order made under it,

(b)   Chapter 1 of Part 3 of the Pensions Act 2008 and any regulations or order made under it,

(c)   any provision corresponding to the provisions mentioned in paragraph (a) or (b) in force in Northern Ireland.]

(2)   For the purposes of this Act, the parties to a marriage shall be held to cohabit with one another only when they are in fact living together as man and wife.

29   Citation, commencement and extent

(1)   This Act may be cited as the Family Law (Scotland) Act 1985.

(2)   This Act shall come into operation on such day as the Secretary of State may appoint by order made by statutory instrument, and different days may be appointed for different purposes.

(3)   An order under subsection (2) above may contain such transitional

provisions and savings as appear to the Secretary of State necessary or expedient in connection with the provisions brought into force (whether wholly or partly) by the order.

(4) So much of section 28 of, and Schedule 1 to, this Act as affects the operation of the Maintenance Orders Act 1950 and the Maintenance Orders (Reciprocal Enforcement) Act 1972 shall extend to England and Wales and to Northern Ireland as well as to Scotland, but save as aforesaid this Act shall extend to Scotland only.

CHILD ABDUCTION AND CUSTODY ACT 1985
(1985, c 60)

PART I
INTERNATIONAL CHILD ABDUCTION

1 The Hague Convention

(1) In this Part of this Act 'the Convention' means the Convention on the Civil Aspects of International Child Abduction which was signed at The Hague on 25th October 1980.

(2) Subject to the provisions of this Part of this Act, the provisions of that Convention set out in Schedule 1 to this Act shall have the force of law in the United Kingdom.

2 Contracting States

(1) For the purposes of the Convention as it has effect under this Part of this Act the Contracting States other than the United Kingdom shall be those for the time being specified by an Order in Council under this section.

(2) An Order in Council under this section shall specify the date of the coming into force of the Convention as between the United Kingdom and any State specified in the Order; and, except where the Order otherwise provides, the Convention shall apply as between the United Kingdom and that State only in relation to wrongful removals or retentions occurring on or after that date.

(3) Where the Convention applies, or applies only, to a particular territory or particular territories specified in a declaration made by a Contracting State under Article 39 or 40 of the Convention references to that State in subsections (1) and (2) above shall be construed as references to that territory or those territories.

3 Central Authorities

(1) Subject to subsection (2) below, the functions under the Convention of a Central Authority shall be discharged—
    (a) in England and Wales [. . .] by the Lord Chancellor; and
    (b) in Scotland by the Secretary of State [; and
    (c) in Northern Ireland by the Department of Justice in Northern Ireland.]

(2) Any application made under the Convention by or on behalf of a person outside the United Kingdom may be addressed to the Lord Chancellor as the Central Authority in the United Kingdom,

(3) Where any such application relates to a function to be discharged under subsection (1) above by [an authority ('the responsible authority') other than the authority to which the application is addressed, the authority to which the application is addressed shall transmit it to the responsible authority.]

4 Judicial authorities

The courts having jurisdiction to entertain applications under the Convention shall be—
    (a) in England and Wales or in Northern Ireland the High Court; and
    (b) in Scotland the Court of Session.

5   Interim powers

Where an application has been made to a court in the United Kingdom under the Convention, the court may, at any time before the application is determined, give such interim directions as it thinks fit for the purpose of securing the welfare of the child concerned or of preventing changes in the circumstances relevant to the determination of the application.

6   Reports

Where the Lord Chancellor [, the Department of Justice in Northern Ireland] or the Secretary of State is requested to provide information relating to a child under Article 7(d) of the Convention he may—

(a)   request a local authority or [an officer of the service] to make a report to him in writing with respect to any matter which appears to him to be relevant;

(b)   request the Department of Health and Social Services for Northern Ireland to arrange for a suitably qualified person to make such a report to him;

(c)   request any court to which a written report relating to the child has been made to send him a copy of the report;

and such a request shall be duly complied with.

7   Proof of documents and evidence

(1)   For the purposes of Article 14 of the Convention a decision or determination of a judicial or administrative authority outside the United Kingdom may be proved by a duly authenticated copy of the decision or determination; and any document purporting to be such a copy shall be deemed to be a true copy unless the contrary is shown.

(2)   For the purposes of subsection (1) above a copy is duly authenticated if it bears the seal, or is signed by a judge or officer, of the authority in question.

(3)   For the purposes of Articles 14 and 30 of the Convention any such document as is mentioned in Article 8 of the Convention, or a certified copy of any such document, shall be sufficient evidence of anything stated in it.

8   Declarations by United Kingdom courts

The High Court or Court of Session may, on an application made for the purposes of Article 15 of the Convention by any person appearing to the court to have an interest in the matter, make a declaration or declarator that the removal of any child from, or his retention outside, the United Kingdom was wrongful within the meaning of Article 3 of the Convention.

9   Suspension of court's powers in cases of wrongful removal

The reference in Article 16 of the Convention to deciding on the merits of rights of custody shall be construed as a reference to—

(a)   making, varying or revoking a custody order, or [a supervision order under section 31 of the Children Act 1989 or Article 50 of the Children (Northern Ireland) Order 1995]

[(aa) enforcing under section 29 of the Family Law Act 1986 a custody order within the meaning of Chapter V of Part I of that Act;]

(b)   registering or enforcing a decision under Part II of this Act;

[(ba)   registering or enforcing a decision under the Convention on Jurisdiction, Applicable Law, Recognition, Enforcement and Co-operation in respect of Parental Responsibility and Measures for the Protection of Children that was signed at The Hague on 19 October 1996 ('the 1996 Convention'), except where provisions of the 1996 Convention are invoked in accordance with Article 50 of the 1996 Convention;]

[. . .]

[(d)   making, varying, amending or revoking a permanence order under section 80 of the Adoption and Children (Scotland) Act 2007 (including a deemed permanence order having effect by virtue of article 13(1) or 14(2) of the

Adoption and Children (Scotland) Act 2007 (Commencement No 4, Transitional and Savings Provisions) Order 2009 (SSI 2009/267))].
    [. . .]

10 Rules of court

(1) An authority having power to make rules of court may make such provision for giving effect to this Part of this Act as appears to that authority to be necessary or expedient.

(2) Without prejudice to the generality of subsection (1) above, rules of court may make provision—

(a) with respect to the procedure on applications for the return of a child and with respect to the documents and information to be furnished and the notices to be given in connection with any such application;

(b) for the transfer of any such application between the appropriate courts in the different parts of the United Kingdom;

(c) for the giving of notices by or to a court for the purposes of the provisions of Article 16 of the Convention and section 9 above and generally as respects proceedings to which those provisions apply;

(d) for enabling a person who wishes to make an application under the Convention in a Contracting State other than the United Kingdom to obtain from any court in the United Kingdom an authenticated copy of any decision of that court relating to the child to whom the application is to relate.

11 Cost of applications

The United Kingdom having made such a reservation as is mentioned in the third paragraph of Article 26 of the Convention, the costs mentioned in that paragraph shall not be borne by any Minister or other authority in the United Kingdom except so far as they fall to be so borne [by virtue of—

[(a) the provision of any civil legal services (within the meaning of Part 1 of the Legal Aid, Sentencing and Punishment of Offenders Act 2012) under arrangements made for the purposes of that Part of that Act, or]

(b) the grant of legal aid or legal advice and assistance under] the Legal Aid (Scotland) Act 1967, Part I of the Legal Advice and Assistance Act 1972 or the Legal Aid Advice and Assistance (Northern Ireland) Order 1981.

PART II
RECOGNITION AND ENFORCEMENT OF CUSTODY DECISIONS

12 The European Convention

(1) In this Part of this Act 'the Convention' means the European Convention on Recognition and Enforcement of Decisions concerning Custody of Children and on the Restoration of Custody of Children which was signed in Luxembourg on 20th May 1980.

(2) Subject to the provisions of this Part of this Act, the provisions of that Convention set out in Schedule 2 to this Act (which include Articles 9 and 10 as they have effect in consequence of a reservation made by the United Kingdom under Article 17) shall have the force of law in the United Kingdom.

13 Contracting States

(1) For the purposes of the Convention as it has effect under this Part of this Act the Contracting States other than the United Kingdom shall be those for the time being specified by an Order in Council under this section.

(2) An Order in Council under this section shall specify the date of the coming into force of the Convention as between the United Kingdom and any State specified in the Order.

(3) Where the Convention applies, or applies only, to a particular territory or particular territories specified by a Contracting State under Article 24 or 25 of the

Convention references to that State in subsections (1) and (2.) above shall be construed as references to that territory or those territories.

14 Central Authorities

(1) Subject to subsection (2) below, the functions under the Convention of a Central Authority shall be discharged—

    (a)   in England and Wales [. . .] by the Lord Chancellor; and

    (b)   in Scotland by the Secretary of State [; and

    (c)   in Northern Ireland by the Department of Justice in Northern Ireland.]

(2) Any application made under the Convention by or on behalf of a person outside the United Kingdom may be addressed to the Lord Chancellor as the Central Authority in the United Kingdom.

[(3) Where any such application relates to a function to be discharged under subsection (1) above by an authority ('the responsible authority') other than the authority to which the application is addressed, the authority to which the application is addressed shall transmit it to the responsible authority.]

15 Recognition of decisions

(1) Articles 7 and 12 of the Convention shall have effect in accordance with this section.

(2) A decision to which either of those Articles applies which was made in a Contracting State other than the United Kingdom shall be recognised in each part of the United Kingdom as if made by a court having jurisdiction to make it in that part but—

    (a)   the appropriate court in any part of the United Kingdom may, on the application of any person appearing to it to have an interest in the matter, declare on any of the grounds specified in Article 9 or 10 of the Convention that the decision is not to be recognised in any part of the United Kingdom; and

    (b)   the decision shall not be enforceable in any part of the United Kingdom unless registered in the appropriate court under section 16 below.

(3) The references in Article 9(1)(c) of the Convention to the removal of the child are to his improper removal within the meaning of the Convention.

16 Registration of decisions

(1) A person on whom any rights are conferred by a decision relating to custody made by an authority in a Contracting State other than the United Kingdom may make an application for the registration of the decision in an appropriate court in the United Kingdom.

(2) The Central Authority in the United Kingdom shall assist such a person in making such an application if a request for such assistance is made by him or on his behalf by the Central Authority of the Contracting State in question.

(3) An application under subsection (1) above or a request under subsection (2) above shall be treated as a request for enforcement for the purposes of Articles 10 and 13 of the Convention.

(4) The High Court or Court of Session shall refuse to register a decision if—

    (a)   the court is of the opinion that on any of the grounds specified in Article 9 or 10 of the Convention the decision should not be recognised in any part of the United Kingdom;

    (b)   the court is of the opinion that the decision is not enforceable in the Contracting State where it was made and is not a decision to which Article 12 of the Convention applies; or

    (c)   an application in respect of the child under Part I of this Act is pending.

[(5) Where an authority mentioned in subsection (1) of section 14 above is requested to assist in making an application under this section to the appropriate court in a part of the United Kingdom ('the relevant part of the United Kingdom') other than the part in relation to which the authority has functions under that subsection, the authority shall transmit the request to the authority which has functions under that subsection in relation to the relevant part of the United Kingdom.]

(6)   In this section 'decision relating to custody' has the same meaning as in the Convention.

17   Variation and revocation of registered decisions

(1)   Where a decision which has been registered under section 16 above is varied or revoked by an authority in the Contracting State in which it was made, the person on whose behalf the application for registration of the decision was made shall notify the court in which the decision is registered of the variation or revocation.

(2)   Where a court is notified under subsection (1) above of the revocation of a decision, it shall—

(a)   cancel the registration, and

(b)   notify such persons as may be prescribed by rules of court of the cancellation,

(3)   Where a court is notified under subsection (1) above of the variation of a decision, it shall—

(a)   notify such persons as may be prescribed by rules of court of the variation, and

(b)   subject to any conditions which may be so prescribed, vary the registration.

(4)   The court in which a decision is registered under section 16 above may also, on the application of any person appearing to the court to have an interest in the matter, cancel or vary the registration if it is satisfied that the decision has been revoked or, as the case may be, varied by an authority in the Contracting State in which it was made.

18   Enforcement of decisions

Where a decision relating to custody has been registered under section 16 above, the court in which it is registered shall have the same powers for the purpose of enforcing the decision as if it had been made by that court; and proceedings for or with respect to enforcement may be taken accordingly.

19   Interim powers

Where an application has been made to a court for the registration of a decision under section 16 above or for the enforcement of such a decision, the court may, at any time before the application is determined, give such interim directions as it thinks fit for the purpose of securing the welfare of the child concerned or of preventing changes in the circumstances relevant to the determination of the application or, in the case of an application for registration, to the determination of any subsequent application for the enforcement of the decision.

20   Suspension of court's powers

(1)   Where it appears to any court in which such proceedings as are mentioned in subsection (2) below are pending in respect of a child that—

(a)   an application has been made for the registration of a decision in respect of the child under section 16 above (other than a decision mentioned in subsection (3) below) or that such a decision is registered; and

(b)   the decision was made in proceedings commenced before the proceedings which are pending,

the powers of the court with respect to the child in those proceedings shall be restricted as mentioned in subsection (2) below unless, in the case of an application for registration, the application is refused.

(2)   Where subsection (1) above applies the court shall not—

(a)   in the case of custody proceedings, make, vary or revoke any custody order, or [a supervision order under section 31 of the Children Act 1989 or article 50 of the Children (Northern Ireland) Order 1995; or (aa) in the case of proceedings under section 29 of the Family Law Act 1986 for the enforcement of a custody order within the meaning of Chapter V of Part I of that Act, enforce that order.]

[. . .]

[(d) in the case of proceedings for the making, varying, amending or revoking of a permanence order under section 80 of the Adoption and Children (Scotland) Act 2007 (including a deemed permanence order having effect by virtue of article 13(1) or 14(2) of the Adoption and Children (Scotland) Act 2007 (Commencement No 4, Transitional and Savings Provisions) Order 2009 (SSI 2009/267)), make, vary, amend or revoke such an order;]

[. . .]

[(2A) Where it appears to the Secretary of State—

(a) that an application has been made for the registration of a decision in respect of a child under section 16 above (other than a decision mentioned in subsection (3) below); or

(b) that such a decision is registered,

the Secretary of State shall not make, vary or revoke any custody order in respect of the child unless, in the case of an application for registration, the application is refused.]

(3) The decision referred to in subsection (1) [or (2A)] above is a decision which is only a decision relating to custody within the meaning of section 16 of this Act by virtue of being a decision relating to rights of access.

(4) Paragraph (b) of Article 10(2) of the Convention shall be construed as referring to custody proceedings within the meaning of this Act.

(5) This section shall apply to a children's hearing as it does to a court.

[(6) In subsection (5), 'children's hearing' is to be construed in accordance with section 5 of the Children's Hearings (Scotland) Act 2011.]

21 Reports

Where the Lord Chancellor [, the Department of Justice in Northern Ireland] or the Secretary of State is requested to make enquiries about a child under Article 15(1)(b) of the Convention he may—

(a) request a local authority or [an officer of the service] to make a report to him in writing with respect to any matter relating to the child concerned which appears to him to be relevant;

(b) request the Department of Health and Social Services for Northern Ireland to arrange for a suitably qualified person to make such a report to him;

(c) request any court to which a written report relating to the child has been made to send him a copy of the report;

and any such request shall be duly complied with.

22 Proof of documents and evidence

(1) In any proceedings under this Part of this Act a decision of an authority outside the United Kingdom may be proved by a duly authenticated copy of the decision; and any document purporting to be such a copy shall be deemed to be a true copy unless the contrary is shown.

(2) For the purposes of subsection (1) above a copy is duly authenticated if it bears the seal, or is signed by a judge or officer, of the authority in question.

(3) In any proceedings under this Part of this Act any such document as is mentioned in Article 13 of the Convention, or a certified copy of any such document, shall be sufficient evidence of anything stated in it.

23 Decisions of United Kingdom courts

(1) Where a person on whom any rights are conferred by a decision relating to custody made by a court in the United Kingdom makes an application to the Lord Chancellor [, the Department of Justice in Northern Ireland] or the Secretary of State under Article 4 of the Convention with a view to securing its recognition or

enforcement in another Contracting State, the Lord Chancellor [, the Department of Justice in Northern Ireland] or the Secretary of State may require the court which made the decision to furnish him with all or any of the documents referred to in Article 13(1)(b), (c) and (d) of the Convention.

(2)   Where in any custody proceedings a court in the United Kingdom makes a decision relating to a child who has been removed from the United Kingdom, the court may also, on an application made by any person for the purposes of Article 12 of the Convention, declare the removal to have been unlawful if it is satisfied that the applicant has an interest in the matter and that the child has been taken from or sent or kept out of the United Kingdom without the consent of the person (or, if more than one, all the persons) having the right to determine the child's place of residence under the law of the part of the United Kingdom in which the child was habitually resident.

(3)   In this section 'decision relating to custody' has the same meaning as in the Convention.

24   Rules of court

(1)   An authority having power to make rules of court may make such provision for giving effect to this Part of this Act as appears to that authority to be necessary or expedient.

(2)   Without prejudice to the generality of subsection (1) above, rules of court may make provision—

(a)   with respect to the procedure on applications to a court under any provision of this Part of this Act and with respect to the documents and information to be furnished and the notices to be given in connection with any such application;

(b)   for the transfer of any such application between the appropriate courts in the different parts of the United Kingdom;

(c)   for the giving of directions requiring the disclosure of information about any child who is the subject of proceedings under this Part of this Act and for safeguarding its welfare.

[24A   Power to order disclosure of child's whereabouts

(1)   Where—

(a)   in proceedings for the return of a child under Part I of this Act; or

(b)   on an application for the recognition, registration or enforcement of a decision in respect of a child under Part II of this Act,

there is not available to the court adequate information as to where the child is, the court may order any person who it has reason to believe may have relevant information to disclose it to the court.

(2)   A person shall not be excused from complying with an order under subsection (1) above by reason that to do so may incriminate him or his spouse [or civil partner] of an offence; but a statement or admission made in compliance with such an order shall not be admissible in evidence against either of them in proceedings for any offence other than perjury.]

PART III
SUPPLEMENTARY

25   Termination of existing custody orders, etc

(1)   Where—

(a)   an order is made for the return of a child under Part I of this Act; or

(b)   a decision with respect to a child (other than a decision mentioned in subsection (2) below) is registered under section 16 of this Act,

any custody order relating to him shall cease to have effect.

(2)   The decision referred to in subsection (1)(b) above is a decision which is

only a decision relating to custody within the meaning of section 16 of this Act by virtue of being a decision relating to rights of access.

[. . .]

26   Expenses

There shall be paid out of money provided by Parliament—

(a)   any expenses incurred by the Lord Chancellor or the Secretary of State by virtue of this Act; and

(b)   any increase attributable to this Act in the sums so payable under any other Act.

27   Interpretation

(1)   In this Act 'custody order' means [(unless the contrary intention appears)] any such order or authorisation as is mentioned in Schedule 3 to this Act and 'custody proceedings' means proceedings in which an order within paragraphs 1, 2, 5, 6, 8 or 9 of that Schedule may be made [. . .] varied or revoked.

(2)   For the purposes of this Act 'part of the United Kingdom' means England and Wales, Scotland or Northern Ireland and 'the appropriate court', in relation to England and Wales or Northern Ireland means the High Court and, in relation to Scotland, the Court of Session.

(3)   In this Act 'local authority' means—

(a)   in relation to England and Wales, the council of a non-metropolitan county, a metropolitan district, a London borough or the Common Council of the City of London; and

(b)   in relation to Scotland, a [. . .] council [constituted under section 2 of the Local Government Etc (Scotland) Act 1994].

[(4)   In this Act a decision relating to rights of access in England and Wales or Scotland or Northern Ireland means a decision as to the contact which a child may, or may not, have with any person.

(5)   In this Act 'officer of the service' has the same meaning as in the Criminal Justice and Court Services Act 2000.]

28   Application as respects British Islands and colonies

(1)   Her Majesty may by Order in Council direct that any of the provisions of this Act specified in the Order shall extend, subject to such modifications as may be specified in the Order, to—

(a)   the Isle of Man,

(b)   any of the Channel Islands, and

(c)   any colony.

(2)   Her Majesty may by Order in Council direct that this Act shall have effect in the United Kingdom as if any reference in this Act, or in any amendment made by this Act, to any order which may be made, or any proceedings which may be brought or any other thing which may be done in, or in any part of, the United Kingdom included a reference to any corresponding order which may be made or, as the case may be, proceedings which may be brought or other thing which may be done in any of the territories mentioned in subsection (1) above.

(3)   An Order in Council under this section may make such consequential, incidental and supplementary provision as Her Majesty considers appropriate.

(4)   An Order in Council under this section shall be subject to annulment in pursuance of a resolution of either House of Parliament.

29   Short title, commencement and extent

(1)   This Act may be cited as the Child Abduction and Custody Act 1985.

(2)   This Act shall come into force on such day as may be appointed by an order made by statutory instrument by the Lord Chancellor and the Lord Advocate; and different days may be so appointed for different provisions.

(3)   This Act extends to Northern Ireland.

SCHEDULES

SCHEDULE 1
CONVENTION ON THE CIVIL ASPECTS OF INTERNATIONAL CHILD ABDUCTION

Section 1(2)

CHAPTER 1—SCOPE OF THE CONVENTION

Article 3

The removal or the retention of a child is to be considered wrongful where—

(a)   it is in breach of rights of custody attributed to a person, an institution or any other body, either jointly or alone, under the law of the State in which the child was habitually resident immediately before the removal or retention; and

(b)   at the time of removal or retention those rights were actually exercised, either jointly or alone, or would have been so exercised but for the removal or retention.

The rights of custody mentioned in sub-paragraph (a) above may arise in particular by operation of law or by reason of a judicial or administrative decision, or by reason of an agreement having legal effect under the law of that State.

Article 4

The Convention shall apply to any child who was habitually resident in a Contracting State immediately before any breach of custody or access rights. The Convention shall cease to apply when the child attains the age of sixteen years.

Article 5

For the purposes of this Convention—

(a)   'rights of custody' shall include rights relating to the care of the person of the child and, in particular, the right to determine the child's place of residence;

(b)   'rights of access' shall include the right to take a child for a limited period of time to a place other than the child's habitual residence.

CHAPTER II—CENTRAL AUTHORITIES

Article 7

Central Authorities shall co-operate with each other and promote co-operation amongst the competent authorities in their respective States to secure the prompt return of children and to achieve the other objects of this Convention.

In particular, either directly or through any intermediary, they shall take all appropriate measures—

(a)   to discover the whereabouts of a child who has been wrongfully removed or retained;

(b)   to prevent further harm to the child or prejudice to interested parties by taking or causing to be taken provisional measures;

(c)   to secure the voluntary return of the child or to bring about an amicable resolution of the issues;

(d)   to exchange, where desirable, information relating to the social background of the child;

(e)   to provide information of a general character as to the law of their State in connection with the application of the Convention;

(f)   to initiate or facilitate the institution of judicial or administrative proceedings with a view to obtaining the return of the child and, in a proper case, to make arrangements for organizing or securing the effective exercise of rights of access;

(g)   where the circumstances so require, to provide or facilitate the provision of legal aid and advice, including the participation of legal counsel and advisers;

(h)   to provide such administrative arrangements as may be necessary and appropriate to secure the safe return of the child;

(i)   to keep each other informed with respect to the operation of this Convention and, as far as possible, to eliminate any obstacles to its application.

CHAPTER III—RETURN OF CHILDREN

Article 8

Any person, institution or other body claiming that a child has been removed or retained in breach of custody rights may apply either to the Central Authority of the child's habitual residence or to the Central Authority of any other Contracting State for assistance in securing the return of the child.

The application shall contain—

(a)   information concerning the identity of the applicant, of the child and of the person alleged to have removed or retained the child;

(b)   where available, the date of birth of the child;

(c)   the grounds on which the applicant's claim for return of the child is based;

(d)   all available information relating to the whereabouts of the child and the identity of the person with whom the child is presumed to be.

The application may be accompanied or supplemented by—

(e)   an authenticated copy of any relevant decision or agreement;

(f)   a certificate or an affidavit emanating from a Central Authority, or other competent authority of the State of the child's habitual residence, or from a qualified person, concerning the relevant law of that State;

(g)   any other relevant document.

Article 9

If the Central Authority which receives an application referred to in Article 8 has reason to believe that the child is in another Contracting State, it shall directly and without delay transmit the application to the Central Authority of that Contracting State and inform the requesting Central Authority, or the applicant, as the case may be.

Article 10

The Central Authority of the State where the child is shall take or cause to be taken all appropriate measures in order to obtain the voluntary return of the child.

Article 11

The judicial or administrative authorities of Contracting States shall act expeditiously in proceedings for the return of children.

If the judicial or administrative authority concerned has not reached a decision within six weeks from the date of commencement of the proceedings, the applicant or the Central Authority of the requested State, on its own initiative or if asked by the Central Authority of the requesting State, shall have the right to request a statement of the reasons for the delay. If a reply is received by the Central Authority of the requested State, that Authority shall transmit the reply to the Central Authority of the requesting State, or to the applicant, as the case may be.

Article 12

Where a child has been wrongfully removed or retained in terms Article 3 and, at the date of the commencement of the proceedings before the judicial or administrative authority of the Contracting State where the child is, a period of less than one year has elapsed from the date of the wrongful removal or retention, the authority concerned shall order the return of the child forthwith.

The judicial or administrative authority, even where the proceedings have been commenced after the expiration of the period of one year referred to in the preceding paragraph, shall also order the return of the child, unless it is demonstrated that the child is now settled in its new environment.

Where the judicial or administrative authority in the requested state has reason to believe that the child has been taken to another State, it may stay the proceedings or dismiss the application for the return of the child.

Article 13

Notwithstanding the provisions of the preceding Article, the judicial or administrative authority of the requested State is not bound to order the return of the child if the person, institution or other body which opposes its return establishes that—

(a)   the person, institution or other body having the care of the person of the child was not actually exercising the custody rights at the time of removal or retention, or had consented to or subsequently acquiesced in the removal or retention; or

(b)   there is a grave risk that his or her return would expose the child to physical or psychological harm or otherwise place the child in an intolerable situation.

The judicial or administrative authority may also refuse to order the return of the child if it finds that the child objects to being returned and has attained an age and degree of maturity at which it is appropriate to take account of its views.

In considering the circumstances referred to in this Article, the judicial and administrative authorities shall take into account the information relating to the social background of the child provided by the Central Authority or other competent authority of the child's habitual residence.

Article 14

In ascertaining whether there has been a wrongful removal or retention within the meaning of Article 3, the judicial or administrative authorities of the requested State may take notice directly of the law of, and of judicial or administrative decisions, formally recognised or not in the State of the habitual residence of the child, without recourse to the specific procedures for the proof of that law or for the recognition of foreign decisions which would otherwise be applicable.

Article 15

The judicial or administrative authorities of a Contracting State may, prior to the making of an order for the return of the child request that the applicant obtain from the authorities of the State of the habitual residence of the child a decision or other determination that the removal or retention was wrongful within the meaning of Article 3 of the Convention, where such a decision or determination may be obtained in that State. The Central Authorities of the Contracting States shall so far as practicable assist applicants to obtain such a decision or determination.

Article 16

After receiving notice of a wrongful removal or retention of a child in the sense of Article 3, the judicial or administrative authorities of the Contracting State to which the child has been removed or in which it has been retained shall not decide on the merits of rights of custody until it has been determined that the child is not to be returned under this Convention or unless an application under this Convention is not lodged within a reasonable time following receipt of the notice.

Article 17

The sole fact that a decision relating to custody has been given in or is entitled to recognition in the requested State shall not be a ground for refusing to return a child under this Convention, but the judicial or administrative authorities of the requested State may take account of the reasons for that decision in applying this Convention.

Article 18

The provisions of this Chapter do not limit the power of a judicial or administrative authority to order the return of the child at any time.

Article 19

A decision under this Convention concerning the return of the child shall not be taken to be a determination on the merits of any custody issue.

CHAPTER IV—RIGHTS OF ACCESS

Article 21

An application to make arrangements for organising or securing the effective exercise of rights of access may be presented to the Central Authorities of the Contracting States in the same way as an application for the return of a child.

The Central Authorities are bound by the obligations of co-operation which are set forth in Article 7 to promote the peaceful enjoyment of access rights and the fulfilment of any conditions to which the exercise of those rights may be subject. The Central Authorities shall take steps to remove, as far as possible, all obstacles to the exercise of such rights. The Central Authorities, either directly or through intermediaries, may initiate or assist in the institution of proceedings with a view to organising or protecting these rights and securing respect for the conditions to which the exercise of these rights may be subject.

CHAPTER V—GENERAL PROVISIONS

Article 22

No security, bond or deposit, however described, shall be required to guarantee the payment of costs and expenses in the judicial or administrative proceedings falling within the scope of this Convention.

Article 24

Any application, communication or other document sent to the Central Authority of the requested State shall be in the original language, and shall be accompanied by a translation into the official language or one of the official languages of the requested State or, where that is not feasible, a translation into French or English.

Article 26

Each Central Authority shall bear its own costs in applying this Convention.

Central Authorities and other public services of Contracting States shall not impose any charges in relation to applications submitted under this Convention. In particular, they may not require any payment from the applicant towards the costs and expenses of the proceedings or, where applicable, those arising from the participation of legal counsel or advisers. However, they may require the payment of the expenses incurred or to be incurred in implementing the return of the child.

However, a Contracting State may, by making a reservation in accordance with Article 42, declare that it shall not be bound to assume any costs referred to in the preceding paragraph resulting from the participation of legal counsel or advisers or from court proceedings, except insofar as those costs may be covered by its system of legal aid and advice.

Upon ordering the return of a child or issuing an order concerning rights of access under this Convention, the judicial or administrative authorities may, where appropriate, direct the person who removed or retained the child, or who prevented the exercise of rights of access, to pay necessary expenses incurred by or on behalf of the applicant, including travel expenses, any costs incurred or payments made for locating the child, the costs of legal representation of the applicant, and those of returning the child.

Article 27

When it is manifest that the requirements of this Convention are not fulfilled or that the application is otherwise not well founded, a Central Authority is not bound to accept the application. In that case, the Central Authority shall forthwith inform the applicant or the Central Authority through which the application was submitted, as the case may be, of its reasons.

Article 28

A Central Authority may require that the application be accompanied by a written authorisation empowering it to act on behalf of the applicant, or to designate a representative so to act.

Article 29

This Convention shall not preclude any person, institution or body who claims that there has been a breach of custody or access rights within the meaning of Article 3 or 21 from applying directly to the judicial or administrative authorities of a Contracting State, whether or not under the provisions of this Convention.

Article 30

Any application submitted to the Central Authorities or directly to the judicial or administrative authorities of a Contracting State in accordance with the terms of this Convention, together with documents and any other information appended thereto or provided by a Central Authority, shall be admissible in the courts or administrative authorities of the Contracting States.

Article 31

In relation to a State which in matters of custody of children has two or more systems of law applicable in different territorial units—

(a) any reference to habitual residence in that State shall be construed as referring to habitual residence in a territorial unit of that State;

(b) any reference to the law of the State of habitual residence shall be construed as referring to the law of the territorial unit in that State where the child habitually resides.

Article 32

In relation to a State which in matters of custody of children has two or more systems of law applicable to different categories of persons, any reference to the law of that State shall be construed as referring to the legal system specified by the law of that State.

SCHEDULE 2
EUROPEAN CONVENTION ON RECOGNITION AND ENFORCEMENT ON DECISIONS CONCERNING CUSTODY OF CHILDREN

Section 12(2)

Article 1

For the purposes of this Convention:

  (a) 'child' means a person of any nationality, so long as he is under 16 years of age and has not the right to decide on his own place of residence under the law of his habitual residence, the law of his nationality or the internal law of the State addressed;

  (b) 'authority' means a judicial or administrative authority;

  (c) 'decision relating to custody' means a decision of an authority in so far as it relates to the care of the person of the child, including the right to decide on the place of his residence, or to the right of access to him.

  (d) 'improper removal' means the removal of a child across an international frontier in breach of a decision relating to his custody which has been given in a Contracting State and which is enforceable in such a State; 'improper removal' also includes:

    (i) the failure to return a child across an international frontier at the end of a period of the exercise of the right of access to this child or at the end of any other temporary stay in a territory other than that where the custody is exercised;

    (ii) a removal which is subsequently declared unlawful within the meaning of Article 12.

Article 4

  (1) Any person who has obtained in a Contracting State a decision relating to the custody of a child and who wishes to have that decision recognised or enforced in another Contracting State may submit an application for this purpose to the central authority in any Contracting State.

  (2) The application shall be accompanied by the documents mentioned in Article 13.

  (3) The central authority receiving the application, if it is not the central authority in the State addressed, shall send the documents directly and without delay to that central authority.

  (4) The central authority receiving the application may refuse to intervene where it is manifestly clear that the conditions laid down by this Convention are not satisfied.

  (5) The central authority receiving the application shall keep the applicant informed without delay of the progress of his application.

Article 5

  (1) The central authority in the State addressed shall take or cause to be taken without delay all steps which it considers to be appropriate, if necessary by instituting proceedings before its competent authorities, in order:

(a)   to discover the whereabouts of the child;

(b)   to avoid, in particular by any necessary provisional measures, prejudice to the interests of the child or of the applicant;

(c)   to secure the recognition or enforcement of the decision;

(d)   to secure the delivery of the child to the applicant where enforcement is granted;

(e)   to inform the requesting authority of the measures taken and their results.

(2)   Where the central authority in the State addressed has reason to believe that the child is in the territory of another Contracting State it shall send the documents directly and without delay to the central authority of that State.

(3)   With the exception of the cost of repatriation, each Contracting State undertakes not to claim any payment from an applicant in respect of any measures taken under paragraph (1) of this Article by the central authority of that State on the applicant's behalf, including the costs of proceedings and, where applicable, the costs incurred by the assistance of a lawyer.

(4)   If recognition or enforcement is refused, and if the central authority of the State addressed considers that it should comply with a request by the applicant to bring in that State proceedings concerning the substance of the case, that authority shall use its best endeavours to secure the representation of the applicant in the proceedings under conditions no less favourable than those available to a person who is resident in and a national of that State and for this purpose it may, in particular, institute proceedings before its competent authorities.

Article 7

A decision relating to custody given in a Contracting State shall be recognised and, where it is enforceable in the State of origin, made enforceable in every other Contracting State.

Article 9

(1)   [Recognition and enforcement may be refused] if:

(a)   in the case of a decision given in the absence of the defendant or his legal representative, the defendant was not duly served with the document which instituted the proceedings or an equivalent document in sufficient time to enable him to arrange his defence; but such a failure to effect service cannot constitute a ground for refusing recognition or enforcement where service was not effected because the defendant had concealed his whereabouts from the person who instituted the proceedings in the State of origin;

(b)   in the case of a decision given in the absence of the defendant or his legal representative, the competence of the authority giving the decision was not founded:

(i)   on the habitual residence of the defendant; or

(ii)   on the last common habitual residence of the child's parents, at least one parent being still habitually resident there; or

(iii)   on the habitual residence of the child;

(c)   the decision is incompatible with a decision relating to custody which became enforceable in the State addressed before the removal of the child, unless the child has had his habitual residence in the territory of the requesting State for one year before his removal.

(3)   In no circumstances may the foreign decision be reviewed as to its substance.

Article 10

(1) [Recognition and enforcement may also be refused] on any of the following grounds:

(a) if it is found that the effects of the decision are manifestly incompatible with the fundamental principles of the law relating to the family and children in the State addressed;

(b) if it is found that by reason of a change in the circumstances including the passage of time but not including a mere change in the residence of the child after an improper removal, the effects of the original decision are manifestly no longer in accordance with the welfare of the child;

(c) if at the time when the proceedings were instituted in the State of origin:

(i) the child was a national of the State addressed or was habitually resident there and no such connection existed with the State of origin;

(ii) the child was a national both of the State of origin and of the State addressed and was habitually resident in the State addressed;

(d) if the decision is incompatible with a decision given in the State addressed or enforceable in that State after being given in a third State, pursuant to proceedings begun before the submission of the request for recognition or enforcement, and if the refusal is in accordance with the welfare of the child.

(2) Proceedings for recognition or enforcement may be adjourned on any of the following grounds:

(a) if an ordinary form of review of the original decision has been commenced;

(b) if proceedings relating to the custody of the child, commenced before the proceedings in the State of origin were instituted, are pending in the State addressed;

(c) if another decision concerning the custody of the child is the subject of proceedings for enforcement or of any other proceedings concerning the recognition of the decision.

Article 11

(1) Decisions on rights of access and provisions of decisions relating to custody which deal with the rights of access shall be recognised and enforced subject to the same conditions as other decisions relating to custody.

(2) However, the competent authority of the State addressed may fix the conditions for the implementation and exercise of the right of access taking into account, in particular, undertakings given by the parties on this matter.

(3) Where no decision on the right of access has been taken or where recognition or enforcement of the decision relating to custody is refused, the central authority of the State addressed may apply to its competent authorities for a decision on the right of access if the person claiming a right of access so requests.

Article 12

Where, at the time of the removal of a child across an international frontier, there is no enforceable decision given in a Contracting State relating to his custody, the provisions of this Convention shall apply to any subsequent decision, relating to the custody of that child and declaring the removal to be unlawful, given in a Contracting State at the request of any interested person.

Article 13

(1) A request for recognition or enforcement in another Contracting State of a decision relating to custody shall be accompanied by:

(a) a document authorising the central authority of the State addressed to act on behalf of the applicant or to designate another representative for that purpose;

(b) a copy of the decision which satisfies the necessary conditions of authenticity;

(c) in the case of a decision given in the absence of the defendant or his legal representative, a document which establishes that the defendant was duly served with the document which instituted the proceedings or an equivalent document;

(d) if applicable, any document which establishes that, in accordance with the law of the State of origin, the decision is enforceable;

(e) if possible, a statement indicating the whereabouts or likely whereabouts of the child in the State addressed;

(f) proposals as to how the custody of the child should be restored.

Article 15

(1) Before reaching a decision under paragraph (1)(b) of Article 10, the authority concerned in the State addressed:

(a) shall ascertain the child's views unless this is impracticable having regard in particular to his age and understanding; and

(b) may request that any appropriate enquiries be carried out.

(2) The cost of enquiries in any Contracting State shall be met by the authorities of the State where they are carried out.

Requests for enquiries and the results of enquiries may be sent to the authority concerned through the central authorities.

Article 16

(1) In relation to a State which has in matters of custody two or more systems of law of territorial application:

(a) reference to the law of a person's habitual residence or to the law of a person's nationality shall be construed as referring to the system of law determined by the rules in force in that State or, if there are no such rules, to the system of law with which the person concerned is most closely connected;

(b) reference to the State of origin or to the State addressed shall be construed as referring, as the case may be, to the territorial unit where the decision was given or to the territorial unit where recognition or enforcement of the decision or restoration of custody is requested.

(2) Paragraph (1)(a) of this Article also applies mutatis mutandis to States which have in matters of custody two or more systems of law of personal application.

SCHEDULE 3
CUSTODY ORDER   Section 27(1)

Part II
Scotland

5. An order made by a court of civil jurisdiction in Scotland under any enactment or rule of law with respect to the [residence,] custody, care or control of a child [or contact with,] or access to a child, excluding—

(i)   an order placing a child under the supervision of a local authority;
[. . .]
(iii)   an order relating to the [guardianship] of a child;
(iv)   an order made under section [86 of the Children (Scotland) Act 1995];
[. . .]
(vi)   an order made in proceedings under this Act;
[(vii)   an adoption order (as defined in section 28(1) of the Adoption and Children (Scotland) Act 2007 (asp 4));
(viii)   a permanence order (as defined in subsection (2) of section 80 of that Act) which includes provision such as is mentioned in paragraph (c) of that subsection.]
[(ix)   an order made, or warrant or authorisation granted, under or by virtue of the Children's Hearings (Scotland) Act 2011 to remove the child to a place of safety or to secure accommodation (those expressions having the meanings given by section 202(1) of that Act), to keep the child at such a place or in such accommodation, or to prevent the removal of the child from a place where the child is being accommodated (or an order continuing, varying or discharging any order, warrant or authorisation so made or granted).]
[6.   A compulsory supervision order (as defined in section 83 of the Children's Hearings (Scotland) Act 2011) and any order made by a court in England and Wales or in Northern Ireland which, by virtue section 190 of that Act has effect as if it were a compulsory supervision order.]
[. . .]

LAW REFORM (PARENT AND CHILD) (SCOTLAND) ACT 1986
(1986, c 9)

1   [Abolition of status of illegitimacy]
(1)   [No person whose status is governed by Scots law shall be illegitimate; and accordingly the fact that a person's parents are not or have not been married to each other shall be left out of account in—
(a)   determining the person's legal status; or
(b)   establishing the legal relationship between the person and any other person.]
(2)   [. . .] Any reference (however expressed) in any enactment or deed to any relative shall, unless the contrary intention appears in the enactment or deed, be construed in accordance with subsection (1) above.
[. . .]
(4)   Nothing in this section shall apply to the construction or effect of—
(a)   any enactment passed or made before the commencement of section 21 of the Family Law (Scotland) Act 2006 (asp 2);
(b)   any deed executed before such commencement.
[. . .]
[(5)   In subsection (4), 'enactment' includes an Act of the Scottish Parliament.
(6)   It shall no longer be competent to bring an action for declarator of legitimacy, legitimation or illegitimacy.]
[. . .]

5   Presumptions
(1)   A man shall be presumed to be the father of a child—
(a)   if he was married to [or in a civil partnership with] the mother of the child at any time in the period beginning with the conception and ending with the birth of the child;
(b)   where paragraph (a) above does not apply, if both he and the mother of the child have acknowledged that he is the father and he has been registered as such in any register kept under section 13 (register of births and still-births) or

section 44 (register of corrections, etc) of the Registration of Births, Deaths and Marriages (Scotland) Act 1965 or in any corresponding register kept under statutory authority in any part of the United Kingdom other than Scotland.

(2) Subsection (1)(a) above shall apply [—

(a) in the case of a void, voidable or irregular marriage as it applies in the case of a valid and regular marriage,

(b) in the case of a void or voidable civil partnership as it applies in the case of a valid civil partnership.]

(3) Without prejudice to the effect under any rule of law which a decree of declarator in an action to which section 7 of this Act applies may have in relation to the parties, a decree of declarator in such an action shall give rise to a presumption to the same effect as the decree; and any such presumption shall displace any contrary presumption howsoever arising.

(4) Any presumption under this section may be rebutted by proof on a balance of probabilities.

6   Determination of parentage by blood sample

(1) This section applies where, for the purpose of obtaining evidence relating to the determination of parentage in civil proceedings, a [sample of blood or other body fluid or of body tissue] is sought by a party to the proceedings or by a curator *ad litem*.

(2) Where [such] a sample is sought from a child [under the age of 16 years], consent to the taking of the sample may be given by [any person having parential responsibilities (within the meaning of section 1(3) of the Children (Scotland) Act 1995) in relation to him or having] care and control of him.

(3) Where [such] a sample is sought from any person who is incapable of giving consent, the court may consent to the taking of the sample where—

(a) there is no person who is entitled to give such consent, or

(b) there is such a person, but it is not reasonably practicable to obtain his consent in the circumstances, or he is unwilling to accept the responsibility of giving or withholding consent.

(4) The court shall not consent under subsection (3) above to the taking of [such] a sample from any person unless the court is satisfied that the taking of the sample would not be detrimental to the person's health.

7   Actions for declarator

(1) An action for declarator of parentage [or non-parentage] may be brought in the Court of Session or the sheriff court.

(2) Such an action may be brought in the Court of Session if and only if the child was born in Scotland or the alleged or presumed parent or the child—

(a) is domiciled in Scotland on the date when the action is brought;

(b) was habitually resident in Scotland for not less than one year immediately preceding that date; or

(c) died before that date and either—

(i) was at the date of death domiciled in Scotland; or

(ii) had been habitually resident in Scotland for not less than one year immediately preceding the date of death.

(3) Such an action may be brought in the sheriff court if and only if—

(a) the child was born in the sheriffdom, or

(b) an action could have been brought in the Court of Session under subsection (2) above and the alleged or presumed parent or the child was habitually resident in the sheriffdom on the date when the action is brought or on the date of his death.

[. . .]

(5) Nothing in any rule of law or enactment shall prevent the court making in any proceedings an incidental finding as to parentage [or non-parentage] for the purposes of those proceedings.

(6) In this section 'the alleged or presumed parent' includes a person who claims or is alleged to be or not to be the parent.

8 Interpretation

In this Act, unless the context otherwise requires, the following expressions shall have the following meanings respectively assigned to them—

'action for declarator' includes an application for declarator contained in other proceedings [but does not include an appeal under section 20(1)(a) or (b) (Appeals) of the Child Support Act 1991 made to the court by virtue of an order made under section 45 (Jurisdiction of the courts in certain proceedings) of that Act];

[. . .]

'the court' means the Court of Session or the sheriff;

[. . .]

'deed' means any disposition, contract, instrument or writing whether *inter vivos* or *mortis causa*;

'non-parentage' means that a person is not or was not the parent, or is not or was not the child, of another person;

'parent' includes natural parent;

'parentage' means that a person is or was the parent, or is or was the child, of another person;

[. . .]

9 Savings and supplementary provisions

(1) Nothing in this Act shall—

[. . .]

(b) [subject to subsection (1A) below,] except to the extent that Schedules 1 and 2 to this Act otherwise provide, affect the law relating to adoption of children;

(c) apply to any title, coat of arms, honour or dignity transmissible on the death of the holder thereof or affect the succession thereto or the devolution thereof [(including, in particular, the competence of bringing an action of declarator of legitimacy, legitimation or illegitimacy in connection with such succession or devolution);

(ca) affect the functions of the Lord Lyon King of Arms so far as relating to the granting of arms;]

(d) affect the right of legitim out of, or the right of succession to, the estate of any person who died before the commencement of this Act.

[(1A) Subsections (1) and (2) of section 1 of this Act shall apply in relation to adopted children.]

(2) The court may at any time vary or recall any order made under section 3 of this Act or consent given by it under section 6 of this Act.

FAMILY LAW ACT 1986
(1986, c 55)

PART I
CHILD CUSTODY

Chapter III
Jurisdiction of Courts in Scotland

8 Jurisdiction in independent proceedings

A court in Scotland may entertain an application for a [Part I order] otherwise than in matrimonial [or civil partnership] proceedings only if it has jurisdiction under section 9, 10, 12 or 15(2) of this Act.

9   Habitual residence
Subject to section 11 of this Act, an application for a [Part I order] otherwise than
in matrimonial [or civil partnership] proceedings may be entertained by—
    (a)   the Court of Session if, on the date of the application, the child concerned
is habitually resident in Scotland;
    (b)   the sheriff if, on the date of the application, the child concerned is habi-
tually resident in the sheriffdom.

10   Presence of child
Subject to section 11 of this Act, an application for a [Part I order] otherwise than
in matrimonial [or civil partnership] proceedings may be entertained by—
    (a)   the Court of Session if, on the date of the application, the child concerned—
        (i)   is present in Scotland; and
        (ii)   is not habitually resident in any part of the United Kingdom;
    (b)   the sheriff if, on the date of the application,—
        (i)   the child is present in Scotland;
        (ii)   the child is not habitually resident in any part of the United Kingdom;
and
        (iii)   either the pursuer or the defender in the application is habitually
resident in the sheriffdom.

11   Provisions supplementary to sections 9 and 10
    (1)   Subject to subsection (2) below, the jurisdiction of the court to entertain an
application for a [Part I order] with respect to a child by virtue of section 9, 10 or
15(2) of this Act is excluded if, on the date of the application, matrimonial [or civil
partnership] proceedings are continuing in a court in any part of the United
Kingdom in respect of the marriage [or civil partnership] of the parents of the
child.
    (2)   Subsection (1) above shall not apply in relation to an application for a
[Part I order] if the court in which the matrimonial [or civil partnership] proceedings are continuing has made one of the following orders, that is to say—
    (a)   an order under section [2A(4)], 13(6) or [19A(4)] of this Act (not being an
order made by virtue of section 13(6)(a)(ii)); or
    (b)   an order under section 5(2), 14(2) or 22(2) of this Act which is recorded
as made for the purpose of enabling [Part I proceedings with respect to] the
child concerned to be taken in Scotland or, as the case may be, in another court
in Scotland, and that order is in force.

12   Emergency jurisdiction
Notwithstanding that any other court, whether within or outside Scotland, has jurisdiction to entertain an application for a [Part I order], the Court of Session or the
sheriff shall have jurisdiction to entertain such an application if—
    (a)   the child concerned is present in Scotland or, as the case may be, in the
sheriffdom on the date of the application; and
    (b)   the Court of Session or sheriff considers that, for the protection of the
child, it is necessary to make such an order immediately.

13   Jurisdiction ancillary to matrimonial proceedings
    (1)   The jurisdiction of a court in Scotland to entertain an application for a
[Part I order] in matrimonial [or civil partnership] proceedings shall be modified
by the following provisions of this section.
    [(2)   A court in Scotland shall not have jurisdiction—
    (a)   after the dismissal of matrimonial proceedings or after decree of absolvi-
tor is granted therein; or
    (b)   after the dismissal of civil partnership proceedings,
to entertain an application for a Part 1 order in those proceedings unless the

application therefor was made on or before such dismissal or the granting of the decree of absolvitor.]

(3) Where, after a decree of separation has been granted, an application is made in the separation process for a [Part I order], a court in Scotland shall not have jurisdiction to entertain that application if, on the date of the application, proceedings for divorce or nullity of marriage [or proceedings for dissolution or nullity of civil partnership] in respect of the marriage [or civil partnership] concerned are continuing in another court in the United Kingdom.

(4) A court in Scotland shall not have jurisdiction to entertain an application for the variation of a [Part I order] made [in matrimonial [or civil partnership] proceedings where the court has refused to grant the principal remedy sought in the proceedings] if, on the date of the application, matrimonial [or civil partnership] proceedings in respect of the marriage [or civil partnership] concerned are continuing in another court in the United Kingdom.

(5) Subsections (3) and (4) above shall not apply if the court in which the other proceedings there referred to are continuing has made—

(a) an order under section [2A(4)] or [19A(4)] of this Act or under subsection (6) below (not being an order made by virtue of paragraph (a)(ii) of that subsection), or

(b) an order under section 5(2), 14(2) or 22(2) of this Act which is recorded as made for the purpose of enabling [Part I proceedings with respect to] the child concerned to be taken in Scotland or, as the case may be, in another court in Scotland, and that order is in force.

(6) A court in Scotland which has jurisdiction in matrimonial [or civil partnership] proceedings to entertain an application for a [Part I order] with respect to a child may make an order declining such jurisdiction if—

(a) it appears to the court with respect to that child that—

(i) but for section 11(1) of this Act, another court in Scotland would have jurisdiction to entertain an application for a [Part I order], or

(ii) but for section 3(2), 6(3), 20(2) or 23(3) of this Act, a court in another part of the United Kingdom would have jurisdiction to make a [Part I order] or an order varying a [Part I order]; and

(b) the court considers that it would be more appropriate for [Part I matters relating to] that child to be determined in that other court or part.

(7) The court may recall an order made under subsection (6) above.

14 Power of court to refuse application or sist proceedings

(1) A court in Scotland which has jurisdiction to entertain an application for a [Part I order] may refuse the application in any case where the matter in question has already been determined in other proceedings.

(2) Where, at any stage of the proceedings on an application made to a court in Scotland for a [Part I order], it appears to the court—

(a) that proceedings with respect to the matters to which the application relates are continuing outside Scotland or in another court in Scotland;

(b) that it would be more appropriate for those matters to be determined in proceedings outside Scotland or in another court in Scotland and that such proceedings are likely to be taken there, or

[. . .]

[(d) that it should exercise its powers under Article 8 of the Hague Convention (request to authority in another Contracting State to assume jurisdiction),]

the court may sist the proceedings on that application [or (as the case may be) exercise its powers under [. . .] Article 8 of the Hague Convention] [. . .].

[(3) The court may recall a sist granted in order for it to exercise its powers under Article 8 of the Hague Convention, and withdraw any request made by it to an authority in another Contracting State to assume jurisdiction, if—

(a)   the authority in the other Contracting State does not assume jurisdiction within the period for which the court granted the sist, or

(b)   the parties do not, within the period specified by the court, request the authority in the other Contracting State to assume jurisdiction.]

15   Duration, variation and recall of orders

(1)   Where, after the making by a court in Scotland of a [Part I order] ('the existing order') with respect to a child,—

(a)   a [Part I order], or an order varying a [Part I order], competently made by another court in any part of the United Kingdom with respect to that child; or

(b)   an order [relating to the parental responsibilities or parental rights in relation to] that child which is made outside the United Kingdom and recognised in Scotland by virtue of section 26 of this Act [. . .],

comes into force, the existing order shall cease to have effect so far as it makes provision for any matter for which the same or different provision is made by the order of the other court in the United Kingdom or, as the case may be, the order so recognised.

(2)   Subject to sections 11(1) and 13(3) and (4) of this Act, a court in Scotland which has made a [Part I order] ('the original order') may, notwithstanding that it would no longer have jurisdiction to make the original order, make an order varying or recalling the original order; but if the original order has by virtue of subsection (1) above ceased to have effect so far as it makes provision for any matter, the court shall not have power to vary that order under this subsection so as to make provision for that matter.

(3)   In subsection (2) above, an order varying an original order means any [Part I order] made with respect to the same child as the original order was made.

(4)   [Where, by virtue of subsection (1) above, a child is to live with a different person], then, if there is in force an order made by a court in Scotland [. . .] providing for the supervision of that child by a local authority, that order shall cease to have effect.

16   Tutory and curatory

(1)   Subject to subsections (2) and (3) below, an application made after the commencement of this Part for an order relating to the [guardianship] of a [child] may be entertained by—

(a)   the Court of Session if, on the date of the application, the pupil or minor is habitually resident in Scotland,

(b)   the sheriff if, on the date of the application, the pupil or minor is habitually resident in the sheriffdom.

(2)   Subsection (1) above shall not apply to an application for the appointment or removal of a [judicial factor] or of a curator bonis or any application made by such factor or curator.

(3)   Subsection (1) above is without prejudice to any other ground of jurisdiction on which the Court of Session or the sheriff may entertain an application mentioned therein.

(4)   Provision may be made by act of sederunt prescribing, in relation to orders relating to the [guardianship] of a [child], what constitutes an application for the purposes of this Chapter.

17   Orders for delivery of child

(1)   [. . .], an application by one parent of a child for an order for the delivery of the child from the other parent, where the order is not sought to implement a [Part I order], may be entertained by the Court of Session or a sheriff if, but only if, the Court of Session or, as the case may be, the sheriff would have jurisdiction under this Chapter to make a [Part I order] with respect to the child concerned.

[. . .]

(3)   Subsection (1) above shall apply to an application by one party to a marriage for an order for the delivery of the child concerned from the other party
where the child [, although not a child of both parties to the marriage, is a child of
the family of those parties] as it applies to an application by one parent of a child
for an order for the delivery of the child from the other parent.

[(4)   In subsection (3) above, 'child of the family' means any child who has been
treated by both parties as a child of their family, except a child who has been
placed with those parties as foster parents by a local authority or a voluntary
organisation.]

[17A   The provisions of this Chapter are subject to [. . .] the Hague Convention.]

18   Interpretation of Chapter III

(1)   In this Chapter—
'child' means a person who has not attained the age of sixteen;
['civil partnership proceedings' means proceedings for dissolution or nullity of a
civil partnership or for the separation of the partners in a civil partnership;]
   'matrimonial proceedings' means proceedings for divorce, nullity of marriage or
judicial separation.
(2)   In this Chapter, 'the date of the application' means, where two or more
applications are pending, the date of the first of those applications; and, for the
purposes of this subsection, an application is pending until a [Part I order] or, in
the case of an application mentioned in section 16(1) of this Act, an order relating
to the [guardianship of a child], has been granted in pursuance of the application
or the court has refused to grant such an order.

Chapter V
Recognition and Enforcement

[26   Recognition: special Scottish rule

[(1)   An order relating to parental responsibilities or parental rights in relation
to a child which is made outside the United Kingdom shall be recognised in
Scotland if the order was made in the country where the child was habitually
resident.]
[. . .]

HUMAN FERTILISATION AND EMBRYOLOGY ACT 1990
(1990, c 37)

Principal terms used

1   Meaning of 'embryo', 'gamete' and associated expressions

(1)   In this Act (except in section 4A or in the term 'human admixed
embryo')—
   (a)   embryo means a live human embryo and does not include a human
   admixed embryo (as defined by section 4A(6)), and
   (b)   references to an embryo include an egg that is in the process of fertilisation or is undergoing any other process capable of resulting in an embryo.]
(2)   This Act, so far as it governs bringing about the creation of an embryo,
applies only to bringing about the creation of an embryo outside the human body;
and in this Act—
   [(a)   references to embryos the creation of which was brought about in vitro
   (in their application to those where fertilisation or any other process by which
   an embryo is created is complete) are to those where fertilisation or any other

process by which the embryo was created began outside the human body whether or not it was completed there, and]

(b) references to embryos taken from a woman do not include embryos whose creation was brought about *in vitro*.

(3) This Act, so far as it governs the keeping or use of an embryo, applies only to keeping or using an embryo outside the human body.

(4) [In this Act (except in section 4A)—

(a) references to eggs are to live human eggs, including cells of the female germ line at any stage of maturity, but (except in subsection (1)(b)) not including eggs that are in the process of fertilisation or are undergoing any other process capable of resulting in an embryo,

(b) references to sperm are to live human sperm, including cells of the male germ line at any stage of maturity, and

(c) references to gametes are to be read accordingly.]

[(5) For the purposes of this Act, sperm is to be treated as partner-donated sperm if the donor of the sperm and the recipient of the sperm declare that they have an intimate physical relationship.]

[(6) If it appears to the Secretary of State necessary or desirable to do so in the light of developments in science or medicine, regulations may provide that in this Act (except in section 4A) 'embryo', 'eggs', 'sperm' or 'gametes' includes things specified in the regulations which would not otherwise fall within the definition.

(7) Regulations made by virtue of subsection (6) may not provide for anything containing any nuclear or mitochondrial DNA that is not human to be treated as an embryo or as eggs, sperm or gametes.]

2 Other terms

(1) In this Act—

'the Authority' means the Human Fertilisation and Embryology Authority estab-lished under section 5 of this Act,

['basic partner treatment services' means treatment services that are provided for a woman and a man together without using—

(a) the gametes of any other person, or

(b) embryos created outside the woman's body,]

[. . .]

'directions' means directions under section 23 of this Act,

['distribution', in relation to gametes or embryos intended for human appli-cation, means transportation or delivery, and related terms are to be interpreted accordingly,

'human application' means use in a human recipient,]

'licence' means a licence under Schedule 2 to this Act and, in relation to a licence, 'the person responsible' has the meaning given by section 17 of this Act,

'non-medical fertility services' means any services that are provided, in the course of a business, for the purpose of assisting women to carry children, but are not medical, surgical or obstetric services,

['nuclear DNA', in relation to an embryo, includes DNA in the pronucleus of the embryo,]

'processing', in relation to gametes or embryos intended for human application, means any operation involved in their preparation, manipulation or packaging, and related terms are to be interpreted accordingly,

['procurement', in relation to gametes or embryos intended for human application, means any process by which they are made available, and related terms are to be interpreted accordingly,

'serious adverse event' means—

(a) any untoward occurrence which may be associated with the procure-ment, testing, processing, storage or distribution of gametes or embryos intended for human application and which, in relation to a donor of gametes or a person who receives treatment services or non-medical fertility services—

    (i)   might lead to the transmission of a communicable disease, to death, or life-threatening, disabling or incapacitating conditions, or

    (ii)   might result in, or prolong, hospitalisation or illness, or

  (b)   any type of gametes or embryo misidentification or mix-up,

'serious adverse reaction' means an unintended response, including a communicable disease, in a donor of gametes intended for human application or a person who receives treatment services or non-medical fertility services, which may be associated with the procurement or human application of gametes or embryos and which is fatal, life-threatening, disabling, incapacitating or which results in, or prolongs, hospitalisation or illness,

'store', in relation to gametes [, embryos or human admixed embryos], means preserve, whether by cryopreservation or in any other way, and 'storage' and 'stored' are to be interpreted accordingly,

['tissue establishment' means a tissue bank or a unit of a hospital or another body which procures, tests, processes, preserves, stores or distributes human tissues and cells,]

'traceability' means the ability—

  (a)   to identify and locate gametes and embryos during any step from procurement to use for human application or disposal,

  (b)   to identify the donor and recipient of particular gametes, embryos [or human admixed embryos],

  (c)   to identify any person who has carried out any activity in relation to particular gametes or embryos, and

  (d)   to identify and locate all relevant data relating to products and materials coming into contact with particular gametes or embryos and which can affect their quality or safety,]

'treatment services' means medical, surgical or obstetric services provided to the public or a section of the public for the purpose of assisting women to carry children.

(2)   References in this Act to keeping, in relation to embryos [, gametes or human admixed embryos] include keeping while preserved [in storage].

[(2A)   For the purposes of this Act, a person who, from any premises, controls the provision of services for transporting gametes or embryos is to be taken to distribute gametes or embryos on those premises.

(2B)   In this Act, any reference to a requirement of a provision of the first, second or third Directive [is to be read as a reference to a requirement which that provision would require to be imposed if the provision formed part of domestic law].]

(3)   For the purposes of this Act, a woman is not to be treated as carrying a child until the embryo has become implanted.

Information

[31 Register of information

(1)   The Authority shall keep a register which is to contain any information which falls within subsection (2) and which—

  (a)   immediately before the coming into force of section 24 of the Human Fertilisation and Embryology Act 2008, was contained in the register kept under this section by the Authority, or

  (b)   is obtained by the Authority.

(2)   Subject to subsection (3), information falls within this subsection if it relates to—

  (a)   the provision for any identifiable individual of treatment services other than basic partner treatment services,

  (b)   the procurement or distribution of any sperm, other than sperm which is partner-donated sperm and has not been stored, in the course of providing non-medical fertility services for any identifiable individual,

    (c)   the keeping of the gametes of any identifiable individual or of an embryo taken from any identifiable woman,

    (d)   the use of the gametes of any identifiable individual other than their use for the purpose of basic partner treatment services, or

    (e)   the use of an embryo taken from any identifiable woman,

or if it shows that any identifiable individual is a relevant individual.

(3) Information does not fall within subsection (2) if it is provided to the Authority for the purposes of any voluntary contact register as defined by section 31ZF(1).

(4) In this section 'relevant individual' means an individual who was or may have been born in consequence of—

    (a)   treatment services, other than basic partner treatment services, or

    (b)   the procurement or distribution of any sperm (other than partner-donated sperm which has not been stored) in the course of providing non-medical fertility services.]

[31ZA   Request for information as to genetic parentage etc

(1)   A person who has attained the age of 16 ('the applicant') may by notice to the Authority require the Authority to comply with a request under subsection (2).

(2)   The applicant may request the Authority to give the applicant notice stating whether or not the information contained in the register shows that a person ('the donor') other than a parent of the applicant would or might, but for the relevant statutory provisions, be the parent of the applicant, and if it does show that—

    (a)   giving the applicant so much of that information as relates to the donor as the Authority is required by regulations to give (but no other information), or

    (b)   stating whether or not that information shows that there are other persons of whom the donor is not the parent but would or might, but for the relevant statutory provisions, be the parent and if so—

        (i)   the number of those other persons,

        (ii)   the sex of each of them, and

        (iii)   the year of birth of each of them.

(3)   The Authority shall comply with a request under subsection (2) if—

    (a)   the information contained in the register shows that the applicant is a relevant individual, and

    (b)   the applicant has been given a suitable opportunity to receive proper counselling about the implications of compliance with the request.

(4)   Where a request is made under subsection (2)(a) and the applicant has not attained the age of 18 when the applicant gives notice to the Authority under subsection (1), regulations cannot require the Authority to give the applicant any information which identifies the donor.

(5)   Regulations cannot require the Authority to give any information as to the identity of a person whose gametes have been used or from whom an embryo has been taken if a person to whom a licence applied was provided with the information at a time when the Authority could not have been required to give information of the kind in question.

(6)   The Authority need not comply with a request made under subsection (2)(b) by any applicant if it considers that special circumstances exist which increase the likelihood that compliance with the request would enable the applicant—

    (a)   to identify the donor, in a case where the Authority is not required by regulations under subsection (2)(a) to give the applicant information which identifies the donor, or

    (b)   to identify any person about whom information is given under subsection (2)(b).

(7)   In this section—
'relevant individual' has the same meaning as in section 31;
'the relevant statutory provisions' means sections 27 to 29 of this Act and sections 33 to 47 of the Human Fertilisation and Embryology Act 2008.]

[31ZB   Request for information as to intended spouse etc

(1)   Subject to subsection (4), a person ('the applicant') may by notice to the Authority require the Authority to comply with a request under subsection (2).

(2)   The applicant may request the Authority to give the applicant notice stating whether or not information contained in the register shows that, but for the relevant statutory provisions, the applicant would or might be related to a person specified in the request ('the specified person') as—

(a)   a person whom the applicant proposes to marry,

(b)   a person with whom the applicant proposes to enter into a civil partnership, or

(c)   a person with whom the applicant is in an intimate physical relationship or with whom the applicant proposes to enter into an intimate physical relationship.

(3)   Subject to subsection (5), the Authority shall comply with a request under subsection (2) if—

(a)   the information contained in the register shows that the applicant is a relevant individual,

(b)   the Authority receives notice in writing from the specified person consenting to the request being made and that notice has not been withdrawn, and

(c)   the applicant and the specified person have each been given a suitable opportunity to receive proper counselling about the implications of compliance with the request.

(4)   A request may not be made under subsection (2)(c) by a person who has not attained the age of 16.

(5)   Where a request is made under subsection (2)(c) and the specified person has not attained the age of 16 when the applicant gives notice to the Authority under subsection (1), the Authority must not comply with the request.

(6)   Where the Authority is required under subsection (3) to comply with a request under subsection (2), the Authority must take all reasonable steps to give the applicant and the specified person notice stating whether or not the information contained in the register shows that, but for the relevant statutory provisions, the applicant and the specified person would or might be related.

(7)   In this section—
'relevant individual' has the same meaning as in section 31;
'the relevant statutory provisions' has the same meaning as in section 31ZA.]

[31ZC   Power of Authority to inform donor of request for information

(1)   Where—

(a)   the Authority has received from a person ('the applicant') a notice containing a request under subsection (2)(a) of section 31ZA, and

(b)   compliance by the Authority with its duty under that section has involved or will involve giving the applicant information relating to a person other than the parent of the applicant who would or might, but for the relevant statutory provisions, be a parent of the applicant ('the donor'),

the Authority may notify the donor that a request under section 31ZA(2)(a) has been made, but may not disclose the identity of the applicant or any information relating to the applicant.

(2)   In this section 'the relevant statutory provisions' has the same meaning as in section 31ZA.]

[31ZD   Provision to donor of information about resulting children

(1)   This section applies where a person ('the donor') has consented under Schedule 3 (whether before or after the coming into force of this section) to—

(a)   the use of the donor's gametes, or an embryo the creation of which was brought about using the donor's gametes, for the purposes of treatment services provided under a licence, or

(b)   the use of the donor's gametes for the purposes of non-medical fertility services provided under a licence.

(2)   In subsection (1)—

(a)   'treatment services' do not include treatment services provided to the donor, or to the donor and another person together, and

(b)   'non-medical fertility services' do not include any services involving partner-donated sperm.

(3)   The donor may by notice request the appropriate person to give the donor notice stating—

(a)   the number of persons of whom the donor is not a parent but would or might, but for the relevant statutory provisions, be a parent by virtue of the use of the gametes or embryos to which the consent relates,

(b)   the sex of each of those persons, and

(c)   the year of birth of each of those persons.

(4)   Subject to subsections (5) to (7), the appropriate person shall notify the donor whether the appropriate person holds the information mentioned in subsection (3) and, if the appropriate person does so, shall comply with the request.

(5)   The appropriate person need not comply with a request under subsection (3) if the appropriate person considers that special circumstances exist which increase the likelihood that compliance with the request would enable the donor to identify any of the persons falling within paragraphs (a) to (c) of subsection (3).

(6)   In the case of a donor who consented as described in subsection (1)(a), the Authority need not comply with a request made to it under subsection (3) where the person who held the licence referred to in subsection (1)(a) continues to hold a licence under paragraph 1 of Schedule 2, unless the donor has previously made a request under subsection (3) to the person responsible and the person responsible—

(a)   has notified the donor that the information concerned is not held, or

(b)   has failed to comply with the request within a reasonable period.

(7)   In the case of a donor who consented as described in subsection (1)(b), the Authority need not comply with a request made to it under subsection (3) where the person who held the licence referred to in subsection (1)(b) continues to hold a licence under paragraph 1A of Schedule 2, unless the donor has previously made a request under subsection (3) to the person responsible and the person responsible—

(a)   has notified the donor that the information concerned is not held, or

(b)   has failed to comply with the request within a reasonable period.

(8)   In this section 'the appropriate person' means—

(a)   in the case of a donor who consented as described in paragraph (a) of subsection (1)—

(i) where the person who held the licence referred to in that paragraph continues to hold a licence under paragraph 1 of Schedule 2, the person responsible, or

(ii) the Authority, and

(b)   in the case of a donor who consented as described in paragraph (b) of subsection (1)—

(i) where the person who held the licence referred to in that paragraph continues to hold a licence under paragraph 1A of Schedule 2, the person responsible, or

(ii) the Authority.

(9) In this section 'the relevant statutory provisions' has the same meaning as in section 31ZA.]

[31ZE **Provision of information about donor-conceived genetic siblings**

(1) For the purposes of this section two relevant individuals are donor-conceived genetic siblings of each other if a person ('the donor') who is not the parent of either of them would or might, but for the relevant statutory provisions, be the parent of both of them.

(2) Where—

(a) the information on the register shows that a relevant individual ('A') is the donor-conceived genetic sibling of another relevant individual ('B'),

(b) A has provided information to the Authority ('the agreed information') which consists of or includes information which enables A to be identified with the request that it should be disclosed to—

(i) any donor-conceived genetic sibling of A, or

(ii) such siblings of A of a specified description which includes B, and

(c) the conditions in subsection (3) are satisfied,

then, subject to subsection (4), the Authority shall disclose the agreed information to B.

(3) The conditions referred to in subsection (2)(c) are—

(a) that each of A and B has attained the age of 18,

(b) that B has requested the disclosure to B of information about any donor-conceived genetic sibling of B, and

(c) that each of A and B has been given a suitable opportunity to receive proper counselling about the implications of disclosure under subsection (2).

(4) The Authority need not disclose any information under subsection (2) if it considers that the disclosure of information will lead to A or B identifying the donor unless—

(a) the donor has consented to the donor's identity being disclosed to A or B, or

(b) were A or B to make a request under section 31ZA(2)(a), the Authority would be required by regulations under that provision to give A or B information which would identify the donor.

(5) In this section—

'relevant individual' has the same meaning as in section 31;

'the relevant statutory provisions' has the same meaning as in section 31ZA.]

[31ZF **Power of Authority to keep voluntary contact register**

(1) In this section and section 31ZG, a 'voluntary contact register' means a register of persons who have expressed their wish to receive information about any person to whom they are genetically related as a consequence of the provision to any person of treatment services in the United Kingdom before 1 August 1991.

(2) The Authority may—

(a) set up a voluntary contact register in such manner as it thinks fit,

(b) keep a voluntary contact register in such manner as it thinks fit,

(c) determine criteria for eligibility for inclusion on the register and the particulars that may be included,

(d) charge a fee to persons who wish their particulars to be entered on the register,

(e) arrange for samples of the DNA of such persons to be analysed at their request,

(f) make such arrangements as it thinks fit for the disclosure of information on the register between persons who appear to the Authority to be genetically related, and

(g) impose such conditions as it thinks fit to prevent a person ('A') from disclosing information to a person to whom A is genetically related ('B') where that information would identify any person who is genetically related to both A and B.

(3)   The Authority may make arrangements with any person by whom a voluntary contact register is kept before the commencement of this section for the supply by that person to the Authority of the information contained in the register maintained by that person.]

[31ZG   Financial assistance for person setting up or keeping voluntary contact register

(1)   The Authority may, instead of keeping a voluntary contact register, give financial assistance to any person who sets up or keeps a voluntary contact register.

(2)   Financial assistance under subsection (1) may be given in any form, and in particular, may be given by way of—

(a)   grants,

(b)   loans,

(c)   guarantees, or

(d)   incurring expenditure for the person assisted.

(3)   Financial assistance under subsection (1) may be given on such terms and conditions as the Authority considers appropriate.

(4)   A person receiving assistance under subsection (1) must comply with the terms and conditions on which it is given, and compliance may be enforced by the Authority.]

[31A   The Authority's register of licences

(1)   The Authority shall keep a register recording the grant, suspension or revocation of—

(a)   every licence under paragraph 1 or 2 of Schedule 2 authorising activities in relation to gametes or embryos intended for use for human application,

(b)   every licence under paragraph 1A of Schedule 2 [, and]

[(c)   every licence under paragraph 3 of Schedule 2 authorising activities in connection with the derivation from embryos of stem cells that are intended for human application.]

(2)   The register shall specify, in relation to each such licence—

(a)   the activities authorised,

(b)   the address of the premises to which the licence relates,

(c)   the name of the person responsible and [the name of the holder of the licence (if different)], and

(d)   any variations made.

(3)   The Authority shall make such of the information included in the register as it considers appropriate available to the public in such manner as it considers appropriate.]

[31B   The Authority's register of serious adverse events and serious adverse reactions

(1)   The Authority shall keep a register containing information provided to it under this Act about any serious adverse event or serious adverse reaction.

(2)   The Authority shall make such of the information included in the register as it considers appropriate available to the public in such manner as it considers appropriate.]

32   Information to be provided to Registrar General

(1)   This section applies where a claim is made before the Registrar General that a [person] is or is not the [parent] of a child and it is necessary or desirable for the purpose of any function of the Registrar General to determine whether the claim is or may be well-founded.

(2)   The Authority shall comply with any request made by the Registrar

General by notice to the Authority to disclose whether any information on the register kept in pursuance of section 31 of this Act tends to show [that the person may be a parent of the child by virtue of any of the statutory provisions] and, if it does, disclose that information.

   [(2A)   In subsection (2) 'the relevant statutory provisions' means—

       (a)   section 28 of this Act, and

       (b)   sections 35 to 47 of the Human Fertilisation and Embryology Act 2008.]

   (3)   In this section and section [33A] of this Act, 'the Registrar General' means the Registrar General for England and Wales, the Registrar General of Births, Deaths and Marriages for Scotland or the Registrar General for Northern Ireland, as the case may be.

[33A   Disclosure of information

   (1)   No person shall disclose any information falling within section 31(2) which the person obtained (whether before or after the coming into force of section 24 of the Human Fertilisation and Embryology Act 2008) in the person's capacity as—

       (a)   a member or employee of the Authority,

       (b)   any person exercising functions of the Authority by virtue of section 8B or 8C of this Act (including a person exercising such functions by virtue of either of those sections as a member of staff or as an employee),

       (c)   any person engaged by the Authority to provide services to the Authority,

       (d)   any person employed by, or engaged to provide services to, a person mentioned in paragraph (c),

       (e)   a person to whom a licence applies,

       (f)   a person to whom a third party agreement applies, or

       (g)   a person to whom directions have been given.

   (2)   Subsection (1) does not apply where—

       (a)   the disclosure is made to a person as a member or employee of the Authority or as a person exercising functions of the Authority as mentioned in subsection (1)(b),

       (b)   the disclosure is made to or by a person falling within subsection (1)(c) for the purpose of the provision of services which that person is engaged to provide to the Authority,

       (c)   the disclosure is made by a person mentioned in subsection (1)(d) for the purpose of enabling a person falling within subsection (1)(c) to provide services which that person is engaged to provide to the Authority,

       (d)   the disclosure is made to a person to whom a licence applies for the purpose of that person's functions as such,

       (e)   the disclosure is made to a person to whom a third party agreement applies for the purpose of that person's functions under that agreement,

       (f)   the disclosure is made in pursuance of directions given by virtue of section 24,

       (g)   the disclosure is made so that no individual can be identified from the information,

       (h)   the disclosure is of information other than identifying donor information and is made with the consent required by section 33B,

       (i)   the disclosure—

           (i)   is made by a person who is satisfied that it is necessary to make the disclosure to avert an imminent danger to the health of an individual ('P'),

           (ii)   is of information falling within section 31(2)(a) which could be disclosed by virtue of paragraph (h) with P's consent or could be disclosed to P by virtue of subsection (5), and

           (iii)   is made in circumstances where it is not reasonably practicable to obtain P's consent,

(j)   the disclosure is of information which has been lawfully made available to the public before the disclosure is made,

(k)   the disclosure is made in accordance with sections 31ZA to 31ZE,

(l)   the disclosure is required or authorised to be made—

(i)   under regulations made under section 33D, or

(ii)   in relation to any time before the coming into force of the first regulations under that section, under regulations made under section 251 of the National Health Service Act 2006,

(m)   the disclosure is made by a person acting in the capacity mentioned in subsection (1)(a) or (b) for the purpose of carrying out the Authority's duties under section 8A,

(n)   the disclosure is made by a person acting in the capacity mentioned in subsection (1)(a) or (b) in pursuance of an order of a court under section 34 or 35,

(o)   the disclosure is made by a person acting in the capacity mentioned in subsection (1)(a) or (b) to the Registrar General in pursuance of a request under section 32,

(p)   the disclosure is made by a person acting in the capacity mentioned in subsection (1)(a) or (b) to any body or person discharging a regulatory function for the purpose of assisting that body or person to carry out that function,

(q)   the disclosure is made for the purpose of establishing in any proceedings relating to an application for an order under subsection (1) of section 54 [or subsection (1) of section 54A] of the Human Fertilisation and Embryology Act 2008 whether the condition specified in paragraph (a) or (b) of that subsection is met,

(r)   the disclosure is made under section 3 of the Access to Health Records Act 1990,

(s)   the disclosure is made under Article 5 of the Access to Health Records (Northern Ireland) Order 1993, or

(t)   the disclosure is made necessarily for—

(i)   the purpose of the investigation of any offence (or suspected offence), or

(ii)   any purpose preliminary to proceedings, or for the purposes of, or in connection with, any proceedings.

(3)   Subsection (1) does not apply to the disclosure of information in so far as—

(a)   the information identifies a person who, but for sections 27 to 29 of this Act or sections 33 to 47 of the Human Fertilisation and Embryology Act 2008, would or might be a parent of a person who instituted proceedings under section 1A of the Congenital Disabilities (Civil Liability) Act 1976, and

(b)   the disclosure is made for the purpose of defending such proceedings, or instituting connected proceedings for compensation against that parent.

(4)   Paragraph (t) of subsection (2), so far as relating to disclosure for the purpose of the investigation of an offence or suspected offence, or for any purpose preliminary to, or in connection with proceedings, does not apply—

(a)   to disclosure of identifying donor information, or

(b)   to disclosure, in circumstances in which subsection (1) of section 34 of this Act applies, of information relevant to the determination of the question mentioned in that subsection, made by any person acting in a capacity mentioned in any of paragraphs (c) to (g) of subsection (1).

(5)   Subsection (1) does not apply to the disclosure to any individual of information which—

(a)   falls within subsection (2) of section 31 of this Act by virtue of any of paragraphs (a) to (e) of that subsection, and

(b)   relates only to that individual or, in the case of an individual who is treated together with, or gives a notice under section 37 or 44 of the Human

Fertilisation and Embryology Act 2008 in respect of, another, only to that individual and that other.

(6)   In subsection (2)—

(a)   in paragraph (p) 'regulatory function' has the same meaning as in section 32 of the Legislative and Regulatory Reform Act 2006, and

(b)   in paragraph (t) references to 'proceedings' include any formal procedure for dealing with a complaint.

(7)   In this section 'identifying donor information' means information enabling a person to be identified as a person whose gametes were used in accordance with consent given under paragraph 5 of Schedule 3 for the purposes of treatment services or non-medical fertility services in consequence of which an identifiable individual was, or may have been, born.]

[33B   Consent required to authorise certain disclosures

(1)   This section has effect for the purposes of section 33A(2)(h).

(2)   Subject to subsection (5), the consent required by this section is the consent of each individual who can be identified from the information.

(3)   Consent in respect of a person who has not attained the age of 18 years ('C') may be given—

(a)   by C, in a case where C is competent to deal with the issue of consent, or

(b)   by a person having parental responsibility for C, in any other case.

(4)   Consent to disclosure given at the request of another shall be disregarded unless, before it is given, the person requesting it takes reasonable steps to explain to the individual from whom it is requested the implications of compliance with the request.

(5)   In the case of information which shows that any identifiable individual ('A') was, or may have been, born in consequence of treatment services, the consent required by this section does not include A's consent if the disclosure is necessarily incidental to the disclosure of information falling within section 31(2)(a).

(6)   The reference in subsection (3) to parental responsibility is—

(a)   in relation to England and Wales, to be read in accordance with the Children Act 1989;

(b)   in relation to Northern Ireland, to be read in accordance with the Children (Northern Ireland) Order 1995;

(c)   in relation to Scotland, to be read as a reference to parental responsibilities and parental rights within the meaning of the Children (Scotland) Act 1995.]

[33C   Power to provide for additional exceptions from section 33A(1)

(1)   Regulations may provide for additional exceptions from section 33A(1).

(2)   No exception may be made under this section for—

(a)   disclosure of a kind mentioned in paragraph (a) or (b) of subsection (4) of section 33A, or

(b)   disclosure in circumstances in which section 32 of this Act applies of information having the tendency mentioned in subsection (2) of that section, made by any person acting in a capacity mentioned in any of paragraphs (c) to (g) of subsection (1) of section 33A.]

[33D   Disclosure for the purposes of medical or other research

(1)   Regulations may—

(a)   make such provision for and in connection with requiring or regulating the processing of protected information for the purposes of medical research as the Secretary of State considers is necessary or expedient in the public interest or in the interests of improving patient care, and

(b)   make such provision for and in connection with requiring or regulating the processing of protected information for the purposes of any other research as the Secretary of State considers is necessary or expedient in the public interest.

(2) Regulations under subsection (1) may, in particular, make provision—

(a) for requiring or authorising the disclosure or other processing of protected information to or by persons of any prescribed description subject to compliance with any prescribed conditions (including conditions requiring prescribed undertakings to be obtained from such persons as to the processing of such information),

(b) for securing that, where prescribed protected information is processed by a person in accordance with the regulations, anything done by that person in so processing the information must be taken to be lawfully done despite any obligation of confidence owed by the person in respect of it,

(c) for requiring fees of a prescribed amount to be paid to the Authority in prescribed circumstances by persons in relation to the disclosure to those persons of protected information under those regulations,

(d) for the establishment of one or more bodies to exercise prescribed functions in relation to the processing of protected information under those regulations,

(e) as to the membership and proceedings of any such body, and

(f) as to the payment of remuneration and allowances to any member of any such body and the reimbursement of expenses.

(3) Where regulations under subsection (1) require or regulate the processing of protected information for the purposes of medical research, such regulations may enable any approval given under regulations made under section 251 of the National Health Service Act 2006 (control of patient information) to have effect for the purposes of the regulations under subsection (1) in their application to England and Wales.

(4) Subsections (1) to (3) are subject to subsections (5) to (8).

(5) Regulations under subsection (1) may not make any provision requiring or authorising the disclosure or other processing, for any purpose, of protected information, where that information is information from which an individual may be identified, if it would be reasonably practicable to achieve that purpose otherwise than pursuant to such regulations, having regard to the cost of and technology available for achieving that purpose.

(6) Regulations under this section may not make provision for or in connection with the processing of protected information in a manner inconsistent with any provision made by or under the Data Protection Act 1998.

(7) Subsection (6) does not affect the operation of provisions made under subsection (2)(b).

(8) Before making any regulations under this section the Secretary of State shall consult such bodies appearing to the Secretary of State to represent the interests of those likely to be affected by the regulations as the Secretary of State considers appropriate.

(9) In this section—

'prescribed' means prescribed by regulations made by virtue of this section,

'processing', in relation to information, means the use, disclosure, or obtaining of the information or the doing of such other things in relation to it as may be prescribed for the purposes of this definition, and

'protected information' means information falling within section 31(2).]

34 Disclosure in interests of justice

(1) Where in any proceedings before a court the question whether a person is or is not the parent of a child by virtue of sections 27 to 29 of this Act [or sections 33 to 47 of the Human Fertilisation and Embryology Act 2008] falls to be determined, the court may on the application of any party to the proceedings make an order requiring the Authority—

(a)   to disclose whether or not any information relevant to that question is contained in the register kept in pursuance of section 31 of this Act, and

(b)   if it is, to disclose so much of it as is specified in the order,

but such an order may not require the Authority to disclose any information falling within section 31(2) [(c) to (e)] of this Act.

(2)   The court must not make an order under subsection (1) above unless it is satisfied that the interests of justice require it to do so, taking into account—

(a)   any representations made by any individual who may be affected by the disclosure, and

(b)   the welfare of the child, if under 18 years old, and of any other person under that age who may be affected by the disclosure.

(3)   If the proceedings before the court are civil proceedings, it—

(a)   may direct that the whole or any part of the proceedings on the application for an order under subsection (2) above shall be heard in camera, and

(b)   if it makes such an order, may then or later direct that the whole or any part of any later stage of the proceedings shall be heard in camera.

(4)   An application for a direction under subsection (3) above shall be heard in camera unless the court otherwise directs.

35   Disclosure in interests of justice: congenital disabilities, etc

(1)   Where for the purpose of instituting proceedings under section 1 of the Congenital Disabilities (Civil Liability) Act 1976 (civil liability to child born disabled) it is necessary to identify a person who would or might be the parent of a child but for [the relevant statutory provisions], the court may, on the application of the child, make an order requiring the Authority to disclose any information contained in the register kept in pursuance of section 31 of this Act identifying that person.

(2)   Where, for the purposes of any action for damages in Scotland (including any such action which is likely to be brought) in which the damages claimed consist of or include damages or solatium in respect of personal injury (including any disease and any impairment of physical or mental condition), it is necessary to identify a person who would or might be the parent of a child but for [the relevant statutory provisions], the court may, on the application of any party to the action or, if the proceedings have not been commenced, the prospective pursuer, make an order requiring the Authority to disclose any information contained in the register kept in pursuance of section 31 of this Act identifying that person.

[(2A)   In subsections (1) and (2) 'the relevant statutory provisions' means—

(a)   sections 27 to 29 of this Act, and

(b)   sections 33 to 47 of the Human Fertilisation and Embryology Act 2008.]

(3)   Subsections (2) to (4) of section 34 of this Act apply for the purposes of this section as they apply for the purposes of that.

[. . .]

LAW REFORM (MISCELLANEOUS PROVISIONS) (SCOTLAND) ACT 1990
(1990, c 40)

Blood and other samples in civil proceedings

70   Blood and other samples in civil proceedings

(1)   In any civil proceedings to which this section applies, the court may (whether or not on application made to it) request a party to the proceedings—

(a)   to provide a sample of blood or other body fluid or of body tissue for the purpose of laboratory analysis;

(b)   to consent to the taking of such a sample from a child in relation to whom the party has power to give such consent.

(2)   Where a party to whom a request under subsection (1) above has been made refuses or fails—

(a) to provide or, as the case may be, to consent to the taking of, a sample as requested by the court, or

(b) to take any step necessary for the provision or taking of such a sample, the court may draw from the refusal or failure such adverse inference, if any, in relation to the subject matter of the proceedings as seems to it to be appropriate.

(3) In section 6 of the Law Reform (Parent and Child) (Scotland) Act 1986 (determination of parentage by blood sample)—

(a) in subsection (1), for the words 'blood sample' there shall be substituted 'sample of blood or other body fluid or of body tissue'; and

(b) in each of subsections (2), (3) and (4), for the words 'a blood' there shall be substituted 'such a'.

(4) This section applies to any civil proceedings brought in the Court of Session or the sheriff court—

(a) on or after the date of the commencement of this section; or

(b) before the said date in a case where the proof has not by that date begun.

CHILD SUPPORT ACT 1991
(1991, c 48)

The basic principles

1   The duty to maintain

(1) For the purposes of this Act, each parent of a qualifying child is responsible for maintaining him.

(2) For the purposes of this Act, [a non-resident parent] shall be taken to have met his responsibility to maintain any qualifying child of his by making periodical payments of maintenance with respect to the child of such amount, and at such intervals, as may be determined in accordance with the provisions of this Act.

(3) Where a maintenance [calculation] made under this Act requires the making of periodical payments, it shall be the duty of the [non-resident] parent with respect to whom the [calculation] was made to make those payments.

2   Welfare of children: the general principle

Where, in any case which falls to be dealt with under this Act, the [Secretary of State] [. . .] is considering the exercise of any discretionary power conferred by this Act, [the Secretary of State] shall have regard to the welfare of any child likely to be affected by [the] decision.

3   Meaning of certain terms used in this Act

(1) A child is a 'qualifying child' if—

(a) one of his parents is, in relation to him, [a non-resident parent]; or

(b) both of his parents are, in relation to him, [non-resident] parents.

(2) The parent of any child is a '[non-resident parent'], in relation to him, if—

(a) that parent is not living in the same household with the child; and

(b) the child has his home with a person who is, in relation to him, a person with care.

(3) A person is a 'person with care', in relation to any child, if he is a person—

(a) with whom the child has his home;

(b) who usually provides day to day care for the child (whether exclusively or in conjunction with any other person); and

(c) who does not fall within a prescribed category of person.

(4) The Secretary of State shall not, under subsection (3)(c), prescribe as a category—

(a) parents;

(b) guardians;

(c) persons [named, in a child arrangements order] under section 8 of the Children Act 1989 [as persons with whom a child is to live;]

(d)   in Scotland, persons [with whom a child is to live by virtue of a residence order under section 11 of the Children (Scotland) Act 1995].

(5)   For the purposes of this Act there may be more than one person with care
in relation to the same qualifying child.

(6)   Periodical payments which are required to be paid in accordance with a
[maintenance calculation] are referred to in this Act as 'child support maintenance'.

(7)   Expressions are defined in this section only for the purposes of this Act.

4   Child support maintenance

(1)   A person who is, in relation to any qualifying child or any qualifying
children, either the person with care or the [non-resident] parent may apply to the
[Secretary of State] for a [maintenance calculation] to be made under this Act with
respect to that child, or any of those children.

(2)   Where a maintenance [calculation] has been made in response to an application under this section the [Secretary of State] may, if the person with care [. . .]
applies to [the Secretary of State] under this subsection, arrange for—

(a)   the collection of the child support maintenance payable in accordance
with the [calculation];

(b)   the enforcement of the obligation to pay child support maintenance in
accordance with the [calculation].

[(2A)   The [Commission] may only make arrangements under subsection
(2)(a) if—

(a)   the non-resident parent agrees to the arrangements, or

(b)   the [Commission] is satisfied that without the arrangements child support maintenance is unlikely to be paid in accordance with the calculation.]

(3)   Where an application under subsection (2) for the enforcement of the obligation mentioned in subsection (2)(b) authorises the [Secretary of State] to take
steps to enforce that obligation whenever [the Secretary of State] considers it necessary to do so, the [Secretary of State] may act accordingly.

(4)   A person who applies to the [Secretary of State] under this section shall, so
far as that person reasonably can, comply with such regulations as may be made
by the Secretary of State with a view to the [Secretary of State] [. . .] being provided with the information which is required to enable—

(a)   the [non-resident parent to be identified or] traced (where that is necessary);

(b)   the amount of child support maintenance payable by the [non-resident]
parent to be [calculated]; and

(c)   that amount to be recovered from the [non-resident] parent.

(5)   Any person who has applied to the [Secretary of State] under this section
may at any time request [the Secretary of State] to cease acting under this section.

(6)   It shall be the duty of the [Secretary of State] to comply with any request
made under subsection (5) (but subject to any regulations made under subsection
(8)).

(7)   The obligation to provide information which is imposed by subsection (4)—

(a)   shall not apply in such circumstances as may be prescribed; and

(b)   may, in such circumstances as may be prescribed, be waived by the
[Secretary of State].

(8)   The Secretary of State may by regulations make such incidental, supplemental or transitional provision as he thinks appropriate with respect to cases in
which he is requested to cease to act under this section.

[. . .]

[(10)   No application may be made at any time under this section with respect
to a qualifying child or any qualifying children if—

(a)   there is in force a written maintenance agreement made before 5th April
1993, or a maintenance order [made before a prescribed date] in respect of that

child or those children and the person who is, at that time, the [non-resident] parent; or

[(aa)   a maintenance order made on or after the date prescribed for the purposes of paragraph (a) is in force in respect of them, but has been so for less than the period of one year beginning with the date on which it was made; or]

[(ab)   a maintenance agreement—

(i)   made on or after the date prescribed for the purposes of paragraph (a); and

(ii)   registered for execution in the Books of Council and Session or the sheriff court books,

is in force in respect of them, but has been so for less than the period of one year beginning with the date on which it was made.]

[. . .]

5   Child support maintenance: supplemental provisions

(1)   Where—

(a)   there is more than one person with care of a qualifying child; and

(b)   one or more, but not all, of them have parental responsibility for . . . the child;

no application may be made for a maintenance [calculation] with respect to the child by any of those persons who do not have parental responsibility for . . . the child.

(2)   Where more than one application for a maintenance [calculation] is made with respect to the child concerned, only one of them may be proceeded with.

(3)   The Secretary of State may by regulations make provision as to which of two or more applications for a maintenance [calculation] with respect to the same child is to be proceeded with.

[. . .]

7   Right of child in Scotland to apply for [calculation]

(1)   A qualifying child who has attained the age of 12 years and who is habitually resident in Scotland may apply to the [Secretary of State] for a maintenance [calculation] to be made with respect to him if—

(a)   no such application has been made by a person who is with respect to that child, a person with care or a [non-resident] parent. [. . .]

(2)   An application made under subsection (1) shall authorise the [Secretary of State] to make a maintenance [calculation] with respect to any other children of the [non-resident] parent who are qualifying children in the care of the same person as the child making the application.

(3)   Where a maintenance [calculation] has been made in response to an application under this section the [Secretary of State] may, if the person with care [. . .] or the child concerned applies to [the Secretary of State] under this subsection, arrange for—

(a)   the collection of the child support maintenance payable in accordance with the [calculation].

(b)   the enforcement of the obligation to pay child support maintenance in accordance with the [calculation].

[(3A)   The [Commission] may only make arrangements under subsection (3)(a) if—

(a)   the non-resident parent agrees to the arrangements, or

(b)   the [Commission] is satisfied that without the arrangements child support maintenance is unlikely to be paid in accordance with the calculation.]

(4)   Where an application under subsection (3) for the enforcement of the obligation mentioned in subsection (3)(b) authorises the [Secretary of State] to take steps to enforce that obligation whenever [the Secretary of State] considers it necessary to do so, the [Secretary of State] may act accordingly.

(5)   Where a child has asked the [Secretary of State] to proceed under this

section, the person with care of the child, the [non-resident] parent and the child concerned shall, so far as they reasonably can, comply with such regulations as may be made by the Secretary of State with a view to the [Secretary of State] [. . .] being provided with the information which is required to enable—

(a)   the [non-resident] parent to be traced (where that is necessary);

(b)   the amount of child support maintenance payable by the [non-resident] parent to be [calculated]; and

(c)   that amount to be recovered from the [non-resident] parent.

(6)   The child who has made the application (but not the person having care of him) may at any time request the [Secretary of State] to cease acting under this section.

(7)   It shall be the duty of the [Secretary of State] to comply with any request made under subsection (6) (but subject to any regulations made under subsection (9)).

(8)   The obligation to provide information which is imposed by subsection (5)—

(a)   shall not apply in such circumstances as may be prescribed by the Secretary of State; and

(b)   may, in such circumstances as may be so prescribed, be waived by the [Secretary of State].

(9)   The Secretary of State may by regulations make such incidental, supplemental or transitional provision as he thinks appropriate with respect to cases in which he is requested to cease to act under this section.

(10)   No application may be made at any time under this section by a qualifying child if—

[(a)] there is in force a written maintenance agreement made before 5th April 1993, or a maintenance order [made before a prescribed date] in respect of that child and the person who is, at that time, the [non-resident parent; or

(b)   a maintenance order made on or after the date prescribed for the purposes of paragraph (a) is in force in respect of them, but has been so for less than the period of one year beginning with the date on which it was made.]

[(c)   a maintenance agreement—

(i)   made on or after the date prescribed for the purposes of paragraph (a); and

(ii)   registered for execution in the Books of Council and Session or the sheriff court books,

is in force in respect of them, but has been so for less than the period of one year beginning with the date on which it was made.]

8   Role of the courts with respect to maintenance for children

(1)   This subsection applies in any case where [the Secretary of State] would have jurisdiction to make a maintenance [calculation] with respect to a qualifying child and [a non-resident parent] of his on an application duly made by a person entitled to apply for such [a calculation] with respect to that child.

(2)   Subsection (1) applies even though the circumstances of the case are such that [the Secretary of State] would not make [a calculation] if it were applied for.

(3)   [Except as provided in subsection (3A)] in any case where subsection (1) applies, no court shall exercise any power which it would otherwise have to make, vary, or revive any maintenance order in relation to the child and [non-resident parent] concerned.

[(3A)   Unless a maintenance calculation has been made with respect to the child concerned, subsection (3) does not prevent a court from varying a maintenance order in relation to that child and the non-resident parent concerned—

(a)   if the maintenance order was made on or after the date prescribed for the purposes of section 4(10)(a) or 7(10)(a); or

(b)   where the order was made before then, in any case in which section 4(10) or 7(10) prevents the making of an application for a maintenance calculation with respect to or by that child.]

(4)   Subsection (3) does not prevent a court from revoking a maintenance order.

(5)   The Lord Chancellor or in relation to Scotland the Lord Advocate may by order provide that, in such circumstances as may be specified by the order, this section shall not prevent a court from exercising any power which it has to make a maintenance order in relation to a child if—

(a)   a written agreement (whether or not enforceable) provides for the making, or securing, by [a non-resident parent] of the child of periodical payments to or for the benefit of the child; and

(b)   the maintenance order which the court makes is, in all material respects, in the same terms as that agreement.

[(5A)   The Lord Chancellor may make an order under subsection (5) only with the concurrence of the Lord Chief Justice.]

(6)   This section shall not prevent a court from exercising any power which it has to make a maintenance order in relation to a child if—

(a)   a maintenance [calculation] is in force with respect to the child;

[(b)   the non-resident parent's [gross] weekly income exceeds the figure referred to in paragraph 10(3) of Schedule 1 (as it has effect from time to time pursuant to regulations made under paragraph 10A(1)(b));]

(c)   the court is satisfied that the circumstances of the case make it appropriate for the [non-resident] parent to make or secure the making of periodical payments under a maintenance order in addition to the child support maintenance payable by him in accordance with the maintenance [calculation].

(7)   This section shall not prevent a court from exercising any power which it has to make a maintenance order in relation to a child if—

(a)   the child is, will be or (if the order were to be made) would be receiving instruction at an educational establishment or undergoing training for a trade, profession or vocation (whether or not while in gainful employment); and

(b)   the order is made solely for the purposes of requiring the person making or securing the making of periodical payments fixed by the order to meet some or all of the expenses incurred in connection with the provision of the instruction or training.

(8)   This section shall not prevent a court from exercising any power which it has to make a maintenance order in relation to a child if—

(a)   [an allowance under Part 4 of the Welfare Reform Act 2012 (personal independence payment) or] in respect of him; or

(b)   no such allowance is paid but he is disabled,

and the order is made solely for the purpose of requiring the person making or securing the making of periodical payments fixed by the order to meet some or all of any expenses attributable to the child's disability.

(9)   For the purposes of subsection (8), a child is disabled if he is blind, deaf or dumb or is substantially and permanently handicapped by illness, injury, mental disorder or congenital deformity or such other disability as may be prescribed.

(10)   This section shall not prevent a court from exercising any power which it has to make a maintenance order in relation to a child if the order is made against a person with care of the child.

(11)   In this Act 'maintenance order', in relation to any child, means an order which requires the making or securing of periodical payments to or for the benefit of the child and which is made under—

(a)   Part II of the Matrimonial Causes Act 1973;
(b)   the Domestic Proceedings and Magistrates' Courts Act 1978;
(c)   Part III of the Matrimonial and Family Proceedings Act 1984;
(d)   the Family Law (Scotland) Act 1985;
(e)   Schedule 1 to the Children Act 1989;

[(ea) Schedule 5, 6 or 7 to the Civil Partnership Act 2004; or]

(f)   any other prescribed enactment,

and includes any order varying or reviving such an order.

[(12)   The Lord Chief Justice may nominate a judicial office holder (as defined in section 109(4) of the Constitutional Reform Act 2005) to exercise his functions under this section.]

9   Agreements about maintenance

(1)   In this section 'maintenance agreement' means any agreement for the making, or for securing the making, of periodical payments by way of maintenance, or in Scotland aliment, to or for the benefit of any child.

(2)   Nothing in this Act shall be taken to prevent any person from entering into a maintenance agreement.

[(2A)   The [Secretary of State] may, with a view to reducing the need for applications under sections 4 and 7—

(a)   take such steps as [the Secretary of State] considers appropriate to encourage the making and keeping of maintenance agreements, and

(b)   in particular, before accepting an application under those sections, invite the applicant to consider with the [Secretary of State] whether it is possible to make such an agreement.]

(3)   [Subject to section 4(10)(a) [and (ab)] and section 7(10),] the existence of a maintenance agreement shall not prevent any party to the agreement or any other person, from applying for a maintenance [calculation] with respect to any child to or for whose benefit periodical payments are to be made or secured under the agreement.

(4)   Where any agreement contains a provision which purports to restrict the right of any person to apply for a maintenance [calculation] that provision shall be void.

(5)   Where section 8 would prevent any court from making a maintenance order in relation to a child and [non-resident] parent of his, no court shall exercise any power that it has to vary any agreement so as—

(a)   to insert a provision requiring that [non-resident] parent to make or secure the making of periodical payments by way of maintenance, or in Scotland aliment, to or for the benefit of that child; or

(b)   to increase the amount payable under such a provision.

[(6)   In any case in which section 4(10) or 7(10) prevents the making of an application for a maintenance [calculation] [. . .] subsection (5) shall have effect with the omission of paragraph (b).]

10   Relationship between [maintenance calculations] and certain court orders and related matters

(1)   Where an order of a kind prescribed for the purposes of this subsection is in force with respect to any qualifying child with respect to whom a maintenance [calculation] is made, the order—

(a)   shall, so far as it relates to the making or securing of periodical payments, cease to have effect to such extent as may be determined in accordance with regulations made by the Secretary of State; or

(b)   where the regulations so provide, shall, so far as it so relates, have effect subject to such modifications as may be so determined.

(2)   Where an agreement of a kind prescribed for the purposes of this subsection is in force with respect to any qualifying child with respect to whom a maintenance [calculation] is made, the agreement—

(a)   shall, so far as it relates to the making or securing of periodical payments, be unenforceable to such extent as may be determined in accordance with regulations made by the Secretary of State; or

(b)   where the regulations so provide, shall, so far as it so relates, have effect subject to such modifications as may be so determined.

(3)   Any regulations under this section may, in particular, make such provision with respect to—

(a)   any case where any person with respect to whom an order or agreement of a kind prescribed for the purposes of subsection (1) or (2) has effect applies to the prescribed court, before the end of the prescribed period, for the order or agreement to be varied in the light of the maintenance [calculation] and of the provisions of this Act;

(b)   the recovery of any arrears under the order or agreement which fell due before the coming into force of the maintenance [calculation]

as the Secretary of State considers appropriate and may provide that, in prescribed circumstances, an application to any court which is made with respect to an order of a prescribed kind relating to the making or securing of periodical payments to or for the benefit of a child shall be treated by the court as an application for the order to be revoked.

(4)   The Secretary of State may by regulations make provision for—

(a)   notification to be given by [the Secretary of State] to the prescribed person in any case where [the Secretary of State] considers that the making of a maintenance [calculation] has affected, or is likely to affect, any order of a kind prescribed for the purposes of this subsection;

(b)   notification to be given by the prescribed person to the [Secretary of State] in any case where a court makes an order which it considers has affected, or is likely to affect, a maintenance [calculation].

(5)   Rules [of court may require] any person who, in prescribed circumstances, makes an application to [the family court] for a maintenance order to furnish the court with a statement in a prescribed form, and signed by [an officer of the Secretary of State] as to whether or not, at the time when the statement is made, there is a maintenance [calculation] in force with respect to that person or the child concerned.

In this subsection—

'maintenance order' means an order of a prescribed kind for the making or securing of periodical payments to or for the benefit of a child; and

'prescribed' means prescribed by the rules.

Special cases

42   Special cases

(1)   The Secretary of State may by regulations provide that in prescribed circumstances a case is to be treated as a special case for the purposes of this Act.

(2)   Those regulations may, for example, provide for the following to be special cases—

(a)   each parent of a child is [a non-resident] parent in relation to the child;

(b)   there is more than one person who is a person with care in relation to the same child;

(c)   there is more than one qualifying child in relation to the same [non-resident] parent but the person who is the person with care in relation to one of those children is not the person who is the person with care in relation to all of them;

(d)   a person is [a non-resident] parent in relation to more than one child and the other parent of each of those children is not the same person;

(e)   the person with care has care of more than one qualifying child and there is more than one [non-resident] parent in relation to those children;

(f)   a qualifying child has his home in two or more separate households;

[(g)   the same persons are the parents of two or more children and each parent is—

(i)   a non-resident parent in relation to one or more of the children, and

(ii)   a person with care in relation to one or more of the children.]

(3)   The Secretary of State may by regulations make provision with respect to special cases.

(4)   Regulations made under subsection (3) may, in particular—

(a)   modify any provision made by or under this Act, in its application to any special case or any special case falling within a prescribed category;

(b)   make new provision for any such case; or

(c)   provide for any prescribed provision made by or under this Act not to apply to any such case.

43   Recovery of child support maintenance by deduction from benefit

[(1)   The power of the Secretary of State to make regulations under section 5 of the Social Security Administration Act 1992 by virtue of subsection (1)(p) of that section may be exercised with a view to securing the making of payments in respect of child support maintenance by a non resident parent.

(2)   The reference in subsection (1) to the making of payments in respect of child support maintenance includes the recovery of—

(a)   arrears of child support maintenance, and

(b)   fees payable under section 6 of the Child Maintenance and Other Payments Act 2008.]

[(3)   For the purposes of this section, the benefits to which section 5 of the 1992 Act applies are to be taken as including war disablement pensions and war widows' pensions (within the meaning of section 150 of the Social Security Contributions and Benefits Act 1992 (interpretation)).]

[43A   Recovery of arrears from deceased's estate

(1)   The Secretary of State may by regulations make provision for the recovery from the estate of a deceased person of arrears of child support maintenance for which the deceased person was liable immediately before death.

(2)   Regulations under subsection (1) may, in particular—

(a)   make provision for arrears of child support maintenance for which a deceased person was so liable to be a debt payable by the deceased's executor or administrator out of the deceased's estate to the [Secretary of State];

(b)   make provision for establishing the amount of any such arrears;

(c)   make provision about procedure in relation to claims under the regulations.

(3)   Regulations under subsection (1) may include provision for proceedings (whether by appeal or otherwise) to be instituted, continued or withdrawn by the deceased's executor or administrator.]

Jurisdiction

44   Jurisdiction

(1)   [The Secretary of State] shall have jurisdiction to make a maintenance [calculation] with respect to a person who is—

(a)   a person with care;

(b)   a [non-resident] parent; or

(c)   a qualifying child,

only if that person is habitually resident in the United Kingdom [except in the case of a non-resident parent who falls within subsection (2A)].

(2)   Where the person with care is not an individual subsection (1) shall have effect as if paragraph (a) were omitted,

[(2A)   A non-resident parent falls within this subsection if he is not habitually resident in the United Kingdom, but is—

(a)   employed in the civil service of the Crown, including Her Majesty's Diplomatic Service and Her Majesty's Overseas Civil Service;

(b)   a member of the naval, military or air forces of the Crown, including any person employed by an association established for the purposes of Part XI of the Reserve Forces Act 1996;

(c)   employed by a company of a prescribed description [registered under the Companies Act 2006]; or

(d)   employed by a body of a prescribed description.]

[. . .]

[(4)   The [Secretary of State] does not have jurisdiction under this section if the exercise of jurisdiction would be contrary to the jurisdictional requirements of the Maintenance Regulation.

(5)   In subsection (4) 'the Maintenance Regulation' means Council Regulation (EC) No 4/2009 including as applied in relation to Denmark by virtue of the Agreement made on 19th October 2005 between the European Community and the Kingdom of Denmark.]

45   Jurisdiction of courts in certain proceedings under this Act

(1)   The Lord Chancellor or, in relation to Scotland, the Lord Advocate may by order make such provision as he considers necessary to secure that appeals, or such class of appeals as may be specified in the order—

(a)   shall be made to a court instead of being made to [the First-tier Tribunal]; or

(b)   shall be so made in such circumstances as may be so specified.

(2)   In subsection (1), 'court' means—

(a)   in relation to England and Wales the High Court [or the family court]; and

(b)   in relation to Scotland, the Court of Session or the sheriff.

[. . .]

(7)   Any order under subsection (1) [. . .] may make—

(a)   such modifications of any provision of this Act or of any other enactment; and

(b)   such transitional provision,

as the Minister making the order considers appropriate in consequence of any provision made by the order.

Miscellaneous and supplemental

. . .

54   Interpretation

[(1)]   In this Act—

['application for a variation' means an application under section 28A or 28G;]

'Benefits Acts' means the [Social Security Contributions and Benefits Act 1992 and the Social Security Administration Act 1992];

[. . .]

['charging order' has the same meaning as in section 1 of the Charging Orders Act 1979;]

'child benefit' has the same meaning as in the Child Benefit Act 1975;

[. . .]

'child support maintenance' has the meaning given in section 3(6);

[. . .]

[. . .]

'deduction from earnings order' has the meaning given in section 31(2);

['default maintenance decision' has the meaning given in section 12;]

['deposit-taker' means a person who, in the course of a business, may lawfully accept deposits in the United Kingdom;]

'disability living allowance' has the same meaning as in the [Benefit Acts];

[. . .]

'general qualification' shall be construed in accordance with section 71 of the Courts and Legal Services Act 1990 (qualification for judicial appointments);
[. . .]
'interim maintenance [decision]' has the meaning given in section 12;
'liability order' has the meaning given in [section 32M(2)];
'maintenance agreement' has the meaning given in section 9(1);
'maintenance [calculation]' means [a calculation] of maintenance made under this Act and, except in prescribed circumstances, includes [a default maintenance decision and an interim maintenance decision];
'maintenance order' has the meaning given in section 8(11);
[. . .]
'non-resident parent', has the meaning given in section 3(2);
'parent', in relation to any child, means any person who is in law the mother or father of the child;
[. . .]
'parent with care' means a person who is, in relation to a child, both a parent and a person with care;]
['parental responsibility', in the application of this Act—(a) to England and Wales, has the same meaning as in the Children Act 1989; and (b) to Scotland, shall be construed as a reference to 'parental responsibilities' within the meaning given by section 1(3) of the Children (Scotland) Act 1995;]
'person with care' has the meaning given in section 3(3);
'prescribed' means prescribed by regulations made by the Secretary of State;
'qualifying child' has the meaning given in section 3(1);
['voluntary payment' has the meaning given in section 28J.]
[(2)   The definition of 'deposit-taker' in subsection (1) is to be read with—
(a)   section 22 of the Financial Services and Markets Act 2000;
(b)   any relevant order under that section; and
(c)   Schedule 2 to that Act.]

[55   Meaning of 'child'
(1)   In this Act, 'child' means (subject to subsection (2)) a person who—
(a)   has not attained the age of 16, or
(b)   has not attained the age of 20 and satisfies such conditions as may be prescribed.
(2)   A person who is or has been party to a marriage or civil partnership is not a child for the purposes of this Act.
(3)   For the purposes of subsection (2), 'marriage' and 'civil partnership' include a void marriage and a void civil partnership respectively.]

AGE OF LEGAL CAPACITY (SCOTLAND) ACT 1991
(1991, c 50)

1   Age of legal capacity
(1)   As from the commencement of this Act—
(a)   a person under the age of 16 years shall, subject to section 2 below, have no legal capacity to enter into any transaction;
(b)   a person of or over the age of 16 years shall have legal capacity to enter into any transaction.
(2)   Subject to section 8 below, any reference in any enactment to a pupil (other than in the context of education or training) or to a person under legal disability or incapacity by reason of nonage shall, insofar as it relates to any time after the commencement of this Act, be construed as a reference to a person under the age of 16 years.
(3)   Nothing in this Act shall—

(a)   apply to any transaction entered into before the commencement of this Act;

(b)   confer any legal capacity on any person who is under legal disability or incapacity other than by reason of nonage;

(c)   affect the delictual or criminal responsibility of any person;

(d)   affect any enactment which lays down an age limit expressed in years for any particular purpose;

(e)   prevent any person under the age of 16 years from receiving or holding any right, title or interest;

(f)   affect any existing rule of law or practice whereby—

(i)   any civil proceedings may be brought or defended, or any step in civil proceedings may be taken in the name of a person under the age of 16 years [in relation to whom there is no person entitled to act as his legal representative (within the meaning of Part I of the Children (Scotland) Act 1995), or where there is such a person] is unable (whether by reason of conflict of interest or otherwise) or refuses to bring or defend such proceedings or take such step;

(ii)   the court may, in any civil proceedings, appoint a curator *ad litem* to a person under the age of 16 years;

(iii)   the court may, in relation to the approval of an arrangement under section 1 of the Trusts (Scotland) Act 1961, appoint a curator *ad litem* to a person of or over the age of 16 years but under the age of 18 years;

(iv)   the court may appoint a curator bonis to any person;

(g)   prevent any person under the age of 16 years from [exercising parental responsibilities and parental rights (within the meaning of sections 1(3) and 2(4) respectively of the Children (Scotland) Act 1995) in relation to any child of his].

(4)   Any existing rule of law relating to the legal capacity of minors and pupils which is inconsistent with the provisions of this Act shall cease to have effect.

(5)   Any existing rule of law relating to reduction of a transaction on the ground of minority and lesion shall cease to have effect.

2   Exceptions to general rule

(1)   A person under the age of 16 years shall have legal capacity to enter into a transaction—

(a)   of a kind commonly entered into by persons of his age and circumstances, and

(b)   on terms which are not unreasonable.

(2)   A person of or over the age of 12 years shall have testamentary capacity, including legal capacity to exercise by testamentary writing any power of appointment.

(3)   A person of or over the age of 12 years shall have legal capacity to consent to the making of an adoption order in relation to him. [. . .]

(4)   A person under the age of 16 years shall have legal capacity to consent on his own behalf to any surgical, medical or dental procedure or treatment where, in the opinion of a qualified medical practitioner attending him, he is capable of understanding the nature and possible consequences of the procedure or treatment.

[(4ZA)   For the purposes of subsection (4), the storage of gametes in accordance with the Human Fertilisation and Embryology Act 1990 is to be treated as a medical procedure.

(4ZB)   A person under the age of 16 years shall have legal capacity to consent to the use of the person's human cells in accordance with Schedule 3 to the Human Fertilisation and Embryology Act 1990 for the purposes of a project of research where the person is capable of understanding the nature of the research; and in this subsection 'human cells' has the same meaning as in that Schedule.]

[(4A)   A person under the age of 16 years shall have legal capacity to instruct a solicitor, in connection with any civil matter, where that person has a general understanding of what it means to do so; and without prejudice to the generality of this subsection a person 12 years of age or more shall be presumed to be of sufficient age and maturity to have such understanding.

(4B) A person who by virtue of subsection (4A) above has legal capacity to instruct a solicitor shall also have legal capacity to sue, or to defend, in any civil proceedings.

(4C) Subsections (4A) and (4B) above are without prejudice to any question of legal capacity arising in connection with any criminal matter.]

(5) Any transaction—

(a) which a person under the age of 16 years purports to enter into after the commencement of this Act, and

(b) in relation to which that person does not have legal capacity by virtue of this section,

shall be void.

3 Setting aside of transactions

(1) A person under the age of 21 years ('the applicant') may make application to the court to set aside a transaction which he entered into while he was of or over the age of 16 years but under the age of 18 years and which is a prejudicial transaction.

(2) In this section 'prejudicial transaction' means a transaction which—

(a) an adult, exercising reasonable prudence, would not have entered into in the circumstances of the applicant at the time of entering into the transaction, and

(b) has caused or is likely to cause substantial prejudice to the applicant.

(3) Subsection (1) above shall not apply to—

(a) the exercise of testamentary capacity;

(b) the exercise by testamentary writing of any power of appointment;

(c) the giving of consent to the making of an adoption order;

(d) the bringing or defending of, or the taking of any step in, civil proceedings;

(e) the giving of consent to any surgical, medical or dental procedure or treatment;

(f) a transaction in the course of the applicant's trade, business or profession;

(g) a transaction into which any other party was induced to enter by virtue of any fraudulent misrepresentation by the applicant as to age or other material fact;

(h) a transaction ratified by the applicant after he attained the age of 18 years and in the knowledge that it could be the subject of an application to the court under this section to set it aside; or

(j) a transaction ratified by the court under section 4 below.

(4) Where an application to set aside a transaction can be made or could have been made under this section by the person referred to in subsection (1) above, such application may instead be made by that person's executor, trustee in bankruptcy, trustee acting under a trust deed for creditors or curator bonis at any time prior to the date on which that person attains or would have attained the age of 21 years.

(5) An application under this section to set aside a transaction may be made—

(a) by an action in the Court of Session or the sheriff court, or

(b) by an incidental application in other proceedings in such court,

and the court may make an order setting aside the transaction and such further order, if any, as seems appropriate to the court in order to give effect to the rights of the parties.

4 Ratification by court of proposed transaction

(1) Where a person of or over the age of 16 years but under the age of 18 years

proposes to enter into a transaction which, if completed, could be the subject of an application to the court under section 3 above to set aside, all parties to the proposed transaction may make a joint application to have it ratified by the court.

(2)   The court shall not grant an application under this section if it appears to the court that an adult, exercising reasonable prudence and in the circumstances of the person referred to in subsection (1) above, would not enter into the transaction.

(3)   An application under this section shall be made by means of a summary application—

(a)   to the sheriff of the sheriffdom in which any of the parties to the proposed transaction resides, or

(b)   where none of the said parties resides in Scotland, to the sheriff at Edinburgh,

and the decision of the sheriff on such application shall be final.

5   Guardians of persons under 16

(1)   Except insofar as otherwise provided in Schedule 1 to this Act, as from the commencement of this Act any reference in any rule of law, enactment or document to the tutor of a pupil child shall be construed as a reference to [a person entitled to act as a child's legal representative (within the meaning of Part I of the Children (Scotland) Act 1995), and any reference to the tutory of such a child shall be construed as a reference to the entitlement to act as a child's legal representative enjoyed by a person by, under or by virtue of the said Part I].

(2)   Subject to section 1(3)(f) above, as from the commencement of this Act no guardian of a person under the age of 16 years shall be appointed as such except under [section 7 of the Children (Scotland) Act 1995].

(3)   As from the commencement of this Act, no person shall, by reason of age alone, be subject to the curatory of another person.

(4)   As from the commencement of this Act, no person shall be appointed as *factor loco tutoris*.

6   Attainment of age

(1)   The time at which a person attains a particular age expressed in years shall be taken to be the beginning of the relevant anniversary of the date of his birth.

(2)   Where a person has been born on 29th February in a leap year, the relevant anniversary in any year other than a leap year shall be taken to be 1st March.

(3)   The provisions of this section shall apply only to a relevant anniversary which occurs after the commencement of this Act.

[. . .]

8   Transitional provision

Where any person referred to in section 6(4)(b), 17(3), 18(3) or 18A(2) of the Prescription and Limitation (Scotland) Act 1973 as having been under legal disability by reason of nonage was of or over the age of 16 years but under the age of 18 years immediately before the commencement of this Act, any period prior to such commencement shall not be reckoned as, or as part of, the period of 5 years, or (as the case may be) 3 years, specified respectively in section 6, 17, 18 or 18A of that Act.

9   Interpretation

In this Act, unless the context otherwise requires—

'existing' means existing immediately before the commencement of this Act;

[. . .]

'transaction' means a transaction having legal effect, and includes—

(a)   any unilateral transaction;

(b)   the exercise of testamentary capacity;

(c)   the exercise of any power of appointment;

(d)   the giving by a person of any consent having legal effect;

(e)   the bringing or defending of, or the taking of any step in, civil proceedings;

(f)   acting as arbiter or trustee;

(g)   acting as an instrumentary witness.

10   Amendments and repeals

(1)   The enactments mentioned in Schedule 1 to this Act shall have effect subject to the amendments therein specified.

(2)   The enactments specified in Schedule 2 to this Act are repealed to the extent specified in the third column of that Schedule.

11   Short title, commencement and extent

(1)   This Act may be cited as the Age of Legal Capacity (Scotland) Act 1991.

(2)   This Act shall come into force at the end of the period of two months beginning with the date on which it is passed.

(3)   This Act shall extend to Scotland only.

CIVIL EVIDENCE (FAMILY MEDIATION) (SCOTLAND) ACT 1995
(1995, c 6)

1   Inadmissibility in civil proceedings of information as to what occurred during family mediation

(1)   Subject to section 2 of this Act, no information as to what occurred during family mediation to which this Act applies shall be admissible as evidence in any civil proceedings.

(2)   This Act applies to family mediation—

(a)   between two or more individuals relating to—

(i)   the residence of a child;

(ii)   the regulation of personal relations and direct contact between a child and any other person;

(iii)   the control, direction or guidance of a child's upbringing;

(iv)   the guardianship or legal representation of a child; or

(v)   any other matter relating to a child's welfare;

(b)   between spouses or former spouses concerning matters arising out of the breakdown or termination of their marriage;

(c)   between parties to a purported marriage concerning matters arising out of the breakdown or annulment of their purported marriage;

[(cc)   between partners in a civil partnership or persons in a purported civil partnership concerning matters arising out of the breakdown or termination of their relationship;]

(d)   between co-habitants or former co-habitants concerning matters arising out of the breakdown or termination of their relationship; or

(e)   of such other description as the Secretary of State may prescribe,

which is conducted by a person accredited as a mediator in family mediation to an organisation which is concerned with such mediation and which is approved for the purposes of this Act by the Lord President of the Court of Session.

(3)   The Lord President of the Court of Session may—

(a)   in approving an organisation under subsection (2) above, specify the period for which the approval is granted;

(b)   if he thinks fit, withdraw the approval at any time.

(4)   A certificate by the Lord President approving an organisation under subsection (2) above shall be—

(a)   in such form as may be prescribed by Act of Sederunt; and

(b)   admissible as evidence in any civil proceedings and sufficient evidence of the matters contained therein.

(5)   A document purporting to be a certificate by the Lord President for the purposes of this Act shall be accepted by the court as such unless the contrary is proved.

(6)   The Lord President may, in connection with the performance of any of his functions under this Act, require an organisation which is seeking, or has been granted, approval under subsection (2) above to provide him with such information as he thinks fit.

(7)   For the purposes of subsection (2)(d) above, 'co-habitants' means—

[(a)]   a man and a woman who are not married to each other but who are living together as if they were husband and wife [, or

(b)   two persons who are not civil partners of each other but are living together as if they were civil partners.]

(8)   In this Act, 'civil proceedings' does not include an arbitration or proceedings before a tribunal or inquiry.

(9)   In this section and section 2 of this Act, any reference to what occurred during family mediation shall include a reference to what was said, written or observed during such mediation.

2 Exceptions to general rule of inadmissibility

(1)   Nothing in section 1 of this Act shall prevent the admissibility as evidence in civil proceedings—

(a)   of information as to any contract entered into during family mediation or of the fact that no contract was entered into during such mediation;

(b)   where any contract entered into as a result of family mediation is challenged in those civil proceedings, of information as to what occurred during family mediation which relates to the subject matter of that challenge;

(c)   of information as to what occurred during family mediation if every participant (other than the mediator) in that mediation agrees that the information should be admitted as evidence; or

(d)   of information as to what occurred during family mediation if those civil proceedings are proceedings—

(i)   (whether under any enactment or otherwise) relating to a child's care or protection to which a local authority or a voluntary organisation is a party;

[. . .]

(iii)   [for the making of an adoption order (as defined in section 28(1) of the Adoption and Children (Scotland) Act 2007)];

[(iiia)   under Part 5 or, as the case may be, any of Parts 8 to 16 of the Children's Hearings (Scotland) Act 2011 (asp 1) before, or relating to, a children's hearing, before a sheriff or before a justice of the peace;

(iiib)   on any appeal arising from such proceedings as are mentioned in sub-paragraph (iiia);]

[. . .]

(v)   against one of the participants, or the mediator, in a family mediation in respect of damage to property, or personal injury, alleged to have been caused by that participant or, as the case may be, mediator during family mediation; or

(vi)   arising from the family mediation and to which the mediator is a party.

(2)   For the purposes of this section—

(a)   an individual, spouse, former spouse, party to a purported marriage, or co-habitant referred to in section 1(2) of this Act; and

(b)   insofar as the family mediation includes any of the matters mentioned in section 1(2)(a) of this Act, a child who—

(i) is the subject of such a family mediation; and

(ii) at the time the family mediation took place was capable of understanding the nature and significance of the matters to which the information which is sought to be admitted as evidence relates,

shall be regarded as a participant in the family mediation.

(3) Notwithstanding anything in the Age of Legal Capacity (Scotland) Act 1991, any child who is regarded as a participant in family mediation by virtue of subsection (2) above shall have legal capacity to agree that information should be admitted as evidence.

(4) The Secretary of State may prescribe other persons or classes of person who shall be regarded for the purposes of this section as participants in a family mediation.

3 Short title, construction, commencement and extent

(1) This Act may be cited as the Civil Evidence (Family Mediation) (Scotland) Act 1995.

(2) In this Act, 'prescribe', except in relation to an Act of Sederunt, means prescribe by regulations made by statutory instrument subject to annulment in pursuance of a resolution of either House of Parliament.

(3) This Act shall come into force on such day as the Lord Advocate may by order made by statutory instrument appoint; and such order may include such transitional or incidental provisions as appear to him to be necessary or expedient.

(4) This Act extends to Scotland only.

CHILDREN (SCOTLAND) ACT 1995
(1995, c 36)

PART I
PARENTS, CHILDREN AND GUARDIANS

Parental responsibilities and parental rights

1 Parental responsibilities

(1) Subject to section 3(1)(b) [and (d)] and (3) of this Act, a parent has in relation to his child the responsibility—

(a) to safeguard and promote the child's health, development and welfare;

(b) to provide, in a manner appropriate to the stage of development of the child—

(i) direction;

(ii) guidance,

to the child;

(c) if the child is not living with the parent, to maintain personal relations and direct contact with the child on a regular basis; and

(d) to act as the child's legal representative,

but only in so far as compliance with this section is practicable and in the interests of the child.

(2) 'Child' means for the purposes of—

(a) paragraphs (a), (b)(i), (c) and (d) of subsection (1) above, a person under the age of sixteen years;

(b) paragraph (b)(ii) of that subsection, a person under the age of eighteen years.

(3) The responsibilities mentioned in paragraphs (a) to (d) of subsection (1) above are in this Act referred to as 'parental responsibilities'; and the child, or any person acting on his behalf, shall have title to sue, or to defend, in any proceedings as respects those responsibilities.

(4) The parental responsibilities supersede any analogous duties imposed on a parent at common law; but this section is without prejudice to any other duty so

imposed on him or to any duty imposed on him by, under or by virtue of any other provision of this Act or of any other enactment.

2 Parental rights

(1)   Subject to section 3(1)(b) [and (d)] and (3) of this Act, a parent, in order to enable him to fulfil his parental responsibilities in relation to his child, has the right—

(a)   to have the child living with him or otherwise to regulate the child's residence;

(b)   to control, direct or guide, in a manner appropriate to the stage of development of the child, the child's upbringing;

(c)   if the child is not living with him, to maintain personal relations and direct contact with the child on a regular basis; and

(d)   to act as the child's legal representative.

(2)   Subject to subsection (3) below, where two or more persons have a parental right as respects a child, each of them may exercise that right without the consent of the other or, as the case may be, of any of the others, unless any decree or deed conferring the right, or regulating its exercise, otherwise provides.

(3)   Without prejudice to any court order, no person shall be entitled to remove a child habitually resident in Scotland from, or to retain any such child outwith, the United Kingdom without the consent of a person described in subsection (6) below.

(4)   The rights mentioned in paragraphs (a) to (d) of subsection (1) above are in this Act referred to as 'parental rights'; and a parent, or any person acting on his behalf, shall have title to sue, or to defend, in any proceedings as respects those rights.

(5)   The parental rights supersede any analogous rights enjoyed by a parent at common law; but this section is without prejudice to any other right so enjoyed by him or to any right enjoyed by him by, under or by virtue of any other provision of this Act or of any other enactment.

(6)   The description of a person referred to in subsection (3) above is a person (whether or not a parent of the child) who for the time being has and is exercising in relation to him a right mentioned in paragraph (a) or (c) of subsection (1) above; except that, where both the child's parents are persons so described, the consent required for his removal or retention shall be that of them both.

(7)   In this section, 'child' means a person under the age of sixteen years.

3 Provisions relating both to parental responsibilities and to parental rights

(1)   Notwithstanding section 1(1) of the Law Reform (Parent and Child) (Scotland) Act 1986 (provision for disregarding whether a person's parents are not, or have not been, married to one another in establishing the legal relationship between him and any other person)—

(a)   a child's mother has parental responsibilities and parental rights in relation to him whether or not she is or has been married to [or in a civil partnership with] his father; and

(b)   without prejudice to any arrangements which may be made under subsection (5) below and subject to any agreement which may be made under section 4 of this Act, his father has such responsibilities and rights in relation to him only if—

[(i)] married to [or in a civil partnership with] the mother at the time of the child's conception or subsequently [; or

(ii)   where not married to [or in a civil partnership with] the mother at that time or subsequently, the father is registered as the child's father under any of the enactments mentioned in subsection (1A).]

[(c)   without prejudice to any arrangements which may be made under subsection (5) below, where a child has a parent by virtue of section 42 of the

Human Fertilisation and Embryology Act 2008, that parent has parental responsibilities and parental rights in relation to the child;

(d) without prejudice to any arrangements which may be made under subsection (5) below and subject to any agreement which may be made under section 4A(1) of this Act, where a child has a parent by virtue of section 43 of the Human Fertilisation and Embryology Act 2008, that parent has parental responsibilities and parental rights in relation to the child if she is registered as a parent of the child under any of the enactments mentioned in subsection (3A).]

[(1A)   Those enactments are—

(a)   section 18(1)(a), (b)(i) and (c) and (2)(b) of the Registration of Births, Deaths and Marriages (Scotland) Act 1965;

(b)   sections 10(1)(a) to (e) and 10A(1)(a) to (e) of the Births and Deaths Registration Act 1953; and

(c)   article 14(3)(a) to (e) of the Births and Deaths Registration (Northern Ireland) Order 1976.]

(2)   For the purposes of subsection (1)(b) above, the father shall be regarded as having been—

[(a)   married to the mother at any time when he was a party to a purported marriage with her which was—

(i)   voidable; or

(ii)   void but believed by them (whether by error of fact or law) in good faith at that time to be valid;

(b)   in a civil partnership with the mother at any time when he was a party to a purported civil partnership with her which was—

(i)   voidable; or

(ii)   void but believed by them (whether by error of fact or law) in good faith at that time to be valid.]

(3)   Subsection (1) above is without prejudice to any order made under section 11 of this Act or section 3(1) of the said Act of 1986 (provision analogous to the said section 11 but repealed by this Act) or to any other order, disposal or resolution affecting parental responsibilities or parental rights; and nothing in subsection (1) above or in this Part of this Act shall affect any other—

(a)   enactment (including any other provision of this Act or of that Act); or

(b)   rule of law,

by, under or by virtue of which a person may have imposed on him (or be relieved of) parental responsibilities or may be granted (or be deprived of) parental rights.

[(3A)   Those enactments are—

(a)   paragraphs (a), (b) and (d) of section 18B(1) and section 18B(3)(a) of the Registration of Births, Deaths and Marriages (Scotland) Act 1965;

(b)   paragraphs (a), (b) and (c) of section 10(1B) and of section 10A(1B) of the Births and Deaths Registration Act 1953;

(c)   sub-paragraphs (a), (b) and (c) of Article 14ZA(3) of the Births and Deaths Registration (Northern Ireland) Order 1976.]

(4)   The fact that a person has parental responsibilities or parental rights in relation to a child shall not entitle that person to act in any way which would be incompatible with any court order relating to the child or the child's property, or with any [compulsory supervision order or interim compulsory supervision order (as defined in sections 83 and 86 respectively of the Children's Hearings (Scotland) Act 2011 (asp 1)) that is in force in relation to the child.]

(5)   Without prejudice to [sections 4(1) and 4A(1)] of this Act, a person who has parental responsibilities or parental rights in relation to a child shall not abdicate those responsibilities or rights to anyone else but may arrange for some or all of them to be fulfilled or exercised on his behalf, and without prejudice to that generality any such arrangement may be made with a person

who already has parental responsibilities or parental rights in relation to the child concerned.

(6)   The making of an arrangement under subsection (5) above shall not affect any liability arising from a failure to fulfil parental responsibilities; and where any arrangements so made are such that the child is a foster child for the purposes of the Foster Children (Scotland) Act 1984, those arrangements are subject to the provisions of that Act.

4   Acquisition of parental rights and responsibilities by natural father

(1)   Where a child's mother has not been deprived of some or all of the parental responsibilities and parental rights in relation to him and, by virtue of subsection (1)(b) of section 3 of this Act, his father has no parental responsibilities or parental rights in relation to him, the father and mother, whatever age they may be, may by agreement provide that, as from the appropriate date, the father shall have the parental responsibilities and parental rights which (in the absence of any order under section 11 of this Act affecting those responsibilities and rights) he would have if married to the mother.

(2)   No agreement under subsection (1) above shall have effect unless—
   (a)   in a form prescribed by the Secretary of State; and
   (b)   registered in the Books of Council and Session while the mother still has the parental responsibilities and parental rights which she had when the agreement was made.

(3)   The date on which such registration as is mentioned in subsection (2)(b) above takes place shall be the 'appropriate date' for the purposes of subsection (1) above.

(4)   An agreement which has effect by virtue of subsection (2) above shall, subject only to section 11(11) of this Act, be irrevocable.

[4A   Acquisition of parental responsibilities and parental rights by second female parent by agreement with mother

(1)   Where—
   (a)   a child's mother has not been deprived of some or all of the parental responsibilities and parental rights in relation to the child; and
   (b)   the child has a parent by virtue of section 43 of the Human Fertilisation and Embryology Act 2008 and that parent is not registered as such under any of the enactments mentioned in section 3(3A),
the mother and the other parent may by agreement provide that, as from the appropriate date, the other parent shall have the parental responsibilities and rights (in the absence of any order under section 11 of this Act affecting responsibilities and rights) as if the other parent were treated as a parent by virtue of section 42 of that Act of 2008.

(2)   Section 4(2), (3) and (4) applies in relation to an agreement under subsection (1) of this section as it applies in relation to an agreement under subsection (1) of section 4.]

5   Care or control of child by person without parental responsibilities or parental rights

(1)   Subject to subsection (2) below, it shall be the responsibility of a person who has attained the age of sixteen years and who has care or control of a child under that age, but in relation to him either has no parental responsibilities or parental rights or does not have the parental responsibility mentioned in section 1(1)(a) of this Act, to do what is reasonable in all the circumstances to safeguard the child's health, development and welfare; and in fulfilling his responsibility under this section the person may in particular, even though he does not have the parental right mentioned in section 2(1)(d) of this Act, give consent to any surgical, medical or dental treatment or procedure where—

(a)   the child is not able to give such consent on his own behalf, and
(b)   it is not within the knowledge of the person that a parent of the child
would refuse to give the consent in question.

(2)   Nothing in this section shall apply to a person in so far as he has care or
control of a child in a school ('school' having the meaning given by section 135(1)
of the Education (Scotland) Act 1980).

6   Views of children

(1)   A person shall, in reaching any major decision which involves—
(a)   his fulfilling a parental responsibility or the responsibility mentioned in
section 5(1) of this Act; or
(b)   his exercising a parental right or giving consent by virtue of that section,
have regard so far as practicable to the views (if he wishes to express them) of the
child concerned, taking account of the child's age and maturity, and to those of
any other person who has parental responsibilities or parental rights in relation to
the child (and wishes to express those views); and without prejudice to the generality of this subsection a child twelve years of age or more shall be presumed to be
of sufficient age and maturity to form a view.

(2)   A transaction entered into in good faith by a third party and a person acting as legal representative of a child shall not be challengeable on the ground only
that the child, or a person with parental responsibilities or parental rights in relation to the child, was not consulted or that due regard was not given to his views
before the transaction was entered into.

Guardianship

7   Appointment of guardians

(1)   A child's parent may appoint a person to be guardian of the child in the
event of the parent's death; but—
(a)   such appointment shall be of no effect unless—
(i)   in writing and signed by the parent; and
(ii)   the parent, at the time of death, was entitled to act as legal representative of the child (or would have been so entitled if he had survived until after
the birth of the child); and
(b)   any parental responsibilities or parental rights (or the right to appoint a
further guardian under this section) which a surviving parent has in relation to
the child shall subsist with those which, by, under or by virtue of this Part of
this Act, the appointee so has.

(2)   A guardian of a child may appoint a person to take his place as guardian in
the event of the guardian's death; but such appointment shall be of no effect
unless in writing and signed by the person making it.

(3)   An appointment as guardian shall not take effect until accepted, either
expressly or impliedly by acts which are not consistent with any other intention.

(4)   If two or more persons are appointed as guardians, any one or more of
them shall, unless the appointment expressly provides otherwise, be entitled to
accept office even if both or all of them do not accept office.

(5)   Subject to any order under section 11 or 86 of this Act, a person appointed
as a child's guardian under this section shall have, in respect of the child, the
responsibilities imposed, and the rights conferred, on a parent by sections 1 and 2
of this Act respectively; and sections 1 and 2 of this Act shall apply in relation to a
guardian as they apply in relation to a parent.

(6)   Without prejudice to the generality of subsection (1) of section 6 of this Act,
a decision as to the appointment of a guardian under subsection (1) or (2) above
shall be regarded for the purposes of that section (or of that section as applied by
subsection (5) above) as a major decision which involves exercising a parental
right.

8   Revocation and other termination of appointment

(1)   An appointment made under section 7(1) or (2) of this Act revokes an earlier such appointment (including one made in an unrevoked will or codicil) made by the same person in respect of the same child, unless it is clear (whether as a result of an express provision in the later appointment or by any necessary implication) that the purpose of the later appointment is to appoint an additional guardian.

(2)   Subject to subsections (3) and (4) below, the revocation of an appointment made under section 7(1) or (2) of this Act (including one made in an unrevoked will or codicil) shall not take effect unless the revocation is in writing and is signed by the person making the revocation.

(3)   An appointment under section 7(1) or (2) of this Act (other than one made in a will or codicil) is revoked if, with the intention of revoking the appointment, the person who made it—

(a)   destroys the document by which it was made; or

(b)   has some other person destroy that document in his presence.

(4)   For the avoidance of doubt, an appointment made under section 7(1) or (2) of this Act in a will or codicil is revoked if the will or codicil is revoked.

(5)   Once an appointment of a guardian has taken effect under section 7 of this Act, then, unless the terms of the appointment provide for earlier termination, it shall terminate only by virtue of—

(a)   the child concerned attaining the age of eighteen years;

(b)   the death of the child or the guardian; or

(c)   the termination of the appointment by a court order under section 11 of this Act.

Administration of child's property

9   Safeguarding of child's property

(1)   Subject to section 13 of this Act, this section applies where—

(a)   property is owned by or due to a child;

(b)   the property is held by a person other than a parent or guardian of the child; and

(c)   but for this section, the property would be required to be transferred to a parent having parental responsibilities in relation to the child or to a guardian for administration by that parent or guardian on behalf of the child.

(2)   Subject to subsection (4) below, where this section applies and the person holding the property is an executor or trustee, then—

(a)   if the value of the property exceeds £20,000, he shall; or

(b)   if that value is not less than £5,000 and does not exceed £20,000, he may, apply to the Accountant of Court for a direction as to the administration of the property.

(3)   Subject to subsection (4) below, where this section applies and the person holding the property is a person other than an executor or trustee, then, if the value of the property is not less than £5,000, that person may apply to the Accountant of Court for a direction as to the administration of the property.

(4)   Where the parent or guardian mentioned in subsection (1)(c) above has been appointed a trustee under a trust deed to administer the property concerned, subsections (2) and (3) above shall not apply, and the person holding the property shall transfer it to the parent or guardian.

(5)   On receipt of an application under subsection (2) or (3) above, the Accountant of Court may do one, or (in so far as the context admits) more than one, of the following—

(a)   apply to the court for the appointment of a judicial factor (whether or not the parent or guardian mentioned in subsection (1)(c) above) to administer all or part of the property concerned and in the event of the court making such an appointment shall direct that the property, or as the case may be part, concerned be transferred to the factor;

   (b)   direct that all or part of the property concerned be transferred to himself;

   (c)   direct that all or, in a case where the parent or guardian so mentioned has not been appointed by virtue of paragraph (a) above, part of the property concerned be transferred to the parent or guardian,
to be administered on behalf of the child.

   (6)   A direction under subsection (5)(c) above may include such conditions as the Accountant of Court considers appropriate, including in particular a condition—

   (a)   that in relation to the property concerned no capital expenditure shall be incurred without his approval; or

   (b)   that there shall be exhibited annually to him the securities and bank books which represent the capital of the estate.

   (7)   A person who has applied under subsection (2) or (3) above for a direction shall not thereafter transfer the property concerned except in accordance with a direction under subsection (5) above.

   (8)   The Secretary of State may from time to time prescribe a variation in any sum referred to in subsections (2) and (3) above.

   (9)   In this section 'child' means a person under the age of sixteen years who is habitually resident in Scotland.

10   Obligations and rights of person administering child's property

   (1)   A person acting as a child's legal representative in relation to the administration of the child's property—

   (a)   shall be required to act as a reasonable and prudent person would act on his own behalf, and

   (b)   subject to any order made under section 11 of this Act, shall be entitled to do anything which the child, if of full age and capacity, could do in relation to that property;
and subject to subsection (2) below, on ceasing to act as legal representative, shall be liable to account to the child for his intromissions with the child's property.

   (2)   No liability shall be incurred by virtue of subsection (1) above in respect of funds which have been used in the proper discharge of the person's responsibility to safeguard and promote the child's health, development and welfare.

Court orders

11   Court orders relating to parental responsibilities etc

   (1)   In the relevant circumstances in proceedings in the Court of Session or sheriff court, whether those proceedings are or are not independent of any other action, an order may be made under this subsection in relation to—

   (a)   parental responsibilities;
   (b)   parental rights;
   (c)   guardianship; or
   (d)   subject to section 14(1) and (2) of this Act, the administration of a child's property.

   (2)   The court may make such order under subsection (1) above as it thinks fit; and without prejudice to the generality of that subsection may in particular so make any of the following orders—

   (a)   an order depriving a person of some or all of his parental responsibilities or parental rights in relation to a child;
   (b)   an order—
      (i)   imposing upon a person (provided he is at least sixteen years of age or is a parent of the child) such responsibilities; and
      (ii)   giving that person such rights;
   (c)   an order regulating the arrangements as to—
      (i)   with whom; or

(ii) if with different persons alternately or periodically, with whom during what periods,
a child under the age of sixteen years is to live (any such order being known as a 'residence order');

(d) an order regulating the arrangements for maintaining personal relations and direct contact between a child under that age and a person with whom the child is not, or will not be, living (any such order being known as a 'contact order');

(e) an order regulating any specific question which has arisen, or may arise, in connection with any of the matters mentioned in paragraphs (a) to (d) of subsection (1) of this section (any such order being known as a 'specific issue order');

(f) an interdict prohibiting the taking of any step of a kind specified in the interdict in the fulfillment of parental responsibilities or the exercise of parental rights relating to a child or in the administration of a child's property;

(g) an order appointing a judicial factor to manage a child's property or remitting the matter to the Accountant of Court to report on suitable arrangements for the future management of the property; or

(h) an order appointing or removing a person as guardian of the child.

[(2A) An order doing any of the things mentioned in subsection (2) is to be regarded as an order in relation to at least one of the matters mentioned in subsection (1).]

(3) The relevant circumstances mentioned in subsection (1) above are—

(a) that application for an order under that subsection is made by a person who—

(i) not having, and never having had, parental responsibilities or parental rights in relation to the child, claims an interest;

(ii) has parental responsibilities or parental rights in relation to the child;
[. . .]

[(aa) that application for a contact order is made with the leave of the court by a person whose parental responsibilities or parental rights in relation to the child were extinguished on the making of an adoption order;

(ab) that application for an order under subsection (1) above [. . .] is made by a person who has had, but for a reason other than is mentioned in subsection (4) below, no longer has, parental responsibilities or parental rights in relation to the child;]

(b) that although [no application for an order under subsection (1) above] has been made, the court (even if it declines to make any other order) considers it should make such an order.

(4) The reasons referred to in subsection (3)[ab] above are that the parental responsibilities or parental rights have been—

(a) extinguished on the making of an adoption order;
[. . .]

(c) extinguished by virtue of [section 55(1) of the Human Fertilisation and Embryology Act 2008 (parental orders: supplementary provision)] on the making of a parental order under [section 54 [or 54A] of that Act].
[. . .]

(5) In subsection (3)(a) [and (ab)] above 'person' includes (without prejudice to the generality of that subsection) the child concerned; but it does not include a local authority.

(6) In [subsections (3)(aa) and] (4) above—
[. . .] 'adoption order' [has the meaning given by section 119 of the Adoption and Children (Scotland) Act 2007] [. . .].

(7) Subject to subsection (8) below, in considering whether or not to make an order under subsection (1) above and what order to make, the court—

(a) shall regard the welfare of the child concerned as its paramount consideration and shall not make any such order unless it considers that it would be better for the child that the order be made than that none should be made at all, and

(b) taking account of the child's age and maturity, shall so far as practicable—

(i) give him an opportunity to indicate whether he wishes to express his views;

(ii) if he does so wish, give him an opportunity to express them; and

(iii) have regard to such views as he may express.

[(7A) In carrying out the duties imposed by subsection (7)(a) above, the court shall have regard in particular to the matters mentioned in subsection (7B) below.

(7B) Those matters are—

(a) the need to protect the child from—

(i) any abuse; or

(ii) the risk of any abuse,

which affects, or might affect, the child;

(b) the effect such abuse, or the risk of such abuse, might have on the child;

(c) the ability of a person—

(i) who has carried out abuse which affects or might affect the child; or

(ii) who might carry out such abuse,

to care for, or otherwise meet the needs of, the child; and

(d) the effect any abuse, or the risk of any abuse, might have on the carrying out of responsibilities in connection with the welfare of the child by a person who has (or, by virtue of an order under subsection (1), would have) those responsibilities.

(7C) In subsection (7B) above—

'abuse' includes—

(a) violence, harassment, threatening conduct and any other conduct giving rise, or likely to give rise, to physical or mental injury, fear, alarm or distress;

(b) abuse of a person other than the child; and

(c) domestic abuse;

'conduct' includes—

(a) speech; and

(b) presence in a specified place or area.

(7D) Where—

(a) the court is considering making an order under subsection (1) above; and

(b) in pursuance of the order two or more relevant persons would have to co-operate with one another as respects matters affecting the child,

the court shall consider whether it would be appropriate to make the order.

(7E) In subsection (7D) above, 'relevant person', in relation to a child, means—

(a) a person having parental responsibilities or parental rights in respect of the child; or

(b) where a parent of the child does not have parental responsibilities or parental rights in respect of the child, a parent of the child.]

(8) The court shall, notwithstanding subsection (7) above, endeavour to ensure that any order which it makes, or any determination by it not to make an order, does not adversely affect the position of a person who has, in good faith and for value, acquired any property of the child concerned, or any right or interest in such property.

(9) Nothing in paragraph (b) of subsection (7) above requires a child to be legally represented, if he does not wish to be, in proceedings in the course of which the court implements that paragraph.

(10) Without prejudice to the generality of paragraph (b) of subsection (7) above, a child twelve years of age or more shall be presumed to be of sufficient

age and maturity to form a view for the purposes both of that paragraph and of subsection (9) above.

(11)   An order under subsection (1) above shall have the effect of depriving a person of a parental responsibility or parental right only in so far as the order expressly so provides and only to the extent necessary to give effect to the order; but in making any such order as is mentioned in paragraph (a) or (b) of subsection (2) above the court may revoke any agreement which, in relation to the child concerned, has effect by virtue of section 4(2) [or 4A(2)] of this Act.

(12)   Where the court makes a residence order which requires that a child live with a person who, immediately before the order is made does not have in relation to the child all the parental responsibilities mentioned in paragraphs (a), (b) and (d) of section 1(1), and the parental rights mentioned in paragraphs (b) and (d) of section 2(1), of this Act (those which he does not so have being in this subsection referred to as the 'relevant responsibilities and rights') that person shall, subject to the provisions of the order or of any other order made under subsection (1) above, have the relevant responsibilities and rights while the residence order remains in force.

(13)   Any reference in this section to an order includes a reference to an interim order or to an order varying or discharging an order.

[11A   Restriction on making of orders under section 11

(1)   Subsection (2) applies where a permanence order (as defined in section 80(2) of the Adoption and Children (Scotland) Act 2007 (asp 4)) is in force in respect of a child.

(2)   The court may not, under subsection (1) of section 11 of this Act, make an order such as is mentioned in any of paragraphs (a) to (e) of subsection (2) of that section.]

12   Restrictions on decrees for divorce, separation or annulment affecting children

(1)   In any action for—

[(a)]   divorce, judicial separation or declarator of nullity of marriage, [or

(b)   dissolution or declarator of nullity of a civil partnership or separation of civil partners,]

the court shall, where this section applies, consider (in the light of such information as is before the court as to the arrangements which have been, or are proposed to be, made for the upbringing of each child by virtue of which it applies) whether to exercise with respect to him the powers conferred by section 11 [of this Act or section 62 of the Children's Hearings (Scotland) Act 2011].

(2)   Where, in any case to which this section applies, the court is of the opinion that—

(a)   the circumstances of the case require, or are likely to require, it to exercise any power under section 11 [of this Act or section 62 of the Children's Hearings (Scotland) Act 2011] with respect to the child concerned;

(b)   it is not in a position to exercise that power without giving further consideration to the case; and

(c)   there are exceptional circumstances which make it desirable in the interests of that child that it should not grant decree in the action until it is in a position to exercise such a power,

it shall postpone its decision on the granting of decree in the action until it is in such a position.

(3)   This section applies where a child of the family has not reached the age of sixteen years at the date when the question first arises as to whether the court should give such consideration as is mentioned in subsection (1) above.

[(4) In this section 'child of the family', in relation to the parties to a marriage or civil partnership, means a child—

(a)   of both of them; or

(b)   who has been treated by both of them as a child of their family, not
being a child who is placed with them as foster parents by a local authority or
voluntary organisation.]

13   Awards of damages to children

(1)   Where in any court proceedings a sum of money becomes payable to, or for
the benefit of, a child under the age of sixteen years, the court may make such
order relating to the payment and management of the sum for the benefit of the
child as it thinks fit.

(2)   Without prejudice to the generality of subsection (1) above, the court may
in an order under this section—

(a)   appoint a judicial factor to invest, apply or otherwise deal with the
money for the benefit of the child concerned;

(b)   order the money to be paid—

   (i)   to the sheriff clerk or the Accountant of Court; or

   (ii)   to a parent or guardian of that child,

to be invested, applied or otherwise dealt with, under the directions of the court,
for the benefit of that child; or

(c)   order the money to be paid directly to that child.

(3)   Where payment is made to a person in accordance with an order under this
section, a receipt given by him shall be a sufficient discharge of the obligation to
make the payment.

Jurisdiction and choice of law

14   Jurisdiction and choice of law in relation to certain matters

(1)   The Court of Session shall have jurisdiction to entertain an application for
an order relating to the administration of a child's property if the child is habitually resident in, or the property is situated in, Scotland.

(2)   A sheriff shall have jurisdiction to entertain such an application if the child
is habitually resident in, or the property is situated in, the sheriffdom.

(3)   Subject to subsection (4) below, any question arising under this Part of this
Act—

(a)   concerning—

   (i)   parental responsibilities or parental rights; or

   (ii)   the responsibilities or rights of a guardian,

in relation to a child shall, in so far as it is not also a question such as is
mentioned in paragraph (b) below, be determined by the law of the place of the
child's habitual residence at the time when the question arises;

(b)   concerning the immediate protection of a child shall be determined by
the law of the place where the child is when the question arises; and

(c)   as to whether a person is validly appointed or constituted guardian of a
child shall be determined by the law of the place of the child's habitual residence on the date when the appointment was made (the date of death of the
testator being taken to be the date of appointment where an appointment was
made by will), or the event constituting the guardianship occurred.

(4)   Nothing in any provision of law in accordance with which, under subsection (3) above, a question which arises in relation to an application for, or the
making of, an order under subsection (1) of section 11 of this Act falls to be determined, shall affect the application of subsection (7) of that section.

Interpretation

15   Interpretation of Part I

(1)   In this Part of this Act—

'child' means, where the expression is not otherwise defined, a person under the
age of eighteen years;

'contact order' has the meaning given by section 11(2)(d) of this Act;

'parent', in relation to any person, means, subject to [Chapter 3 of Part 1 of the Adoption and Children (Scotland) Act 2007] and sections 27 to 30 of the Human Fertilisation and Embryology Act 1990 [and Part 2 of the Human Fertilisation and Embryology Act 2008] and any regulations made under [section 55(1) of that Act of 2008], someone, of whatever age, who is that person's genetic father or mother;

'parental responsibilities' has the meaning given by section 1(3) of this Act;

'parental rights' has the meaning given by section 2(4) of this Act;

'residence order' has the meaning given by section 11(2)(c) of this Act;

'specific issue order' has the meaning given by section 11(2)(e) of this Act; and

'transaction' has the meaning given by section 9 of the Age of Legal Capacity (Scotland) Act 1991 (except that, for the purposes of subsection (5)(b) below, paragraph (d) of the definition in question shall be disregarded).

(2)   No provision in this Part of this Act shall affect any legal proceedings commenced, or any application made to a court, before that provision comes into effect; except that where, before section 11 of this Act comes into force, there has been final decree in a cause in which, as respects a child, an order for custody or access, or an order which is analogous to any such order as is mentioned in subsection (2) of that section, has been made, any application on or after the date on which the section does come into force for variation or recall of the order shall proceed as if the order had been made under that section.

(3)   In subsection (2) above, the reference to final decree is to a decree or interlocutor which, taken by itself or along with previous interlocutors, disposes of the whole subject matter of the cause.

(4)   Any reference in this Part of this Act to a person—

    (a)   having parental rights or responsibilities;

    (b)   acting as a legal representative; or

    (c)   being appointed a guardian,

is to a natural person only.

(5)   Any reference in this Part of this Act to a person acting as the legal representative of a child is a reference to that person, in the interests of the child—

    (a)   administering any property belonging to the child; and

    (b)   acting in, or giving consent to, any transaction where the child is incapable of so acting or consenting on his own behalf.

(6)   Where a child has legal capacity to sue, or to defend, in any civil proceedings, he may nevertheless consent to be represented in those proceedings by any person who, had the child lacked that capacity, would have had the responsibility to act as his legal representative.

[(7)   No provision in this Part of this Act shall permit a person to give a consent to the storage of gametes under the Human Fertilisation and Embryology Act 1990 on behalf of a child.]

PART II

PROMOTION OF CHILDREN'S WELFARE BY LOCAL AUTHORITIES AND BY CHILDREN'S HEARINGS ETC

Chapter 1
Support for Children and their Families

Introductory

16   Welfare of child and consideration of his views

(1)   Where under or by virtue of this Part of this Act, [. . .] a court determines, any matter with respect to a child the welfare of that child throughout his childhood shall be [. . .] its paramount consideration.

(2)   In the circumstances mentioned in subsection (4) below, [. . .] the sheriff, taking account of the age and maturity of the child concerned, shall so far as practicable—

(a)   give him an opportunity to indicate whether he wishes to express his views;

(b)   if he does so wish, give him an opportunity to express them; and

(c)   have regard to such views as he may express;

and without prejudice to the generality of this subsection a child twelve years of age or more shall be presumed to be of sufficient age and maturity to form a view.

(3)   In the circumstances mentioned in subsection (4) [. . .] of this section, no [. . .] order so mentioned shall be made with respect to the child concerned unless [. . .] the sheriff considers, that it would be better for the child that the [. . .] order be made than that none should be made at all.

(4)   [The circumstances to which subsection (2) above refers are that the sheriff is considering whether to make, order or discharge an exclusion order.]

(5)   If, for the purpose of protecting members of the public from serious harm (whether or not physical harm)—

[. . .]

(b)   a court considers it necessary to make a determination under or by virtue of [Chapters 1 or 3] of this Part of this Act which (but for this paragraph) would not be consistent with its affording such paramountcy, it may make that determination.

17   Duty of local authority to child looked after by them

(1)   Where a child is looked after by a local authority they shall, in such manner as the Secretary of State may prescribe—

(a)   safeguard and promote his welfare (which shall, in the exercise of their duty to him be their paramount concern);

(b)   make such use of services available for children cared for by their own parents as appear to the authority reasonable in his case;

(c)   take such steps to promote, on a regular basis, personal relations and direct contact between the child and any person with parental responsibilities in relation to him as appear to them to be, having regard to their duty to him under paragraph (a) above, both practicable and appropriate; and

[(d)   take such steps to promote, on a regular basis, personal relations and direct contact between the child and any person mentioned in subsection (1A) as appear to them to be appropriate having regard to their duty to the child under paragraph (a).]

[(1A)   The persons referred to in subsection (1)(d) are—

(a)   a sibling of the child, and

(b)   any other person with whom the child has lived and with whom the child has an ongoing relationship with the character of a relationship between siblings.

(1B)   For the purposes of subsection (1A), two people are siblings if they have at least one parent in common.]

(2)   The duty under paragraph (a) of subsection (1) above includes, without prejudice to that paragraph's generality, the duty of providing advice and assistance with a view to preparing the child for when he is no longer looked after by a local authority.

(3)   Before making any decision with respect to a child whom they are looking after, or proposing to look after, a local authority shall, so far as is reasonably practicable, ascertain the views of—

(a)   the child;

(b)   his parents;

(c)   any person who is not a parent of his but who has parental rights in relation to him;

[(ca) any person mentioned in subsection (1A); and]

(d)   any other person whose views the authority consider to be relevant,
regarding the matter to be decided.

(4)   In making any such decision a local authority shall have regard so far as
practicable—

(a)   to the views (if he wishes to express them) of the child concerned, taking
account of his age and maturity;

(b)   to such views of any person mentioned in subsection (3)(b) to (d) above
as they have been able to ascertain; and

(c)   to the child's religious persuasion, racial origin and cultural and linguistic background.

(5)   If, for the purpose of protecting members of the public from serious harm
(whether or not physical harm) a local authority consider it necessary to exercise,
in a manner which (but for this paragraph) would not be consistent with their
duties under this section, their powers with respect to a child whom they are looking after, they may do so.

(6)   Any reference in this Chapter of this Part to a child who is 'looked after' by
a local authority, is to a child—

(a)   for whom they are providing accommodation under section 25 of this
Act;

[(b)   who is subject to a compulsory supervision order or an interim compulsory supervision order and in respect of whom they are the implementation
authority (within the meaning of the Children's Hearings (Scotland) Act
2011);]

[. . .]

(d)   who is subject to an order in accordance with which, by virtue of
regulations made under section 33(1) of this Act [or section 190 of the Children's
Hearings (Scotland) Act 2011 (asp 1) (effect of Orders made outwith Scotland)],
they have [responsibilities as respects the child] [; or

(e)   in respect of whom a permanence order has, on an application by them
under section 80 of the Adoption and Children (Scotland) Act 2007 (asp 4), been
made and has not ceased to have effect.]

(7)   Regulations made by the Secretary of State under subsection (1) above may,
without prejudice to the generality of that subsection, include—

(a)   provision as to the circumstances in which the child may be cared for by
the child's own parents; and

(b)   procedures which shall be followed in the event of the child's death.

18   Duty of persons with parental responsibilities to notify change of address to local authority looking after child

(1)   Where a child is being looked after by a local authority, each natural
person who has parental responsibilities in relation to the child shall, without
unreasonable delay, inform that authority whenever the person changes his
address.

(2)   A person who knowingly fails to comply with the requirement imposed by
subsection (1) above shall be liable on summary conviction to a fine of level 1 on
the standard scale; but in any proceedings under this section it shall be a defence
that—

(a)   the change was to the same address as that to which another person who
at that time had parental responsibilities in relation to the child was changing;
and

(b)   the accused had reasonable cause to believe that the other person had
informed the authority of the change of address of them both.

Provision of services

[. . .]

20 Publication of information about services for children

(1) A local authority shall, within such period after the coming into force of this section as the Secretary of State may direct, and thereafter from time to time, prepare and publish information—

(a) about relevant services which are provided by them for or in respect of children (including, without prejudice to that generality, services for or in respect of disabled children or children otherwise affected by disability) in their area or by any other local authority for those children; and

(b) where they consider it appropriate, about services which are provided by voluntary organisations and by other persons for those children, being services which the authority have power to provide and which, were they to do so, they would provide as relevant services.

[(2) In subsection (1) above, 'relevant services' means services provided by a local authority under or by virtue of—

(a) this Part of this Act;

(b) the Children's Hearings (Scotland) Act 2011;

(c) Part 12 of the Children and Young People (Scotland) Act 2014; or

(d) any of the enactments mentioned in section 5(1B)(a) to (n), (r) or (t) of the Social Work (Scotland) Act 1968.]

21 Co-operation between authorities

(1) Where it appears to a local authority that an appropriate person could, by doing certain things, help in the exercise of any of their functions under this Part of this Act, they may, specifying what those things are, request the help of that person.

(2) For the purposes of subsection (1) above, persons who are appropriate are—

(a) any other local authority;

(b) a health board constituted under section 2 of the National Health Service (Scotland) Act 1978;

(c) a national health service trust established under section 12A of that Act; and

(d) any person authorised by the Secretary of State for the purposes of this section;

and an appropriate person receiving such a request shall comply with it provided that it is compatible with their own statutory or other duties and obligations and (in the case of a person not a natural person) does not unduly prejudice the discharge of any of their functions.

22 Promotion of welfare of children in need

(1) A local authority shall—

(a) safeguard and promote the welfare of children in their area who are in need; and

(b) so far as is consistent with that duty, promote the upbringing of such children by their families,

by providing a range and level of services appropriate to the children's needs.

(2) In providing services under subsection (1) above, a local authority shall have regard so far as practicable to each child's religious persuasion, racial origin and cultural and linguistic background.

(3) Without prejudice to the generality of subsection (1) above—

(a) a service may be provided under that subsection—

(i) for a particular child;

(ii) if provided with a view to safeguarding or promoting his welfare, for his family; or

    (iii) if provided with such a view, for any other member of his family; and

    (b)   the services mentioned in that subsection may include giving assistance in kind or, in exceptional circumstances, in cash.

(4)   Assistance such as is mentioned in subsection (3)(b) above may be given unconditionally or subject to conditions as to the repayment, in whole or in part, of it or of its value; but before giving it, or imposing such conditions, the local authority shall have regard to the means of the child concerned and of his parents and no condition shall require repayment by a person at any time when in receipt of—

    [(za) universal credit under Part 1 of the Welfare Reform Act 2012;]

    (a)   income support or [working families tax] credit payable under the Social Security Contributions and Benefits Act 1992; or

    [(aa) any element of child tax credit other than the family element or working tax credit; or]

    (b)   an income-based jobseeker's allowance payable under the Jobseekers Act 1995 [; or

    (c)   an income-related allowance under Part 1 of the Welfare Reform Act 2007 (employment and support allowance).]

23 Children affected by disability

(1)   Without prejudice to the generality of subsection (1) of section 22 of this Act, services provided by a local authority under that subsection shall be designed—

    (a)   to minimise the effect on any—

        (i)   disabled child who is within the authority's area, of his disability; and

        (ii) child who is within that area and is affected adversely by the disability of any other person in his family, of that other person's disability; and

    (b)   to give those children the opportunity to lead lives which are as normal as possible.

(2)   For the purposes of this Chapter of this Part a person is disabled if he is chronically sick or disabled or suffers from mental disorder (within the meaning of the Mental Health (Scotland) Act 1984).

(3)   [Where requested to do so by—

    (a)   a child's parent or guardian; or

    (b)   a mental health officer (as defined in section 329 of the Mental Health (Care and Treatment) (Scotland) Act 2003 (asp 13)) who—

        (i) has responsibility under that Act or the Criminal Procedure (Scotland) Act 1995 (c 46) for a child's case; and

        (ii) makes the request for the purposes of either of those Acts,

a local authority shall, for the purpose of facilitating the discharge of such duties as the authority may have under section 22(1) of this Act (whether or not by virtue of subsection (1) above) as respects the child, carry out an assessment of the child, or of any other person in the child's family, to determine the needs of the child, or of any other person in the child's family, to determine the needs of the child in so far as attributable to his disability or to that of the other person.]

    [(4)   In determining the needs of a child under subsection (3) above, the local authority shall take account—

    [(a) if an adult carer provides, or intends to provide, care for the child, of the care provided by that carer,

    (aa) if a young carer provides, or intends to provide, care for the child, of the care provided by that carer,]

    (b)   in so far as it is reasonable and practicable to do so, of—

        (i) the views of the parent or guardian of the child, and the child,

        [. . .]

provided that the parent, guardian, [or child] in question has a wish, or as the case may be, a capacity, to express a view.]

[(5) In subsection (4)(a) and (aa), the reference to the care provided by a carer means—

(a) in the case of an adult carer who has an adult carer support plan, the information about that care set out in that plan,

(b) in the case of a young carer who has a young carer statement, the information about that care set out in that statement.

(6) In—

(a) determining the needs of a child under subsection (3),

(b) deciding whether to provide any services under section 22(1), and

(c) deciding how any such services are to be provided,

a local authority must take account of the views of the carer, in so far as it is reasonable and practicable to do so.

(7) In this section—

'adult carer' and 'adult carer support plan' have the meanings given by the Carers (Scotland) Act 2016,

'young carer' and 'young carer statement' have the meanings given by the Carers (Scotland) Act 2016.]

[23A Sections 17, 22 and 26A: consideration of wellbeing

(1) This section applies where a local authority is exercising a function under or by virtue of section 17, 22 or 26A of this Act.

(2) The local authority must have regard to the general principle that functions should be exercised in relation to children and young people in a way which is designed to safeguard, support and promote their wellbeing.

(3) For the purpose of subsection (2) above, the local authority is to assess the wellbeing of a child or young person by reference to the extent to which the matters listed in section 96(2) of the 2014 Act are or, as the case may be, would be satisfied in relation to the child or young person.

(4) In assessing the wellbeing of a child or young person as mentioned in subsection (3) above, a local authority is to have regard to the guidance issued under section 96(3) of the 2014 Act.

(5) In this section, 'the 2014 Act' means the Children and Young People (Scotland) Act 2014.]

[. . .]

25 Provision of accommodation for children, etc

(1) A local authority shall provide accommodation for any child who, residing or having been found within their area, appears to them to require such provision because—

(a) no-one has parental responsibility for him;

(b) he is lost or abandoned; or

(c) the person who has been caring for him is prevented, whether or not permanently and for whatever reason, from providing him with suitable accommodation or care.

(2) Without prejudice to subsection (1) above, a local authority may provide accommodation for any child within their area if they consider that to do so would safeguard or promote his welfare.

(3) A local authority may provide accommodation for any person within their area who is at least eighteen years of age but not yet twenty-one, if they consider that to do so would safeguard or promote his welfare.

(4) A local authority providing accommodation under subsection (1) above for a child who is ordinarily resident in the area of another local authority shall notify the other authority, in writing, that such provision is being made; and the

other authority may at any time take over the provision of accommodation for
the child.

(5) Before providing a child with accommodation under this section, a local
authority shall have regard, so far as practicable, to his views (if he wishes to
express them), taking account of his age and maturity; and without prejudice to
the generality of this subsection a child twelve years of age or more shall be presumed to be of sufficient age and maturity to form a view.

(6) Subject to subsection (7) below—

(a) a local authority shall not provide accommodation under this section for
a child if any person who—

(i) has parental responsibilities in relation to him and the parental rights
mentioned in section 2(1)(a) and (b) of this Act; and

(ii) is willing and able either to provide, or to arrange to have provided,
accommodation for him,

objects; and

(b) any such person may at any time remove the child from accommodation
which has been provided by the local authority under this section.

(7) Paragraph (a) of subsection (6) above does not apply—

(a) as respects any child who, being at least sixteen years of age, agrees to be
provided with accommodation under this section; or

(b) where a residence order has been made in favour of one or more persons
and that person has, or as the case may be those persons have, agreed that the
child should be looked after in accommodation provided by, or on behalf of, the
local authority;

and paragraph (b) of that subsection does not apply where accommodation has
been provided for a continuous period of at least six months (whether by a single
local authority or, by virtue of subsection (4) above, by more than one local authority), unless the person removing the child has given the local authority for the
time being making such provision at least fourteen days' notice in writing of his
intention to remove the child.

(8) In this Part of this Act, accommodation means, except where the context
otherwise requires, accommodation provided for a continuous period of more than
twenty-four hours.

**26 Manner of provision of accommodation to child looked after by local
authority**

(1) A local authority may provide accommodation for a child looked after by
them by—

(a) placing him with—

(i) a family (other than such family as is mentioned in paragraph (a) or
(b) of the definition of that expression in section 93(1) of this Act);

(ii) a relative of his; or

(iii) any other suitable person. [. . .]

(b) maintaining him in a residential establishment; or

(c) making such other arrangements as appear to them to be appropriate,
including (without prejudice to the generality of this paragraph) making use of
such services as are referred to in section 17(1)(b) of this Act.

(2) A local authority may arrange for a child whom they are looking after—

(a) to be placed, under subsection (1)(a) above, with a person in England
and Wales or in Northern Ireland; or

(b) to be maintained in any accommodation in which—

(i) a local authority in England and Wales could maintain him by virtue
of section 23(2)(b) to (e) of the Children Act 1989; or

(ii) an authority within the meaning of the Children (Northern Ireland)
Order 1995 could maintain him by virtue of Article 27(2)(b) to (e) of that Order.

[26A   Provision of continuing care: looked after children

(1)   This section applies where an eligible person ceases to be looked after by a local authority.

(2)   An 'eligible person' is a person who—

(a)   is at least sixteen years of age, and

(b)   is not yet such higher age as may be specified.

(3)   Subject to subsection (5) below, the local authority must provide the person with continuing care.

(4)   'Continuing care' means the same accommodation and other assistance as was being provided for the person by the authority, in pursuance of this Chapter of this Part, immediately before the person ceased to be looked after.

(5)   The duty to provide continuing care does not apply if—

(a)   the accommodation the person was in immediately before ceasing to be looked after was secure accommodation,

(b)   the accommodation the person was in immediately before ceasing to be looked after was a care placement and the carer has indicated to the authority that the carer is unable or unwilling to continue to provide the placement, or

(c)   the local authority considers that providing the care would significantly adversely affect the welfare of the person.

(6)   A local authority's duty to provide continuing care lasts, subject to subsection (7) below, until the expiry of such period as may be specified.

(7)   The duty to provide continuing care ceases if—

(a)   the person leaves the accommodation of the person's own volition,

(b)   the accommodation ceases to be available, or

(c)   the local authority considers that continuing to provide the care would significantly adversely affect the welfare of the person.

(8)   For the purposes of subsection (7)(b) above, the situations in which accommodation ceases to be available include—

(a)   in the case of a care placement, where the carer indicates to the authority that the carer is unable or unwilling to continue to provide the placement,

(b)   in the case of a residential establishment provided by the local authority, where the authority closes the establishment,

(c)   in the case of a residential establishment provided under arrangements made by the local authority, where the arrangements come to an end.

(9)   The Scottish Ministers may by order—

(a)   make provision about when or how a local authority is to consider whether subsection (5)(c) or (7)(c) above is the case,

(b)   modify subsection (5) above so as to add, remove or vary a situation in which the duty to provide continuing care does not apply,

(c)   modify subsection (7) or (8) above so as to add, remove or vary a situation in which the duty to provide continuing care ceases.

(10)   If a local authority becomes aware that a person who is being provided with continuing care has died, the local authority must as soon as reasonably practicable notify—

(a)   the Scottish Ministers, and

(b)   Social Care and Social Work Improvement Scotland.

(11)   An order under this section—

(a)   may make different provision for different purposes,

(b)   is subject to the affirmative procedure.

(12)   Before making an order under this section, the Scottish Ministers must consult—

(a)   each local authority, and

(b)   such other persons as they consider appropriate.

(13)   In this section—

'carer', in relation to a care placement, means the family or persons with whom the placement is made, 'care placement' means a placement such as is mentioned in section 26(1)(a) of this Act,

'specified' means specified by order made the Scottish Ministers.]

27 Day care for pre-school and other children

(1) Each local authority shall provide such day care for children in need within their area who—

    (a) are aged five or under; and

    (b) have not yet commenced attendance at a school,

as is appropriate; and they may provide such day care for children within their area who satisfy the conditions mentioned in paragraphs (a) and (b) but are not in need.

[(1A) A local authority must, at least once every two years—

    (a) consult such persons as appear to be representative of parents of children in need within their area who satisfy the conditions mentioned in paragraphs (a) and (b) of subsection (1) above about how they should provide day care for such children in pursuance of that subsection; and

    (b) after having had regard to the views expressed, prepare and publish their plans for how they intend to provide day care for such children in pursuance of that subsection.

(1B) A local authority must, at least once every two years—

    (a) consult such persons as appear to be representative of parents of children within their area who satisfy the conditions mentioned in paragraphs (a) and (b) of subsection (1) above but are not in need about whether and if so how they should provide day care for such children under that subsection; and

    (b) after having had regard to the views expressed, prepare and publish their plans in relation to the provision of day care for such children under that subsection.]

(2) A local authority may provide facilities (including training, advice, guidance and counselling) for those—

    (a) caring for children in day care; or

    (b) who at any time accompany such children while they are in day care.

(3) Each local authority shall provide for children in need within their area who are in attendance at a school such care—

    (a) outside school hours; or

    (b) during school holidays,

as is appropriate; and they may provide such care for children within their area who are in such attendance but are not in need.

[(3A) A local authority must, at least once every two years—

    (a) consult such persons as appear to be representative of parents of children in need within their area who are in attendance at a school about how they should provide appropriate care for such children in pursuance of subsection (3) above; and

    (b) after having had regard to the views expressed, prepare and publish their plans for how they intend to provide appropriate care for such children in pursuance of that subsection.

(3B) A local authority must, at least once every two years—

    (a) consult such persons as appear to be representative of parents of children within their area who are in attendance at a school but are not in need about whether and if so how they should provide appropriate care for such children under subsection (3) above; and

    (b) after having had regard to the views expressed, prepare and publish plans in relation to the provision of appropriate care for such children in their area under that subsection.

(3C) The Scottish Ministers may by order modify subsection (1A), (1B),

(3A) or (3B) above so as to vary the regularity within which a local authority must consult and plan in pursuance of that subsection.

(3D) An order made under subsection (3C) above is subject to the negative procedure.]

(4) In this section—

'day care' means any form of care provided for children during the day, whether or not it is provided on a regular basis; and

'school' has the meaning given by section 135(1) of the Education (Scotland) Act 1980.

28 Removal of power to arrange for emigration of children

Section 23 of the Social Work (Scotland) Act 1968 (which provides a power for local authorities and voluntary associations, with the consent of the Secretary of State, to make arrangements for the emigration of children in their care) shall cease to have effect.

Advice and assistance for young persons formerly looked after by local authorities

29 After-care

(1) A local authority shall, unless they are satisfied that his welfare does not require it, advise, guide and assist any person in their area [who is at least sixteen] but not yet nineteen years of age who, [either—

(a) was (on his sixteenth birthday or at any subsequent time) but is no longer looked after by a local authority; or

(b) is of such other description of person formerly but no longer looked after by a local authority as the Scottish Ministers may specify by order.]

[(1A) An order under subsection (1)(b) above is subject to the affirmative procedure.]

(2) If a person within the area of a local authority is at least nineteen, but is less than [twenty-six], years of age and is otherwise a person such as is described in subsection (1) above, he may by application to the authority request that they provide him with advice, guidance and assistance [. . .].

[(2A) Subsections (1) and (2) above do not apply to a person during any period when the person is being provided with continuing care under section 26A of this Act.]

(3) [Subject to section 73(2) of the Regulation of Care (Scotland) Act 2001 (asp 8)], assistance given under subsection (1) [above or (5A) or (5B) below] may include assistance in kind or in cash.

(4) Where a person—

(a) [who is at least sixteen years of] age ceases to be looked after by a local authority; or

(b) described in subsection (1) above is being provided with advice, guidance or assistance by a local authority,

they shall, if he proposes to reside in the area of another local authority, inform that other local authority accordingly provided that he consents to their doing so.

[(5) It is the duty of each local authority, in relation to any person to whom they have a duty under subsection (1) above or who makes an application under subsection (2) above, to carry out an assessment of the person's needs.

[(5A) After carrying out an assessment under subsection (5) above in pursuance of an application made by a person under subsection (2) above, the local authority—

(a) must, if satisfied that the person has any eligible needs which cannot be met other than by taking action under this subsection, provide the person with such advice, guidance and assistance as it considers necessary for the purposes of meeting those needs; and

(b)   may otherwise provide such advice, guidance and assistance as it considers appropriate having regard to the person's welfare.

[(5B)   A local authority may (but is not required to) continue to provide advice, guidance and assistance to a person in pursuance of subsection (5A) after the person reaches the age of twenty-six.]

(6)   Each local authority shall establish a procedure for considering representations (including complaints) made to them by any person mentioned in subsection (1) or (2) above about the discharge of their functions under the provisions of subsections (1) to [(5B)] above.

(7)   In subsection (1) above, the reference to having been 'looked after by a local authority' shall be construed as including having been looked after by a local authority in England and Wales, and subsection (4) of section 105 of the Children Act 1989 (c 41) (construction of references to a child looked after by a local authority) shall apply for the purposes of this subsection as it applies for the purposes of that Act ('local authority in England and Wales' being construed in accordance with subsection (1) of that section).]

[(8)   For the purposes of subsection (5A)(a) above, a person has 'eligible needs' if the person needs care, attention or support of such type as the Scottish Ministers may by order specify.

(9)   An order made under subsection (8) is subject to the affirmative procedure.

(10)   If a local authority becomes aware that a person who is being provided with advice, guidance or assistance by them under this section has died, the local authority must as soon as reasonably practicable notify—

(a)   the Scottish Ministers; and

(b)   Social Care and Social Work Improvement Scotland.]

30   Financial assistance towards expenses of education or training and removal of power to guarantee indentures etc

(1)   Without prejudice to section 12 of the Social Work (Scotland) Act 1968 (general social welfare services of local authorities), a local authority may make—

(a)   grants to any relevant person in their area to enable him to meet expenses connected with his receiving education or training; and

(b)   contributions to the accommodation and maintenance of any such person in any place near where he may be—

(i)   employed, or seeking employment; or

(ii)   receiving education or training.

(2)   [A] person is a relevant person for the purposes of subsection (1) above if—

(a)   he is [at least sixteen years of] age but not yet [twenty-six] years of age; and

[(b)   he either—

(i)   was (on his sixteenth birthday or at any subsequent time) but is no longer looked after by a local authority; or

(ii)   is of such other description of person formerly but no longer looked after by a local authority as the Scottish Ministers may specify by order.

(2A)   An order made under subsection (2)(b)(ii) above is subject to the affirmative procedure.]

[. . .]

Miscellaneous and general

31   Review of case of child looked after by local authority

(1)   Without prejudice to their duty under section 17(1)(a) of this Act, it shall be the duty of a local authority who are looking after a child to review his case at such intervals as may be prescribed by the Secretary of State.

(2)   The Secretary of State may prescribe—

(a)   different intervals in respect of the first such review and in respect of subsequent reviews;

(b)   the manner in which cases are to be reviewed under this section;

(c)   the considerations to which the local authority are to have regard in reviewing cases under this section.

32   Removal of child from residential establishment

A local authority, notwithstanding any agreement made in connection with the placing of a child in a residential establishment under this Chapter, or Chapter 4, of this Part of this Act by them—

(a)   may, at any time; and

(b)   shall, if requested to do so by the person responsible for the establishment,

remove a child so placed.

33   Effect of orders etc made in different parts of the United Kingdom

(1)   The Secretary of State may make regulations providing for a prescribed order which is made by a court in England and Wales or in Northern Ireland, if that order appears to him to correspond generally to an order of a kind which may be made under this Part of this Act [. . .], to have effect in prescribed circumstances and for prescribed purposes of the law of Scotland as if it were an order of that kind [. . .].

(2)   The Secretary of State may make regulations providing—

(a)   for a prescribed order made under this Part of this Act by a court in Scotland;

[. . .]

if that order [. . .] appears to him to correspond generally to an order of a kind which may be made under any provision of law in force in England and Wales or in Northern Ireland, to have effect in prescribed circumstances and for prescribed purposes of the law of England and Wales, or as the case may be of Northern Ireland, as if it were an order of that kind.

(3)   Regulations under subsection (1) or (2)(a) above may provide for the order given effect for prescribed purposes to cease to have effect for those purposes, or for the purposes of the law of the place where the order was made, if prescribed conditions are satisfied.

[. . .]

(5)   Regulations under this section may modify any provision of—

(a)   the Social Work (Scotland) Act 1968 or this Act in any application which the Acts may respectively have, by virtue of the regulations, in relation to an order made otherwise than in Scotland;

(b)   the Children Act 1989 or the Children and Young Persons Act 1969 [or sections 63 to 67 of and Schedules 6 and 7 to the Powers of Criminal Courts (Sentencing) Act 2000] in any application which those Acts may respectively have, by virtue of the regulations, in relation to an order prescribed under subsection (2)(a) above [. . .]; or

(c)   the Children (Northern Ireland) Order 1995 or the Children and Young Persons Act (Northern Ireland) 1968 in any application which they may respectively have, by virtue of the regulations, in relation to an order so prescribed [. . .].

[. . .]

36   Welfare of certain children in hospitals and nursing homes etc

(1)   Where a child is provided with residential accommodation by a person mentioned in subsection (3) below and it appears to the person that the child either—

(a)   has had no parental contact for a continuous period of three months or more; or

(b)   is likely to have no parental contact for a period which, taken with any immediately preceding period in which the child has had no such contact, will constitute a continuous period of three months or more,

the person shall (whether or not the child has been, or will be, so accommodated throughout the continuous period) so notify the local authority in whose area the accommodation is provided.

(2)   A local authority receiving notification under subsection (1) above shall—

(a)   take such steps as are reasonably practicable to enable them to determine whether the child's welfare is adequately safeguarded and promoted while he is so accommodated; and

(b)   consider the extent to which (if at all) they should exercise any of their functions under this Act with respect to the child.

(3)   The persons are—

(a)   any health board constituted under section 2 of the National Health Service (Scotland) Act 1978;

(b)   any national health service trust established under section 12A of that Act;

[(c)   any person providing—
(i)   an independent hospital;
(ii)   a private psychiatric hospital;
(iii)   an independent clinic; or
(iv)   an independent medical agency,

within the meaning given to those expressions by section 10F(2) of the National Health Service (Scotland) Act 1978 (c 29); and

(d)   any person providing a care home service (as defined by paragraph 2 of schedule 12 to the Public Services Reform (Scotland) Act 2010).]

(4)   For the purposes of subsection (1) above, a child has parental contact only when in the presence of a person having parental responsibilities in relation to him.

(5)   A person duly authorised by a local authority may in the area of that authority, at all reasonable times, enter for the purposes of subsection (2) above or of determining whether there has been compliance with subsection (1) above any such place as is mentioned in sub-paragraph (i) or (ii) of subsection (3)(c) above and may for those purposes inspect any records or registers relating to that place; and subsections (2A) to (2D) and (4) of section 6 of the Social Work (Scotland) Act 1968 (exercise of powers of entry and inspection) [(as in force immediately prior to their repeal by section 8 of the Joint Inspection of Children's Services and Inspection of Social Work Services (Scotland) Act 2006)] shall apply in respect of a person so authorised as they [applied] in respect of a person duly authorised under subsection (1) of that section.

[. . .]

38   Short-term refuges for children at risk of harm

(1)   Where a child appears—

(a)   to a local authority to be at risk of harm, they may at the child's request—

(i)   provide him with refuge in a residential establishment both controlled or managed by them and designated by them for the purposes of this paragraph; or

(ii)   arrange for a person whose household is approved by virtue of section 5(3)(b) of the Social Work (Scotland) Act 1968 (provision for securing that persons are not placed in any household unless the household has prescribed approval) and is designated by them for the purposes of this paragraph to provide him with refuge in that household,

for a period which does not exceed the relevant period;

(b)   to a person who [provides a care home service (as defined by [paragraph 2 of schedule 12 to the Public Services Reform (Scotland) Act 2010])] or to any person for the time being employed in the management of the accommodation in question, to be at risk of harm, the person to whom the child so appears may at the child's request provide him with refuge, for a period which does not exceed the relevant period, in the accommodation but shall do so only if and to the extent that the local authority within whose area the accommodation is situated have given their approval to the use of the accommodation (or a part of the accommodation) for the purposes of this paragraph.

(2)   The Secretary of State may by regulations make provision as to—

(a)   designation, for the purposes of paragraph (a) of subsection (1) above, of establishments and households;

(b)   application for, the giving of and the withdrawal of, approval under paragraph (b) of subsection (1) above;

(c)   requirements (if any) which must be complied with while any such approval remains in force;

(d)   the performance by a person mentioned in the said paragraph (b) of anything to be done by him under that paragraph;

(e)   the performance by a local authority of their functions under this section; and

(f)   the giving, to such persons or classes of person as may be specified in the regulations, of notice as to the whereabouts of a child provided with refuge under this section,

and regulations made under this subsection may include such incidental and supplementary provisions as he thinks fit.

(3)   While a child is being provided with refuge under, and in accordance with regulations made under, this section, none of the enactments mentioned in subsection (4) below shall apply in relation to him unless the commencement of the period of refuge has followed within two days of the termination of a prior period of refuge so provided to him by any person.

(4)   The enactments are—

(a)   section 89 of this Act and, so far as it applies in relation to anything done in Scotland, section [171 of the Children's Hearings (Scotland) Act 2011]; and

(b)   section 32(3) of the Children and Young Persons Act 1969 (compelling, persuading, inciting or assisting any person to be absent from detention etc), so far as it applies in relation to anything done in Scotland.

(5)   References in this section to the relevant period shall be construed as references either to a period which does not exceed seven days or, in such exceptional circumstances as the Secretary of State may prescribe, to a period which does not exceed fourteen days.

(6)   A child who is provided with refuge for a period by virtue of such arrangements as are mentioned in subsection (1)(a) above shall not be regarded as a foster child for the purposes of the Foster Children (Scotland) Act 1984 by reason only of such provision.

Chapter 3
Protection and Supervision of Children

. . .

75   Powers of Secretary of State with respect to secure accommodation

(1)   The Secretary of State may by regulations make provision with respect to the placing in secure accommodation of any child—

[. . .]

(b)   who is not subject to a [compulsory supervision order, interim compulsory supervision order, medical examination order or warrant to secure attendance (all within the meaning of the Children's Hearings (Scotland) Act 2011)] but who is being looked after by a local authority in pursuance of such enactments as may be specified in the regulations.

(2)   Regulations under subsection (1) above may—

(a)   specify the circumstances in which a child may be so placed under the regulations;

(b)   make provision to enable a child who has been so placed or any relevant person to require that the child's case be brought before a children's hearing within a shorter period than would apply under regulations made under subsection (3) below; and

(c)   specify different circumstances for different cases or classes of case.

[(2A)   In subsection (2), 'relevant person' has the meaning given by section 200 of the Children's Hearings (Scotland) Act 2011 and includes a person deemed to be a relevant person by virtue of section 81(3), 160(4)(b) or 164(6) of that Act.]

(3)   Subject to subsection (4) below and without prejudice to subsection (2)(b) above, the Secretary of State may prescribe—

(a)   the maximum period during which a child may be kept under this Act in secure accommodation without the authority of a children's hearing or of the sheriff;

(b)   the period within which a children's hearing shall be arranged to consider the case of a child placed in secure accommodation by virtue of regulations made under this section (and different periods may be so prescribed in respect of different cases or classes of case).

[(4)   A child may not be kept in secure accommodation by virtue of regulations made under this section for a period exceeding 66 days from the day when the child was first taken to the secure accommodation.]

[. . .]

(6)   The Secretary of State may by regulations make provision for the procedures to be applied in placing children in secure accommodation; and without prejudice to the generality of this subsection, such regulations may—

(a)   specify the duties of the Principal Reporter in relation to the placing of children in secure accommodation;

(b)   make provision for the referral of cases to a children's hearing for review; and

(c)   make provision for any person with parental responsibilities in relation to the child to be informed of the placing of the child in secure accommodation.

Exclusion orders

76   Exclusion orders

(1)   Subject to subsections (3) to (9) below, where on the application of a local authority the sheriff is satisfied, in relation to a child, that the conditions mentioned in subsection (2) below are met, he may grant an order under this section (to be known as 'an exclusion order') excluding from the child's family home any person named in the order (in this Part of this Act referred to as the 'named person').

(2)   The conditions are—

(a)   that the child has suffered, is suffering, or is likely to suffer, significant harm as a result of any conduct, or any threatened or reasonably apprehended conduct, of the named person;

(b)   that the making of an exclusion order against the named person—

(i)   is necessary for the protection of the child, irrespective of whether the child is for the time being residing in the family home; and

(ii)   would better safeguard the child's welfare than the removal of the child from the family home; and

(c)   that, if an order is made, there will be a person specified in the application who is capable of taking responsibility for the provision of appropriate care for the child and any other member of the family who requires such care and who is, or will be, residing in the family home (in this section, sections 77 to 79 and section 91(3)(f) of this Act referred to as an 'appropriate person').

(3)   No application under subsection (1) above for an exclusion order shall be finally determined under this section unless—

(a)   the named person has been afforded an opportunity of being heard by, or represented before, the sheriff, and

(b)   the sheriff has considered any views expressed by any person on whom notice of the application has been served in accordance with rules making such provision as is mentioned in section 91(3)(d) of this Act.

(4)   Where, on an application under subsection (1) above, the sheriff—

(a)   is satisfied as mentioned in that subsection; but

(b)   the conditions mentioned in paragraphs (a) and (b) of subsection (3) above for the final determination of the application are not fulfilled,

he may grant an interim order, which shall have effect as an exclusion order pending a hearing by the sheriff under subsection (5) below held within such period as may be specified in rules made by virtue of section 91(3)(e) of this Act.

(5)   The sheriff shall conduct a hearing under this subsection within such period as may be specified in rules made by virtue of section 91(3)(e) of this Act, and, if satisfied at that hearing as mentioned in subsection (1) above, he may, before finally determining the application, confirm or vary the interim order, or any term or condition on which it was granted, or may recall such order.

(6)   Where the conditions mentioned in paragraphs (a) and (b) of subsection (3) above have been fulfilled, the sheriff may, at any point prior to the final determination of the application, grant an interim order.

(7)   An order under subsection (5) or (6) above shall have effect as an exclusion order pending the final determination of the application.

(8)   Where—

(a)   an application is made under subsection (1) above; and

(b)   the sheriff considers that the conditions for making a child protection order under [Part 5 of the Children's Hearings (Scotland) Act 2011] are satisfied,

he may make [child protection order] as if the application had been duly made by the local authority under that [Part] rather than under this section.

(9)   The sheriff shall not make an exclusion order if it appears to him that to do so would be unjustifiable or unreasonable, having regard to—

(a)   all the circumstances of the case, including without prejudice to the generality of this subsection the matters specified in subsection (10) below; and

(b)   any requirement such as is specified in subsection (11) below and the likely consequences in the light of that requirement of the exclusion of the named person from the family home.

(10)   The matters referred to in subsection (9)(a) above are—

(a)   the conduct of the members of the child's family (whether in relation to each other or otherwise);

(b)   the respective needs and financial resources of the members of that family;

(c)   the extent (if any) to which—

(i)   the family home; and

(ii)   any relevant item in that home,

is used in connection with a trade, business or profession by any member of the family.

(11)   The requirement referred to in subsection (9)(b) above is a requirement

that the named person (whether alone or with any other person) must reside in the family home, where that home—

(a)   [is on or comprised in a lease constituting a 1991 Act tenancy within the meaning of the Agricultural Holdings (Scotland) Act 2003 (asp 11) or in a lease constituting a short limited duration tenancy or a limited duration tenancy (within the meaning of that Act)]; or

(b)   is let, or is a home in respect of which possession is given, to the named person (whether alone or with any other person) by an employer as an incident of employment.

(12)   In this Part of this Act—

'caravan' has the meaning given to it by section 29(1) of the Caravan Sites and Control of Development Act 1960;

'exclusion order', includes an interim order granted under subsection (4) above and such an order confirmed or varied under subsection (5) above and an interim order granted under subsection (6) above; except that in subsection (3) above and in section 79 of this Act, it does not include an interim order granted under subsection (4) above;

'family' has the meaning given in section 93(1) of this Act;

'family home' means any house, caravan, houseboat or other structure which is used as a family residence and in which the child ordinarily resides with any person described in subsection (13) below and the expression includes any garden or other ground or building attached to and usually occupied with, or otherwise required for the amenity or convenience of, the house, caravan, houseboat or other structure.

(13)   The description of person referred to in the definition of 'family home' in subsection (12) above, is a person who has parental responsibilities in relation to the child, or who ordinarily (and other than by reason only of his employment) has charge of, or control over him.

77   Effect of, and orders etc ancillary to, exclusion order

(1)   An exclusion order shall, in respect of the home to which it relates, have the effect of suspending the named person's rights of occupancy (if any) and shall prevent him from entering the home, except with the express permission of the local authority which applied for the order.

(2)   The sheriff, on the application of the local authority, may, if and in so far as he thinks fit, when making an exclusion order do any of the things mentioned in subsection (3) below.

(3)   The things referred to in subsection (2) above are—

(a)   grant a warrant for the summary ejection of the named person from the home;

(b)   grant an interdict prohibiting the named person from entering the home without the express permission of the local authority;

(c)   grant an interdict prohibiting the removal by the named person of any relevant item specified in the interdict from the home, except either—

(i)   with the written consent of the local authority, or of an appropriate person; or

(ii)   by virtue of a subsequent order of the sheriff,

(d)   grant an interdict prohibiting the named person from entering or remaining in a specified area in the vicinity of the home;

(e)   grant an interdict prohibiting the taking by the named person of any step of a kind specified in the interdict in relation to the child;

(f)   make an order regulating the contact between the child and the named person,

and the sheriff may make any other order which he considers is necessary for the proper enforcement of a remedy granted by virtue of paragraph (a), (b) or (c) of this subsection.

(4)   No warrant, interdict or order (except an interdict granted by virtue of paragraph (b) of subsection (3) above) shall be granted or made under sub-section (2) above if the named person satisfies the sheriff that it is unnecessary to do so.

(5)   Where the sheriff grants a warrant of summary ejection under subsection (2) above in the absence of the named person, he may give directions as to the preservation of any of that person's goods and effects which remain in the family home.

(6)   The sheriff may make an order of the kind specified in subsection (3)(f) above irrespective of whether there has been an application for such an order.

(7)   On the application of either the named person or the local authority, the sheriff may make the exclusion order, or any remedy granted under subsection (2) above, subject to such terms and conditions as he considers appropriate.

(8)   In this Part of this Act references to a 'relevant item' are references to any item within the home which both—

(a)   is owned or hired by any member of the family concerned or an appro-priate person or is being acquired by any such member or person under a hire purchase agreement or conditional sale agreement; and

(b)   is reasonably necessary to enable the home to be used as a family residence,

but does not include any such vehicle, caravan or houseboat or such other structure so used as is mentioned in the definition of 'family home' in section 76 (12) of this Act.

78   Powers of arrest etc in relation to exclusion order

(1)   The sheriff may, whether or not on an application such as is mentioned in subsection (2) below, attach a power of arrest to any interdict granted under section 77(2) of this Act by virtue of subsection (3) of that section.

(2)   A local authority may at any time while an exclusion order has effect apply for such attachment of a power of arrest as is mentioned in subsection (1) above.

(3)   A power of arrest attached to an interdict by virtue of subsection (1) above shall not have effect until such interdict, together with the attached power of arrest, is served on the named person.

(4)   If, by virtue of subsection (1) above, a power of arrest is attached to an interdict, the local authority shall, as soon as possible after the interdict, together with the attached power of arrest, is served on the named person, ensure that there is delivered [to the chief constable of the Police Service of Scotland] a copy of the application for the interdict and of the interlocutor granting the interdict to-gether with a certificate of service of the interdict and, where the application to attach the power of arrest was made after the interdict was granted, a copy of that application and of the interlocutor above granting it and a certificate of service of the interdict together with the attached power of arrest.

(5)   Where any interdict to which a power of arrest is attached by virtue of sub-section (1) above is varied or recalled, the person who applied for the variation or recall shall ensure that there is delivered to [the chief constable of the Police Service of Scotland] a copy of the application for such variation or recall and of the interlocutor granting the variation or recall.

(6)   A constable may arrest without warrant the named person if he has reason-able cause for suspecting that person to be in breach of an interdict to which a power of arrest has been attached by virtue of subsection (1) above.

(7)   Where a person has been arrested under subsection (6) above, the constable in charge of a police station may—

(a)   if satisfied there is no likelihood of that person further breaching the interdict to which the power of arrest was attached under subsection (1) above, liberate him unconditionally; or

(b)   refuse to liberate that person.

(8)   Such a refusal to liberate an arrested person as is mentioned in subsection (7)(b) above, and the detention of that person until his appearance in court by virtue of either subsection (11) below, or any provision of the Criminal Procedure (Scotland) Act [1995], shall not subject that constable to any claim whatsoever.

(9)   Where a person has been liberated under subsection (7)(a) above, the facts and circumstances which gave rise to the arrest shall be reported to the procurator fiscal forthwith.

(10)   Subsections (11) to (13) below apply only where—

(a)   the arrested person has not been released under subsection (7)(a) above; and

(b)   the procurator fiscal decides that no criminal proceedings are to be taken in respect of the facts and circumstances which gave rise to the arrest.

(11)   A person arrested under subsection (6) above shall, wherever practicable, be brought before the sheriff sitting as a court of summary criminal jurisdiction for the district in which he was arrested not later than in the course of the first day after the arrest such day not being a Saturday, a Sunday or a court holiday pre-scribed for that court under [section 8 of the said Act of 1995], on which the sheriff is not sitting for the disposal of criminal business.

(12)   Subsections (1), [(2) and (4) of section 15 of the said Act of 1995] (intimation to a person named by the person arrested) shall apply to a person arrested under subsection (6) above as they apply to a person who has been arres-ted in respect of an offence.

(13)   Where a person is brought before the sheriff under subsection (11) above—

(a)   the procurator fiscal shall present to the court a petition containing—

(i)   a statement of the particulars of the person arrested under subsection (6) above;

(ii)   a statement of the facts and circumstances which gave rise to that arrest; and

(iii)   a request that the person be detained for a further period not exceeding two days;

(b)   the sheriff, if it appears to him that—

(i)   the statement referred to in paragraph (a)(ii) above discloses a *prima facie* breach of interdict by the arrested person;

(ii)   proceedings for breach of interdict will be taken; and

(iii)   there is a substantial risk of violence by the arrested person against any member of the family, or an appropriate person, resident in the family home,

may order the arrested person to be detained for a period not exceeding two days; and

(c)   the sheriff shall, in any case in which paragraph (b) above does not apply, order the release of the arrested person from custody (unless that person is in custody in respect of some other matter);

and in computing the period of two days referred to in paragraphs (a) and (b) above, no account shall be taken of a Saturday, a Sunday or any holiday in the court in which proceedings for breach of interdict will require to be raised.

(14)   Where a person—

(a)   is liberated under subsection (7)(a) above; or

(b)   is to be brought before the sheriff under subsection (11) above,

the procurator fiscal shall at the earliest opportunity, and, in the case of a person to whom paragraph (b) above applies, before that person is brought before the sheriff, take all reasonable steps to intimate to—

(i)   the local authority which made the application for the interdict;

(ii) an appropriate person who will reside in, or who remains in residence in, the family home mentioned in the order; and

(iii) any solicitor who acted for the appropriate person when the interdict was granted or to any other solicitor who the procurator fiscal has reason to believe acts for the time being for that person,

that he has decided that no criminal proceedings should be taken in respect of the facts and circumstances which gave rise to the arrest of the named person.

79 Duration, variation and recall of exclusion order

(1) Subject to subsection (2) below, an exclusion order shall cease to have effect on a date six months after being made.

(2) An exclusion order shall cease to have effect on a date prior to the date mentioned in subsection (1) above where—

(a) the order contains a direction by the sheriff that it shall cease to have effect on that prior date;

(b) the sheriff, on an application under subsection (3) below, recalls the order before the date so mentioned; or

(c) any permission given by a third party to the spouse or partner of the named person, or to an appropriate person, to occupy the home to which the order relates is withdrawn.

(3) The sheriff may, on the application of the local authority, the named person, an appropriate person or the spouse or partner of the named person, if that spouse or partner is not excluded from the family home and is not an appropriate person, vary or recall an exclusion order and any warrant, interdict, order or direction granted or made under section 77 of this Act.

(4) For the purposes of this section, partners are persons who live together in a family home as if they were husband and wife.

80 Exclusion orders: supplementary provisions

(1) The Secretary of State may make regulations with respect to the powers, duties and functions of local authorities in relation to exclusion orders.

(2) An application for an exclusion order, or under section 79(3) of this Act for the variation or recall of such an order or of any thing done under section 77(2) of this Act, shall be made to the sheriff for the sheriffdom within which the family home is situated.

Chapter 4
Parental Responsibilities Orders, etc

Miscellaneous

[. . .]

91 Procedural rules in relation to certain applications etc

(1) All proceedings to which this section applies are civil proceedings for the purposes of section 32 of the Sheriff Courts (Scotland) Act 1971 (power of Court of Session to regulate civil procedure in the sheriff court).

(2) Any reference in this Part of this Act to regulation or prescription by rules in relation to any proceedings to which this section applies shall be construed, unless the context otherwise requires, as a reference to regulation or prescription by rules made under the said section 32.

(3) Without prejudice to the generality of the said section 32, rules may make provision as to—

[. . .]

(d) the persons to whom notice of an application for an exclusion order or, under section 79(3) of this Act, for the recall or variation of such an order or of anything done under section 77(2) of this Act shall be given;

    (e) the period within which a hearing shall be held under subsection (5) of section 76 of this Act after the granting of an order under subsection (4) of that section;

    (f) the service of any exclusion order on the named person and the appropriate person within such period as may be specified in the rules.

(4) In relation to any proceedings to which this section applies, rules may permit a party to such proceedings, in such circumstances as may be specified in the rules, to be represented by a person who is neither an advocate nor a solicitor.

(5) This section applies to any application made to the sheriff, and any other proceeding before the sheriff (whether on appeal or otherwise), under any provision of this Part of this Act.

Interpretation of Part II

93 Interpretation of Part II

(1) In this Part of this Act, unless the context otherwise requires,—

'accommodation' shall be construed in accordance with section 25(8) of this Act;

[. . .]

'children's hearing' shall be construed in accordance with [section 5 of the Children's Hearings (Scotland) Act 2011];

[. . .]

'constable' means a constable of a police force within the meaning of the Police (Scotland) Act 1967;

'contact order' has the meaning given by section 11(2)(d) of this Act;

'disabled' has the meaning given by section 23(2) of this Act;

. . .

'exclusion order' has the meaning given by section 76(12) of this Act;

'family', in relation to a child, includes—

    (a) any person who has parental responsibility for the child; and

    (b) any other person with whom the child has been living;

'local authority' means a council constituted under section 2 of the Local Government etc (Scotland) Act 1994;

[. . .]

'parental responsibilities' has the meaning given by section 1(3) of this Act;

[. . .]

'parental rights' has the meaning given by section 2(4) of this Act;

[. . .]

'residence order' has the meaning given by section 11(2)(c) of this Act;

'residential establishment'—

    (a) in relation to a place in Scotland, means an establishment (whether managed by a local authority, by a voluntary organisation or by any other person) which provides residential accommodation for children for the purposes of this Act or the Social Work (Scotland) Act 1968;

    (b) in relation to a place in England and Wales, means a community home, voluntary home or [private] children's home (within the meaning of the Children Act 1989); and

    (c) in relation to a place in Northern Ireland, means

      [(i) a private children's home within the meaning of the Children (Northern Ireland) Order 1995 (SI 1995/755),

      (ii) an authority home provided under Part VII of that Order, or

      (iii) a voluntary home provided under Part VIII of that Order,]

'school age' shall be construed in accordance with section 31 of the Education (Scotland) Act 1980;

'secure accommodation' means accommodation provided [for the purpose of restricting the liberty of children which—

(a)   in Scotland, is provided in a residential establishment approved in accordance with regulations made under section 78(2) of the Public Services Reform (Scotland) Act 2010 (asp 8),

(b)   in England, is provided in a children's home (within the meaning of the Care Standards Act 2000 (c 14) ('the 2000 Act')) in respect of which a person is registered under Part 2 of that Act, except that before the coming into force of section 107(2) of the Health and Social Care (Community Health Standards) Act 2003 (c 43), 'secure accommodation' means accommodation in relation to England which—

(i)   is provided in a children's home (within the meaning of the 2000 Act) in respect of which a person is registered under Part 2 of that Act, and

(ii)   is approved by the Secretary of State for the purpose of restricting the liberty of children,

(c)   in Wales, is provided in a children's home (within the meaning of the 2000 Act) in respect of which a person is registered under Part 2 of that Act,]

[. . .]

'voluntary organisation' means a body (other than a public or local authority) whose activities are not carried on for profit; and

[. . .]

(2)   For the purposes of—

(a)   Chapter 1 and this Chapter (except this section) of this Part [and section 44], 'child' means a person under the age of eighteen years; and

(b)   [Chapter 2 (except section 44) and Chapter 3 [. . .]] of this Part— 'child' means—

[(i)   in relation to section 75, a person under the age of 18 years,

(ii)   in relation to any other section, a person under the age of 16 years;]

and for the purposes of the application of those Chapters to a person who has failed to attend school regularly without reasonable excuse includes a person who is over sixteen years of age but is not over school age; and

[. . .]

(3)   Where, in the course of any proceedings under Chapter 2 or 3 of this Part, a child ceases to be a child within the meaning of subsection (2) above, the provisions of those Chapters of this Part and of any statutory instrument made under those provisions shall continue to apply to him as if he had not so ceased to be a child.

(4)   Any reference in this Part of this Act to a child—

(a)   being 'in need', is to his being in need of care and attention because—

(i)   he is unlikely to achieve or maintain, or to have the opportunity of achieving or maintaining, a reasonable standard of health or development unless there are provided for him, under or by virtue of this Part, services by a local authority;

(ii)   his health or development is likely significantly to be impaired, or further impaired, unless such services are so provided;

(iii)   he is disabled; or

(iv)   he is affected adversely by the disability of any other person in his family;

(b)   who is 'looked after' by a local authority, shall be construed in accordance with section 17(6) of this Act.

(5)   Any reference to any proceedings under this Part of this Act, whether on an application or on appeal, being heard by the sheriff, shall be construed as a reference to such proceedings being heard by the sheriff in chambers.

. . .

PART IV
GENERAL AND SUPPLEMENTAL

99 Registration of births by persons who are themselves children

(1) In paragraph (a) of section 14(1) of the Registration of Births, Deaths and Marriages (Scotland) Act 1965 (duty of father and mother to give information of particulars of birth), for the words 'father or mother of the child' substitute 'child's father or mother (whether or not they have attained the age of sixteen years)'.

(2) Where, at any time after the coming into force of the Age of Legal Capacity (Scotland) Act 1991 but before the coming into force of subsection (1) above, a person mentioned in the said paragraph (a) who had not at that time attained the age of sixteen years purported to fulfil the duty mentioned in the said section 14(1), he shall be presumed to have had legal capacity to fulfil that duty.

(3) [amends Registration of Births, Deaths and Marriages (Scotland) Act 1965]

(4) Where, at any time after the coming into force of the Age of Legal Capacity (Scotland) Act 1991 but before the coming into force of subsection (3) above, a person who had not at that time attained the age of sixteen years made a request, declaration, statutory declaration or application mentioned in subsection (1) or (2) of the said section 18 in relation to a child in respect of whose birth an entry was consequently made under the said subsection (1) in a register of births, or as the case may be under the said subsection (2) in the Register of Corrections etc, the person shall be presumed to have had legal capacity to make the request, declaration, statutory declaration, or application in question.

101 Panels for curators *ad litem*, reporting officers and safeguarders

[(1) The Scottish Ministers may by regulations make provision for the establishment of one or more of each of the following—

(a) a panel of persons from which curators *ad litem* may be appointed [by virtue of section 108 of the Adoption and Children (Scotland) Act 2007] [. . .];

(b) a panel of persons from which reporting officers may be appointed under either of those sections;

[. . .]

(2) Regulations under subsection (1) above may provide, without prejudice to the generality of that subsection—

(a) for the appointment, qualifications and training of persons who may be appointed to [those panels]; and

(b) for the management and organisation of persons available for appointment from [those panels].

[(3) Regulations under subsection (1) above may provide—

(a) for the defrayment by local authorities of expenses incurred by members of any panel established by virtue of that subsection; and

(b) for the payment by local authorities of fees and allowances for such members.

[101A Register for child welfare reporters

(1) A court may only appoint as a child welfare reporter a person who is included on the register maintained in accordance with subsection (2).

(2) The Scottish Ministers must establish and maintain a register of persons who may be appointed to act as a child welfare reporter.

(3) The Scottish Ministers may by regulations make provision for or in connection with—

(a) the requirements that a person must satisfy in order to be included, and remain, on the register (including requirements as to training and qualifications),

(b)   the processes for including a person on, and removing a person from, the register (including appeal rights),

(c)   the process for how, and by whom, a registered person is to be selected as the appointed child welfare reporter in a case,

(d)   the remuneration by the Scottish Ministers of child welfare reporters, including expenses and outlays,

(e)   the operation and management of the register.

(4) Before making, revising or revoking regulations under subsection (3), the Scottish Ministers must consult persons with lived experience of—

(a)   domestic abuse,

(b)   court-ordered contact.

(5)   Regulations under subsection (3) are subject to the negative procedure.]

[101B   Register of curators ad litem for the purposes of section 11D

(1)   The Scottish Ministers must establish and maintain a register of persons who may be appointed to act as a curator ad litem in accordance with section 11D.

(2)   The Scottish Ministers may by regulations make provision for or in connection with—

(a)   the requirements that a person must satisfy in order to be included, and remain, on the register (including requirements as to training and qualifications),

(b)   the processes for including a person on, and removing a person from, the register (including appeal rights),

(c)   the process for how, and by whom, a registered person is to be selected as the appointed curator ad litem in a case,

(d)   the remuneration by the Scottish Ministers of curators ad litem appointed in accordance with section 11D, including expenses and outlays (such as counsel's fees),

(e)   the operation and management of the register.

(3)   Regulations under subsection (2) are subject to the negative procedure.]

[101C   Contact services: regulation

(1)   The Scottish Ministers may by regulations make provision about the regulation of a contact service provided in relation to the requirements of a contact order.

(2)   Regulations under subsection (1) may in particular—

(a)   make provision for the minimum standards to be met by contact service providers, including qualifications and training of staff,

(b)   make provision for the registration of contact service providers that meet those minimum standards and, for those that do not, the refusal of registration or removal from the register (including appeal rights),

(c)   make provision for minimum standards to be met by contact centres (including standards in respect of accommodation),

(d)   make provision for the registration of contact centres that meet those minimum standards and, for those that do not, the refusal of registration or removal from the register (including appeal rights),

(e)   make provision about the conditions on which a regulated contact service provider may, in accordance with the regulations, provide a contact service at a place that is not registered as a contact centre (including conditions about the minimum standards for accommodation at a place if it is to be used for that purpose),

(f)   appoint a person or persons for the purposes of administering the registration of contact service providers and contact centres,

(g)   confer functions on the appointed person or persons,

(h)   determine the fees payable in connection with the registration of a contact service provider or contact centre.

(3)   Functions conferred by virtue of subsection (2)(g) may include—

(a)   inspecting contact centres, regulated contact service providers and contact service providers applying for registration,

(b)   having risk assessments of contact centres undertaken by persons trained in undertaking such assessments,

(c)   issuing reports on the inspection of contact centres, regulated contact service providers and contact service providers applying for registration,

(d)   issuing reports on any failure, or possible failure, by a contact service provider to comply with the provider's duties under the Equality Act 2010, and in particular any duty to make reasonable adjustments to premises in order to facilitate their use by disabled people,

(e)   refusing to register contact service providers and contact centres, and removing from a register regulated contact service providers and contact centres, that do not meet the minimum standards.

(4)   Regulations under subsection (1)—

(a)   may make such modifications to other enactments as the Scottish Ministers consider appropriate for the purposes of, or in connection with, or for giving full effect to the regulations,

(b)   are subject to the affirmative procedure.

(5)   In this section—

'contact centre' means a place that is used for the provision of a contact service,

'contact service' means the facilitation of contact between a child and a person with whom the child is not, or will not be, living (including the handover of the child to that person),

'enactment' includes an enactment comprised in, or in an instrument made under, an Act of the Scottish Parliament,

'regulated contact service' means a contact service that—

(a)   is provided by a regulated contact service provider, and

(b)   is either—

(i)   provided at a place that is registered as a contact centre in accordance with regulations under subsection (1), or

(ii)   provided in circumstances in which the provider may, in accordance with regulations under subsection (1), provide the service at a place that is not registered as a contact centre,

'regulated contact service provider' means an organisation that is registered in accordance with regulations under subsection (1) to provide contact services.]

[. . .]

103   Interpretation, rules, regulations and Parliamentary control

(1)   Any reference in this Act, or in any enactment amended by this Act, to a person having, or to there being vested in him, parental responsibilities or parental rights shall, unless the context otherwise requires, be construed as a reference to his having, or to there being so vested, any of those rights or as the case may be responsibilities.

(2)   Any reference in this Act to something being 'prescribed' is, unless the context otherwise requires, a reference to its being prescribed by regulations; and any power conferred by this Act on the Secretary of State or the Lord Advocate to make rules or regulations shall be exercisable by statutory instrument which shall be subject to annulment in pursuance of a resolution of either House of Parliament.

(3)   Rules or regulations made under this Act—

(a)   may make different provision for different cases or classes of case; and

(b)   may exclude certain cases or classes of case.

105   Extent, short title, minor and consequential amendments, repeals and commencement

(1)   This Act, which subject to subsections (8) to (10) below extends to Scotland only—

(a)   may be cited as the Children (Scotland) Act 1995; and

(b)   except for subsections (1), (2) and (6) to (10) of this section, shall come into force on such day as the Secretary of State may by order made by statutory instrument appoint;

and different days may be appointed under paragraph (b) above for different purposes.

(2) An order under subsection (1)(b) above may contain such transitional and consequential provisions and savings as appear to the Secretary of State to be necessary or expedient in connection with the provisions brought into force.

(3) The transitional provisions and savings contained in Schedule 3 to this Act shall have effect but are without prejudice to sections 16 and 17 of the Interpretation Act 1978 (effect of repeals).

(4) Schedule 4 to this Act, which contains minor amendments and amendments consequential upon the provisions of this Act, shall have effect.

(5) The enactments mentioned in Schedule 5 to this Act (which include spent provisions) are hereby repealed to the extent specified in the third column of that Schedule.

(6) The Secretary of State may by order made by statutory instrument make such further amendments or repeals, in such enactments as may be specified in the order, as appear to him to be necessary or expedient in consequence of any provision of this Act.

(7) A statutory instrument containing an order under subsection (6) above shall be subject to annulment in pursuance of a resolution of either House of Parliament.

(8) Sections 18, 26(2), 33, [. . .] 93 and 104 of this Act and this section extend to England and Wales, and those sections and this section (except section 70(4)) also extend to Northern Ireland; but—

(a) subsection (4) of this section so extends—

(i) to England and Wales, only in so far as it relates to paragraphs 8, 10, 19, 31, 37, 41(1), (2) and (7) to (9), 48 to 52, 54 and 55 of Schedule 4; and

(ii) to Northern Ireland, only in so far as it relates to paragraphs 31, 37, 41(1); (2) and (7) to (9), 54, 55 and 58 of that Schedule; and

(b) subsection (5) of this section so extends—

(i) to England and Wales, only in so far as it relates to the entries in Schedule 5 in respect of Part V of the Social Work (Scotland) Act 1968, the Maintenance Orders (Reciprocal Enforcement) Act 1972, section 35(4)(c) of the Family Law Act 1986, the Children Act 1989, the Child Support Act 1991 and the Education Act 1993; and

(ii) to Northern Ireland, only in so far as it relates to the entries in that Schedule in respect of Part V of the Social Work (Scotland) Act 1968, the Maintenance Orders (Reciprocal Enforcement) Act 1972 and section 35(4)(c) of the Family Law Act 1986.

(9) This section, so far as it relates to the repeal of Part V of the Social Work (Scotland) Act 1968, also extends to the Channel Islands.

[. . .]

CRIMINAL LAW (CONSOLIDATION) (SCOTLAND) ACT 1995
(1995, c 39)

PART I
SEXUAL OFFENCES

Incest and related offences

1 Incest

(1) Any male person who has sexual intercourse with a person related to him in a degree specified in column 1 of the Table set out at the end of this subsection, or any female person who has sexual intercourse with a person related to her in a

degree specified in column 2 of that Table, shall be guilty of incest, unless the accused proves that he or she—

(a)   did not know and had no reason to suspect that the person with whom he or she had sexual intercourse was related in a degree so specified; or

(b)   did not consent to have sexual intercourse, or to have sexual intercourse with that person; or

(c)   was married to that person, at the time when the sexual intercourse took place, by a marriage entered into outside Scotland and recognised as valid by Scots law.

Table
Degrees of Relationship

Column 1	Column 2

1. Relationships by consanguinity

Mother	Father
Daughter	Son
Grandmother	Grandfather
Grand-daughter	Grandson
Sister	Brother
Aunt	Uncle
Niece	Nephew
Great grandmother	Great grandfather
Great grand-daughter	Great grandson

2. Relationships by adoption

Adoptive mother or former adoptive mother.	Adoptive father or former adoptive father.
Adopted daughter or former adopted daughter.	Adopted son or former adopted son.

[3. Relationships by virtue of Part 2 of the Human Fertilisation and Embryology Act 2008

Mother	Father
Daughter	Son
Second female parent by virtue of section 42 or 43 of that Act.]	

(2)   For the purpose of this section, a degree of relationship exists in the case of a degree specified in paragraph 1 of the Table—

(a)   whether it is of the full blood or the half blood; and

(b)   even where traced through or to any person whose parents are not or have not been married to one another.

(3)   For the avoidance of doubt sexual intercourse between persons who are not related to each other in a degree referred to in subsection (1) above is not incest.

2   Intercourse with step-child

Any step-parent or former step-parent who has sexual intercourse with his or her step-child or former step-child shall be guilty of an offence if that step-child is either under the age of 21 years or has at any time before attaining the age of 18 years lived in the same household and been treated as a child of his or her family, unless the accused proves that he or she—

(a) did not know and had no reason to suspect that the person with whom he or she had sexual intercourse was a step-child or former step-child; or

(b) believed on reasonable grounds that that person was of or over the age of 21 years; or

(c) did not consent to have sexual intercourse, or to have sexual intercourse with that person; or

(d) was married to that person, at the time when the sexual intercourse took place, by a marriage entered into outside Scotland and recognised as valid by Scots law.

Procuring, prostitution etc

7 Procuring

(1) Any person who procures or attempts to procure—

(a) any woman under 21 years of age or girl to have unlawful sexual intercourse with any other person or persons in any part of the world; or

(b) any woman or girl to become a common prostitute in any part of the world; or

(c) any woman or girl to leave the United Kingdom, with intent that she may become an inmate of or frequent a brothel elsewhere; or

(d) any woman or girl to leave her usual place of abode in the United Kingdom, with intent that she may, for the purposes of prostitution, become an inmate of or frequent a brothel in any part of the world,

shall be liable on conviction on indictment to imprisonment for a term not exceeding two years or on summary conviction to imprisonment for a term not exceeding three months.

[. . .]

(4) A constable may arrest without a warrant any person whom he has good cause to suspect of having committed, or of attempting to commit, any offence under subsection (1) above.

10 Seduction, prostitution, etc, of girl under 16

(1) If any person having parental responsibilities (within the meaning of section 1(3) of the Children (Scotland) Act 1995), in relation to, or having charge or care of a girl under the age of 16 years causes or encourages—

(a) the seduction or prostitution of;

(b) unlawful sexual intercourse with; or

(c) the commission of an indecent assault upon,

her he shall be liable on conviction on indictment to imprisonment for a term not exceeding two years or on summary conviction to imprisonment for a term not exceeding three months.

(2) For the purposes of this section, a person shall be deemed to have caused or encouraged the matters mentioned in paragraphs (a) to (c) of subsection (1) above upon a girl who has been seduced or indecently assaulted, or who has had unlawful sexual intercourse or who has become a prostitute, if he has knowingly allowed her to consort with, or to enter or continue in the employment of, any prostitute or person of known immoral character.

(3) Subsections (1) and (2) above shall apply to a contravention of [sections 19 to 26 and 29 to 36 of the Sexual Offences (Scotland) Act 2009 (certain sexual offences relating to children)] in like manner as they apply to an indecent assault, and any reference to the commission of such an assault or to being indecently assaulted shall be construed accordingly.

(4) Where on the trial of any offence under this Part of this Act it is proved to the satisfaction of the court that the seduction or prostitution of a girl under the age of 16 years has been caused, encouraged or favoured by her father, mother or guardian it shall be in the power of the court to divest such person of all authority over her, and to appoint any person or persons willing to take charge of such girl

to be her guardian until she has attained the age of 21 years, or such lower age as the court may direct.

(5)　The High Court of Justiciary shall have the power from time to time to rescind or vary an order under subsection (4) above by the appointment of any other person or persons as such guardian, or in any other respect.

11　Trading in prostitution and brothel-keeping

(1)　Every male person who—

(a)　knowingly lives wholly or in part on the earnings of prostitution; or

(b)　in any public place persistently solicits or importunes for immoral purposes,

shall be [guilty of an offence and liable to the penalties set out in subsection (1A)].

[(1A)　A person—

(a)　guilty of the offence set out in subsection (1)(a) is liable—

(i)　on conviction on indictment, to imprisonment for a term not exceeding seven years, to a fine, or to both,

(ii)　on summary conviction, to imprisonment for a term not exceeding 12 months, to a fine not exceeding the statutory maximum, or to both,

(b)　guilty of the offence set out in subsection (1)(b) is liable—

(i)　on conviction on indictment, to imprisonment for a term not exceeding two years,

(ii)　on summary conviction, to imprisonment for a term not exceeding 12 months.

(2)　If it is made to appear to a court of summary jurisdiction by information on oath that there is reason to suspect that any house or any part of a house is used by a female for purposes of prostitution, and that any male person residing in or frequenting the house is living wholly or in part on the earnings of the prostitute, the court may issue a warrant authorising a constable to enter and search the house and to arrest that male person.

(3)　Where a male person is proved to live with or to be habitually in the company of a prostitute, or is proved to have exercised control, direction or influence over the movements of a prostitute in such a manner as to show that he is aiding, abetting or compelling her prostitution with any other person, or generally, he shall, unless he can satisfy the court to the contrary, be deemed to be knowingly living on the earnings of prostitution.

(4)　Every female who is proved to have, for the purposes of gain, exercised control, direction or influence over the movements of a prostitute in such a manner as to show that she is aiding, abetting or compelling her prostitution with any other person, or generally, shall be liable to the penalties set out in [subsection (1A)(a) above].

(5)　Any person who—

(a)　keeps or manages or acts or assists in the management of a brothel; or

(b)　being the tenant, lessee, occupier or person in charge of any premises, knowingly permits such premises or any part thereof to be used as a brothel or for the purposes of habitual prostitution; or

(c)　being the lessor or landlord of any premises, or the agent of such lessor or landlord, lets the same or any part thereof with the knowledge that such premises or some part thereof are or is to be used as a brothel, or is wilfully a party to the continued use of such premises or any part thereof as a brothel,

shall be guilty of an offence.

[(6)　A person guilty of an offence under subsection (5) is liable—

(a)　on conviction on indictment, to imprisonment for a term not exceeding seven years, to a fine, or to both,

(b)　on summary conviction, to imprisonment for a term not exceeding 12 months, to a fine not exceeding the statutory maximum, or to both.

12　Allowing child to be in brothel

(1)　If any person having parental responsibilities (within the meaning of section 1(3) of the Children (Scotland) Act 1995), in relation to, or having charge or care of a child who has attained the age of four years and is under the age of 16 years, allows that child to reside in or to frequent a brothel, he shall be liable on conviction on indictment, or on summary conviction, to a fine not exceeding level 2 on the standard scale or alternatively, or in default of payment of such a fine, or in addition thereto, to imprisonment for a term not exceeding six months.

(2)   Nothing in this section shall affect the liability of a person to be indicted under section 9 of this Act, but upon the trial of a person under that section it shall be lawful for the jury, if they are satisfied that he is guilty of an offence under this section, to find him guilty of that offence.

[12A   Sections 11(5) and 12: further provision

(1)   Premises shall be treated for the purposes of sections 11(5) and 12 of this Act as a brothel if people resort to them for the purposes of homosexual acts in circumstances in which resort to them for heterosexual practices would have led to the premises being treated as a brothel for the purposes of those sections.

(2)   For the purposes of this section, a homosexual act is an act of engaging in sexual activity by one male person with another male person; and an activity is sexual in any case if a reasonable person would, in all the circumstances of the case, consider it to be sexual.]

PRIVATE INTERNATIONAL LAW (MISCELLANEOUS PROVISIONS) ACT 1995
(1995, c 42)

7   Validity and effect in Scots law of potentially polygamous marriages

(1)   A person domiciled in Scotland does not lack capacity to enter into a marriage by reason only that the marriage is entered into under a law which permits polygamy.

(2)   For the avoidance of doubt, a marriage valid by the law of Scotland and entered into—

(a)   under a law which permits polygamy; and

(b)   at a time when neither party to the marriage is already married,

has, so long as neither party marries a second spouse during the subsistence of the marriage, the same effects for all purposes of the law of Scotland as a marriage entered into under a law which does not permit polygamy.

PROTECTION FROM HARASSMENT ACT 1997
(1997, c 40)

Scotland

8   Harassment

(1)   Every individual has a right to be free from harassment and, accordingly, a person must not pursue a course of conduct which amounts to harassment of another and—

(a)   is intended to amount to harassment of that person; or

(b)   occurs in circumstances where it would appear to a reasonable person that it would amount to harassment of that person.

[(1A)   Subsection (1) is subject to section 8A.]

(2)   An actual or apprehended breach of subsection (1) may be the subject of a claim in civil proceedings by the person who is or may be the victim of the course of conduct in question; and any such claim shall be known as an action of harassment.

(3)   For the purposes of this section—

'conduct' includes speech;

'harassment' of a person includes causing the person alarm or distress; and a course of conduct must involve conduct on at least two occasions.

(4)   It shall be a defence to any action of harassment to show that the course of conduct complained of—

(a)   was authorised by, under or by virtue of any enactment or rule of law;
(b)   was [engaged in] for the purpose of preventing or detecting crime; or
(c)   was, in the particular circumstances, reasonable.

(5)   In an action of harassment the court may, without prejudice to any other remedies which it may grant—

(a)   award damages;
(b)   grant—
     (i)   interdict or interim interdict;
     (ii)   if it is satisfied that it is appropriate for it to do so in order to protect the person from further harassment, an order, to be known as a 'non-harassment order', requiring the defender to refrain from such conduct in relation to the pursuer as may be specified in the order for such period (which includes an indeterminate period) as may be so specified,

but a person may not be subjected to the same prohibitions in an interdict or interim interdict and a non-harassment order at the same time.

(6)   The damages which may be awarded in an action of harassment include damages for any anxiety caused by the harassment and any financial loss resulting from it.

(7)   Without prejudice to any right to seek review of any interlocutor, a person against whom a non-harassment order has been made, or the person for whose protection the order was made, may apply to the court by which the order was made for revocation of or a variation of the order and, on any such application, the court may revoke the order or vary it in such manner as it considers appropriate.

[. . .]

[8A   Harassment amounting to domestic abuse

(1)   Every individual has a right to be free from harassment and, accordingly, a person must not engage in conduct which amounts to harassment of another and—

(a)   is intended to amount to harassment of that person; or
(b)   occurs in circumstances where it would appear to a reasonable person that it would amount to harassment of that person.

(2)   Subsection (1) only applies where the conduct referred to amounts to domestic abuse.

(3)   Subsections (2) to (7) of section 8 apply in relation to subsection (1) as they apply in relation to subsection (1) of that section but with the following modifications—

(a)   in subsections (2) and (4), the words 'course of' are omitted;
(b)   for subsection (3) there is substituted—
     '(3)   For the purposes of this section—
     "conduct"—
          (a)   may involve behaviour on one or more than one occasion; and
          (b)   includes—
               (i)   speech; and
               (ii)   presence in any place or area; and
     "harassment" of a person includes causing the person alarm or distress.'.]

9   Breach of non-harassment order

(1)   Any person who is found to be in breach of a non-harassment order made under section 8 [or section 8A] is guilty of an offence and liable—

(a)   on conviction on indictment, to imprisonment for a term not exceeding five years or to a fine, or to both such imprisonment and such fine; and

(b)   on summary conviction, to imprisonment for a period not exceeding six months or to a fine not exceeding the statutory maximum, or to both such imprisonment and such fine.

(2)   A breach of a non-harassment order shall not be punishable other than in accordance with subsection (1).

[(3)   A constable may arrest without warrant any person he reasonably believes is committing or has committed an offence under subsection (1).

(4)   Subsection (3) is without prejudice to any power of arrest conferred by law apart from that subsection.]

PROTECTION FROM ABUSE (SCOTLAND) ACT 2001
(2001, asp 14)

1   Attachment of power of arrest to interdict

(1)   A person who is applying for, or who has obtained, an interdict for the purpose of protection against abuse may apply to the court for a power of arrest to be attached to the interdict under this Act.

[(1A)   In the case of an interdict which is—

(a)   a matrimonial interdict (as defined by section 14(2) of the Matrimonial Homes (Family Protection) (Scotland) Act 1981) which is ancillary to—

(i)   an exclusion order within the meaning of section 4(1) of that Act; or

(ii)   an interim order under section 4(6) of that Act; or

(b)   a relevant interdict (as defined by section 113(2) of the Civil Partnership Act 2004) which is ancillary to—

(i)   an exclusion order within the meaning of section 104(1) of that Act; or

(ii)   an interim order under section 104(6) of that Act,

the court must, on an application under subsection (1), attach a power of arrest to the interdict.]

(2)   [In the case of any other interdict] the court must, on such application, attach a power of arrest to the interdict if satisfied that—

(a)   the interdicted person has been given an opportunity to be heard by, or represented before, the court;

(b)   [. . .] and

(c)   attaching the power of arrest is necessary to protect the applicant from a risk of abuse in breach of the interdict.

(3)   The court, on attaching a power of arrest, must specify a date of expiry for the power, being a date not later than three years after the date when the power is attached.

2   Duration, extension and recall

(1)   A power of arrest comes into effect only when it has been served on the interdicted person along with such documents as may be prescribed.

(2)   A power of arrest ceases to have effect—

(a)   on the date of expiry specified by the court;

(b)   when it is recalled by the court; or

(c)   when the interdict to which the power is attached is varied or recalled, whichever is the earliest.

(3)   The duration of a power of arrest must, on the application of the person who obtained it, be extended by the court, if satisfied that—

(a)   the interdicted person has been given an opportunity to be heard by, or represented before, the court; and

(b)   the extension is necessary to protect the applicant from a risk of abuse in breach of the interdict.

(4)   The court, on extending the duration of a power of arrest, must specify a

new date of expiry for the power, being a date not later than three years after the date when the extension is granted.

(5)   Where the duration of a power of arrest has been extended—

(a)   the extension comes into effect only when it has been served on the interdicted person along with such documents as may be prescribed; and

(b)   subsection (2) applies as if the date referred to in paragraph (a) of that subsection were the new date of expiry specified by the court in granting the extension.

(6)   Subsections (3), (4) and (5) apply to further extensions as they apply to an initial extension.

(7)   A power of arrest must be recalled by the court if—

(a)   the person who obtained it applies for recall; or

(b)   the interdicted person applies for recall and the court is satisfied that—

(i)   the person who obtained the power has been given an opportunity to be heard by, or represented before, the court; and

(ii)   the power is no longer necessary to protect that person from a risk of abuse in breach of the interdict.

3   Notification to police

(1)   As soon as possible after—

(a)   a power of arrest has been served;

(b)   an extension of the duration of a power of arrest has been served;

(c)   a recall of a power of arrest has been granted; or

(d)   the relevant interdict has been varied or recalled,

the person who has obtained such power, extension, variation or recall, or such other person as may be prescribed, must deliver such documents as may be prescribed to the chief constable of [the Police Service of Scotland].

(2)   In this section 'relevant interdict' means the interdict to which the power of arrest is or was attached.

4   Powers and duties of police

(1)   Where a power of arrest attached to an interdict has effect a constable may arrest the interdicted person without warrant if the constable—

(a)   has reasonable cause for suspecting that person of being in breach of the interdict; and

(b)   considers that there would, if that person were not arrested, be a risk of abuse or further abuse by that person in breach of the interdict.

(2)   A person who is arrested under subsection (1) must be [. . .] detained until—

[. . .]

(b)   brought before a court under section 5.

[. . .]

(6)   When a person has been arrested under this section the facts and circumstances giving rise to the arrest must be reported to the procurator fiscal as soon as is practicable.

5   Court appearance

(1)   [Where a person is detained under section 4(2), the] person must wherever practicable be brought before the sheriff sitting as a court of summary criminal jurisdiction for the district in which the person was arrested not later than in the course of the first day after the arrest, such day not being a Saturday, a Sunday or a court holiday for that court.

(2)   Nothing in subsection (1) prevents the detained person from being brought before the sheriff on a Saturday, a Sunday or a court holiday if the sheriff is sitting on such a day for the disposal of criminal business.

[(2A) Subsections (3) to (5) apply where, on being brought before the sheriff under this section, the detained person is not accused on petition or charged on complaint with an offence in respect of the facts and circumstances giving rise to the arrest.]

(3) When the detained person is brought before the sheriff under this section the procurator fiscal must present to the court a petition—

(a) giving particulars of the detained person;

(b) stating the facts and circumstances which gave rise to the arrest;

(c) giving any information known to the procurator fiscal about the circumstances which gave rise to the interdict and the attachment of the power of arrest;

(d) giving any other information known to the procurator fiscal and relevant to an assessment of the risk of abuse or further abuse in breach of the interdict; and

(e) requesting the court to consider whether, on the information presented, a further period of detention is justified.

(4) If it appears to the sheriff, after affording the detained person the opportunity to make representations, that—

(a) the information presented to the court discloses a prima facie breach of the interdict by that person; and

(b) there would, if further detention were not ordered, be a substantial risk of abuse or further abuse by that person in breach of the interdict, the sheriff may order that person to be detained for a further period not exceeding 2 days.

(5) If the sheriff does not order further detention the detained person must, unless in custody in respect of any other matter, be released from custody.

[. . .]

7 Interpretation

In this Act, unless the context otherwise requires—

'abuse' includes violence, harassment, threatening conduct, and any other conduct giving rise, or likely to give rise, to physical or mental injury, fear, alarm or distress;

'conduct' includes—

(a) speech; and

(b) presence in a specified place or area;

'court' means the Court of Session or a sheriff;

'documents' includes documents in electronic form;

'interdict' includes interim interdict;

'interdicted person' means—

(a) in section 1, the person against whom the power of arrest is sought (being the person or one of the persons prohibited by the interdict mentioned in subsection (1) of that section); and

(b) in sections 2 and 4, the person against whom the power of arrest has been granted;

'parental responsibilities and rights' has the same meaning as in the Children (Scotland) Act 1995 (c 36);

'person' means natural person;

'power of arrest' means a power of arrest under this Act; and

'prescribed' means prescribed by rules of court.

8 Short title and commencement

(1) This Act may be cited as the Protection from Abuse (Scotland) Act 2001.

(2) This Act comes into force at the end of the period of three months beginning with the date of Royal Assent.

COMMISSIONER FOR CHILDREN AND YOUNG PEOPLE (SCOTLAND) ACT 2003
(2003, asp 17)

The Commissioner

1 Establishment

(1) There is to be a Commissioner for Children and Young People in Scotland.

(2) Schedule 1 makes further provision about the Commissioner.

2 Appointment

(1) The Commissioner is to be an individual appointed by Her Majesty on the nomination of the Parliament.

(2) A person is disqualified from appointment as the Commissioner if that person is, at the date when the appointment is to take effect, or in the year prior to that date has been—

  (a) a member of the Parliament;

  (b) a member of the House of Commons; or

  (c) a member of the European Parliament.

(3) The Commissioner is to be appointed for such period, not exceeding [eight] years, as the Parliamentary corporation may determine.

(4) [A person who has been appointed Commissioner is ineligible for re-appointment at any time].

3 Removal

(1) The Commissioner may be removed from office by Her Majesty if—

  (a) the Commissioner so requests; or

  (b) [subsection (2) applies].

[(2) This subsection applies if—

  (a) the Parliamentary corporation is satisfied that the Commissioner has breached the terms and conditions of appointment and the Parliament resolves that the Commissioner should be removed from office for that breach, or

  (b) the Parliament resolves that it has lost confidence in the Commissioner's willingness, suitability or ability to perform the functions of the Commissioner,

and, in either case, the resolution is voted for by a number of members not fewer than two thirds of the total number of seats for members of the Parliament.]

Functions

4 Promoting and safeguarding rights

(1) The general function of the Commissioner is to promote and safeguard the rights of children and young people.

(2) In exercising that general function the Commissioner is, in particular, to—

  (a) promote awareness and understanding of the rights of children and young people;

  (b) keep under review the law, policy and practice relating to the rights of children and young people with a view to assessing the adequacy and effectiveness of such law, policy and practice;

  (c) promote best practice by service providers; and

  (d) promote, commission, undertake and publish research on matters relating to the rights of children and young people.

5 United Nations Convention and equal opportunities

(1) In exercising functions under this Act, the Commissioner must comply with subsections (2) to (4).

(2) The Commissioner must have regard to any relevant provisions of the United Nations Convention on the Rights of the Child.

(3) The Commissioner must, in particular—

(a) regard, and encourage others to regard, the best interests of children and young people as a primary consideration; and

(b) have regard to, and encourage others to have regard to, the views of children and young people on all matters affecting them, due allowance being made for age and maturity.

(4) The Commissioner must act in a manner which encourages equal opportunities and, in particular, the observance of the equal opportunity requirements.

6 Involving children and young people

(1) The Commissioner must encourage the involvement of children and young people in the work of the Commissioner.

(2) The Commissioner must, in particular, take reasonable steps to—

(a) ensure that children and young people are made aware of—

(i) the functions of the Commissioner;

(ii) the ways in which they may communicate with the Commissioner; and

(iii) the ways in which the Commissioner may respond to any issues which they raise;

(b) consult children and young people on the work to be undertaken by the Commissioner; and

(c) consult organisations working with and for children and young people on the work to be undertaken by the Commissioner.

(3) In carrying out the duties under subsections (1) and (2) the Commissioner must pay particular attention to groups of children and young people who do not have other adequate means by which they can make their views known.

(4) The Commissioner must prepare and keep under review a strategy for involving children and young people in the work of the Commissioner in accordance with this section.

7 Carrying out investigations

[(1) The Commissioner may carry out an investigation into—

(a) whether, by what means and to what extent a service provider has regard to the rights, interests and views of children and young people in making decisions or taking actions that affect those children and young people (such an investigation being called a 'general investigation');

(b) whether, by what means and to what extent a service provider had regard to the rights, interests and views of a child or young person in making a decision or taking an action that affected that child or young person (such an investigation being called an 'individual investigation').

(2) The Commissioner may carry out a general investigation only if the Commissioner, having considered the available evidence on, and any information received about, the matter, is satisfied on reasonable grounds that the matter to be investigated raises an issue of particular significance to—

(a) children and young people generally; or

(b) particular groups of children and young people.

[(2A) The Commissioner may carry out an investigation only if the Commissioner, having considered the available evidence on, and any information received about, the matter, is satisfied on reasonable grounds that the investigation would not duplicate work that is properly the function of another person.]

(3) The Commissioner may not carry out an investigation—

(a) if it would relate to a reserved matter;

[. . .]

(c)　so far as it would relate to—

(i) the making of decisions or taking of action in particular legal proceedings before a court or tribunal; or

(ii) a matter which is the subject of legal proceedings before a court or tribunal.

[(4)　Subsection (5) applies in relation to a matter about which the Commissioner may carry out an individual investigation.

(5)　Where the Commissioner considers that the matter may be capable of being resolved without an investigation, the Commissioner may with a view to securing that outcome take such steps as the Commissioner considers appropriate.]

8　Initiation and conduct of investigation

(1)　Before taking any steps in the conduct of an investigation, the Commissioner must—

(a)　draw up terms of reference for the investigation; and

[(b)　take such steps as appear to the Commissioner to be appropriate with a view to bringing notice of the investigation and terms of reference to the attention of persons likely to be affected by it.]

(2)　[A general] investigation is to be conducted in public except to the extent that the Commissioner considers that the taking of evidence in private is necessary or appropriate.

[(3)　An individual investigation is to be conducted in private.]

9　Investigations: witnesses and documents

(1)　The Commissioner may require any person—

(a)　to give evidence on any matter within the terms of reference of an investigation; or

(b)　to produce documents in the custody or control of that person which have a bearing on any such matter.

(2)　The Commissioner may not impose such a requirement on any person whom the Parliament could not require, under section 23 of the Scotland Act, to attend its proceedings for the purpose of giving evidence or to produce documents.

(3)　Schedule 2 makes further provision with respect to witnesses and documents and the sanctions for non-compliance with a requirement under this section.

Reports

10　Annual report

(1)　The Commissioner must lay before the Parliament annually a report on the exercise of the Commissioner's functions [during the reporting year].

(2)　The report must include—

(a)　a review of issues identified by the Commissioner in [the reporting year] as being relevant to children and young people;

(b)　a review of the Commissioner's activity in [the reporting year], including the steps taken to fulfil each of the Commissioner's functions;

(c)　any recommendations by the Commissioner arising out of such activity; and

(d)　an overview of work to be undertaken by the Commissioner in the year following [the reporting year], including the strategy for involving children and young people in the work of the Commissioner.

[(3)　The report must be laid before the Parliament within 7 months after the end of the reporting year.

(4)　In preparing the report, the Commissioner must comply with any direction given by the Parliamentary corporation as to the form and content of the report.

(5)　In this section 'reporting year' means the year beginning on 1 April.]

11   Reports on investigations

(1)   The Commissioner must, at the conclusion of any investigation, [prepare] a report of the investigation.

(2)   The report must contain any recommendations by the Commissioner arising out of the investigation.

[(2A)   In relation to any such recommendation, the report may include a requirement to respond.

(2B)   A requirement to respond is a requirement that the service provider provides, within such period as the Commissioner reasonably requires, a statement in writing to the Commissioner setting out—

(a)   what the service provider has done or proposes to do in response to the recommendation; or

(b)   if the service provider does not intend to do anything in response to the recommendation, the reasons for that.]

(3)   A report of an investigation into the activities of a person named in, or identifiable from, the report may be [finalised] only if that person has, where this is reasonable and practicable, been given a copy of the draft report and an opportunity to make representations on it.

[(4)   The Commissioner must lay before the Parliament the report of a general investigation.

(5)   The Commissioner may lay before the Parliament the report of an individual investigation.]

[(6)   Where a report of an investigation includes a requirement to respond, the Commissioner must give a copy of the report to the service provider.]

12   Other reports to Parliament

The Commissioner may lay before the Parliament such other reports on the exercise of the Commissioner's functions as the Commissioner considers necessary or appropriate.

13   Anonymity for children and young people

The Commissioner must ensure that, so far as reasonable and practicable having regard to the subject matter, a report under this Act does not name or identify any child or young person, or group of children or young people, referred to in it.

14   Publication

(1)   The Commissioner must publish any report laid before the Parliament under this Act.

(2)   The Commissioner may publish any other report relating to the exercise of the Commissioner's functions.

(3)   Where the Commissioner publishes a report which is not specifically designed for children or young people the Commissioner must also publish a child friendly version of the report.

[14AA   Publication of responses to recommendations of investigations

(1)   The Commissioner must publish any statement provided in response to a requirement to respond to a recommendation arising out of a general investigation.

(2)   Subsection (1) does not apply if, or to the extent that, the Commissioner considers publication to be inappropriate.

(3)   The Commissioner may publish any statement provided in response to a requirement to respond to a recommendation arising out of an individual investigation.

(4)   The Commissioner must ensure that, so far as reasonable and practicable having regard to the subject matter, the version of the statement which is published under subsection (1) or (3) does not name or identify any child or young person, or group of children or young people, referred to in it.

(5)   The Commissioner may, in such manner as the Commissioner considers appropriate, publicise a failure to comply with a requirement to respond.]

[14A   Strategic plans

(1)   The Commissioner must, in respect of each 4 year period, lay before the Parliament a plan (referred to in this section as a 'strategic plan') setting out how the Commissioner proposes to perform the Commissioner's functions during the 4 year period.

(2)   A strategic plan must, in particular, set out—

(a)   the Commissioner's objectives and priorities during the 4 year period,

(b)   how the Commissioner proposes to achieve them,

(c)   a timetable for doing so, and

(d)   estimates of the costs of doing so.

(3)   Before laying a strategic plan before the Parliament, the Commissioner must provide a draft of it to and invite, and (if any are given) consider, comments on it from—

(a)   the Parliamentary corporation, and

(b)   such other persons as the Commissioner thinks appropriate.

(4)   The reference in subsection (3)(b) to other persons includes a committee of the Parliament.

(5)   The Commissioner must lay each strategic plan before the Parliament not later than the beginning of the 4 year period to which the plan relates.

(6)   The Commissioner must arrange for the publication of each strategic plan laid before the Parliament.

(7)   The Commissioner may, at any time during a 4 year period, review the strategic plan for the period and lay a revised strategic plan before the Parliament.

(8)   Subsections (2) to (7) apply to a revised strategic plan as they apply to a strategic plan.

(9)   In that application, the reference in subsection (5) to the 4 year period is a reference to the period to which the revised strategic plan relates.

(10)   In this section, '4 year period' means the period of 4 years beginning on 1 April next following the coming into force of this section and each subsequent period of 4 years.]

Defamation

15   Protection from actions of defamation

(1)   For the purposes of the law of defamation—

(a)   any statement made by the Commissioner or any of the Commissioner's staff—

(i)   in conducting an investigation under this Act;

(ii)   in communicating with any person for the purposes of such an investigation;

(iii)   in a report published under this Act,

has absolute privilege;

(b)   any other statement made by the Commissioner or any of the Commissioner's staff in pursuance of the purposes of this Act has qualified privilege; and

(c)   any statement made to the Commissioner or any of the Commissioner's staff in pursuance of those purposes has qualified privilege.

(2)   In subsection (1), 'statement' has the same meaning as in the Defamation Act 1996 (c 31).

Interpretation, commencement and short title

16   Interpretation

(1)   In this Act, unless the context otherwise requires—

'action' includes failure to act and related expressions are to be construed accordingly;

'best practice' means such practice in relation to the rights of children and young people as appears to the Commissioner to be desirable;

'child friendly version', in relation to a report, means a version or summary which is specifically designed to take account, so far as practicable, of the age, understanding and usual language of any children or young people by whom it is intended that the report should be read;

'children and young people' means natural persons in Scotland who are under the age of 18 years or, if they have at any time been in the care of, or looked after by, a local authority or Northern Ireland authority, under the age of 21 years; and related expressions have corresponding meanings;

'Commissioner' means the Commissioner for Children and Young People in Scotland;

'equal opportunities' and 'equal opportunity requirements' have the same meaning as in Section L2 of Part II of Schedule 5 to the Scotland Act;

'local authority' means any council of a county, city, town, burgh, borough, district, island or other local government area in Scotland, England or Wales;

'looked after', in relation to a local authority in Scotland, has the same meaning as in section 17(6) of the Children (Scotland) Act 1995 (c 36), in relation to a local authority in England and Wales, has the same meaning as in section 22(1) of the Children Act 1989 (c 41) and in relation to a Northern Ireland authority, has the same meaning as in article 25(1) of the Children (Northern Ireland) Order 1995 (SI 1995/755);

'Northern Ireland authority' means any authority (including any Health and Social Services Board or trust) in Northern Ireland;

'Scotland Act' means the Scotland Act 1998 (c 46);

'Scottish Law Officer' means the Lord Advocate or the Solicitor General for Scotland;

'service provider' means any person providing services for children and young people but does not include a parent or guardian exercising the responsibilities imposed or the rights conferred by sections 1 and 2 of the Children (Scotland) Act 1995 (c 36); and

'terms' includes conditions.

(2) Any reference in this Act to the United Nations Convention on the Rights of the Child is to that Convention read subject to any reservations, objections or interpretative declarations by the United Kingdom for the time being in force.

17 Commencement and short title

(1) The provisions of this Act, except for—

(a) sections 1 to 3 and section 16;

(b) schedule 1; and

(c) this section,

come into force at the end of the period of six months beginning with the date of Royal Assent.

(2) This Act may be cited as the Commissioner for Children and Young People (Scotland) Act 2003.

SCHEDULES

SCHEDULE 1
THE COMMISSIONER FOR CHILDREN AND YOUNG PEOPLE IN SCOTLAND
(introduced by section 1)

Status

1.—(1) Neither the Commissioner nor any member of the Commissioner's staff is to be regarded as a servant or agent of the Crown or as having any status, immunity or privilege of the Crown.

(2) The Commissioner's property is not to be regarded as property of, or property held on behalf of, the Crown.

[(3) The Commissioner is, as such, to be regarded as a juristic person distinct from the natural person holding the office.]

Independence

2.—(1) The Commissioner is not, except as provided in the provisions of this Act listed in sub-paragraph (2), subject to the direction or control of—

(a) any member of the Parliament;

(b) any member of the Scottish Executive; or

(c) the Parliamentary corporation.

(2) The listed provisions are sections 2(3) [3(1)(b) and 10(4) and paragraphs 4, 6(2A) and (3), 6A, 7, 7A, 7B(3), 9A] and 10 of this schedule and paragraph 8 of schedule 2.

Validity of actings

3. The validity of any actings of the Commissioner is not affected by—

(a) any defect in the nomination by the Parliament for the Commissioner's appointment; or

(b) any disqualification from appointment as Commissioner.

Remuneration and terms of appointment

4.—(1) The Commissioner is entitled to—

(a) a salary of such amount; and

(b) such allowances,

as the Parliamentary corporation may determine.

[(1A) The Commissioner ceases to hold office as Commissioner on becoming—

(a) a member of the Parliament,

(b) a member of the House of Commons, or

(c) a member of the European Parliament.]

(2) The appointment of the Commissioner is otherwise on such terms [and conditions] as the Parliamentary corporation may determine.

[(3) The terms and conditions may, without prejudice to section 2(2) or sub-paragraph (1A) of this paragraph—

(a) prohibit the Commissioner from holding any other specified office, employment or appointment or engaging in any other specified occupation,

(b) provide that the Commissioner's holding of any such office, employment or appointment or engagement in any such occupation is subject to the approval of the Parliamentary corporation.

(4) In sub-paragraph (3)(b), 'specified' means specified in the terms and conditions or within a description so specified.]

Pensions etc

5.—(1) The Parliamentary corporation may make arrangements for the payment of pensions, allowances and gratuities to, or in respect of, any person who has ceased to hold the office of Commissioner.

(2) The Parliamentary corporation may, in particular—

(a) make contributions or payments towards provision for such pensions, allowances or gratuities; and

(b) establish and administer one or more pension schemes.

[*Subsequent appointments etc*

5A.—(1) A person who has ceased being the Commissioner ('the former Commissioner') may not, without the approval of the Parliamentary corporation—

(a) be employed or appointed in any other capacity by the Commissioner,

(b) be an employee or appointee of—

(i)   any person in relation to whom, or

(ii)   any body in relation to which,

an investigation under this Act has been carried out or continued by the former Commissioner when Commissioner, or hold office in any such body, or

(c)   hold any other office, employment or appointment or engage in any other occupation, being an office, employment, appointment or occupation which, by virtue of paragraph 4(3)(a), that former Commissioner could not have held or, as the case may be, engaged in when Commissioner.

(2)   The restriction in sub-paragraph (1)—

(a)   starts when the person ceases to be the Commissioner, and

(b)   ends on the expiry of the financial year next following the one in which it started.]

General powers

6.—(1)   The Commissioner has a general power to do anything necessary or expedient for the purposes of, or in connection with, the exercise of the Commissioner's functions.

(2)   In particular, the Commissioner may enter into contracts and acquire and dispose of [land and other] property.

[(2A)   The exercise of the power to acquire or dispose of land is subject to the approval of the Parliamentary corporation.]

(3)   The Commissioner may [determine and charge reasonable sums for anything done or provided by the Commissioner in the performance of, or in connection with, the Commissioner's functions].

[(3A)   Any sums received by the Commissioner by virtue of sub-paragraph (3) are to be retained by the Commissioner and applied to meet expenditure incurred in doing or providing whatever is charged for.]

[. . .]

[Location of office

6A. The Commissioner must comply with any direction given by the Parliamentary corporation as to the location of the Commissioner's office.]

Staff

7.—(1)   The Commissioner may, with the consent of the Parliamentary corporation as to numbers, appoint staff to assist in carrying out the Commissioner's functions.

(2)   The Commissioner may, with the consent of the Parliamentary corporation, determine the terms [and conditions] of appointment of such staff, including arrangements for the payment of pensions, allowances or gratuities to, or in respect of, any person who has ceased to be a member of staff of the Commissioner.

[Sharing of premises, staff, services and other resources

7A.   The Commissioner must comply with any direction given by the Parliamentary corporation as to the sharing of premises, staff, services or other resources with any other officeholder or any public body.

Advisers and other services

7B.—(1)   The Commissioner may obtain advice, assistance or any other service from any person who, in the opinion of the Commissioner, is qualified to give it.

(2)   The Commissioner may pay to that person such fees and allowances as the Commissioner determines.

(3)   Any payment under sub-paragraph (2) is subject to the approval of the Parliamentary corporation.]

Delegation of authority

8.   The Commissioner may authorise any person to exercise functions on behalf of the Commissioner to the extent specified in the authorisation, but any such delegation of authority does not affect the responsibility of the Commissioner for the exercise of the functions.

Financial provision

9.—[(1)]   The Parliamentary corporation is to pay—

(a)   the salary and allowances of the Commissioner; and

(b)   any expenses properly incurred by the Commissioner in the exercise of the Commissioner's functions [so far as not met out of sums received and applied by the Commissioner under paragraph 6(3A).

[(2)   Sub-paragraph (1)(b) does not require the Parliamentary corporation to pay any expenses incurred by the Commissioner which exceed or are otherwise not covered by a budget or, as the case may be, revised budget approved under paragraph 9A.

(3)   However, the Parliamentary corporation may pay those expenses.

(4)   The Parliamentary corporation is to indemnify the Commissioner in respect of any liabilities incurred by the Commissioner in the exercise of the Commissioner's functions.]

[*Budget*

9A.—(1)   The Commissioner must, before the start of each financial year, prepare proposals for the Commissioner's use of resources and expenditure during the year (a 'budget') and, by such date as the Parliamentary corporation determines, send the budget to the Parliamentary corporation for approval.

(2)   The Commissioner may, in the course of a financial year, prepare a revised budget for the remainder of the year and send it to the Parliamentary corporation for approval.

(3)   In preparing a budget or revised budget, the Commissioner must ensure that the resources of the Commissioner will be used economically, efficiently and effectively.

(4)   A budget or revised budget must contain a statement that the Commissioner has complied with the duty under sub-paragraph (3).]

Accountable officer

10.—(1)   The Parliamentary corporation is to designate the Commissioner or a member of the Commissioner's staff as the accountable officer for the purposes of this paragraph.

(2)   The functions of the accountable officer are—

(a)   signing the accounts of the expenditure and receipts of the Commissioner;

(b)   ensuring the propriety and regularity of the finances of the Commissioner;

(c)   ensuring that the resources of the Commissioner are used economically, efficiently and effectively; and

(d)   where the accountable officer is not the Commissioner, the duty set out in sub-paragraph (4).

(3)   The accountable officer is answerable to the Parliament for the exercise of those functions.

(4)   The duty referred to in sub-paragraph (2)(d) is a duty, where the accountable officer is required to act in some way but considers that to do so would be inconsistent with the proper performance of the functions specified in sub-paragraph (2)(a) to (c), to—

(a)   obtain written authority from the Commissioner before taking the action; and

(b)   send a copy of that authority as soon as possible to the Auditor General for Scotland.

Accounts and audit

11.—(1)   The Commissioner must keep proper accounts at all times and prepare annual accounts in respect of each financial year.

(2)   The Commissioner must send a copy of the annual accounts to the Auditor General for Scotland for auditing.

(3)   The financial year of the Commissioner is—

(a)   the period beginning with the date on which the first Commissioner is appointed and ending with the 31st of March next following that date; and

(b)   each successive period of twelve months ending with the 31st of March.

(4)   If requested by any person, the Commissioner must make available at any reasonable time, and without charge, in printed or electronic form, the audited accounts, so that they may be inspected by that person.

Appointment of acting Commissioner

12.—(1)   Where there is no Commissioner for the time being, or the Commissioner is unable to act, the Parliamentary corporation may appoint a person (whether or not a member of the Commissioner's staff) to discharge the Commissioner's functions until a new Commissioner is appointed or the Commissioner is again able to act; and a person so appointed is referred to in this Act as the 'acting Commissioner'.

(2)   A person who is disqualified from appointment as the Commissioner is also disqualified from appointment as acting Commissioner.

(3)   While holding office as such, the acting Commissioner is governed by the provisions of this Act, other than paragraphs 3(a) and 5 of this schedule, applying to the Commissioner.

VULNERABLE WITNESSES (SCOTLAND) ACT 2004
(2004, asp 3)

PART 2
CIVIL PROCEEDINGS

Evidence of children and other vulnerable witnesses: special measures

11   Interpretation of this Part

(1)   For the purposes of this Part of this Act, a person who is giving or is to give evidence in or for the purposes of any civil proceedings is a vulnerable witness if—

(a)   the person is under the age of [18] on the date of commencement of the proceedings (such a vulnerable witness being referred to in this Part as a 'child witness'),

(b)   where the person is not a child witness, there is a significant risk that the quality of the evidence to be given by the person will be diminished by reason of—

(i)   mental disorder (within the meaning of section 328 of the Mental Health (Care and Treatment) (Scotland) Act 2003 (asp 13)), or

(ii)   fear or distress in connection with giving evidence in the proceedings [, or

[(c)   the person is of such description or is a witness in such proceedings as the Scottish ministers may by order subject to the affirmation procedure prescribe].

(2)   In considering whether a person is a vulnerable witness by virtue of subsection (1)(b) above, the court must take into account—

(a)   the nature and circumstances of the alleged matter to which the proceedings relate,

(b)   the nature of the evidence which the person is likely to give,

(c)   the relationship (if any) between the person and any party to the proceedings,

(d)   the person's age and maturity,

(e)   any behaviour towards the person on the part of—

(i)   any party to the proceedings,

(ii)   members of the family or associates of any such party,

(iii)   any other person who is likely to be a party to the proceedings or a witness in the proceedings, and

(f)   such other matters, including—

(i)   the social and cultural background and ethnic origins of the person,

(ii)   the person's sexual orientation,

(iii)   the domestic and employment circumstances of the person,

(iv)   any religious beliefs or political opinions of the person, and

(v)   any physical disability or other physical impairment which the person has,

as appear to the court to be relevant.

(3)   For the purposes of subsection (1)(a) above, proceedings are taken to have commenced when the petition, summons, initial writ or other document initiating the proceedings is served, and, where the document is served on more than one person, the proceedings shall be taken to have commenced when the document is served on the first person on whom it is served.

(4)   In subsection (1)(b), the reference to the quality of evidence is to its quality in terms of completeness, coherence and accuracy.

(5)   In this Part—

['the 2011 Act' means the Children's Hearings (Scotland) Act 2011,]

'child witness notice' has the meaning given in section 12(2),

'civil proceedings' includes, in addition to such proceedings in any of the ordinary courts of law, [relevant proceedings],

'court' is to be construed in accordance with the meaning of 'civil proceedings',

['relevant proceedings' means proceedings under Part 10 of the 2011 Act (other than section 98 or 99),]

'special measure' means any of the special measures set out in, or prescribed under, section 18,

'vulnerable witness application' has the meaning given in section 12(6)(a).

12   Orders authorising the use of special measures for vulnerable witnesses

(1)   Where a child witness is to give evidence in or for the purposes of any civil proceedings, the court must, before the proof or other hearing at which the child is to give evidence, make an order—

(a)   authorising the use of such special measure or measures as the court considers to be the most appropriate for the purpose of taking the child witness's evidence, or

(b)   that the child witness is to give evidence without the benefit of any special measure.

(2)   The party citing or intending to cite a child witness must lodge with the court a notice (referred to in this Part as a 'child witness notice')—

(a)   specifying the special measure or measures which the party considers to be the most appropriate for the purpose of taking the child witness's evidence, or

(b)   if the party considers that the child witness should give evidence without the benefit of any special measure, stating that fact,

and the court must have regard to the child witness notice in making an order under subsection (1) above.

(3)   If a child witness notice specifies any of the following special measures, namely—

(a) the use of a live television link in accordance with section 20 where the place from which the child witness is to give evidence by means of the link is another part of the court building in which the court-room is located,

(b) the use of a screen in accordance with section 21, or

(c) the use of a supporter in accordance with section 22 in conjunction with either of the special measures referred to in paragraphs (a) and (b) above,

that special measure is, for the purposes of subsection (1)(a) above, to be taken to be the most appropriate for the purposes of taking the child witness's evidence.

(4) The court may make an order under subsection (1)(b) above only if satisfied—

(a) that the child witness has expressed a wish to give evidence without the benefit of any special measure and that it is appropriate for the child witness so to give evidence, or

(b) that—

(i) the use of any special measure for the purpose of taking the evidence of the child witness would give rise to a significant risk of prejudice to the fairness of the proceedings or otherwise to the interests of justice, and

(ii) that risk significantly outweighs any risk of prejudice to the interests of the child witness if the order is made.

(5) Subsection (6) below applies in relation to a person other than a child witness who is to give evidence in or for the purpose of any civil proceedings (referred to in this section as 'the witness').

(6) The court may—

(a) on an application (referred to in this Part as a 'vulnerable witness application') made to it by the party citing or intending to cite the witness, and

(b) if satisfied that the witness is a vulnerable witness,

make an order authorising the use of such special measure or measures as the court considers most appropriate for the purpose of taking the witness's evidence.

(7) In deciding whether to make an order under subsection (6) above, the court must—

(a) have regard to—

(i) the possible effect on the witness if required to give evidence without the benefit of any special measure, and

(ii) whether it is likely that the witness would be better able to give evidence with the benefit of a special measure, and

(b) take into account the matters specified in section 11(2)(a) to (f).

[(8) In the case of relevant proceedings, the child witness notice or vulnerable witness application—

(a) must be lodged or made before the commencement of the hearing at which the child or, as the case may be, vulnerable witness is to give evidence,

(b) on cause shown, may be lodged or made after the commencement of that hearing.]

13 Review of arrangements for vulnerable witnesses

(1) In any civil proceedings in which a person who is giving or is to give evidence (referred to in this section as 'the witness') appears to the court to be a vulnerable witness, the court may at any stage in the proceedings (whether before or after the commencement of the proof or other hearing at which the witness is giving or is to give evidence or before or after the witness has begun to give evidence)—

(a) on the application of the party citing or intending to cite the witness, or

(b) of its own motion,

review the current arrangements for taking the witness's evidence and make an order under subsection (2) below.

(2) The order which may be made under this subsection is—

(a) where the current arrangements for taking the witness's evidence include the use of a special measure or combination of special measures authorised by an order under section 12 or under this subsection (referred to as the 'earlier order'), an order varying or revoking the earlier order, or

(b)   where the current arrangements for taking the witness's evidence do not include any special measure, an order authorising the use of such special measure or measures as the court considers most appropriate for the purpose of taking the witness's evidence.

(3)   An order under subsection (2)(a) above varying an earlier order may—

(a)   add to or substitute for any special measure authorised by the earlier order such other special measure as the court considers most appropriate for the purpose of taking the witness's evidence, or

(b)   where the earlier order authorises the use of a combination of special measures for that purpose, delete any of the special measures so authorised.

(4)   The court may make an order under subsection (2)(a) above revoking an earlier order only if satisfied that—

(a)   the witness has expressed a wish to give or, as the case may be, continue to give evidence without the benefit of any special measure and that it is appropriate for the witness so to give evidence, or

(b)   that—

(i)   the use, or continued use, of the special measure for the purpose of taking the witness's evidence would give rise to a significant risk of prejudice to the fairness of the proceedings or otherwise to the interests of justice, and

(ii)   that risk significantly outweighs any risk of prejudice to the interests of the witness if the order is made.

(5)   Subsection (7) of section 12 applies to the making of an order under subsection (2)(b) of this section as it applies to the making of an order under subsection (6) of that section but as if the references to the witness were to the witness within the meaning of this section.

(6)   In this section, 'current arrangements' means the arrangements in place at the time the review under this section is begun.

14   [Amends Court of Session Act 1988.]

15   Vulnerable witnesses: supplementary provision

(1)   Subsection (2) below applies where—

(a)   a party is considering for the purposes of a child witness notice or a vulnerable witness application which of the special measures is or are the most appropriate for the purpose of taking the evidence of the person to whom the notice or application relates, or

(b)   the court is making an order under section 12(1) or (6) or 13(2).

(2)   The party or, as the case may be, the court must—

(a)   have regard to the best interests of the witness, and

(b)   take account of any views expressed by—

(i)   the witness (having regard, where the witness is a child witness, to the witness's age and maturity), and

(ii)   where the witness is a child witness, the witness's parent.

(3)   For the purposes of subsection (2)(b) above, where the witness is a child witness—

(a)   the witness is to be presumed to be of sufficient age and maturity to form a view if aged 12 or older, and

(b)   in the event that any views expressed by the witness are inconsistent with any views expressed by the witness's parent, the views of the witness are to be given greater weight.

(4)   In this section—

'parent', in relation to a child witness, means any person having parental responsibilities within the meaning of section 1(3) of the Children (Scotland) Act 1995 (c 36) in relation to the child witness 'the witness' means—

(a)   in the case referred to in subsection (1)(a) above, the person to whom the child witness notice or vulnerable witness application relates,

(b)   in the case referred to in subsection (1)(b) above, the person to whom the order would relate.

16   Party to proceedings as a vulnerable witness

Where a child witness or other person who is giving or is to give evidence in or for the purposes of any civil proceedings (referred to in this section as 'the witness') is a party to the proceedings—

(a)   sections 12 and 13 have effect in relation to the witness as if references in those sections to the party citing or intending to cite the witness were references to the witness, and

(b)   section 15 has effect in relation to the witness as if—

(i)   in subsection (1), paragraph (a) were omitted, and

(ii)   in subsection (2), the words 'The party or, as the case may be,' were omitted.

[16A   Relevant proceedings: Principal Reporter's power to act for party to proceedings

(1)   Subsection (2) applies where a child witness or other person who is giving or is to give evidence in or for the purposes of relevant proceedings (referred to in this section as 'the party') is a party to the proceedings.

(2)   The Principal Reporter may, on the party's behalf—

(a)   lodge a child witness notice under section 12(2),

(b)   make a vulnerable witness application for an order under section 12(6),

(c)   make an application under section 13(1)(a) for review of the current arrangements for taking a witness's evidence.]

17   Crown application and saving provision

(1)   Sections 11 to 15 of this Act apply to the Crown.

(2)   Nothing in section 12 or 13 of this Act affects any power or duty which a court has otherwise than by virtue of those sections to make or authorise any special arrangements for taking the evidence of any person in any civil proceedings.

18   The special measures

(1)   The special measures which may be authorised to be used by virtue of section 12 or 13 of this Act for the purpose of taking the evidence of a vulnerable witness are—

(a)   taking of evidence by a commissioner in accordance with section 19,

(b)   use of a live television link in accordance with section 20,

(c)   use of screen in accordance with section 21,

(d)   use of a supporter in accordance with section 22, and

(e)   such other measures as the Scottish Ministers may, by order made by statutory instrument, prescribe.

(2)   An order under subsection (1)(e) above is not to be made unless a draft of the statutory instrument containing the order has been laid before and approved by a resolution of the Scottish Parliament.

19   Taking of evidence by a commissioner

(1)   Where the special measure to be used is taking of evidence by a commissioner, the court must appoint a commissioner to take the evidence of the vulnerable witness in respect of whom the special measure is to be used.

(2)   Proceedings before a commissioner appointed under subsection (1) above must be recorded by video recorder.

(3)   A party to the proceedings—

(a) must not, except by leave of the court, be present in the room where such proceedings are taking place, but

(b) is entitled by such means as seem suitable to the court to watch and hear the proceedings.

(4) The recording of the proceedings made in pursuance of subsection (2) above is to be received in evidence without being sworn to by witnesses.

20 Live television link

(1) Where the special measure to be used is a live television link, the court must make such arrangements as seem to it appropriate for the vulnerable witness in respect of whom the special measure is to be used to give evidence by means of such a link.

(2) Where—

(a) the live television link is to be used in proceedings in a sheriff court, but

(b) that court lacks accommodation or equipment necessary for the purpose of receiving such a link,

the sheriff may by order transfer the proceedings to any sheriff court in the same sheriffdom which has such accommodation or equipment available.

(3) An order may be made under subsection (2) above—

(a) at any stage in the proceedings (whether before or after the commencement of the proof or other hearing at which the vulnerable witness is to give evidence), or

(b) in relation to a part of the proceedings.

21 Screens

(1) Where the special measure to be used is a screen, the screen must be used to conceal the parties to the proceedings from the sight of the vulnerable witness in respect of whom the special measure is to be used.

(2) However, the court must make arrangements to ensure that the parties are able to watch and hear the vulnerable witness giving evidence.

(3) Subsections (2) and (3) of section 20 apply for the purposes of use of a screen under this section as they apply for the purposes of use of a live television link under that section but as if—

(a) references to the live television link were references to the screen, and

(b) the reference to receiving such a link were a reference to the use of a screen.

22 Supporters

(1) Where the special measure to be used is a supporter, another person ('the supporter') nominated by or on behalf of the vulnerable witness in respect of whom the special measure is to be used may be present alongside the witness for the purpose of providing support whilst the witness is giving evidence.

(2) Where the person nominated as the supporter is to give evidence in the proceedings, that person may not act as the supporter at any time before giving evidence.

(3) The supporter must not prompt or otherwise seek to influence the vulnerable witness in the course of giving evidence.

[22A Giving evidence in chief in the form of a prior statement

(1) This section applies to proceedings in relation to—

(a) an application made by virtue of section 93 or 94 of the 2011 Act to determine whether the ground mentioned in section 67(2)(j) of that Act is established, or

(b) an application under section 110 of that Act for review of a finding that the ground mentioned in section 67(2)(j) of that Act is established.

(2) The special measures which may be authorised by virtue of section 12 or 13 for the purpose of taking the evidence of a vulnerable witness at a hearing to consider such an application include (in addition to those listed in section 18(1)) the

giving of evidence in chief in the form of a prior statement in accordance with subsections (3) to (10).

(3)   Where that special measure is to be used, a statement made by the vulnerable witness (a 'prior statement') may be lodged in evidence for the purposes of this section by or on behalf of the party citing the vulnerable witness.

(4)   A prior statement is admissible as the witness's evidence in chief, or as part of the witness's evidence in chief, without the witness being required to adopt or otherwise speak to the statement in giving evidence.

(5)   A prior statement is admissible as evidence of any matter stated in it of which direct oral evidence by the vulnerable witness would be admissible if given at the hearing.

(6)   A prior statement is admissible under this section only if—
    (a)   it is contained in a document, and
    (b)   at the time the statement was made, the vulnerable witness would have been a competent witness for the purposes of the hearing.

(7)   Subsection (6) does not apply to a prior statement—
    (a)   contained in a precognition on oath, or
    (b)   made in other proceedings (whether criminal or civil and whether taking place in the United Kingdom or elsewhere).

(8)   A prior statement of a type mentioned in subsection (7) is not admissible for the purposes of this section unless it is authenticated in such manner as may be prescribed by regulations made by statutory instrument by the Scottish Ministers.

(9)   This section does not affect the admissibility of any statement made by any person which is admissible otherwise than by virtue of this section.

(10)   In this section—
'document' has the meaning given by section 262(3) of the Criminal Procedure (Scotland) Act 1995 (c 46),
   'statement'—
    (a)   includes—
       (i)   any representation, however made or expressed, of fact or opinion, and
       (ii)   any part of a statement, but
    (b)   does not include a statement in a precognition other than a precognition on oath.

(11)   For the purposes of this section, a statement is contained in a document where the person who makes it—
    (a)   makes the statement in the document personally,
    (b)   makes a statement which is, with or without the person's knowledge, embodied in a document by whatever means or by any person who has direct personal knowledge of the making of the statement, or
    (c)   approves a document as embodying the statement.

(12)   A statutory instrument containing regulations under subsection (8) is subject to annulment in pursuance of a resolution of the Scottish Parliament.]

ANTISOCIAL BEHAVIOUR ETC (SCOTLAND) ACT 2004
(2004, asp 8)

PART 9
PARENTING ORDERS

Applications

102   Applications

(1)   The court may make a parenting order in respect of a parent of a child where—
    (a)   subsection (2) or (3) applies; and
    (b)   the Scottish Ministers have notified the court that the local authority for

the area in which the parent ordinarily resides has made arrangements that would enable the order to be complied with.

(2)   This subsection applies where—

(a)   the application for the order is made by the appropriate local authority; and

(b)   the court is satisfied that—

(i)   the behaviour condition; or

(ii)   the conduct condition,

is met.

(3)   This subsection applies where—

(a)   the application for the order is made by the Principal Reporter, and

(b)   the court is satisfied that—

(i)   the behaviour condition;

(ii)   the conduct condition; or

(iii)   the welfare condition,

is met.

(4)   The behaviour condition is—

(a)   that the child has engaged in antisocial behaviour; and

(b)   that the making of the order is desirable in the interests of preventing the child from engaging in further such behaviour.

(5)   The conduct condition is—

(a)   that the child has engaged in criminal conduct; and

(b)   that the making of the order is desirable in the interests of preventing the child from engaging in further such conduct.

(6)   The welfare condition is that the making of the order is desirable in the interests of improving the welfare of the child.

(7)   For the purposes of subsection (5), a child engages in criminal conduct if the child engages in conduct that constitutes a criminal offence (or would do so if the child had attained the age of 8 years).

(8)   An application under this section shall be made by summary application to the sheriff of the sheriffdom where the parent ordinarily resides.

(9)   Before an application is made under this section—

(a)   by a local authority, it shall consult the Principal Reporter;

(b)   by the Principal Reporter, the Principal Reporter shall consult the appropriate local authority.

(10)   In this section, 'appropriate local authority' means the local authority for the area where the child ordinarily resides.

Parenting orders

103   Parenting orders

(1)   A parenting order is an order requiring the specified person—

(a)   to comply, during a specified period—

(i)   beginning with the making of the order; and

(ii)   not exceeding 12 months,

with such requirements as are specified; and

(b)   subject to subsection (2), to attend, during a specified period—

(i)   falling within the specified period mentioned in paragraph (a); and

(ii)   not exceeding 3 months,

such counselling or guidance sessions as may be directed by a supervising officer appointed by the relevant local authority.

(2)   Where a parenting order has been made in respect of the person on a previous occasion in the interests of the child in whose interests the order is to be made, the order need not include a requirement under subsection (1)(b).

(3)   The Scottish Ministers may by order amend the number of months mentioned in—

(a) subsection (1)(a)(ii); and
(b) subsection (1)(b)(ii).
(4) In subsection (1), 'specified' means specified in the order.

Matters following making of order

104 Notification of making of order

(1) The clerk of the court by which a parenting order is made shall cause a copy of the order to be—
(a) given to the person specified in the order; or
(b) sent to the person so specified by registered post or the recorded delivery service.
(2) A certificate of posting of a letter sent under subsection (1)(b) issued by the postal operator concerned shall be sufficient evidence of the sending of the letter on the day specified in such certificate.
(3) In subsection (2), 'postal operator' has the meaning given by section 125(1) of the Postal Services Act 2000 (c 26).

105 Review of order

(1) On the application of a relevant applicant the court that made a parenting order may, if it considers that it would be appropriate to do so—
(a) revoke the order; or
(b) vary the order by—
(i) deleting any of the requirements specified in the order;
(ii) adding a new requirement;
(iii) altering the period specified for the purpose of section 103(1)(b).
(2) In subsection (1), 'relevant applicant' means—
(a) the person specified in the order;
(b) the child in respect of whom the order was made;
(c) the local authority for the area in which the person specified in the order ordinarily resides.
(3) Before an application is made under subsection (1) by a local authority, it shall consult the Principal Reporter.
(4) Where an application under subsection (1) for the revocation or, as the case may be, variation, of a parenting order is refused, another such application by the same applicant under that subsection for revocation or, as the case may be, variation, may be made only with the consent of the court that made the order.
(5) Where the court that made a parenting order is satisfied that—
(a) the person specified in the order proposes to change, or has changed, the person's place of ordinary residence; and
(b) it is appropriate to make an order specifying the sheriff of another sheriffdom as the court that may entertain applications under subsection (1),
it may make such an order; and in such a case, this section shall be read as if references to the court that made the order were references to that sheriff.

106 Appeals

An interlocutor—
(a) varying, or refusing to vary a parenting order; or
(b) making a parenting order under section 13,
is an appealable interlocutor.

107 Failure to comply with order

(1) If the person specified in a parenting order fails without reasonable excuse to comply with—
(a) any requirement specified in the order; or
(b) any direction given under the order,

the person shall be guilty of an offence.

(2)   A person guilty of an offence under subsection (1) shall be liable on summary conviction to a fine not exceeding level 3 on the standard scale.

(3)   In determining the sentence to be imposed on a person guilty of an offence under subsection (1) a court shall take into consideration the welfare of any child in respect of whom the person is a parent.

General requirements

108   Procedural requirements

(1)   Before making, varying or revoking a parenting order, a court shall—

(a)   having regard to the age and maturity of the child, so far as practicable—

(i)   give the child an opportunity to indicate whether the child wishes to express views; and

(ii)   if the child so wishes, give the child an opportunity to express those views;

(b)   give the parent the opportunity to be heard;

(c)   obtain information about the family circumstances of the parent and the likely effect of the order on those circumstances.

(2)   Before making a parenting order, the court shall explain in ordinary language—

(a)   the effect of the order and of the requirements proposed to be included in it;

(b)   the consequences of failing to comply with the order;

(c)   the powers the court has under section 81; and

(d)   the entitlement of the parent to appeal against the making of the order.

(3)   Before varying or revoking a parenting order, the court shall explain in ordinary language the effect of the variation or, as the case may be, revocation.

(4)   Subsections (1A) and (1B) apply only where the parent is present in court.

(5)   Failure to comply with subsection (1A) or (1B) shall not affect the validity of the order made.

(6)   Without prejudice to the generality of subsection (1)(a), a child who is at least 12 years of age shall be presumed to be of sufficient age and maturity to form a view.

109   General considerations relating to making, varying and revoking order

(1)   Where a court is determining whether to make, vary or revoke a parenting order its paramount consideration shall be the welfare of the child.

(2)   Where a court is determining whether to make a parenting order it shall have regard to—

(a)   such views as the child has expressed in relation to that matter by virtue of paragraph (a) of subsection (1) of section 108;

(b)   the information obtained in relation to that matter by virtue of paragraph (c) of that subsection;

(c)   whether (and if so the extent to which) the parent has, at any time that appears to the court to be relevant, taken relevant voluntary steps; and

(d)   any other behaviour of the parent that appears to the court to be relevant.

(3)   Where a court is determining whether to vary or revoke a parenting order it shall have regard to—

(a)   such views as the child has expressed in relation to that matter by virtue of paragraph (a) of subsection (1) of section 108;

(b)   the information obtained in relation to that matter by virtue of paragraph (c) of that subsection; and

(c)   any behaviour of the parent that appears to the court to be relevant.

(4)   In subsection (2)(c) 'relevant voluntary steps' means—

(a)   where the court is determining whether to—

(i)   make a parenting order under section 13; or

(ii)   make a parenting order under subsection (1) of section 102 in respect
of the condition mentioned in subsection (4) of that section,
voluntary steps intended to be in the interests of preventing the child from
engaging in antisocial behaviour;

(b)   where the court is determining whether to make a parenting order under
subsection (1) of section 102 in respect of the condition mentioned in subsection
(5) of that section, voluntary steps intended to be in the interests of preventing
the child from engaging in criminal conduct;

(c)   where the court is determining whether to make a parenting order under
subsection (1) of section 102 in respect of the condition mentioned in subsection
(6) of that section, voluntary steps intended to be in the interests of improving
the welfare of the child.

110   Account to be taken of religion, work and education

(1)   A court shall ensure that the requirements of a parenting order made by it
avoid, so far as practicable—

(a)   any conflict with the religious beliefs of the person specified in the order; and

(b)   any interference with times at which that person normally works (or
carries out voluntary work) or attends an educational establishment.

(2)   The supervising officer appointed by a local authority in respect of a
parenting order shall ensure that the directions given by the officer avoid, so far as
practicable, the matters mentioned in subsection (1)(a) and (b).

Miscellaneous

111   Restriction on reporting proceedings relating to parenting orders

(1)   Subject to subsection (2), a person shall be guilty of an offence if the person
publishes, anywhere in the world, any matter in respect of relevant proceedings
which is intended, or likely to, identify—

(a)   the parent concerned in the proceedings (the 'person concerned');

(b)   any address as being that of the person concerned;

(c)   the child concerned in the proceedings;

(d)   any other child—

(i)   who is a member of the same household as the person concerned; or

(ii)   of whom the person concerned is a parent; or

(e)   any—

(i)   address; or

(ii)   school,

as being that of a child mentioned in paragraph (c) or (d).

(2)   In relevant proceedings, the court may, in the interests of justice, order that
subsection (1) shall not apply to the proceedings to such extent as the court considers appropriate.

(3)   A person guilty of an offence under subsection (1) shall be liable on
summary conviction to a fine not exceeding level 4 on the standard scale.

(4)   It shall be a defence for a person charged with an offence under subsection
(1) to show that the person—

(a)   did not know; and

(b)   had no reason to suspect,

that the published matter was intended, or was likely, to identify the person concerned, child, address or school (as the case may be).

(5)   Section 46 of the Children and Young Persons (Scotland) Act 1937 (c 37)
shall apply in relation to relevant proceedings only in respect of a person concerned in the proceedings as a witness.

(6)   A child in whose interests a parenting order has been made shall be regarded as a person who falls within subsection (1)(a) of section 47 of the Criminal
Procedure (Scotland) Act 1995 (c 46) for the purposes of that section in its

application to proceedings in respect of the commission of an offence under section 83(1) in respect of that order.

(7) In this section—

'programme service' has the meaning given by section 201 of the Broadcasting Act 1990 (c 42);

'publishes' includes—

(a) causing to be published; and

(b) publishing in a programme service,

and 'published' shall be construed accordingly; and

'relevant proceedings' means—

(a) proceedings before a sheriff for the purpose of considering whether to make a parenting order under section 13(1);

(b) proceedings before a sheriff on an application for the making of a parenting order under section 102(1);

(c) proceedings before a sheriff on an application for the variation, or revocation, of a parenting order under section 105(1);

(d) proceedings before a sheriff for the purpose of considering whether to make an order under section 105(5);

(e) an appeal arising from proceedings such as are mentioned in paragraphs (a) to (d).

112 Conduct of proceedings by reporters

(1) The Scottish Ministers may by regulations empower a reporter, whether or not the reporter is an advocate or solicitor, to conduct proceedings—

(a) before a sheriff—

(i) on an application by the Principal Reporter for the making of a parenting order;

(ii) on an application for the variation, or revocation, of a parenting order made on the application of the Principal Reporter, under section 105(1); or

(iii) for the purpose of considering whether to make an order under section 105(5) in respect of a parenting order made on the application of the Principal Reporter; or

(b) before [the Sheriff Appeal Court], on any appeal arising from proceedings such as are mentioned in paragraph (a).

(2) Regulations under subsection (1) may prescribe such requirements as the Scottish Ministers think fit as to—

(a) qualifications;

(b) training; or

(c) experience,

necessary for a reporter to be so empowered.

(3) In this section 'reporter' means—

(a) the Principal Reporter; and

(b) any [person employed by the Scottish Children's Reporter Administration to whom there is delegated, under paragraph 10 of schedule 3 to the Children's Hearings (Scotland) Act 2011 (asp 1), any function of the Principal Reporter.]

113 Initial investigations by Principal Reporter

(1) For the purpose of determining whether to make an application for the making of a parenting order under section 102, the Principal Reporter may make such investigations as the Principal Reporter considers appropriate.

(2) On a request made by the Principal Reporter for the purpose mentioned in subsection (1), a local authority shall supply to the Principal Reporter a report on—

(a) the child in relation to whom the Principal Reporter is determining whether to make the application;

(b)   the parent in relation to whom the Principal Reporter is determining whether to make the application; and

(c)   such circumstances concerning—

(i)   the child; and

(ii)   the parent,

as appear to the Principal Reporter to be relevant.

114   Power of court to direct reporter to consider application for parenting order
Where, in any proceedings (other than proceedings under section 4 or 102), it appears to a court that it might be appropriate for a parenting order to be made in respect of a parent of a child, the court may require the Principal Reporter to consider whether to apply under section 102 for such an order.

115   Guidance about parenting orders
A person (other than a court) shall, in discharging functions by virtue of section 13 or this Part, have regard to any guidance given by the Scottish Ministers about—

(a)   the discharge of those functions; and

(b)   matters arising in connection with the discharge of those functions.

[. . .]

Interpretation

117   Interpretation of Part 9
In this Part—

'child' means a person who is under the age of 16 years;

['parent' means—

(a)   any parent enjoying parental responsibilities or parental rights under Part 1 of the Children (Scotland) Act 1995,

(b)   any individual in whom parental responsibilities or parental rights are vested by, under or by virtue of that Act,

(c)   any individual in whom parental responsibilities or parental rights are vested by, under or by virtue of a permanence order (as defined in section 80(2) of the Adoption and Children (Scotland) Act 2007), and

(d)   any individual who appears to be an individual who ordinarily (and other than by reason only of the individual's employment) has charge of, or control over, the child;]

'parenting order' has the meaning given by section 103(1).

GENDER RECOGNITION ACT 2004
(2004, c 7)

Applications for gender recognition certificate

1   Applications
(1)   A person of either gender who is aged at least 18 may make an application for a gender recognition certificate on the basis of—

(a)   living in the other gender, or

(b)   having changed gender under the law of a country or territory outside the United Kingdom.

(2)   In this Act 'the acquired gender', in relation to a person by whom an application under subsection (1) is or has been made, means—

(a)   in the case of an application under paragraph (a) of that subsection, the gender in which the person is living, or

(b)   in the case of an application under paragraph (b) of that subsection, the gender to which the person has changed under the law of the country or territory concerned.

(3)   An application under subsection (1) is to be determined by a Gender Recognition Panel.

(4)   Schedule 1 (Gender Recognition Panels) has effect.

2   Determination of applications

(1)   In the case of an application under section 1(1)(a), the Panel must grant the application if satisfied that the applicant—

(a)   has or has had gender dysphoria,

(b)   has lived in the acquired gender throughout the period of two years ending with the date on which the application is made,

(c)   intends to continue to live in the acquired gender until death, and

(d)   complies with the requirements imposed by and under section 3.

(2)   In the case of an application under section 1(1)(b), the Panel must grant the application if satisfied—

(a)   that the country or territory under the law of which the applicant has changed gender is an approved country or territory, and

(b)   that the applicant complies with the requirements imposed by and under section 3.

(3)   The Panel must reject an application under section 1(1) if not required by subsection (1) or (2) to grant it.

[(3A)   This section does not apply to an application under section 1(1)(a) which states that it is an application for a certificate to be granted in accordance with section 3A.]

[(3B)   This section does not apply to an application under section 1(1)(a) which states that it is an application for a certificate to be granted in accordance with section 3C.]

[(3C)   This section does not apply to an application under section 1(1)(a) which states that it is an application for a certificate to be granted in accordance with section 3E.]

(4)   In this Act 'approved country or territory' means a country or territory prescribed by order made by the Secretary of State after consulting the Scottish Ministers and the Department of Finance and Personnel in Northern Ireland.

3   Evidence

(1)   An application under section 1(1)(a) must include either—

(a)   a report made by a registered medical practitioner practising in the field of gender dysphoria and a report made by another registered medical practitioner (who may, but need not, practise in that field), or

(b)   a report made by a [registered psychologist] practising in that field and a report made by a registered medical practitioner (who may, but need not, practise in that field).

(2)   But subsection (1) is not complied with unless a report required by that subsection and made by—

(a)   a registered medical practitioner, or

(b)   a [registered] psychologist,

practising in the field of gender dysphoria includes details of the diagnosis of the applicant's gender dysphoria.

(3)   And subsection (1) is not complied with in a case where—

(a)   the applicant has undergone or is undergoing treatment for the purpose of modifying sexual characteristics, or

(b)   treatment for that purpose has been prescribed or planned for the applicant,

unless at least one of the reports required by that subsection includes details of it.

(4)   An application under section 1(1)(a) must also include a statutory

declaration by the applicant that the applicant meets the conditions in section 2(1)(b) and (c).

(5) An application under section 1(1)(b) must include evidence that the applicant has changed gender under the law of an approved country or territory.

(6) Any application under section 1(1) must include—

(a) a statutory declaration as to whether or not the applicant is married [or a civil partner],

(b) any other information or evidence required by an order made by the Secretary of State, and

(c) any other information or evidence which the Panel which is to determine the application may require,

and may include any other information or evidence which the applicant wishes to include.

[(6A) If the applicant is married, an application under section 1(1) must include a statutory declaration as to whether the marriage is a marriage under the law of England and Wales, of Scotland, of Northern Ireland, or of a country or territory outside the United Kingdom.

[(6AA) If the applicant is a civil partner, an application under section 1(1) must include a statutory declaration as to whether the civil partnership is a civil partnership under the law of England and Wales, of Scotland or of Northern Ireland, or is an overseas relationship that is treated as a civil partnership by virtue of Chapter 2 of Part 5 of the Civil Partnership Act 2004.]

[(6B) If the applicant is married [or a civil partner], and the marriage [or civil partnership] is a protected marriage [or a protected civil partnership], an application under section 1(1) must also include—

(a) a statutory declaration by the applicant's spouse [or civil partner] that the spouse [or partner] consents to the marriage [or partnership] after the issue of a full gender recognition certificate ('a statutory declaration of consent') (if the spouse [or partner] has made such a declaration), or

(b) a statutory declaration by the applicant that the applicant's spouse [or civil partner] has not made a statutory declaration of consent (if that is the case).

(6C) If an application includes a statutory declaration of consent by the applicant's spouse [or civil partner], the Gender Recognition Panel must give the spouse [or partner] notice that the application has been made.]

[(6D) If the applicant is a party to a protected Scottish marriage, an application under section 1(1) must also include—

(a) a statutory declaration by the applicant that the applicant wishes the marriage to continue after the issue of a full gender recognition certificate (if that is the case), and

(b) either—

(i) a statutory declaration by the applicant's spouse that the spouse consents to the marriage continuing after the issue of a full gender recognition certificate ('a statutory declaration of consent') (if the spouse has made such a declaration), or

(ii) a statutory declaration by the applicant that no such declaration by the applicant's spouse is included.

(6E) If an application includes a statutory declaration of consent by the applicant's spouse under subsection (6D)(b)(i), the Gender Recognition Panel must give the spouse notice that the application has been made.

(6F) If the applicant is a party to a protected Scottish civil partnership, an application under section 1(1) must also include a statutory declaration as to where the civil partnership was registered and, if the civil partnership was registered outside the United Kingdom, that details of the civil partnership have been sent to the Registrar General for Scotland.]

[(6G) If the applicant is a party to a protected Scottish civil partnership, an application under section 1(1) must also include—

(a)   a statutory declaration by the applicant that the applicant wishes the civil partnership to continue after the issue of a full gender recognition certificate (if that is the case), and

(b)   either—

(i)   a statutory declaration by the applicant's civil partner that the civil partner consents to the civil partnership continuing after the issue of a full gender recognition certificate ('a statutory declaration of consent') (if the civil partner has made such a declaration), or

(ii)   a statutory declaration by the applicant that no such declaration by the applicant's civil partner is included.

(6H)   If an application includes a statutory declaration of consent by the applicant's civil partner under subsection (6G)(b)(i), the Gender Recognition Panel must give the civil partner notice that the application has been made.]

(7)   The Secretary of State may not make an order under subsection (6)(b) without consulting the Scottish Ministers and the Department of Finance and Personnel in Northern Ireland.

(8)   If the Panel which is to determine the application requires information or evidence under subsection (6)(c) it must give reasons for doing so.

[(9)   This section does not apply to an application under section 1(1)(a) which states that it is an application for a certificate to be granted in accordance with section 3A.]

[(10)   This section does not apply to an application under section 1(1)(a) which states that it is an application for a certificate to be granted in accordance with section 3C.]

[(11)   This section does not apply to an application under section (1)(1)(a) which states that it is an application for a certificate to be granted in accordance with section 3E.]

[3A   Alternative grounds for granting applications

(1)   This section applies to an application under section 1(1)(a) which states that it is an application for a certificate to be granted in accordance with this section.

(2)   The Panel must grant the application if satisfied that the applicant complies with the requirements imposed by and under section 3B and meets the conditions in subsections (3) to (6).

(3)   The first condition is that the applicant was a party to a protected marriage or a protected civil partnership on or before the date the application was made.

(4)   The second condition is that the applicant—

(a)   was living in the acquired gender six years before the commencement of section 12 of the Marriage (Same Sex Couples) Act 2013,

(b)   continued to live in the acquired gender until the date the application was made, and

(c)   intends to continue to live in the acquired gender until death.

(5)   The third condition is that the applicant—

(a)   has or has had gender dysphoria, or

(b)   has undergone surgical treatment for the purpose of modifying sexual characteristics.

(6)   The fourth condition is that the applicant is ordinarily resident in England, Wales or Scotland.

(7)   The Panel must reject the application if not required by subsection (2) to grant it.]

[(8)   Where the applicant—

(a)   is a party to a protected marriage under the law of Northern Ireland, or

(b)   is a party to a protected civil partnership that is a civil partnership under the law of Northern Ireland, or

(c)   is ordinarily resident in Northern Ireland,

subsection (4)(a) has effect as for the words after 'was living in the acquired gender' there were substituted 'on 13 January 2014'.]

[3B Evidence for granting applications on alternative grounds
(1) This section applies to an application under section 1(1)(a) which states that it is an application for a certificate to be granted in accordance with section 3A.
(2) The application must include either—
(a) a report made by a registered medical practitioner, or
(b) a report made by a registered psychologist practising in the field of gender dysphoria.
(3) If the application is based on the applicant having or having had gender dysphoria—
(a) the reference in subsection (2) to a registered medical practitioner is to one practising in the field of gender dysphoria, and
(b) that subsection is not complied with unless the report includes details of the diagnosis of the applicant's gender dysphoria.
(4) Subsection (2) is not complied with in a case where—
(a) the applicant has undergone or is undergoing treatment for the purpose of modifying sexual characteristics, or
(b) treatment for that purpose has been prescribed or planned for the applicant,
unless the report required by that subsection includes details of it.
(5) The application must also include a statutory declaration by the applicant that the applicant meets the conditions in section 3A(3) and (4).
(6) The application must include—
(a) a statutory declaration as to whether or not the applicant is married or a civil partner,
(b) any other information or evidence required by an order made by the Secretary of State, and
(c) any other information or evidence which the Panel which is to determine the application may require,
and may include any other information or evidence which the applicant wishes to include.
(7) If the applicant is married, the application must include a statutory declaration as to whether the marriage is a marriage under the law of England and Wales, of Scotland, of Northern Ireland, or of a country or territory outside the United Kingdom.
[(7A) If the applicant is a civil partner, the application must include a statutory declaration as to whether the civil partnership is a civil partnership under the law of England and Wales, of Scotland, or of Northern Ireland, or is an overseas relationship that is treated as a civil partnership by virtue of Chapter 2 of Part 5 of the Civil Partnership Act 2004.]
(8) If the applicant is married [or a civil partner], and the marriage [or civil partnership] is a protected marriage [or a protected civil partnership], the application must also include—
(a) a statutory declaration of consent by the applicant's spouse [or civil partner] (if the spouse [or partner] has made such a declaration), or
(b) a statutory declaration by the applicant that the applicant's spouse [or civil partner] has not made a statutory declaration of consent (if that is the case).
(9) If the application includes a statutory declaration of consent by the applicant's spouse [or civil partner], the Panel must give the spouse [or partner] notice that the application has been made.
(10) If the Panel which is to determine the application requires information or evidence under subsection (6)(c) it must give reasons for doing so.]

[3C   Alternative grounds for granting applications: Scotland

(1)   This section applies to an application under section 1(1)(a) which states that it is an application for a certificate to be granted in accordance with this section.

(2)   The Panel must grant the application if satisfied that the applicant complies with the requirements imposed by and under section 3D and meets the conditions in subsections (3) to (6).

(3)   The first condition is that the applicant was a party to a protected Scottish marriage or a protected Scottish civil partnership on or before the date the application was made.

(4)   The second condition is that the applicant—

(a)   was living in the acquired gender six years before the commencement of section 29 of the Marriage and Civil Partnership (Scotland) Act 2014,

(b)   continued to live in the acquired gender until the date the application was made, and

(c)   intends to continue to live in the acquired gender until death.

(5)   The third condition is that the applicant—

(a)   has or has had gender dysphoria, or

(b)   has undergone—

(i)   surgical treatment, or

(ii)   such other treatment as the Scottish Ministers may by order prescribe,

for the purpose of modifying sexual characteristics.

(6)   The fourth condition is that the applicant is ordinarily resident in Scotland.

(7)   Before making an order under subsection (5)(b)(ii) the Scottish Ministers must consult the following persons on a copy of the proposed draft order—

(a)   the Gender Recognition Panel,

(b)   such other persons as the Scottish Ministers consider appropriate.

(8)   An order under subsection (5)(b)(ii)—

(a)   may make different provision for different cases or circumstances,

(b)   may amend any enactment (including this Act).

(9)   The Panel must reject the application if not required by subsection (2) to grant it.]

[3D   Evidence for granting applications on alternative grounds: Scotland

(1)   This section applies to an application under section 1(1)(a) which states that it is an application for a certificate to be granted in accordance with section 3C.

(2)   The application must include either—

(a)   a report made by a registered medical practitioner, or

(b)   a report made by a registered psychologist practising in the field of gender dysphoria.

(3)   If the application is based on the applicant having or having had gender dysphoria—

(a)   the reference in subsection (2) to a registered medical practitioner is to one practising in the field of gender dysphoria, and

(b)   that subsection is not complied with unless the report includes details of the diagnosis of the applicant's gender dysphoria.

(4)   Subsection (2) is not complied with in a case where—

(a)   the applicant has undergone or is undergoing treatment for the purpose of modifying sexual characteristics, or

(b)   treatment for that purpose has been prescribed or planned for the applicant,

unless the report required by that subsection includes details of it.

(5)   The application must also include a statutory declaration by the applicant that the applicant meets the conditions in section 3C(3) and (4).

(6)   The application must include—

(a)   a statutory declaration as to whether or not the applicant is married or a civil partner,

(b)   any other information or evidence required by an order made by the Scottish Ministers, and

(c)   any other information or evidence which the Panel which is to determine the application may require,

and may include any other information or evidence which the applicant wishes to include.

[(7)   If the applicant is—

(a)   married, the application must include a statutory declaration as to whether the marriage is a protected Scottish marriage,

(b)   a party to a civil partnership, the application must include a statutory declaration as to whether the civil partnership is a protected Scottish civil partnership.]

(8)   If the applicant is married, and the marriage is a protected Scottish marriage, the application must also include—

(a)   a statutory declaration of consent (within the meaning of section 3(6D)(b)(i)) by the applicant's spouse (if the spouse has made such a declaration), or

(b)   a statutory declaration by the applicant that no such declaration by the applicant's spouse is included.

[(8A)   If the applicant is a party to a protected Scottish civil partnership, the application must also include—

(a)   a statutory declaration of consent (within the meaning of section 3(6G)(b) (i)) by the applicant's civil partner (if the civil partner has made such a declaration), or

(b)   a statutory declaration by the applicant that no such declaration by the applicant's civil partner is included.]

(9)   If the application includes a statutory declaration of consent by the applicant's spouse [or (as the case may be) civil partner], the Panel must give the spouse [or civil partner] notice that the application has been made.

(10)   If the Panel which is to determine the application requires information or evidence under subsection (6)(c) it must give reasons for doing so.']

4   Successful applications

(1)   If a Gender Recognition Panel grants an application under section 1(1) it must issue a gender recognition certificate to the applicant.

[(1A)   The certificate is to be a full gender recognition certificate if the applicant is neither married nor in a civil partnership.]

[(2)   The certificate is [also] to be a full gender recognition certificate if—

[. . .]

(b)   the applicant is a party to a protected marriage and the applicant's spouse consents to the marriage continuing after the issue of a full gender recognition certificate, or

(c)   the applicant is a party to a protected civil partnership and [the applicant's civil partner consents to the civil partnership continuing after the issue of a full gender recognition certificate].

(3)   The certificate is to be an interim gender recognition certificate if—

(a)   the applicant is a party to a protected marriage and the applicant's spouse does not consent to the marriage continuing after the issue of a full gender recognition certificate,

(b)   [subject to subsection (3C)(a),] the applicant is a party to a marriage that is not a protected marriage,

(c)   the applicant is a party to a protected civil partnership and the other party to the civil partnership [does not consent to the civil partnership continuing after the issue of a full gender recognition certificate, or]

[. . .]

(e)   [subject to subsection [(3C)(c)],] the applicant is a party to a civil partnership that is not a protected civil partnership.

[(3A)   If a Gender Recognition Panel issues a full gender recognition certificate under this section to an applicant who is a party to a protected marriage [or a protected civil partnership], the Panel must give the applicant's spouse [or civil partner] notice of the issue of the certificate.]

[. . .]

[(3C)   The certificate is also to be a full gender recognition certificate if—

(a)   the applicant is a party to a protected Scottish marriage and both parties to the marriage consent to the marriage continuing after the issue of a full gender recognition certificate, or

[. . .]

(c)   the applicant is a party to a protected Scottish civil partnership and both parties to the partnership consent to it continuing after the issue of a full gender recognition certificate.

(3D)   The certificate is to be an interim gender recognition certificate if—

(a)   the applicant is a party to a protected Scottish marriage and either party to the marriage does not consent to the marriage continuing after the issue of a full gender recognition certificate,

(b)   subject to subsection (2)(b), the applicant is a party to a marriage which is not a protected Scottish marriage,

(ba)   the applicant is a party to a protected Scottish civil partnership and either party to the partnership does not consent to it continuing after the issue of a full gender recognition certificate,

[. . .], or

(e)   subject to subsection (2)(c), the applicant is a party to a civil partnership which is not a protected Scottish civil partnership.

(3E)   If a Gender Recognition Panel issues a full gender recognition certificate under this section to an applicant who is a party to a protected Scottish marriage, the Panel must give the applicant's spouse notice of the issue of the certificate.

[(3EA)   If a Gender Recognition Panel issues a full gender recognition certificate under this section to an applicant who is a party to a protected Scottish civil partnership, the Panel must give the applicant's civil partner notice of the issue of the certificate.]

[. . .]

(4)   Schedule 2 (annulment or dissolution of marriage after issue of interim gender recognition certificate) has effect.

(5)   The Secretary of State may, after consulting the Scottish Ministers and the Department of Finance and Personnel in Northern Ireland, specify the content and form of gender recognition certificates.

[Issue of full certificate after interim certificate: applicant married [or a civil partner]]

[4A   Married person [or civil partner] with interim certificate: issue of full certificate

(1)   A Gender Recognition Panel must issue a full gender recognition certificate to a person [if subsection (2) applies].

(2)   [This subsection applies if], on an application by the person, the Panel is satisfied that—

(a)   an interim gender recognition certificate has been issued to the person;

(b)   the person was a party to a protected marriage [or a protected civil partnership] at the time when the interim gender recognition certificate was issued;

(c)   the person is a party to a protected marriage [or a protected civil partnership]; and

(d)   the person's spouse [or civil partner] now consents to the marriage [or civil partnership] continuing after the issue of the full gender recognition certificate.

[. . .]

(4)   If, on an application under subsection (2) [. . .], the Panel is not satisfied as mentioned in that subsection, the Panel must reject the application.

(5)   An application under subsection (2) must be made within the period of six months beginning with the day on which the interim gender recognition certificate is issued.

[. . .]

(7)   An application under subsection (2) [. . .] must include a statutory declaration of consent made by the person's spouse [or civil partner].

[. . .]

(9)   If an application is made under [subsection (2)], the Gender Recognition Panel must give the applicant's spouse [or civil partner]—

(a)   notice of the application; and

(b)   if the Panel grants the application, notice of the issue of the full gender recognition certificate.]

[. . .]

[4B   Application under section 4A: death of spouse [or civil partner]

(1)   In a case where an application is made under section 4A(2) [. . .] and the applicant's spouse [or civil partner] dies before the application is determined—

(a)   the application is to be treated as an application, made under section 5(2) in a case where a spouse has died [or under section 5A(2) in a case where a civil partner has died], for a full gender recognition certificate to be issued; and

(b)   that application is to be treated as having been made at the time when the application under section 4A was made.

(2)   The Gender Recognition Panel determining the application must specify the period within which the applicant is to produce the required evidence in support of the new application.

(3)   In this section—

'new application' means the application under section 5(2) [or (as the case may be) section 5A(2)] which the person is, by virtue of subsection (1), treated as having made;

'required evidence' means the evidence required by section 5(4) [or (as the case may be) section 5A(4).]

[4C   Married person [or civil partner] with interim certificate: issue of full certificate (Scotland)

(1)   A Gender Recognition Panel must issue a full gender recognition certificate to a person [if, on an application by the person ('the applicant'), the Panel is satisfied that the conditions set out in subsection (1A) are met].

[(1A)   The conditions referred to in subsection (1) are—

(a)   an interim gender recognition certificate has been issued to the applicant,

(b)   when the interim gender recognition certificate was issued, the applicant and another person ('P') were the parties to—

(i)   a protected Scottish marriage, or

(ii)   a protected Scottish civil partnership,

(c)   the applicant and P are still, or have since become, the parties to—

(i)   a protected Scottish marriage, or

(ii)   a protected Scottish civil partnership, and

(d)   P consents to the marriage or civil partnership continuing after the issue of a full gender recognition certificate.]

[. . .]

(4)   If, on an application under subsection (1), the Panel is not satisfied as mentioned in that subsection, the Panel must reject the application.

(5)   An application under subsection (1) must be made within the period of six

months beginning with the day on which the interim gender recognition certificate is issued.

[. . .]

(7)　An application under subsection (1) must include a statutory declaration of consent (within the meaning of section 3(6D)(b)(i) [or (6G)(b)(i)]) made by the person's spouse [or (as the case may be) civil partner].

[. . .]

(9)　If an application is made under this section, the Panel must give the applicant's spouse [or (as the case may be) civil partner]—

(a)　notice of the application, and

(b)　if the Panel grants the application, notice of the issue of the full gender recognition certificate.]

[4D　Application under section 4C: death of spouse [or civil partner]

(1)　In a case where an application is made under section [4C] and the applicant's spouse [or (as the case may be) civil partner] dies before the application is determined—

(a)　the application is to be treated as an application, made under section 5(2) in a case where a spouse [or civil partner] has died, for a full gender recognition certificate to be issued, and

(b)　that application is to be treated as having been made at the time when the application under section 4C was made.

(2)　The Gender Recognition Panel determining the application must specify the period within which the applicant is to produce the required evidence in support of the new application.

(3)　In this section—

'new application' means the application under section 5(2) which the person is, by virtue of subsection (1), treated as having made,

'required evidence' means the evidence required by section 5(4).]

[4E　Married person [or civil partner] with interim certificate: issue of full certificate on application to the sheriff (Scotland)

(1)　A person may make a summary application to the sheriff for the issue of a full gender recognition certificate where—

(a)　an interim gender recognition certificate has been issued to the person,

[(b)　the person and another person ('P') are the parties to—

(i)　a protected Scottish marriage, or

(ii)　a protected Scottish civil partnership,]

(c)　the person is not in possession of a statutory declaration by [P] that [P] consents to the marriage [or (as the case may be) civil partnership] continuing after the issue of a full gender recognition certificate.

(2)　The sheriff must grant an application made under subsection (1) if the sheriff is satisfied that—

[(a)　at the time when the interim gender recognition certificate was issued, the applicant and P were the parties to—

(i)　a protected Scottish marriage, or

(ii)　a protected Scottish civil partnership,

(b)　the applicant and P are still, or have since become, the parties to—

(i)　a protected Scottish marriage, or

(ii)　a protected Scottish civil partnership,] and

(c)　the application was made within the period of six months beginning with the day on which the interim gender recognition certificate was issued.

(3)　If an application is made under this section, the sheriff must give the applicant's spouse [or (as the case may be) civil partner]—

(a)　notice of the application, and

(b)　if the sheriff grants the application, notice of the issue of the full gender recognition certificate.

(4)   Where the sheriff issues a full gender recognition certificate, the sheriff must send a copy to the Gender Recognition Panel.]

[. . .]

5   [Issue of full certificates where applicant has been married]

(1)   A court which—

(a)   makes absolute a decree of nullity granted on the ground that an interim gender recognition certificate has been issued to a party to the marriage, or

(b)   (in Scotland) grants a decree of divorce on that ground, must, on doing so, issue a full gender recognition certificate to that party and send a copy to the Secretary of State.

[(1A)   Subsection (1) does not apply where a full gender recognition certificate has already been issued, to the party to whom the interim gender recognition certificate was issued, by the sheriff under section 4E.]

(2)   If an interim gender recognition certificate has been issued to a person and either—

(a)   the person's marriage is dissolved or annulled (otherwise than on the ground mentioned in subsection (1)) in proceedings instituted during the period of six months beginning with the day on which it was issued, or

(b)   the person's spouse dies within that period,

the person may make an application for a full gender recognition certificate at any time within the period specified in subsection (3) (unless the person is again married [or is a civil partner]).

(3)   That period is the period of six months beginning with the day on which the marriage is dissolved or annulled or the death occurs.

(4)   An application under subsection (2) must include evidence of the dissolution or annulment of the marriage and the date on which proceedings for it were instituted, or of the death of the spouse and the date on which it occurred.

(5)   An application under subsection (2) is to be determined by a Gender Recognition Panel.

(6)   The Panel—

(a)   must grant the application if satisfied that the applicant [is neither married nor a civil partner], and

(b)   otherwise must reject it.

(7)   If the Panel grants the application it must issue a full gender recognition certificate to the applicant.

[5A   Issue of full certificates where applicant has been a civil partner

(1)   A court which—

(a)   makes final a nullity order made on the ground that an interim gender recognition certificate has been issued to a civil partner, or

(b)   (in Scotland) grants a decree of dissolution on that ground,

must, on doing so, issue a full gender recognition certificate to that civil partner and send a copy to the Secretary of State.

[(1A)   Subsection (1) does not apply where a full gender recognition certificate has already been issued, to the party to whom the interim gender recognition certificate was issued, by the sheriff under section 4E.]

(2)   If an interim gender recognition certificate has been issued to a person and either—

(a)   the person's civil partnership is dissolved or annulled (otherwise than on the ground mentioned in subsection (1)) in proceedings instituted during the period of six months beginning with the day on which it was issued, or

(b)   the person's civil partner dies within that period,

the person may make an application for a full gender recognition certificate at any time within the period specified in subsection (3) (unless the person is again a civil partner or is married).

(3)   That period is the period of six months beginning with the day on which the civil partnership is dissolved or annulled or the death occurs.

(4)   An application under subsection (2) must include evidence of the dissolution or annulment of the civil partnership and the date on which proceedings for it were instituted, or of the death of the civil partner and the date on which it occurred.

(5)   An application under subsection (2) is to be determined by a Gender Recognition Panel.

(6)   The Panel—

(a)   must grant the application if satisfied that the applicant is neither a civil partner nor married, and

(b)   otherwise must reject it.

(7)   If the Panel grants the application it must issue a full gender recognition certificate to the applicant.]

[Other provision about applications and certificates

[. . .]

6 [Errors]

[(1)   Where a gender recognition certificate has been issued to a person, the person or the Secretary of State may make an application for—

(a)   an interim gender recognition certificate, on the ground that a full gender recognition certificate has incorrectly been issued instead of an interim certificate;

(b)   a full gender recognition certificate, on the ground that an interim gender recognition certificate has incorrectly been issued instead of a full certificate; or

(c)   a corrected certificate, on the ground that the certificate which has been issued contains an error.]

(2)   If the certificate was issued by a court the application is to be determined by the court but in any other case it is to be determined by a Gender Recognition Panel.

(3)   The court or Panel—

(a)   [must grant the application if satisfied that the ground on which the application is made is correct, and]

(b)   otherwise must reject it.

(4)   If the court or Panel grants the application it must issue [a correct, or a corrected] gender recognition certificate to the applicant.

7 Applications: supplementary

(1)   An application to a Gender Recognition Panel under section 1(1), [4A, 4C, [. . .],] 5(2)[, 5A(2)] or 6(1) must be made in a form and manner specified by the Secretary of State after consulting the Scottish Ministers and the Department of Finance and Personnel in Northern Ireland.

(2)   The applicant must pay to the Secretary of State a non-refundable fee of an amount prescribed by order made by the Secretary of State unless the application is made in circumstances in which, in accordance with provision made by the order, no fee is payable; and fees of different amounts may be prescribed for different circumstances.

8 Appeals etc

(1)   An applicant to a Gender Recognition Panel under section 1(1), [4A, 4C, [. . .],] 5(2)[, 5A(2)] or 6(1) may appeal to the High Court[, family court] or Court of Session on a point of law against a decision by the Panel to reject the application.

(2)   An appeal under subsection (1) must be heard in private if the applicant so requests.

(3)   On such an appeal the court must—
    (a)   allow the appeal and issue the certificate applied for,
    (b)   allow the appeal and refer the matter to the same or another Panel for re-
consideration, or
    (c)   dismiss the appeal.
(4)   If an application under section 1(1) is rejected, the applicant may not make
another application before the end of the period of six months beginning with the
date on which it is rejected.
(5)   If an application under section 1(1), [4A, 4C, 4E, [. . .],] 5(2)[, 5A(2)] or 6(1)
is granted but the Secretary of State considers that its grant was secured by fraud,
the Secretary of State may refer the case to the High Court [, family court] or Court
of Session.
    [(5A)   If an application under section 1(1), 4A, 5(2), 5A(2) or 6(1) is granted, the
applicant's spouse [or civil partner] may apply to the High Court or Court of Session to quash the decision to grant the application on the grounds that its grant
was secured by fraud.]
    [(5B)   If an application under section 1(1), 4C, 4E, [. . .], 5(2), 5A(2) or 6(1) is
granted, the applicant's spouse or civil partner may apply to the Court of Session
to quash the decision to grant the application on the grounds that its grant was
secured by fraud.]
(6)   On a reference under subsection (5) [or an application under subsection
(5B)] the court—
    (a)   must either quash or confirm the decision to grant the application, and
    (b)   if it quashes it, must revoke the gender recognition certificate issued on
the grant of the application and may make any order which it considers appropriate in consequence of, or otherwise in connection with, doing so.

Consequences of issue of gender recognition certificate etc

9   General
(1)   Where a full gender recognition certificate is issued to a person, the person's gender becomes for all purposes the acquired gender (so that, if the acquired
gender is the male gender, the person's sex becomes that of a man and, if it is the
female gender, the person's sex becomes that of a woman).
(2)   Subsection (1) does not affect things done, or events occurring, before the
certificate is issued; but it does operate for the interpretation of enactments passed,
and instruments and other documents made, before the certificate is issued (as
well as those passed or made afterwards).
(3)   Subsection (1) is subject to provision made by this Act or any other enactment or any subordinate legislation.

10   Registration
(1)   Where there is a UK birth register entry in relation to a person to whom a
full gender recognition certificate is issued, the Secretary of State must send a copy
of the certificate to the appropriate Registrar General.
    [(1A)   Where a full gender recognition certificate is issued to a person who is a
party to—
    (a)   a marriage under the law of England and Wales, or
    (b)   a civil partnership under that law,
the Secretary of State must send a copy of the certificate to the Registrar General
for England and Wales.]
    [(1B)   Where a full gender recognition certificate is issued by a Gender Recogni-
tion Panel or the sheriff to a person who is a party to a protected Scottish marriage
or a protected Scottish civil partnership, the Panel must send a copy of the certificate to the Registrar General for Scotland.]
    [(1C)   Where a full gender recognition certificate is issued to a person who is a
party to—

(a)   a marriage under the law of Northern Ireland, or

(b)   a civil partnership under the law of Northern Ireland,

the Secretary of State must send a copy of the certificate to the Registrar General
for Northern Ireland.]

(2)   In this Act 'UK birth register entry', in relation to a person to whom a full
gender recognition certificate is issued, means—

(a)   an entry of which a certified copy is kept by a Registrar General, or

(b)   an entry in a register so kept,

containing a record of the person's birth or adoption (or, if there would otherwise
be more than one, the most recent).

(3)   'The appropriate Registrar General' means whichever of—

(a)   the Registrar General for England and Wales,

(b)   the Registrar General for Scotland, or

(c)   the Registrar General for Northern Ireland,

keeps a certified copy of the person's UK birth register entry or the register containing that entry.

(4)   Schedule 3 (provisions about registration) has effect.

11   Marriage

Schedule 4 (amendments of marriage law) has effect.

[11A   Change in gender of party to marriage

(1)   This section applies in relation to a protected marriage if (by virtue of
section 4(2)(b) or 4A) a full gender recognition certificate is issued to a party to the
marriage.

(2)   The continuity of the protected marriage is not affected by the relevant
change in gender.

(3)   If the protected marriage is a foreign marriage—

(a)   the continuity of the marriage continues by virtue of subsection (2) notwithstanding any impediment under the proper law of the marriage;

(b)   the proper law of the marriage is not affected by its continuation by
virtue of subsection (2).

(4)   In this section—

'foreign marriage' means a marriage under the law of a country or territory outside the United Kingdom;

'impediment' means anything which affects the continuation of a marriage
merely by virtue of the relevant change in gender;

'proper law', in relation to a protected marriage, means the law of the country or
territory under which the marriage was entered into;

'relevant change in gender' means the change or changes of gender occurring by
virtue of the issue of the full gender recognition certificate or certificates.]

[11B   Change in gender of civil partner

(1)   This section applies in relation to a protected civil partnership if (by virtue
of section 4(2)(c) or 4A) a full gender recognition certificate is issued to a party to
the partnership.

(2)   The continuity of the protected civil partnership is not affected by the relevant change in gender.

(3)   If the protected civil partnership is a protected overseas relationship, the
continuity of the civil partnership continues by virtue of subsection (2) notwithstanding any impediment under the relevant law.

(4)   In this section—

'impediment' means anything which would affect the continuation of the overseas relationship merely by virtue of the relevant change in gender,

'relevant change in gender' means the change or changes in gender occurring by
virtue of the issue of the full gender recognition certificate or certificates,

'relevant law', in relation to the protected overseas relationship in question, has the same meaning as in Chapter 2 of Part 5 of the Civil Partnership Act 2004.]

[11C Continuity of marriage: Scotland

(1) This section applies in relation to a protected Scottish marriage if (by virtue of section 4(3C)(a), 4C or 4E) a full gender recognition certificate is issued to a party to the marriage.

(2) The continuity of the protected Scottish marriage is not affected by the issuing of a full gender recognition certificate.]

[11D Continuity of civil partnership: Scotland

The continuity of a protected Scottish civil partnership is not affected by the issuing of [a full gender recognition certificate to either (or both) of the civil partners.]]

12 Parenthood

The fact that a person's gender has become the acquired gender under this Act does not affect the status of the person as the father or mother of a child.

15 Succession etc

The fact that a person's gender has become the acquired gender under this Act does not affect the disposal or devolution of property under a will or other instrument made before the appointed day.

16 Peerages etc

The fact that a person's gender has become the acquired gender under this Act—

(a) does not affect the descent of any peerage or dignity or title of honour, and

(b) does not affect the devolution of any property limited (expressly or not) by a will or other instrument to devolve (as nearly as the law permits) along with any peerage or dignity or title of honour unless an intention that it should do so is expressed in the will or other instrument.

17 Trustees and personal representatives

(1) A trustee or personal representative is not under a duty, by virtue of the law relating to trusts or the administration of estates, to enquire, before conveying or distributing any property, whether a full gender recognition certificate has been issued to any person or revoked (if that fact could affect entitlement to the property).

(2) A trustee or personal representative is not liable to any person by reason of a conveyance or distribution of the property made without regard to whether a full gender recognition certificate has been issued to any person or revoked if the trustee or personal representative has not received notice of the fact before the conveyance or distribution.

(3) This section does not prejudice the right of a person to follow the property, or any property representing it, into the hands of another person who has received it unless that person has purchased it for value in good faith and without notice.

18 Orders where expectations defeated

(1) This section applies where the disposition or devolution of any property under a will or other instrument (made on or after the appointed day) is different from what it would be but for the fact that a person's gender has become the acquired gender under this Act.

(2) A person may apply to the High Court or Court of Session for an order on the ground of being adversely affected by the different disposition or devolution of the property.

(3)   The court may, if it is satisfied that it is just to do so, make in relation to any person benefiting from the different disposition or devolution of the property such order as it considers appropriate.

(4)   An order may, in particular, make provision for—
    (a)   the payment of a lump sum to the applicant,
    (b)   the transfer of property to the applicant,
    (c)   the settlement of property for the benefit of the applicant,
    (d)   the acquisition of property and either its transfer to the applicant or its settlement for the benefit of the applicant.

(5)   An order may contain consequential or supplementary provisions for giving effect to the order or for ensuring that it operates fairly as between the applicant and the other person or persons affected by it; and an order may, in particular, confer powers on trustees.

20   Gender-specific offences

(1)   Where (apart from this subsection) a relevant gender-specific offence could be committed or attempted only if the gender of a person to whom a full gender recognition certificate has been issued were not the acquired gender, the fact that the person's gender has become the acquired gender does not prevent the offence being committed or attempted.

(2)   An offence is a 'relevant gender-specific offence' if—
    (a)   either or both of the conditions in subsection (3) are satisfied, and
    (b)   the commission of the offence involves the accused engaging in sexual activity.

(3)   The conditions are—
    (a)   that the offence may be committed only by a person of a particular gender, and
    (b)   that the offence may be committed only on, or in relation to, a person of a particular gender,
and the references to a particular gender include a gender identified by reference to the gender of the other person involved.

21   Foreign gender change and marriage

(1)   A person's gender is not to be regarded as having changed by reason only that it has changed under the law of a country or territory outside the United Kingdom.
    [. . .]
[(6)   Nothing in this section prevents the exercise of any right which forms part of retained EU law by virtue of section 3 or 4 of the European Union (Withdrawal) Act 2018.]

Supplementary

22   Prohibition on disclosure of information

(1)   It is an offence for a person who has acquired protected information in an official capacity to disclose the information to any other person.

(2)   'Protected information' means information which relates to a person who has made an application under section 1(1) and which—
    (a)   concerns that application or any application by the person [under any other section of this Act], or
    (b)   if the application under section 1(1) is granted, otherwise concerns the person's gender before it becomes the acquired gender.

(3)   A person acquires protected information in an official capacity if the person acquires it—
    (a)   in connection with the person's functions as a member of the civil service, a constable or the holder of any other public office or in connection with the functions of a local or public authority or of a voluntary organisation,

(b)   as an employer, or prospective employer, of the person to whom the information relates or as a person employed by such an employer or prospective employer, or

(c)   in the course of, or otherwise in connection with, the conduct of business or the supply of professional services.

(4)   But it is not an offence under this section to disclose protected information relating to a person if—

(a)   the information does not enable that person to be identified,

(b)   that person has agreed to the disclosure of the information,

(c)   the information is protected information by virtue of subsection (2)(b) and the person by whom the disclosure is made does not know or believe that a full gender recognition certificate has been issued,

(d)   the disclosure is in accordance with an order of a court or tribunal,

(e)   the disclosure is for the purpose of instituting, or otherwise for the purposes of, proceedings before a court or tribunal,

(f)   the disclosure is for the purpose of preventing or investigating crime,

(g)   the disclosure is made to the Registrar General for England and Wales, the Registrar General for Scotland or the Registrar General for Northern Ireland,

(h)   the disclosure is made for the purposes of the social security system or a pension scheme,

(i)   the disclosure is in accordance with provision made by an order under subsection (5), or

(j)   the disclosure is in accordance with any provision of, or made by virtue of, an enactment other than this section.

(5)   The Secretary of State may by order make provision prescribing circumstances in which the disclosure of protected information is not to constitute an offence under this section.

(6)   The power conferred by subsection (5) is exercisable by the Scottish Ministers (rather than the Secretary of State) where the provision to be made is within the legislative competence of the Scottish Parliament.

(7)   An order under subsection (5) may make provision permitting—

(a)   disclosure to specified persons or persons of a specified description,

(b)   disclosure for specified purposes,

(c)   disclosure of specified descriptions of information, or

(d)   disclosure by specified persons or persons of a specified description.

(8)   A person guilty of an offence under this section is liable on summary conviction to a fine not exceeding level 5 on the standard scale.

23   Power to modify statutory provisions

(1)   The Secretary of State may by order make provision for modifying the operation of any enactment or subordinate legislation in relation to—

(a)   persons whose gender has become the acquired gender under this Act, or

(b)   any description of such persons.

(2)   The power conferred by subsection (1) is exercisable by the Scottish Ministers (rather than the Secretary of State) where the provision to be made is within the legislative competence of the Scottish Parliament.

(3)   The appropriate Northern Ireland department may by order make provision for modifying the operation of any enactment or subordinate legislation which deals with a transferred matter in relation to—

(a)   persons whose gender has become the acquired gender under this Act, or

(b)   any description of such persons.

(4)   In subsection (3)—

'the appropriate Northern Ireland department', in relation to any enactment or subordinate legislation which deals with a transferred matter, means the Northern Ireland department which has responsibility for that matter, 'deals with' is to be construed in accordance with section 98(2) and (3) of the Northern Ireland Act 1998 (c 47), and

'transferred matter' has the meaning given by section 4(1) of that Act.

(5)   Before an order is made under this section, appropriate consultation must be undertaken with persons likely to be affected by it.

24   Orders and regulations

(1)   Any power of the Secretary of State [. . .] the Scottish Ministers or a Northern Ireland department to make an order under this Act includes power to make any appropriate incidental, supplementary, consequential or transitional provision or savings.

(2)   Any power of the Secretary of State [. . .] or the Scottish Ministers to make an order under this Act, and any power of the Registrar General for England and Wales or the Registrar General for Scotland to make regulations under this Act, is exercisable by statutory instrument.

(3)   No order may be made under section 2 [. . .] unless a draft of the statutory instrument containing the order has been laid before, and approved by a resolution of, each House of Parliament.

(4)   A statutory instrument containing an order made by the Secretary of State under section 7, 22 or 23 is subject to annulment in pursuance of a resolution of either House of Parliament.

(5)   A statutory instrument containing an order made by the Scottish Ministers under section [3D(6)(b),] 22 or 23 is subject to annulment in pursuance of a resolution of the Scottish Parliament.

[(5A)   Regulations made by the Registrar General for Scotland under paragraph 20A of Schedule 3 are subject to the negative procedure.

(5B)   An order under section 3C(5)(b)(ii) [. . .] is subject to the affirmative procedure.]

(6)   Any power of a Northern Ireland department to make an order or regulations under this Act is exercisable by statutory rule for the purposes of the Statutory Rules (Northern Ireland) Order 1979 (SI 1979/1573 (NI 12)).

(7)   Orders and regulations made by a Northern Ireland department under this Act are subject to negative resolution (within the meaning of section 41(6) of the Interpretation Act (Northern Ireland) 1954 (c 33 (NI))).

25   Interpretation

[(1)]   In this Act—

'the acquired gender' is to be construed in accordance with section 1(2),

'approved country or territory' has the meaning given by section 2(4),

'the appointed day' means the day appointed by order under section 26,

[. . .]

'enactment' includes an enactment contained in an Act of the Scottish Parliament or in any Northern Ireland legislation,

'full gender recognition certificate' and 'interim gender recognition certificate' mean the certificates issued as such under section 4[, 4C, 4E, 4F, 5, [or 5A]] and 'gender recognition certificate' means either of those sorts of certificate,

'gender dysphoria' means the disorder variously referred to as gender dysphoria, gender identity disorder and transsexualism,

'Gender Recognition Panel' (and 'Panel') is to be construed in accordance with Schedule 1,

['protected civil partnership' [means—

(a)   a civil partnership under the law of England and Wales or under the law of Northern Ireland, or

(b)   an overseas relationship that is treated as a civil partnership by virtue of Chapter 2 of Part 5 of the Civil Partnership Act 2004,

and 'protected overseas relationship' means a protected civil partnership within paragraph (b),]

'protected marriage' means—
    (a)   a marriage under the law of England and Wales, or
    (b)   a marriage under the law of a country or territory outside the United Kingdom,]
['protected Scottish civil partnership' means a civil partnership registered in Scotland,
    'protected Scottish marriage' means a marriage solemnised in Scotland,]
['registered psychologist' means a person registered in the part of the register maintained under the [Health and Social Work Professions Order 2001] which relates to practitioner psychologists,]
['statutory declaration of consent' has the meaning given by section 3(6B)(a),]
'subordinate legislation' means an Order in Council, an order, rules, regulations, a scheme, a warrant, bye-laws or any other instrument made under an enactment, and
'UK birth register entry' has the meaning given by section 10(2).
[(2) A civil partnership which was registered outside the United Kingdom under an Order in Council made under Chapter 1 of Part 5 of the Civil Partnership Act 2004 is to be treated for the purposes of this Act as having been registered in Scotland if—
    (a)   the parties to the civil partnership elected Scotland as the relevant part of the United Kingdom under the Order, and
    (b)   details of the civil partnership have been sent to the Registrar General for Scotland.
(3) A marriage which was registered outside the United Kingdom under the Foreign Marriage Act 1892 (other than a marriage registered by virtue of section 18 of that Act) is to be treated for the purposes of this Act as having been solemnised in Scotland if details of the marriage have been sent to the Registrar General for Scotland.
(4) A marriage which was solemnised outside the United Kingdom and registered under an Order in Council made under the Registration of Births, Deaths and Marriages (Special Provisions) Act 1957 is to be treated for the purposes of this Act as having been solemnised in Scotland if details of the marriage have been sent to the Registrar General for Scotland.
(5) A consular marriage in relation to which the relevant part of the United Kingdom is Scotland is to be treated for the purposes of this Act as having been solemnised in Scotland.
(6) In subsection (5)—
'consular marriage' means a marriage solemnised in accordance with Part 1 of Schedule 6 to the Marriage (Same Sex Couples) Act 2013 and any Order in Council made under it,
'relevant part of the United Kingdom', in relation to such a marriage, means the part of the United Kingdom determined in accordance with paragraph 1(2)(b) of that Part of that Schedule for the purposes of the marriage.]

. . .

28 Extent
    (2) The following provisions extend only to Scotland—
        (a)   section 24(5),
        (b)   Part 2 of Schedule 2,
        (c)   Part 2 of Schedule 3, and
        (d)   Part 2 of Schedule 4.
    (3) The following provisions extend only to England and Wales and Scotland—
        (a)   paragraphs 12, 14 and 16 of Schedule 5, and
        (b)   Part 1 of Schedule 6.

29 Short title

(1)   This Act may be cited as the Gender Recognition Act 2004.

(2)   Nothing in this Act shall impose any charge on the people or on public funds, or vary the amount or incidence of or otherwise alter any such charge in any manner, or affect the assessment, levying, administration or application of any money raised by any such charge.

SCHEDULE 3
REGISTRATION

Section 10

PART 2
Scotland

Introductory

12.   In this Part—

'the Registrar General' means the Registrar General for Scotland, and 'the 1965 Act' means the Registration of Births, Deaths and Marriages (Scotland) Act 1965 (c 49).

Gender Recognition Register

13.—(1)   The Registrar General must maintain, in the General Register Office of Births, Deaths and Marriages in Scotland, a register to be called the Gender Recognition Register.

(2)   In this Part 'the Gender Recognition Register' means the register maintained under sub-paragraph (1).

(3)   The form in which the Gender Recognition Register is maintained is to be determined by the Registrar General.

(4)   The Gender Recognition Register is not to be open to public inspection or search.

Entries in Gender Recognition Register

14.—(1)   If the Registrar General receives under section 10(1) a copy of a full gender recognition certificate issued to a person, the Registrar General must—

(a)   make an entry in the Gender Recognition Register containing such particulars as may be prescribed in relation to the person's birth and any other prescribed matter, and

(b)   otherwise than by annotating in any way the birth register, make traceable the connection between the UK birth register entry and the entry in the Gender Recognition Register.

(2)   Sub-paragraph (1) does not apply if the gender recognition certificate was issued after an application under section 6(1) and that sub-paragraph has already been complied with in relation to the person.

(3)   Information kept by the Registrar General for the purposes of sub-paragraph (1)(b) is not to be open to public inspection or search.

(4)   'Prescribed' means prescribed by regulations made by the Registrar General with the approval of the Scottish Ministers.

Indexing of entries in Gender Recognition Register

15.—(1)   The Registrar General must make arrangements for each entry made in the Gender Recognition Register to be included in an index of such entries kept in the General Register Office of Births, Deaths and Marriages in Scotland.

(2)   Whenever the Registrar General causes a search to be made under subsection (2)(a) of section 38 of the 1965 Act (search of indexes of entries in the

registers of births, deaths and marriages) on behalf of any person, he must also, without payment of any fee additional to the fee or fees prescribed under that section—

    (a)   cause a search to be made of the index of entries in the Gender Recognition Register on behalf of that person, and

    (b)   issue to that person an extract of any such entry provided that (disregarding, for the purposes of subsection (4)(j) of section 22, this paragraph) disclosure of the entry to the person would not constitute an offence under that section.

Extracts of entries in Gender Recognition Register

16.—(1)   This paragraph applies in respect of an extract issued under paragraph 15(2)(b).

(2)   Except as regards the sex and name of the person to whom it relates, the extract must have the form and content it would have had had it been an extract from the register of births of the entry relating to that person.

(3)   The extract must not disclose the fact that the entry is contained in the Gender Recognition Register.

Abbreviated certificates of birth compiled from Gender Recognition Register

17.   Where an abbreviated certificate of birth under section [39E] of the 1965 Act is compiled from the Gender Recognition Register, the certificate must not disclose that fact.

Gender Recognition Register: correction, re-registration etc

18.   Section 18A(2) (decrees of parentage and non-parentage), section 20(1) [. . .] (re-registration in certain cases), section 42(1) and (5) (correction of errors), section 43(1), (2) and (5) to (9) (recording change of name or surname) and section 44 (Register of Corrections etc) of the 1965 Act apply in relation to the Gender Recognition Register as they apply in relation to the register of births.

Revocation of gender recognition certificate etc

19.—(1)   This paragraph applies if, after an entry has been made in the Gender Recognition Register in relation to a person, the High Court or the Court of Session makes an order under section 8(6) quashing the decision to grant the person's application under section 1(1)[, [4C, 4E, [. . .],] 5(2) or 5A(2)].

(2)   The High Court or the Court of Session must inform the Registrar General.

(3)   Subject to any appeal, the Registrar General must cancel the entry in the Gender Recognition Register.

Authentication and admissibility

20.   [Sections 41 and 41A] of the 1965 Act (authentication of extracts etc and their admissibility as evidence) [apply] in relation to the Gender Recognition Register as in relation to the registers kept under the provisions of that Act.

[20A.—(1)   The Registrar General may, with the approval of the Scottish Ministers, make regulations about—

    (a)   the registration of qualifying Scottish marriages, and

    (b)   the registration of qualifying Scottish civil partnerships.

(2)   Regulations under sub-paragraph (1) may in particular make provision for fees to be payable in respect of things done under the regulations.

(3)   Regulations under sub-paragraph (1) may make different provision for different cases or circumstances.

(4)   In this paragraph—

'qualifying Scottish civil partnership' means a civil partnership registered in

Scotland in a case where a full gender recognition certificate has been issued to [one, or each,] of the civil partners,

'qualifying Scottish marriage' means a marriage solemnised in Scotland in a case where a full gender recognition certificate has been issued to one, or each, of the spouses.]

CIVIL PARTNERSHIP ACT 2004
(2004, c 33)

PART 1
INTRODUCTION

1   Civil partnership

(1)   A civil partnership is a relationship between two people [. . .] ('civil partners')—

    (a)   which is formed when they register as civil partners of each other—

        (i)   in England or Wales (under Part 2),

        (ii)   in Scotland (under Part 3),

        (iii)   in Northern Ireland (under Part 4), or

        (iv)   outside the United Kingdom under an Order in Council made under Chapter 1 of Part 5 (registration at British consulates etc or by armed forces personnel), or

    (b)   which they are treated under Chapter 2 of Part 5 as having formed (at the time determined under that Chapter) by virtue of having registered an overseas relationship.

(2)   Subsection (1) is subject to the provisions of this Act under or by virtue of which a civil partnership is void.

(3)   A civil partnership ends only

    (a)   on death, dissolution or annulment [, or

    (b)   in the case of a civil partnership formed as mentioned in subsection (1) (a)(i) or (iv), on the conversion of the civil partnership into a marriage under section 9 of the Marriage (Same Sex Couples) Act 2013.]

[(3A)   Subsection (3) is subject to section 11(2)(a) of the Marriage and Civil Partnership (Scotland) Act 2014 (ending of certain civil partnerships on marriage under Scots law).]

(4)   The references in subsection (3) to dissolution and annulment are to dissolution and annulment having effect under or recognised in accordance with this Act.

(5)   References in this Act to an overseas relationship are to be read in accordance with Chapter 2 of Part 5.

PART 3
CIVIL PARTNERSHIP: SCOTLAND

CHAPTER 1
Formation and Eligibility

85   Formation of civil partnership by registration

(1)   For the purposes of section 1, two people are to be regarded as having registered as civil partners of each other once each of them has signed the civil partnership schedule, in the presence of—

    (a)   each other,

    (b)   two witnesses both of whom have attained the age of 16, and

    [(c)   the approved celebrant or, as the case may be, the authorised registrar].

(2)   But the two people must be eligible to be so registered.

(3) Subsection (1) applies regardless of whether subsection (4) is complied with.

(4) After the civil partnership schedule has been signed under subsection (1), it must also be signed, in the presence of the civil partners and each other by—

(a) each of the two witnesses, and

(b) [the approved celebrant or, as the case may be,] the authorised registrar.

86 Eligibility

(1) Two people are not eligible to register in Scotland as civil partners of each other if—

[. . .]

(b) they are related in a forbidden degree,

(c) either has not attained the age of 16,

(d) either is married or already in civil partnership, or

(e) either is incapable of—

(i) understanding the nature of civil partnership, or

(ii) validly consenting to its formation.

[(2) Subject to subsection (3), a person is related to another person in a forbidden degree if related to that person in a degree specified in Schedule 10.]

(3) [A person who is related to another person in a degree specified in paragraph 2 of Schedule 10 (relations by affinity) is not related to that person] in a forbidden degree if—

(a) both persons have attained the age of 21, and

(b) the younger has not at any time before attaining the age of 18 lived in the same household as the elder and been treated by the elder as a child of the elder's family.

[(3A) For the purposes of paragraph 2 of Schedule 10, 'spouse' means—

(a) in the case of a marriage between persons of different sexes, a wife in relation to her husband or a husband in relation to his wife, and

(b) in the case of a marriage between persons of the same sex, one of the parties to the marriage in relation to the other.]

[(4) Paragraph 2 of Schedule 10 has effect subject to the modifications specified in subsection (5) in the case of a person (here the 'relevant person') whose gender has become the acquired gender under the Gender Recognition Act 2004 (c 7).

(5) The reference in [subsection (3A)(a) as it applies to] that paragraph to—

(a) a [. . .] wife of the relevant person includes any [. . .] husband of the relevant person, and

(b) a [. . .] husband of the relevant person includes any [. . .] wife of the relevant person.]

[(5A) This section and Schedule 10 have effect as if any reference in that Schedule to a [parent] within any of the degrees of relationship specified [. . .] included a woman who is a parent of a child by virtue of section 42 or 43 of the Human Fertilisation and Embryology Act 2008 (c 22).]

[. . .]

(8) References in this section and in Schedule 10 to relationships and degrees of relationship are to be construed in accordance with section 1(1) of the Law Reform (Parent and Child) (Scotland) Act 1986 (c 9).

(9) For the purposes of this section, a degree of relationship specified in paragraph 1 of Schedule 10 exists whether it is of the full blood or the half blood.

(10) [Amends Adoption (Scotland) Act 1978.]

CHAPTER 2
Registration

87 Appointment of authorised registrars

For the purpose of affording reasonable facilities throughout Scotland for [civil] registration as civil partners, the Registrar General—

(a)   is to appoint such number of district registrars as he thinks necessary, and

(b)   may, in respect of any district for which he has made an appointment under paragraph (a), appoint one or more assistant registrars,

as persons who may carry out such registration (in this Part referred to as 'authorised registrars').

88   Notice of proposed civil partnership

(1)   In order to register as civil partners, each of the intended civil partners must submit to the district registrar a notice, in the prescribed form [. . .] of intention to enter civil partnership (in this Part referred to as a 'notice of proposed civil partnership').

(2)   [Each of the intended civil partners must also pay the prescribed fee and submit the following documents—

(a)   that person's birth certificate,]

(b)   if that person has previously been married or in civil partnership and—

(i)   the marriage or civil partnership has been dissolved, a copy of the decree of divorce or dissolution, or

(ii)   the other party to that marriage or civil partnership has died, the death certificate of that other party, and

(c)   if that person has previously ostensibly been married or in civil partnership but decree of annulment has been obtained, a copy of that decree.

[(2A)   If an intended civil partner is a relevant national as defined in section 30A(ab)(i) or (ii) the intended civil partner must also submit—

(a)   where the intended civil partner falls within section 30A(ab)(i), an electronic certificate which confirms that the leave referred to in that provision has been granted; or

(b)   where the intended civil partner falls within section 30A(ab)(ii)—

(i)   a certificate of application which confirms that the application referred to in regulation 4 of the Citizens' Rights (Application Deadline and Temporary Protection) (EU Exit) Regulations 2020 has been made; and

(ii)   evidence that the relevant period referred to in regulation 4 of those Regulations has not expired.]

(3)   If a person is unable to submit a certificate or decree required by subsection (2) he may instead make a declaration to that effect, stating what the reasons are; and he must provide the district registrar with such—

(a)   information in respect of the matters to which the certificate or document would have related, and

(b)   documentary evidence in support of that information, as the district registrar may require.

(4)   If a document submitted under subsection (2) or (3) is in a language other than English, the person submitting it must [, unless subsection (4A) applies,] attach to the document a translation of it in English, certified by the translator as a correct translation.

[(4A)   This subsection applies where—

(a)   the document submitted is accompanied by a multilingual standard form issued by an authority in a Member State of the European Union in accordance with Regulation (EU) 2016/1191 of the European Parliament and of the Council, and

(b)   the district registrar considers that the information included in the multilingual standard form is sufficient for processing the document.]

(5)   A person submitting a notice under subsection (1) must make and [attest in the prescribed manner] the necessary declaration (the form for which must be included in any form prescribed for the notice).

[(5A)   Regulations prescribing the form of the notice of proposed civil partnership may make provision for the notice to be electronic rather than paper-based.]

(6) The necessary declaration is a declaration that the person submitting the notice believes that the intended civil partners are eligible to be in civil partnership with each other.

[(7) In this section, 'the district registrar' means—

(a) where the civil partnership is to be registered in a registration district, the district registrar for that district,

(b) where the civil partnership is to be registered in Scottish waters—

(i) in the case where the civil partnership is to be registered by an approved celebrant, the district registrar for any registration district,

(ii) in the case where the civil partnership is to be registered by an authorised registrar, the district registrar for the registration district of the proposed authorised registrar.]

[(8) A district registrar to whom a notice under subsection (1) is submitted may require the person submitting the notice to provide the district registrar with specified nationality evidence relating to each of the intended civil partners.

(9) A requirement under subsection (8) may be imposed at any time—

(a) on or after the submitting of the notice under subsection (1), but

(b) before the district registrar completes the civil partnership schedule.

(10) In subsection (8), 'specified nationality evidence' means such evidence of that person's nationality as may be specified in guidance issued by the Registrar General.]

[88A Additional information if party not relevant national

(1) This section applies to a notice of proposed civil partnership submitted to a district registrar in accordance with section 88 if one, or each, of the parties to the proposed civil partnership is not a relevant national.

(2) For each party to the proposed civil partnership who is not a relevant national, the notice must be accompanied by whichever of statements A, B or C is applicable to that person.

(3) Statement A is a statement that the person has the appropriate immigration status.

(4) Statement B is a statement that the person holds a relevant visa in respect of the proposed civil partnership.

(5) Statement C is a statement that the person neither—

(a) has the appropriate immigration status, nor

(b) holds a relevant visa in respect of the proposed civil partnership.

(6) If the notice is accompanied by the statement referred to in the first column of an entry in this table, the notice must also be accompanied by the information and photographs referred to in the second column of that entry (insofar as that entry is applicable to the parties to the proposed civil partnership)—

If the notice is accompanied by this statement . . .	. . . the notice shall also be accompanied by . . .
Statement A (in respect of one or both of the parties to the proposed civil partnership)	For each party in respect of whom statement A is made, details of the particular immigration status which that party has
Statement B (in respect of one or both of the parties to the proposed civil partnership)	1. For each party, a specified photograph of that party 2. For each party in respect of whom statement B is made, details of the relevant visa which that party has

If the notice is accompanied by this statement . . .	. . . the notice shall also be accompanied by . . .
Statement C (in respect of one or both of the parties to the proposed civil partnership)	1. For each party, a specified photograph of that party 2. For each party, the usual address of that party 3. For each party who has previously used any name or names other than the person's name stated in the civil partnership notice, a statement of the other name or names 4. For each party who currently uses, or has previously used, an alias or aliases, a statement of the alias or aliases

(7) If the notice is accompanied by more than one of statements A, B and C, subsection (6) must be complied with in relation to each of those statements; but where the notice is accompanied by statements B and C, subsection (6) does not require the notice to be accompanied by more than one specified photograph of each party.

(8) If the notice is accompanied by statement C for a party to the proposed civil partnership—

    (a) the notice may also be accompanied by a statement ('statement D') of that person's immigration position in the United Kingdom;

    (b) if the notice is accompanied by statement D for a party to the proposed civil partnership, the person may provide the district registrar with details of his immigration position in the United Kingdom; and

    (c) if any such details are provided, the district registrar must record them.

(9) In this section and section 88B—

    (a) a reference—

        (i) to a person having the appropriate immigration status, or

        (ii) to a person holding a relevant visa,

is to be construed in accordance with section 49 of the 2014 Act;

    (b) a reference to the particular immigration status which a person has is a reference to the immigration status set out in any of paragraphs (a) to (c) of section 49(2) of that Act which the person has;

    (c) a reference to a person's immigration position in the United Kingdom includes a reference to the person's not being entitled to be in the United Kingdom.

(10) In this section 'specified photograph' means a photograph that is in accordance with regulations made by the Secretary of State under section 54(2) of, and paragraph 3 of Schedule 5 to, the 2014 Act (and for this purpose 'photograph' includes other kinds of images).]

[88B   Additional evidence if party not relevant national

(1) If a notice of proposed civil partnership to which section 88A applies ('the notice') is accompanied by statement A (referred to in section 88A(3)), and accordingly is also accompanied by details of the particular immigration status which a party to the proposed civil partnership has, the notice must also be accompanied by specified evidence of that status.

(2) If the notice is accompanied by statement B (referred to in section 88A(4)), the notice must also be accompanied by specified evidence of the holding of the relevant visa by the party to the proposed civil partnership.

(3) If, in accordance with section 88A(6), the notice is accompanied by the

usual address of a party to the proposed civil partnership, the notice must also be accompanied by specified evidence that it is that party's usual address.

(4) If the notice is accompanied by statement D (referred to in section 88A(8)), the notice may also be accompanied by evidence of the person's immigration position in the United Kingdom.

(5) If subsection (1) or (2) applies to the notice, and the notice is not accompanied by the specified evidence required by that subsection, the notice must be accompanied by—

(a) photographs and addresses of the kinds referred to in paragraphs 1 and 2 in the relevant entry in section 88A(6);

(b) as respects the usual address of each party that is provided in accordance with sub-paragraph (a), specified evidence that the address provided is that party's usual address; and

(c) names and aliases of the kinds referred to in paragraphs 3 and 4 in the relevant entry in section 88A(6) (insofar as those paragraphs are applicable to the proposed civil partnership).

(6) In this section—

'relevant entry in section 88A(6)' means the second column of the last entry in the table in section 88A(6);

'specified evidence' means evidence that is in accordance with regulations made by the Secretary of State under section 54(2) of, and paragraph 3 of Schedule 5 to, the 2014 Act.]

[88C Declaration to accompany information and evidence

Where the notice of proposed civil partnership is accompanied by—

(a) information provided in accordance with section 88A, and

(b) information and evidence provided in accordance with section 88B,

that information and evidence must also be accompanied by a declaration in writing and signed by the party who makes it that the party believes all of the information and evidence accompanying the notice to be true.]

[88D Rejection of false information or evidence

(1) A district registrar may reject—

(a) any evidence relating to a party's nationality provided in accordance with section 88(8),

(b) any information or photograph provided under section 88A or 88B, or

(c) any evidence provided under section 88B,

if (in particular) the district registrar has reasonable grounds for suspecting that the information, photograph or evidence is false.

(2) If the district registrar rejects any information, photograph or evidence, the district registrar may proceed under this Act as if the rejected information, photograph or evidence had not been provided.

(3) This section does not limit the powers of the district registrar to reject anything provided under any other enactment.

(4) In this section 'enactment' includes an enactment comprised in, or an instrument made under, an Act of the Scottish Parliament.]

[88E Notice of proposed civil partnership: treated as not given

(1) Where any of the requirements imposed by or under any of the provisions of this Act mentioned in subsection (2) is applicable but not complied with by either or both parties to the proposed civil partnership, the parties are to be taken not to have submitted notice under section 88.

(2) The provisions are—

(a) section 88(8);

(b) section 88A(2) to (7);

(c) section 88B(3) or (5);

(d) paragraph 9 of Schedule 23.]

[88F   Referral of proposed civil partnership to the Secretary of State

(1)   On every occasion when notice of proposed civil partnership is submitted under section 88, a district registrar must decide whether or not each of the parties to the proposed civil partnership is an exempt person.

(2)   But this section does not apply if section 96 applies to the proposed civil partnership.

(3)   In making a decision under subsection (1) about a party to a proposed civil partnership, a district registrar may rely on any advice given in relation to that decision by the Secretary of State.

(4)   In a case where—

  (a)   section 88A applies to the notice of proposed civil partnership, and

  (b)   specified evidence required by section 88B(1) or (2) in relation to a party to the proposed civil partnership is not produced in accordance with that section,

the district registrar must decide that that party to the proposed civil partnership is not an exempt person.

(5)   If the district registrar decides that either of the parties is not an exempt person, or that both of the parties are not exempt persons, the registrar must—

  (a)   refer the proposed civil partnership to the Secretary of State;

  (b)   notify the parties to the proposed civil partnership that the proposed civil partnership must be referred to the Secretary of State;

  (c)   give the parties to the proposed civil partnership prescribed information about—

    (i)   the effects of the referral;

    (ii)   the requirement under regulations to notify the Secretary of State of changes of address.

(6)   The district registrar must act in accordance with regulations when complying with the duty in subsection (5)(a) to refer a proposed civil partnership to the Secretary of State.

(7)   If the district registrar refers the proposed civil partnership to the Secretary of State, this Act has effect in relation to the proposed civil partnership subject to the modifications in Schedule 10A.

(8)   In this section—

  (a)   a reference to a person being an exempt person has the same meaning as in section 49 of the 2014 Act;

  (b)   'prescribed information' means information prescribed in regulations;

  (c)   'regulations' means regulations made by the Secretary of State under section 54(2) of, and Schedule 5 to, the 2014 Act.]

89   Civil partnership notice book

(1)   On receipt of a notice of proposed civil partnership, the district registrar is to enter in a book (to be known as 'the civil partnership book') supplied to him for that purpose by the Registrar General such particulars, extracted from the notice, as may be prescribed and the date of receipt by him of that notice.

(2)   The form and content of any page of that book is to be prescribed.

[(3)   In this section and sections 90, 91, 92 and 94, 'the district registrar' means—

  (a)   where the civil partnership is to be registered in a registration district, the district registrar for that district,

  (b)   where the civil partnership is to be registered in Scottish waters—

    (i)   in the case where the civil partnership is to be registered by an approved celebrant, the district registrar to whom the civil partnership notices were submitted,

    (ii)   in the case where the civil partnership is to be registered by an authorised registrar, the district registrar for the registration district of the proposed authorised registrar.]

[(4)   Subsection (1) is subject to section 88E.]

90 Publicisation

(1) Where notices of a proposed civil partnership are [received by] [the district registrar], he must, as soon as practicable after [such receipt] (or, if the two documents are not [received] on the same day, after [the first is received]), publicise the relevant information and send it to the Registrar General who must also publicise   it.

(2) 'The relevant information' means—

(a) the names of the intended civil partners, and

(b) the date on which it is intended to register them as civil partners of each other, being a date more than [28 days] after publicisation by the district registrar under subsection (1).

(3) Paragraph (b) of subsection (2) is subject to section [91(1)].

(4) The manner in which and means by which relevant information is to be publicised are to be prescribed.

91 Early registration

[(1)] [Where the district registrar] who receives a request in writing from one or both of two intended civil partners that they should be registered as civil partners of each other on a date specified in the request (being a date [28 days] or fewer after publicisation by the district registrar under subsection (1) of section 90 [the district registrar]) may, provided that he is authorised to do so by the Registrar General, fix that date as the date for registration; and if a date is so fixed, paragraph (b) of subsection (2) of that section is to be construed as if it were a reference to that date.

[(1A) Unless subsection (1B) applies, if a proposed civil partnership is referred to the Secretary of State under section 88F ('the referred civil partnership') the Registrar General may not authorise the district registrar to fix the specified date mentioned in subsection (1) as the date for registration of the referred civil partnership without the consent of the Secretary of State.

(1B) This subsection applies if the request made under subsection (1) is made because a party to the referred civil partnership is gravely ill and not expected to recover.]

[(2) For the purposes of subsection (1), a request which is made by electronic means is to be treated as in writing if it is received in a form which is legible and capable of being used for subsequent reference.]

92 Objections to registration

(1) Any person may at any time before the registration in Scotland of two people as civil partners of each other submit in writing an objection to such registration to the district registrar.

[(1A) For the purpose of subsection (1), an objection which is submitted to the registrar by electronic means is to be treated as in writing if it is received in a form which is legible and capable of being used for subsequent reference.]

(2) But where the objection is that the intended civil partners are not eligible to be in civil partnership with each other because either is incapable of—

(a) understanding the nature of civil partnership, or

(b) validly consenting to its formation,

it shall [not be treated as submitted until there has also been produced to the registrar] a supporting certificate [attested in the prescribed manner] by a registered medical practitioner.

(3) A person claiming that he may have reason to submit such an objection may, free of charge and at any time when the registration office [of the district registrar] is open for public business, inspect any relevant entry in the civil partnership book.

(4) Where the district registrar receives an objection in accordance with subsection (1) he must—

(a) in any case where he is satisfied that the objection relates to no more than a misdescription or inaccuracy in a notice submitted under section 88(1)—

    (i) notify the intended civil partners of the nature of the objection and make such enquiries into the matter mentioned in it as he thinks fit, and

    (ii) subject to the approval of the Registrar General, make any necessary correction to any document relating to the proposed civil partnership, or

(b) in any other case—

    (i) at once notify the Registrar General of the objection,

    (ii) pending consideration of the objection by the Registrar General, suspend the completion or issue of the civil partnership schedule in respect of the proposed civil partnership [, and

    (iii) where, in the case of a civil partnership to be registered by an approved celebrant, the civil partnership schedule has already been issued to the parties, if possible notify that celebrant of the objection and advise the celebrant not to register the civil partnership pending consideration of the objection.]

(5) If the Registrar General is satisfied, on consideration of an objection of which he has received notification under subsection (4)(b)(i) that—

(a) there is a legal impediment to registration, he must direct the district registrar [to take all reasonable steps to ensure that the registration of the civil partnership does not take place and must notify, or direct the district registrar to notify, the intended civil partners] accordingly, or

(b) there is no such impediment, he must inform the district registrar to that effect.

(6) For the purposes of this section and section 94, there is a legal impediment to registration where the intended civil partners are not eligible to be in civil partnership with each other.

93 [Place of civil registration of civil partnerships]

(1) Two people may be registered [by an authorised registrar] as civil partners of each [other—

(a) at the registration office of the authorised registrar,

(b) at an appropriate place in the registration district of the authorised registrar, or

(c) with the approval of the Registrar General, at—

    (i) the registration office of another authorised registrar,

    (ii) an appropriate place in the registration district of another authorised registrar, or

    (iii) an appropriate place in Scottish waters.]

[(1A) In this section—

'appropriate place' means a place which—

(a) the parties to the intended civil partnership and the local registration authority agree is to be the place of registration, and

(b) is not religious premises,

'local registration authority' means—

(a) the local registration authority for the registration district which includes the place, or

(b) where the place is in Scottish waters, the local registration authority for the authorised registrar's registration district,

'religious premises' means premises which—

(a) are used solely or mainly for religious purposes, or

(b) have been so used and have not subsequently been used solely or mainly for other purposes.]

[. . .]

(4) 'Local registration authority' has the meaning given by section 5(3) of the 1965 Act.

[(5) 'Scottish waters' has the meaning given by section 26(2) of the Marriage (Scotland) Act 1977 (c 15).]

[93A Date and place of registration of religious or belief civil partnerships

(1) A religious or belief civil partnership may be registered only on the date and at the place specified in the civil partnership schedule.

(2) But if, for any reason, the civil partnership cannot be registered on that date or at that place and a new date or place is fixed for the registration, the district registrar must—

(a) issue another civil partnership schedule under section 94(2) in place of that already issued, specifying the new date or place, or

(b) substitute, or direct the approved celebrant to substitute, the new date or place in the civil partnership schedule already issued.

(3) Subsection (2) does not apply where—

(a) the new date is more than 3 months after the date for the registration specified in the civil partnership schedule already issued, or

(b) the new place is in a different registration district, is in Scottish waters instead of a registration district or is in a registration district instead of Scottish waters.

(4) In a case falling within subsection (3)(a) or (b) the Registrar General may, according to the circumstances—

(a) direct the district registrar—

(i) to issue another civil partnership schedule under section 94(2) in place of that already issued, specifying the new date or place, or

(ii) to substitute, or direct the approved celebrant to substitute, the new date or place in the civil partnership schedule already issued,

(whichever the Registrar General considers the more appropriate), or

(b) direct each party to the civil partnership to submit to the district registrar a new notice of proposed civil partnership.]

94 The civil partnership schedule

[(1)] Where—

(a) the district registrar has received a notice of proposed civil partnership in respect of each of the intended civil partners and—

(i) is satisfied that there is no legal impediment to their registration as civil partners of each other, or

(ii) as the case may be, is informed under section 92(5)(b) that there is no such impediment,

(b) the [28 days] mentioned in paragraph (b) of section 90(2) have expired (or as the case may be the date which, by virtue of section [91(1)], that paragraph is to be construed as a reference to has been reached), and

(c) the period which has elapsed since the day of receipt of the notices by him (or, if the two notices were not received on the same day, since the day of receipt of the later) does not exceed 3 months, he is to complete a civil partnership schedule in the prescribed form.

[(2) In the case of a civil partnership to be registered by an approved celebrant, the civil partnership schedule completed in accordance with subsection (1) is to be issued by the district registrar to one or both of the parties to the intended civil partnership.

(3) The district registrar may not issue the civil partnership schedule on a date earlier than 7 days before the date of the intended civil partnership unless authorised to do so by the Registrar General.]

[94A Notice of proposed civil partnership: false information or evidence

(1) A district registrar may refuse to complete a civil partnership schedule under section 94 in a case where—

(a)   a civil partnership notice has been submitted under section 88(1), and

(b)   the district registrar has reasonable grounds for suspecting that a relevant decision was made incorrectly because of the provision of false information or evidence in or accompanying that notice.

(2)   If the district registrar refuses to complete a civil partnership schedule under subsection (1), the parties to the proposed civil partnership are to be taken not to have submitted a notice of proposed civil partnership under section 88; but that does not prevent criminal proceedings from being brought against either party, or any other person, in relation to the submission of notice.

(3)   This section is without prejudice to any other powers of district registrars to refuse to complete a civil partnership schedule.

(4)   In this section—

'evidence' includes a photograph or other image;

'exempt person' has the same meaning as in section 88F;

'relevant decision' means a decision of a district registrar that a party to the proposed civil partnership is an exempt person.]

[94A   Persons who may register civil partnerships

(1)   A civil partnership [between persons of the same sex] may be registered by and only by—

(a)   a person who is—

(i)   a celebrant of a religious or belief body prescribed by regulations made by the Scottish Ministers, or who, not being a celebrant, is recognised by a religious or belief body so prescribed as entitled to register civil partnerships [between persons of the same sex] on its behalf,

(ii)   registered under section 94B [to register civil partnerships between persons of the same sex], or

(iii)   temporarily authorised under section 94E [to register civil partnerships between persons of the same sex], or

(b)   a person who is a district registrar or assistant registrar appointed under section 87.

(2)   The Scottish Ministers may prescribe a religious or belief body under subsection (1)(a)(i) only if—

(a)   the body requests them to do so, and

(b)   the Scottish Ministers are satisfied that the body meets the qualifying requirements.

[(2A)   A civil partnership between persons of different sexes may be registered by and only by—

(a)   a person who is—

(i)   a celebrant of a religious or belief body prescribed by regulations made by the Scottish Ministers, or who, not being a celebrant, is recognised by a religious or belief body so prescribed as entitled to register civil partnerships between persons of different sexes on its behalf,

(ii)   registered under section 94B to register civil partnerships between persons of different sexes, or

(iii)   temporarily authorised under section 94E to register civil partnerships between persons of different sexes, or

(b)   a person who is a district registrar or assistant registrar appointed under section 87.

(2B)   The Scottish Ministers may prescribe a religious or belief body under subsection (2A)(a)(i) only if—

(a)   the body requests them to do so, and

(b)   the Scottish Ministers are satisfied that the body meets the qualifying requirements.]

(3)   For the avoidance of doubt, nothing in subsection (1)(a) [, (2)(a), (2A)(a) or (2B)(a)]—

(a) imposes a duty on any religious or belief body to make a request referred to in subsection (2)(a) [or subsection (2B)(a)],

(b) imposes a duty on any such body to nominate under section 94B any of its members to be registered as empowered to register civil partnerships [between persons of the same sex or between persons of different sexes],

(c) imposes a duty on any person to apply for temporary authorisation under section 94E to register civil partnerships [between persons of the same sex or between persons of different sexes],

(d) imposes a duty on any person who is an approved celebrant in relation to civil partnerships to register civil partnerships [between persons of the same sex or between persons of different sexes].

(4) In this Part—

(a) any such person as is mentioned in subsection (1)(a) [or (2A)(a)] is referred to as an 'approved celebrant',

(b) a civil partnership registered by an approved celebrant is referred to as a 'religious or belief civil partnership',

(c) a civil partnership registered by an authorised registrar is referred to as a 'civil registration'.

(5) In [subsections (2)(b) and (2B)(b)], the 'qualifying requirements' are such requirements as may be set out in regulations made by the Scottish Ministers.]

[94B Registration of nominated persons as celebrants

(1) A religious or belief body, not being prescribed by virtue of section 94A(1)(a)(i), may nominate to the Registrar General any of its members who it desires should be registered under this section as empowered to register civil partnerships [between persons of the same sex].

[(1A) A religious or belief body, not being prescribed by virtue of section 94A(2A)(a)(i), may nominate to the Registrar General any of its members who it desires should be registered under this section as empowered to register civil partnerships between persons of different sexes.]

(2) The Registrar General must reject a nomination under subsection (1) [or (1A)] if in the Registrar General's opinion—

(a) the nominating body is not a religious or belief body,

(b) the nominee is not a fit and proper person to register a civil partnership,

(c) there are already registered under this section sufficient members of the same body as the nominee to meet the needs of that body [in relation to registering civil partnerships between persons of the same sex or, as the case may be, civil partnerships between persons of different sexes], or

(d) the nominating body does not meet the qualifying requirements.

(3) In subsection (2)(d), the 'qualifying requirements' are such requirements as may be set out in regulations made by the Scottish Ministers.

(4) Where the Registrar General accepts a nomination made under subsection (1), the Registrar General—

(a) must determine the period during which the nominee is empowered to register civil partnerships, being a period of not more than 3 years,

(b) may determine that the nominee is empowered to register civil partnerships only in such area or place as the Registrar General may specify, and

(c) may make acceptance of the nominee's registration subject to such other conditions as the Registrar General thinks fit.

(5) Nothing in subsection (4)(a) prevents the Registrar General from accepting a further nomination of that nominee, in accordance with this section, to take effect at any time after the end of the period determined by the Registrar General under subsection (4)(a).

(6) The Registrar General must—

(a) if accepting a nomination made under subsection (1) [or (1A)]—

(i) so inform the nominee and the nominating body, specifying the period during which the acceptance has effect and any condition to which the acceptance is subject,

(ii) enter the name of the nominee, the nominating body and such other particulars as the Registrar General thinks fit in a register which the Registrar General must establish and maintain and which must be made available for public inspection at all reasonable times free of charge,

(b) if rejecting a nomination made under subsection (1) or (1A), by notice in writing inform the nominating body of the reasons for that rejection.

[(6A) The register mentioned in subsection (6)(a)(ii) is to be in two parts—

(a) the first part containing the details mentioned in subsection (6)(a)(ii) in relation to persons nominated by religious or belief bodies to register civil partnerships between persons of the same sex, and

(b) the second part containing those details in relation to persons nominated by religious or belief bodies to register civil partnerships between persons of different sexes.]

(7) For the purposes of subsection (6)(b), notice which is given by electronic means is to be treated as in writing if it is received in a form which is legible and capable of being used for subsequent reference.

(8) If the nominating body is aggrieved by a rejection under this section it may, within 28 days of receiving notice of the rejection, appeal to the Scottish Ministers.

(9) On any such appeal the Scottish Ministers may—

(a) direct the Registrar General to accept the nomination, or

(b) confirm the rejection of the nomination,

and must inform the nominating body of their decision and the reason for it; and their decision is final.

(10) If a reason given for confirming the rejection of a nomination is that the nominating body is not a religious or belief body, the body may, within 42 days of receiving notice of the confirmation, appeal against the decision to the Court of Session and seek the determination of that court as to whether the body is a religious or belief body.

(11) If—

(a) the Court determines that the nominating body is a religious or belief body, and

(b) the reason mentioned in subsection (10) was the only reason given for confirming the rejection of the nomination,

the Registrar General must give effect to the determination as if it were a direction under subsection (9)(a) to accept the nomination.]

[94C Removal of celebrant's name from register

(1) Subject to the provisions of this section, the Registrar General may remove the name of a person registered under section 94B from the register on the ground that—

(a) the person has requested that the person's name should be so removed,

(b) the body which nominated the person under section 94B(1) [or (1A)] no longer desires that the person should be so registered,

(c) the person—

(i) has, while registered as an approved celebrant, been convicted of an offence under this Part,

(ii) has, for the purpose of profit or gain, been carrying on a business of registering civil partnerships,

(iii) is not a fit and proper person to register civil partnerships, or

(iv) for any other reason, should not be registered as an approved celebrant.

(2) The Registrar General may not remove the name of a person from the

register on any ground mentioned in subsection (1)(c) unless the Registrar General has given the person at least 21 days notice in writing of the intention to do so.

(3) For the purposes of subsection (2), notice which is given by electronic means is to be treated as in writing if it is received in a form which is legible and capable of being used for subsequent reference.

(4) The Registrar General must—

(a) in the notice given under subsection (2), specify the ground of removal and call upon the person to give any reasons, within the period specified in the notice, why the person's name should not be removed from the register, and

(b) consider any representations made within that period by the person.

(5) Where a person's name has been removed from the register on any of the grounds mentioned in paragraph (c) of subsection (1), the person or the body which nominated the person under section 94B(1) [or (1A)] may, if aggrieved by the removal, within 28 days of receiving notice of the removal appeal to the Scottish Ministers.

(6) On an appeal under subsection (5) the Scottish Ministers may give any direction they think proper to the Registrar General as to the removal from, or restoration to, the register of the person's name; and such direction is final.

(7) Where a person has received a notice in pursuance of subsection (2), the person must not register a civil partnership unless and until the person's name is restored to the register or, as the case may be, the Registrar General has decided not to remove the person's name from the register.]

[94D Alterations to register maintained under section 94B

(1) A body registered in pursuance of section 94B(6)(a)(ii) must notify the Registrar General of any of the following events (if practicable, within 21 days of its occurrence)—

(a) any change in the name or the address of the body or any amalgamation with any other religious or belief body, giving the name and address of any approved celebrant who is a member of the body so registered,

(b) the death of an approved celebrant who is a member of the body so registered,

(c) any change of name, address or designation of an approved celebrant who is a member of the body so registered,

(d) the cessation of an approved celebrant who is a member of the body so registered from exercising the functions of an approved celebrant, giving the person's name and address.

(2) The Registrar General must, on receipt of any such notification, make whatever alteration to the register maintained under section 94B the Registrar General considers necessary or desirable.]

[94E Temporary authorisation of celebrants

(1) The Registrar General may, in accordance with such terms and conditions as may be specified in the authorisation, grant to any member of a religious or belief body a temporary written authorisation to register—

(a) a civil partnership or partnerships specified in the authorisation, or

(b) civil partnerships during such period as is specified in the authorisation.

(2) The Registrar General may grant an authorisation to a person under subsection (1) only if satisfied that the religious or belief body of which the person is a member meets the qualifying requirements.

[(2A) An authorisation under subsection (1)(b) may be granted in relation to—

(a) civil partnerships between persons of the same sex only,

(b) civil partnerships between persons of different sexes only, or

(c) both.]

(3) The Registrar General may grant an authorisation to a person under

subsection (1)(b) [in relation to civil partnerships between persons of the same sex] only if the religious or belief body of which the person is a member—

(a) is prescribed by virtue of section 94A(1)(a)(i), or

(b) has nominated members (whether or not including that person) under section 94B(1).

[(3A) The Registrar General may grant an authorisation to a person under subsection (1)(b) in relation to civil partnerships between persons of different sexes only if the religious or belief body of which the person is a member—

(a) is prescribed by virtue of section 94A(2A)(a)(i), or

(b) has nominated members (whether or not including that person) under section 94B(1A).]

(4) In subsection (2), the 'qualifying requirements' are such requirements as may be set out in regulations made by the Scottish Ministers.

(5) For the purposes of subsection (1), an authorisation which is issued by electronic means is to be treated as written if it is received in a form which is legible and capable of being used for subsequent reference.]

95 Further provision as to registration

(1) Before the persons present sign in accordance with section 85 [the approved celebrant or, as the case may be,] the authorised registrar is to require the intended civil partners to confirm that (to the best of their knowledge) the particulars set out in the civil partnership schedule are correct.

[(1A) In the case of a religious or belief civil partnership, the parties to the civil partnership must, within 3 days of signing the civil partnership schedule in accordance with section 85(4), deliver the civil partnership schedule, or send it by post or arrange that it is delivered, to the district registrar.]

(2) As soon as practicable [after—

(a) in the case of a civil registration, the civil partnership schedule has been signed in accordance with section 85, or

(b) in the case of a religious or belief civil partnership, the district registrar receives the civil partnership schedule,

the district registrar] must cause those particulars to be entered in a register (to be known as the 'civil partnership register') supplied to him for that purpose by the Registrar General.

(3) The form and content of any page of that register is to be prescribed.

[(3A) The district registrar must not enter the particulars set out in the civil partnership schedule relating to a religious or belief civil partnership in the civil partnership register unless and until the registrar receives a duly signed civil partnership schedule in respect of that civil partnership.

(3B) Where the Registrar General is satisfied that—

(a) a civil partnership has been properly registered, and

(b) the civil partnership schedule in respect of the civil partnership has been duly signed but has been lost or destroyed,

the Registrar General may direct the district registrar to complete an exact copy of the original civil partnership schedule and, so far as practicable, to arrange for its signature by those persons who signed the original schedule.

(3C) As soon as possible after the copy schedule has been signed, the district registrar must cause the particulars as set out in it to be entered into the civil partnership register.]

(4) A fee payable by the intended civil partners for their [civil] registration as civil partners of each other is to be prescribed.

[95ZA Registrar's power to require delivery of civil partnership schedule

(1) Where the civil partnership schedule is not delivered to the district registrar within 21 days from the date of registration as entered in the schedule, the registrar may serve a notice in the prescribed form on either of the parties to the civil

partnership requiring that party within 8 days from the date of service to deliver the schedule, or send it by post, to the registrar.

(2) If a person on whom a notice has been served under subsection (1) fails to comply with the notice, the district registrar may serve on the person a second notice in the prescribed form requiring the person to attend personally at the registration office of the district registrar, within 8 days from the date of service of the second notice, for the purpose of delivering the civil partnership schedule to the district registrar to enable the registrar to enter the civil partnership in the civil partnership register.]

[95A Validity following entry in civil partnership register

(1) Subsection (2) applies where the particulars set out in a civil partnership schedule signed in accordance with section 85 are entered in the civil partnership register in pursuance of section 95(2 [or (3C)]).

(2) The validity of the registration as civil partners to which the schedule relates is not to be questioned in any legal proceedings on the ground of failure to comply with a requirement or restriction imposed by or under this Part.

(3) Subsection (2)—
    (a) is subject to section 85(2), and
    (b) does not prejudice section 100.]

96 Civil partnership with former spouse

(1) Where an intended civil partner has a full gender recognition certificate issued under section 5(1) of the Gender Recognition Act 2004 (c 7) and the other intended civil partner was the other party in the proceedings in which the certificate was issued, the procedures for their registration as civil partners of each other may—
    (a) if they so elect, and
    (b) if each of them submits a notice under section 88(1) within 30 days after
the certificate is issued,
be expedited as follows.

(2) The registration may take place on any of the 30 days immediately following—
    (a) that on which the notices are submitted, or
    (b) (if the two notices are not submitted on the same day) that on which the
later is submitted.

(3) And accordingly there are to be disregarded—
    (a) in section 90—
        (i) in subsection (2)(b), the words from 'being' to the end, and
        (ii) subsection (3),
    (b) section [91(1)], and
    (c) in section 94, [subsection (1)(b)].

97 Certificates of no impediment for Part 2 purposes

(1) This section applies where—
    (a) two people propose to register as civil partners of each other under Chapter 1 of Part 2, and
    (b) one of them ('A') resides in Scotland but the other ('B') resides in England or Wales.

(2) A may submit a notice of intention to register under section 88 as if A and B intended to register as civil partners in the district in which A resides.

(3) If the district registrar is satisfied (after consultation, if he considers it necessary, with the Registrar General) that there is no impediment (in terms of section 92(6)) to A registering as B's civil partner, he must issue a certificate to A in the prescribed form that there is not known to be any such impediment.

(4) But the certificate may not be issued to A earlier than [28 days] after the

receipt (as entered in the civil partnership notice book) of the notice under subsection (2) unless—

(a)   the circumstances are as mentioned in section 96(1), and

(b)   A makes an election for the certificate to be issued as soon as possible.

(5)   Any person may, at any time before a certificate is issued under subsection (3), submit to the district registrar an objection in writing to its issue.

[(5A)   For the purposes of subsection (5), an objection which is submitted by electronic means is to be treated as in writing if it is received in a form which is legible and capable of being used for subsequent reference.]

(6)   Any objection made under subsection (5) must be taken into account by the district registrar in deciding whether he is satisfied that there is no legal impediment to A registering as B's civil partner.

[97A   Second civil partnership registration

(1)   Subsection (2) applies where—

(a)   two people have registered a specified relationship (within the meaning of section 213) or a relationship which meets the general conditions (within the meaning of section 214), whether before or after section 8 of the Civil Partnership (Scotland) Act 2020 comes into force, and

(b)   that relationship would result in them being treated as having formed a civil partnership under the law of Scotland (by virtue of section 1(1)(b) and Chapter 2 of Part 5) but for the fact that they cannot prove that the relationship has been registered as mentioned in section 212(1)(b).

(2)   An authorised registrar may, on an application made by the parties to the relationship, subject to the approval of the Registrar General and to subsection (3), register their civil partnership as if they had not already registered that relationship with each other.

(3)   Sections 85 to 100 apply for the purpose of registering a civil partnership under this section as they apply to registering a civil partnership under section 1, subject to the modifications set out in subsections (4) to (11).

(4)   Section 85 (formation of civil partnership by registration) applies as if the words 'the approved celebrant or, as the case may be,', in both places where they occur, were omitted.

(5)   Section 86 (eligibility) does not apply in respect of the parties already being in civil partnership with each other.

(6)   Section 88 (notice of proposed civil partnership) applies as if after subsection (1) there were inserted—

'(1A)   Both parties must submit to the authorised registrar a statutory declaration—

(a)   stating that they have previously registered their relationship, and

(b)   specifying the date, place and country or territory at which, and the circumstances in which, they did so.'.

(7)   Section 93A does not apply.

(8)   Section 94 (the civil partnership schedule) applies as if after subsection (1) there were inserted—

'(1A)   In the case of a civil partnership to be registered under section 97A, the civil partnership schedule is to contain such modifications as the Registrar General may direct to indicate that the parties have previously entered into a civil partnership with each other.'.

(9)   Section 94A (persons who may register civil partnerships) applies as if subsections (1)(a), (2), (2A)(a), (2B), (3), (4)(a) and (b) and (5) were omitted.

(10)   Sections 94B to 94E do not apply.

(11)   Section 95 (further provision as to registration) applies as if after subsection (2) there were inserted—

'(2A)   As soon as practicable after the civil partnership schedule has been signed in accordance with section 85, the authorised registrar must make an endorsement on it in the following terms—

"This civil partnership registration was carried out under section 97A of the Civil Partnership Act 2004, following a statutory declaration by the parties that they registered a relationship with each other on [*date*] at [*place*] in [*country or territory*].'"]

[98   Application of certain provisions to civil partnership

(1)   The following sections of the 1965 Act apply in relation to the civil partnership register as they apply in relation to the registers of births, marriages and deaths—

    (a)   section 34 (examination and transmission of registers),

    (b)   section 38(1) and (2) (search of indexes kept by Registrar General),

    (c)   section 39C (provision of information to district registrars), and

    (d)   section 44 (Register of Corrections Etc).

[. . .].

99   Correction of errors in civil partnership register

(1)   No alteration is to be made in the civil partnership register except as authorised by or under this or any other Act ('Act' including an Act of the Scottish Parliament).

(2)   Any clerical error in the register or error in it of a kind prescribed may be corrected by the district registrar.

(3)   The Registrar General may authorise district examiners ('district examiner' having the meaning given by section 2(1) of the 1965 Act) to correct any error in the register of a type specified by him which they discover during an examination under section 34 of the 1965 Act.

100   Offences

(1)   A person ('A') commits an offence who [purports to register] in Scotland as the civil partner of another person ('B') knowing that either or both—

    (a)   A is already married to or in civil partnership with a person other than B, or

    (b)   B is already married to or in civil partnership with a person other than A.

(2)   A person commits an offence who knowingly—

    (a)   falsifies or forges any civil partnership document (that is to say, any document issued or made, or purporting to be issued or made, or required, under this Part),

    (b)   uses, or gives or sends to any person as genuine, any false or forged civil partnership document,

    (c)   being [an approved celebrant or, as the case may be,] an authorised registrar, purports to register two people as civil partners of each other before any civil partnership schedule available to him at the time of registration has been duly completed,

    (d)   not being [an approved celebrant or, as the case may be,] an authorised registrar, conducts himself in such a way as to lead intended civil partners to believe that he is authorised to register them as civil partners of each other,

    (e)   being [an approved celebrant or, as the case may be,] an authorised registrar, purports to register two people as civil partners of each other without both of them being present, or

    (f)   being an authorised registrar, purports to register two people as civil partners of each other in a place other than a registration office or [in accordance with section 93].

(3)   A person guilty of an offence under subsection (1) or (2) is liable—

(a)   on conviction on indictment, to imprisonment for a term not exceeding 2 years or to a fine (or both);

(b)   on summary conviction, to imprisonment for a term not exceeding 3 months or to a fine not exceeding [the statutory maximum] (or both).

[(3A)   A person commits an offence if the person—

(a)   registers a civil partnership in an area or place in which by virtue of section 94B(4)(b) the person is not permitted to register a civil partnership,

(b)   registers a civil partnership in contravention of section 94C(7),

(c)   being a person temporarily authorised under section 94E—

    (i)   if authorised under subsection (1)(a) of that section, registers a civil partnership not specified in the authorisation,

    (ii)   if authorised under subsection (1)(b) of that section, registers a civil partnership outwith the period specified in the authorisation,

    (iii)   in either case, registers a civil partnership otherwise than in accordance with such terms and conditions as may be specified in the authorisation,

(d)   being a party to a civil partnership, fails to comply with a notice served under section 95ZA(2).

(3B)   A person guilty of an offence under subsection (3A) is liable on summary conviction to a fine not exceeding level 3 on the standard scale.]

(4)   Summary proceedings for an offence under subsection (1) [, (2) or (3A)] may be commenced at any time within 3 months after evidence sufficient in the opinion of the Lord Advocate to justify the proceedings comes to his knowledge or within 12 months after the offence is committed (whichever period last expires).

(5)   Subsection (3) of section 136 of the Criminal Procedure (Scotland) Act 1995 (c 46) (time limits) has effect for the purposes of this section as it has for the purposes of that section.

CHAPTER 3
Occupancy Rights and Tenancies

Occupancy rights

101   Occupancy rights

(1)   Where, apart from the provisions of this Chapter, one civil partner in a civil partnership is entitled, or permitted by a third party, to occupy a family home of the civil partnership (that civil partner being referred in this Chapter as an 'entitled partner') and the other civil partner is not so entitled or permitted (a 'non-entitled partner'), the non-entitled partner has, subject to the provisions of this Chapter, the following rights—

(a)   if in occupation, a right to continue to occupy the family home;

(b)   if not in occupation, a right to enter into and occupy the family home.

(2)   The rights conferred by subsection (1) to continue to occupy or, as the case may be, to enter and occupy the family home include, without prejudice to their generality, the right to do so together with any child of the family.

(3)   In subsection (1), an 'entitled partner' includes a civil partner who is entitled, or permitted by a third party, to occupy the family home along with an individual who is not the other civil partner only if that individual has waived a right of occupation in favour of the civil partner so entitled or permitted.

(4)   If the entitled partner refuses to allow the non-entitled partner to exercise the right conferred by subsection (1)(b), the non-entitled partner may exercise that right only with the leave of the Court of Session or the sheriff under section 103(3) or (4).

(5)   A non-entitled partner may renounce in writing the rights mentioned in paragraphs (a) and (b) of subsection (1) only—

(a)   in a particular family home, or

(b)   in a particular property which it is intended by the civil partners will become their family home.

(6)   A renunciation under subsection (5) has effect only if, at the time of making the renunciation, the non-entitled partner swears or affirms before a notary public that it is made freely and without coercion of any kind.

[(6A)   Subject to subsection (5), if—

(a)   there has been no cohabitation between an entitled partner and a non-entitled partner during a continuous period of two years, and

(b)   during that period the non-entitled partner has not occupied the family home,

the non-entitled partner shall, on the expiry of that period, cease to have occupancy rights in the family home.

(6B)   A non-entitled partner who has ceased to have occupancy rights by virtue of subsection (6A) may not apply to the court for an order under section 103(1).]

(7)   In this Part—

'child of the family' means [any child or grandchild of either civil partner, and any person who has been brought up or treated by either civil partner as if the person were a child of that partner, whatever the age of such a child, grandchild or person], and

'family' means the civil partners in the civil partnership, together with any child [, grandchild or person so treated] by them.

(8)   In subsection (6), 'notary public' includes any person duly authorised, by the law of the country other than Scotland in which the swearing or affirmation takes place, to administer oaths or receive affirmations in that other country.

102   Occupancy: subsidiary and consequential rights

(1)   For the purpose of securing the occupancy rights of a non-entitled partner, that partner is, in relation to a family home, entitled without the consent of the entitled partner—

(a)   to make any payment due by the entitled partner in respect of rent, rates, secured loan instalments, interest or other outgoings (not being outgoings on repairs or improvements);

(b)   to perform any other obligation incumbent on the entitled partner (not being an obligation in respect of non-essential repairs or improvements);

(c)   to enforce performance of an obligation by a third party which that third party has undertaken to the entitled partner to the extent that the entitled partner may enforce such performance;

(d)   to carry out such essential repairs as the entitled partner may carry out;

(e)   to carry out such non-essential repairs or improvements as may be authorised by an order of the court, being such repairs or improvements as the entitled partner may carry out and which the court considers to be appropriate for the reasonable enjoyment of the occupancy rights;

(f)   to take such other steps, for the purpose of protecting the occupancy rights of the non-entitled partner, as the entitled partner may take to protect the occupancy rights of the entitled partner.

(2)   Any payment made under subsection (1)(a) or any obligation performed under subsection (1)(b) has effect in relation to the rights of a third party as if the payment were made or the obligation were performed by the entitled partner; and the performance of an obligation which has been enforced under subsection (1)(c) has effect as if it had been enforced by the entitled partner.

(3)   Where there is an entitled and a non-entitled partner, the court, on the application of either of them, may, having regard in particular to the respective

financial circumstances of the partners, make an order apportioning expenditure
incurred or to be incurred by either partner—

    (a)   without the consent of the other partner, on any of the items mentioned
in paragraphs (a) and (d) of subsection (1);

    (b)   with the consent of the other partner, on anything relating to a family
home.

(4)   Where both partners are entitled, or permitted by a third party, to occupy a
family home—

    (a)   either partner is entitled, without the consent of the other partner, to
carry out such non-essential repairs or improvements as may be authorised
by an order of the court, being such repairs or improvements as the court
considers to be appropriate for the reasonable enjoyment of the occupancy
rights;

    (b)   the court, on the application of either partner, may, having regard in par-
ticular to the respective financial circumstances of the partners, make an order
apportioning expenditure incurred or to be incurred by either partner, with or
without the consent of the other partner, on anything relating to the family
home.

(5)   Where one partner ('A') owns or hires, or is acquiring under a hire-
purchase or conditional sale agreement, furniture and plenishings in a family
home—

    (a)   the other partner may, without the consent of A—

        (i)   make any payment due by A which is necessary, or take any other
step which A is entitled to take, to secure the possession or use of any such
furniture and plenishings (and any such payment is to have effect in relation
to the rights of a third party as if it were made by A), or

        (ii)   carry out such essential repairs to the furniture and plenishings as A is
entitled to carry out;

    (b)   the court, on the application of either partner, may, having regard in par-
ticular to the respective financial circumstances of the partners, make an order
apportioning expenditure incurred or to be incurred by either partner—

        (i)   without the consent of the other partner, in making payments under a
hire, hire-purchase or conditional sale agreement, or in paying interest charges
in respect of the furniture and plenishings, or in carrying out essential repairs
to the furniture and plenishings, or

        (ii)   with the consent of the other partner, on anything relating to the
furniture or plenishings.

(6)   An order under subsection (3), (4)(b) or (5)(b) may require one partner
to make a payment to the other partner in implementation of the apportionment.

(7)   Any application under subsection (3), (4)(b) or (5)(b) is to be made within 5
years after the date on which any payment in respect of such incurred expenditure
was made.

(8)   Where—

    (a)   the entitled partner is a tenant of a family home,

    (b)   possession of it is necessary in order to continue the tenancy, and

    (c)   the entitled partner abandons such possession,
the tenancy is continued by such possession by the non-entitled partner.

(9)   In this section 'improvements' includes alterations and enlargement.

103   Regulation by court of rights of occupancy of family home

(1)   [Subject to section 101(6A),] where there is an entitled and a non-entitled
partner, or where both partners are entitled, or permitted by a third party, to
occupy a family home, either partner may apply to the court for an order—

    (a)   declaring the occupancy rights of the applicant partner;

    (b)   enforcing the occupancy rights of the applicant partner;

    (c)   restricting the occupancy rights of the non-applicant partner;

    (d)   regulating the exercise by either partner of his or her occupancy rights;

    (e)   protecting the occupancy rights of the applicant partner in relation to the other partner.

(2) Where one partner owns or hires, or is acquiring under a hire-purchase or conditional sale agreement, furniture and plenishings in a family home and the other partner has occupancy rights in that home, that other person may apply to the court for an order granting to the applicant the possession or use in the family home of any such furniture and plenishings; but, subject to section 102, an order under this subsection does not prejudice the rights of any third party in relation to the non-performance of any obligation under such hire-purchase or conditional sale agreement.

(3) The court is to grant an application under subsection (1)(a) if it appears to the court that the application relates to a family home; and, on an application under any of paragraphs (b) to (e) of subsection (1) or under subsection (2), the court may make such order relating to the application as appears to it to be just and reasonable having regard to all the circumstances of the case including—

    (a)   the conduct of the partners, whether in relation to each other or otherwise,

    (b)   the respective needs and financial resources of the partners,

    (c)   the needs of any child of the family,

    (d)   the extent (if any) to which—

        (i)   the family home, and

        (ii)   in relation only to an order under subsection (2), any item of furniture and plenishings referred to in that subsection, is used in connection with a trade, business or profession of either partner, and

    (e)   whether the entitled partner offers or has offered to make available to the non-entitled partner any suitable alternative accommodation.

(4) Pending the making of an order under subsection (3), the court, on the application of either partner, may make such interim order as it considers necessary or expedient in relation to—

    (a)   the residence of either partner in the home to which the application relates,

    (b)   the personal effects of either partner or of any child of the family, or

    (c)   the furniture and plenishings,

but an interim order may be made only if the non-applicant partner has been afforded an opportunity of being heard by or represented before the court.

(5) The court is not to make an order under subsection (3) or (4) if it appears that the effect of the order would be to exclude the non-applicant partner from the family home.

(6) If the court makes an order under subsection (3) or (4) which requires the delivery to one partner of anything which has been left in or removed from the family home, it may also grant a warrant authorising a [judicial officer] to enter the family home or other premises occupied by the other partner and to search for and take possession of the thing required to be delivered, (if need be by opening shut and lockfast places) and to deliver the thing in accordance with the order.

(7) A warrant granted under subsection (6) is to be executed only after expiry of such period as the court is to specify in the order for delivery.

(8) Where it appears to the court—

    (a)   on the application of a non-entitled partner, that the applicant has suffered a loss of occupancy rights or that the quality of the applicant's occupation of a family home has been impaired, or

    (b)   on the application of a partner who has been given the possession or use of furniture and plenishings by virtue of an order under subsection (3), that the applicant has suffered a loss of such possession or use or that the quality of the applicant's possession or use of the furniture and plenishings has been impaired, in consequence of any act or default on the part of the other partner which was intended to result in such loss or impairment, it may order that other partner to pay to the applicant such compensation as it considers just and reasonable in respect of that loss or impairment.

(9)   A partner may renounce in writing the right to apply under subsection (2) for the possession or use of any item of furniture and plenishings.

104   Exclusion orders

(1)   Where there is an entitled and non-entitled partner, or where both partners are entitled, or permitted by a third party, to occupy a family home, either partner, whether or not that partner is in occupation at the time of the application, may apply to the court for an order (in this Chapter referred to as 'an exclusion order') suspending the occupancy rights of the other partner ('the non-applicant partner') in a family home.

(2)   Subject to subsection (3), the court is to make an exclusion order if it appears to it that to do so is necessary for the protection of the applicant or any child of the family from any conduct, or threatened or reasonably apprehended conduct, of the non-applicant partner which is or would be injurious to the physical or mental health of the applicant or child.

(3)   The court is not to make an exclusion order if it appears to it that to do so would be unjustified or unreasonable—

(a)   having regard to all the circumstances of the case including the matters specified in paragraphs (a) to (e) of section 103(3), and

(b)   where the family home—

(i)   is, or is part of, an agricultural holding within the meaning of section 1 of the Agricultural Holdings (Scotland) Act 1991 (c 55), or

(ii)   is let, or is a home in respect of which possession is given, to the non-applicant partner or to both partners by an employer as an incident of employment,

having regard to any requirement that the non-applicant partner, or, as the case may be, both partners must reside in the family home and to the likely consequences of the exclusion of the non-applicant partner from the family home.

(4)   In making an exclusion order the court is, on the application of the applicant partner—

(a)   to grant a warrant for the summary ejection of the non-applicant partner from the family home unless the non-applicant partner satisfies the court that it is unnecessary for it to grant such a remedy,

(b)   to grant an interdict prohibiting the non-applicant partner from entering the family home without the express permission of the applicant, and

(c)   to grant an interdict prohibiting the removal by the non-applicant partner, except with the written consent of the applicant or by a further order of the court, of any furniture and plenishings in the family home unless the non-applicant partner satisfies the court that it is unnecessary for it to grant such a remedy.

(5)   In making an exclusion order the court may—

(a)   grant an interdict prohibiting the non-applicant partner from entering or remaining in a specified area in the vicinity of the family home;

(b)   where the warrant for the summary ejection of the non-applicant partner has been granted in that partner's absence, give directions as to the preservation of that partner's goods and effects which remain in the family home;

(c)   on the application of either partner, make the exclusion order or the warrant or interdict mentioned in paragraph (a), (b) or (c) of subsection (4) or paragraph (a) of this subsection subject to such terms and conditions as the court may prescribe;

(d)   on the application of either partner, make such other order as it considers necessary for the proper enforcement of an order made under subsection (4) or paragraph (a), (b) or (c).

(6)   Pending the making of an exclusion order, the court may, on the application of the applicant partner, make an interim order suspending the occupancy rights of the non-applicant partner in the family home to which the application for the exclusion order relates; and subsections (4) and (5) apply to such an interim order as they apply to an exclusion order.

(7)   But an interim order may be made only if the non-applicant partner has been afforded an opportunity of being heard by or represented before the court.

(8)   Without prejudice to subsections (1) and (6), where both partners are entitled, or permitted by a third party, to occupy a family home, it is incompetent for one partner to bring an action of ejection from the family home against the other partner.

105   Duration of orders under sections 103 and 104

(1)   The court may, on the application of either partner, vary or recall any order made by it under section 103 or 104.

(2)   Subject to subsection (3), any such order, unless previously so varied or recalled, ceases to have effect—

   (a)   on the dissolution of the civil partnership,

   (b)   subject to section 106(1), where there is an entitled and non-entitled partner, on the entitled partner ceasing to be an entitled partner in respect of the family home to which the order relates, or

   (c)   where both partners are entitled, or permitted by a third party, to occupy the family home, on both partners ceasing to be so entitled or permitted.

(3)   Without prejudice to the generality of subsection (2), an order under section 103(3) or (4) which grants the possession or use of furniture and plenishings ceases to have effect if the furniture and plenishings cease to be permitted by a third party to be retained in the family home.

106   Continued exercise of occupancy rights after dealing

(1)   Subject to subsection (3)—

   (a)   the continued exercise of the rights conferred on a non-entitled partner by the provisions of this Chapter in respect of a family home are not prejudiced by reason only of any dealing of the entitled partner relating to that home, and

   (b)   a third party is not by reason only of such a dealing entitled to occupy that home or any part of it.

[(1A)   The occupancy rights of a non-entitled partner in relation to a family home shall not be exercisable in relation to the home where, following a dealing of the entitled partner relating to the home—

   (a)   a person acquires the home, or an interest in it, in good faith and for value from a person other than the person who is or, as the case may be, was the entitled partner, or

   (b)   a person derives title to the home from a person who acquired title as mentioned in paragraph (a).]

(2)   In this section and section 107—

'dealing' includes the grant of a heritable security and the creation of a trust but does not include a conveyance under section 80 of the Lands Clauses Consolidation Act 1845 (c 18);

'entitled partner' does not include a civil partner who, apart from the provisions of this Chapter—

   (a)   is permitted by a third party to occupy a family home, or

   (b)   is entitled to occupy a family home along with an individual who is not the other civil partner whether or not that individual has waived a right of occupation in favour of the civil partner so entitled, ('non-entitled partner' being construed accordingly).

(3)   This section does not apply in any case where—

(a)   the non-entitled partner in writing either—

(i)   consents or has consented to the dealing (any consent being in such form as the Scottish Ministers may, by regulations made by statutory instrument, prescribe), or

(ii)   renounces or has renounced occupancy rights in relation to the family home or property to which the dealing relates,

(b)   the court has made an order under section 107 dispensing with the consent of the non-entitled partner to the dealing,

(c)   the dealing occurred, or implements a binding obligation entered into by the entitled partner, before the registration of the civil partnership,

(d)   the dealing occurred, or implements a binding obligation entered into, before the commencement of this section,

(e)   the dealing comprises a [transfer for value] to a third party who has acted in good faith, if there is produced to the third party by the [transferor—

(i)   a written declaration signed by the transferor, or a person acting on behalf of the transferor under a power of attorney or as a guardian (within the meaning of the Adults with Incapacity (Scotland) Act 2000 (asp 4)), that the subjects of the transfer are not, or were not at the time of the dealing, a family home in relation to which a civil partner or the transferor has or had occupancy rights, or

(ii)   a renunciation of occupancy rights or consent to the dealing which bears to have been properly made or given by the non-entitled partner or a person acting on behalf of the non-entitled partner under a power of attorney or as a guardian (within the meaning of the Adults with Incapacity (Scotland) Act 2000 (asp 4)).]

(f)   the entitled partner has permanently ceased to be entitled to occupy the family home, and at any time after that a continuous period of [2] years has elapsed during which the non-entitled partner has not occupied the family home.

(4)   For the purposes of subsection (3)(e), the time of the dealing, in the case of the sale of an interest in heritable property, is the date of delivery to the purchaser of the deed transferring title to that interest.

107   Dispensation with civil partner's consent to dealing

(1)   [Subject to subsections (1A) and (1C),] the court may, on the application of an entitled partner or any other person having an interest, make an order dispensing with the consent of a non-entitled partner to a dealing which has taken place or a proposed dealing, if—

(a)   such consent is unreasonably withheld,

(b)   such consent cannot be given by reason of physical or mental disability, or

(c)   the non-entitled partner cannot be found after reasonable steps have been taken to trace that partner.

[(1A)   Subsection (1B) applies if, in relation to a proposed sale—

(a)   negotiations with a third party have not begun, or

(b)   negotiations have begun but a price has not been agreed.

(1B)   An order under subsection (1) dispensing with consent may be made only if—

(a)   the price agreed for the sale is no less than such amount as the court specifies in the order, and

(b)   the contract for the sale is concluded before the expiry of such period as may be so specified.

(1C)   Subsection (1D) applies if the proposed dealing is the grant of a heritable security.

(1D)   An order under subsection (1) dispensing with consent may be made only if—

(a)   the heritable security is granted for a loan of no more than such amount as the court specifies in the order, and

(b)   the security is executed before the expiry of such period as may be so specified.]

(2)   For the purposes of subsection (1)(a), a non-entitled partner has unreasonably withheld consent to a dealing which has taken place or a proposed dealing, where it appears to the court either—

(a)   that the non-entitled partner—

(i)   has led the entitled partner to believe that the non-entitled partner would consent to the dealing, and

(ii)   would not be prejudiced by any change in the circumstances of the case since the conduct which gave rise to that belief occurred, or

(b)   that the entitled partner has, having taken all reasonable steps to do so, been unable to obtain an answer to a request for consent.

(3)   The court, in considering whether to make an order under subsection (1), is to have regard to all the circumstances of the case including the matters specified in paragraphs (a) to (e) of section 103(3).

[(3A)   If the court refuses an application for an order under subsection (1), it may make an order requiring a non-entitled partner who is or becomes the occupier of the family home—

(a)   to make such payments to the owner of the home in respect of that partner's occupation of it as may be specified in the order,

(b)   to comply with such other conditions relating to that partner's occupation of the family home as may be so specified.]

(4)   Where—

(a)   an application is made for an order under this section, and

(b)   an action is or has been raised by a non-entitled partner to enforce occupancy rights,

the action is to be sisted until the conclusion of the proceedings on the application.

108   Interests of heritable creditors

(1)   The rights of a third party with an interest in the family home as a creditor under a secured loan in relation to the non-performance of any obligation under the loan are not prejudiced by reason only of the occupancy rights of the non-entitled partner; but where a non-entitled partner has or obtains occupation of a family home and—

(a)   the entitled partner is not in occupation, and

(b)   there is a third party with such an interest in the family home,

the court may, on the application of the third party, make an order requiring the non-entitled partner to make any payment due by the entitled partner in respect of the loan.

(2)   This section does not apply to secured loans in respect of which the security was granted prior to the commencement of section 13 of the Law Reform (Miscellaneous Provisions) (Scotland) Act 1985 (c 73) unless the third party in granting the secured loan acted in good faith and there was produced to the third party by the entitled partner—

(a)   [a written declaration signed] by the entitled partner declaring that there is no non-entitled partner, or

(b)   a renunciation of occupancy rights or consent to the taking of the loan which bears to have been properly made or given by the non-entitled partner.

(3)   This section does not apply to secured loans in respect of which the security was granted after the commencement of section 13 of the Law Reform (Miscellaneous Provisions) (Scotland) Act 1985 (c 73) unless the third party in granting the secured loan acted in good faith and there was produced to the third party by the grantor—

(a)   [a written declaration signed] by the grantor declaring that the security subjects are not or were not at the time of the granting of the security a family home in relation to which a civil partner of the grantor has or had occupancy rights, or

(b)   a renunciation of occupancy rights or consent to the granting of the security which bears to have been properly made or given by the non-entitled partner.

(4)   For the purposes of subsections (2) and (3), the time of granting a security, in the case of a heritable security, is the date of delivery of the deed creating the security.

109   Provisions where both civil partners have title

(1)   Subject to subsection (2), where, apart from the provisions of this Chapter, both civil partners are entitled to occupy a family home—

(a)   the rights in that home of one civil partner are not prejudiced by reason only of any dealing of the other civil partner, and

(b)   a third party is not by reason only of such a dealing entitled to occupy that home or any part of it.

(2)   Sections 106(3) and 107 and the definition of 'dealing' in section 106(2) apply for the purposes of subsection (1) as they apply for the purposes of section 106(1) but subject to the following modifications—

(a)   any reference to the entitled partner and to the non-entitled partner is to be construed as a reference to a civil partner who has entered into, or as the case may be proposes to enter into, a dealing and to the other civil partner respectively, and

(b)   in paragraph (b) of section 107(4) the reference to occupancy rights is to be construed as a reference to any rights in the family home.

110   Rights of occupancy in relation to division and sale

Where a civil partner brings an action for the division and sale of a family home owned in common with the other civil partner, the court, after having regard to all the circumstances of the case including—

(a)   the matters specified in paragraphs (a) to (d) of section 103(3), and

(b)   whether the civil partner bringing the action offers or has offered to make available to the other civil partner any suitable alternative accommodation, may refuse to grant decree in that action or may postpone the granting of decree for such period as it considers reasonable in the circumstances or may grant decree subject to such conditions as it may prescribe.

111   Adjudication

(1)   Where a family home as regards which there is an entitled partner and a non-entitled partner is adjudged, the Court of Session, on the application of the non-entitled partner made within 40 days after the date of the decree of adjudication, may—

(a)   order the reduction of the decree, or

(b)   make such order as it thinks appropriate to protect the occupancy rights of the non-entitled partner,

if satisfied that the purpose of the diligence was wholly or mainly to defeat the occupancy rights of the non-entitled partner.

(2)   Section 106(2) applies in construing 'entitled partner' and 'non-entitled partner' for the purposes of subsection (1).

[111A   Effect of court action under section 103, 104 or 105 on reckoning of periods in sections 101 and 106

(1)   Subsection (2) applies where an application is made under section 103(1), 104(1) or 105(1).

(2)   In calculating the period of two years mentioned in section 101(6A)(a) or 106(3)(f), no account shall be taken of the period mentioned in subsection (3).

(3)   The period is the period beginning with the date on which the application is made and—

(a)   in the case of an application under section 103(1) or 104(1), ending on the date on which—

(i)   an order under section 103(3) or, as the case may be, 104(2) is made, or

(ii)   the application is otherwise finally determined or abandoned,

(b)   in the case of an application under section 105(1), ending on the date on which—

(i)   the order under section 103(3) or, as the case may be, 104(2) is varied or recalled, or

(ii)   the application is otherwise finally determined or abandoned.]

Transfer of tenancy

112   Transfer of tenancy

(1)   The court may, on the application of a non-entitled partner, make an order transferring the tenancy of a family home to that partner and providing, subject to subsection (12), for the payment by the non-entitled partner to the entitled partner of such compensation as seems to it to be just and reasonable in all the circumstances of the case.

(2)   In an action—

(a)   for dissolution of a civil partnership, the Court of Session or the sheriff,

(b)   for declarator of nullity of a civil partnership, the Court of Session,

may, on granting decree or within such period as the court may specify on granting decree, make an order granting an application under subsection (1).

(3)   In determining whether to grant an application under subsection (1), the court is to have regard to all the circumstances of the case including the matters specified in paragraphs (a) to (e) of section 103(3) and the suitability of the applicant to become the tenant and the applicant's capacity to perform the obligations under the lease of the family home.

(4)   The non-entitled partner is to serve a copy of an application under subsection (1) on the landlord and, before making an order under subsection (1), the court is to give the landlord an opportunity of being heard by it.

(5)   On the making of an order granting an application under subsection (1), the tenancy vests in the non-entitled partner without intimation to the landlord, subject to all the liabilities under the lease (other than liability for any arrears of rent for the period before the making of the order).

(6)   The arrears mentioned in subsection (5) are to remain the liability of the original entitled partner.

(7)   The clerk of court is to notify the landlord of the making of an order granting an application under subsection (1).

(8)   It is not competent for a non-entitled partner to apply for an order under subsection (1) where the family home—

(a)   is let to the entitled partner by the entitled partner's employer as an incident of employment, and the lease is subject to a requirement that the entitled partner must reside there,

(b)   is or is part of an agricultural holding,

(c)   is on, or pertains to—

(i)   a croft,

(ii)   the subject of a cottar, or

(iii)   the holding of a landholder or of a statutory small tenant,

(d)   is let on a long lease, or

(e)   is part of the tenancy land of a tenant-at-will.

(9)   In subsection (8)—

'agricultural holding' has the same meaning as in section 1 of the Agricultural Holdings (Scotland) Act 1991 (c 55),

'cottar' has the same meaning as in section 12(5) of the Crofters (Scotland) Act 1993 (c 44), 'croft' has the same meaning as in that Act of 1993,

'holding', in relation to a landholder and a statutory small tenant,

'landholder' and 'statutory small tenant' have the same meanings respectively as in sections 2(1), 2(2) and 32(1) of the Small Landholders (Scotland) Act 1911 (c 49),

'long lease' has the same meaning as in section [9(2) of the Land Registration etc (Scotland) Act 2012], and

'tenant-at-will' has the same meaning as in section 20(8) of that Act of 1979.

(10)   Where both civil partners are joint or common tenants of a family home, the court may, on the application of one of the civil partners, make an order vesting the tenancy in that civil partner solely and providing, subject to subsection (12), for the payment by the applicant to the other partner of such compensation as seems just and reasonable in the circumstances of the case.

(11)   Subsections (2) to (9) apply for the purposes of an order under subsection (10) as they apply for the purposes of an order under subsection (1) but subject to the following modifications—

    (a)   in subsection (3), for 'tenant' there is substituted 'sole tenant';

    (b)   in subsection (4), for 'non-entitled' there is substituted 'applicant';

    (c)   in subsection (5), for 'non-entitled' there is substituted 'applicant',

    (d)   in subsection (6), for 'liability of the original entitled partner' there is substituted 'joint and several liability of both partners';

    (e)   in subsection (8)—

      (i)   for 'a non-entitled' there is substituted 'an applicant',

      (ii)   for paragraph (a) there is substituted—

'(a) is let to both partners by their employer as an incident of employment, and the lease is subject to a requirement that both partners must reside there;', and

      (iii)   paragraphs (c) and (e) are omitted.

(12)   Where the family home is a Scottish secure tenancy within the meaning of the Housing (Scotland) Act 2001 (asp 10), no account is to be taken, in assessing the amount of any compensation to be awarded under subsection (1) or (10), of the loss, by virtue of the transfer of the tenancy of the home, of a right to purchase the home under Part 3 of the Housing (Scotland) Act 1987 (c 26).

CHAPTER 4
Interdicts

113   Civil partners: competency of interdict

(1)   It shall not be incompetent for the Court of Session or the sheriff to entertain an application by one civil partner in a civil partnership for a relevant interdict by reason only that the civil partners are living together in civil partnership.

(2)   In subsection (1) [. . .] 'relevant interdict' means an interdict, including an interim interdict, which—

    (a)   restrains or prohibits any conduct of one civil partner towards the other civil partner or a child of the family, or

    (b)   [subject to subsection (3), prohibits a civil partner from entering or remaining in—

      (i)   a family home,

      (ii)   any other residence occupied by the applicant civil partner,

      (iii)   any place of work of the applicant civil partner,

      (iv)   any school attended by a child in the permanent or temporary care of the applicant civil partner.]

[(3)   Subsection (4) applies if in relation to a family home the non-applicant civil partner—

    (a)   is an entitled partner, or

(b)   has occupancy rights.

(4)   Except where subsection (5) applies, the court may not grant a relevant interdict prohibiting the non-applicant civil partner from entering or remaining in the family home.

(5)   This subsection applies if—

(a)   the interdict is ancillary to an exclusion order, or

(b)   by virtue of section 101(4), the court refuses leave to exercise occupancy rights.

(6)   In this section [. . .], 'applicant civil partner' means the civil partner who has applied for the interdict; and 'non-applicant civil partner' is to be construed accordingly.]

[. . .]

CHAPTER 5
Dissolution, Separation and Nullity

Dissolution and separation

117   Dissolution

(1)   An action for the dissolution of a civil partnership may be brought in the Court of Session or in the sheriff court.

(2)   In such an action the court may grant decree, if, but only if, it is established that—

(a)   the civil partnership has broken down irretrievably, or

(b)   [subject to subsection (3A),] an interim gender recognition certificate under the Gender Recognition Act 2004 (c 7) has, after the date of registration of the civil partnership, been issued to either of the civil partners.

(3)   The irretrievable breakdown of a civil partnership is taken to be established if—

(a)   since the date of registration of the civil partnership the defender has at any time behaved (whether or not as a result of mental abnormality and whether such behaviour has been active or passive) in such a way that the pursuer cannot reasonably be expected to cohabit with the defender,

[. . .]

(c)   there has been no cohabitation between the civil partners at any time during a continuous period of [one year] after the date of registration of the civil partnership and immediately preceding the bringing of the action and the defender consents to the granting of decree of dissolution of the civil partnership, or

(d)   there has been no cohabitation between the civil partners at any time during a continuous period of [two] years after that date and immediately preceding the bringing of the action.

[(3A)   Subsection (2)(b)—

(a)   does not apply where, under the Gender Recognition Act 2004, a Gender Recognition Panel issues a full gender recognition certificate to the person to whom the interim gender recognition certificate was issued, but

(b)   continues to apply despite a full gender recognition certificate being issued to that person by the sheriff under section 4E of that Act.]

(4)   Provision is to be made by act of sederunt—

(a)   for the purpose of ensuring that, in an action to which paragraph (c) of subsection (3) relates, the defender has been given such information as enables that civil partner to understand—

(i)   the consequences of consenting to the granting of decree, and

(ii)   the steps which must be taken to indicate such consent, and

(b)   as to the manner in which the defender in such an action is to indicate such consent, and any withdrawal of such consent, and where the defender has indicated (and not withdrawn) such consent in the prescribed manner, that indication is sufficient evidence of such consent.

(5) Provision is to be made by act of sederunt for the purpose of ensuring that, where in an action for the dissolution of a civil partnership the defender is suffering from mental illness, the court appoints a curator ad litem to the defender.

[. . .]

(8) In an action for dissolution of a civil partnership the standard of proof required to establish the ground of action is on balance of probability.

118 Encouragement of reconciliation

(1) At any time before granting decree in an action by virtue of paragraph (a) of section 117(2) for dissolution of a civil partnership, if it appears to the court that there is a reasonable prospect of a reconciliation between the civil partners it must continue, or further continue, the action for such period as it thinks proper to enable attempts to be made to effect such a reconciliation.

(2) If during any such continuation the civil partners cohabit with one another, no account is to be taken of such cohabitation for the purposes of that action.

119 Effect of resumption of cohabitation

[. . .]

(3) In considering whether any period mentioned in paragraph (c) or (d) of section 117(3) has been continuous, no account is to be taken of any period or periods not exceeding 6 months in all during which the civil partners cohabited with one another; but no such period or periods during which the civil partners cohabited with one another is to count as part of the period of non-cohabitation required by any of those paragraphs.

120 Separation

(1) An action for the separation of the civil partners in a civil partnership may be brought in the Court of Session or in the sheriff court.

(2) In such an action the court may grant decree if satisfied that the circumstances set out in any of paragraphs (a) to (d) of section 117(3) are established.

121 Dissolution following on decree of separation

(1) The court may grant decree in an action for the dissolution of a civil partnership even though decree of separation has previously been granted to the pursuer on the same, or substantially the same, facts as those averred in support of that action; and in any such action the court may treat an extract decree of separation lodged in process as sufficient proof of the facts under which that decree was granted.

(2) Nothing in this section entitles a court to grant decree of dissolution of a civil partnership without receiving evidence from the pursuer.

[121A Postponement of decree of dissolution where religious impediment to marry exists

(1) Notwithstanding that irretrievable breakdown of a civil partnership has been established in an action for dissolution, the court may—

(a) on the application of a party ('the applicant'), and

(b) if satisfied—

(i) that subsection (2) applies, and

(ii) that it is just and reasonable to do so,

postpone the grant of decree in the action until it is satisfied that the other party has complied with subsection (3).

(2) This subsection applies where—

(a) the applicant is prevented from entering into a religious marriage by virtue of a requirement of the religion of that marriage, and

(b) the other party can act so as to remove, or enable or contribute to the removal of, the impediment which prevents that marriage.

(3) A party complies with this subsection by acting in the way described in subsection (2)(b).

(4) The court may, whether or not on the application of a party and notwithstanding that subsection (2) applies, recall a postponement under subsection (1).

(5) The court may, before recalling a postponement under subsection (1), order the other party to produce a certificate from the relevant religious body confirming that the other party has acted in the way described in subsection (2)(b).

(6) For the purposes of subsection (5), a religious body is 'relevant' if the applicant considers the body competent to provide the confirmation referred to in that subsection.

(7) In this section—

'religious marriage' means a marriage solemnised by a marriage celebrant of a specified religious body, and 'religion of that marriage' is to be construed accordingly,

'specified' means specified by regulations made by the Scottish Ministers.

(8) Any reference in this section to a marriage celebrant of a specified religious body is a reference to—

(a) a minister, clergyman, pastor or priest of such a body,

(b) a person who has, on the nomination of such a body, been registered under section 9 of the Marriage (Scotland) Act 1977 as empowered to solemnise marriages,

(c) any person who is recognised by such a body as entitled to solemnise marriages on its behalf.]

122 Registration of [*dissolutions and declarators of nullity*] of civil partnership

(1) The Registrar General is to maintain at the General Register Office a register of decrees of dissolution [*and declarator of nullity*] of civil partnership (a register which shall be known as the 'Register of Dissolutions of Civil Partnership').

(2) The Registrar General is to cause to be made and kept at the General Register Office an alphabetical index of the entries in that register.

(3) The register is to be in such form as may be prescribed.

(4) On payment to him of such fee or fees as may be prescribed, the Registrar General must, at any time when the General Register Office is open for that purpose—

(a) cause a search of the index to be made on behalf of any person or permit any person to search the index himself,

(b) issue to any person an extract of any entry in the register which that person may require.

(5) An extract of any entry in the register is to be sufficient evidence of the decree of dissolution [*or, as the case may be, of the declarator of nullity of civil partnership*] to which it relates.

(6) The Registrar General may—

(a) delete,

(b) amend, or

(c) substitute another entry for,

any entry in the register.

[(7) Section 39C of the 1965 Act applies in relation to the Register of Dissolutions of Civil Partnership as it applies in relation to the Register of Divorces.]

Nullity

123 Nullity

[(1)] Where two people register in Scotland as civil partners of each other, the civil partnership is void if, and only if—

(a) they were not eligible to do so,

(b) though they were so eligible, either of them did not [. . .] consent to its formation, [or

(c)   at the time of registration one of them who was capable of consenting to the formation of the civil partnership purported to give consent but did so by reason only of duress or error.]

[(2)   In this section 'error' means—

(a)   error as to the nature of civil partnership, or

(b)   a mistaken belief held by a person ('A') that the other person with whom A purported to register a civil partnership was the person with whom A had agreed to register a civil partnership.]

124   Validity of civil partnerships registered outside Scotland

(1)   Where two people register as civil partners of each other in England and Wales—

(a)   the civil partnership is void if it would be void in England and Wales under section 49, and

(b)   the civil partnership is voidable if it would be voidable there under section 50(1)(a), (b), (c) or (e).

(2)   Where two people register as civil partners of each other in Northern Ireland, the civil partnership is—

(a)   void, if it would be void in Northern Ireland under section 173, and

(b)   voidable, if it would be voidable there under section 174(1)(a), (b), (c) or (e).

(3)   Subsection (4) applies where two people register as civil partners of each other under an Order in Council under—

(a)   section 210 (registration at British consulates etc), or

(b)   section 211 (registration by armed forces personnel), ('the relevant section').

(4)   The civil partnership is—

(a)   void, if—

(i)   the condition in subsection (2)(a) or (b) of the relevant section is not met, or

(ii)   a requirement prescribed for the purposes of this paragraph by an Order in Council under the relevant section is not complied with, and

(b)   voidable, if—

(i)   the appropriate part of the United Kingdom is England and Wales and the circumstances fall within section 50(1)(a), (b), (c) or (e), or

(ii)   the appropriate part of the United Kingdom is Northern Ireland and the circumstances fall within section 174(1)(a), (b), (c) or (e).

(5)   The appropriate part of the United Kingdom is the part by reference to which the condition in subsection (2)(b) of the relevant section is met.

(6)   Subsections (7) and (8) apply where two people have registered an apparent or alleged overseas relationship.

(7)   The civil partnership is void if—

(a)   the relationship is not an overseas relationship, or

(b)   (even though the relationship is an overseas relationship), the parties are not treated under Chapter 2 of Part 5 as having formed a civil partnership.

(8)   The civil partnership is voidable if—

(a)   the overseas relationship is voidable under the relevant law,

(b)   where either of the parties was domiciled in England and Wales at the time when the overseas relationship was registered, the circumstances fall within section 50(1)(a), (b), (c) or (e), or

(c)   where either of the parties was domiciled in Northern Ireland at the time when the overseas relationship was registered, the circumstances fall within section 174(1)(a), (b), (c) or (e).

(9)   Section 51 or (as the case may be) section 175 applies for the purposes of—

(a)   subsections (1)(b), (2)(b) and (4)(b),

(b)   subsection (8)(a), in so far as applicable in accordance with the relevant law, and

(c)   subsection (8)(b) and (c).

(10)   In subsections (8)(a) and (9)(b) 'the relevant law' means the law of the country or territory where the overseas relationship was registered (including its rules of private international law).

(11)   For the purposes of subsections (8) and (9)(b) and (c), references in sections 50 and 51 or (as the case may be) sections 174 and 175 to the formation of the civil partnership are to be read as references to the registration of the overseas relationship.

Financial provision after overseas proceedings

125   Financial provision after overseas dissolution or annulment
Schedule 11 relates to applications for financial provision in Scotland after a civil partnership has been dissolved or annulled in a country or territory outside the British Islands.

CHAPTER 6
Miscellaneous and Interpretation

Miscellaneous

126   Regulations
(1)   In this Chapter and in Chapters 2 [(except in section 88F)] and 5, 'prescribed' means prescribed by regulations made by the Registrar General.

(2)   Regulations so made may make provision (including provision as to fees) supplementing, in respect of the provision of services by or on behalf of the Registrar General or by local registration authorities (as defined by section 5(3) of the 1965 Act), the provisions of Chapter 2 of this Part.

(3)   Any power to make regulations under subsection (1) or (2) is exercisable by statutory instrument; and no such regulations are to be made except with the approval of the Scottish Ministers.

(4)   A statutory instrument containing regulations under subsection (1) or (2), or regulations under section [94A(1)(a)(i), (2A)(a)(i) or (5), 94B(3), 94E(4), 106(3)(a)(i) or 12A(7)], is subject to annulment in pursuance of a resolution of the Scottish Parliament.

127   Attachment
Where an attachment has been executed of furniture and plenishings of which the debtor's civil partner has the possession or use by virtue of an order under section 103(3) or (4), the sheriff, on the application of that civil partner made within 40 days after the execution of the attachment, may—
    (a)   declare the attachment null, or
    (b)   make such order as he thinks appropriate to protect such possession or use by that civil partner,
if satisfied that the purpose of the attachment was wholly or mainly to prevent such possession or use.

128   Promise or agreement to enter into civil partnership
No promise or agreement to enter into civil partnership creates any rights or obligations under the law of Scotland; and no action for breach of such a promise or agreement may be brought in any court in Scotland, whatever the law applicable to the promise or agreement.

[. . .]

131   Succession: legal rights arising by virtue of civil partnership
(1)   Where a person dies survived by a civil partner then, unless the circumstance is as mentioned in subsection (2), the civil partner has right to half of the moveable net estate belonging to the deceased at the time of death.

(2)   That circumstance is that the person is also survived by issue, in which case

the civil partner has right to a third of that moveable net estate and those issue have right to another third of it.

(3) In this section—

'issue' means issue however remote, and

'net estate' has the meaning given by section 36(1) (interpretation) of the Succession (Scotland) Act 1964 (c 41).

(4) Every testamentary disposition executed after the commencement of this section by which provision is made in favour of the civil partner of the testator and which does not contain a declaration to the effect that the provision so made is in full and final satisfaction of the right to any share in the testator's estate to which the civil partner is entitled by virtue of subsection (1) or (2), has effect (unless the disposition contains an express provision to the contrary) as if it contained such a declaration.

(5) In section 36(1) of the Succession (Scotland) Act 1964 (c 41), in the definition of 'legal rights', for 'and legitim' substitute 'legitim and rights under section 131 of the Civil Partnership Act 2004'.

132   Assurance policies

Section 2 of the Married Women's Policies of Assurance (Scotland) Act 1880 (c 26) (which provides that a policy of assurance may be effected in trust for a person's spouse, children or spouse and children) applies in relation to a policy of assurance—

    (a)   effected by a civil partner (in this section referred to as 'A') on A's own life, and

    (b)   expressed upon the face of it to be for the benefit of A's civil partner, or of A's children, or of A's civil partner and children,

as it applies in relation to a policy of assurance effected as, and expressed upon the face of it to be for such benefit as, is mentioned in that section.

134   General provisions as to fees

(1) Subject to such exceptions as may be prescribed, a district registrar may refuse to comply with any application voluntarily made to him under this Part until the appropriate fee, if any, provided for by or under this Part is paid to him; and any such fee, if not prepaid, is recoverable by the registrar to whom it is payable.

(2) Circumstances, of hardship or otherwise, may be prescribed in which fees provided for by or under this Part may be remitted by the Registrar General.

Interpretation

135   Interpretation of this Part

[(1)] In this Part, unless the context otherwise requires—

'the 1965 Act' means the Registration of Births, Deaths and Marriages (Scotland) Act 1965 (c 49);

['2014 Act' means the Immigration Act 2014;]

['approved celebrant' has the meaning given by section 94A(4)(c);]

'authorised registrar' has the meaning given by section 87;

'caravan' means a caravan which is mobile or affixed to land;

'child of the family' has the meaning given by section 101(7);

'civil partnership book' has the meaning given by section 89;

'civil partnership register' has the meaning given by section 95(2);

'civil partnership schedule' has the meaning given by section 94;

['civil registration' has the meaning given by section 94A(4)(c);]

'the court' means the Court of Session or the sheriff;

'district' means a registration district as defined by section 5(1) of the 1965 Act;

'district registrar' has the meaning given by section 7(12) of the 1965 Act;

'entitled partner' and 'non-entitled partner', subject to sections 106(2) and 111(2), have the meanings respectively assigned to them by section 101(1);

'exclusion order' has the meaning given by section 104(1);

'family' has the meaning given by section 101(7);

'family home' means [, subject to subsection (2),] any house, caravan, houseboat or other structure which has been provided or has been made available by one or both of the civil partners as, or has become, a family residence and includes any garden or other ground or building [. . .] usually occupied with, or otherwise required for the amenity or convenience of, the house, caravan, houseboat or other structure but does not include a residence provided or made available by [a person for one] civil partner to reside in, whether with any child of the family or not, separately from the other civil partner;

'furniture and plenishings' means any article situated in a family home of civil partners which—

(a)   is-owned or hired by either civil partner or is being acquired by either civil partner under a hire-purchase agreement or conditional sale agreement, and

(b)   is reasonably necessary to enable the home to be used as a family residence,

but does not include any vehicle, caravan or houseboat or such other structure as is mentioned in the definition of 'family home';

'notice of proposed civil partnership' has the meaning given by section 88(1);

'occupancy rights' means the rights conferred by section 101(1);

'Registrar General' means the Registrar General of Births, Deaths and Marriages for Scotland;

'registration office' means a registration office provided under section 8(1) of the 1965 Act;

['relevant national' has the same meaning as in section 30A;]

['religious or belief body' means an organised group of people—

(a)   which meets regularly for religious worship, or

(b)   the principal object (or one of the principal objects) of which is to uphold or promote philosophical beliefs and which meets regularly for that purpose;

'religious or belief civil partnership' has the meaning given by section 94A(4)(b);]

'tenant' includes—

(a)   a sub-tenant,

(b)   a statutory tenant as defined in section 3 of the Rent (Scotland) Act 1984 (c 58), and

(c)   a statutory assured tenant as defined in section 16(1) of the Housing (Scotland) Act 1988 (c 43),

and 'tenancy' is to be construed accordingly.

[(2) If—

(a)   the tenancy of a family home is transferred from one civil partner to the other by agreement or under any enactment, and

(b)   following the transfer, the civil partner to whom the tenancy was transferred occupies the home but the other civil partner does not,

the home shall, on such transfer, cease to be a family home.]

136   The expression 'relative' in the 1965 Act

In section 56(1) of the 1965 Act (interpretation), in the definition of 'relative', at the end insert ', a civil partner and anyone related to the civil partner of the person as regards whom the expression is being construed'.

PART 5

CIVIL PARTNERSHIP FORMED OR DISSOLVED ABROAD ETC

Jurisdiction of Scottish courts

225   Jurisdiction of Scottish courts

(1)   The Court of Session has jurisdiction to entertain an action for the dissolu-

tion of a civil partnership or for separation of civil partners if (and only if) [either civil partner]—

[(a)   is domiciled in Scotland on the date when proceedings are begun, or

(b)   was habitually resident in Scotland throughout the period of one year ending with that date, or]

(c)   the following conditions are met—

(i)   the two people concerned registered as civil partners of each other in Scotland,

(ii)   no court has, or is recognised as having, jurisdiction [. . .], and

(iii)   it appears to the court to be in the interests of justice to assume jurisdiction in the case.

(2)   The sheriff has jurisdiction to entertain an action for the dissolution of a civil partnership or for separation of civil partners if (and only if) the requirements of paragraph (a) or (b) of subsection (1) are met and either civil partner—

(a)   was resident in the sheriffdom for a period of 40 days ending with the date when the action is begun, or

(b)   had been resident in the sheriffdom for a period of not less than 40 days ending not more than 40 days before that date and has no known residence in Scotland at that date.

(3)   The Court of Session has jurisdiction to entertain an action for declarator of nullity of a civil partnership if (and only if)—

[(a)   either of the ostensible civil partners—

(i)   is domiciled in Scotland on the date when the proceedings are begun or was habitually resident in Scotland throughout the period of one year ending with that date, or

(ii)   died before that date and either was at death domiciled in Scotland or had been habitually resident in Scotland throughout the period of one year ending with the date of death, or]

[. . .]

(c)   the following conditions are met—

(i)   the two people concerned registered as civil partners of each other in Scotland,

(ii)   no court has, or is recognised as having, jurisdiction [. . .], and

(iii)   it appears to the court to be in the interests of justice to assume jurisdiction in the case.

[(3A)   The sheriff has jurisdiction to entertain an action for declarator of nullity of a civil partnership if (and only if)—

(a)   the requirements as to domicile or habitual residence that would apply were the action to have been begun in the Court of Session under subsection (3) (other than paragraph (c)) are met, and

(b)   either of the ostensible civil partners—

(i)   was resident in the sheriffdom for a period of 40 days ending with the date when the action is begun, or

(ii)   had been resident in the sheriffdom for a period of not less than 40 days ending not more than 40 days before that date and has no known residence in Scotland at that date.]

(4)   At any time when proceedings are pending in respect of which a court has jurisdiction by virtue of any of subsections (1) to [(3A)] (or this subsection) it also has jurisdiction to entertain other proceedings, in respect of the same civil partnership (or ostensible civil partnership), for dissolution, separation or [. . .] declarator of nullity, even though that jurisdiction would not be exercisable under any of subsections (1) [to (3A)].

226   Sisting of proceedings

(1)   Rules of court may make provision in relation to civil partnerships corresponding to the provision made in relation to marriages by Schedule 3 to the

Domicile and Matrimonial Proceedings Act 1973 (c 45) (sisting of Scottish consistorial actions).

(2)   The rules may in particular make provision—

(a)   for the provision of information by the pursuer and by any other person who has entered appearance in an action where proceedings relating to the same civil partnership (or ostensible civil partnership) are continuing in another jurisdiction, and

(b)   for an action to be sisted where there are concurrent proceedings elsewhere in respect of the same civil partnership (or ostensible civil partnership).

227   Scottish ancillary and collateral orders

(1)   This section applies where after the commencement of this Act an application is competently made to the Court of Session or the sheriff for the making, or the variation or recall, of an order which is ancillary or collateral to an action for—

(a)   the dissolution of a civil partnership,

(b)   the separation of civil partners, or

(c)   declarator of nullity of a civil partnership.

(2)   And the section applies whether the application is made in the same proceedings or in other proceedings and whether it is made before or after the pronouncement of a final decree in the action.

[. . .]

(3)   If the court has or, as the case may be, had jurisdiction to entertain the action, it has jurisdiction to entertain [the application.

[. . .]

[(3B)   If the application or part of it relates to a matter [in relation to which Article 18 of the 2007 Hague Convention applies, the court may not entertain the application or that part of it except where permitted by Article 18].]

(4)   Where the Court of Session has jurisdiction by virtue of this section to entertain an application for the variation or recall, as respects any person, of an order made by it and the order is one to which section 8 (variation and recall by the sheriff of certain orders made by the Court of Session) of the Law Reform (Miscellaneous Provisions) (Scotland) Act 1966 (c 19) applies, then for the purposes of any application under that section for the variation or recall of the order in so far as it relates to the person, the sheriff (as defined in that section) has jurisdiction to exercise the power conferred on him by that section.

(5)   The reference in subsection (1) to an order which is ancillary or collateral is to an order relating to children, aliment, financial provision or expenses.

[(6)   In this section 'the 2007 Hague Convention' means that Convention on the International Recovery of Child Support and Other Forms of Family Maintenance concluded on 23 November 2007 at the Hague.]

PART 6
RELATIONSHIPS ARISING THROUGH CIVIL PARTNERSHIP

246   Interpretation of statutory references to stepchildren etc

(1)   In any provision to which this section applies, references to a stepchild or step-parent of a person (here, 'A'), and cognate expressions, are to be read as follows—

A's stepchild includes a person who is the child of A's civil partner (but is not A's child);

A's step-parent includes a person who is the civil partner of A's parent (but is not A's parent);

A's stepdaughter includes a person who is the daughter of A's civil partner (but is not A's daughter);

A's stepson includes a person who is the son of A's civil partner (but is not A's son);

A's stepfather includes a person who is the civil partner of A's father (but is not A's parent);

A's stepmother includes a person who is the civil partner of A's mother (but is not A's parent);

A's stepbrother includes a person who is the son of the civil partner of A's parent (but is not the son of either of A's parents);

A's stepsister includes a person who is the daughter of the civil partner of A's parent (but is not the daughter of either of A's parents).

(2) For the purposes of any provision to which this section applies—

'brother-in-law' includes civil partner's brother,

'daughter-in-law' includes daughter's civil partner,

'father-in-law' includes civil partner's father,

'mother-in-law' includes civil partner's mother,

'parent-in-law' includes civil partner's parent,

'sister-in-law' includes civil partner's sister, and

'son-in-law' includes son's civil partner.

247 Provisions to which section 246 applies: Acts of Parliament etc

(1) Section 246 applies to—

(a) any provision listed in Schedule 21 (references to stepchildren, in-laws etc in existing Acts),

(b) except in so far as otherwise provided, any provision made by a future Act, and

(c) except in so far as otherwise provided, any provision made by future subordinate legislation.

(2) A Minister of the Crown may by order—

(a) amend Schedule 21 by adding to it any provision of an existing Act;

(b) provide for section 246 to apply to prescribed provisions of existing subordinate legislation.

(3) The power conferred by subsection (2) is also exercisable—

(a) by the Scottish Ministers, in relation to a relevant Scottish provision;

(b) by a Northern Ireland department, in relation to a provision which deals with a transferred matter;

(c) by the National Assembly for Wales, if the order is made by virtue of subsection (2)(b) and deals with matters with respect to which functions are exercisable by the Assembly.

(4) Subject to subsection (5), the power to make an order under subsection (2) is exercisable by statutory instrument.

(5) Any power of a Northern Ireland department to make an order under subsection (2) is exercisable by statutory rule for the purposes of the Statutory Rules (Northern Ireland) Order 1979 (SI 1979/1573 (NI 12)).

(6) A statutory instrument containing an order under subsection (2) made by a Minister of the Crown is subject to annulment in pursuance of a resolution of either House of Parliament.

(7) A statutory instrument containing an order under subsection (2) made by the Scottish Ministers is subject to annulment in pursuance of a resolution of the Scottish Parliament.

(8) A statutory rule containing an order under subsection (2) made by a Northern Ireland department is subject to negative resolution (within the meaning of section 41(6) of the Interpretation Act (Northern Ireland) 1954 (c 33 (NI)).

(9) In this section—

'Act' includes an Act of the Scottish Parliament;

'existing Act' means an Act passed on or before the last day of the Session in which this Act is passed;

'existing subordinate legislation' means subordinate legislation made before the day on which this section comes into force;

'future Act' means an Act passed after the last day of the Session in which this Act is passed;

'future subordinate legislation' means subordinate legislation made on or after the day on which this section comes into force;

'Minister of the Crown' has the same meaning as in the Ministers of the Crown Act 1975 (c 26);

'prescribed' means prescribed by the order;

'relevant Scottish provision' means a provision that would be within the legislative competence of the Scottish Parliament if it were included in an Act of that Parliament;

'subordinate legislation' has the same meaning as in the Interpretation Act 1978 (c 30) except that it includes an instrument made under an Act of the Scottish Parliament;

'transferred matter' has the meaning given by section 4(1) of the Northern Ireland Act 1998 (c 47) and 'deals with' in relation to a transferred matter is to be construed in accordance with section 98(2) and (3) of the 1998 Act.

PART 7
MISCELLANEOUS

249 Immigration control and formation of civil partnerships
Schedule 23 contains provisions relating to the formation of civil partnerships in the United Kingdom by persons subject to immigration control.

253 Civil partners to have unlimited insurable interest in each other
(1)   Where two people are civil partners, each of them is to be presumed for the purposes of section 1 of the Life Assurance Act 1774 (c 48) to have an interest in the life of the other.

(2)   For the purposes of section 3 of the 1774 Act, there is no limit on the amount of value of the interest.

PART 8
SUPPLEMENTARY

258 Regulations and orders
(1)   This section applies to any power conferred by this Act to make regulations or an order (except a power of a court to make an order).

(2)   The power may be exercised so as to make different provision for different cases and different purposes.

(3)   The power includes power to make any supplementary, incidental, consequential, transitional, transitory or saving provision which the person making the regulations or order considers expedient.

259 Power to make further provision in connection with civil partnership
(1)   A Minister of the Crown may by order make such further provision (including supplementary, incidental, consequential, transitory, transitional or saving provision) as he considers appropriate—

    (a)   for the general purposes, or any particular purpose, of this Act,

    (b)   in consequence of any provision made by or under this Act, or

    (c)   for giving full effect to this Act or any provision of it.

(2)   The power conferred by subsection (1) is also exercisable—

    (a)   by the Scottish Ministers, in relation to a relevant Scottish provision;

    (b)   by a Northern Ireland department, in relation to a provision which deals with a transferred matter;

    (c)   by the National Assembly for Wales, in relation to a provision which is made otherwise than by virtue of subsection (3) and deals with matters with respect to which functions are exercisable by the Assembly.

(3)   An order under subsection (1) may—

(a)   amend or repeal any enactment contained in an Act passed on or before the last day of the Session in which this Act is passed, including an enactment conferring power to make subordinate legislation where the power is limited by reference to persons who are or have been parties to a marriage;

(b)   amend, repeal or (as the case may be) revoke any provision contained in Northern Ireland legislation passed or made on or before the last day of the Session in which this Act is passed, including a provision conferring power to make subordinate legislation where the power is limited by reference to persons who are or have been parties to a marriage;

(c)   amend, repeal or (as the case may be) revoke any Church legislation.

(4)   An order under subsection (1) may—

(a)   provide for any provision of this Act which comes into force before another such provision has come into force to have effect, until that other provision has come into force, with such modifications as are specified in the order;

(b)   amend or revoke any subordinate legislation.

(5)   The power to make an order under subsection (1) is not restricted by any other provision of this Act.

(6)   Subject to subsection (7), the power to make an order under subsection (1) is exercisable by statutory instrument.

(7)   Any power of a Northern Ireland department to make an order under this section is exercisable by statutory rule for the purposes of the Statutory Rules (Northern Ireland) Order 1979 (SI 1979/1573 (NI 12)).

(8)   An order under subsection (1) which contains any provision (whether alone or with other provisions) made by virtue of subsection (3) may not be made—

(a)   by a Minister of the Crown, unless a draft of the statutory instrument containing the order has been laid before, and approved by a resolution of, each House of Parliament;

(b)   by the Scottish Ministers, unless a draft of the statutory instrument containing the order has been laid before, and approved by a resolution of, the Scottish Parliament;

(c)   by a Northern Ireland department, unless a draft of the statutory rule containing the order has been laid before, and approved by a resolution of, the Northern Ireland Assembly.

(9)   A statutory instrument containing an order under subsection (1) to which subsection (8) does not apply—

(a)   if made by a Minister of the Crown, is subject to annulment in pursuance of a resolution of either House of Parliament;

(b)   if made by the Scottish Ministers, is subject to annulment in pursuance of a resolution of the Scottish Parliament.

(10)   A statutory rule made by a Northern Ireland department and containing an order to which subsection (8) does not apply is subject to negative resolution (within the meaning of section 41(6) of the Interpretation Act (Northern Ireland) 1954 (c 33 (NI))).

(11)   In this section—

'Act' includes an Act of the Scottish Parliament;

'Church legislation' has the same meaning as in section 255;

'Minister of the Crown' has the same meaning as in the Ministers of the Crown Act 1975 (c 26);

'relevant Scottish provision' means a provision that would be within the legislative competence of the Scottish Parliament if it were included in an Act of that Parliament;

'subordinate legislation' has the same meaning as in the Interpretation Act 1978 (c 30) except that it includes any instrument made under an Act of the Scottish Parliament and any instrument within the meaning of section 1(c) of the Interpretation Act (Northern Ireland) 1954 (c 33 (NI));

'transferred matter' has the meaning given by section 4(1) of the Northern Ireland Act 1998 (c 47) and 'deals with' in relation to a transferred matter is to be construed in accordance with section 98(2) and (3) of the 1998 Act.

260 Community obligations and civil partners

(1) Subsection (2) applies where any person, by Order in Council or regulations under section 2(2) of the European Communities Act 1972 (c 68) (general implementation of Treaties)—

(a) is making provision for the purpose of implementing, or for a purpose concerning, a Community obligation of the United Kingdom which relates to persons who are or have been parties to a marriage, or

(b) has made such provision and it has not been revoked.

(2) The appropriate person may by Order in Council or (as the case may be) by regulations make provision in relation to persons who are or have been civil partners in a civil partnership that is the same or similar to the provision referred to in subsection (1).

(3) 'Marriage' and 'civil partnership' include a void marriage and a void civil partnership respectively.

(4) 'The appropriate person' means—

(a) if subsection (1)(a) applies, the person making the provision referred to there;

(b) if subsection (1)(b) applies, any person who would have power to make the provision referred to there if it were being made at the time of the exercise of the power under subsection (2).

(5) The following provisions apply in relation to the power conferred by subsection (2) to make an Order in Council or regulations as they apply in relation to the power conferred by section 2(2) of the 1972 Act to make an Order in Council or regulations—

(a) paragraph 2 of Schedule 2 to the 1972 Act (procedure etc in relation to making of Orders in Council and regulations: general);

(b) paragraph 15(3)(c) of Schedule 8 to the Scotland Act 1998 (c 46) (modifications of paragraph 2 in relation to Scottish Ministers and to Orders in Council made on the recommendation of the First Minister);

(c) paragraph 3 of Schedule 2 to the 1972 Act (modifications of paragraph 2 in relation to Northern Ireland departments etc) and the Statutory Rules (Northern Ireland) Order 1979 (SI 1979/1573 (NI 12)) (treating the power conferred by subsection (2) as conferred by an Act passed before 1st January 1974 for the purposes of the application of that Order);

(d) section 29(3) of the Government of Wales Act 1998 (c 38) (modifications of paragraph 2 in relation to the National Assembly for Wales).

261 *[Minor and consequential amendments, repeals and revocations]*

262 Extent

(2) Part 3 (civil partnership: Scotland), including Schedules 10 and 11, extends to Scotland only.

(4) In Part 5 (civil partnerships formed or dissolved abroad etc)—

(b) sections 225 to 227 extend to Scotland only;

(5) In Part 6—

(a) any amendment made by virtue of section 247(1)(a) and Schedule 21 has the same extent as the provision subject to the amendment;

(8) Schedule 28 extends to Scotland only.

263   *[Commencement]*

264   **Short title**

This Act may be cited as the Civil Partnership Act 2004.

[SCHEDULE 10
FORBIDDEN DEGREES OF RELATIONSHIP: SCOTLAND

(introduced by section 86)

1. Relationships by consanguinity
Parent
Child
Grandparent
Grandchild
Sibling
Aunt or uncle
Niece or nephew
Great-grandparent
Great-grandchild

2. Relationships by affinity referred to in section 86(3)
Child of former spouse
Child of former civil partner
Former spouse of parent
Former civil partner of parent
Former spouse of grandparent
Former civil partner of grandparent
Grandchild of former spouse
Grandchild of former civil partner.]

[SCHEDULE 10A
MODIFICATIONS OF PROPOSED CIVIL PARTNERSHIP REFERRED UNDER
SECTION 88F

Introduction

1.—(1)   These are the modifications subject to which this Act has effect if the district registrar refers a proposed civil partnership to the Secretary of State.

(2)   In this Schedule 'referred civil partnership' means the proposed civil partnership referred to the Secretary of State.

No civil partnership schedule to be completed until decision about investigation etc

2.—(1)   The duty under section 94 (civil partnership schedule)(5) to complete a civil partnership schedule in respect of the referred civil partnership does not apply unless and until one of the following events occurs.

(2)   Event 1 occurs if—

(a)   the Secretary of State gives the district registrar the section 48 notice, and

(b)   the notice is of a decision not to investigate whether the referred civil partnership is a sham.

(3)   Event 2 occurs if—

(a)   the relevant statutory period ends, and

(b)   the Secretary of State has not given the district registrar the section 48 notice.

(4)   Event 3 occurs if—

(a)   the Secretary of State gives the district registrar the section 48 notice,

(b)   that notice is of a decision to investigate whether the referred civil partnership is a sham,

(c)   the Secretary of State gives the district registrar the section 50 notice, and

(d)   that notice is of a decision that both of the parties to the referred civil partnership have complied with the investigation.

(5)   Event 4 occurs if—

(a)   the 70 day period ends, and

(b)   the Secretary of State has not given the district registrar the section 50 notice.

(6)   Event 5 occurs if the Secretary of State gives the district registrar notice that the duty under section 94 is applicable.

(7)   The Secretary of State may give a notice for that purpose only if—

(a)   the Secretary of State has given the district registrar the section 48 notice,

(b)   that notice is of a decision to investigate whether the referred civil partnership is a sham,

(c)   the Secretary of State has given the district registrar the section 50 notice, and

(d)   that notice is of a decision that one or both of the parties to the referred civil partnership have not complied with the investigation.

(8)   This paragraph applies in addition to any other requirements applicable to the completion of the civil partnership schedule.

(9)   This paragraph is subject to paragraph 4.

(10)   In this paragraph—

'70 day period' has the same meaning as in section 50(11) of the 2014 Act;

'relevant statutory period' has the same meaning as in section 62(6) of the 2014 Act;

'section 48 notice' means notice under section 48(8D)(7) of the 2014 Act;

'section 50 notice' means notice under section 50(7) of the 2014 Act.

Civil partnership to be investigated: extension of 28 day period to 70 days

3.—(1)   The modifications in this paragraph have effect if the Secretary of State gives the district registrar notice under section 48(8D) of the 2014 Act of a decision to investigate whether the referred civil partnership is a sham.

(2)   Section 91(1)(8) has effect as if—

(a)   for the words from 'being' to 'section 90' there were substituted 'being a date before the expiry of the relevant 70 day period', and

(b)   the words from '; and if a date' to the end were omitted.

(3)   Section 94(9) has effect as if for paragraph (b) there were substituted—

'(b)   the relevant 70 day period has expired,'.'

(4)   In sections 91 and 94 (as modified by this paragraph) and in paragraph 4 'relevant 70 day period' means the period—

(a)   beginning the day after the particulars of the proposed civil partnership are entered in the civil partnership book in accordance with section 89 (civil partnership notice book), and

(b)   ending at the end of the period of 70 days beginning with that day.

(5)   This paragraph is subject to paragraph 4.

Effect of reducing statutory period

4.—(1)   Where—

(a)   either—

(i)   a district registrar is authorised to fix a date for the date of registration of the referred civil partnership that is 28 days or fewer after publicisation by the district registrar under section 90(1), or

(ii)   in the case of a referred civil partnership to which paragraph 3 applies, the district registrar is authorised to fix a date for the date of registration before the expiry of the relevant 70 day period, and

(b)   the authorisation mentioned in sub-paragraph (i) or, as the case may be, (ii) of paragraph (a) is given at a time when the duty under section 94 to complete a civil partnership schedule in respect of the referred civil partnership has not arisen in accordance with paragraph 2,

the duty under section 94 to complete the civil partnership schedule arises on the giving of the authorisation, subject to any other requirements applicable to the completion of the schedule being met.

(2)   But the requirements of paragraph 2 are not applicable in such a case.

(3)   The Secretary of State is not prevented from deciding to conduct, conducting, or continuing, an investigation if the civil partnership schedule is completed as mentioned in sub-paragraph (1).

(4)   But in such a case, nothing in the 2014 Act requires the Secretary of State to decide whether to conduct, or to continue, an investigation.

(5)   In this paragraph 'investigation' means an investigation, conducted following a decision by the Secretary of State under section 48 of the 2014 Act, whether a proposed civil partnership is a sham.]

SCHEDULE 11
FINANCIAL PROVISION IN SCOTLAND AFTER OVERSEAS PROCEEDINGS
Section 125

PART 1
Introductory

1 (1)   This Schedule applies where—

(a)   a civil partnership has been dissolved or annulled in a country or territory outside the British Islands by means of judicial or other proceedings (here the 'overseas proceedings'), and

(b)   the dissolution or annulment (here the 'overseas determination') is entitled to be recognised as valid in Scotland.

(2)   This Schedule applies even if the date of the overseas determination is earlier than the date on which this Schedule comes into force.

PART 2
Circumstances in which Court may entertain Application for Financial Provision

2 (1)   Subject to [sub-paragraphs (3A) and (4)], if the jurisdictional requirements and the conditions set out in sub-paragraphs (2) and (3), respectively, are satisfied, the court may entertain an application by one of the former civil partners or former ostensible civil partners, (here 'A') for an order for financial provision.

(2)   The jurisdictional requirements are—

(a)   that A is domiciled or habitually resident in Scotland when the application is made,

(b)   that the other former civil partner, or former ostensible civil partner, (here 'B')—

(i)   is domiciled or habitually resident in Scotland when the application is made,

(ii)   was domiciled or habitually resident in Scotland when A and B last lived together in civil partnership, or

(iii)   when the application is made is an owner or tenant of, or has a beneficial interest in, property in Scotland which has at some time been a family home of A and B, and

(c)   where the court is the sheriff, that when the application is made either—

(i)   A or B is habitually resident in the sheriffdom, or

(ii)   property mentioned in sub-paragraph (2)(b)(iii) is wholly or partially in the sheriffdom.

(3)   The conditions are that—

(a)   B initiated the overseas proceedings,

(b)   the application is made within 5 years after the overseas determination takes effect,

(c)   the civil partnership (or ostensible civil partnership) had a substantial connection with Scotland,

(d)   A and B are alive when the application is made, and

(e)   (taking Part 3 of this Act to have been in force) a court in Scotland would have had jurisdiction to entertain an action for dissolution or annulment of the civil partnership, if such an action had been brought immediately before the overseas determination took effect.

[(3A)   If an application or part of an application relates to a matter where jurisdiction falls to be determined by reference to the jurisdictional requirements of the Maintenance Regulation and Schedule 6 to the Civil Jurisdiction and Judgments (Maintenance) Regulations 2011—

(a)   those requirements are to be satisfied in respect of the application, or that part of it, instead of the requirements set out in sub-paragraph (2), and

(b)   the condition mentioned in sub-paragraph (3)(c) does not apply.]

[. . .]

[(5)   In this paragraph 'the Maintenance Regulation' means Council Regulation (EC) No 4/2009 including as applied in relation to Denmark by virtue of the Agreement made on 19th October 2005 between the European Community and the Kingdom of Denmark.]

PART 3

Disposal of Applications

3 (1)   Subject to sub-paragraphs (2) to (5), Scots law applies in relation to an application made under paragraph 2 as it would apply were the application made in an action in Scotland for, as the case may be, dissolution or annulment of a civil partnership.

(2)   In disposing of an application made under paragraph 2 the court must exercise its powers so as to place A and B, in so far as it is reasonable and practicable to do so, in the financial position in which they would have been had that application been disposed of, in such an action in Scotland, on the date when the overseas determination took effect.

(3)   In determining what is reasonable and practicable for the purposes of sub-paragraph (2), the court must have regard in particular to—

(a)   A and B's respective resources, both present and foreseeable, at the date the application is disposed of,

(b)   any order made by a foreign court in or in connection with the overseas proceedings, being an order—

(i)   for the making of financial provision, in whatever form, by A for B or by B for A, or

(ii)   for the transfer of property from A to B or from B to A.

(4)   Subject to sub-paragraph (5), the court may make an order for an interim award of a periodical allowance where—

(a)   it appears from A's averments that in the disposal of the application an order for financial provision is likely to be made, and

(b)   the court considers that such an interim award is necessary to avoid hardship to A.

(5)   Where but for paragraph 2(2)(b)(iii) the court would not have jurisdiction to entertain the application, the court may make no order for financial provision other than an order—

(a)   relating to the former family home or its furniture and plenishings, or

(b)   that B must pay A a capital sum not exceeding the value of B's interest in the former family home and its furniture and plenishings.

PART 4

The Expression 'Order for Financial Provision'

4   In this Schedule, 'order for financial provision' means any one or more of the orders specified in section 8(1) of the Family Law (Scotland) Act 1985 (c 37) or an order under section 111.

FAMILY LAW (SCOTLAND) ACT 2006
(2006, asp 2)

Marriage

3 Abolition of marriage by cohabitation with habit and repute

(1)   The rule of law by which marriage may be constituted by cohabitation with habit and repute shall cease to have effect.

(2)   Nothing in subsection (1) shall affect the application of the rule in relation to cohabitation with habit and repute where the cohabitation with habit and repute—

(a)   ended before the commencement of this section ('commencement');

(b)   began before, but ended after, commencement; or

(c)   began before, and continues after, commencement.

(3)   Nothing in subsection (1) shall affect the application of the rule in relation to cohabitation with habit and repute where—

(a)   the cohabitation with habit and repute began after commencement; and

(b)   the conditions in subsection (4) are met.

(4)   Those conditions are—

(a)   that the cohabitation with habit and repute was between two persons, one of whom, ('A'), is domiciled in Scotland;

(b)   that the person with whom A was cohabiting, ('B'), died domiciled in Scotland;

(c)   that, before the cohabitation with habit and repute began, A and B purported to enter into a marriage ('the purported marriage') outwith the United Kingdom;

(d)   that, in consequence of the purported marriage, A and B believed themselves to be married to each other and continued in that belief until B's death;

(e)   that the purported marriage was invalid under the law of the place where the purported marriage was entered into; and

(f)   that A became aware of the invalidity of the purported marriage only after B's death.

4 Extension of jurisdiction of sheriff

In subsection (1) of section 5 of the Sheriff Courts (Scotland) Act 1907 (c 51) (extension of jurisdiction), the words '(except declarators of marriage or nullity of marriage)' shall be repealed.

14 Collusion no longer to be bar to divorce

(1)   Any rule of law by which collusion between parties is a bar to their divorce shall cease to have effect.

(2)   [*Amends Divorce (Scotland) Act 1976.*]

Domicile of persons under 16

22 Domicile of persons under 16

(1)   Subsection (2) applies where—

(a)   the parents of a child are domiciled in the same country as each other; and

(b)   the child has a home with a parent or a home (or homes) with both of them.

(2)   The child shall be domiciled in the same country as the child's parents.

(3)   Where subsection (2) does not apply, the child shall be domiciled in the country with which the child has for the time being the closest connection.

(4)   In this section, 'child' means a person under 16 years of age.

Cohabitation

25   Meaning of 'cohabitant' in sections 26 to 29

(1)   In sections 26 to 29, 'cohabitant' means either member of a couple consisting of—

(a)   a man and a woman who are (or were) living together as if they were husband and wife; or

(b)   two persons of the same sex who are (or were) living together as if they were civil partners.

(2)   In determining for the purposes of any of sections 26 to 29 whether a person ('A') is a cohabitant of another person ('B'), the court shall have regard to—

(a)   the length of the period during which A and B have been living together (or lived together);

(b)   the nature of their relationship during that period; and

(c)   the nature and extent of any financial arrangements subsisting, or which subsisted, during that period.

(3)   In subsection (2) and section 28, 'court' means Court of Session or sheriff.

26   Rights in certain household goods

(1)   Subsection (2) applies where any question arises (whether during or after the cohabitation) as to the respective rights of ownership of cohabitants in any household goods.

(2)   It shall be presumed that each cohabitant has a right to an equal share in household goods acquired (other than by gift or succession from a third party) during the period of cohabitation.

(3)   The presumption in subsection (2) shall be rebuttable.

(4)   In this section, 'household goods' means any goods (including decorative or ornamental goods) kept or used at any time during the cohabitation in any residence in which the cohabitants are (or were) cohabiting for their joint domestic purposes; but does not include—

(a)   money;

(b)   securities;

(c)   any motor car, caravan or other road vehicle; or

(d)   any domestic animal.

27   Rights in certain money and property

(1)   Subsection (2) applies where, in relation to cohabitants, any question arises (whether during or after the cohabitation) as to the right of a cohabitant to—

(a)   money derived from any allowance made by either cohabitant for their joint household expenses or for similar purposes; or

(b)   any property acquired out of such money.

(2)   Subject to any agreement between the cohabitants to the contrary, the money or property shall be treated as belonging to each cohabitant in equal shares.

(3)   In this section 'property' does not include a residence used by the cohabitants as the sole or main residence in which they live (or lived) together.

28   Financial provision where cohabitation ends otherwise than by death

(1)   Subsection (2) applies where cohabitants cease to cohabit otherwise than by reason of the death of one (or both) of them.

(2)   On the application of a cohabitant (the 'applicant'), the appropriate court may, after having regard to the matters mentioned in subsection (3)—

(a)   make an order requiring the other cohabitant (the 'defender') to pay a capital sum of an amount specified in the order to the applicant;

(b)   make an order requiring the defender to pay such amount as may be specified in the order in respect of any economic burden of caring, after the end of the cohabitation, for a child of whom the cohabitants are the parents;

(c)   make such interim order as it thinks fit.

(3)   Those matters are—
   (a)   whether (and, if so, to what extent) the defender has derived economic advantage from contributions made by the applicant; and
   (b)   whether (and, if so, to what extent) the applicant has suffered economic disadvantage in the interests of—
      (i)   the defender; or
      (ii)   any relevant child.
(4)   In considering whether to make an order under subsection (2)(a), the appropriate court shall have regard to the matters mentioned in subsections (5) and (6).
(5)   The first matter is the extent to which any economic advantage derived by the defender from contributions made by the applicant is offset by any economic disadvantage suffered by the defender in the interests of—
   (a)   the applicant; or
   (b)   any relevant child.
(6)   The second matter is the extent to which any economic disadvantage suffered by the applicant in the interests of—
   (a)   the defender; or
   (b)   any relevant child,
is offset by any economic advantage the applicant has derived from contributions made by the defender.
(7)   In making an order under paragraph (a) or (b) of subsection (2), the appropriate court may specify that the amount shall be payable—
   (a)   on such date as may be specified;
   (b)   in instalments.
(8)   Any application under this section shall be made not later than one year after the day on which the cohabitants cease to cohabit.
(9)   In this section—
'appropriate court' means—
   (a)   where the cohabitants are a man and a woman, the court which would have jurisdiction to hear an action of divorce in relation to them if they were married to each other;
   (b)   where the cohabitants are of the same sex, the court which would have jurisdiction to hear an action for the dissolution of the civil partnership if they were civil partners of each other;
'child' means a person under 16 years of age;
'contributions' includes indirect and non-financial contributions (and, in particular, any such contribution made by looking after any relevant child or any house in which they cohabited); and
'economic advantage' includes gains in—
   (a)   capital;
   (b)   income; and
   (c)   earning capacity;
and 'economic disadvantage' shall be construed accordingly.
(10)   For the purposes of this section, a child is 'relevant' if the child is—
   (a)   a child of whom the cohabitants are the parents;
   (b)   a child who is or was accepted by the cohabitants as a child of the family.

29   Application to court by survivor for provision on intestacy
(1)   This section applies where—
   (a)   a cohabitant (the 'deceased') dies intestate; and
   (b)   immediately before the death the deceased was—
      (i)   domiciled in Scotland; and
      (ii)   cohabiting with another cohabitant (the 'survivor').
(2)   Subject to subsection (4), on the application of the survivor, the court may—

(a)　after having regard to the matters mentioned in subsection (3), make an order—

　　(i)　for payment to the survivor out of the deceased's net intestate estate of a capital sum of such amount as may be specified in the order;

　　(ii)　for transfer to the survivor of such property (whether heritable or moveable) from that estate as may be so specified;

(b)　make such interim order as it thinks fit.

(3)　Those matters are—

(a)　the size and nature of the deceased's net intestate estate;

(b)　any benefit received, or to be received, by the survivor—

　　(i)　on, or in consequence of, the deceased's death; and

　　(ii)　from somewhere other than the deceased's net intestate estate;

(c)　the nature and extent of any other rights against, or claims on, the deceased's net intestate estate; and

(d)　any other matter the court considers appropriate.

(4)　An order or interim order under subsection (2) shall not have the effect of awarding to the survivor an amount which would exceed the amount to which the survivor would have been entitled had the survivor been the spouse or civil partner of the deceased.

(5)　An application under this section may be made to—

(a)　the Court of Session;

(b)　a sheriff in the sheriffdom in which the deceased was habitually resident at the date of death;

(c)　if at the date of death it is uncertain in which sheriffdom the deceased was habitually resident, the sheriff at Edinburgh.

(6)　[Subject to section 29A, any] application under this section shall be made before the expiry of the period of 6 months beginning with the day on which the deceased died.

(7)　In making an order under paragraph (a)(i) of subsection (2), the court may specify that the capital sum shall be payable—

(a)　on such date as may be specified;

(b)　in instalments.

(8)　In making an order under paragraph (a)(ii) of subsection (2), the court may specify that the transfer shall be effective on such date as may be specified.

(9)　If the court makes an order in accordance with subsection (7), it may, on an application by any party having an interest, vary the date or method of payment of the capital sum.

(10)　In this section—

'intestate' shall be construed in accordance with section 36(1) of the Succession (Scotland) Act 1964 (c 41);

'legal rights' has the meaning given by section 36(1) of the Succession (Scotland) Act 1964 (c 41);

'net intestate estate' means so much of the intestate estate as remains after provision for the satisfaction of—

(a)　inheritance tax;

(b)　other liabilities of the estate having priority over legal rights and the prior rights of a surviving spouse or surviving civil partner; and

(c)　the legal rights, and the prior rights, of any surviving spouse or surviving civil partner; and

'prior rights' has the meaning given by section 36(1) of the Succession (Scotland) Act 1964 (c 41).

Private international law

38　Validity of marriages

(1)　Subject to [section 13(1) of, and Schedule 6 to, the Marriage (Same Sex

Couples) Act 2013 and any Orders in Council made under that Schedule], the question whether a marriage is formally valid shall be determined by the law of the place where the marriage was celebrated.

(2) The question whether a person who enters into a marriage—

(a) had capacity; or

(b) consented,

to enter into it shall, subject to subsections (3) and (4) and to section 50 of the Family Law Act 1986 (c 55) (non-recognition of divorce or annulment in another jurisdiction no bar to remarriage), be determined by the law of the place where, immediately before the marriage, that person was domiciled.

(3) If a marriage entered into in Scotland is void under a rule of Scots internal law, then, notwithstanding subsection (2), that rule shall prevail over any law under which the marriage would be valid.

(4) The capacity of the person to enter into the marriage shall not be determined under the law of the place where, immediately before the marriage, the person was domiciled in so far as it would be contrary to public policy in Scotland for such capacity to be so determined.

(5) If the law of the place in which a person is domiciled requires a person under a certain age to obtain parental consent before entering into a marriage, that requirement shall not be taken to affect the capacity of a person to enter into a marriage in Scotland unless failure to obtain such consent would render invalid any marriage that the person purported to enter into in any form anywhere in the world.

39 Matrimonial property

(1) Any question in relation to the rights of spouses to each other's immoveable property arising by virtue of the marriage shall be determined by the law of the place in which the property is situated.

(2) Subject to subsections (4) and (5), if spouses are domiciled in the same country, any question in relation to the rights of the spouses to each other's moveable property arising by virtue of the marriage shall be determined by the law of that country.

(3) Subject to subsections (4) and (5), if spouses are domiciled in different countries then, for the purposes of any question in relation to the rights of the spouses to each other's moveable property arising by virtue of the marriage, the spouses shall be taken to have the same rights to such property as they had immediately before the marriage.

(4) Any question in relation to—

(a) the use or occupation of a matrimonial home which is moveable; or

(b) the use of the contents of a matrimonial home (whether the home is moveable or immoveable),

shall be determined by the law of the country in which the home is situated.

(5) A change of domicile by a spouse (or both spouses) shall not affect a right in moveable property which, immediately before the change, has vested in either spouse.

(6) This section shall not apply—

(a) in relation to the law on aliment, financial provision on divorce, transfer of property on divorce or succession;

(b) to the extent that spouses agree otherwise.

(7) In this section, 'matrimonial home' has the same meaning as in section 22 of the 1981 Act.

40 Aliment

Subject to the Maintenance Orders (Reciprocal Enforcement) Act 1972 (c 18), a court in Scotland shall apply Scots internal law in any action for aliment which comes before it.

41 Effect of parents' marriage in determining status to depend on law of domicile

Any question arising as to the effect on a person's status of—

(a)   the person's parents being, or having been, married to each other; or

(b)   the person's parents not being, or not having been, married to each other,

shall be determined by the law of the country in which the person is domiciled at the time at which the question arises.

Declarator of freedom and putting to silence: action no longer competent

42 Action for declarator of freedom and putting to silence to cease to be competent

It shall not be competent to raise an action for declarator of freedom and putting to silence.

General

43 Interpretation

In this Act—

'the 1976 Act' means the Divorce (Scotland) Act 1976 (c 39); and

'the 1981 Act' means the Matrimonial Homes (Family Protection) (Scotland) Act 1981 (c 59).

44 Ancillary provision

(1)   The Scottish Ministers may by order made by statutory instrument make such consequential, transitional or saving provision as they consider appropriate for the purposes of, in consequence of or for giving full effect to this Act or any provision of it.

(2)   An order under subsection (1) may modify any enactment (including this Act).

(3)   The power conferred by subsection (1) on the Scottish Ministers to make orders may be exercised so as to make different provision for different purposes.

(4)   A statutory instrument containing an order under subsection (1) shall, subject to subsection (5), be subject to annulment in pursuance of a resolution of the Scottish Parliament.

(5)   A statutory instrument containing an order under subsection (1) which includes provision modifying an Act or an Act of the Scottish Parliament shall not be made unless a draft of the instrument has been laid before, and approved by resolution of, the Scottish Parliament.

45 [*Minor and consequential amendments and repeals*]

46 Short title and commencement

(1)   This Act may be cited as the Family Law (Scotland) Act 2006.

(2)   The provisions of this Act (except this section) shall come into force on such day as the Scottish Ministers may by order made by statutory instrument appoint.

(3)   An order under subsection (2) may—

(a)   appoint different days for different purposes; and

(b)   include such transitional or saving provision as the Scottish Ministers consider necessary or expedient in connection with the coming into force of the provisions brought into force.

ADOPTION AND CHILDREN (SCOTLAND) ACT 2007
(2007, asp 4)

PART 1
ADOPTION

Chapter 1
The Adoption Service

The adoption service

1   Duty of local authority to provide adoption service

(1)   Each local authority must—

(a)   to the extent that it already provides an adoption service in its area, continue to do so, and

(b)   to the extent that it does not provide such a service in its area, provide such a service there.

(2)   In this Act, 'adoption service' means services designed to meet the needs, in relation to adoption, of persons mentioned in subsection (3).

(3)   Those persons are—

(a)   children who may be adopted,

(b)   persons who have been adopted,

(c)   parents and guardians of children mentioned in paragraph (a),

(d)   natural parents of persons who have been adopted,

(e)   persons who, before the placing of a child for adoption or the adoption of a child, treated the child as their child,

(f)   siblings (whether of the whole-blood or half-blood), natural grandparents and former guardians of—

(i)   children mentioned in paragraph (a), or

(ii)   persons mentioned in paragraph (b),

(g)   persons who may adopt a child,

(h)   persons who have adopted a child,

(i)   in relation to persons mentioned in paragraph (g) or (h), children of, or children treated as children of, such persons, and

(j)   any other persons who are—

(i)   affected by the placing, or proposed placing, of a child for adoption, or

(ii)   affected by an adoption.

(4)   An adoption service includes, in particular, services consisting of or including—

(a)   arrangements for assessing children who may be adopted,

(b)   arrangements for assessing prospective adopters,

(c)   arrangements for placing children for adoption,

(d)   the provision of information about adoption to any of the persons mentioned in subsection (3), and

(e)   adoption support services.

(5)   In this Act, 'adoption support services' means services consisting of or including the provision of—

(a)   counselling to any of the persons mentioned in subsection (3),

(b)   guidance about adoption to such persons,

(c)   any other assistance in relation to the adoption process that the local authority providing an adoption service in a particular case considers appropriate in the circumstances of that case.

2   Carrying out of duties imposed by section 1

(1)   For the purpose of carrying out the duties imposed by section 1(1) efficiently and effectively, a local authority must have regard to—

(a)   the other services that it provides in its area in carrying out the functions of a local authority under any of the enactments mentioned in section 5(1B) of the Social Work (Scotland) Act 1968 (c 49) (power of the Scottish Ministers to issue certain directions) including, in particular, those functions in so far as they relate to children, and

(b)   any registered adoption service provided there.

(2)   A local authority may carry out the duties imposed by section 1(1) by securing the provision of its adoption service by a registered adoption service.

(3)   In this section, 'registered adoption service' means an adoption service provided as mentioned in [paragraph 8(1)(b) of schedule 12 to the Public Services Reform (Scotland) Act 2010] and registered under [Part 5] of that Act.

3   Adoption service: regulations

The Scottish Ministers may by regulations—

(a)   amend subsection (4) or (5) of section 1 by—
  (i)   adding further services,
  (ii)   modifying the services mentioned in those subsections,
(b)   make further provision about adoption services.

[. . .]

5   Guidance

(1)   Subsection (2) applies where a local authority is carrying out its function under section 1 to continue to provide, or to provide, an adoption service or to secure the provision of such a service.

(2)   The local authority must have regard to any guidance given by the Scottish Ministers.

(3)   Guidance such as is mentioned in subsection (2) may, in particular, contain provision in relation to—

(a)   how a local authority should assess (or reassess) the needs of a person for adoption support services,
(b)   how the power conferred by section 9(1)(b) should be exercised,
(c)   the classes of person in relation to whom that power should be exercised,
(d)   how responsibility for the provision of an adoption service should be transferred from one local authority to another.

(4)   The Scottish Ministers may vary or revoke any guidance such as is mentioned in subsection (2).

6   [Assistance in carrying out functions under section 1]

(1)   Where it appears to a local authority that an appropriate person could assist the authority in carrying out any of its functions under section 1 [. . .], it may require the person to assist the authority in the way specified in the requirement.

(2)   An appropriate person need not comply with a requirement made by virtue of subsection (1) if—

(a)   it would not be reasonably practicable to do so,
(b)   doing so would be incompatible with the person's functions (whether statutory or otherwise), or
(c)   where the person is not a natural person, doing so would unduly prejudice the carrying out of such functions.

(3)   For the purposes of this section, a person is 'appropriate' if the person is—

(a)   another local authority,
(b)   a Health Board constituted under section 2 of the National Health Service (Scotland) Act 1978 (c 29),
(c)   such other person as may be prescribed by regulations made by the Scottish Ministers.

[. . .]

8 Adoption agencies: regulations about carrying out of functions

(1) The Scottish Ministers may make regulations for any purpose relating to the carrying out of its functions by a registered adoption service.

(2) The Scottish Ministers may make regulations with respect to the carrying out by local authorities of their functions in relation to adoption.

(3) Regulations under this section may in particular make provision for or in connection with—

(a) specifying circumstances in which a local authority proposing to make arrangements for the adoption of a child must apply for a permanence order which includes provision granting authority for the child to be adopted,

(b) requiring such an application to be made within a period specified in the regulations.

Adoption support services

9 Assessment of needs for adoption support services

(1) A local authority—

(a) must, on the request of a person mentioned in any of paragraphs (a) to (i) of subsection (3) of section 1, make an assessment of the needs of the person for adoption support services,

(b) may, on the request of a person mentioned in paragraph (j) of that subsection, make an assessment of the needs of the person for such services.

(2) Where a local authority makes an assessment of the needs of a person for adoption support services under subsection (1), the authority must decide whether the needs of the person call for the provision of such services.

(3) A local authority making an assessment of needs under subsection (1) must—

(a) do so in such manner as may be prescribed by regulations made by the Scottish Ministers, and

(b) have regard to such matters as may be so prescribed.

10 Provision of services

(1) On the request of a person mentioned in subsection (3) of section 1, a local authority must provide [. . .] services of a type mentioned in paragraph (d) of subsection (4) of that section to the person.

(2) On the request of a person mentioned in paragraph (a), (c) or (g) of subsection (3) of section 1, a local authority—

(a) must provide [. . .] services of a type mentioned in paragraphs (a) to (c) of subsection (4) of that section to the person, and

(b) may, without prejudice to subsection (4)(a), provide adoption support services to the person.

(3) For the purposes of subsection (2), it is immaterial whether the local authority has made an assessment of the needs of the person under section 9(1)(a).

(4) Where a local authority decides under section 9(2) that the provision of adoption support services is called for in respect of—

(a) a person mentioned in any of paragraphs (a) to (i) of subsection (3) of section 1, the authority must provide the services to the person,

(b) a person mentioned in paragraph (j) of that subsection, the authority may provide the services to the person.

11 Urgent provision

(1) If in the opinion of a local authority a person mentioned in subsection (3) of section 1 requires adoption support services as a matter of urgency, nothing in section 9 prevents the authority from providing, or arranging for the provision of, those services for the person without first carrying out an assessment under that section of the person's needs for adoption support services.

(2) If by virtue of subsection (1) a local authority provides, or arranges for the provision of, adoption support services the authority must, as soon as is reasonably practicable after such provision, make an assessment of the person's needs for adoption support services.

12 Power to provide payment to person entitled to adoption support service

(1) Subsection (2) applies where a local authority—

(a) has, in respect of a person, an obligation to provide, or secure the provision of, an adoption support service under this Part, or

(b) has a power so to provide and determines it should provide.

(2) Subject to subsection (4), the authority may, after having regard to the matters mentioned in subsection (3), provide the person with a payment instead of the service.

(3) Those matters are—

(a) the person's eligibility for assistance from any other body,

(b) where the person is so eligible, the availability to the person of that assistance at the time when the service might have been provided to the person by the authority,

(c) the ability of the authority to provide, or secure the provision of, the service, and

(d) the person's need for the service.

(4) A payment under subsection (2) may be made subject to such conditions (including conditions as to repayment) as the authority considers reasonable.

(5) In imposing conditions under subsection (4), the authority must have regard to the person's eligibility for assistance from any other body.

Regulations

13 Regulations

(1) The Scottish Ministers may by regulations make provision for or in connection with—

(a) determining in circumstances specified in the regulations which local authority is, or may become, responsible for—

(i) the provision of an adoption service,

(ii) the making of an assessment of needs under section 9(1)(a),

(b) determining the time at which, and the circumstances in which, a local authority's duty to provide an adoption service ends,

(c) specifying the circumstances in which a local authority may continue to provide an adoption service after the time determined by virtue of paragraph (b) has passed,

(d) specifying the arrangements a local authority may make when a person in respect of whom the authority provides, or has a power or a duty to provide, an adoption service moves outwith the authority's area,

(e) specifying the persons with whom such arrangements may be made,

(f) assessing the needs for adoption support services of persons who have moved or who intend to move—

(i) from one local authority area to another,

(ii) from outwith Scotland to Scotland.

(2) The power conferred by subsection (1) may be exercised so as to make different provision for different adoption services.

[Chapter 1A
Scotland's Adoption Register

[13A Scotland's Adoption Register

(1) The Scottish Ministers must make arrangements for the establishment and

maintenance of a register to be known as Scotland's Adoption Register for the purposes of facilitating adoption (referred to in this Chapter as 'the Register').

(2) The Scottish Ministers may by regulations—

(a) prescribe information relating to adoption which is, or types of information relating to adoption which are, to be included in the Register, which may include information relating to—

(i) children who adoption agencies consider ought to be placed for adoption,

(ii) persons considered by adoption agencies as suitable to have a child placed with them for adoption,

(iii) matters relating to such children or persons which arise after information about them is included in the Register,

(iv) children outwith Scotland who may be suitable for adoption,

(v) prospective adopters outwith Scotland,

(b) provide for how information is to be retained in the Register,

(c) make such further provision in relation to the Register as they consider appropriate.

(3) The Register is not to be open to public inspection or search.

(4) Information is to be kept in the Register in any form the Scottish Ministers consider appropriate.]

[13B Registration organisation

(1) Arrangements made by the Scottish Ministers under section 13A(1) may in particular—

(a) authorise an organisation to perform the Scottish Ministers' functions in respect of the Register (other than functions of making subordinate legislation),

(b) provide for payments to be made by the Scottish Ministers to an organisation so authorised.

(2) The Scottish Ministers must publish arrangements under section 13A(1) so far as they authorise an organisation as mentioned in subsection (1)(a).

(3) An organisation authorised in pursuance of subsection (1) (a 'registration organisation') must perform functions delegated to it in accordance with any directions (general or specific) given by the Scottish Ministers.]

[13C Supply of information for the Register

(1) An adoption agency must provide the Scottish Ministers with such information as may be prescribed in regulations made under section 13A(2) about—

(a) children who it considers ought to be placed for adoption or persons who were included in the Register as such children,

(b) persons who it considers as suitable to have a child placed with them for adoption or persons who were included in the Register as such persons.

(2) Regulations made under section 13A(2) may—

(a) provide that information is to be provided to a registration organisation in pursuance of subsection (1) instead of to the Scottish Ministers,

(b) provide for how and by when information is to be provided in pursuance of subsection (1),

(c) prescribe circumstances in which an adoption agency, despite subsection (1), is not to disclose information of the type prescribed for the purposes of that subsection.]

[13D Disclosure of information

(1) It is an offence to disclose any information derived from the Register other than in accordance with regulations made under section 13A(2) in pursuance of this section.

(2) Regulations made under section 13A(2) may authorise the Scottish Ministers or a registration organisation to disclose information derived from the Register—

    (a)   to an adoption agency for the purposes of helping it—
        (i)   to find persons with whom it would be appropriate to place a child for whom the agency is acting, or
        (ii)   to find a child who is appropriate for adoption by persons for whom the agency is acting,
    (b)   to any person (whether or not established or operating in Scotland) specified in the regulations—
        (i)   for any purpose connected with the performance of functions by the Scottish Ministers or a registration organisation in pursuance of this Chapter,
        (ii)   for the purpose of enabling the information to be entered in a register which is maintained in respect of England, Wales or Northern Ireland and which contains information about children who are suitable for adoption or prospective adopters,
        (iii)   for the purpose of enabling or assisting that person to perform any functions which relate to adoption,
        (iv)   for use for statistical or research purposes, or
        (v)   for any other purpose relating to adoption.
  (3)   Regulations made under section 13A(2) may—
    (a)   set out terms and conditions on which information may be disclosed in pursuance of this section,
    (b)   specify steps to be taken by an adoption agency in respect of information received in pursuance of subsection (2),
    (c)   authorise an adoption agency to disclose information derived from the Register for purposes relating to adoption.
  (4)   Subsection (1) does not apply to a disclosure of information by or with the authority of the Scottish Ministers.
  (5)   A person who is guilty of an offence under subsection (1) is liable on summary conviction to imprisonment for a term not exceeding 3 months, or a fine not exceeding level 5 on the standard scale, or both.]

[13E   Fees and other payments
Regulations made under section 13A(2) may prescribe—
    (a)   a fee which is to be paid by an adoption agency when providing information in pursuance of section 13C(1),
    (b)   a fee which is to be paid to the Scottish Ministers or a registration organisation in respect of a disclosure of information made in pursuance of section 13D(2), (3)(c) or (4),
    (c)   such other fees to be paid by adoption agencies, or payments to be made by them, in relation to the Register as the Scottish Ministers consider appropriate.]

[13F   Use of an organisation as agency for payments
  (1)   The Scottish Ministers may by regulations authorise a registration organisation or any other person to act as agent for the payment or receipt of sums payable by adoption agencies to other adoption agencies and may require adoption agencies to pay or receive such sums through the organisation.
  (2)   A registration organisation or other person authorised under subsection (1) is to perform the functions exercisable by virtue of that subsection in accordance with any directions (general or specific) given by the Scottish Ministers.]

[13G Supplementary
Nothing authorised or required to be done by virtue of this Chapter constitutes an offence under section 72(2) or 75(1).']]

. . .

Chapter 2
The Adoption Process

Preliminary

14 Considerations applying to the exercise of powers
(1) Subsections (2) to (4) apply where a court or adoption agency is coming to a decision relating to the adoption of a child.
(2) The court or adoption agency must have regard to all the circumstances of the case.
(3) The court or adoption agency is to regard the need to safeguard and promote the welfare of the child throughout the child's life as the paramount consideration.
(4) The court or adoption agency must, so far as is reasonably practicable, have regard in particular to—
  (a) the value of a stable family unit in the child's development,
  (b) the child's ascertainable views regarding the decision (taking account of the child's age and maturity),
  (c) the child's religious persuasion, racial origin and cultural and linguistic background, and
  (d) the likely effect on the child, throughout the child's life, of the making of an adoption order.
(5) Where an adoption agency is placing a child for adoption it must have regard, so far as is reasonably practicable, to the views of the parents, guardians and other relatives of the child.
(6) In carrying out the duties imposed on it by subsections (2) to (4) an adoption agency must, before making any arrangements for the adoption of a child, consider whether adoption is likely best to meet the needs of the child or whether there is some better practical alternative for the child.
(7) If an adoption agency concludes that there is an alternative such as is mentioned in subsection (6), it must not make arrangements for the adoption of the child.
(8) Without prejudice to the generality of subsection (4)(b), a child who is aged 12 or over is presumed to be of sufficient age and maturity to form a view for the purposes of that subsection.

Pre-adoption requirements

15 Child to live with adopters before adoption order made
(1) Where—
  (a) subsection (2) applies, an adoption order may not be made in relation to a child unless the conditions in subsection (3) are met,
  (b) subsection (2) does not apply, an adoption order may not be made in relation to the child unless the condition in subsection (4) is met.
(2) This subsection applies if—
  (a) the person applying for the adoption order (the 'applicant'), or one of the applicants, is a parent, step-parent or relative of the child, or
  (b) the child was placed with the applicant, or applicants, by an adoption agency.
(3) The conditions are—
  (a) that the child is at least 19 weeks old, and
  (b) that at all times during the period of 13 weeks immediately preceding the making of the order the child's home was with the applicants.
(4) The condition is that at all times during the period of 12 months immediately preceding the making of the order the child's home was with the applicants.

(5) In relation to—

(a) an adoption proposed to be effected by a Convention adoption order, or

(b) an adoption of a child habitually resident outwith the British Islands which is proposed to be effected by an adoption order other than a Convention adoption order, subsection (3)(b) has effect as if the reference to a period of 13 weeks were a reference to a period of 6 months.

16 Home visits

(1) Where a child was placed for adoption with the applicants by an adoption agency, an adoption order may not be made unless the appropriate court is satisfied that the condition in subsection (2) is met.

(2) The condition is that sufficient opportunities to see the child with the applicant or, in the case of an application by two applicants, both of them together in the home environment have been given to the agency.

(3) Where the child was not placed for adoption with the applicants by an adoption agency, an adoption order may not be made unless the appropriate court is satisfied that the condition in subsection (4) is met.

(4) The condition is that sufficient opportunities to see the child with the applicant or, in the case of an application by two applicants, both of them together in the home environment have been given—

(a) where the home is in Scotland, to the local authority within whose area the home is situated,

(b) where the home is outwith Scotland, to any local authority.

17 Reports where child placed by agency

(1) Subsection (2) applies where an application for an adoption order relates to a child placed for adoption by an adoption agency.

(2) The agency must—

(a) submit to the court a report on—

(i) the suitability of the applicants, and

(ii) any other matters relevant to the operation of section 14, and

(b) assist the court in any manner the court directs.

18 Notification to local authority of adoption application

(1) Subsection (2) applies where a child was not placed for adoption with the applicants by an adoption agency.

(2) An adoption order may not be made in relation to the child unless the applicants have, at least 3 months before the date of the order, given notice to the appropriate local authority of their intention to apply for the order.

(3) In subsection (2), 'appropriate local authority' means—

(a) where the applicants have their home in Scotland, the local authority within whose area the home is situated,

(b) where they have their home outwith Scotland, any local authority.

19 Notice under section 18: local authority's duties

(1) This section applies where a local authority receives a notice under section 18 in respect of a child.

(2) On receipt of the notice the authority must—

(a) investigate the matter, and

(b) submit to the court a report of the investigation.

(3) The local authority must in particular investigate—

(a) so far as is reasonably practicable, the suitability of the applicants and any other matters relevant to the operation of section 14 in relation to the application,

(b) whether there has been a contravention of section 75 in relation to the child, and

(c) whether there has been a failure to comply with section 76(2) in relation to the child.

(4) If the authority knows that the child is being looked after by another local

authority, it must, before the expiry of the period of 7 days beginning with the day on which it receives the notice, give the other authority a copy of the notice.

Restrictions on removal of children placed for adoption

20 Restrictions on removal: child placed for adoption with consent

(1) Subsection (2) applies where—

(a) an adoption agency has placed a child for adoption with persons ('prospective adopters'), and

(b) each parent or guardian of the child has, in accordance with such provision as may be made by regulations by the Scottish Ministers, consented to the placement (whether or not each parent or guardian knows the identity of the prospective adopters).

(2) A parent or guardian of the child must not remove the child from the care of the prospective adopters without the leave of—

(a) the adoption agency, or

(b) the appropriate court.

(3) A person who removes a child in contravention of this section commits an offence and is liable on summary conviction to imprisonment for a term not exceeding 3 months or a fine not exceeding level 5 on the standard scale or both.

21 Restrictions on removal: notice of intention to adopt given

(1) Subsection (2) applies where—

(a) persons ('prospective adopters') give notice under section 18(2) in relation to a child, and

(b) during the period of 5 years immediately preceding the giving of notice, the child's home has been with the prospective adopters.

(2) Except where subsection (3) applies, a person may not remove the child from the care of the prospective adopters during the period beginning with the giving of notice and ending with the relevant act.

(3) This subsection applies if—

(a) the prospective adopters consent to the removal,

(b) a court having jurisdiction to make adoption orders grants leave for the removal,

(c) the child is arrested, or

(d) the removal is authorised by virtue of any enactment.

(4) For the purposes of subsection (2), 'relevant act' means—

(a) where before the expiry of the 3 month period the prospective adopters apply for an adoption order in relation to the child to whom the notice relates, the making of the application for the adoption order,

(b) where the prospective adopters do not apply for an adoption order before the expiry of that period, the expiry of that period.

(5) In this section, '3 month period' means the period of 3 months beginning with the day on which the local authority receives the notice.

(6) If during—

(a) the 3 month period, or

(b) the period of 28 days beginning with the expiry of the 3 month period, the prospective adopters give a further notice under section 18(2) to a local authority in respect of the same child, subsection (2) does not apply.

(7) A person who removes a child in contravention of this section commits an offence and is liable on summary conviction to imprisonment for a term not exceeding 3 months or a fine not exceeding level 5 on the standard scale or both.

22 Restrictions on removal: application for adoption order pending

(1) Subsection (2) applies where—

(a) an application for an adoption order in relation to a child has been made to, but not determined by, the appropriate court, and

(b)   during the period of 5 years immediately preceding the making of the application, the child's home has been with the persons applying for the order (the 'prospective adopters').

(2)   Except where subsection (3) applies, a person may not remove the child from the care of the prospective adopters.

(3)   This subsection applies if—

(a)   the prospective adopters consent to the removal,

(b)   the court determining the application grants leave for the removal,

(c)   the child is arrested, or

(d)   the removal is authorised by virtue of any enactment.

(4)   A person who removes a child in contravention of this section commits an offence and is liable on summary conviction to imprisonment for a term not exceeding 3 months or a fine not exceeding level 5 on the standard scale or both.

23   Restrictions on removal of child looked after by local authority

(1)   Subsection (2) applies where—

(a)   section 21(1) or 22(1) applies,

(b)   before the child's home came to be with the prospective adopters, the child was looked after by a local authority, and

(c)   the child continues to be looked after by a local authority.

(2)   Except where subsection (3) applies, the local authority must not remove the child from the care of the prospective adopters.

(3)   This subsection applies if—

(a)   the removal is made in accordance with section 25 or 26,

(b)   an appropriate court grants leave for the removal, [. . .]

(c)   the removal is authorised by virtue of Chapter [. . .] 3 of Part II of the 1995 Act [, or

(d)   the removal is authorised by an order or warrant under the Children's Hearings (Scotland) Act 2011.]

Return of children

24   Return of child removed in breach of certain provisions

(1)   The relevant court may, on the application of a person from whose care a child has been removed in breach of any of the relevant provisions, order the person who has so removed the child to return the child to the applicant.

(2)   The relevant court may, on the application of a person who has reasonable grounds for believing that another person is intending to remove a child from the applicant's care in breach of any of the relevant provisions, by order direct that other person not to remove the child from the applicant's care in breach of the provision concerned.

(3)   The 'relevant court' is—

(a)   if there is pending in respect of the child an application for an adoption order or a permanence order, the court in which the application is pending,

(b)   in any other case—

(i)   the Court of Session, or

(ii)   the sheriff court of the sheriffdom within which the applicant resides.

(4)   The relevant provisions are—

(a)   sections 20, 21, 22 and 23,

(b)   sections 30, 34, 35 and 36 of the 2002 Act,

(c)   Articles 28 and 29 of the Northern Ireland Order.

25   Return of child placed for adoption by adoption agency

(1)   This section applies where—

(a)   in pursuance of arrangements made by an adoption agency or a registered adoption society for the adoption of a child by persons (the 'prospective adopters'), the child has been placed with the prospective adopters, and

(b)   no adoption order has been made in relation to the child on the application of the prospective adopters.

(2)   The prospective adopters may give notice to the agency or society of their intention not to retain the care of the child.

(3)   The agency or society may give notice to the prospective adopters of its intention not to allow the child to remain in the care of the prospective adopters.

(4)   If an application for an adoption order in relation to the child has been made by the prospective adopters, notice under subsection (3) may be given only with leave of the court which is hearing the application.

(5)   Subsection (6) applies where—

(a)   notice is given by virtue of subsection (2) or (3), or

(b)   an application for an adoption order made by the prospective adopters is refused or withdrawn.

(6)   The prospective adopters must, before the expiry of the relevant period, return the child to—

(a)   the agency or, as the case may be, society, or

(b)   a person nominated by the agency or, as the case may be, society for the purposes of this section.

(7)   In subsection (6), 'relevant period' means—

(a)   in the case mentioned in paragraph (a) of subsection (5), the period of 7 days beginning with the day on which notice was given,

(b)   in the case mentioned in paragraph (b) of that subsection—

(i)   the period of 7 days beginning with the day on which the application was refused or withdrawn, or

(ii)   if, before the expiry of the period mentioned in sub-paragraph (i), the court makes an order extending that period for a period (not exceeding 6 weeks) specified in the order, the period so specified.

(8)   A person who fails to return a child in contravention of this section commits an offence and is liable on summary conviction to imprisonment for a term not exceeding 3 months or a fine not exceeding level 5 on the standard scale or both.

(9)   The court by which a person is convicted by virtue of subsection (8) may order that the child in respect of whom the offence is committed be returned to the child's parent or guardian or, as the case may be, the adoption agency or registered adoption society.

Adoption not proceeding: arrangements

26   Looked after children: adoption not proceeding

(1)   This section applies where—

(a)   persons ('prospective adopters') give notice under section 18(2) in relation to a child,

(b)   the child has a home with the prospective adopters,

(c)   the child was not placed with the prospective adopters in pursuance of arrangements made by an adoption agency or a registered adoption society for the adoption of the child by the prospective adopters, and

(d)   the child is being looked after by a local authority (the 'relevant local authority').

(2)   The prospective adopters may give notice to the relevant local authority of their intention not to retain the care of the child.

(3)   The authority may give notice to the prospective adopters of its intention not to allow the child to remain in the care of the prospective adopters.

(4)   Where notice is given by virtue of subsection (2) or (3) the prospective adopters must, before the expiry of the period of 7 days beginning with the day on which notice is given, deliver the child to—

(a)   the authority, or

(b)   person nominated by the authority for the purposes of this section.

(5)   If an application for an adoption order in relation to the child has been made by the prospective adopters, notice under subsection (3) may be given only with leave of the court which is hearing the application.

(6)   If an application for an adoption order in relation to the child is refused or withdrawn, the child—

(a)   must be delivered to the relevant local authority only if the authority requires it, and

(b)   where such a requirement is made, must be delivered before the expiry of the period of 7 days beginning with the day on which the requirement is made.

(7)   Where an application by the prospective adopters for an adoption order in relation to the child has been made but not disposed of, any right of the relevant local authority to require the child to be delivered otherwise than by virtue of this section is suspended.

(8)   A person who fails to deliver a child in contravention of this section commits an offence and is liable on summary conviction to imprisonment for a term not exceeding 3 months or a fine not exceeding level 5 on the standard scale or both.

(9)   The court by which a person is convicted by virtue of subsection (8) may order that the child in respect of whom the offence is committed be delivered to the child's parent or guardian or, as the case may be, the relevant local authority.

[. . .]

Contravention of sections 30 to 36 of 2002 Act

27   Contravention of sections 30 to 36 of 2002 Act

(1)   A person who contravenes any of the provisions of the 2002 Act mentioned in subsection (2) commits an offence and is liable on summary conviction to imprisonment for a term not exceeding 3 months or a fine not exceeding level 5 on the standard scale or both.

(2)   Those provisions are—

(a)   section 30(1), (2) and (3) (removal of child placed or who may be placed for adoption),

(b)   sections 32(2)(b), 33(2) and 35(2) (return of child by prospective adopters),

(c)   section 34(1) (removal of child in contravention of placement order),

(d)   section 36(1) (removal of child in non-agency case), and

(e)   section 36(5) (return of child to parent or guardian).

The making of adoption orders

28   Adoption orders

(1)   An adoption order is an order made by the appropriate court on an application under section 29 or 30 vesting the parental responsibilities and parental rights in relation to a child in the adopters or adopter.

(2)   The court must not make an adoption order unless it considers that it would be better for the child that the order be made than not.

(3)   An adoption order may contain such terms and conditions as the court thinks fit.

(4)   An adoption order may be made in respect of a person aged 18 or over if the application for the order was made when the person was under 18.

(5)   An adoption order may be made in respect of a child who is subject to a permanence order.

(6)   An adoption order may be made even if the child to be adopted is already an adopted child.

(7)   An adoption order may not be made in respect of a person who is or has been—

(a)   married, or

(b)   a civil partner.

29   Adoption by certain couples

(1)   Where—

(a)   each member of a relevant couple is aged 21 or over,

(b)   neither member of the couple is a parent of the child to be adopted, and

(c)   one of the conditions in subsection (2) is met,

an adoption order may be made on the application of the couple.

(2)   Those conditions are—

(a)   that a member of the couple is domiciled in a part of the British Islands,

(b)   that each member of the couple has been habitually resident in a part of the British Islands for a period of at least one year ending with the date of the application.

(3)   A couple is 'relevant' for the purposes of this section if its members are—

(a)   persons who are married to each other,

(b)   persons who are civil partners of each other,

(c)   persons who are living together as if husband and wife in an enduring family relationship, or

(d)   persons who are living together as if civil partners in an enduring family relationship.

(4)   In this section 'parent', in relation to the child to be adopted, means a parent who has any parental responsibilities or parental rights in relation to the child.

30   Adoption by one person

(1)   An adoption order may be made on the application of a person ('A') if—

(a)   A is aged 21 or over,

(b)   subsection (2), (3), (4) or (5) applies,

(c)   one of the conditions in subsection (6) is met, and

(d)   where A is a natural parent of the child to be adopted, subsection (7) applies.

(2)   This subsection applies if A is not a member of a relevant couple.

(3)   This subsection applies if—

(a)   A and another person ('B') are a relevant couple,

(b)   B is aged 18 or over,

(c)   B is a parent of the child to be adopted, and

(d)   B—

(i)   is domiciled in a part of the British Islands, or

(ii)   has been habitually resident in a part of the British Islands for a period of at least one year ending with the date of the application.

(4)   This subsection applies if—

(a)   A and B are—

(i)   married to each other, or

(ii)   civil partners of each other,

(b)   B is not a parent of the child to be adopted, and

(c)   the court is satisfied that—

(i)   B cannot be found,

(ii)   A and B have separated and are living apart and the separation is likely to be permanent, or

(iii)   B is by reason of ill-health (whether physical or mental) incapable of making an application for an adoption order.

(5)   This subsection applies if—

(a)   A and B are a relevant couple by virtue of being members of a couple falling within paragraph (c) or (d) of subsection (3) of section 29,

(b)   B is not a parent of the child to be adopted, and

(c)   the court is satisfied that B is by reason of ill-health (whether physical or mental) incapable of making an application for an adoption order.

(6)   Those conditions are—

(a)   that A is domiciled in a part of the British Islands,

(b)   that A has been habitually resident in a part of the British Islands for a period of at least one year ending with the date of the application.

(7)   This subsection applies if the court is satisfied that—

(a)   the other natural parent is dead,

(b)   the other natural parent cannot be found,

(c)   by virtue of [the provisions specified in subsection (7A), there is no other parent], or

(d)   the exclusion of the other natural parent from the application for adoption is justified on some other ground.

[(7A)   The provisions referred to in subsection (7)(c) are—

(a)   section 28 of the Human Fertilisation and Embryology Act 1990 (disregarding subsections (5A) to (5I) of that section), or

(b)   sections 34 to 47 of the Human Fertilisation and Embryology Act 2008 (disregarding sections 39, 40 and 46 of that Act).]

(8)   In subsections (3)(c), (4)(b) and (5)(b), 'parent' has the meaning given by section 29(4).

31   Parental etc consent

(1)   An adoption order may not be made unless one of the five conditions is met.

(2)   The first condition is that, in the case of each parent or guardian of the child, the appropriate court is satisfied—

(a)   that the parent or guardian understands what the effect of making an adoption order would be and consents to the making of the order (whether or not the parent or guardian knows the identity of the persons applying for the order), or

(b)   that the parent's or guardian's consent to the making of the adoption order should be dispensed with on one of the grounds mentioned in subsection (3).

(3)   Those grounds are—

(a)   that the parent or guardian is dead,

(b)   that the parent or guardian cannot be found or is incapable of giving consent,

(c)   that subsection (4) or (5) applies,

(d)   that, where neither of those subsections applies, the welfare of the child otherwise requires the consent to be dispensed with.

(4)   This subsection applies if the parent or guardian—

(a)   has parental responsibilities or parental rights in relation to the child other than those mentioned in sections 1(1)(c) and 2(1)(c) of the 1995 Act,

(b)   is, in the opinion of the court, unable satisfactorily to—

(i)   discharge those responsibilities, or

(ii)   exercise those rights, and

(c)   is likely to continue to be unable to do so.

(5)   This subsection applies if—

(a)   the parent or guardian has, by virtue of the making of a relevant order, no parental responsibilities or parental rights in relation to the child, and

(b)   it is unlikely that such responsibilities will be imposed on, or such rights given to, the parent or guardian.

(6)   In subsection (5)(a), 'relevant order' means a permanence order which does

not include provision granting authority for the child to whom the order relates to be adopted.

(7) The second condition is that a permanence order granting authority for the child to be adopted is in force.

(8) The third condition is that each parent or guardian of the child has consented under section 20 of the 2002 Act (advance consent to adoption), has not withdrawn the consent and does not oppose the making of the adoption order.

(9) The fourth condition is that—

(a) the child has been placed for adoption by an adoption agency (within the meaning of section 2(1) of the 2002 Act) with the prospective adopters in whose favour the adoption order is proposed to be made,

(b) the child was placed for adoption—

(i) under section 19 of the 2002 Act (placing children with parental consent) with the consent of each parent or guardian and the consent of the mother was given when the child was at least 6 weeks old, or

(ii) under an order made under section 21 of the 2002 Act (placement orders) and the child was at least 6 weeks old when the order was made, and

(c) no parent or guardian of the child opposes the making of the adoption order.

(10) The fifth condition is that an order under Article 17(1) or 18(1) of the Northern Ireland Order (orders declaring children free for adoption) is in force in relation to the child.

(11) Consent is ineffective for the purposes of subsection (2)(a) if given by the mother less than 6 weeks after the child's birth.

(12) A parent or guardian may not oppose the making of an adoption order under subsection (8) or (9) without leave of the court.

(13) The court must not give leave under subsection (12) unless satisfied that there has been a change of circumstances since the consent of the parent or guardian was given or, as the case may be, the order under section 21 of the 2002 Act was made.

(14) The withdrawal of—

(a) any consent to the placement of a child for adoption under section 19, or under an order under section 21, of the 2002 Act, or

(b) any consent given under section 20 of that Act,

is ineffective if the consent is given after an application for an adoption order is made.

(15) In subsections (2) and (3), 'parent', in relation to the child to be adopted, means—

(a) a parent who has any parental responsibilities or parental rights in relation to the child, or

(b) a parent who, by virtue of a permanence order which does not include provision granting authority for the child to be adopted, has no such responsibilities or rights.

32 Consent of child aged 12 or over

(1) Except where subsection (2) applies, an adoption order may not be made in respect of a child who is aged 12 or over unless the child consents.

(2) This subsection applies where the court is satisfied that the child is incapable of consenting to the order.

33 Restrictions on making orders

(1) Except where subsection (2) applies, the court may not hear an application for an adoption order in relation to a child where a previous application falling

within subsection (3) made in relation to the child by the same persons was refused by any court.

(2) This subsection applies where—

(a) in refusing the previous application, the court directed that this section should not apply, or

(b) it appears to the court that, because of a change in circumstances, or for any other reason, it is proper to hear the application.

(3) An application falls within this subsection if it is an application for—

(a) an adoption order,

(b) an adoption order as defined in section 46(1) of the 2002 Act,

(c) an order made, or having effect as if made, under Article 12 of the Northern Ireland Order,

(d) an order for adoption made in the Isle of Man,

(e) an order for adoption made in any of the Channel Islands.

34 Contravention of section 72 no bar to making order

The court may make an adoption order in relation to a child even where it is found that the applicants have, as respects the child, contravened section 72.

Effect of order on existing rights etc

35 Effect of order on existing rights etc

(1) Where an adoption order is made on the application of a member of a relevant couple by virtue of subsection (3) of section 30, the making of the order—

(a) does not affect any parental responsibilities and parental rights which immediately before the making of the order were vested in the other member of the relevant couple,

(b) does not extinguish any duty owed to the child by that other member—

(i) to pay or provide aliment in respect of any period occurring after the making of the order,

(ii) to make any payment arising out of parental responsibilities and parental rights in respect of such a period.

(2) Otherwise, the making of an adoption order—

(a) extinguishes any parental responsibilities and parental rights relating to the child which immediately before the making of the order were vested in any person,

(b) subject to subsection (3), extinguishes any duty owed to the child immediately before the making of the order—

(i) to pay or provide aliment in respect of any period occurring after the making of the order,

(ii) to make any payment arising out of parental responsibilities and parental rights in respect of such a period.

(3) The making of an adoption order does not extinguish a duty arising under a deed or agreement—

(a) which constitutes a trust, or

(b) which expressly provides that the duty is not to be extinguished by the making of an adoption order.

(4) An adoption order does not affect parental responsibilities and parental rights so far as they relate to any period before the making of the order.

Revocation of supervision requirement

36 [Revocation of compulsory supervision order on making of adoption order]

(1) Subsection (2) applies where—

(a) the child to be adopted is subject to a [compulsory supervision order], and

(b) the appropriate court is satisfied that, were it to make an adoption order in relation to the child, [it would no longer be necessary that, for the protection, guidance, treatment or control of the child, the child be subject to the compulsory supervision order.]

(2) The court must make an order providing that, on the making of the adoption order, the [compulsory supervision order] ceases to have effect.

Adoption records

37 Information to be kept about adoptions

The Scottish Ministers may make regulations for or in connection with specifying—

(a) the information which an adoption agency must keep in relation to adoptions, and

(b) the form and manner in which it must keep the information.

38 Disclosure of information kept under relevant enactment

(1) The Scottish Ministers may by regulations make provision for or in connection with the disclosure by adoption agencies to adopted persons and other persons of a description or descriptions specified in the regulations of information kept by virtue of a relevant enactment.

(2) Regulations under subsection (1) may in particular include provision—

(a) in circumstances specified in the regulations, conferring discretion on adoption agencies as to whether to disclose or withhold information,

(b) specifying conditions which are to apply in relation to the disclosure of information, or information of a type so specified, to adopted persons of a description or descriptions so specified,

(c) specifying circumstances in which information should not be disclosed to adopted persons of a description or descriptions so specified,

(d) about the review of decisions of adoption agencies in connection with—

(i) the disclosure of information,

(ii) the conditions applicable to such disclosure.

(3) In this section, 'relevant enactment' means—

(a) section 37, or

(b) any other enactment (whether or not in force) which imposes a requirement (however expressed) to keep records relating to adoptions.

Chapter 3
Status of Adopted Children

39 Meaning of 'adoption' in Chapter 3

(1) In this Chapter, 'adoption' means—

(a) adoption by an adoption order,

(b) adoption by an adoption order as defined in section 46(1) of the 2002 Act,

(c) adoption by an order made, or having effect as if made, under Article 12 of the Northern Ireland Order,

(d) adoption by an order made in the Isle of Man or any of the Channel Islands,

(e) a Convention adoption,

(f) an overseas adoption, or

(g) an adoption recognised by the law of Scotland and effected under the law of any other country;

and related expressions are to be interpreted accordingly.

(2) References in this Chapter to adoption do not include an adoption effected before the day on which this chapter comes into force.

(3) Any reference in an enactment to an adopted person within the meaning of

this Chapter includes a reference to an adopted child within the meaning of Part IV of the Adoption (Scotland) Act 1978 (c 28).

40 Status conferred by adoption

(1) An adopted person is to be treated in law as if born as the child of the adopters or adopter.

(2) If an adopted person is adopted—

(a) by a relevant couple, or

(b) by virtue of section 30(3), by a member of a relevant couple, the adopted person is to be treated as the child of the couple concerned.

(3) An adopted person adopted by virtue of section 30(3) by a member of a relevant couple is to be treated in law as not being the child of any person other than the adopter and the other member of the couple.

(4) Otherwise, an adopted person is to be treated in law as not being the child of any person other than the adopters or adopter.

(5) Subsections (3) and (4) do not affect any reference in this Act to a person's natural parent or to any other natural relationship.

(6) Subsection (7) applies where, in the case of a person adopted under a Convention adoption, the Court of Session is satisfied, on an application under this section—

(a) that under the law of the country in which the adoption was effected the adoption is not a full adoption,

(b) that—

(i) the consents mentioned in Article 4(c) and (d) of the Convention have not been given for a full adoption, or

(ii) the United Kingdom is not the receiving State (within the meaning of Article 2 of the Convention), and

(c) that it would be more favourable to the person for a direction to be given under that subsection.

(7) The court may direct that subsection (4)—

(a) is not to apply, or

(b) is not to apply to such extent as may be specified in the direction.

(8) In subsection (6), 'full adoption' means an adoption by virtue of which the person falls to be treated in law as if the person were not the child of any person other than the adopters or adopter.

(9) This section has effect from the date of the adoption.

(10) Subject to the provisions of this Chapter, this section—

(a) applies for the interpretation of enactments or instruments passed or made before as well as after the adoption and so applies subject to any contrary indication, and

(b) has effect as respects things done, or events occurring, on or after the adoption.

41 Miscellaneous enactments

(1) Subject to subsection (2), section 40 does not apply—

(a) for the purposes of determining the forbidden degrees of consanguinity and affinity in respect of the law relating to marriage or to the eligibility of persons to register as civil partners of each other, or

(b) in respect of the crime of incest.

(2) On the making of an adoption order, the adopter and the person adopted are deemed, for all time coming, to be within the forbidden degrees in respect of the law relating to marriage, to such eligibility and to incest.

(3) Section 40 does not apply for the purposes of any provision of—

(a) the British Nationality Act 1981 (c 61),

(b) the Immigration Act 1971 (c 77),

(c) any instrument having effect under either of those Acts, or

(d) any other law for the time being in force which determines British citizenship, British overseas territories citizenship or British Overseas Citizenship.

42 Pensions

Section 40 does not affect entitlement to a pension which is payable to or for the benefit of a person and is in payment at the time of the person's adoption.

43 Insurance

(1) Subsections (2) and (3) apply where a child is adopted whose natural parent has effected an insurance with—

    (a) a friendly society,

    (b) a collecting society, or

    (c) an industrial insurance company,

for the payment on the death of the child of money for funeral expenses.

(2) The rights and liabilities under the policy are by virtue of the adoption transferred to the adoptive parents.

(3) For the purposes of the enactments relating to such societies and companies, the adoptive parents are to be treated as the person who took out the policy.

(4) Where the adoption is effected by an order made by virtue of section 30(3), the references in subsections (2) and (3) to the adoptive parents are to be read as references to the adopter and the other member of the relevant couple.

44 Succession and inter vivos deeds

Section 40 does not affect the law relating to adopted persons in respect of—

    (a) succession to an intestate or testate estate, and

    (b) the disposal of property by virtue of an inter vivos deed.

Chapter 4

Adoption Support Plans

Adoption support plans

45 Adoption support plans

(1) This section applies where—

    (a) a local authority has, by virtue of section 9(1), assessed the needs of a person for adoption support services and decides that the provision of such services is called for in respect of the person, and

    (b) the person is a member of a relevant family.

(2) Subject to subsection (4), the authority must prepare an adoption support plan in respect of each member of the relevant family.

(3) An adoption support plan must, in relation to the person it concerns ('the person')—

    (a) specify the needs of the person identified as a result of an assessment carried out by virtue of section 9(1),

    (b) record details of the adoption support services the provision of which the authority decides is called for by virtue of section 9(2),

    (c) specify any other needs of the person identified by the authority,

    (d) set out how the needs mentioned in paragraphs (a) and (c) may be met by the provision of adoption support services,

    (e) record details of any previous assessment of needs in respect of the person carried out by virtue of section 9(1),

    (f) record details of any assessment of needs in respect of the person made under section 12A(1) of the Social Work (Scotland) Act 1968 (c 49),

    (g) where the person has been adopted, record details of any care plan prepared by a local authority in respect of the person under regulations made under section 17 of the 1995 Act,

    (h) record details of any adoption support services which—

        (i) were provided to the person before the plan was prepared, or

(ii) are being provided to the person when the plan is prepared,

(i)   specify any other matter which, in the opinion of the local authority preparing the plan, is relevant to the provision of adoption support services to the person, and

(j)   where there is no information to be included in the plan under any of paragraphs (a) to (i), record that fact.

(4)   The authority may, with the consent of each member of the relevant family aged 12 or over, prepare a single adoption support plan in respect of all members of the relevant family instead of preparing adoption support plans in respect of each of them.

(5)   Subsection (3) applies to a single adoption support plan prepared under subsection (4) as if—

(a)   for the words 'the person it concerns ("the person")' there were substituted 'each member of the relevant family it concerns',

(b)   for the words 'the person' in paragraphs (a), (c), (e), (f), (h) and (i) there were substituted 'each member',

(c)   for the words 'the person' in paragraph (g), where they first occur, there were substituted 'a member of the relevant family', and

(d)   for the words 'the person' in that paragraph, where they second occur, there were substituted 'that member'.

(6)   If in the opinion of the authority a member of the relevant family aged 12 or over is incapable of giving consent under subsection (4), the requirement to obtain such consent does not apply in relation to the member.

(7)   In this section, 'relevant family' means—

(a)   a child who is placed for adoption,

(b)   the person or persons with whom a child is placed for adoption,

(c)   a child who has been adopted,

(d)   the person who has, or persons who have, adopted that child,

(e)   any—

(i)   child of a person or persons mentioned in paragraph (b) or (d),

(ii)   other child who has been treated by the person or persons as a child of the person or persons, living in the same household as the person or persons.

46 Duration

(1)   An adoption support plan ceases to have effect on the occurrence of whichever of the events in subsection (2) first occurs.

(2)   Those events are—

(a)   the preparation of a further adoption support plan in respect of the member or, as the case may be, members of the relevant family in relation to whom the adoption support plan was prepared,

(b)   the date on which an appropriate child reaches the age of 18.

(3)   In this section, 'appropriate child' means a child—

(a)   who has been placed for adoption, or

(b)   who has been adopted,

and who is a member of the relevant family in relation to which, or to any members of which, the adoption support plan was prepared.

47 Family member's right to require review of plan

(1)   This section applies where an adoption support plan is in force in respect of a member of a relevant family or, as the case may be, a relevant family.

(2)   Subject to subsection (4), the person to whom the plan relates or, as the case may be, a member of the relevant family to which the plan relates (in either case, the 'relevant member') may, if the relevant member believes the local authority is not complying with any of its obligations mentioned in the plan, require the authority to review the plan.

(3) The authority may, in reviewing the plan, carry out a reassessment of the needs of the relevant member for adoption support services.

(4) A relevant member (other than the person or persons with whom the child has been placed for adoption or the person who has, or persons who have, adopted the child) may not make a requirement under subsection (2) unless, in the opinion of the local authority, the member is capable of understanding the need for adoption support services.

(5) After reviewing the plan, the local authority must vary the plan to reflect any changes in—

    (a) the needs of any relevant member for adoption support services identified as a result of a reassessment of needs made under subsection (3),

    (b) the adoption support services the local authority will provide.

(6) In this section, any references to a reassessment of needs of a person include, where no assessment has been carried out by virtue of section 9(1)(a) in relation to the person, references to an assessment of needs of the person.

48 Other cases where authority under duty to review plan

(1) This section applies where an adoption support plan is in force.

(2) The local authority must review the plan—

    (a) from time to time, and

    (b) at any time when the authority becomes aware of a change in the circumstances of a relevant member.

(3) In reviewing the plan, the authority may make a reassessment of the needs of any relevant member.

(4) After reviewing the plan, the authority must vary the plan to reflect any changes in—

    (a) the needs of any relevant member for adoption support services identified as a result of a reassessment of needs made under subsection (3),

    (b) the adoption support services the local authority will provide.

(5) In this section—

    (a) any references to a reassessment of needs of a person are to be construed in accordance with subsection (6) of section 47,

    (b) 'relevant member' has the same meaning as in that section.

Reassessment

49 Reassessment of needs for adoption support services

(1) This section applies where an adoption support plan is in force.

(2) Any relevant member aged 12 or over may require the local authority which prepared the plan to make a reassessment of the member's needs for adoption support services.

(3) The authority, having regard to the results of that reassessment, must decide whether the needs of the member call for the provision of such services.

(4) Where the authority decides, by virtue of subsection (3), that the provision of adoption support services is called for, the authority must provide the services.

(5) Where the authority provides adoption support services under subsection (4), it must vary the adoption support plan to reflect any changes in the services the authority will provide.

(6) A relevant member (other than the person or persons with whom the child has been placed for adoption or the person who has, or persons who have, adopted the child) may not require a reassessment to be made under subsection (2) unless, in the opinion of the local authority, the member is capable of understanding the need for adoption support services.

(7) Where a local authority is making a reassessment of needs under this section, it must—

    (a) do so in such manner as may be prescribed by regulations made by the Scottish Ministers, and

    (b) have regard to such matters as may be so prescribed.

(8) In this section—

    (a) any references to a reassessment of needs of a person are to be construed in accordance with subsection (6) of section 47,

    (b) 'relevant member' has the same meaning as in that section.

Directions

50 Implementation of plans: directions

(1) The Scottish Ministers may give directions of a general or specific nature to a local authority as to the implementation of adoption support plans.

(2) A direction under subsection (1) may not require an authority—

    (a) to provide or, as the case may be, continue to provide, or

    (b) withhold provision of,

a particular adoption support service.

(3) The Scottish Ministers may vary or revoke any direction under subsection (1).

Guidance

51 Guidance

(1) In preparing or reviewing adoption support plans, a local authority must have regard to any guidance issued by the Scottish Ministers.

(2) The Scottish Ministers may vary or revoke any such guidance.

Regulations

52 Regulations about reviews of adoption support plans

The Scottish Ministers may by regulations make provision for or in connection with specifying the way in which reviews of adoption support plans are to be carried out.

Chapter 5
Registration

53 Adopted Children Register and index

(1) The Registrar General must continue to maintain—

    (a) a register to be called the Adopted Children Register, and

    (b) an index of the Adopted Children Register.

(2) No entries may be made in the Adopted Children Register other than entries—

    (a) directed to be made in it by adoption orders, or

    (b) required to be made under schedule 1.

(3) The provisions of the Registration of Births, Deaths and Marriages (Scotland) Act 1965 (c 49) with regard to the correction of errors in entries apply in relation to entries in the Adopted Children Register as they apply in relation to entries in any register of births.

(4) Schedule 1 (which makes provision about registration of adoptions and the amendment of adoption orders) has effect.

54 Searches and extracts

(1) The terms, conditions and regulations as to payment of fees, form and authentication of documents and otherwise applicable under the Registration of Births, Deaths and Marriages (Scotland) Act 1965 (c 49) in respect of—

(a)   searches in indexes kept by virtue of that Act by the Registrar General, and

(b)   the supply from the General Register Office of extracts of entries in the registers of births, deaths and marriages,

apply in respect of searches in the index of the Adopted Children Register and supplies of extracts of entries in the Adopted Children Register.

(2)   Where a person makes a request in accordance with those terms, conditions and regulations (including paying such fee as may be prescribed by those regulations), the Registrar General is, if the General Register Office is open for the purpose, to—

(a)   search (or permit the person to search) the index of the Adopted Children Register, and

(b)   issue to the person an extract of an entry in the register.

55   Connections between the register and birth records

(1)   The Registrar General must make traceable the connection between any entry in the register of births which, by virtue of paragraph 2(2) of schedule 1 or any enactment at the time in force, has been marked 'Adopted' and any corresponding entry in the Adopted Children Register.

(2)   Information kept by the Registrar General for the purposes of subsection (1) is not to be open to public inspection or search.

(3)   The Registrar General may disclose any such information only in accordance with subsection (4).

(4)   Information is disclosed in accordance with this subsection if disclosed—

(a)   under an order of the Court of Session or a sheriff,

(b)   to an adopted person who is aged 16 or over and to whom the information relates, or

(c)   to a local authority, Board, registered adoption society or relevant adoption society which is providing counselling for any such adopted person.

(5)   Where the Registrar General discloses information in accordance with subsection (4)(b), the Registrar must inform the adopted person that counselling services are available for the person—

(a)   if the person is in Scotland, from any local authority in Scotland,

(b)   if the person is in England and Wales, from any local authority in England and Wales,

(c)   if the person is in Northern Ireland, from any Board,

(d)   if the person is in the United Kingdom and the person's adoption was arranged by—

(i)   a registered adoption service, from that service,

(ii)   a registered adoption society, from that society, or

(iii)   relevant adoption society, from that society.

(6)   Where—

(a)   in accordance with subsection (4) information is disclosed to an adopted person who is in Scotland, or

(b)   such a person applies for information under—

(i)   Schedule 2 to the 2002 Act, or

(ii)   Article 54 of the Northern Ireland Order,

any body mentioned in subsection (7) from which the adopted person requests counselling must provide counselling for the person.

(7)   Those bodies are—

(a)   any local authority in Scotland,

(b)   any registered adoption service, or

(c)   any registered adoption society or relevant adoption society in so far as (by virtue of section 76(2)) that society is acting as an adoption society in Scotland.

(8)   In this section—

'Board' means a Health and Social Services Board established under Article 16 of the Health and Personal Social Services (Northern Ireland) Order 1972 (SI 1972/1265),

'local authority', in relation to England and Wales, means—

(a) any unitary authority, or

(b) any county council so far as it is not a unitary authority, 'relevant adoption society'means an adoption society registered under Article 4 of the Northern Ireland Order.

56 Admissibility of extracts as evidence

(1) An extract of an entry in the Adopted Children Register issued by virtue of section 54(2)(b) is sufficient evidence of the adoption to which it relates.

(2) Where an entry in the Adopted Children Register contains a record of—

(a) the date of birth, or

(b) the country of the birth,

of the adopted person, an extract of the entry issued by virtue of that section is sufficient evidence of that date or, as the case may be, country.

57 Interpretation of Chapter 5

(1) In this Chapter, 'Registrar General' means the Registrar General of Births, Deaths and Marriages for Scotland.

(2) Any register, index or record maintained by virtue of section 53 or 55 or schedule 1 may be maintained in any form that the Registrar General considers appropriate.

(3) References (however expressed) to entries in such a register, or to their amendment, cancellation or marking, are to be read accordingly.

Chapter 6
Adoptions With a Foreign Element

Restrictions on movement of children

58 Restriction on bringing children into the United Kingdom

(1) This section applies where a person who is habitually resident in the British Islands (the 'British resident')—

(a) brings, or causes another to bring, a child who is habitually resident outwith the British Islands into the United Kingdom for the purpose of adoption by the British resident, or

(b) at any time brings, or causes another to bring, into the United Kingdom a child adopted by the British resident under an external adoption effected within the period of 12 months ending with that time.

(2) In subsection (1), the references to adoption, or a child adopted, by the British resident include a reference to adoption, or a child adopted, by the British resident and another person.

(3) This section does not apply if the child is intended to be adopted under a Convention adoption order.

(4) An external adoption means an adoption, other than a Convention adoption, of a child effected under the law of any country or territory outwith the British Islands, whether or not the adoption is—

(a) an adoption within the meaning of Chapter 3, or

(b) a full adoption (as defined in section 40(8)).

(5) Regulations may require a person intending to bring, or to cause another to bring, a child into the United Kingdom in circumstances where this section applies—

(a) to apply to an adoption agency in the prescribed manner for an assessment of the person's suitability to adopt the child, and

(b)   to give the agency any information it may require for the purpose of the assessment.

(6)   Regulations may require prescribed conditions to be met in respect of a child brought into the United Kingdom in circumstances where this section applies.

(7)   In relation to a child brought into the United Kingdom for adoption in circumstances where this section applies, regulations may provide for any provision of Chapter 2 to apply with modifications or not to apply.

(8)   Regulations may provide for this section not to apply if—

   (a)   the adopters or, as the case may be, prospective adopters of the child in question are—

      (i)   natural parents,

      (ii)   natural relatives, or

      (iii)   guardians,

of the child (or one of them is), or

   (b)   the British resident in question is a step-parent of the child,

and any prescribed conditions are met.

(9)   On the occasion of the first exercise of the power to make regulations under subsection (8)—

   (a)   the regulations must not be made unless a draft of the regulations has been approved by a resolution of the Scottish Parliament, and

   (b)   accordingly section 117(4) does not apply to the statutory instrument containing the regulations.

(10)   In this section, 'prescribed' means prescribed by regulations and 'regulations' means regulations made by the Scottish Ministers.

59   Preliminary order where child to be adopted abroad

(1)   The appropriate court may, on an application by persons ('the prospective adopters') who the court is satisfied intend to adopt a child under the law of a country or territory outwith the British Islands, make an order vesting parental responsibilities and parental rights in relation to the child in the prospective adopters.

(2)   If the court is satisfied that the prospective adopters would meet the requirements as to domicile, or habitual residence, in Scotland which they would require to meet if an adoption order were to be made on their application, the court may not make an order under this section.

(3)   An order under this section may not be made unless any requirements prescribed by regulations by the Scottish Ministers are satisfied.

(4)   An application for an order under this section may not be made unless at all times during the period of 10 weeks immediately preceding the application the child's home was with the prospective adopters.

(5)   Section 35 has effect in relation to an order under this section as it has effect in relation to adoption orders.

(6)   The Scottish Ministers may by regulations provide for any provision of this Act which relates to adoption orders to apply, with or without modifications, to orders under this section.

60   Restriction on removal of children for adoption outwith Great Britain

(1)   A person who takes or sends a protected child out of Great Britain to any place outwith the British Islands with a view to the adoption of the child by any person commits an offence.

(2)   A person who makes or takes part in any arrangements for transferring the care of a protected child to another person, knowing that the other person intends to take or send the child out of Great Britain in circumstances which would constitute an offence under subsection (1), commits an offence.

(3)   No offence is committed under subsection (1) if the child is taken or sent out of Great Britain under the authority of an order under—

(a)   section 59,

(b)   section 84 of the 2002 Act, or

(c)   Article 57 of the Northern Ireland Order.

(4)   A person is deemed to take part in arrangements for transferring the care of a child to another person for the purpose mentioned in subsection (2) if the person—

(a)   facilitates the placing of the child in the care of the other person,

(b)   initiates or takes part in negotiations the purpose or effect of which is—

(i)   the making of such arrangements, or

(ii)   the conclusion of an agreement to transfer the care of the child,

for the purpose mentioned in that subsection, or

(c)   causes any person to initiate or take part in any such negotiations.

(5)   The Scottish Ministers may by regulations provide for subsections (1) to (3) to apply with modifications, or not to apply, if—

(a)   the prospective adopters are—

(i)   parents,

(ii)   relatives, or

(iii)   guardians,

of the child (or one of them is), or

(b)   the prospective adopter is a step-parent of the child,

and any conditions prescribed by the regulations are met.

(6)   On the occasion of the first exercise of the power to make regulations under subsection (5)—

(a)   the regulations must not be made unless a draft of the regulations has been approved by a resolution of the Scottish Parliament, and

(b)   accordingly section 117(4) does not apply to the statutory instrument containing the regulations.

(7)   In any proceedings under this section—

(a)   a report by a British consular officer or a deposition made before, and authenticated under the signature of, such an officer is (if proved that the officer or deponent cannot be found in the United Kingdom) sufficient evidence of the matters stated in the report or deposition, and

(b)   it is not necessary to prove the signature or official character of the person who bears to have signed the report or deposition.

(8)   A person who commits an offence under this section is liable on summary conviction to imprisonment for a term not exceeding 3 months or a fine not exceeding level 5 on the standard scale or both.

(9)   In subsections (1) and (2), 'protected child' means a child who is—

(a)   habitually resident in the United Kingdom, or

(b)   a Commonwealth citizen.

61   Regulations under section 58: offences

(1)   If a person brings, or causes another to bring, a child into the United Kingdom at any time in circumstances where section 58 applies, the person commits an offence—

(a)   if the person has not complied with any requirement imposed by virtue of subsection (5) of that section, or

(b)   if the person has not met any condition which the person is required to meet by virtue of subsection (6) of that section,

before that time, or before any later time which may be prescribed by regulations made by the Scottish Ministers.

(2)   A person who commits an offence under subsection (1) is liable—

(a)   on summary conviction to imprisonment for a term not exceeding 6 months or a fine not exceeding the statutory maximum or both,

(b)   on conviction on indictment to imprisonment for a term not exceeding 12 months, or a fine or both.

Adoptions from abroad: special restrictions

62   Declaration of special restrictions on adoptions from abroad

(1)   This section applies if the Scottish Ministers have reason to believe that, because of practices taking place in a country or territory outwith the British Islands (the 'relevant country') in connection with the adoption of children, it would be contrary to public policy to further the bringing of children into the United Kingdom in the cases mentioned in subsection (2).

(2)   Those cases are—

   (a)   that a British resident wishes to bring, or cause another to bring, a child who is not a British resident into the United Kingdom for the purpose of adoption by the British resident and, in connection with the proposed adoption, there have been, or would have to be, proceedings in the relevant country or dealings with authorities or agencies there, or

   (b)   that a British resident wishes to bring, or cause another to bring, into the United Kingdom a child adopted by the British resident under an adoption effected, within the period of 12 months ending with the date of the bringing in, under the law of the relevant country.

(3)   The Scottish Ministers may by order declare, in relation to any relevant country, that special restrictions are to apply for the time being in relation to the bringing in of children in the cases mentioned in subsection (2).

(4)   The Scottish Ministers must, as respects each relevant country in relation to which such a declaration has effect for the time being (a 'restricted country'), publish reasons for making the declaration in relation to the country.

(5)   The Scottish Ministers must publish a list of restricted countries ('the restricted list') and keep the list up to date.

(6)   The reasons and the restricted list are to be published in whatever way the Scottish Ministers think appropriate for bringing them to the attention of adoption agencies and members of the public.

(7)   In this section, 'British resident' means a person habitually resident in the British Islands.

(8)   Any reference in this section to adoption by a British resident includes adoption by a British resident and another person.

63   Review

(1)   The Scottish Ministers must keep under review, in relation to each restricted country, whether it should continue to be a restricted country.

(2)   If the Scottish Ministers determine, in relation to a restricted country, that there is no longer a reason to believe what is mentioned in subsection (1) of section 62, they must by order revoke the order containing the declaration made in relation to it under subsection (3) of that section.

(3)   In this section, 'restricted country' has the same meaning as in section 62.

64   The special restrictions

(1)   The special restrictions mentioned in subsection (3) of section 62 are that the Scottish Ministers are not to take any step which they might otherwise have taken in connection with furthering the bringing of a child into the United Kingdom in the cases mentioned in subsection (2) of that section (whether or not that step is provided for by virtue of any enactment).

(2)   Nothing in subsection (1) prevents the Scottish Ministers from taking those steps if, in any particular case, the prospective adopters or, as the case may be, the adopters satisfy the Scottish Ministers that they should take those steps despite the special restrictions.

(3)   The Scottish Ministers may make regulations providing for—

   (a)   the procedure to be followed by them in determining whether or not they are satisfied as mentioned in subsection (2),

(b)   matters which they are to take into account when making such a determination (whether or not they also take other matters into account).

65   Imposition of extra conditions in certain cases

(1)   The Scottish Ministers may make regulations providing—

(a)   for them to specify in the restricted list, in relation to any restricted country, a step which is not otherwise provided for by virtue of any enactment but which, by virtue of the arrangements between the United Kingdom and that country, the Scottish Ministers normally take in connection with the bringing in of a child where that country is concerned, and

(b)   that, if such a step has been so specified in relation to a restricted country, one or more conditions specified in the regulations are to be met in respect of a child brought into the United Kingdom in either of the cases mentioned in section 62(2) (reading the reference there to the 'relevant country' as being to the restricted country in question).

(2)   Those conditions are in addition to any provided for by virtue of—

(a)   section 58, or

(b)   any other enactment.

(3)   A person who brings, or causes another to bring, a child into the United Kingdom commits an offence if the person has not met any condition which the person is required to meet by virtue of subsection (1)(b).

(4)   Subsection (3) does not apply if the step specified in the restricted list in relation to any country had already been taken before the publication of the restricted list.

(5)   A person who commits an offence under subsection (3) is liable—

(a)   on summary conviction to imprisonment for a term not exceeding 6 months or a fine not exceeding the statutory maximum or both,

(b)   on conviction on indictment to imprisonment for a term not exceeding 12 months or a fine or both.

(6)   In this section, 'restricted country' and 'restricted list' have the same meanings as in section 62.

Charging

66   Power to charge

(1)   This section applies to adoptions to which—

(a)   section 58 applies, or

(b)   regulations made under section 1 of the Adoption (Intercountry Aspects) Act 1999 (c 18) apply.

(2)   The Scottish Ministers may charge a fee to adopters for services provided or to be provided by them in relation to adoptions to which this section applies.

(3)   The Scottish Ministers may determine the level of fee as they see fit and may, in particular—

(a)   charge a flat fee or charge different fees in different cases or descriptions of case,

(b)   in any case or description of case, waive a fee.

(4)   The Scottish Ministers must secure that, taking one financial year with another, the income from fees under this section does not exceed the total cost to them of providing the services in relation to which the fees are imposed.

(5)   In this section, 'financial year' means a period of 12 months ending with 31 March.

(6)   Any references in this section—

(a)   to adoptions include prospective adoptions, and

(b)   to adopters include prospective adopters.

Overseas adoptions etc

67   Meaning of 'overseas adoption'

(1)   In this Act, 'overseas adoption'—

(a)   means an adoption of a description specified in regulations made by the Scottish Ministers (being a description of adoptions effected under the law of any country or territory outwith the British Islands), but

(b)   does not include a Convention adoption.

(2)   The Scottish Ministers may by regulations prescribe the requirements that ought to be met by an adoption of any description effected after the coming into force of the regulations for it to be an overseas adoption for the purposes of this Act.

(3)   At any time when regulations under subsection (2) are in force, the Scottish Ministers must exercise their power under subsection (1) so as to secure that adoptions of any description effected after the coming into force of the regulations are not overseas adoptions for the purposes of this Act if they consider that such adoptions are not likely, within a reasonable time, to meet the requirements prescribed under subsection (2).

(4)   Regulations under subsection (1) may contain provision as to the manner in which evidence of any overseas adoption may be given.

(5)   In this section, 'adoption' means the adoption of a child or of a person who was a child at the time the adoption was applied for.

68   Annulment and recognition

(1)   The Court of Session may, on an application under this subsection, by order annul a Convention adoption or a Convention adoption order on the ground that the adoption or, as the case may be, order is contrary to public policy.

(2)   The Court of Session may, on an application under this subsection—

(a)   order that an overseas adoption or a determination is to cease to be valid in Great Britain on the ground that the adoption or, as the case may be, determination is contrary to public policy or that the authority which purported to authorise the adoption or make the determination was not competent to entertain the case,

(b)   decide the extent, if any, to which a determination has been affected by a subsequent determination.

(3)   The Court of Session may, in any proceedings in that court, decide that an overseas adoption or a determination is, for the purposes of those proceedings, to be treated as invalid in Great Britain on either of the grounds mentioned in subsection (2)(a).

(4)   An order or decision of the High Court on an application under section 89(2) of the 2002 Act is to be recognised and to have effect as if it were an order or decision of the Court of Session on an application under subsection (2).

(5)   Except as provided by this section, the validity of a Convention adoption, a Convention adoption order, an overseas adoption or a determination is not to be questioned in proceedings in any court in Scotland.

(6)   In this section 'determination' means such a determination as is mentioned in section 70.

69   Section 68: supplementary provision

(1)   Any application for—

(a)   an order under section 68, or

(b)   a decision under subsection (2)(b) of that section,

is to be made in the manner prescribed in regulations made by the Scottish Ministers and within such period as may be so prescribed.

(2)   No application is to be made under section 68(1) in respect of an adoption unless immediately before the application is made—

(a)   the person adopted was habitually resident in Scotland, or

(b)   the persons on whose application the adoption order was made were habitually resident there.

(3)   In deciding in pursuance of section 68 whether such an authority as is mentioned in section 70 was competent to hear a particular case, a court is to be bound by any finding of fact made by the authority and stated by the authority to be so made for the purpose of determining whether the authority was competent to hear the case.

70   Effect of determinations and orders made outwith Scotland

(1)   Subsection (2) applies where—

(a)   an authority of a Convention country (other than the United Kingdom) having power under the law of that country—

(i)   to authorise, or review the authorisation of, a Convention adoption, or

(ii)   to give or review a decision revoking or annulling such an adoption or a Convention adoption order, or

(b)   an authority of a relevant territory having power under the law of that territory—

(i)   to authorise, or review the authorisation of, a Convention adoption or an adoption effected in that territory, or

(ii)   to give or review a decision revoking or annulling such an adoption or a Convention adoption order,

makes a determination ('the relevant determination') in the exercise of that power.

(2)   Subject to section 68 and any subsequent determination having effect under this subsection, the relevant determination has effect in Scotland for the purpose of effecting, confirming or terminating the adoption in question or confirming its termination as the case may be.

(3)   In subsection (1), 'relevant territory' means—

(a)   any of the Channel Islands,

(b)   the Isle of Man, or

(c)   any British overseas territory (within the meaning of the British Nationality Act 1981 (c 61)).

(4)   Section 35 applies in relation to an order under Article 17 (freeing child for adoption with parental agreement) or 18 (freeing child for adoption without parental agreement) of the Northern Ireland Order as if it were an adoption order.

(5)   Sections 35(2) and (3) and 43 apply in relation to a child who is the subject of an order which—

(a)   is similar to an order under section 59, and

(b)   is made (whether before or after this Act has effect) in a part of the British Islands,

as those sections apply in relation to a child who is the subject of an adoption order.

Chapter 7
Miscellaneous

Adoption allowances

71   Adoption allowances schemes

(1)   Subject to subsection (3), an adoption agency which is—

(a)   a local authority must, within such period after the coming into force of this section as the Scottish Ministers may by order direct, prepare an adoption allowances scheme,

(b)   a registered adoption service may prepare such a scheme.

(2)   An adoption allowances scheme is a scheme for or in connection with the payment by the agency of allowances to any person who has adopted, or intends to adopt, a child in any case where arrangements for the adoption were made or, as the case may be, are to be made by the agency.

(3) The Scottish Ministers may by regulations make provision for or in connection with adoption allowances schemes.

(4) Regulations under subsection (3) may in particular make provision for or in connection with specifying—

(a) the procedure to be followed by an agency in determining whether a person should be paid an allowance,

(b) the circumstances in which an allowance may be paid,

(c) the factors to be taken into account in determining the amount of an allowance,

(d) the procedure for review, variation and termination of allowances,

(e) the information about allowances which is to be supplied by an agency to a person who intends to adopt a child, and

(f) the procedure to be followed by an agency in preparing, modifying or revoking an adoption allowances scheme.

Prohibited payments

72 Prohibition of certain payments

(1) This section applies to any payment (other than an excepted payment) which is made to any person for or in consideration of—

(a) the adoption by that person of a child,

(b) the giving by that person of any consent required in connection with the adoption of a child,

(c) the transfer by that person of the care of a child with a view to the adoption of the child, or

(d) the making by that person of any arrangements for the adoption of a child.

(2) Any person who—

(a) makes any payment to which this section applies,

(b) agrees or offers to make any such payment,

(c) receives, or agrees to receive, any such payment, or

(d) attempts to obtain any such payment,

commits an offence.

(3) A person who commits an offence under subsection (2) is liable on summary conviction to imprisonment for a term not exceeding 3 months or a fine not exceeding level 5 on the standard scale or both.

(4) Where a person is convicted of an offence under subsection (2), the court may, without prejudice to any power which it has to make any other order in relation to the child as respects whom the offence was committed, order the child to be removed to a place of safety until—

(a) the child can be returned to the child's parent or guardian, or

(b) other arrangements can be made for the child.

(5) In this section—

'payment' includes reward,

'place of safety' has the meaning given by section [202(1) of the Children's Hearings (Scotland) Act 2011.]

73 Excepted payments

(1) A payment is an excepted payment if it is made by virtue of, or in accordance with, provision made by virtue of this Act, the 2002 Act or the Northern Ireland Order.

(2) A payment is an excepted payment if—

(a) it is made to an adoption agency by—

(i) a parent or guardian of the child, or

(ii) a person who adopts, or proposes to adopt, a child,

in respect of expenses reasonably incurred by the agency in connection with the adoption, or proposed adoption, of the child,

(b) it is made in respect of any legal or medical expenses incurred or to be incurred by any person in connection with an application which the person has made, or proposes to make, for an adoption order or an order under section 59,

(c) it is authorised by the court to which an application for an adoption order is made,

(d) it is made by an adoption agency to another adoption agency in consideration of placing the child for adoption,

(e) it is made by an adoption agency to a voluntary organisation for the time being approved for the purposes of this paragraph by the Scottish Ministers as a fee for the services of the organisation in putting the agency in touch with another adoption agency with a view to the making of arrangements between the adoption agencies for the adoption of a child.

(3) In this section, 'payment' includes reward.

Disclosure of medical information about parents

74 Disclosure of medical information about parents

(1) The Scottish Ministers may by regulations make provision for or in connection with disclosure of information about the health of the natural parents of a child who is to be, may be or has been adopted ('the relevant child').

(2) In making regulations under subsection (1), the Scottish Ministers must secure that a person to whom information is disclosed by virtue of the regulations has a duty of confidentiality in relation to the information.

(3) Notwithstanding subsection (2), regulations under subsection (1) may include provision enabling a person to whom information is disclosed by virtue of the regulations, in such circumstances and to such an extent as may be specified in the regulations, to disclose the information to—

(a) the relevant child,

(b) persons who are to or may adopt, or have adopted, the relevant child.

(4) Regulations under subsection (1) may, in particular, include provision for or in connection with specifying—

(a) the descriptions of person by whom, and to whom, information may be disclosed,

(b) the circumstances in which information may be disclosed,

(c) the type of information which may, or may not, be disclosed,

(d) the circumstances in which consent to disclosure of information need not be obtained,

(e) the processing of information by a person to whom information is disclosed.

(5) In subsection (4)(e), 'processing' has the same meaning as in [Parts 5 to 7 of the Data Protection Act 2018 (see section 3(4) and (14) of that Act)].

Restrictions on arranging adoptions and placing for adoption

75 Restriction on arranging adoptions and placing children

(1) Subject to subsection (2), a person other than an adoption agency who—

(a) makes arrangements for the adoption of a child, or

(b) places a child for adoption,

commits an offence.

(2) Subsection (1) does not apply if the person proposing to adopt the child or, as the case may be, the person with whom the child is placed is—

(a) a parent of the child,

(b) any other relative of the child, or

(c) where a parent of the child is a member of a relevant couple, the other member of the couple.

(3) A person who receives a child placed in contravention of subsection (1)

knowing that the placement is with a view to the person's adopting the child commits an offence.

(4)   A person who takes part in the management or control of a body of persons—

(a)   which exists wholly or partly for the purpose of making arrangements for the adoption of children, and

(b)   which is not an adoption agency,

commits an offence.

(5)   A person who commits an offence under this section is liable on summary conviction to imprisonment for a term not exceeding 3 months or a fine not exceeding level 5 on the standard scale or both.

(6)   In any proceedings for an offence under subsection (4), proof of—

(a)   things done, or

(b)   words written, spoken or published,

by any person taking part in the management or control of the body of persons, or in making arrangements for the adoption of children on behalf of the body, is sufficient evidence of the purpose for which that body exists.

(7)   It is immaterial whether the actions mentioned in paragraphs (a) and (b) of subsection (6) are carried out in the presence of a party to the proceedings.

76   Adoption societies which are not registered adoption services

(1)   Subsection (2) applies where—

(a)   an adoption society is—

(i)   a registered adoption society, or

(ii)   registered as respects Northern Ireland under Part III of the Health and Personal Social Services (Quality, Improvement and Regulation) (Northern Ireland) Order 2003 (SI 2003/431), and

(b)   the society is not a registered adoption service.

(2)   Except to the extent that the society considers it necessary to do so in the interests of a person mentioned in section 3(1) of [the 2002] Act or, as the case may be, Article 3 of the Northern Ireland Order, it must not act as an adoption society in Scotland.

Effect of orders, and placing for adoption, under 2002 Act

77   Effect of certain orders made in England and Wales

(1)   An adoption order (within the meaning of section 46(1) of the 2002 Act) has effect in Scotland as it has in England and Wales but as if any reference to the parental responsibility for the child were to the parental responsibilities and parental rights in relation to the child.

(2)   An order made under section 21 of that Act (placement orders), and the variation or revocation of such an order under section 23 or 24 of that Act, have effect in Scotland as they have in England and Wales but as if any reference to the parental responsibility for the child were to the parental responsibilities and parental rights in relation to the child.

78   Effect of placing for adoption etc under 2002 Act

(1)   If—

(a)   a child is placed for adoption under section 19 of the 2002 Act (placing children with parental consent), or

(b)   an adoption agency is authorised to place a child for adoption under that section,

sections 25 (parental responsibility) and 28(2) to (4) (further consequences of placement) of that Act have effect in Scotland as they have in England and Wales but with the modifications specified in subsection (2).

(2)   Those modifications are—

(a)   in section 25, any reference to the parental responsibility for the child is to be read as a reference to the parental responsibilities and parental rights in relation to the child, and

(b)   in section 28(2), the reference to the court is to be read as a reference to the appropriate court.

79   Further consequences of placement and placement orders

(1)   Subsection (2) applies where—

(a)   a child is placed for adoption under section 19 of the 2002 Act (placing children with parental consent), or

(b)   an adoption agency is authorised to place a child for adoption under that section.

(2)   No order under subsection (1) of section 11 of the 1995 Act (court orders relating to parental responsibilities etc) of a kind mentioned in subsection (2)(c) (residence orders) of that section may be made in respect of the child.

(3)   On the making of an order under section 21 of the 2002 Act (a 'placement order') in respect of a child, any order under subsection (1) of section 11 of the 1995 Act of a kind mentioned in subsection (2)(c) to (f) (residence orders, contact orders, specific issue orders and interdicts in relation to parental responsibilities) of that section in respect of the child ceases to have effect.

(4)   Where a placement order is in force—

(a)   no such order as is mentioned in subsection (3) of this section, and

(b)   no order under section [36 of the Children's Hearings (Scotland) Act 2011] (child assessment orders),

may be made in respect of the child.

PART 2
PERMANENCE ORDERS

The making of permanence orders

80   Permanence orders

(1)   The appropriate court may, on the application of a local authority, make a permanence order in respect of a child.

(2)   A permanence order is an order consisting of—

(a)   the mandatory provision,

(b)   such of the ancillary provisions as the court thinks fit, and

(c)   if the conditions in section 83 are met, provision granting authority for the child to be adopted.

(3)   In making a permanence order in respect of a child, the appropriate court must secure that each parental responsibility and parental right in respect of the child vests in a person.

81   Permanence orders: mandatory provision

(1)   The mandatory provision is provision vesting in the local authority for the appropriate period—

(a)   the responsibility mentioned in section 1(1)(b)(ii) of the 1995 Act (provision of guidance appropriate to child's stage of development) in relation to the child, and

(b)   the right mentioned in section 2(1)(a) of that Act (regulation of child's residence) in relation to the child.

(2)   In subsection (1) 'the appropriate period' means—

(a)   in the case of the responsibility referred to in subsection (1)(a), the period beginning with the making of the permanence order and ending with the day on which the child reaches the age of 18,

(b) in the case of the right referred to in subsection (1)(b), the period beginning with the making of the permanence order and ending with the day on which the child reaches the age of 16.

82 Permanence orders: ancillary provisions

(1) The ancillary provisions are provisions—

(a) vesting in the local authority for the appropriate period—

(i) such of the parental responsibilities mentioned in section 1(1)(a), (b)(i) and (d) of the 1995 Act, and

(ii) such of the parental rights mentioned in section 2(1)(b) and (d) of that Act,

in relation to the child as the court considers appropriate,

(b) vesting in a person other than the local authority for the appropriate period—

(i) such of the parental responsibilities mentioned in section 1(1) of that Act, and

(ii) such of the parental rights mentioned in section 2(1)(b) to (d) of that Act,

in relation to the child as the court considers appropriate,

(c) extinguishing any parental responsibilities which, immediately before the making of the order, vested in a parent or guardian of the child, and which—

(i) by virtue of section 81(1)(a) or paragraph (a)(i), vest in the local authority, or

(ii) by virtue of paragraph (b)(i), vest in a person other than the authority,

(d) extinguishing any parental rights in relation to the child which, immediately before the making of the order, vested in a parent or guardian of the child, and which—

(i) by virtue of paragraph (a)(ii), vest in the local authority, or

(ii) by virtue of paragraph (b)(ii), vest in a person other than the authority,

(e) specifying such arrangements for contact between the child and any other person as the court considers appropriate and to be in the best interests of the child, and

(f) determining any question which has arisen in connection with—

(i) any parental responsibilities or parental rights in relation to the child, or

(ii) any other aspect of the welfare of the child.

(2) In subsection (1), 'the appropriate period' means—

(a) in the case of the responsibility mentioned in section 1(1)(b)(ii) of the 1995 Act, the period beginning with the making of the permanence order and ending with the day on which the child reaches the age of 18,

(b) in any other case, the period beginning with the making of the permanence order and ending with the day on which the child reaches the age of 16.

83 Order granting authority for adoption: conditions

(1) The conditions referred to in section 80(2)(c) are—

(a) that the local authority has, in the application for the permanence order, requested that the order include provision granting authority for the child to be adopted,

(b) that the court is satisfied that the child has been, or is likely to be, placed for adoption,

(c) that, in the case of each parent or guardian of the child, the court is satisfied—

(i) that the parent or guardian understands what the effect of making an adoption order would be and consents to the making of such an order in relation to the child, or

(ii) that the parent's or guardian's consent to the making of such an order should be dispensed with on one of the grounds mentioned in subsection (2), (d)　that the court considers that it would be better for the child if it were to grant authority for the child to be adopted than if it were not to grant such authority.

(2)　Those grounds are—

(a)　that the parent or guardian is dead,

(b)　that the parent or guardian cannot be found or is incapable of giving consent,

(c)　that subsection (3) or (4) applies,

(d)　that, where neither of those subsections applies, the welfare of the child otherwise requires the consent to be dispensed with.

(3)　This subsection applies if the parent or guardian—

(a)　has parental responsibilities or parental rights in relation to the child other than those mentioned in sections 1(1)(c) and 2(1)(c) of the 1995 Act,

(b)　is, in the opinion of the court, unable satisfactorily to—

(i)　discharge those responsibilities, or

(ii)　exercise those rights, and

(c)　is likely to continue to be unable to do so.

(4)　This subsection applies if—

(a)　the parent or guardian has, by virtue of the making of a permanence order which does not include provision granting authority for the child to be adopted, no parental responsibilities or parental rights in relation to the child, and

(b)　it is unlikely that such responsibilities will be imposed on, or such rights given to, the parent or guardian.

(5)　In subsections (1)(c) and (2), 'parent', in relation to the child in respect of whom the permanence order is to be made, means—

(a)　a parent who has any parental responsibilities or parental rights in relation to the child, or

(b)　a parent who, by virtue of a permanence order which does not include provision granting authority for the child to be adopted, has no such responsibilities or rights.

84　Conditions and considerations applicable to making of order

(1)　Except where subsection (2) applies, a permanence order may not be made in respect of a child who is aged 12 or over unless the child consents.

(2)　This subsection applies where the court is satisfied that the child is incapable of consenting to the order.

(3)　The court may not make a permanence order in respect of a child unless it considers that it would be better for the child that the order be made than that it should not be made.

(4)　In considering whether to make a permanence order and, if so, what provision the order should make, the court is to regard the need to safeguard and promote the welfare of the child throughout childhood as the paramount consideration.

(5)　Before making a permanence order, the court must—

(a)　after taking account of the child's age and maturity, so far as is reasonably practicable—

(i)　give the child the opportunity to indicate whether the child wishes to express any views, and

(ii)　if the child does so wish, give the child the opportunity to express them,

(b)　have regard to—

(i)　any such views the child may express,

(ii)　the child's religious persuasion, racial origin and cultural and linguistic background, and

(iii)　the likely effect on the child of the making of the order, and

(c)   be satisfied that—
    (i)   there is no person who has the right mentioned in subsection (1)(a) of section 2 of the 1995 Act to have the child living with the person or otherwise to regulate the child's residence, or
    (ii)   where there is such a person, the child's residence with the person is, or is likely to be, seriously detrimental to the welfare of the child.

(6)   A child who is aged 12 or over is presumed to be of sufficient age and maturity to form a view for the purposes of subsection (5)(a).

85   Child in respect of whom order may be made

(1)   A permanence order may be made in respect of a child who is an adopted child.

(2)   A permanence order may not be made in respect of a child who is or has been—
    (a)   married,
    (b)   a civil partner.

86   Representations

(1)   In any proceedings relating to an application for a permanence order, the appropriate court must permit any person mentioned in subsection (2) who wishes to make representations to the court to do so.

(2)   Those persons are—
    (a)   the local authority making the application,
    (b)   the child or the child's representative,
    (c)   any person who has parental responsibilities or parental rights in relation to the child,
    (d)   any other person who claims an interest.

Effect of order

87   Effect of order on existing parental right

The making of a permanence order extinguishes the parental right mentioned in subsection (1)(a) of section 2 of the 1995 Act of—
    (a)   a parent of the child in respect of whom the order is made,
    (b)   guardian of such a child,
which, immediately before the making of the order, vested in the parent or, as the case may be, guardian.

88   Effect of order on existing orders

(1)   This section applies where—
    (a)   parental responsibilities or parental rights in relation to a child vest in a person by virtue of—
        (i)   a permanence order, or
        (ii)   an order under section 11 of the 1995 Act (court orders relating to parental responsibilities etc),
('the existing order'), and
    (b)   the appropriate court intends to make a permanence order ('the new order') as respects the child.

(2)   On the making of the new order, the existing order is revoked.

(3)   In making the new order, the court must secure that the parental responsibilities or parental rights vesting by virtue of the existing order vest in a person under the new order.

Revocation of supervision requirement

89   [Revocation of compulsory supervision order on making of permanence order]

(1)   Subsection (2) applies where—

(a)   the child in respect of whom a permanence order is to be made is subject to a [compulsory supervision order], and

(b)   the appropriate court is satisfied that, were it to make a permanence order in respect of the child, [it would no longer be necessary that, for the protection, guidance, treatment or control of the child, the child be subject to the compulsory supervision order.]

(2)   The court must make an order providing that, on the making of the permanence order, the [compulsory supervision order] ceases to have effect.

Precedence

90   Precedence of [certain other orders]

(1)   Subsection (2) applies where a local authority has, by virtue of a permanence order, parental responsibilities or parental rights in relation to a child.

(2)   The local authority must not act in any way which would be incompatible with—

(a)   any other court order of which the authority is aware relating to the child or the child's property,

(b)   any [compulsory supervision order or interim compulsory supervision order] to which the child is subject.

Exercise of parental right under order

91   Exercise of parental right under order

(1)   Subsection (2) applies where—

(a)   two or more persons have a parental right in relation to a child, and

(b)   by virtue of paragraph (a) or (b) of subsection (1) of section 82, the right vests in one of them or, as the case may be, two or more of them.

(2)   Each of the persons mentioned in subsection (1)(a) may exercise the right without the consent of the other or, as the case may be, any of the others.

(3)   Subsection (2) does not apply where an order vesting the right, or regulating its exercise, provides otherwise.

Variation

92   Variation of ancillary provisions in order

(1)   This section applies where a permanence order which includes ancillary provisions is in force.

(2)   The appropriate court may, on an application by a person mentioned in subsection (3), vary such of the ancillary provisions as the court considers appropriate.

(3)   Those persons are—

(a)   the local authority on whose application the permanence order was made,

(b)   if the child in respect of whom the order was made is—

(i)   aged 12 or over, or

(ii)   under the age of 12 but, in the court's opinion (taking account of the child's age and maturity), capable of understanding the effect of the order, that child,

(c)   any person in whom parental responsibilities and parental rights are vested by virtue of the order,

(d)   any person in whom were vested, immediately before the making of the order, any parental responsibilities or parental rights which, by virtue of the making of the order, vest in another person,

(e)   any person in whom were vested, immediately before a variation by virtue of this section of the order, parental responsibilities or parental rights which, by virtue of the variation, vest in another person,

(f) any other person who claims an interest.

(4) Subsection (5) applies where the court exercises its power under subsection (2) to vary the ancillary provisions so as to vest, by virtue of paragraph (a) or (b) of subsection (1) of section 82, in a person a parental responsibility or a parental right which, immediately before the variation, vested in another person.

(5) The court may include in the order as varied provision extinguishing the responsibility or right of that other person.

(6) Subsections (4), (5)(a) and (b) and (6) of section 84 apply to the variation of a permanence order under this section as they apply to the making of such an order.

(7) In subsections (1) and (2), 'ancillary provisions' has the same meaning as in section 82.

(8) In this section, 'vary' includes add to, omit, or amend; and 'variation' is to be construed accordingly.

93 Amendment of order to grant authority for child to be adopted

(1) This section applies where—

(a) a permanence order in respect of a child is in force, and

(b) the order does not include provision granting authority for the child to be adopted.

(2) On the application of the local authority on whose application the order was made, the appropriate court may amend the order so as to include provision granting authority for the child to be adopted if (and only if)—

(a) the court is satisfied that the child has been placed for adoption, or is likely to be placed for adoption,

(b) the court is satisfied that the condition in subsection (3) or subsection (4) is met, and

(c) the court considers that it would be better for the child that authority for the child to be adopted is granted than that it should not be granted.

(3) The condition is that each parent or guardian of the child understands what the effect of making an adoption order would be and consents to the making of such an order in relation to the child.

(4) The condition is that the consent of each parent or guardian should be dispensed with on any of the grounds mentioned in section 83.

(5) Subsections (4), (5)(a) and (b) and (6) of section 84 apply to the amendment of a permanence order under this section as they apply to the making of such an order.

(6) In subsections (3) and (4)—

'guardian', in relation to a child in respect of whom a permanence order to which this section applies is in force, means a guardian—

(a) who has any parental responsibilities or parental rights in relation to the child, or

(b) who, by virtue of the making of a previous such order, no longer has any such responsibilities or rights,

'parent', in relation to a child in respect of whom a permanence order to which this section applies is in force, means a parent—

(a) who has any parental responsibilities or parental rights in relation to the child, or

(b) who, by virtue of the making of a previous such order, no longer has any such responsibilities or rights.

94 Proceedings

(1) In any proceedings for variation of a permanence order by the local authority on whose application the order was granted, the appropriate court must permit any person who is affected by the order, and who wishes to make representations to the court, to do so.

(2) In any proceedings for variation of a permanence order by a person other

than the local authority on whose application the order was granted, the appropriate court must permit any person mentioned in subsection (3) who wishes to make representations to the court to do so.

(3) Those persons are—

(a) the local authority on whose application the permanence order was made,

(b) if the child in respect of whom the original order was made is—

(i) aged 12 or over, or

(ii) under the age of 12 but, in the court's opinion (taking account of the child's age and maturity), is capable of understanding the effect of the order, that child,

(c) any person who has parental responsibilities or parental rights in relation to the child,

(d) any person on whom a duty was imposed, or power conferred, by the order,

(e) any person in whom were vested, immediately before the making of the order, any parental responsibilities or parental rights which, by virtue of the making of the order, vest in another person,

(f) any person in whom were vested, immediately before a variation by virtue of section 92 of the order, parental responsibilities or parental rights which, by virtue of the variation, vest in another person, and

(g) any other person who claims an interest.

(4) A person other than the local authority on whose application a permanence order was granted may not apply to the court for a variation of the order without first obtaining the leave of the court.

(5) If the court is satisfied—

(a) that there has been a material change in the circumstances directly relating to any of the order's provisions, or

(b) that for any other reason it is proper to allow the application to be made, it must grant that leave.

(6) In determining whether there has been a material change in circumstances, the court must have regard, in particular, to any aspect of—

(a) the welfare of the child in respect of whom the permanence order was made, and

(b) the circumstances of—

(i) a parent, or the parents, of the child,

(ii) the child's guardian, or

(iii) any person mentioned in paragraph (e) or (f) of subsection (3).

(7) In subsection (1), the reference to variation of a permanence order includes a reference to amendment of the order to include provision granting authority for the child to whom the order relates to be adopted.

Orders and supervision requirements

95 Duty of children's hearing to prepare report for court

(1) Subsection (2) applies where—

(a) an application is made for a permanence order, or variation of such an order, in respect of a child,

(b) the application has not been determined (or, as the case may be, withdrawn or abandoned), and

(c) a children's hearing proposes to [make or vary (other than by interim variation, as defined in section 140 of the Children's Hearings (Scotland) Act 2011 (asp 1)) a compulsory supervision order in respect of the child.]

(2) The children's hearing must prepare for the court to which the application has been made a report containing such information as the Scottish Ministers may by regulations prescribe.

(3) In subsection (1)(a), the reference to variation of a permanence order

includes a reference to amendment of the order to include provision granting authority for the child to whom the order relates to be adopted.

96 [Application: effect on compulsory supervision order]

(1) Subsection (2) applies where an application is made for a permanence order, or variation of such an order, in respect of a child.

(2) A [compulsory supervision order may not be made or varied (other than by interim variation, as defined in section 140 of the Children's Hearings (Scotland) Act 2011 (asp 1)) in respect of the child] until the application is determined (or, as the case may be, withdrawn or abandoned).

(3) Subsection (2) does not apply if the court to which the application is made refers the child's case to the Principal Reporter (whether following receipt of a report under section 95 or otherwise).

(4) In subsection (1), the reference to variation of a permanence order includes a reference to amendment of the order to include provision granting authority for the child to whom the order relates to be adopted.

[. . .]

97 [Interim orders and revocation of compulsory supervision order]

(1) Subsection (2) applies where an application is made for a permanence order, or variation of such an order, in respect of a child.

(2) The appropriate court may make such interim order as it thinks fit.

(3) Subsection (4) applies where—

(a) the child in respect of whom an interim order is to be made is subject to a [compulsory supervision order], and

(b) the court is satisfied that, were it to make an interim order in relation to the child, [it would no longer be necessary that, for the protection, guidance, treatment or control of the child, the child be subject to the compulsory supervision order.]

(4) The court must make an order providing that, on the making of the interim order, the [compulsory supervision order] ceases to have effect.

(5) If—

(a) the child in respect of whom an interim order is made is subject to a [compulsory supervision order], and

(b) the provisions of the [interim order conflict, or are otherwise inconsistent, with the compulsory supervision order,] the provisions of the [interim] order prevail.

(6) In subsection (1), the reference to variation of a permanence order includes a reference to amendment of the order to include provision granting authority for the child to whom the order relates to be adopted.

Revocation and variation

98 Revocation

(1) The appropriate court may, on an application by a person mentioned in subsection (2), revoke a permanence order if satisfied that it is appropriate to do so in all the circumstances of the case, including, in particular—

(a) a material change in the circumstances directly relating to any of the order's provisions,

(b) any wish by the parent or guardian of the child in respect of whom the order was made to have reinstated any parental responsibilities or parental rights vested in another person by virtue of the order.

(2) Those persons are—

(a) the local authority on whose application the order was made,

(b) any other person affected by the order who has obtained the leave of the court to apply for revocation of the order.

(3) Subsections (4), (5)(a) and (b) and (6) of section 84 apply to the revocation

of a permanence order under this section as they apply to the making of such an order.

99   Duty of local authority to apply for variation or revocation

(1)   Subsection (2) applies where a local authority on whose application a permanence order was made determines that—

(a)   there has been a material change in the circumstances directly relating to any of the order's provisions, and

(b)   in consequence of that change, the order ought to be varied or revoked.

(2)   The authority must, as soon as is reasonably practicable, apply to the appropriate court for variation or, as the case may be, revocation of the order.

(3)   In this section, 'variation', in relation to the permanence order, includes amendment of the order so as to include provision granting authority for the child to whom the order relates to be adopted; and 'varied' is to be construed accordingly.

100   Revocation: order under section 11 of 1995 Act

(1)   Subsection (2) applies where the appropriate court revokes a permanence order in respect of a child.

(2)   The court must consider whether to make an order under section 11of the 1995 Act—

(a)   imposing on a person specified in the order parental responsibilities in relation to the child, and

(b)   giving to such a person parental rights in relation to the child.

Notification requirements

101   Local authority to give notice of certain matters

(1)   This section applies where—

(a)   a permanence order includes provision granting authority for the child to be adopted,

(b)   after the order is made or, as the case may be, amended under section 93(2) so as to include that provision, an event mentioned in subsection (2) occurs, and

(c)   the order has not been revoked under section 98(1).

(2)   Those events are—

(a)   the child is placed for adoption,

(b)   an adoption order is made in respect of the child,

(c)   the child ceases to be placed for adoption otherwise than on the making of an adoption order.

(3)   As soon as is reasonably practicable after the occurrence of the event, the local authority on whose application the permanence order was made must give notice of the event to any person falling within subsection (4).

(4)   A person falls within this subsection if—

(a)   the person consented under section 83(1)(c)(i) or 93(3) to the making of the order,

(b)   the person's consent to the making of the order was dispensed with under section 83(1)(c)(ii) or 93(4).

(5)   The local authority need not comply with the requirement imposed by subsection (3) in relation to a person if the person has given notice to that effect to the authority.

Effect of subsequent adoption order on permanence order

102   Effect of subsequent adoption order on permanence order

(1)   Subsection (2) applies where—

(a)   a permanence order is in force in respect of a child, and

(b)   an adoption order is made in respect of the child.

(2) The permanence order ceases to have effect on the making of the adoption order.

Restriction on making certain orders under 1995 Act

103 *[Amends Children (Scotland) Act 1995]*

Rules of procedure

104 Permanence orders: rules of procedure

(1) Provision may be made by rules of court in respect of—

(a) applications for permanence orders,

(b) applications for variation, or revocation, of permanence orders,

(c) applications for leave to apply for such variation or revocation.

(2) In the case of an application for a permanence order containing a request that the order include provision granting authority for the child to be adopted, or an application made by virtue of section 93(2), rules must require—

(a) any person mentioned in subsection (3)(a) to be notified of the matters mentioned in subsection (4), and

(b) the person mentioned in subsection (3)(b) (if he can be found) to be notified of the matters mentioned in paragraphs (a) and (b) of subsection (4).

(3) Those persons are—

(a) every person who can be found and whose consent to the making of the order is required to be given or dispensed with under this Act or, if no such person can be found, any relative prescribed by the rules who can be found,

(b) if the father of the child in relation to whom the order is to be made does not have, and has never had, parental responsibilities or parental rights in relation to the child, the father of the child.

(4) Those matters are—

(a) that the application has been made,

(b) the date on which, and place where, the application will be heard,

(c) the fact that the person is entitled to be heard on the application,

(d) the fact that, unless the person wishes, or the court requires, the person need not attend the hearing.

(5) In subsection (1), any references to an application for variation of a permanence order include references to an application to amend the order to include provision granting authority for the child to whom the order relates to be adopted.

PART 3

MISCELLANEOUS

Provisions applicable to adoption orders and permanence orders

105 Notification of proposed application for order

(1) Subsection (2) applies where—

(a) a local authority—

(i) proposes to make an application for a permanence order in respect of a child, or

(ii) becomes aware that an application for an adoption order in respect of a child in its area has been, or is to be, made,

(b) the father of the child is not married to the mother of the child on the relevant date,

(c) the father, never having had parental responsibilities or parental rights in relation to the child, does not have such responsibilities or rights on the relevant date, and

(d) the authority—

(i) knows the identity and whereabouts of the father, or

     (ii) can, by taking such reasonable and practicable steps as are appropriate in the circumstances of the case, ascertain that information.

(2) The local authority must, on or after the relevant date—

    (a)   give notice to the father that—

       (i) it proposes to apply for a permanence order,

      (ii) an application for an adoption order has been made, or

     (iii) an application for an adoption order is to be made,

as the case may be, and

    (b)   provide the father with prescribed information relating to the processes for applying for the order in question.

(3) Where a local authority is required to give notice under subsection (2)(a)(i), it must give the notice at least 4 weeks before the application for the permanence order is made.

(4) Where a local authority is required to give notice under sub-paragraph (ii) or (iii) of subsection (2)(a), it must give the notice as soon as is reasonably practicable after it becomes aware that the application for an adoption order has been or, as the case may be, is to be made.

(5) In this section—

    (a) 'relevant date' means—

       (i) the date on which the local authority determines it will make the application mentioned in sub-paragraph (i) of subsection (1)(a), or

      (ii) the date on which the authority becomes aware of the application mentioned in sub-paragraph (ii) of that subsection,

as the case may be,

    (b) 'prescribed' means prescribed by regulations made by the Scottish Ministers.

106 [Child subject to compulsory supervision order: duty to refer to Principal Reporter]

(1) Subsection (2) applies where—

    (a)   a child is subject to a [compulsory supervision order],

    (b)   a registered adoption service is satisfied that the best interests of the child would be served by placing the child for adoption, and

    (c)   it intends to place the child for adoption.

(2) The registered adoption service must refer the child's case to the Principal Reporter.

(3) The Scottish Ministers may make regulations specifying by reference to the occurrence of an event or events described in the regulations the period of time during which a referral under this section is to be made.

    [. . .]

107 [Amends Children (Scotland) Act 1995]

108 Rules: appointment of curators ad litem and reporting officers

(1) In the case of an application for a relevant order in relation to a child, rules of court must provide for the appointment, in such cases as are prescribed by the rules—

    (a)   of a person to act as curator ad litem of the child on the hearing of the application, with the duty of safeguarding the interests of the child in such manner as may be so prescribed,

    (b)   of a person to act as reporting officer for the purpose of witnessing agreements to adoption and performing such other duties as may be so prescribed.

(2) Rules may in particular make provision—

    (a)   enabling the reporting officer to be appointed before the application is made, (b)　enabling the court to appoint the same person to be curator ad litem and reporting officer.

(3)　Rules may not make provision for—

(a)　the appointment of a person who is employed by an adoption agency which has placed a child for adoption to act as curator ad litem or reporting officer for the purposes of an application for an adoption order in respect of the child,

(b)　the appointment of a person who is employed by a local authority which is making (or has made) an application for a permanence order to act as curator ad litem or reporting officer for the purposes of the application.

(4)　A relevant order means—

(a)　an adoption order,

(b)　a permanence order, or

(c)　an order under section 59.

109　Proceedings to be in private

(1)　Any proceedings before the court relating to applications under any of the provisions mentioned in subsection (2) must be heard and determined in private unless the court otherwise directs.

(2)　Those provisions are—

(a)　section 24,

(b)　section 29,

(c)　section 30,

(d)　section 59,

(e)　section 80,

(f)　section 92,

(g)　section 93,

[(ga)　section 98, and]

(h)　section 99.

Care allowances: regulations

110　Allowances for care of certain children: regulations

(1)　The Scottish Ministers may by regulations make provision about payments by a local authority in respect of a child who falls within subsection (2).

(2)　A child falls within this subsection if—

(a)　the child is placed by the authority under section 26(1)(a) of the 1995 Act,

(b)　the child is required by virtue of [a compulsory supervision order] to reside with a person other than a parent of the child, or

(c)　were the child not residing with a relative, the authority would be required by section 25(1) of that Act to provide accommodation for the child.

(3)　Regulations under subsection (1) may in particular include provision for or in connection with—

(a)　specifying descriptions of person to whom payments may be made,

(b)　specifying circumstances in which payments may be made,

(c)　specifying rates of payment to be payable in such circumstances as may be specified in the regulations,

(d)　where a rate is so specified—

(i)　requiring local authorities to pay at least that rate in the circumstances so specified,

(ii)　recommending that local authorities pay at least that rate ('the recommended rate') in the circumstances so specified,

(e)　where a recommended rate is payable, requiring local authorities which pay less than that rate to publish, in such manner as may be so specified, their reasons for doing so.

(4)　A child does not cease to fall within paragraph (a) of subsection (2) by reason only of the making of a permanence order vesting parental responsibilities in a person who is a member of the family with whom the child was placed.

(5)   A child does not fall within paragraph (c) of subsection (2) if the relative is a guardian of the child.

(6)   It is immaterial for the purposes of paragraph (c) of subsection (2) whether the relative has any parental rights or parental responsibilities in relation to the child.

Evidence and notices

111   Evidence of consent

(1)   If a document signifying any consent which is required by this Act to be given is witnessed in accordance with rules of court, it is sufficient evidence of the signature of the person by whom it was executed.

(2)   A document signifying any such consent which purports to be witnessed in accordance with rules is to be presumed to be so witnessed and to have been executed and witnessed on the date and at the place specified in the document unless the contrary is shown.

112   Service of notices etc

Any notice or information required to be given under this Act may be given by post.

113   Admissibility of certain documents as evidence

Any document which is receivable as evidence of any matter—

(a)   in England and Wales under section 77(4) and (5) of the 2002 Act, or

(b)   in Northern Ireland under Article 63(1) of the Northern Ireland Order,

is sufficient evidence in Scotland of the matter to which it relates.

PART 4
GENERAL

114   Rules of procedure

(1)   Provision may be made by rules of court in respect of any matter to be prescribed by rules made by virtue of this Act and dealing generally with all matters of procedure.

(2)   In the case of an application for an adoption order, the rules must require—

(a)   any person mentioned in subsection (3) to be notified of the matters mentioned in subsection (4), and

(b)   the person mentioned in subsection (5) (if he can be found) to be notified of the matters mentioned in paragraphs (a) and (b) of subsection (4).

(3)   Those persons are—

(a)   every person who can be found and whose consent to the making of the order is required to be given or dispensed with under this Act or, if no such person can be found, any relative prescribed by rules who can be found,

(b)   every person who has consented to the making of the order under section 20 of the 2002 Act (and has not withdrawn the consent) unless the person has given a notice under subsection (4)(a) of that section which has effect,

(c)   every person who, if leave were given under section 31(12), would be entitled to oppose the making of the order.

(4)   Those matters are—

(a)   that the application has been made,

(b)   the date on which, and place where, the application will be heard,

(c)   the fact that the person is entitled to be heard on the application, and

(d)   the fact that, unless the person wishes, or the court requires, the person need not attend the hearing.

(5)   The person is the father of the child to be adopted if he does not have, and has never had, parental responsibilities or parental rights in relation to the child.

(6)   In the case of an application under section 59, rules of court must require

every person who can be found, and whose consent to the making of the order would be required if the application were for an adoption order (other than a Convention adoption order) to be notified of the matters mentioned in subsection (4).

115   Offences by bodies corporate and partnerships

(1)   Where an offence under this Act committed by a body corporate is proved to have been committed with the consent or connivance of, or to be attributable to any neglect on the part of, a relevant person, the relevant person as well as the body corporate is guilty of the offence and is liable to be proceeded against and punished accordingly.

(2)   Where the affairs of a body corporate are managed by its members, subsection (1) applies in relation to the acts and defaults of a member in connection with the member's functions of management as if the member were a relevant person.

(3)   Where an offence under this Act committed by a partnership is proved to have been committed with the consent or connivance of, or to be attributable to any neglect on the part of, a partner, the partner as well as the partnership is guilty of the offence and is liable to be proceeded against and punished accordingly.

(4)   In this section, 'relevant person', in relation to a body corporate, means a director, manager, secretary or other similar officer of the body, or a person purporting to act in any such capacity.

116   Ancillary provision

(1)   The Scottish Ministers may by order make such incidental, supplementary, consequential, transitory, transitional or saving provision as they consider necessary for the purposes of, in consequence of or for giving full effect to this Act or any provision of it.

(2)   An order under subsection (1) may modify any enactment (including this Act).

117   Orders and regulations

(1)   Any power conferred by this Act on the Scottish Ministers or the Registrar General to make orders or regulations is exercisable by statutory instrument.

(2)   Any power conferred by this Act on the Scottish Ministers or the Registrar General to make orders or regulations—

(a)   may be exercised so as to make different provision for different purposes,

(b)   includes power to make such incidental, supplementary, consequential, transitory, transitional or saving provision as the Scottish Ministers consider appropriate or, as the case may be, the Registrar General considers appropriate.

(3)   Any power conferred by this Act on the Scottish Ministers to make orders or regulations (as well as being exercisable in relation to all cases to which it extends) may be exercised in relation to—

(a)   those cases subject to specified exceptions, or

(b)   a particular case or class of case.

(4)   Subject to subsection (5), a statutory instrument containing an order or regulations made under this Act (other than an order under section 121) is subject to annulment in pursuance of a resolution of the Scottish Parliament.

(5)   A statutory instrument containing—

(a)   regulations under—

(i)   section 3 which includes provision amending subsection (4) or (5) of section 1,

[(ia)   section 13A(2),

(ib)   section 13F(1),]

(ii)   section 38(1),

(iii)   section 74(1),

(b)   an order under section 116(1) which includes provision modifying an Act or an Act of the Scottish Parliament,

is not to be made unless a draft of the instrument has been laid before, and approved by resolution of, the Scottish Parliament.

(6)   In this section, 'Registrar General' has the meaning given by section 57(1).

118   Meaning of 'appropriate court'

(1)   In this Act, 'appropriate court', as respects any application made by virtue of this Act, is to be construed as follows.

(2)   If the application relates to a child who is in Scotland when the application is made, the appropriate court is—

(a)   the Court of Session, or

(b)   the sheriff court of the sheriffdom within which the child is.

(3)   If—

(a)   the application is for—

(i)   an adoption order, or

(ii)   a permanence order seeking provision granting authority for the child to whom the order relates to be adopted, and

(b)   the child is not in Scotland when the application is made,

the appropriate court is the Court of Session.

119   Interpretation

(1)   In this Act, unless the context otherwise requires—

'the 1995 Act' means the Children (Scotland) Act 1995 (c 36),

'the 2002 Act' means the Adoption and Children Act 2002 (c 38),

'the Northern Ireland Order' means the Adoption (Northern Ireland) Order 1987 (SI 1987/2203),

'adoption agency'—

(a)   means—

(i)   a local authority, or

(ii)   a registered adoption service, and

(b)   in sections [13A, 13D, 13F,] 15, 17, 18, 20, 58 and 75 includes—

(i)   an adoption agency within the meaning of section 2(1) of the 2002 Act (adoption agencies in England and Wales), and

(ii)   an adoption agency within the meaning of Article 3 of the Northern Ireland Order (adoption agencies in Northern Ireland),

'adoption order' has the meaning given by section 28(1),

'adoption society' means a body of persons whose functions consist of or include the making of arrangements for or in connection with the adoption of children,

'adoption support services' has the meaning given by section 1(5),

'applicant', in sections 16 to 19 and 34, has the meaning given by section 15(2),

'British Islands' means the United Kingdom, the Channel Islands and the Isle of Man,

'child' means a person who is under the age of 18,

['compulsory supervision order' has the meaning given by section 83 of the Children's Hearings (Scotland) Act 2011,]

[. . .]

'the Convention' means the Convention on Protection of Children and Co-operation in respect of Intercountry Adoption, concluded at the Hague on 29th May 1993,

'Convention adoption' means an adoption effected under the law of a Convention country outwith the British Islands and certified in pursuance of Article 23(1) of the Convention,

'Convention adoption order' means an adoption order which, by virtue of regulations under section 1 of the Adoption (Intercountry Aspects) Act 1999 (c 18), is made as a Convention adoption order,

'Convention country' means any country or territory in which the Convention is in force,

'guardian', in relation to a child, means a person appointed by deed or will or by a court of competent jurisdiction to be the guardian of the child,

['interim compulsory supervision order' has the meaning given by section 86 of the Children's Hearings (Scotland) Act 2011,]

'local authority' means a council constituted under section 2 of the Local Government etc (Scotland) Act 1994 (c 39),

'notice' means notice in writing,

'overseas adoption' has the meaning given by section 67,

'parental responsibilities' and 'parental rights' have the meanings respectively given by sections 1(3) and 2(4) of the 1995 Act (analogous expressions being construed accordingly),

'permanence order' has the meaning given by section 80(2),

'registered adoption service' has the meaning given by section 2(3),

'registered adoption society' has the meaning given by section 2(2) of the 2002 Act,

'relative', in relation to a child, means a grandparent, brother, sister, uncle or aunt of the child (in each case, whether or not by affinity, and in the cases of a brother, sister, uncle or aunt, whether of the full-blood or half-blood); and includes a civil partner of any such grandparent, brother, sister, uncle or aunt,

'relevant family' has the meaning given by section 45(7); and 'member', in relation to a relevant family, is to be construed accordingly,

[. . .]

'voluntary organisation' means a body other than a public or local authority the activities of which are not carried on for profit.

(2)   In this Act, unless the context otherwise requires, references to adoption are to the adoption of children, wherever they may be habitually resident, effected under the law of any country or territory, whether within or outwith the British Islands.

(3)   In this Act, references to an adoption service include references to part of such a service.

(4)   In this Act, references, in relation to a child, to being looked after by a local authority are to be construed in accordance with section 17(6) of the 1995 Act.

(5)   In this Act, references to a relevant couple are to be construed in accordance with section 29(3).

(6)   Subject to subsection (7), for the purposes of this Act, a person is deemed to make arrangements for the adoption of a child if—

(a)   the person enters into or makes any agreement or arrangement for, or for facilitating, the adoption of the child by any other person (whether the adoption is effected or intended to be effected in Great Britain or elsewhere),

(b)   the person initiates or takes part in any negotiations the purpose or effect of which is the conclusion of any such agreement or the making of any such arrangement, or

(c)   the person causes another person to act as mentioned in paragraph (a) or (b).

(7)   The making [of an order mentioned in subsection (8)] which, in respect that it provides as to where the child is to reside, facilitates an adoption agency's placing the child for adoption does not constitute the making of such arrangements.

[(8)   The orders are—

(a)   a compulsory supervision order—

(b)   an order varying a compulsory supervision order—

(c)   an interim compulsory supervision order.]

120 Minor and consequential amendments and repeals

(1) Schedule 2 (which contains minor amendments and amendments consequential on the provisions of this Act) has effect.

(2) The enactments mentioned in the first column in schedule 3 (which include enactments that are spent) are repealed to the extent set out in the second column.

121 Short title and commencement

(1) This Act may be cited as the Adoption and Children (Scotland) Act 2007.

(2) The provisions of this Act (except this section and sections 116 and 117) come into force on such day as the Scottish Ministers may by order appoint.

(3) An order under subsection (2) may appoint different days for different purposes.

SCHEDULE 1
REGISTRATION OF ADOPTIONS
(introduced by section 53(4))

Registration of adoption orders

1—(1) Every adoption order must contain a direction to the Registrar General to make in the Adopted Children Register an entry in the form prescribed by regulations made by the Registrar General with the approval of the Scottish Ministers.

(2) For the purposes of compliance with the requirements of sub-paragraph (1)—

(a) where the precise date of the child's birth is not proved to the satisfaction of the court—

(i) the court is to determine the probable date of the child's birth, and

(ii) the date so determined is to be specified in the adoption order as the date of the child's birth,

(b) where the country of birth of the child is not proved to the satisfaction of the court—

(i) if it appears probable that the child was born in a part of the British Islands, the child is to be treated as having been born in Scotland,

(ii) in any other case, the particulars of the country of birth may be omitted from the adoption order and from the entry in the Adopted Children Register,

(c) where—

(i) the application for the adoption order specifies a name (or names) and surname as being those of the child, that name (or those names) and surname are to be recorded in the adoption order as the name (or names) and surname of the child,

(ii) no name (or names) or surname is so specified, the original name (or names) of the child and the surname of the applicant are to be recorded in the adoption order as the name (or names) and surname of the child.

2—(1) Sub-paragraph (2) applies where—

(a) on an application to the appropriate court for an adoption order in respect of a child, the identity of the child with a child to whom an entry in the register of births relates is proved to the satisfaction of the court, and

(b) the child has not previously been the subject of an adoption order made by a court in Scotland under this Act or any enactment at the time in force.

(2) Any adoption order made in pursuance of the application must contain a direction to the Registrar General to secure that the entry in the register of births is marked with the word "Adopted".

3 Where an adoption order is made in respect of a child who has previously been the subject of an adoption order made by a court in Scotland under this Act or any enactment at the time in force, the order must contain a direction to the Registrar General to secure that the previous entry in the Adopted Children Register is marked with the word "Re-adopted".

4—(1)   Where an adoption order is made, the clerk of the court which made the order must secure that the order is communicated to the Registrar General.

(2)   As soon as is reasonably practicable after receipt of the communication, the Registrar General must secure that the direction contained in the order is complied with.

Registration of adoptions in other parts of the British Islands

5—(1)   Sub-paragraphs (2) and (3) apply where the Registrar General is notified by the authority maintaining a register of adoptions in a part of the British Islands outwith Scotland that an order has been made in that part authorising the adoption of a child.

(2)   If an entry in the register of births (and no entry in the Adopted Children Register) relates to the child, the Registrar General must secure that the entry is marked with the word "Adopted" followed by the name, in brackets, of the part of the British Islands in which the order was made.

(3)   If an entry in the Adopted Children Register relates to the child, the Registrar General must mark the entry with the word "Re-adopted" followed by the name, in brackets, of the part of the British Islands in which the order was made.

(4)   Where, after an entry in either of the registers mentioned in sub-paragraphs (2) and (3) has been so marked, the Registrar General is notified by the authority concerned that—

    (a)   the order has been quashed,
    (b)   an appeal against the order has been allowed, or
    (c)   the order has been revoked,

the Registrar General must secure that the marking is cancelled.

(5)   Where the marking of an entry in a register is cancelled under sub-paragraph (4), an extract of the entry is not to be treated as accurate unless both the marking and the cancellation are omitted from it.

(6)   This paragraph applies in relation to orders corresponding to orders under section 59 as it applies in relation to orders authorising the adoption of a child except that any marking of an entry required by virtue of this sub-paragraph is to consist of the words "proposed foreign adoption" or, as the case may require, "proposed foreign re-adoption" followed by the name, in brackets, of the part of the British Islands in which the order was made.

Registration of other adoptions

6—(1)   If the Registrar General is satisfied, on an application under this paragraph, that the Registrar General has sufficient particulars relating to a child adopted under a registrable foreign adoption to enable an entry to be made in the Adopted Children Register for the child, the Registrar General must make the entry accordingly.

(2)   If the Registrar General is also satisfied that an entry in the register of births relates to the child, the Registrar General must secure that the entry in that register is marked "Adopted" or "Re-adopted", as the case may be, followed by the name, in brackets, of the country in which the adoption was effected.

(3)   An application under this paragraph must be made in the prescribed manner by a prescribed person and the applicant must provide the prescribed particulars.

(4)   An entry made in the Adopted Children Register by virtue of this paragraph must be made in the prescribed form.

(5)   In this paragraph—

"prescribed" means prescribed by regulations made by the Registrar General with the approval of the Scottish Ministers,

"registrable foreign adoption" means an adoption which satisfies prescribed requirements and which is—

(a) a Convention adoption, or

(b) an overseas adoption.

Amendment of orders and rectification of registers

7—(1) The court by which an adoption order has been made may, on the application of the adopter or the adopted person, amend the order by the correction of any error in the particulars contained in it.

(2) The court by which an adoption order has been made may, if satisfied on the application of the adopter or the adopted person that before the expiry of the period of one year beginning with the date of the order any new name—

(a) has been given to the adopted person (whether in baptism or otherwise), or

(b) has been taken by the adopted person,

in place of or in addition to a name specified in the particulars required to be entered in the Adopted Children Register in pursuance of the order, amend the order by substituting or, as the case may be, adding that name in those particulars.

(3) The court by which an adoption order has been made may, if satisfied on the application of any person concerned that a direction for the marking of an entry in the register of births or the Adopted Children Register included in the order in pursuance of paragraph 2 or 3 was wrongly so included, revoke that direction.

(4) Where an adoption order is amended or a direction revoked under sub-paragraphs (1) to (3), the clerk of the court must secure that the amendment is communicated in the prescribed manner to the Registrar General.

(5) As soon as is reasonably practicable after receipt of the communication, the Registrar General must secure that—

(a) the entry in the Adopted Children Register is amended accordingly, or

(b) the marking of the entry in the register of births or the Adopted Children Register is cancelled,

as the case may be.

(6) Where an adoption order is quashed or an appeal against an adoption order allowed by any court, the court must give directions to the Registrar General to secure that—

(a) any entry in the Adopted Children Register, and

(b) any marking of an entry in that register or, as the case may be,

the register of births, which was effected in pursuance of the order is cancelled.

(7) Where an adoption order has been amended, any extract of the relevant entry in the Adopted Children Register which may be issued in pursuance of section 54 must be a copy of the entry as amended, without the reproduction of—

(a) any note or marking relating to the amendment, or

(b) any matter cancelled in pursuance of it.

(8) Where the marking of an entry is cancelled, an extract of the entry is not to be treated as accurate unless both the marking and the cancellation are omitted from it.

(9) If the Registrar General is satisfied—

(a) that a registrable foreign adoption (as defined in sub-paragraph (5) of paragraph 6) has ceased to have effect (whether on annulment or otherwise), or

(b) that any entry or mark was erroneously made in pursuance of that paragraph in the Adopted Children Register or the register of births,

the Registrar General may secure that such alterations are made in those registers as the Registrar General considers are required in consequence of the adoption ceasing to have effect or to correct the error.

(10) Where an entry in such a register is amended in pursuance of sub-paragraph (9), an extract of the entry is not to be treated as accurate unless it shows the entry as amended but without indicating that it has been amended.

(11) In this paragraph, "prescribed" means prescribed by regulations made by the Registrar General with the approval of the Scottish Ministers.

Marking of entries on re-registration of birth

8   Without prejudice to any other provision of this Act, where—
    (a)   an entry in the register of births has been marked in accordance with
    paragraph 5 or 6, and
    (b)   the birth is re-registered under section 20(1) of the Registration of Births,
    Deaths and Marriages (Scotland) Act 1965 (c 49),
the entry made on re-registration must be marked in the same way.

HUMAN FERTILISATION AND EMBRYOLOGY ACT 2008
(2008, c 22)

PART 2
PARENTHOOD IN CASES INVOLVING ASSISTED REPRODUCTION

Meaning of 'mother'

33   Meaning of 'mother'
(1)   The woman who is carrying or has carried a child as a result of the placing
in her of an embryo or of sperm and eggs, and no other woman, is to be treated as
the mother of the child.

(2)   Subsection (1) does not apply to any child to the extent that the child is
treated by virtue of adoption as not being the woman's child.

(3)   Subsection (1) applies whether the woman was in the United Kingdom or
elsewhere at the time of the placing in her of the embryo or the sperm and eggs.

Application of sections 35 to 47

34   Application of sections 35 to 47
(1)   Sections 35 to 47 apply, in the case of a child who is being or has been carried by a woman (referred to in those sections as 'W') as a result of the placing in
her of an embryo or of sperm and eggs or her artificial insemination, to determine
who is to be treated as the other parent of the child.

(2)   Subsection (1) has effect subject to the provisions of sections 39, 40 and 46
limiting the purposes for which a person is treated as the child's other parent by
virtue of those sections.

Meaning of 'father'

35   Woman married [to [or civil partner of] a man] at time of treatment
(1)   If—
    (a)   at the time of the placing in her of the embryo or of the sperm and eggs
    or of her artificial insemination, W was a party to a marriage [with a man] [or a
    civil partnership with a man], and
    (b)   the creation of the embryo carried by her was not brought about with the
    sperm of the other party to the marriage [or civil partnership],
then, subject to section 38(2) to (4), the other party to the marriage [or civil partner-
ship] is to be treated as the father of the child unless it is shown that he did not
consent to the placing in her of the embryo or the sperm and eggs or to her artificial insemination (as the case may be).

(2)   This section applies whether W was in the United Kingdom or elsewhere at
the time mentioned in subsection (1)(a).

36   Treatment provided to woman where agreed fatherhood conditions apply
If no man is treated by virtue of section 35 as the father of the child and no woman
is treated by virtue of section 42 as a parent of the child but—
    (a)   the embryo or the sperm and eggs were placed in W, or W was

artificially inseminated, in the course of treatment services provided in the United Kingdom by a person to whom a licence applies,

(b) at the time when the embryo or the sperm and eggs were placed in W, or W was artificially inseminated, the agreed fatherhood conditions (as set out in section 37) were satisfied in relation to a man, in relation to treatment provided to W under the licence,

(c) the man remained alive at that time, and

(d) the creation of the embryo carried by W was not brought about with the man's sperm,

then, subject to section 38(2) to (4), the man is to be treated as the father of the child.

37 The agreed fatherhood conditions

(1) The agreed fatherhood conditions referred to in section 36(b) are met in relation to a man ('M') in relation to treatment provided to W under a licence if, but only if,—

(a) M has given the person responsible a notice stating that he consents to being treated as the father of any child resulting from treatment provided to W under the licence,

(b) W has given the person responsible a notice stating that she consents to M being so treated,

(c) neither M nor W has, since giving notice under paragraph (a) or (b), given the person responsible notice of the withdrawal of M's or W's consent to M being so treated,

(d) W has not, since the giving of the notice under paragraph (b), given the person responsible—

(i) a further notice under that paragraph stating that she consents to another man being treated as the father of any resulting child, or

(ii) a notice under section 44(1)(b) stating that she consents to a woman being treated as a parent of any resulting child, and

(e) W and M are not within prohibited degrees of relationship in relation to each other.

(2) A notice under subsection (1)(a), (b) or (c) must be in writing and must be signed by the person giving it.

(3) A notice under subsection (1)(a), (b) or (c) by a person ('S') who is unable to sign because of illness, injury or physical disability is to be taken to comply with the requirement of subsection (2) as to signature if it is signed at the direction of S, in the presence of S and in the presence of at least one witness who attests the signature.

38 Further provision relating to sections 35 and 36

(1) Where a person is to be treated as the father of the child by virtue of section 35 or 36, no other person is to be treated as the father of the child.

(2) In England and Wales and Northern Ireland, sections 35 and 36 do not affect any presumption, applying by virtue of the rules of common law [or section A1(2) of the Legitimacy Act 1976], that a child is the legitimate child of the parties to a marriage [or civil partnership].

(3) In Scotland, sections 35 and 36 do not apply in relation to any child who, by virtue of any enactment or other rule of law, is treated as the child of the parties to a marriage.

(4) Sections 35 and 36 do not apply to any child to the extent that the child is treated by virtue of adoption as not being the man's child.

39 Use of sperm, or transfer of embryo, after death of man providing sperm

(1) If—

(a) the child has been carried by W as a result of the placing in her of an embryo or of sperm and eggs or her artificial insemination,

(b) the creation of the embryo carried by W was brought about by using the sperm of a man after his death, or the creation of the embryo was brought about using the sperm of a man before his death but the embryo was placed in W after his death,

(c)   the man consented in writing (and did not withdraw the consent)—

(i) to the use of his sperm after his death which brought about the creation of the embryo carried by W or (as the case may be) to the placing in W after his death of the embryo which was brought about using his sperm before his death, and

(ii) to being treated for the purpose mentioned in subsection (3) as the father of any resulting child,

(d)   W has elected in writing not later than the end of the period of 42 days from the day on which the child was born for the man to be treated for the purpose mentioned in subsection (3) as the father of the child, and

(e)   no-one else is to be treated—

(i) as the father of the child by virtue of section 35 or 36 or by virtue of section 38(2) or (3), or

(ii) as a parent of the child by virtue of section 42 or 43 or by virtue of adoption,

then the man is to be treated for the purpose mentioned in subsection (3) as the father of the child.

(2)   Subsection (1) applies whether W was in the United Kingdom or elsewhere at the time of the placing in her of the embryo or of the sperm and eggs or of her artificial insemination.

(3)   The purpose referred to in subsection (1) is the purpose of enabling the man's particulars to be entered as the particulars of the child's father in a relevant register of births.

(4)   In the application of this section to Scotland, for any reference to a period of 42 days there is substituted a reference to a period of 21 days.

40   Embryo transferred after death of [male spouse, civil partnership or intended parent] who did not provide sperm

(1)   If—

(a)   the child has been carried by W as a result of the placing in her of an embryo,

(b)   the embryo was created at a time when W was a party to a marriage [with a man] [or a civil partnership with a man],

(c)   the creation of the embryo was not brought about with the sperm of the other party to the marriage [or civil partnership],

(d)   the other party to the marriage [or civil partnership] died before the placing of the embryo in W,

(e)   the other party to the marriage [or civil partnership] consented in writing (and did not withdraw the consent)—

(i) to the placing of the embryo in W after his death, and

(ii) to being treated for the purpose mentioned in subsection (4) as the father of any resulting child,

(f)   W has elected in writing not later than the end of the period of 42 days from the day on which the child was born for the man to be treated for the purpose mentioned in subsection (4) as the father of the child, and

(g)   no-one else is to be treated—

(i) as the father of the child by virtue of section 35 or 36 or by virtue of section 38(2) or (3), or

(ii) as a parent of the child by virtue of section 42 or 43 or by virtue of adoption,

then the man is to be treated for the purpose mentioned in subsection (4) as the father of the child.

(2)   If—

(a)   the child has been carried by W as a result of the placing in her of an embryo,

(b)   the embryo was not created at a time when W was a party to a marriage or a civil partnership but was created in the course of treatment services provided to W in the United Kingdom by a person to whom a licence applies,

(c)   a man consented in writing (and did not withdraw the consent)—

(i)   to the placing of the embryo in W after his death, and

(ii)   to being treated for the purpose mentioned in subsection (4) as the father of any resulting child,

(d)   the creation of the embryo was not brought about with the sperm of that man,

(e)   the man died before the placing of the embryo in W,

(f)   immediately before the man's death, the agreed fatherhood conditions set out in section 37 were met in relation to the man in relation to treatment proposed to be provided to W in the United Kingdom by a person to whom a licence applies,

(g)   W has elected in writing not later than the end of the period of 42 days from the day on which the child was born for the man to be treated for the purpose mentioned in subsection (4) as the father of the child, and

(h)   no-one else is to be treated—

(i)   as the father of the child by virtue of section 35 or 36 or by virtue of section 38(2) or (3), or

(ii)   as a parent of the child by virtue of section 42 or 43 or by virtue of adoption,

then the man is to be treated for the purpose mentioned in subsection (4) as the father of the child.

(3)   Subsections (1) and (2) apply whether W was in the United Kingdom or elsewhere at the time of the placing in her of the embryo.

(4)   The purpose referred to in subsections (1) and (2) is the purpose of enabling the man's particulars to be entered as the particulars of the child's father in a relevant register of births.

(5)   In the application of this section to Scotland, for any reference to a period of 42 days there is substituted a reference to a period of 21 days.

41   Persons not to be treated as father

(1)   Where the sperm of a man who had given such consent as is required by paragraph 5 of Schedule 3 to the 1990 Act (consent to use of gametes for purposes of treatment services or non-medical fertility services) was used for a purpose for which such consent was required, he is not to be treated as the father of the child.

(2)   Where the sperm of a man, or an embryo the creation of which was brought about with his sperm, was used after his death, he is not, subject to section 39, to be treated as the father of the child.

(3)   Subsection (2) applies whether W was in the United Kingdom or elsewhere at the time of the placing in her of the embryo or of the sperm and eggs or of her artificial insemination.

Cases in which woman to be other parent

42   Woman in civil partnership [or marriage to a woman] at time of treatment

(1)   If at the time of the placing in her of the embryo or the sperm and eggs or of her artificial insemination, W was a party to a civil partnership [with another woman] [or marriage with another woman], then subject to section 45(2) to (4), the other party to the civil partnership [or marriage] is to be treated as a parent of the child unless it is shown that she did not consent to the placing in W of the embryo or the sperm and eggs or to her artificial insemination (as the case may be).

(2) This section applies whether W was in the United Kingdom or elsewhere at the time mentioned in subsection (1).

43 Treatment provided to woman who agrees that second woman to be parent

If no man is treated by virtue of section 35 as the father of the child and no woman is treated by virtue of section 42 as a parent of the child but—

(a) the embryo or the sperm and eggs were placed in W, or W was artificially inseminated, in the course of treatment services provided in the United Kingdom by a person to whom a licence applies,

(b) at the time when the embryo or the sperm and eggs were placed in W, or W was artificially inseminated, the agreed female parenthood conditions (as set out in section 44) were met in relation to another woman, in relation to treatment provided to W under that licence, and

(c) the other woman remained alive at that time,

then, subject to section 45(2) to (4), the other woman is to be treated as a parent of the child.

44 The agreed female parenthood conditions

(1) The agreed female parenthood conditions referred to in section 43(b) are met in relation to another woman ('P') in relation to treatment provided to W under a licence if, but only if,—

(a) P has given the person responsible a notice stating that P consents to P being treated as a parent of any child resulting from treatment provided to W under the licence,

(b) W has given the person responsible a notice stating that W agrees to P being so treated,

(c) neither W nor P has, since giving notice under paragraph (a) or (b), given the person responsible notice of the withdrawal of P's or W's consent to P being so treated,

(d) W has not, since the giving of the notice under paragraph (b), given the person responsible—

(i) a further notice under that paragraph stating that W consents to a woman other than P being treated as a parent of any resulting child, or

(ii) a notice under section 37(1)(b) stating that W consents to a man being treated as the father of any resulting child, and

(e) W and P are not within prohibited degrees of relationship in relation to each other.

(2) A notice under subsection (1)(a), (b) or (c) must be in writing and must be signed by the person giving it.

(3) A notice under subsection (1)(a), (b) or (c) by a person ('S') who is unable to sign because of illness, injury or physical disability is to be taken to comply with the requirement of subsection (2) as to signature if it is signed at the direction of S, in the presence of S and in the presence of at least one witness who attests the signature.

45 Further provision relating to sections 42 and 43

(1) Where a woman is treated by virtue of section 42 or 43 as a parent of the child, no man is to be treated as the father of the child.

(2) In England and Wales and Northern Ireland, sections 42 and 43 do not affect any presumption, applying by virtue of the rules of common law [or section A1(2) of the Legitimacy Act 1976], that a child is the legitimate child of the parties to a marriage [or civil partnership].

(3) In Scotland, sections 42 and 43 do not apply in relation to any child who, by virtue of any enactment or other rule of law, is treated as the child of the parties to a marriage.

(4) Sections 42 and 43 do not apply to any child to the extent that the child is treated by virtue of adoption as not being the woman's child.

46   Embryo transferred after death of [female spouse, civil partner or intended parent]

(1)   If—

(a)   the child has been carried by W as the result of the placing in her of an embryo,

(b)   the embryo was created at a time when W was a party to a civil partnership [with a woman or a marriage with a woman],

(c)   the other party to the civil partnership [or marriage] died before the placing of the embryo in W,

(d)   the other party to the civil partnership [or marriage] consented in writing (and did not withdraw the consent)—

(i)   to the placing of the embryo in W after the death of the other party, and

(ii)   to being treated for the purpose mentioned in subsection (4) as the parent of any resulting child,

(e)   W has elected in writing not later than the end of the period of 42 days from the day on which the child was born for the other party to the civil partnership [or marriage] to be treated for the purpose mentioned in subsection (4) as the parent of the child, and

(f)   no one else is to be treated—

(i)   as the father of the child by virtue of section 35 or 36 or by virtue of section 45(2) or (3), or

(ii)   as a parent of the child by virtue of section 42 or 43 or by virtue of adoption,

then the other party to the civil partnership [or marriage] is to be treated for the purpose mentioned in subsection (4) as a parent of the child.

(2)   If—

(a)   the child has been carried by W as the result of the placing in her of an embryo,

(b)   the embryo was not created at a time when W was a party to a marriage or a civil partnership, but was created in the course of treatment services provided to W in the United Kingdom by a person to whom a licence applies,

(c)   another woman consented in writing (and did not withdraw the consent)—

(i)   to the placing of the embryo in W after the death of the other woman, and

(ii)   to being treated for the purpose mentioned in subsection (4) as the parent of any resulting child,

(d)   the other woman died before the placing of the embryo in W,

(e)   immediately before the other woman's death, the agreed female parenthood conditions set out in section 44 were met in relation to the other woman in relation to treatment proposed to be provided to W in the United Kingdom by a person to whom a licence applies,

(f)   W has elected in writing not later than the end of the period of 42 days from the day on which the child was born for the other woman to be treated for the purpose mentioned in subsection (4) as the parent of the child, and

(g)   no one else is to be treated—

(i)   as the father of the child by virtue of section 35 or 36 or by virtue of section 45(2) or (3), or

(ii)   as a parent of the child by virtue of section 42 or 43 or by virtue of adoption,

then the other woman is to be treated for the purpose mentioned in subsection (4) as a parent of the child.

(3)   Subsections (1) and (2) apply whether W was in the United Kingdom or elsewhere at the time of the placing in her of the embryo.

(4)   The purpose referred to in subsections (1) and (2) is the purpose of enabling

the deceased woman's particulars to be entered as the particulars of the child's other parent in a relevant register of births.

(5) In the application of subsections (1) and (2) to Scotland, for any reference to a period of 42 days there is substituted a reference to a period of 21 days.

47 Woman not to be other parent merely because of egg donation

A woman is not to be treated as the parent of a child whom she is not carrying and has not carried, except where she is so treated—

    (a)   by virtue of section 42 or 43, or

    (b)   by virtue of section 46 (for the purpose mentioned in subsection (4) of that section), or

    (c)   by virtue of adoption.

Effect of sections 33 to 47

48 Effect of sections 33 to 47

(1) Where by virtue of section 33, 35, 36, 42 or 43 a person is to be treated as the mother, father or parent of a child, that person is to be treated in law as the mother, father or parent (as the case may be) of the child for all purposes.

(2) Where by virtue of section 33, 38, 41, 45 or 47 a person is not to be treated as a parent of the child, that person is to be treated in law as not being a parent of the child for any purpose.

(3) Where section 39(1) or 40(1) or (2) applies, the deceased man—

    (a)   is to be treated in law as the father of the child for the purpose mentioned in section 39(3) or 40(4), but

    (b)   is to be treated in law as not being the father of the child for any other purpose.

(4) Where section 46(1) or (2) applies, the deceased woman—

    (a)   is to be treated in law as a parent of the child for the purpose mentioned in section 46(4), but

    (b)   is to be treated in law as not being a parent of the child for any other purpose.

(5) Where any of subsections (1) to (4) has effect, references to any relationship between two people in any enactment, deed or other instrument or document (whenever passed or made) are to be read accordingly.

(6) In relation to England and Wales and Northern Ireland, a child who—

    (a)   has a parent by virtue of section 42, or

    (b)   has a parent by virtue of section 43 who is at any time during the period beginning with the time mentioned in section 43(b) and ending with the time of the child's birth a party to [marriage or] a civil partnership with the child's mother, is the legitimate child of the child's parents.

(7) In relation to England and Wales and Northern Ireland, nothing in the provisions of section 33(1) or sections 35 to 47, read with this section—

    (a)   affects the succession to any dignity or title of honour or renders any person capable of succeeding to or transmitting a right to succeed to any such dignity or title, or

    (b)   affects the devolution of any property limited (expressly or not) to devolve (as nearly as the law permits) along with any dignity or title of honour.

(8) In relation to Scotland—

    (a)   those provisions do not apply to any title, coat of arms, honour or dignity transmissible on the death of its holder or affect the succession to any such title, coat of arms or dignity or its devolution, and

    (b)   where the terms of any deed provide that any property or interest in property is to devolve along with a title, coat of arms, honour or dignity, nothing in those provisions is to prevent that property or interest from so devolving.

References to parties to marriage or civil partnership

49 Meaning of references to parties to a marriage

(1) The references in sections 35 to 47 to the parties to a marriage at any time there referred to—

(a) are to the parties to a marriage subsisting at that time, unless a judicial separation was then in force, but

(b) include the parties to a void marriage if either or both of them reasonably believed at that time that the marriage was valid; and for the purposes of those sections it is to be presumed, unless the contrary is shown, that one of them reasonably believed at that time that the marriage was valid.

(2) In subsection (1)(a) 'judicial separation' includes a legal separation obtained in a country outside the British Islands and recognised in the United Kingdom.

50 Meaning of references to parties to a civil partnership

(1) The references in sections 35 to 47 to the parties to a civil partnership at any time there referred to—

(a) are to the parties to a civil partnership subsisting at that time, unless a separation order was then in force, but

(b) include the parties to a void civil partnership if either or both of them reasonably believed at that time that the civil partnership was valid; and for the purposes of those sections it is to be presumed, unless the contrary is shown, that one of them reasonably believed at that time that the civil partnership was valid.

(2) The reference in section 48(6)(b) to a civil partnership includes a reference to a void civil partnership if either or both of the parties reasonably believed at the time when they registered as civil partners of each other that the civil partnership was valid; and for this purpose it is to be presumed, unless the contrary is shown, that one of them reasonably believed at that time that the civil partnership was valid.

(3) In subsection (1)(a), 'separation order' means—

(a) a separation order under section 37(1)(d) or 161(1)(d) of the Civil Partnership Act 2004,

(b) a decree of separation under section 120(2) of that Act, or

(c) a legal separation obtained in a country outside the United Kingdom and recognised in the United Kingdom.

Further provision about registration by virtue of section 39, 40 or 46

51 Meaning of 'relevant register of births'

For the purposes of this Part a 'relevant register of births', in relation to a birth, is whichever of the following is relevant—

(a) a register of live-births or still-births kept under the Births and Deaths Registration Act 1953,

(b) a register of births or still-births kept under the Registration of Births, Deaths and Marriages (Scotland) Act 1965, or

(c) a register of live-births or still-births kept under the Births and Deaths Registration (Northern Ireland) Order 1976.

52 Late election by mother with consent of Registrar General

(1) The requirement under section 39(1), 40(1) or (2) or 46(1) or (2) as to the making of an election (which requires an election to be made either on or before the day on which the child was born or within the period of 42 or, as the case may be, 21 days from that day) is nevertheless to be treated as satisfied if the required election is made after the end of that period but with the consent of the Registrar General under subsection (2).

(2) The Registrar General may at any time consent to the making of an election after the end of the period mentioned in subsection (1) if, on an application made to him in accordance with such requirements as he may specify, he is satisfied that there is a compelling reason for giving his consent to the making of such an election.

(3) In this section 'the Registrar General' means the Registrar General for England and Wales, the Registrar General of Births, Deaths and Marriages for Scotland or (as the case may be) the Registrar General for Northern Ireland.

Interpretation of references to father etc where woman is other parent

53 Interpretation of references to father etc

(1) Subsections (2) and (3) have effect, subject to subsections (4) and (6), for the interpretation of any enactment, deed or any other instrument or document (whenever passed or made).

(2) Any reference (however expressed) to the father of a child who has a parent by virtue of section 42 or 43 is to be read as a reference to the woman who is a parent of the child by virtue of that section.

(3) Any reference (however expressed) to evidence of paternity is, in relation to a woman who is a parent by virtue of section 42 or 43, to be read as a reference to evidence of parentage.

(4) This section does not affect the interpretation of the enactments specified in subsection (5)(which make express provision for the case where a child has a parent by virtue of section 42 or 43).

(5) Those enactments are—

    (a) the Legitimacy Act (Northern Ireland) 1928,

    (b) the Schedule to the Population (Statistics) Act 1938,

    (c) the Births and Deaths Registration Act 1953,

    (d) the Registration of Births, Deaths and Marriages (Special Provisions) Act 1957,

    (e) Part 2 of the Registration of Births, Deaths and Marriages (Scotland) Act 1965,

    (f) the Congenital Disabilities (Civil Liability) Act 1976,

    (g) the Legitimacy Act 1976,

    (h) the Births and Deaths Registration (Northern Ireland) Order 1976,

    (i) the British Nationality Act 1981,

    (j) the Family Law Reform Act 1987,

    (k) Parts 1 and 2 of the Children Act 1989,

    (l) Part 1 of the Children (Scotland) Act 1995,

    (m) section 1 of the Criminal Law (Consolidation)(Scotland) Act 1995, and

    (n) Parts 2, 3 and 14 of the Children (Northern Ireland) Order 1995.

(6) This section does not affect the interpretation of references that fall to be read in accordance with section 1(2)(a) or (b) of the Family Law Reform Act 1987 or Article 155(2)(a) or (b) of the Children (Northern Ireland) Order 1995 (references to a person whose father and mother were, or were not, married to each other at the time of the person's birth).

Parental orders

54 Parental orders [: two applicants]

(1) On an application made by two people ('the applicants'), the court may make an order providing for a child to be treated in law as the child of the applicants if—

    (a) the child has been carried by a woman who is not one of the applicants, as a result of the placing in her of an embryo or sperm and eggs or her artificial insemination,

    (b) the gametes of at least one of the applicants were used to bring about the creation of the embryo, and

    (c) the conditions in subsections (2) to [(8A)] are satisfied.

(2) The applicants must be—

    (a) husband and wife,

    (b) civil partners of each other, or

    (c) two persons who are living as partners in an enduring family relationship and are not within prohibited degrees of relationship in relation to each other.

(3) Except in a case falling within subsection (11), the applicants must apply for the order during the period of 6 months beginning with the day on which the child is born.

(4) At the time of the application and the making of the order—

    (a) the child's home must be with the applicants, and

    (b) either or both of the applicants must be domiciled in the United Kingdom or in the Channel Islands or the Isle of Man.

(5) At the time of the making of the order both the applicants must have attained the age of 18.

(6) The court must be satisfied that both—

    (a) the woman who carried the child, and

    (b) any other person who is a parent of the child but is not one of the applicants (including any man who is the father by virtue of section 35 or 36 or any woman who is a parent by virtue of section 42 or 43),

have freely, and with full understanding of what is involved, agreed unconditionally to the making of the order.

(7) Subsection (6) does not require the agreement of a person who cannot be found or is incapable of giving agreement; and the agreement of the woman who carried the child is ineffective for the purpose of that subsection if given by her less than six weeks after the child's birth.

(8) The court must be satisfied that no money or other benefit (other than for expenses reasonably incurred) has been given or received by either of the applicants for or in consideration of—

    (a) the making of the order,

    (b) any agreement required by subsection (6),

    (c) the handing over of the child to the applicants, or

    (d) the making of arrangements with a view to the making of the order,

unless authorised by the court.

[(8A) An order relating to the child must not previously have been made under this section or section 54A, unless the order has been quashed or an appeal against the order has been allowed.]

(9) For the purposes of an application under this section—

    (a) in relation to England and Wales [—

        (i) 'the court' means the High Court or the family court, and

        (ii) proceedings on the application are to be 'family proceedings' for the purposes of the Children Act 1989,]

    (b) in relation to Scotland, 'the court' means the Court of Session or the sheriff court of the sheriffdom within which the child is, and

    (c) in relation to Northern Ireland, 'the court' means the High Court or any county court within whose division the child is.

(10) Subsection (1)(a) applies whether the woman was in the United Kingdom or elsewhere at the time of the placing in her of the embryo or the sperm and eggs or her artificial insemination.

(11) An application which—

    (a) relates to a child born before the coming into force of this section, and

    (b) is made by two persons who, throughout the period applicable under subsection (2) of section 30 of the 1990 Act, were not eligible to apply for an order under that section in relation to the child as husband and wife,

may be made within the period of six months beginning with the day on which this section comes into force.

[54A Parental orders: one applicant

(1) On an application made by one person ("the applicant"), the court may make an order providing for a child to be treated in law as the child of the applicant if—

    (a) the child has been carried by a woman who is not the applicant, as a result of the placing in her of an embryo or sperm and eggs or her artificial insemination,

(b)   the gametes of the applicant were used to bring about the creation of the embryo, and

(c)   the conditions in subsections (2) to (8) are satisfied.

(2)   Except in a case falling within subsection (11), the applicant must apply for the order within the period of 6 months beginning with the day on which the child is born.

(3)   At the time of the application and the making of the order—

(a)   the child's home must be with the applicant, and

(b)   the applicant must be domiciled in the United Kingdom or in the Channel Islands or the Isle of Man.

(4)   At the time of the making of the order the applicant must have attained the age of 18.

(5)   The court must be satisfied that both—

(a)   the woman who carried the child, and

(b)   any other person who is a parent of the child but is not the applicant (including any man who is the father by virtue of section 35 or 36 or any woman who is a parent by virtue of section 42 or 43),

have freely, and with full understanding of what is involved, agreed unconditionally to the making of the order.

(6)   Subsection (5) does not require the agreement of a person who cannot be found or is incapable of giving agreement; and the agreement of the woman who carried the child is ineffective for the purpose of that subsection if given by her less than six weeks after the child's birth.

(7)   The court must be satisfied that no money or other benefit (other than for expenses reasonably incurred) has been given or received by the applicant for or in consideration of—

(a)   the making of the order,

(b)   any agreement required by subsection (5),

(c)   the handing over of the child to the applicant, or

(d)   the making of arrangements with a view to the making of the order, unless authorised by the court.

(8)   An order relating to the child must not previously have been made under section 54 or this section, unless the order has been quashed or an appeal against the order has been allowed.

(9)   Section 54(9) applies for the purposes of an application under this section.

(10)   Subsection (1)(a) applies whether the woman was in the United Kingdom or elsewhere at the time of the placing in her of the embryo or the sperm and eggs or her artificial insemination.

(11)   An application which relates to a child born before the coming into force of this section may be made within the period of six months beginning with the day on which this section comes into force.]

55   Parental orders: supplementary provision

(1)   The Secretary of State may by regulations provide—

(a)   for any provision of the enactments about adoption to have effect, with such modifications (if any) as may be specified in the regulations, in relation to orders under section 54 [or 54A], and applications for such orders, as it has effect in relation to adoption, and applications for adoption orders, and

(b)   for references in any enactment to adoption, an adopted child or an adoptive relationship to be read (respectively) as references to the effect of an order under section 54 [or 54A], a child to whom such an order applies and a relationship arising by virtue of the enactments about adoption, as applied by the regulations, and for similar expressions in connection with adoption to be read accordingly.

(2)   The regulations may include such incidental or supplemental provision as appears to the Secretary of State to be necessary or desirable in consequence of any provision made by virtue of subsection (1)(a) or (b).

(3)   In this section 'the enactments about adoption' means—

(a) the Adoption (Scotland) Act 1978,

(b) the Adoption and Children Act 2002,

(c) the Adoption and Children (Scotland) Act 2007, and

(d) the Adoption (Northern Ireland) Order 1987.

Amendments of enactments

56 Amendments relating to parenthood in cases involving assisted reproduction
Schedule 6 contains amendments related to the provisions of this Part.

General

57 Repeals and transitional provision relating to Part 2
(1) Sections 33 to 48 have effect only in relation to children carried by women as a result of the placing in them of embryos or of sperm and eggs, or their artificial insemination (as the case may be), after the commencement of those sections.

(2) Sections 27 to 29 of the 1990 Act (which relate to status) do not have effect in relation to children carried by women as a result of the placing in them of embryos or of sperm and eggs, or their artificial insemination (as the case may be), after the commencement of sections 33 to 48.

(3) Section 30 of the 1990 Act (parental orders in favour of gamete donors) ceases to have effect.

(4) Subsection (3) does not affect the validity of any order made under section 30 of the 1990 Act before the coming into force of that subsection.

58 Interpretation of Part 2
(1) In this Part 'enactment' means an enactment contained in, or in an instrument made under—

(a) an Act of Parliament,

(b) an Act of the Scottish Parliament,

(c) a Measure or Act of the National Assembly for Wales, or

(d) Northern Ireland legislation.

(2) For the purposes of this Part, two persons are within prohibited degrees of relationship if one is the other's parent, grandparent, sister, brother, aunt or uncle; and in this subsection references to relationships—

(a) are to relationships of the full blood or half blood or, in the case of an adopted person, such of those relationships as would subsist but for adoption, and

(b) include the relationship of a child with his adoptive, or former adoptive, parents,

but do not include any other adoptive relationships.

(3) Other expressions used in this Part and in the 1990 Act have the same meaning in this Part as in that Act.

CHILDREN'S HEARINGS (SCOTLAND) ACT 2011
(2011, asp 1)

PART 1
THE NATIONAL CONVENER AND CHILDREN'S HEARINGS SCOTLAND

The National Convener and CHS

1 The National Convener
(1) There is to be an officer to be known as the National Convener of Children's Hearings Scotland (referred to in this Act as 'the National Convener').

(2) The Scottish Ministers are to appoint a person as the first National Convener.

(3)   The Scottish Ministers must take reasonable steps to involve persons who are under 21 years of age in the process for selection of a person for appointment under subsection (2).

(4)   The period for which the person is appointed is 5 years.

(5)   The terms and conditions on which the person holds and vacates office are to be determined by the Scottish Ministers.

2   Children's Hearings Scotland

There is established a body corporate to be known as Children's Hearings Scotland (referred to in this Act as 'CHS').

3   Further provision about National Convener and CHS

Schedule 1 makes further provision about the National Convener and CHS.

The Children's Panel

4   The Children's Panel

(1)   The National Convener must appoint persons to be members of a panel to be known as the Children's Panel.

(2)   The National Convener must endeavour to ensure that—

(a)   the number of persons that the National Convener considers appropriate is appointed, and

(b)   the panel includes persons from all local authority areas.

(3)   Schedule 2 makes further provision about the Children's Panel.

Children's Hearings

5   Children's hearing

A children's hearing consists of three members of the Children's Panel selected in accordance with section 6 for the purpose of carrying out functions conferred on a children's hearing by virtue of this Act or any other enactment.

6   Selection of members of children's hearing

(1)   This section applies where a children's hearing requires to be arranged by virtue of, or for the purposes of, this Act or any other enactment.

(2)   The members of the children's hearing are to be selected by the National Convener.

(3)   The National Convener must ensure that the children's hearing—

(a)   includes both male and female members of the Children's Panel, and

(b)   so far as practicable, consists only of members of the Children's Panel who live or work in the area of the local authority which is the relevant local authority for the child to whom the hearing relates.

(4)   The National Convener may select one of the members of the children's hearing to chair the hearing.

[(5)   In this section 'children's hearing' includes a pre-hearing panel.]

7   Holding of children's hearing

The National Convener must ensure that a children's hearing is held for the purpose of carrying out any function conferred on a children's hearing by virtue of this Act or any other enactment.

8   Provision of advice to children's hearing

(1)   The National Convener may provide advice to children's hearings about any matter arising in connection with the functions conferred on children's hearings by virtue of this Act or any other enactment.

(2)   The National Convener may in particular provide—

(a)   legal advice,

(b)   advice about procedural matters,

(c)   advice about the consequences of decisions of the children's hearing,

    (d)   advice about how decisions of children's hearings are implemented.

(3)   In this section, 'children's hearing' includes pre-hearing panel.

9 Independence of children's hearings

Nothing in this Act authorises the National Convener or the Principal Reporter to direct or guide a children's hearing in carrying out the functions conferred on children's hearings by virtue of this Act or any other enactment.

Power to change National Convener's functions

10 Power to change National Convener's functions

(1)   The Scottish Ministers may by order—

    (a)   confer additional functions on the National Convener,

    (b)   remove functions from the National Convener,

    (c)   transfer functions from another person to the National Convener,

    (d)   transfer functions from the National Convener to another person,

    (e)   specify the manner in which, or period within which, any function conferred on the National Convener by virtue of this Act is to be carried out.

(2)   An order under this section is subject to the super-affirmative procedure (other than an order under subsection (1)(e), which is subject to the affirmative procedure).

Functions of CHS

11 Provision of assistance to National Convener

CHS must—

    (a)   assist the National Convener in carrying out the functions conferred on the National Convener by virtue of this Act or any other enactment,

    (b)   facilitate the carrying out of those functions.

12 Independence of National Convener

(1)   Nothing in this Act authorises CHS or any other person to direct or guide the National Convener in carrying out the functions conferred on the National Convener by virtue of this Act or any other enactment.

(2)   This section is subject to section 10(1)(e).

13 Directions

(1)   The Scottish Ministers may give CHS general or specific directions about the carrying out of its functions.

(2)   CHS must comply with a direction under subsection (1).

(3)   The Scottish Ministers may vary or revoke a direction under subsection (1) by giving a subsequent direction under that subsection.

PART 2
THE PRINCIPAL REPORTER AND THE SCOTTISH CHILDREN'S REPORTER ADMINISTRATION

The Principal Reporter and SCRA

14 The Principal Reporter

There continues to be an officer known as the Principal Reporter.

15 The Scottish Children's Reporter Administration

There continues to be a body corporate known as the Scottish Children's Reporter Administration (in this Act referred to as 'SCRA').

16 Further provision about Principal Reporter and SCRA

Schedule 3 makes further provision about the Principal Reporter and SCRA.

The Principal Reporter

17 Duty as respects location of children's hearing

The Principal Reporter must ensure that, so far as practicable, a children's hearing takes place in the area of the relevant local authority for the child to whom the hearing relates.

18 Power to change Principal Reporter's functions

(1) The Scottish Ministers may by order—

(a) confer additional functions on the Principal Reporter,

(b) remove functions from the Principal Reporter,

(c) transfer functions from another person to the Principal Reporter,

(d) transfer functions from the Principal Reporter to another person,

(e) specify the manner in which, or period within which, any function conferred on the Principal Reporter by virtue of this Act or the Criminal Procedure (Scotland) Act 1995 is to be carried out.

(2) An order under this section is subject to the super-affirmative procedure (other than an order under subsection (1)(e), which is subject to the affirmative procedure).

19 Rights of audience

(1) The Scottish Ministers may by regulations—

(a) empower the Principal Reporter to conduct proceedings which by virtue of this Act require to be conducted before the sheriff or the sheriff principal [or the Sheriff Appeal Court],

(b) prescribe qualifications or experience that must be acquired or training that must be undertaken by the Principal Reporter before conducting such proceedings.

(2) References in subsection (1) to the Principal Reporter include references to a person carrying out a function on behalf of the Principal Reporter by virtue of paragraph 10(1) of schedule 3.

Functions of SCRA

20 Assisting Principal Reporter

SCRA must—

(a) assist the Principal Reporter in carrying out the functions conferred on the Principal Reporter by virtue of this Act or any other enactment, and

(b) facilitate the carrying out of those functions.

21 Provision of accommodation for children's hearings

(1) SCRA must provide suitable accommodation and facilities for children's hearings.

(2) Accommodation and facilities must, so far as practicable, be provided in the area of each local authority.

(3) Accommodation and facilities must be dissociated from courts exercising criminal jurisdiction and police stations.

22 Independence of Principal Reporter

(1) Nothing in this Act authorises SCRA or any other person to direct or guide the Principal Reporter in carrying out the functions conferred on the Principal Reporter by virtue of this Act or any other enactment.

(2) This section is subject to section 18(1)(e).

23 Directions

(1) The Scottish Ministers may give SCRA general or specific directions about the carrying out of its functions.

(2) SCRA must comply with a direction under subsection (1).

(3)   The Scottish Ministers may vary or revoke a direction under subsection (1) by giving a subsequent direction under that subsection.

Transfer of staff, property etc

24   Transfer of staff, property etc
Schedule 4 makes provision about the transfer of staff, property, rights, liabilities and obligations to CHS.

PART 3
GENERAL CONSIDERATIONS

25   Welfare of the child
(1)   This section applies where by virtue of this Act a children's hearing, pre-hearing panel or court is coming to a decision about a matter relating to a child.
(2)   The children's hearing, pre-hearing panel or court is to regard the need to safeguard and promote the welfare of the child throughout the child's childhood as the paramount consideration.

26   Decisions inconsistent with section 25
(1)   A children's hearing or a court may make a decision that is inconsistent with the requirement imposed by section 25(2) if—
    (a)   the children's hearing [, pre-hearing panel] or court considers that, for the purpose of protecting members of the public from serious harm (whether physical or not), it is necessary that the decision be made, and
    (b)   in coming to the decision, the children's hearing [, pre-hearing panel] or court complies with subsection (2).
(2)   The children's hearing [, pre-hearing panel] or court is to regard the need to safeguard and promote the welfare of the child throughout the child's childhood as a primary consideration rather than the paramount consideration.

27   Views of the child
(1)   This section applies where by virtue of this Act a children's hearing [, pre-hearing panel] or the sheriff is coming to a decision about a matter relating to a child.
(2)   This section does not apply where the sheriff is deciding whether to make a child protection order in relation to a child.
(3)   The children's hearing [, pre-hearing panel] or the sheriff must, so far as practicable and taking account of the age and maturity of the child—
    (a)   give the child an opportunity to indicate whether the child wishes to express the child's views,
    (b)   if the child wishes to do so, give the child an opportunity to express them, and
    (c)   have regard to any views expressed by the child.
(4)   Without prejudice to the generality of subsection (3), a child who is aged 12 or over is presumed to be of sufficient age and maturity to form a view for the purposes of that subsection.
(5)   In this section 'coming to a decision about a matter relating to a child', in relation to a children's hearing [, pre-hearing panel], includes—
    (a)   providing advice by virtue of section 50,
    (b)   preparing a report under section 141(2).

28   Children's hearing: pre-condition for making certain orders and warrants
(1)   Subsection (2) applies where a children's hearing is—
    (a)   considering whether to make a compulsory supervision order,
    (b)   considering whether to vary or continue a compulsory supervision order,
    (c)   considering whether to make an interim compulsory supervision order,
    (d)   considering whether to make an interim variation of a compulsory supervision order,

(e)   considering whether to make a medical examination order, or
(f)   considering whether to grant a warrant to secure attendance.
(2)   The children's hearing may make, vary or continue the order or interim variation or grant the warrant, only if the children's hearing considers that it would be better for the child if the order, interim variation or warrant were in force than not.

29   Sheriff: pre-condition for making certain orders and warrants

(1)   Subsection (2) applies where—
(a)   the sheriff is considering making a child assessment order,
(b)   the sheriff is considering making or varying a child protection order,
(c)   by virtue of section 156(1)(b) or (2)(b), the sheriff is considering—
(i)   varying or continuing a compulsory supervision order,
(ii)   making or varying an interim compulsory supervision order or an interim variation of a compulsory supervision order,
(iii)   varying a medical examination order, or
(iv)   granting a warrant to secure attendance,
(d)   the sheriff is otherwise considering—
(i)   making an interim compulsory supervision order or an interim variation of a compulsory supervision order, or
(ii)   granting a warrant to secure attendance, or
(e)   the sheriff is considering extending or varying an interim compulsory supervision order under section 98 or 99.
(2)   The sheriff may make, vary, continue or extend the order or interim variation or grant the warrant, only if the sheriff considers that it would be better for the child if the order, interim variation or warrant were in force than not.

[29A   Duty to consider including contact direction

(1)   A children's hearing must, when making, varying or continuing a compulsory supervision order in relation to a child, consider whether to include in the order a measure of the type mentioned in section 83(2)(g).
(2)   A sheriff must, when varying or continuing a compulsory supervision order in relation to a child, consider whether to include in the order a measure of the type mentioned in section 83(2)(g).]
[(3)   In considering whether to include a measure of the type mentioned in section 83(2)(g), the children's hearing or, as the case may be, the sheriff must in particular consider the inclusion of a measure regulating contact between the child and any person mentioned in subsection (4) with whom the child does not reside.
(4)   The persons referred to in subsection (3) are—
(a)   a relevant person in relation to the child,
(b)   a sibling of the child,
(c)   any other person with whom the child has resided and with whom the child has an ongoing relationship with the character of a relationship between siblings.
(5)   For the purposes of subsection (4), two people are siblings if they have at least one parent in common.]

30   Children's hearing: duty to consider appointing safeguarder

(1)   A children's hearing must consider whether to appoint a person to safeguard the interests of the child to whom the children's hearing relates (a 'safeguarder').
(2)   A children's hearing may appoint a safeguarder at any time when the children's hearing is still deciding matters in relation to the child.
(3)   A children's hearing must record an appointment made under subsection (2).
(4)   If a children's hearing appoints a safeguarder, it must give reasons for its decision.

(5) Subsection (1) does not apply where a safeguarder has already been appointed.

31 Sheriff: duty to consider appointing safeguarder

(1) This section applies where—

(a) proceedings are being taken before the sheriff under Part 10 or 15 in relation to a child, and

(b) a safeguarder has not been appointed for the child in relation to proceedings under those Parts.

(2) The sheriff must consider whether to appoint a safeguarder for the child.

(3) The sheriff may appoint a safeguarder for the child.

(4) A safeguarder appointed under this section is to be treated for the purposes of this Act (other than this section [and section 33]) as having been appointed by a children's hearing by virtue of section 30.

(5) An appointment under subsection (3) must be recorded.

(6) If the sheriff appoints a safeguarder, the sheriff must give reasons for the decision.

PART 4
SAFEGUARDERS

32 The Safeguarders Panel

(1) The Scottish Ministers must establish and maintain a panel of persons (to be known as the Safeguarders Panel) from which any appointment under this Act of a safeguarder is to be made.

(2) The Scottish Ministers may by regulations make provision for or in connection with—

(a) the recruitment and selection of persons who may be appointed as members of the Safeguarders Panel,

(b) the appointment and removal of members of the Safeguarders Panel,

(c) qualifications to be held by members of the Safeguarders Panel,

(d) the training of members and potential members of the Safeguarders Panel,

(e) the payment of expenses, fees and allowances by the Scottish Ministers to members and potential members of the Safeguarders Panel,

(f) the operation and management of the Safeguarders Panel.

(3) For the purpose of complying with the requirements imposed by subsection (1) and regulations under subsection (2), the Scottish Ministers may enter into arrangements (contractual or otherwise) with any person other than CHS or SCRA.

33 Functions of safeguarder

(1) A safeguarder appointed in relation to a child by virtue of section 30 must—

(a) except where subsection (2) [or (3)] applies, on being so appointed, prepare a report setting out anything that, in the opinion of the safeguarder, is relevant to the consideration of the matter before the children's hearing,

(b) so far as reasonably practicable, attend the children's hearing, and

(c) prepare any report that the safeguarder is required to prepare by a children's hearing.

(2) This subsection applies where the children's hearing directs the Principal Reporter under section 93(2)(a) or 94(2)(a) to make an application to the sheriff.

[(3) This subsection applies where the children's hearing was arranged under section 45, 46, 50, 96, 126 or 158.]

34 Safeguarders: regulations

(1) The Scottish Ministers may by regulations make further provision about safeguarders.

(2)   Regulations under this section may in particular make provision for or in connection with—

(a)   imposing additional requirements on safeguarders,

(b)   conferring additional powers (including rights of appeal) on safeguarders,

(c)   the termination of safeguarders' appointments.

PART 5
CHILD ASSESSMENT AND CHILD PROTECTION ORDERS

Child assessment orders

35 Child assessment orders

(1)   A local authority may apply to the sheriff for a child assessment order in respect of a child.

(2)   A child assessment order is an order authorising an officer of a local authority or a person authorised by that officer to carry out (subject to section 186) an assessment of—

(a)   the child's health or development, or

(b)   the way in which the child has been or is being treated or neglected.

(3)   An order may—

(a)   require any person in a position to do so to produce the child to the officer,

(b)   for the purpose of carrying out the assessment, authorise the taking of the child to any place and the keeping of the child at that place or any other place for a period specified in the order,

(c)   where it contains an authorisation of the type mentioned in paragraph (b), include directions about contact between the child and any other person.

(4)   A child assessment order must specify the period during which it has effect.

(5)   That period must—

(a)   begin no later than 24 hours after the order is granted, and

(b)   not exceed 3 days.

36 Consideration by sheriff

(1)   This section applies where an application for a child assessment order in respect of a child is made by a local authority.

(2)   The sheriff may make the order if the sheriff is satisfied that—

(a)   the local authority has reasonable cause to suspect—

(i)   that the child has been or is being treated in such a way that the child is suffering or is likely to suffer significant harm, or

(ii)   that the child has been or is being neglected and as a result of the neglect the child is suffering or is likely to suffer significant harm,

(b)   an assessment of the kind mentioned in section 35(2) is necessary in order to establish whether there is reasonable cause to believe that the child has been or is being so treated or neglected, and

(c)   it is unlikely that the assessment could be carried out, or carried out satisfactorily, unless the order was made.

(3)   The sheriff may, instead of making a child assessment order, make a child protection order if the sheriff considers the conditions in section 38(2) are satisfied.

Child protection orders

37 Child protection orders

(1)   A person may apply to the sheriff for a child protection order in respect of a child.

(2)   A child protection order is an order doing one or more of the following—

(a)   requiring any person in a position to do so to produce the child to a specified person.

(b)   authorising the removal of the child by the specified person to a place of safety and the keeping of the child in that place,

(c)   authorising the prevention of the removal of the child from any place where the child is staying (whether or not the child is resident there),

(d)   authorising the carrying out (subject to section 186) of an assessment of—
(i)   the child's health or development, or
(ii)   the way in which the child has been or is being treated or neglected.

(3)   A child protection order may also include any other authorisation or requirement necessary to safeguard or promote the welfare of the child.

(4)   A child protection order may include an authorisation of the type mentioned in paragraph (d) of subsection (2) only if it also includes an authorisation of a type mentioned in paragraph (b) or (c) of that subsection.

(5)   An application for a child protection order must—
(a)   identify the applicant,
(b)   in so far as is practicable, identify the child in respect of whom the order is sought,
(c)   state the grounds on which the application is made, and
(d)   be accompanied by supporting evidence, whether documentary or otherwise, sufficient to enable the sheriff to determine the application.

(6)   In subsection (2), 'specified' means specified in the order.

Consideration of application by sheriff

38   Consideration by sheriff: application by local authority only

(1)   This section applies where an application for a child protection order in respect of a child is made by a local authority.

(2)   The sheriff may make the order if the sheriff is satisfied that—
(a)   the local authority has reasonable grounds to suspect that—
(i)   the child has been or is being treated in such a way that the child is suffering or is likely to suffer significant harm,
(ii)   the child has been or is being neglected and as a result of the neglect the child is suffering or is likely to suffer significant harm, or
(iii)   the child will be treated or neglected in such a way that is likely to cause significant harm to the child,
(b)   the local authority is making enquiries to allow it to decide whether to take action to safeguard the welfare of the child, or is causing those enquiries to be made,
(c)   those enquiries are being frustrated by access to the child being unreasonably denied, and
(d)   the local authority has reasonable cause to believe that access is required as a matter of urgency.

39   Consideration by sheriff: application by local authority or other person

(1)   This section applies where an application for a child protection order in respect of a child is made by a local authority or other person.

(2)   The sheriff may make the order if the sheriff is satisfied that—
(a)   there are reasonable grounds to believe that—
(i)   the child has been or is being treated in such a way that the child is suffering or is likely to suffer significant harm,
(ii)   the child has been or is being neglected and as a result of the neglect the child is suffering or is likely to suffer significant harm,
(iii)   the child is likely to suffer significant harm if the child is not removed to and kept in a place of safety, or
(iv)   the child is likely to suffer significant harm if the child does not remain

in the place at which the child is staying (whether or not the child is resident there), and

(b)   the order is necessary to protect the child from that harm or from further harm.

Ancillary measures

40   Information non-disclosure directions

(1)   This section applies where the sheriff makes a child protection order in respect of a child.

(2)   The sheriff must consider whether to include an information non-disclosure direction in the order.

(3)   An information non-disclosure direction is a direction that—

(a)   the location of any place of safety at which the child is being kept, and

(b)   any other information specified in the direction relating to the child,

must not be disclosed (directly or indirectly) to any person or class of person specified in the direction.

(4)   An information non-disclosure direction ceases to have effect when—

(a)   it is terminated by a children's hearing under section 47(1)(a)(ii) or the sheriff under section 51(5)(b), or

(b)   the child protection order in which it is included ceases to have effect.

41   Contact directions

(1)   This section applies where the sheriff makes a child protection order in respect of a child.

(2)   The sheriff must consider whether to include a contact direction in the order.

(3)   A contact direction is a direction—

(a)   prohibiting contact between the child and a person mentioned in subsection (4),

(b)   making contact between the child and such a person subject to any conditions which the sheriff considers appropriate to safeguard and promote the welfare of the child,

(c)   making such other provision as the sheriff considers appropriate about contact between the child and such a person.

(4)   The persons are—

(a)   a parent of the child, person with parental responsibilities for the child or other person specified in the direction,

(b)   a person falling within a class of person specified in the direction.

(5)   A contact direction ceases to have effect when—

(a)   it is terminated by a children's hearing under section 47(1)(a)(ii) or the sheriff under section 51(5)(b), or

(b)   the child protection order in which it is included ceases to have effect.

42   Parental responsibilities and rights directions

(1)   A person applying to the sheriff for a child protection order in respect of a child may, at the same time, apply to the sheriff for a parental responsibilities and rights direction.

(2)   A parental responsibilities and rights direction is a direction about the fulfilment of parental responsibilities or exercise of parental rights in relation to—

(a)   the treatment of the child arising out of any assessment authorised by the child protection order, or

(b)   any other matter that the sheriff considers appropriate.

(3)   A parental responsibilities and rights direction ceases to have effect when—

(a)   it is terminated by a children's hearing under section 47(1)(a)(ii) or the sheriff under section 51(5)(b), or

(b)   the child protection order in which it is included ceases to have effect.

Notice of order

43 Notice of child protection order

(1) As soon as practicable after the making of a child protection order, the applicant must give notice to—

    (a) the person specified in the order under section 37(2)(a) (unless the person is the applicant),

    (b) the child in respect of whom it is made,

    (c) each relevant person in relation to the child,

    (d) the relevant local authority for the child (unless the local authority is the applicant),

    (e) the Principal Reporter,

    (f) any other person to whom the applicant is required to give notice under rules of court.

(2) Where the Principal Reporter receives notice under subsection (1)(e), the Principal Reporter must give notice of the making of the order to any person (other than a relevant person in relation to the child) who the Principal Reporter considers to have (or to recently have had) a significant involvement in the upbringing of the child.

Obligations of local authority

44 Obligations of local authority

(1) This section applies where, by virtue of a child protection order, a child is removed to a place of safety provided by a local authority.

(2) Subject to the child protection order, the local authority has the same duties towards the child as the local authority would have by virtue of section 17 of the 1995 Act if the child were looked after by the local authority.

Review by children's hearing of certain orders

45 Review by children's hearing where child in place of safety

(1) This section applies where—

    (a) a child protection order is in force in respect of a child,

    (b) the child has been taken to a place of safety by virtue of the order, and

    (c) the Principal Reporter has not received notice under section 49 of an application to the sheriff to terminate or vary the order.

(2) The Principal Reporter must arrange a children's hearing.

(3) The Principal Reporter must arrange for the children's hearing to take place on the second working day after the day on which the child is taken to the place of safety.

46 Review by children's hearing where order prevents removal of child

(1) This section applies where—

    (a) a child protection order is in force in respect of a child,

    (b) the order authorises the prevention of the removal of the child from a place, and

    (c) the Principal Reporter has not received notice under section 49 of an application to the sheriff to terminate or vary the order.

(2) The Principal Reporter must arrange a children's hearing.

(3) The Principal Reporter must arrange for the children's hearing to take place on the second working day after the day on which the child protection order is made.

Decision of children's hearing

47 Decision of children's hearing

(1) A children's hearing arranged under section 45 or 46 may—

    (a) if it is satisfied that the conditions for making the order are met—

(i)   continue the order, or

(ii)   continue and vary the order (including by terminating, varying or including an information non-disclosure direction, a contact direction or a
parental responsibilities and rights direction), or

(b)   if it is not satisfied that those conditions are met, terminate the order.

(2)   In subsection (1), the 'conditions for making the order' are—

(a)   where the order was made under section 38, the matters mentioned in
subsection (2)(a) to (d) of that section,

(b)   where the order was made under section 39, the matters mentioned in
subsection (2)(a) and (b) of that section.

Variation or termination of order by sheriff

48   Application for variation or termination

(1)   An application may be made by any of the following persons to the sheriff
to vary a child protection order—

(a)   the child in respect of whom the order is made,

(b)   a relevant person in relation to the child,

(c)   a person not falling within paragraph (b) who has (or recently had) a
significant involvement in the upbringing of the child,

(d)   the person who applied for the child protection order,

(e)   the person specified in the child protection order under section 37(2)(a),

(f)   the Principal Reporter,

(g)   any other person prescribed by rules of court.

(2)   An application may be made by any of the persons mentioned in subsection (1)(a) to (g) (other than the Principal Reporter) to the sheriff to terminate a
child protection order.

(3)   An application under this section may be made only—

(a)   before the commencement of a children's hearing arranged under section
45 or 46, or

(b)   if the children's hearing arranged under section 45 or 46 continues the
child protection order (with or without variation), within 2 working days after
the day on which the child protection order is continued.

49   Notice of application for variation or termination

A person applying under section 48 for variation or termination must, as soon as
practicable after making the application, give notice of it to—

(a)   the person who applied for the child protection order (unless the person
is the applicant),

(b)   the person specified in the child protection order under section 37(2)(a)
(unless the person is the applicant),

(c)   the child (unless the child is the applicant),

(d)   each relevant person in relation to the child (unless the relevant person is
the applicant),

(e)   the relevant local authority for the child (unless the local authority is the
applicant),

(f)   the Principal Reporter (unless the Principal Reporter is the applicant),
and

(g)   any other person to whom the applicant is required to give notice under
rules of court.

50   Children's hearing to provide advice to sheriff in relation to application

The Principal Reporter may arrange a children's hearing for the purpose of providing any advice the children's hearing may consider appropriate to assist the
sheriff in the determination of an application under section 48.

51 Determination by sheriff

(1) This section applies where an application is made under section 48 in relation to a child protection order.

(2) The sheriff must, before determining the application, give the following persons an opportunity to make representations—

(a) the applicant,

(b) the child in respect of whom the child protection order is made,

(c) each relevant person in relation to the child,

(d) any person not falling within paragraph (c) who the sheriff considers to have (or to recently have had) a significant involvement in the upbringing of the child,

(e) the applicant for the child protection order,

(f) the relevant local authority for the child (if the authority did not apply for the child protection order),

(g) the Principal Reporter.

(3) The application must be determined within 3 working days after the day on which it is made.

(4) The child protection order ceases to have effect at the end of that period if the application is not determined within that period.

(5) The sheriff may—

(a) terminate the child protection order if the sheriff is not satisfied of—

(i) where the order was made under section 38, the matters mentioned in subsection (2)(a) to (d) of that section, or

(ii) where the order was made under section 39, the matters mentioned in subsection (2)(a) and (b) of that section,

(b) vary the child protection order (including by terminating, varying or including an information non-disclosure direction, a contact direction or a parental responsibilities and rights direction), or

(c) confirm the child protection order.

(6) If the sheriff orders that the child protection order is to be terminated, the order ceases to have effect at the end of the hearing before the sheriff.

Termination of order

52 Automatic termination of order

(1) This section applies where a child protection order contains an authorisation of the type mentioned in section 37(2)(b).

(2) The order ceases to have effect at the end of the period of 24 hours beginning with the making of the order if the person specified in the order under section 37(2)(a) has not attempted to implement it within that period.

(3) The order ceases to have effect at the end of the period of 6 days beginning with the making of the order if the child to whom the order relates has not been removed to a place of safety within that period.

53 Power of Principal Reporter to terminate order

(1) If the Principal Reporter is satisfied that the conditions for the making of a child protection order in respect of a child are no longer satisfied, the Principal Reporter may terminate the order by giving notice to—

(a) the person specified in the order under section 37(2)(a), or

(b) where there is no such person specified, the applicant for the order.

(2) If the Principal Reporter is satisfied that the conditions for including a relevant direction in a child protection order in respect of a child are no longer satisfied, the Principal Reporter may vary the child protection order so as to terminate the direction by giving notice to—

(a) the person specified in the order under section 37(2)(a), or

(b) where there is no such person specified, the applicant for the order.

(3) A relevant direction is—

(a)   an information non-disclosure direction,

(b)   a contact direction,

(c)   a parental responsibilities and rights direction.

(4)   The Principal Reporter may not terminate or vary the order if—

(a)   a children's hearing arranged under section 45 or 46 has commenced, or

(b)   proceedings before the sheriff in relation to an application under section 48 have commenced.

(5)   Where the Principal Reporter terminates or varies a child protection order under subsection (1), the Principal Reporter must notify the sheriff who granted the order.

54   Termination of order after maximum of 8 working days

A child protection order in respect of a child ceases to have effect on the earliest of—

(a)   the beginning of a children's hearing arranged under section 69 in relation to the child,

(b)   the person specified in the order under section 37(2)(a) or, where there is no such person specified, the applicant for the order receiving notice under section 68(3) that the question of whether a compulsory supervision order should be made in respect of the child will not be referred to a children's hearing,

(c)   where the order contains an authorisation of the type mentioned in section 37(2)(b), the end of the period of 8 working days beginning on the day [after the day on which] the child was removed to a place of safety, or

(d)   where the order does not contain such an authorisation, the end of the period of 8 working days beginning on the day [after the day on which] the order was made.

Other emergency measures

55   Application to justice of the peace

(1)   A person may apply to a justice of the peace for an order in respect of a child—

(a)   requiring any person in a position to do so to produce the child to a specified person,

(b)   authorising the removal of the child by the specified person to a place of safety and the keeping of the child in that place,

(c)   authorising the prevention of the removal of the child from any place where the child is staying.

(2)   A justice of the peace may make an order under this section if—

(a)   the justice of the peace is satisfied of—

(i)   in a case where the applicant for the order is a local authority, the matters mentioned in section 38(2)(a) to (d), or

(ii)   in a case where the applicant for the order is a local authority or any other person, the matters mentioned in section 39(2)(a) and (b), and

(b)   the justice of the peace is satisfied that it is not practicable in the circumstances for an application for a child protection order to be made to or considered by the sheriff.

(3)   As soon as practicable after the making of the order, the applicant must inform—

(a)   the Principal Reporter,

(b)   the person specified in the order under subsection (1)(a) (unless the person is the applicant).

(4)   The order ceases to have effect at the end of the period of 12 hours beginning with the making of the order if—

(a)   where the order authorises the removal of the child to a place of safety, the child has not been taken, or is not being taken, to that place within that period,

(b)   where the order authorises the prevention of the removal of the child from a place where the child is staying, arrangements have not been made within that period to prevent that removal.

(5)   Otherwise, the order ceases to have effect on the earlier of—

(a)   the end of the period of 24 hours beginning with the making of the order, or

(b)   the determination by the sheriff of an application to the sheriff for a child protection order in respect of the child.

(6)   The Principal Reporter may, by giving notice to the applicant, terminate the order if—

(a)   the Principal Reporter is satisfied that the conditions for the making of an order under this section are no longer satisfied, or

(b)   the Principal Reporter is satisfied that it is no longer in the best interests of the child for the order to continue to have effect.

(7)   In subsection (1), 'specified' means specified in the order.

56   Constable's power to remove child to place of safety

(1)   A constable may remove a child to a place of safety and keep the child there if—

(a)   the constable is satisfied—

(i)   of the matters mentioned in section 39(2)(a), and

(ii)   that the removal of the child is necessary to protect the child from the harm mentioned there or from further harm, and

(b)   it is not practicable in the circumstances for an application for a child protection order to be made to or considered by the sheriff.

(2)   As soon as practicable after a constable removes a child under this section, the constable must inform the Principal Reporter.

(3)   The child may not be kept in a place of safety under this section for a period of more than 24 hours.

(4)   The child may not be kept in a place of safety under this section if—

(a)   a child protection order is in force in respect of the child, or

(b)   an application has been made to the sheriff for a child protection order or to a justice of the peace for an order under section 55 on the basis of the facts before the constable and that application has been refused.

(5)   The Principal Reporter may, by giving notice to the constable, require the constable to release the child if—

(a)   the Principal Reporter is satisfied that the conditions for placing the child in a place of safety under this section are no longer satisfied, or

(b)   the Principal Reporter is satisfied that it is no longer in the best interests of the child to be kept in a place of safety.

57   Sections 55 and 56: regulations

(1)   The Scottish Ministers may by regulations make further provision in respect of a child removed to or kept in a place of safety—

(a)   under an order under section 55.

(b)   under section 56.

(2)   In particular, the regulations may require notice to be given to a person specified in the regulations of—

(a)   the removal of the child to the place of safety,

(b)   the location of the place of safety,

(c)   an order under section 55 ceasing to have effect by virtue of subsection (4) or (5) of that section.

Implementation of orders: welfare of child

58   Implementation of orders: welfare of child

(1)   An applicant for (and any other person specified in) an order mentioned in

subsection (2) may only take such steps to implement the order as the applicant (or other person) reasonably believes are necessary to safeguard or promote the welfare of the child.

(2)   The orders are—

(a)   a child assessment order,

(b)   a child protection order,

(c)   an order under section 55.

Offences

59   Offences

(1)   A person who intentionally obstructs—

(a)   a person acting under a child assessment order,

(b)   a person acting under a child protection order,

(c)   a person acting under an order under section 55, or

(d)   a constable acting under section 56(1),

commits an offence

(2)   A person guilty of an offence under subsection (1) is liable on summary conviction to a fine not exceeding level 3 on the standard scale.

PART 6

INVESTIGATION AND REFERRAL TO CHILDREN'S HEARING

Provision of information to Principal Reporter

60   Local authority's duty to provide information to Principal Reporter

(1)   If a local authority considers that it is likely that subsection (2) applies in relation to a child in its area, it must make all necessary inquiries into the child's circumstances.

(2)   This subsection applies where the local authority considers—

(a)   that the child is in need of protection, guidance, treatment or control, and

(b)   that it might be necessary for a compulsory supervision order to be made in relation to the child.

(3)   Where subsection (2) applies in relation to a child the local authority must give any information that it has about the child to the Principal Reporter.

61   Constable's duty to provide information to Principal Reporter

(1)   This section applies where a constable considers—

(a)   that a child is in need of protection, guidance, treatment or control, and

(b)   that it might be necessary for a compulsory supervision order to be made in relation to the child.

(2)   The constable must give the Principal Reporter all relevant information which the constable has been able to discover in relation to the child.

(3)   If the constable makes a report under [section 20(1)(d) of the Police and Fire Reform (Scotland) Act 2012] in relation to the child, the constable must also make the report to the Principal Reporter.

62   Provision of information by court

(1)   This section applies where, in the course of relevant proceedings, a court considers that a section 67 ground (other than the ground mentioned in section 67(2)(j)) might apply in relation to a child.

(2)   The court may refer the matter to the Principal Reporter.

(3)   If the court refers the matter under subsection (2) it must give the Principal Reporter a section 62 statement.

(4)   A section 62 statement is a statement—

(a)   specifying which of the section 67 grounds the court considers might apply in relation to the child,

(b)   setting out the reasons why the court considers that the ground might apply, and

(c)   setting out any other information about the child which appears to the court to be relevant.

(5)   In this section 'relevant proceedings' means—

(a)   an action for divorce,

(b)   an action for separation,

(c)   an action for declarator of marriage,

(d)   an action for declarator of nullity of marriage,

(e)   an action for dissolution of a civil partnership,

(f)   an action for separation of civil partners,

(g)   an action for declarator of nullity of a civil partnership,

(h)   an action for declarator of parentage,

(i)   an action for declarator of non-parentage,

(j)   proceedings relating to parental responsibilities or parental rights,

(k)   an application for an adoption order (as defined in section 28(1) of the Adoption and Children (Scotland) Act 2007),

(l)   an application for the making, variation or revocation of a permanence order (as defined in section 80(2) of the Adoption and Children (Scotland) Act 2007) in respect of a child who is not subject to a compulsory supervision order, [. . .]

(m)   proceedings relating to an offence under any of the following sections of the Education (Scotland) Act 1980—

(i)   section 35 (failure by parent to secure regular attendance by child at a public school),

(ii)   section 41 (failure to comply with attendance order),

(iii)   section 42(3) (failure to permit examination of child),

[(n)   an application for the making, variation, recall or extension of—

(i)   a forced marriage protection order (as defined in section 1(6) of the Forced Marriage etc (Protection and Jurisdiction) (Scotland) Act 2011 (asp 15)), or

(ii)   an interim forced marriage protection order (as defined in section 5(2) of that Act),

(o)   civil proceedings in which a court makes an order such as is mentioned in sub-paragraph (i) or (ii) of paragraph (n) by virtue of section 4(1) of that Act (power to make order without application), or

(p)   proceedings relating to an offence under section 9(1) of that Act (offence of breaching order).]

63   Provision of evidence from certain criminal cases

(1)   The Lord Advocate may direct that in any specified case or class of case evidence lawfully obtained in the investigation of a crime or suspected crime must be given to the Principal Reporter.

(2)   The evidence must in that case, or in a case of that class, be given to the Principal Reporter even if the Principal Reporter has not made a request under section 172.

64   Provision of information by other persons

(1)   This section applies where a person considers—

(a)   that a child is in need of protection, guidance, treatment or control, and

(b)   that it might be necessary for a compulsory supervision order to be made in relation to the child.

(2)   The person may give the Principal Reporter all relevant information which the person has in relation to the child.

65   Provision of information by constable: child in place of safety

[(1)   Subsection (2) applies when the Principal Reporter is informed under

subsection (2) of section 53 of the Criminal Justice (Scotland) Act 2016 that a child
is being kept in a place of safety under subsection (3) of that section.]
  (2) The Principal Reporter may direct—
    (a) that the child be released from the place of safety, or
    (b) that the child continue to be kept [in a] place of safety until the Principal
Reporter makes a determination under section 66(2).

Investigation and determination by Principal Reporter

66 Investigation and determination by Principal Reporter
  (1) This section applies where—
    (a) the Principal Reporter receives in relation to a child—
      (i) notice under section 43 of the making of a child protection order,
      (ii) information from a local authority under section 60,
      (iii) information or a report from a constable under section 61,
      (iv) a section 62 statement,
      (v) evidence under section 63,
      (vi) information from a person under section 64,
    [(vii) information [under section 53 of the Criminal Justice (Scotland) Act
2016]], or
    [(viii) a reference from a court under section 48(1) of the Criminal Pro-
cedure (Scotland) Act 1995,]
    (b) it appears to the Principal Reporter that a child might be in need of pro-
tection, guidance, treatment or control.
  (2) The Principal Reporter must determine—
    (a) whether the Principal Reporter considers that a section 67 ground applies
in relation to the child, and
    (b) if so, whether the Principal Reporter considers that it is necessary for a
compulsory supervision order to be made in respect of the child.
  [(2A) In a case where a certificate is supplied under section 48(1) of the Criminal Procedure (Scotland) Act 1995, the Principal Reporter is deemed to have determined under subsection (2)(a) that the Principal Reporter considers that a section
67 ground applies in relation to the child.]
  (3) The Principal Reporter may make any further investigations relating to the
child that the Principal Reporter considers necessary.
  (4) The Principal Reporter may require a local authority to give the Principal
Reporter a report on—
    (a) the child generally,
    (b) any particular matter relating to the child specified by the Principal
Reporter.
  (5) A local authority may include in a report given to the Principal Reporter
under subsection (4) information given to the local authority by another person.
  (6) The report may contain information in addition to any information given to
the Principal Reporter under section 60.

67 Meaning of 'section 67 ground'
  (1) In this Act 'section 67 ground', in relation to a child, means any of the
grounds mentioned in subsection (2).
  (2) The grounds are that—
    (a) the child is likely to suffer unnecessarily, or the health or development of
the child is likely to be seriously impaired, due to a lack of parental care,
    (b) a schedule 1 offence has been committed in respect of the child,
    (c) the child has, or is likely to have, a close connection with a person who
has committed a schedule 1 offence,
    (d) the child is, or is likely to become, a member of the same household as a
child in respect of whom a schedule 1 offence has been committed,

(e)   the child is being, or is likely to be, exposed to persons whose conduct is (or has been) such that it is likely that—

(i)   the child will be abused or harmed, or

(ii)   the child's health, safety or development will be seriously adversely affected,

(f)   the child has, or is likely to have, a close connection with a person who has carried out domestic abuse,

(g)   the child has, or is likely to have, a close connection with a person who has committed an offence under Part 1, 4 or 5 of the Sexual Offences (Scotland) Act 2009,

(h)   the child is being provided with accommodation by a local authority under section 25 of the 1995 Act and special measures are needed to support the child,

(i)   a permanence order is in force in respect of the child and special measures are needed to support the child,

(j)   the child has committed an offence,

(k)   the child has misused alcohol,

(l)   the child has misused a drug (whether or not a controlled drug),

(m)   the child's conduct has had, or is likely to have, a serious adverse effect on the health, safety or development of the child or another person,

(n)   the child is beyond the control of a relevant person,

(o)   the child has failed without reasonable excuse to attend regularly at school,

(p)   the child—

(i)   [has been, is being] or is likely to be, subjected to physical, emotional or other pressure to enter into a [. . .] civil partnership, or

(ii)   is, or is likely to become, a member of the same household as such a child,

[(q)   the child—

(i)   has been, is being or is likely to be forced into a marriage (that expression being construed in accordance with section 1 of the Forced Marriage etc (Protection and Jurisdiction) (Scotland) Act 2011 (asp 15)) or,

(ii)   is, or is likely to become, a member of the same household as such a child.]

(3)   For the purposes of paragraphs (c), (f) and (g) of subsection (2), a child is to be taken to have a close connection with a person if—

(a)   the child is a member of the same household as the person, or

(b)   the child is not a member of the same household as the person but the child has significant contact with the person.

(4)   The Scottish Ministers may by order—

(a)   amend subsection (2) by—

(i)   adding a ground,

(ii)   removing a ground for the time being mentioned in it, or

(iii)   amending a ground for the time being mentioned in it, and

(b)   make such other amendments of this section as appear to the Scottish Ministers to be necessary or expedient in consequence of provision made under paragraph (a).

(5)   An order under subsection (4) is subject to the affirmative procedure.

(6)   In this section—

'controlled drug' means a controlled drug as defined in section 2(1)(a) of the Misuse of Drugs Act 1971,

'permanence order' has the meaning given by section 80(2) of the Adoption and Children (Scotland) Act 2007,

'schedule 1 offence' means an offence mentioned in Schedule 1 to the Criminal

Procedure (Scotland) Act 1995 (offences against children under 17 years of age to which special provisions apply).

68   Determination under section 66: no referral to children's hearing

(1)   This section applies where, having made a determination under section 66(2) in relation to a child, the Principal Reporter considers that—

(a)   none of the section 67 grounds applies in relation to the child, or

(b)   it is not necessary for a compulsory supervision order to be made in respect of the child.

(2)   If the child is being kept in a place of safety under section 65(2)(b) the Principal Reporter must direct that the child be released from the place of safety.

(3)   The Principal Reporter—

(a)   must inform the persons mentioned in subsection (4) of the determination and the fact that the question of whether a compulsory supervision order should be made in respect of the child will not be referred to a children's hearing, and

(b)   may, if the Principal Reporter considers it appropriate, inform any other person of the determination and that fact.

[(3A)   The Principal Reporter may not, under subsection (3)(b), provide information to a person who is entitled to request that information under section 179A(3).]

(4)   Those persons are—

(a)   the child,

(b)   each relevant person in relation to the child,

(c)   the relevant local authority for the child,

(d)   any person specified in a child protection order in force in relation to the child under section 37(2)(a),

(e)   any person who has given the Principal Reporter—

(i)   notice under section 43 of a child protection order,

(ii)   information under section 60, 61, 64 or 66,

(iii)   a report under section 61 or 66,

(iv)   a section 62 statement,

(v)   evidence under section 63, or

(vi)   information under [section 53 of the Criminal Justice (Scotland) Act 2016].

(5)   The Principal Reporter may refer the child to—

(a)   the relevant local authority for the child with a view to the authority providing (or making arrangements for the provision by another person or body of) advice, guidance and assistance to the child and the child's family in accordance with Chapter 1 of Part 2 of the 1995 Act (support for children and their families),

(b)   such other person or body as may be specified by the Scottish Ministers by order for the purposes of this subsection, with a view to that person or body providing advice, guidance and assistance to the child and the child's family.

(6)   After complying with the requirements imposed by subsection (3)(a), the Principal Reporter must not refer the question of whether a compulsory supervision order should be made in respect of the child to a children's hearing unless the Principal Reporter receives new information about the child.

69   Determination under section 66: referral to children's hearing

(1)   This section applies where, having made a determination under section 66(2) in relation to a child, the Principal Reporter considers that it is necessary for a compulsory supervision order to be made in respect of the child.

(2)   The Principal Reporter must arrange a children's hearing for the purpose of deciding whether a compulsory supervision order should be made in respect of the child.

[(3)   If—

(a)   the determination under section 66(2) is made following the Principal

Reporter receiving information under section 53 of the Criminal Justice (Scotland) Act 2016, and

(b) at the time the determination is made the child is being kept in a place of safety,

the children's hearing must be arranged to take place no later than the third day after the Principal Reporter receives the information mentioned in paragraph (a).]

(4) If the Principal Reporter has required a local authority to give the Principal Reporter a report under section 66(4), the Principal Reporter may request additional information from the local authority.

(5) If the Principal Reporter has not required a local authority to give the Principal Reporter a report under section 66(4), the Principal Reporter must require a local authority to give the Principal Reporter a report under that section.

70 Requirement under Antisocial Behaviour etc (Scotland) Act 2004

(1) This section applies where—

(a) under section 12(1A) of the Antisocial Behaviour etc (Scotland) Act 2004 the sheriff requires the Principal Reporter to arrange a children's hearing in respect of a child, and

(b) a compulsory supervision order is not in force in relation to the child.

(2) This Act applies as if—

(a) the requirement of the sheriff were a determination of the sheriff under section 108 that the section 67 ground specified in the statement given to the Principal Reporter under section 12 of the Antisocial Behaviour etc (Scotland) Act 2004 was established in relation to the child, and

(b) the sheriff had directed the Principal Reporter under section 108(2) to arrange a children's hearing.

71 Case remitted under section 49 of Criminal Procedure (Scotland) Act 1995

(1) This section applies where under section 49 of the Criminal Procedure (Scotland) Act 1995—

(a) a court remits a case to the Principal Reporter to arrange for the disposal of the case by a children's hearing, and

(b) a compulsory supervision order is not in force in relation to the child or person whose case is remitted.

(2) A certificate signed by the clerk of the court stating that the child or person whose case is remitted has pled guilty to, or been found guilty of, the offence to which the case relates is conclusive evidence for the purposes of the children's hearing that the offence was committed by the child or person.

(3) This Act applies as if—

(a) the plea of guilty, or the finding of guilt, were a determination of the sheriff under section 108 that the ground in section 67(2)(j) was established in relation to the child, and

(b) the sheriff had directed the Principal Reporter under section 108(2) to arrange a children's hearing.

72 Child in place of safety: Principal Reporter's powers

(1) Subsection (2) applies where—

(a) the Principal Reporter is required by section 69(2) to arrange a children's hearing in relation to a child, and

(b) the child is being kept in a place of safety under section 65(2)(b).

(2) The Principal Reporter may direct—

(a) that the child be released from the place of safety, or

(b) that the child continue to be kept [in a] place of safety until the children's hearing.

PART 7
ATTENDANCE AT CHILDREN'S HEARING

73 Child's duty to attend children's hearing

(1) This section applies where by virtue of this Act a children's hearing is, or is to be, arranged in relation to a child.

(2) The child must attend the children's hearing unless the child is excused under subsection (3) or rules under section 177.

(3) A children's hearing may excuse the child from attending all or part of the children's hearing if the children's hearing is satisfied that—

(a) the hearing relates to the ground mentioned in section 67(2)(b), (c), (d) or (g) and the attendance of the child at the hearing, or that part of the hearing, is not necessary for a fair hearing,

(b) the attendance of the child at the hearing, or that part of the hearing, would place the child's physical, mental or moral welfare at risk, or

(c) taking account of the child's age and maturity, the child would not be capable of understanding what happens at the hearing or that part of the hearing.

(4) Where the children's hearing is a grounds hearing, the children's hearing may excuse the child from attending during an explanation given in compliance with section 90(1) only if it is satisfied that, taking account of the child's age and maturity, the child would not be capable of understanding the explanation.

74 Relevant person's duty to attend children's hearing

(1) This section applies where by virtue of this Act a children's hearing is, or is to be, arranged in relation to a child.

(2) Each relevant person in relation to the child who is notified of the children's hearing by virtue of rules under section 177 must attend the children's hearing unless the relevant person is—

(a) excused under subsection (3) or rules under section 177, or

(b) excluded from the children's hearing under section 76(2).

(3) A children's hearing may excuse a relevant person from attending all or part of the children's hearing if the children's hearing is satisfied that—

(a) it would be unreasonable to require the relevant person's attendance at the hearing or that part of the hearing, or

(b) the attendance of the relevant person at the hearing, or that part of the hearing, is unnecessary for the proper consideration of the matter before the hearing.

(4) A relevant person who is required to attend a children's hearing under subsection (2) and fails to do so commits an offence and is liable on summary conviction to a fine not exceeding level 3 on the standard scale.

75 Power to proceed in absence of relevant person

(1) This section applies where a relevant person in relation to a child is required by section 74(2) to attend a children's hearing and fails to do so.

(2) The children's hearing may, if it considers it appropriate to do so, proceed with the children's hearing in the relevant person's absence.

76 Power to exclude relevant person from children's hearing

(1) This section applies where a children's hearing is satisfied that the presence at the hearing of a relevant person in relation to the child—

(a) is preventing the hearing from obtaining the views of the child, or

(b) is causing, or is likely to cause, significant distress to the child.

(2) The children's hearing may exclude the relevant person from the children's hearing for as long as is necessary.

(3) After the exclusion has ended, the chairing member of the children's hearing must explain to the relevant person what has taken place in the relevant person's absence.

77 Power to exclude relevant person's representative from children's hearing

(1) This section applies where a children's hearing is satisfied that the presence at the hearing of a representative of a relevant person in relation to the child—

(a) is preventing the hearing from obtaining the views of the child, or

(b) is causing, or is likely to cause, significant distress to the child.

(2) The children's hearing may exclude the representative from the children's hearing for as long as is necessary.

(3) After the exclusion has ended, the chairing member of the children's hearing must explain to the representative what has taken place in the representative's absence.

78 Rights of certain persons to attend children's hearing

(1) The following persons have a right to attend a children's hearing—

(a) the child (whether or not the child has been excused from attending),

(b) a person representing the child,

(c) a relevant person in relation to the child (unless that person is excluded under section 76(2)),

(d) a person representing a relevant person in relation to the child (unless that person is excluded under section 77(2)),

(e) the Principal Reporter,

(f) if a safeguarder is appointed under this Act in relation to the child, the safeguarder,

(g) a member of the Administrative Justice and Tribunals Council or the Scottish Committee of that Council (acting in that person's capacity as such),

(h) a member of an area support team (acting in that person's capacity as such),

(i) subject to subsection (5), a representative of a newspaper or news agency.

(2) No other person may attend a children's hearing unless—

(a) the person's attendance at the hearing is considered by the chairing member of the children's hearing to be necessary for the proper consideration of the matter before the children's hearing,

(b) the person is otherwise granted permission to attend by the chairing member of the children's hearing, or

(c) the person is authorised or required to attend by virtue of rules under section 177.

(3) The chairing member may not grant permission to a person under subsection (2)(b) if the child or a relevant person in relation to the child objects to the person attending the children's hearing.

(4) The chairing member must take all reasonable steps to ensure that the number of persons present at a children's hearing at the same time is kept to a minimum.

(5) The children's hearing may exclude a representative of a newspaper or news agency from any part of the hearing where it is satisfied that—

(a) it is necessary to do so to obtain the views of the child, or

(b) the presence of that person is causing, or is likely to cause, significant distress to the child.

(6) Where a person is excluded under subsection (5), after the exclusion has ended, the chairing member may explain to the person, where appropriate to do so, the substance of what has taken place in the person's absence.

[(7) In this section 'children's hearing' includes a pre-hearing panel.]

PART 8

PRE-HEARING PANEL

79 Referral of certain matters for pre-hearing determination

(1) [Subsections (2) to (5) apply] where a children's hearing is to be held in relation to a child by virtue of section 69(2) or Part 9 to 11 or 13.

[(1A) Subsection (5A) applies (in addition to subsections (2) to (5)) where the children's hearing is—

(a) a subsequent children's hearing under Part 11, or

(b) held for the purposes of reviewing a compulsory supervision order.]

(2) The Principal Reporter—

(a) must refer the matter of whether a particular individual should be deemed to be a relevant person in relation to the child for determination by three members of the Children's Panel selected by the National Convener (a 'pre-hearing panel') if requested to do so by—

(i) the individual in question,

(ii) the child, or

(iii) a relevant person in relation to the child,

(b) may refer that matter for determination by a pre-hearing panel on the Principal Reporter's own initiative,

[(ba) must, if requested to do so by an individual, refer for determination by a pre-hearing panel the matter of whether the individual meets the criteria specified in rules under section 177 to be afforded the rights mentioned in subsection (5ZA) in relation to the children's hearing,

(bb) must refer for determination by a pre-hearing panel the matter of whether subsection (2) of section 132A applies to an individual if—

(i) the individual has requested a review of a compulsory supervision order under that section, and

(ii) the Principal Reporter is not satisfied that the subsection applies to the individual.]

(c) may refer a matter of a type mentioned in subsection (3) for determination by a pre-hearing panel—

(i) on the Principal Reporter's own initiative, or

(ii) following a request to the Principal Reporter from the child, a relevant person in relation to the child, or if a safeguarder has been appointed for the child, the safeguarder.

(3) Those matters are—

(a) whether the child should be excused from attending the children's hearing,

(b) whether a relevant person in relation to the child should be excused from attending the children's hearing,

(c) whether it is likely that the children's hearing will consider making a compulsory supervision order including a secure accommodation authorisation in relation to the child,

(d) a matter specified in rules under section 177(2)(a).

(4) For the purposes of subsection (3)(a), the pre-hearing panel may excuse the child from attending the children's hearing only if—

(a) the pre-hearing panel is satisfied that any of paragraphs (a) to (c) of section 73(3) applies, or

(b) the child may be excused under rules under section 177.

(5) For the purposes of subsection (3)(b), the pre-hearing panel may excuse a relevant person in relation to the child from attending the children's hearing only if—

(a) the pre-hearing panel is satisfied that section 74(3)(a) or (b) applies, or

(b) the relevant person may be excused under rules under section 177.

[(5ZA) The rights referred to in subsection (2)(ba) are the following rights, as provided for in rules under section 177 and subject to such conditions and limitations as the rules specify—

(a) the right to be notified of the hearing,

(b) the right to provide a report or other document to the hearing,

(c) the right to be provided with documents specified in the rules,

(d) authorisation to attend the hearing,

　　(e)　the right to be represented at the hearing.]
[(5A)　The Principal Reporter—
　　(a)　must refer the matter of whether an individual deemed to be a relevant person by virtue of section 81 should continue to be deemed to be a relevant person in relation to the child for determination by a pre-hearing panel if requested to do so by—
　　　　(i)　the individual so deemed,
　　　　(ii)　the child, or
　　　　(iii)　a relevant person in relation to the child,
　　(b)　may refer that matter for determination by a pre-hearing panel on the Principal Reporter's own initiative.]
　　(6)　A member of the Children's Panel selected for a pre-hearing panel may (but need not) be a member of the children's hearing.

80　Determination of matter referred under section 79

　　(1)　This section applies where the Principal Reporter refers a matter to a pre-hearing panel under section 79(2) [or (5A)].
　　(2)　The Principal Reporter must arrange a meeting of the pre-hearing panel for a date before the date fixed for the children's hearing.
　　(3)　If it is not practicable for the Principal Reporter to comply with subsection (2), the children's hearing must determine the matter referred at the beginning of the children's hearing.

81　Determination of claim that person be deemed a relevant person

　　(1)　This section applies where a matter mentioned in section 79(2)(a) (a 'relevant person claim') is referred to a meeting of a pre-hearing panel.
　　(2)　Where the relevant person claim is referred along with any other matter, the pre-hearing panel must [, unless that other matter is a matter mentioned in section 79(5A)(a),] determine the relevant person claim before determining the other matter.
　　(3)　The pre-hearing panel must deem the individual to be a relevant person if it considers that the individual has (or has recently had) a significant involvement in the upbringing of the child.
　　(4)　Where the pre-hearing panel deems the individual to be a relevant person, the individual is to be treated as a relevant person for the purposes of Parts 7 to 15, 17 and 18 in so far as they relate to—
　　(a)　the children's hearing,
　　(b)　any subsequent children's hearing under Part 11,
　　(c)　any pre-hearing panel held in connection with a children's hearing mentioned in paragraph (a), (b) or (e),
　　(d)　any compulsory supervision order, interim compulsory supervision order, medical examination order, or warrant to secure attendance made by—
　　　　(i)　a hearing mentioned in paragraph (a) or (b),
　　　　(ii)　the sheriff in any court proceedings falling within paragraph (f),
　　(e)　any children's hearing held for the purposes of reviewing a compulsory supervision order falling within paragraph (d),
　　(f)　any court proceedings held in connection with a hearing mentioned in paragraph (a), (b) or (e),
　　(g)　any court proceedings held in connection with an order or warrant falling within paragraph (d),
　　(h)　the implementation of an order or warrant falling within paragraph (d).
　　(5)　The Scottish Ministers may by order—
　　(a)　amend subsection (3),
　　(b)　in consequence of provision made under paragraph (a), make such other amendments as appear to the Scottish Ministers to be necessary or expedient to—
　　　　(i)　section 43,
　　　　(ii)　section 48,

      (iii) section 51,
      (iv) this section,
    [(iva) section 81A,]
      (v) section 142.

(6) An order under subsection (5) is subject to the affirmative procedure.

(7) Where, by virtue of section 80(3), the children's hearing is to determine the relevant person claim, references in subsections (2) to (4) (other than paragraph (c) of subsection (4)) to the pre-hearing panel are to be read as references to the children's hearing.

[81A Determination that deeming of person as relevant person to end

(1) This section applies where a matter mentioned in section 79(5A)(a) is referred to a meeting of a pre-hearing panel.

(2) Where the matter is referred along with any other matter, the pre-hearing panel must determine it before determining the other matter.

(3) The pre-hearing panel must determine that the individual is no longer to be deemed to be a relevant person if it considers that the individual does not have (and has not recently had) a significant involvement in the upbringing of the child.

(4) Where the pre-hearing panel makes a determination as described in subsection (3), section 81(4) ceases to apply in relation to the individual.

(5) Where, by virtue of section 80(3), the children's hearing is to determine a matter mentioned in section 79(5A)(a), references in subsections (2) to (4) to the pre-hearing panel are to be read as references to the children's hearing.]

[81B Determination of claim that opportunity to participate not afforded

(1) Subsection (2) applies where the Principal Reporter has referred to a meeting of a pre-hearing panel the matter of whether subsection (2) of section 132A applies to an individual, or individuals, who have requested a review of a compulsory supervision order under that section.

(2) The pre-hearing panel must discharge the children's hearing that is to be arranged as a result of the request if—

    (a) there is no reason for the children's hearing to be arranged besides the request from the individual, or individuals, in question, and

    (b) the pre-hearing panel determines—

        (i) that section 132A(2) does not apply to the individual, or

        (ii) where its application to more than one individual is in question, that it applies to none of them.]

82 Appointment of safeguarder

(1) A pre-hearing panel may appoint a safeguarder for the child to whom the children's hearing relates.

(2) A pre-hearing panel must record an appointment made under subsection (1).

(3) If a pre-hearing panel appoints a safeguarder, it must give reasons for the decision.

(4) Subsection (1) does not apply where a safeguarder has already been appointed.

(5) A safeguarder appointed under this section is to be treated for the purposes of this Act (other than this section) as being appointed by a children's hearing by virtue of section 30.

PART 9
CHILDREN'S HEARING

Key definitions

83 Meaning of 'compulsory supervision order'

(1) In this Act, 'compulsory supervision order', in relation to a child, means an order—

(a) including any of the measures mentioned in subsection (2),

(b) specifying a local authority which is to be responsible for giving effect to the measures included in the order (the 'implementation authority'), and

(c) having effect for the relevant period.

(2) The measures are—

(a) a requirement that the child reside at a specified place,

(b) a direction authorising the person who is in charge of a place specified under paragraph (a) to restrict the child's liberty to the extent that the person considers appropriate having regard to the measures included in the order,

(c) a prohibition on the disclosure (whether directly or indirectly) of a place specified under paragraph (a),

(d) a movement restriction condition,

(e) a secure accommodation authorisation,

(f) subject to section 186, a requirement that the implementation authority arrange—

(i) a specified medical or other examination of the child, or

(ii) specified medical or other treatment for the child,

(g) a direction regulating contact between the child and a specified person or class of person,

(h) a requirement that the child comply with any other specified condition,

(i) a requirement that the implementation authority carry out specified duties in relation to the child.

[. . .]

(4) A compulsory supervision order may include a movement restriction condition only if—

(a) one or more of the conditions mentioned in subsection (6) applies, and

(b) the children's hearing or, as the case may be, the sheriff is satisfied that it is necessary to include a movement restriction condition in the order.

(5) A compulsory supervision order may include a secure accommodation authorisation only if—

(a) the order contains a requirement of the type mentioned in subsection (2)(a) which requires the child to reside at—

(i) a residential establishment which contains both secure accommodation and accommodation which is not secure accommodation, or

(ii) two or more residential establishments, one of which contains accommodation which is not secure accommodation,

(b) one or more of the conditions mentioned in subsection (6) applies, and

(c) having considered the other options available (including a movement restriction condition) the children's hearing or, as the case may be, the sheriff is satisfied that it is necessary to include a secure accommodation authorisation in the order.

(6) The conditions are—

(a) that the child has previously absconded and is likely to abscond again and, if the child were to abscond, it is likely that the child's physical, mental or moral welfare would be at risk,

(b) that the child is likely to engage in self-harming conduct,

(c) that the child is likely to cause injury to another person.

(7) In subsection (1), 'relevant period' means the period beginning with the making of the order and ending with—

(a) where the order has not been continued, whichever of the following first occurs—

(i) the day one year after the day on which the order is made,

(ii) the day on which the child attains the age of 18 years,

(b) where the order has been continued, whichever of the following first occurs—

    (i)   the end of the period for which the order was last continued,

    (ii) the day on which the child attains the age of 18 years.

(8)   In subsection (2)—

'medical' includes psychological,

'specified' means specified in the order.

84 Meaning of 'movement restriction condition'

In this Act, 'movement restriction condition', in relation to a child, means—

    (a)   a restriction on the child's movements in a way specified in the movement restriction condition, and

    (b)   a requirement that the child comply with arrangements specified in the movement restriction condition for monitoring compliance with the restriction.

85 Meaning of 'secure accommodation authorisation'

In this Act, 'secure accommodation authorisation', in relation to a child, means an authorisation enabling the child to be placed and kept in secure accommodation within a residential establishment.

86 Meaning of 'interim compulsory supervision order'

(1)   In this Act 'interim compulsory supervision order', in relation to a child, means an order—

    (a)   including any of the measures mentioned in section 83(2),

    (b)   specifying a local authority which is to be responsible for giving effect to the measures included in the order ('the implementation authority'), and

    (c)   having effect for the relevant period.

(2)   An interim compulsory supervision order may, instead of specifying a place or places at which the child is to reside under section 83(2)(a), specify that the child is to reside at any place of safety away from the place where the child predominantly resides.

(3)   In subsection (1), 'relevant period' means the period beginning with the making of the order and ending with whichever of the following first occurs—

    (a)   the next children's hearing arranged in relation to the child,

    (b)   the disposal by the sheriff of an application made by virtue of section 93(2)(a) or 94(2)(a) in relation to the child,

    (c)   a day specified in the order,

    (d)   where the order has not been extended under section 98 or 99, the expiry of the period of 22 days beginning on the day on which the order is made,

    (e)   where the order has been extended (or extended and varied) under section 98 or 99, the expiry of the period of 22 days beginning on the day on which the order is extended.

(4)   Subsections (3) to (6) (except subsection (5)(a)) of section 83 apply to an interim compulsory supervision order as they apply to a compulsory supervision order.

87 Meaning of 'medical examination order'

(1)   In this Act 'medical examination order', in relation to a child, means an order authorising for the relevant period any of the measures mentioned in subsection (2).

(2)   The measures are—

    (a)   a requirement that the child attend or reside at a specified clinic, hospital or other establishment,

    (b)   subject to section 186, a requirement that a specified local authority arrange a specified medical examination of the child,

    (c)   a prohibition on the disclosure (whether directly or indirectly) of a place specified under paragraph (a),

    (d)   a secure accommodation authorisation,

    (e)   a direction regulating contact between the child and a specified person or class of person,

    (f)   any other specified condition appearing to the children's hearing to be appropriate for the purposes of ensuring that the child complies with the order.

(3) A medical examination order may include a secure accommodation authorisation only if—

(a) the order authorises the keeping of the child in a residential establishment,

(b) one of the conditions mentioned in subsection (4) applies, and

(c) having considered the other options available the children's hearing is satisfied that it is necessary to do so.

(4) The conditions are—

(a) that the child has previously absconded and is likely to abscond again and, if the child were to abscond, it is likely that the child's physical, mental or moral welfare would be at risk,

(b) that the child is likely to engage in self-harming conduct,

(c) that the child is likely to cause injury to another person.

(5) In this section—

'medical' includes psychological,

'relevant period', in relation to a medical examination order, means the period beginning with the making of the order and ending with whichever of the following first occurs—

(a) the beginning of the next children's hearing arranged in relation to the child,

(b) a day specified in the order,

(c) the expiry of the period of 22 days beginning on the day on which the order is made,

'specified' means specified in the order.

88 Meaning of 'warrant to secure attendance'

(1) In this Act, 'warrant to secure attendance', in relation to a child, means a warrant effective for the relevant period—

(a) authorising an officer of law—

(i) to search for and apprehend the child,

(ii) to take the child to, and detain the child in, a place of safety,

(iii) to bring the child before the relevant proceedings, and

(iv) so far as is necessary for the execution of the warrant, to break open shut and lockfast places,

(b) prohibiting disclosure (whether directly or indirectly) to any person specified in the warrant of the place of safety.

(2) A warrant to secure attendance may include a secure accommodation authorisation but only if—

(a) the warrant authorises the keeping of the child in a residential establishment,

(b) one or more of the conditions mentioned in subsection (3) applies, and

(c) having considered the other options available the children's hearing or sheriff is satisfied that it is necessary to do so.

(3) The conditions are—

(a) that the child has previously absconded and is likely to abscond again and, if the child were to abscond, it is likely that the child's physical, mental or moral welfare would be at risk,

(b) that the child is likely to engage in self-harming conduct,

(c) that the child is likely to cause injury to another person.

(4) In this section—

'relevant period', in relation to a warrant to secure attendance, means—

(a) where the warrant is granted by a children's hearing, the period beginning with the granting of the warrant and ending with the earlier of—

(i) the beginning of the relevant proceedings, or

(ii) the expiry of the period of 7 days beginning with the day on which the
child is first detained in pursuance of the warrant,
(b)   where the warrant is granted by the sheriff under section 103(7), the
period beginning with the granting of the warrant and ending with the earlier
of—
(i) the beginning of the continued hearing, or
(ii) the expiry of the period of 14 days beginning with the day on which
the child is first detained in pursuance of the warrant,
(c)   where the warrant is granted by the sheriff under any other provision in
respect of attendance at proceedings under Part 10, the period beginning with
the granting of the warrant and ending with the earlier of—
(i) the beginning of the relevant proceedings, or
(ii) the expiry of the period of 14 days beginning with the day on which
the child is first detained in pursuance of the warrant,
(d)   where the warrant is granted by the sheriff in respect of attendance at a
children's hearing arranged by virtue of section 108, 115, 117(2)(b) or 156(3)(a),
the period beginning with the granting of the warrant and ending with the
earlier of—
(i) the beginning of the relevant proceedings, or
(ii) the expiry of the period of 7 days beginning with the day on which the
child is first detained in pursuance of the warrant,
'relevant proceedings', in relation to a warrant to secure attendance, means the
children's hearing or, as the case may be, proceedings before the sheriff in respect
of which it is granted.

Statement of grounds

89 Principal Reporter's duty to prepare statement of grounds

(1)   This section applies where the Principal Reporter is required by virtue of
section 69(2) to arrange a children's hearing in relation to a child.
(2)   The Principal Reporter must prepare the statement of grounds.
(3)   In this Act 'statement of grounds', in relation to a child, means a statement
setting out—
(a)   which of the section 67 grounds the Principal Reporter believes applies
in relation to the child, and
(b)   the facts on which that belief is based.

Grounds hearing

90 Grounds to be put to child and relevant person

(1)   At the opening of a children's hearing arranged by virtue of section 69(2) or
95(2) (the 'grounds hearing') the chairing member must—
[(a)   explain to the child and each relevant person in relation to the child—
(i)   each section 67 ground specified in the statement of grounds, and
(ii)   the supporting facts in relation to that ground,]
(b)   ask them whether they accept that each ground applies in relation to the
child.
[(1A)   In relation to each ground that a person accepts applies in relation to the
child, the chairing member must ask the person whether the person accepts each
of the supporting facts.
(1B)   Where under subsection (1A) any person does not accept all of the supporting
facts in relation to a ground, the ground is taken for the purposes of this Act to be accepted at the grounds hearing only if the grounds hearing considers that—
(a)   the person has accepted sufficient of the supporting facts to support the
conclusion that the ground applies in relation to the child, and
(b)   it is appropriate to proceed in relation to the ground on the basis of only
those supporting facts which are accepted by the child and each relevant person.

(1C)   Where a ground is taken to be accepted for the purposes of this Act by virtue of subsection (1B), the grounds hearing must amend the statement of grounds to delete any supporting facts in relation to the ground which are not accepted by the child and each relevant person.

(1D)   In this section, 'supporting facts', in relation to a section 67 ground, means facts set out in relation to the ground by virtue of section 89(3)(b).]

(2)   This section is subject to section 94.

91   Grounds accepted: powers of grounds hearing

(1)   This section applies where—

(a)   each ground specified in the statement of grounds is accepted, or

(b)   at least one of the grounds specified in the statement of grounds is accepted and the grounds hearing considers that it is appropriate to make a decision on whether to make a compulsory supervision order on the basis of the ground or grounds that have been accepted.

(2)   If the grounds hearing considers that it is appropriate to do so, the grounds hearing may defer making a decision on whether to make a compulsory supervision order until a subsequent children's hearing.

(3)   If the grounds hearing does not exercise the power conferred by subsection (2) the grounds hearing must—

(a)   if satisfied that it is necessary to do so for the protection, guidance, treatment or control of the child, make a compulsory supervision order, or

(b)   if not so satisfied, discharge the referral.

[(3A)   *In deciding whether to exercise the power conferred by subsection (2), the grounds hearing must consider whether to require the Principal Reporter to obtain any report, from any person, which the grounds hearing considers relevant to any matter to be determined by the subsequent children's hearing.*]

(4)   In subsection (1), 'accepted' means accepted by the child and (subject to sections 74 and 75) each relevant person in relation to the child.

92   Powers of grounds hearing on deferral

(1)   This section applies where under section 91(2) the grounds hearing defers making a decision in relation to a child until a subsequent children's hearing.

(2)   If the grounds hearing considers that the nature of the child's circumstances is such that for the protection, guidance, treatment or control of the child it is necessary as a matter of urgency that an interim compulsory supervision order be made, the grounds hearing may make an interim compulsory supervision order in relation to the child.

(3)   If the grounds hearing considers that it is necessary to do so for the purpose of obtaining any further information, or carrying out any further investigation, that is needed before the subsequent children's hearing, the hearing may make a medical examination order.

93   Grounds not accepted: application to sheriff or discharge

(1)   This section applies where—

(a)   at least one of the grounds specified in the statement of grounds is accepted but the grounds hearing does not consider that it is appropriate to make a decision on whether to make a compulsory supervision order on the basis of the ground or grounds that have been accepted, or

(b)   none of the grounds specified in the statement of grounds is accepted.

(2)   The grounds hearing must—

(a)   direct the Principal Reporter to make an application to the sheriff for a determination on whether each ground that is not accepted by the child and (subject to sections 74 and 75) each relevant person in relation to the child is established, or

(b)   discharge the referral.

(3)   Subsections (4) and (5) apply if the grounds hearing gives a direction under subsection (2)(a).

(4) The chairing member must—

(a) explain the purpose of the application to the child and (subject to sections 74 and 75) each relevant person in relation to the child, and

(b) inform the child that the child is obliged to attend the hearing before the sheriff unless excused by the sheriff.

(5) If the grounds hearing considers that the nature of the child's circumstances is such that for the protection, guidance, treatment or control of the child it is necessary as a matter of urgency that an interim compulsory supervision order be made, the grounds hearing may make an interim compulsory supervision order in relation to the child.

(6) An interim compulsory supervision order made under subsection (5) may not include a measure of the kind mentioned in section 83(2)(f)(i).

(7) In subsection (1), 'accepted' means accepted by the child and (subject to sections 74 and 75) each relevant person in relation to the child.

94 Child or relevant person unable to understand grounds

(1) Subsection (2) applies where the grounds hearing is satisfied that the child or a relevant person in relation to the child—

(a) would not be capable of understanding an explanation given in compliance with section 90(1) in relation to a ground, or

(b) has not understood the explanation given in compliance with section 90(1) in relation to a ground.

(2) The grounds hearing must—

(a) direct the Principal Reporter to make an application to the sheriff to determine whether the ground is established, or

(b) discharge the referral in relation to the ground.

(3) In the case mentioned in subsection (1)(a), the chairing member need not comply with section 90(1) in relation to that ground as respects the person who would not be capable of understanding an explanation [given in compliance with section 90(1) in relation to] the ground.

(4) If the grounds hearing gives a direction under subsection (2)(a), the chairing member must—

(a) in so far as is reasonably practicable comply with the requirement in paragraph (a) of section 93(4), and

(b) comply with the requirement in paragraph (b) of that section.

(5) If the grounds hearing gives a direction under subsection (2)(a), section 93(5) applies.

95 Child fails to attend grounds hearing

(1) This section applies where—

(a) a child fails to attend a grounds hearing arranged by virtue of section 69(2) or subsection (2), and

(b) the child was not excused from attending the grounds hearing.

(2) The grounds hearing may require the Principal Reporter to arrange another grounds hearing.

[(3) Subsection (4) applies where under subsection (2) the grounds hearing requires the Principal Reporter to arrange another grounds hearing.

(4) If the grounds hearing considers that the nature of the child's circumstances is such that for the protection, guidance, treatment or control of the child it is necessary as a matter of urgency that an interim compulsory supervision order be made, the grounds hearing may make an interim compulsory supervision order in relation to the child.

(5) An interim compulsory supervision order made under subsection (4) may not include a measure of the kind mentioned in section 83(2)(f)(i).]

Children's hearing to consider need for further interim order

96 Children's hearing to consider need for further interim compulsory supervision order

(1) This section applies where—

(a) under section 93(5) a grounds hearing makes an interim compulsory supervision order in relation to a child, and

(b) the order will cease to have effect before the disposal of the application to the sheriff to which it relates.

(2) The Principal Reporter may arrange a children's hearing for the purpose of considering whether a further interim compulsory supervision order should be made in relation to the child.

(3) If the children's hearing is satisfied that the nature of the child's circumstances is such that for the protection, guidance, treatment or control of the child it is necessary that a further interim compulsory supervision order be made, the children's hearing may make a further interim compulsory supervision order in relation to the child.

(4) The children's hearing may not make a further interim compulsory supervision order in relation to the child if [it would be the third such order made under subsection (3) in consequence of the same interim compulsory supervision order made under section 93(5)].

Application of Part where compulsory supervision order in force

97 Application of Part where compulsory supervision order in force

(1) This Part has effect in relation to a child mentioned in subsection (2) with the modifications set out in subsections (3) to (6).

(2) The child is a child in relation to whom a compulsory supervision order is in force.

(3) References to a decision on whether to make a compulsory supervision order are to be read as references to a decision on whether to review the compulsory supervision order.

(4) Section 91 applies as if for subsections (2) and (3) there were substituted—

'(2) The grounds hearing is to be treated as if it were a hearing to review the compulsory supervision order (and sections 138, 139 and 142 apply accordingly).'.

(5) References to an interim compulsory supervision order are to be read as references to an interim variation of the compulsory supervision order.

(6) Section 96(4) does not apply.

PART 10
PROCEEDINGS BEFORE SHERIFF

Application for extension or variation of interim compulsory supervision order

98 Application for extension or variation of interim compulsory supervision order

(1) This section applies where—

(a) a child is subject to an interim compulsory supervision order ('the current order'), and

(b) [either—

(i) the current order is made under section 93(5) and] by virtue of section 96(4) a children's hearing would be unable to make a further interim compulsory supervision order [, or

(ii) the current order is made under section 100(2).]

(2) The Principal Reporter may, before the expiry of the current order, apply to the sheriff for an extension of the order.

(3)   The Principal Reporter may, at the same time as applying for an extension of the current order, apply to the sheriff for the order to be varied.

(4)   The current order may be extended, or extended and varied, only if the sheriff is satisfied that the nature of the child's circumstances is such that for the protection, guidance, treatment or control of the child it is necessary that the current order be extended or extended and varied.

99   Further extension or variation of interim compulsory supervision order

(1)   This section applies where an interim compulsory supervision order is—

  (a)   extended, or extended and varied, under section 98(4), or

  (b)   further extended, or further extended and varied, under subsection (4).

(2)   The Principal Reporter may, before the expiry of the order, apply to the sheriff for a further extension of the order.

(3)   The Principal Reporter may, at the same time as applying for a further extension of the order, apply to the sheriff for the order to be varied.

(4)   The sheriff may further extend, or further extend and vary, the order if the sheriff is satisfied that the nature of the child's circumstances is such that for the protection, guidance, treatment or control of the child it is necessary that the order be further extended or, as the case may be, further extended and varied.

Power to make interim compulsory supervision order

100   Sheriff's power to make interim compulsory supervision order

(1)   This section applies where—

  (a)   a child is not subject to an interim compulsory supervision order, and

  (b)   an application to the sheriff by virtue of section 93(2)(a) or 94(2)(a) in relation to the child has been made but not determined.

(2)   If the sheriff is satisfied that the nature of the child's circumstances is such that for the protection, guidance, treatment or control of the child it is necessary as a matter of urgency that an interim compulsory supervision order be made, the sheriff may make an interim compulsory supervision order in relation to the child.

Application to establish grounds

101   Hearing of application

(1)   This section applies where an application is made to the sheriff by virtue of section 93(2)(a) or 94(2)(a).

(2)   The application must be heard not later than 28 days after the day on which the application is lodged.

(3)   The application must not be heard in open court.

102   Jurisdiction and standard of proof: offence ground

(1)   This section applies where an application is to be made to the sheriff to determine whether the ground mentioned in section 67(2)(j) is established in relation to a child.

(2)   The application must be made to the sheriff who would have jurisdiction if the child were being prosecuted for the offence or offences.

(3)   The standard of proof in relation to the ground is that which applies in criminal proceedings.

(4)   It is immaterial whether the application also relates to other section 67 grounds.

103   Child's duty to attend hearing unless excused

(1)   This section applies where an application is made to the sheriff by virtue of section 93(2)(a) or 94(2)(a).

(2)   The child to whom the application relates must attend the hearing of the application unless the child is excused from doing so under subsection (3).

(3) The sheriff may excuse the child from attending all or part of the hearing of the application where—

(a) the hearing relates to the ground mentioned in section 67(2)(b), (c), (d) or (g) and the attendance of the child at the hearing, or that part of the hearing, is not necessary for a fair hearing,

(b) the attendance of the child at the hearing, or that part of the hearing, would place the child's physical, mental or moral welfare at risk, or

(c) taking account of the child's age and maturity, the child would not be capable of understanding what happens at the hearing or that part of the hearing.

(4) The child may attend the hearing of the application even if the child is excused from doing so under subsection (3).

(5) If the child is not excused from attending the hearing but the child does not attend the sheriff may grant a warrant to secure attendance in relation to the child.

(6) Subsection (7) applies if—

(a) the hearing of the application is to be continued to another day, and

(b) the sheriff is satisfied that there is reason to believe that the child will not attend on that day.

(7) The sheriff may grant a warrant to secure attendance in relation to the child.

104 Child and relevant person: representation at hearing

(1) This section applies where an application is made to the sheriff by virtue of section 93(2)(a) or 94(2)(a).

(2) The child may be represented at the hearing of the application by another person.

(3) A relevant person in relation to the child may be represented at the hearing of the application by another person.

(4) A person representing the child or relevant person at the hearing need not be a solicitor or advocate.

Ground accepted before application determined

105 Application by virtue of section 93: ground accepted before determination

(1) This section applies where—

(a) an application is made to the sheriff by virtue of section 93(2)(a) in relation to a ground, and

(b) before the application is determined, the ground is accepted by the child and each relevant person in relation to the child who is present at the hearing before the sheriff.

[(1A) The reference in subsection (1)(b) to the ground being accepted is, in relation to a ground which was not accepted by virtue of section 90(1B), a reference to all of the supporting facts in relation to the ground being accepted.]

(2) Unless the sheriff is satisfied in all the circumstances that evidence in relation to the ground should be heard, the sheriff must—

(a) dispense with hearing such evidence, and

(b) determine that the ground is established.

106 Application by virtue of section 94: ground accepted by relevant person before determination

(1) This section applies where—

(a) an application to the sheriff is made by virtue of section 94(2)(a) in relation to a ground on the basis that the child would not understand, or has not understood, an explanation given in compliance with section 90(1)(a), and

(b) before the application is determined the ground is accepted by each relevant person in relation to the child who is present at the hearing before the sheriff.

[(1A) The reference in subsection (1)(b) to the ground being accepted is, in relation to a ground which was not accepted by virtue of section 90(1B), a reference to all of the supporting facts in relation to the ground being accepted.]

(2) The sheriff may determine the application without a hearing unless—

(a) a person mentioned in subsection (3) requests that a hearing be held, or

(b) the sheriff considers that it would not be appropriate to determine the application without a hearing.

(3) The persons are—

(a) the child,

(b) a relevant person in relation to the child,

(c) if a safeguarder has been appointed, the safeguarder,

(d) the Principal Reporter.

(4) If the sheriff determines the application without a hearing, the sheriff must do so before the expiry of the period of 7 days beginning with the day on which the application is made.

Withdrawal of application: termination of orders etc

107 Withdrawal of application: termination of orders etc by Principal Reporter

(1) This section applies where—

(a) an application is made to the sheriff by virtue of section 93(2)(a) or 94(2)(a), and

(b) before the application is determined, due to a change of circumstances or information becoming available to the Principal Reporter, the Principal Reporter no longer considers that any ground to which the application relates applies in relation to the child.

(2) The Principal Reporter must withdraw the application.

(3) If one or more grounds were accepted at the grounds hearing which directed the Principal Reporter to make the application, the Principal Reporter must arrange a children's hearing to decide whether to make a compulsory supervision order in relation to the child.

(4) If none of the grounds was accepted at the grounds hearing, any interim compulsory supervision order or warrant to secure attendance which is in force in relation to the child ceases to have effect on the withdrawal of the application.

Determination of application

108 Determination: ground established

(1) This section applies where the sheriff determines an application made by virtue of section 93(2)(a) or 94(2)(a).

(2) If subsection (4) applies, the sheriff must direct the Principal Reporter to arrange a children's hearing to decide whether to make a compulsory supervision order in relation to the child.

(3) In any other case, the sheriff must—

(a) dismiss the application, and

(b) discharge the referral to the children's hearing.

(4) This subsection applies if—

(a) the sheriff determines that one or more grounds to which the application relates are established, or

(b) one or more other grounds were accepted at the grounds hearing which directed the Principal Reporter to make the application.

(5) In subsection (4)(b), 'accepted' means accepted by the child and (subject to sections 74 and 75) each relevant person in relation to the child.

109 Determination: power to make interim compulsory supervision order etc

(1)   This section applies where the sheriff directs the Principal Reporter to arrange a children's hearing to decide whether to make a compulsory supervision order in relation to the child.

(2)   Subsection (3) applies if immediately before the hearing at which the sheriff determined the application made by virtue of section 93(2)(a) or 94(2)(a) an interim compulsory supervision order was not in force in relation to the child.

(3)   If the sheriff is satisfied that the nature of the child's circumstances is such that for the protection, guidance, treatment or control of the child it is necessary as a matter of urgency that an interim compulsory supervision order be made, the sheriff may make an interim compulsory supervision order in relation to the child.

(4)   Subsection (5) applies if immediately before the hearing at which the sheriff determined the application made by virtue of section 93(2)(a) or 94(2)(a) an interim compulsory supervision order was in force in relation to the child.

(5)   If the sheriff is satisfied that the nature of the child's circumstances is such that for the protection, guidance, treatment or control of the child it is necessary that a further interim compulsory supervision order be made, the sheriff may make a further interim compulsory supervision order in relation to the child.

(6)   If the sheriff is satisfied that there is reason to believe that the child would not otherwise attend the children's hearing, the sheriff may grant a warrant to secure attendance.

(7)   If the sheriff makes an interim compulsory supervision order under subsection (3) or (5) specifying that the child is to reside at a place of safety, the children's hearing must be arranged to take place no later than the third day after the day on which the child begins to reside at the place of safety.

Review of sheriff's determination

110 Application for review of grounds determination

(1)   This section applies where the sheriff makes a determination under section 108 that a section 67 ground (other than the ground mentioned in section 67(2)(j) if the case was remitted to the Principal Reporter under section 49 of the Criminal Procedure (Scotland) Act 1995) is established in relation to a child (a 'grounds determination').

(2)   A person mentioned in subsection (3) may apply to the sheriff for a review of the grounds determination.

(3)   The persons are—

(a)   the person who is the subject of the grounds determination (even if that person is no longer a child),

(b)   a person who is, or was at the time the grounds determination was made, a relevant person in relation to the child.

111 Sheriff: review or dismissal of application

(1)   This section applies where an application is made under section 110.

(2)   If subsection (3) applies the sheriff must review the grounds determination.

(3)   This subsection applies if—

(a)   there is evidence in relation to the ground that was not considered by the sheriff when making the grounds determination,

(b)   the evidence would have been admissible,

(c)   there is a reasonable explanation for the failure to lead that evidence before the grounds determination was made, and

(d)   the evidence is significant and relevant to the question of whether the grounds determination should have been made.

(4)   If subsection (3) does not apply, the sheriff must dismiss the application.

112 Child's duty to attend review hearing unless excused

(1)   This section applies where—

(a)   a hearing is to be held by virtue of section 111(2) for the purpose of reviewing a grounds determination, and

(b)   the person who is the subject of the grounds determination is still a child.

(2)   The child must attend the hearing unless the child is excused by the sheriff on a ground mentioned in section 103(3).

(3)   The child may attend the hearing even if the child is excused under subsection (2).

(4)   If the sheriff is satisfied that there is reason to believe that the child would not otherwise attend the hearing, the sheriff may grant a warrant to secure attendance.

113   Child and relevant person: representation at review hearing

(1)   This section applies where a hearing is to be held by virtue of section 111(2) for the purpose of reviewing a grounds determination.

(2)   The person who is the subject of the grounds determination ('P') may be represented at the hearing by another person.

(3)   A relevant person in relation to P (or, where P is no longer a child, a person who was a relevant person in relation to P at the time the grounds determination was made) may be represented at the hearing by another person.

(4)   A person representing P or the relevant person (or person who was a relevant person) at the hearing need not be a solicitor or advocate.

114   Sheriff's powers on review of grounds determination

(1)   This section applies where the sheriff reviews a grounds determination by virtue of section 111(2).

(2)   If the sheriff is satisfied that the section 67 ground to which the application relates is established, the sheriff must refuse the application.

(3)   If the sheriff determines that the ground to which the application relates is not established, the sheriff must—

(a)   recall the grounds determination, and

(b)   make an order discharging (wholly or to the extent that it relates to the ground) the referral of the child to the children's hearing.

115   Recall: power to refer other grounds

(1)   This section applies where—

(a)   the sheriff makes an order under section 114(3), but

(b)   another section 67 ground specified in the same statement of grounds that gave rise to the grounds determination is accepted or established.

(2)   If the person to whom the grounds determination relates is still a child, the sheriff must direct the Principal Reporter to arrange a children's hearing for the purpose of considering whether a compulsory supervision order should be made in relation to the child.

(3)   If the sheriff is satisfied that the nature of the child's circumstances is such that for the protection, guidance, treatment or control of the child it is necessary as a matter of urgency that an interim compulsory supervision order be made, the sheriff may make an interim compulsory supervision order in relation to the child.

(4)   If the sheriff is satisfied that there is reason to believe that the child would not otherwise attend the children's hearing, the sheriff may grant a warrant to secure attendance.

[(5)   If the sheriff makes an interim compulsory supervision order under subsection (3) specifying that the child is to reside at a place of safety, the children's hearing must be arranged to take place no later than the third day after the day on which the child begins to reside at the place of safety.]

116   Recall: powers where no grounds accepted or established

(1)   This section applies where—

(a)   the sheriff makes an order under section 114(3), and

(b)   none of the other section 67 grounds specified in the statement of grounds that gave rise to the grounds determination is accepted or established.

(2)   If a compulsory supervision order that is in force in relation to the person who is the subject of the grounds determination was in force at the time of the grounds determination, the sheriff must require a review of the compulsory supervision order.

(3)   In any other case, the sheriff must—

(a)   terminate any compulsory supervision order that is in force in relation to the person who is the subject of the grounds determination, and

(b)   if that person is still a child, consider whether the child will require supervision or guidance.

(4)   Where that person is still a child and the sheriff considers that the child will require supervision or guidance, the sheriff must order the relevant local authority for the child to provide it.

(5)   Where the sheriff makes such an order, the relevant local authority for the child must give such supervision or guidance as the child will accept.

117   New section 67 ground established: sheriff to refer to children's hearing

(1)   This section applies where—

(a)   by virtue of section 110 the sheriff is reviewing a grounds determination, and

(b)   the sheriff is satisfied that there is sufficient evidence to establish a section 67 ground that is not specified in the statement of grounds that gave rise to the grounds determination.

(2)   The sheriff must—

(a)   determine that the ground is established, and

(b)   if the person to whom the grounds determination relates is still a child, direct the Principal Reporter to arrange a children's hearing for the purpose of considering whether a compulsory supervision order should be made in relation to the child.

(3)   If the sheriff is satisfied that the nature of the child's circumstances is such that for the protection, guidance, treatment or control of the child it is necessary as a matter of urgency that an interim compulsory supervision order be made, the sheriff may make an interim compulsory supervision order in relation to the child.

(4)   If the sheriff is satisfied that there is reason to believe that the child would not otherwise attend the children's hearing, the sheriff may grant a warrant to secure attendance.

[(5)   If the sheriff makes an interim compulsory supervision order under subsection (3) specifying that the child is to reside at a place of safety, the children's hearing must be arranged to take place no later than the third day after the day on which the child begins to reside at the place of safety.]

Application of Part where compulsory supervision order in force

118   Application of Part where compulsory supervision order in force

(1)   This Part has effect in relation to a child mentioned in subsection (2) with the modifications set out in subsections (3) to (5).

(2)   The child is a child in relation to whom a compulsory supervision order is in force.

(3)   References to an interim compulsory supervision order are to be read as references to an interim variation of the compulsory supervision order.

(4)   References to the sheriff directing the Principal Reporter to arrange a children's hearing to decide whether to make a compulsory supervision order in relation to the child are to be read as references to the sheriff requiring a review of the compulsory supervision order.

(5)   Sections 98 and 99 do not apply.

PART 11
SUBSEQUENT CHILDREN'S HEARINGS

119   Children's hearing following deferral or proceedings under Part 10

(1)   This section applies where a children's hearing is arranged by the Principal Reporter by virtue of section 91(2), 107(3), 108, 115(2) or 117(2)(b) or subsection (2).

(2)   If the children's hearing considers that it is appropriate to do so, the children's hearing may defer making a decision on whether to make a compulsory supervision order until a subsequent children's hearing.

(3)   If the children's hearing does not exercise the power conferred by subsection (2) the children's hearing must—

(a)   if satisfied that it is necessary to do so for the protection, guidance, treatment or control of the child, make a compulsory supervision order, or

(b)   if not so satisfied, discharge the referral.

[(3A)   *In deciding whether to exercise the power conferred by subsection (2), the grounds hearing must consider whether to require the Principal Reporter to obtain any report, from any person, which the grounds hearing considers relevant to any matter to be determined by the subsequent children's hearing.*]

(4)   Subsection (5) applies where—

(a)   the child is excused by virtue of section 73(3) or 79(3)(a) or rules under section 177, or

(b)   a relevant person in relation to the child is excused by virtue of section 74(3) or 79(3)(b) or rules under section 177.

(5)   The children's hearing may, despite the excusal, defer its decision to a subsequent children's hearing under this section without further excusing the person.

120   Powers of children's hearing on deferral under section 119

(1)   This section applies where under subsection (2) of section 119 a children's hearing defers making a decision in relation to a child until a subsequent children's hearing under that section.

(2)   Subsection (3) applies if immediately before the children's hearing which takes place under section 119 an interim compulsory supervision order was not in force in relation to the child.

(3)   If the children's hearing considers that the nature of the child's circumstances is such that for the protection, guidance, treatment or control of the child it is necessary as a matter of urgency to make an interim compulsory supervision order, the children's hearing may make an interim compulsory supervision order in relation to the child.

(4)   Subsection (5) applies if immediately before the children's hearing which takes place under section 119 an interim compulsory supervision order was in force in relation to the child.

(5)   If the children's hearing is satisfied that the nature of the child's circumstances is such that for the protection, guidance, treatment or control of the child it is necessary that a further interim compulsory supervision order be made, the children's hearing may make a further interim compulsory supervision order in relation to the child.

(6)   If the children's hearing considers that it is necessary to do so for the purpose of obtaining any further information, or carrying out any further investigation, that is needed before the subsequent children's hearing, the hearing may make a medical examination order.

PART 12
CHILDREN'S HEARINGS: GENERAL

Views of child

121 Confirmation that child given opportunity to express views before hearing

(1) This section applies where a children's hearing is held in relation to a child by virtue of this Act.

(2) The chairing member of the children's hearing must ask the child whether the documents provided to the child by virtue of rules made under section 177 accurately reflect any views expressed by the child.

(3) The chairing member need not comply with subsection (2) if, taking account of the age and maturity of the child, the chairing member considers that it would not be appropriate to do so.

Children's advocacy services

122 Children's advocacy services

(1) This section applies where a children's hearing is held in relation to a child by virtue of this Act.

(2) The chairing member of the children's hearing must inform the child of the availability of children's advocacy services.

(3) The chairing member need not comply with subsection (2) if, taking account of the age and maturity of the child, the chairing member considers that it would not be appropriate to do so.

(4) The Scottish Ministers may by regulations make provision for or in connection with—

(a) the provision of children's advocacy services,

(b) qualifications to be held by persons providing children's advocacy services,

(c) the training of persons providing children's advocacy services,

(d) the payment of expenses, fees and allowances by the Scottish Ministers to persons providing children's advocacy services.

(5) The Scottish Ministers may enter into arrangements (contractual or otherwise) with any person other than a local authority, CHS or SCRA for the provision of children's advocacy services.

(6) Regulations under this section are subject to the affirmative procedure.

(7) In this section, 'children's advocacy services' means services of support and representation provided for the purposes of assisting a child in relation to the child's involvement in a children's hearing.

Warrants to secure attendance

123 General power to grant warrant to secure attendance

(1) This section applies where in relation to a child—

(a) a children's hearing has been or is to be arranged, or

(b) a hearing is to take place under Part 10.

(2) On the application of the Principal Reporter, any children's hearing may on cause shown grant a warrant to secure the attendance of the child at the children's hearing or, as the case may be, the hearing under Part 10.

Child's age

124 Requirement to establish child's age

(1) This section applies where a children's hearing is held by virtue of this Act.

(2) The chairing member of the children's hearing must ask the person in respect of whom the hearing has been arranged to declare the person's age.

(3)   The person may make another declaration as to the person's age at any time.

(4)   The chairing member need not comply with the requirement in subsection (2) if the chairing member considers that the person would not be capable of understanding the question.

(5)   Any children's hearing may make a determination of the age of a person who is the subject of the hearing.

(6)   A person is taken for the purposes of this Act to be of the age—

(a)   worked out on the basis of the person's most recent declaration, or

(b)   if a determination of age by a children's hearing is in effect, worked out in accordance with that determination.

(7)   Nothing done by a children's hearing in relation to a person is invalidated if it is subsequently proved that the age of the person is not that worked out under subsection (6).

Compulsory supervision orders: review

125   Compulsory supervision order: requirement to review

(1)   This section applies where a children's hearing is making, varying or continuing a compulsory supervision order.

(2)   Where the order being made contains a movement restriction condition (or the order is being varied so as to include such a condition), the children's hearing must require the order to be reviewed by a children's hearing on a day or within a period specified in the order.

(3)   In any other case, the children's hearing may require the order to be so reviewed.

Contact orders and permanence orders

126   Review of contact direction

(1)   This section applies where, in relation to a child—

(a)   a children's hearing—

(i)   makes a compulsory supervision order,

(ii)   makes an interim compulsory supervision order, an interim variation of a compulsory supervision order or a medical examination order which is to have effect for more than 5 working days, or

(iii)   continues or varies a compulsory supervision order under section 138, and

(b)   the order contains (or is varied so as to contain) a measure of the type mentioned in section 83(2)(g) or 87(2)(e) ('a contact direction').

(2)   The Principal Reporter must arrange a children's hearing for the purposes of reviewing the contact direction—

(a)   if an order mentioned in subsection (3) is in force, or

(b)   if requested to do so by an individual who claims that the conditions specified for the purposes of this paragraph in an order made by the Scottish Ministers are satisfied in relation to the individual.

(3)   The orders are—

(a)   a contact order regulating contact between an individual (other than a relevant person in relation to the child) and the child, or

(b)   a permanence order which specifies arrangements for contact between such an individual and the child.

(4)   The children's hearing is to take place no later than 5 working days after the children's hearing mentioned in subsection (1)(a).

(5)   If a children's hearing arranged by virtue of paragraph (b) of subsection (2) considers that the conditions specified for the purposes of that paragraph are not satisfied in relation to the individual, the children's hearing must take no further action.

(6) In any other case, the children's hearing may—

(a) confirm the decision of the children's hearing mentioned in subsection (1)(a), or

(b) vary the compulsory supervision order, interim compulsory supervision order or medical examination order (but only by varying or removing the contact direction).

(7) Sections 73 and 74 do not apply in relation to a children's hearing arranged by virtue of subsection (2).

Referral where failure to provide education for excluded pupil

127 Referral where failure to provide education for excluded pupil

(1) This section applies where it appears to a children's hearing that—

(a) an education authority has a duty under section 14(3) of the Education (Scotland) Act 1980 (education authority's duty to provide education for child excluded from school) in relation to the child to whom the children's hearing relates, and

(b) the authority is failing to comply with the duty.

(2) The children's hearing may require the National Convener to refer the matter to the Scottish Ministers.

(3) If a requirement is made under subsection (2), the National Convener must—

(a) make a referral to the Scottish Ministers, and

(b) give a copy of it to the education authority to which it relates and the Principal Reporter.

Parenting order

128 Duty to consider applying for parenting order

(1) This section applies where a children's hearing constituted for any purpose in respect of a child is satisfied that it might be appropriate for a parenting order to be made in respect of a parent of the child under section 102 of the Antisocial Behaviour etc (Scotland) Act 2004 (the '2004 Act').

(2) The children's hearing may require the Principal Reporter to consider whether to apply under section 102(3) of the 2004 Act for such an order.

(3) The children's hearing must specify in the requirement—

(a) the parent in respect of whom it might be appropriate for the order to be made, and

(b) by reference to section 102(4) to (6) of the 2004 Act, the condition in respect of which the application might be made.

(4) In this section, 'parent' and 'child' have the meanings given by section 117 of the 2004 Act.

PART 13
REVIEW OF COMPULSORY SUPERVISION ORDER

Requirement for review

129 Requirement under Antisocial Behaviour etc (Scotland) Act 2004

(1) Subsection (2) applies where—

(a) under section 12(1A) of the Antisocial Behaviour etc (Scotland) Act 2004 the sheriff requires the Principal Reporter to arrange a children's hearing in respect of a child, and

(b) a compulsory supervision order is in force in relation to the child.

(2) The Principal Reporter must initiate a review of the compulsory supervision order.

130   Case remitted under section 49 of Criminal Procedure (Scotland) Act 1995

(1)   This section applies where, in relation to a child—

(a)   a court remits a case under section 49 of the Criminal Procedure (Scotland) Act 1995 to the Principal Reporter to arrange for the disposal of the case by a children's hearing, and

(b)   a compulsory supervision order is in force in relation to the child.

(2)   The Principal Reporter must initiate a review of the compulsory supervision order.

(3)   A certificate signed by the clerk of the court stating that the child has pled guilty to, or been found guilty of, the offence to which the case relates is conclusive evidence for the purposes of the children's hearing held for the purposes of reviewing the order that the offence was committed by the child.

(4)   This Act applies as if the plea of guilty, or the finding of guilt, were a determination of the sheriff under section 108 that the ground in section 67(2)(j) was established in relation to the child.

131   Duty of implementation authority to require review

(1)   The implementation authority must, by notice to the Principal Reporter, require a review of a compulsory supervision order in relation to a child where the authority is satisfied that one or more of the circumstances set out in subsection (2) exist.

(2)   Those circumstances are—

(a)   the compulsory supervision order ought to be terminated or varied,

(b)   the compulsory supervision order is not being complied with,

(c)   the best interests of the child would be served by the authority making one of the following applications, and the authority intends to make such an application—

(i)   an application under section 80 of the Adoption and Children (Scotland) Act 2007 (the '2007 Act') for a permanence order,

(ii)   an application under section 92 of the 2007 Act for variation of such an order,

(iii)   an application under section 93 of the 2007 Act for amendment of such an order,

(iv)   an application under section 98 of the 2007 Act for revocation of such an order,

(d)   the best interests of the child would be served by the authority placing the child for adoption and the authority intends to place the child for adoption,

(e)   the authority is aware that an application has been made and is pending, or is about to be made, under section 29 or 30 of the 2007 Act for an adoption order in respect of the child.

(3)   The Scottish Ministers may by regulations specify the period within which a requirement under subsection (1) must be made where the implementation authority is satisfied as to the existence of the circumstances mentioned in subsection (2)(a) to (d).

(4)   Different periods may be specified for different circumstances, or classes of circumstances.

(5)   Where an implementation authority is under a duty to require a review under subsection (1) by virtue of being satisfied as to the existence of the circumstances mentioned in subsection (2)(e), the authority must do so as soon as practicable after the authority becomes aware of the application.

132   [Right to require review: child, relevant person afforded opportunity to participate]

(1)   This section applies where a compulsory supervision order is in force in relation to a child.

(2)   The child may by giving notice to the Principal Reporter require a review of the order.

(3)   A relevant person in relation to the child may by giving notice to the Principal Reporter require a review of the order.

[(3A)   An individual who is entitled to do so by subsection (6) may by giving notice to the Principal Reporter require a review of the order.]

(4)   The order may not be reviewed—

(a)   during the period of 3 months beginning with the day on which the order is made,

(b)   if the order is continued or varied, during the period of 3 months beginning with the day on which it is continued or varied.

(5)   The Scottish Ministers may by regulations provide that, despite subsection (4), where the order includes a secure accommodation authorisation, the order may be reviewed during a period specified in the regulations.

[(6)   An individual is entitled to require a review under subsection (3A) if—

(a)   the Principal Reporter was satisfied at the relevant time, or

(b)   a pre-hearing panel or children's hearing determined,

that the individual met the criteria to be afforded an opportunity to participate in relation to the children's hearing that most recently made a decision in respect of the order (whether that was a decision to make, vary or continue it).

(7)   Where a children's hearing is arranged as a result (solely or partly) of an individual requiring a review under subsection (3A), the individual is to be treated as an individual whom a pre-hearing panel has determined meets the criteria to be afforded an opportunity to participate in relation to the children's hearing.

(8)   For the purposes of subsections (6) and (7)—

(a)   'the criteria to be afforded an opportunity to participate' means the criteria specified in rules under section 177 to be afforded the rights mentioned in section 79(5ZA) in relation to a children's hearing,

(b)   'the relevant time' means—

(i)   the time when the children's hearing referred to in subsection (6) began, or

(ii)   if more than one children's hearing is to be regarded as a single children's hearing by virtue of paragraph (c), the time when any one of them began,

(c)   if the children's hearing that most recently made a decision in respect of the order was a subsequent children's hearing arranged as a result of an earlier children's hearing deferring making a decision, they are to be regarded as a single children's hearing.]

[132A   Right of person not afforded opportunity to participate to require review

(1)   The Principal Reporter must initiate a review of a compulsory supervision order in relation to a child if requested to do so by an individual who claims to be an individual to whom subsection (2) applies.

(2)   This subsection applies to an individual if—

(a)   the individual did not attend the children's hearing that most recently made a decision in respect of the order (whether that was a decision to make, vary or continue it), and

(b)   either—

(i)   the conditions in subsection (3) are met, or

(ii)   the conditions in subsection (4) are met.

(3)   The conditions referred to in subsection (2)(b)(i) are—

(a)   neither a pre-hearing panel nor a children's hearing made a determination about whether the individual met the criteria to be afforded an opportunity to participate in relation to the children's hearing referred to in subsection (2)(a),

(b)   it is more likely than not that had a pre-hearing panel or children's hearing made a determination about that matter at the relevant time, it would have determined that the individual met those criteria in relation to the children's hearing, and

(c)   the individual was not afforded the rights mentioned in section 79(5ZA) in relation to the children's hearing as the Principal Reporter either did not consider whether, or was not satisfied that, the individual met those criteria in relation to the children's hearing.

(4)   The conditions referred to in subsection (2)(b)(ii) are—

(a)   the Principal Reporter was satisfied at the relevant time, or a pre-hearing panel or children's hearing determined, that the individual met the criteria to be afforded an opportunity to participate in relation to the children's hearing referred to in subsection (2)(a), and

(b)   the individual was not able to participate properly in the children's hearing's decision making as a result of—

(i)   a material failure to treat the individual, or any representative of the individual, in accordance with the rules, or

(ii)   exceptional circumstances.

(5)   For the purposes of this section—

(a)   'the criteria to be afforded an opportunity to participate' means the criteria specified in the rules to be afforded the rights mentioned in section 79(5ZA) in relation to a children's hearing,

(b)   'the relevant time' means—

(i)   the time when the children's hearing referred to in subsection (2)(a) began, or

(ii)   if more than one children's hearing is to be regarded as a single children's hearing by virtue of paragraph (d), the time when any one of them began,

(c)   'the rules' means rules under section 177,

(d)   if the children's hearing referred to in subsection (2)(a) was a subsequent children's hearing arranged as a result of an earlier children's hearing deferring making a decision, they are to be regarded as a single children's hearing.]

133   Principal Reporter's duty to initiate review
The Principal Reporter must initiate a review of a compulsory supervision order in relation to a child if—

(a)   the order will expire within 3 months, and

(b)   the order would not otherwise be reviewed before it expires.

134   Duty to initiate review if child to be taken out of Scotland
(1)   This section applies where—

(a)   a child is subject to a compulsory supervision order,

(b)   a relevant person in relation to the child proposes to take the child to live outwith Scotland, and

(c)   the proposal is not in accordance with the order or an order under section 11 of the 1995 Act.

(2)   The relevant person must give notice of the proposal to the Principal Reporter and the implementation authority at least 28 days before the day on which the relevant person proposes to take the child to live outwith Scotland.

(3)   If the Principal Reporter receives notice under subsection (2), the Principal Reporter must initiate a review of the compulsory supervision order.

135   Duty to initiate review: secure accommodation authorisation
(1)   Subsection (2) applies where a compulsory supervision order includes a secure accommodation authorisation (which has not ceased to have effect by virtue of section 151(5)).

(2)   The Principal Reporter must initiate a review of the order—

(a)   before the end of the period of 3 months beginning with the day on which the order is made, and

(b)   if the order is varied or continued, before the end of the period of 3 months beginning with the day on which it is varied or continued.

136   Duty to initiate review where child transferred

The Principal Reporter must initiate a review of a compulsory supervision order in relation to a child where the child is transferred under section 143(2).

Functions of Principal Reporter and children's hearing

137   Duty to arrange children's hearing

(1)   This section applies where a compulsory supervision order is in force in relation to a child and—
(a)   a review of the order is required or initiated by virtue of any of—
(i)   sections 107, 108, 115 and 117 (all as modified by section 118),
(ii)   sections 116, 125, 129 to 136 and 146, or
(b)   the child's case is referred to the Principal Reporter under section 96(3) or 106 of the Adoption and Children (Scotland) Act 2007.

(2)   The Principal Reporter must arrange a children's hearing to review the compulsory supervision order.

(3)   If the review is initiated under section 136, the children's hearing must be arranged to take place before the expiry of the period of 3 working days beginning with the day on which the child is transferred.

(4)   The Principal Reporter must require the implementation authority to give the Principal Reporter any reports that the authority has prepared in relation to the child and any other information which the authority may wish to give to assist the children's hearing.

(5)   The Principal Reporter may require the implementation authority to give the Principal Reporter a report on—
(a)   the child generally,
(b)   any particular matter relating to the child specified by the Principal Reporter.

(6)   The implementation authority may include in a report given to the Principal Reporter under subsection (4) or (5) information given to the authority by another person.

138   Powers of children's hearing on review

(1)   This section applies where a children's hearing is carrying out a review of a compulsory supervision order in relation to a child.

(2)   If the children's hearing considers that it is appropriate to do so, the children's hearing may defer making a decision about the compulsory supervision order until a subsequent children's hearing under this section.

(3)   Otherwise, the children's hearing may—
(a)   terminate the compulsory supervision order,
(b)   vary the compulsory supervision order,
(c)   continue the compulsory supervision order for a period not exceeding one year.

[(3A)   *In deciding whether to exercise the power conferred by subsection (2), the grounds hearing must consider whether to require the Principal Reporter to obtain any report, from any person, which the grounds hearing considers relevant to any matter to be determined by the subsequent children's hearing.*]

(4)   The children's hearing may vary or continue a compulsory supervision order only if the children's hearing is satisfied that it is necessary to do so for the protection, guidance, treatment or control of the child.

[. . .]

(6)   If the children's hearing terminates the compulsory supervision order, the children's hearing must—
(a)   consider whether supervision or guidance is needed by the child, and

(b)   if so, make a statement to that effect.

(7)   If the children's hearing states that supervision or guidance is needed by the child, it is the duty of the relevant local authority for the child to give such supervision or guidance as the child will accept.

(8)   Subsection (9) applies where—

(a)   a child or relevant person in relation to the child is excused under section 73(2), 74(2) or 79 from attending the children's hearing, and

(b)   the hearing defers its decision until a subsequent children's hearing.

(9)   The children's hearing need not excuse the child or relevant person in relation to the child from attending the subsequent children's hearing.

139   Powers of children's hearing on deferral under section 138

(1)   This section applies where under subsection (2) of section 138 a children's hearing defers making a decision about the compulsory supervision order in relation to a child until a subsequent children's hearing under that section.

(2)   The children's hearing may continue the compulsory supervision order until the subsequent children's hearing.

(3)   If the children's hearing considers that the nature of the child's circumstances is such that for the protection, guidance, treatment or control of the child it is necessary as a matter of urgency that the compulsory supervision order be varied, the children's hearing may make an interim variation of the compulsory supervision order.

140   Interim variation of compulsory supervision order

(1)   In this Act, 'interim variation', in relation to a compulsory supervision order made in relation to a child, means a variation of the order having effect for the relevant period.

(2)   An interim variation may vary the order so that, instead of specifying a place or places at which the child is to reside under section 83(2)(a), the order specifies that the child is to reside at any place of safety away from the place where the child predominantly resides.

(3)   Section 83(5)(a) does not apply to the varied order.

(4)   In subsection (1), the 'relevant period' means the period beginning with the variation of the order and ending with whichever of the following first occurs—

(a)   the next children's hearing arranged in relation to the child,

(b)   the disposal by the sheriff of [an application made by virtue of section 93(2)(a) or 94(2)(a)] relating to the child,

(c)   a day specified in the variation,

(d)   the expiry of the period of 22 days beginning with the day on which the order is varied.

141   Preparation of report in circumstances relating to permanence order or adoption

(1)   This section applies where a review of a compulsory supervision order in relation to a child is required under subsection (1) of section 131 in the circumstances mentioned in subsection (2)(c), (d) or (e) of that section.

(2)   On determining the review under section 138(3), the children's hearing must prepare a report providing advice about the circumstances to which the review relates for—

(a)   the implementation authority, and

(b)   any court that requires (or may subsequently require) to come to a decision about an application of the type mentioned in section 131(2)(c) or (e).

(3)   The report must be in such form as the Scottish Ministers may determine.

(4)   If an application of the type mentioned in section 131(2)(c) or (e) is (or has been) made, the court must have regard to the report when coming to its decision about the application.

Review of relevant person determination

142 Review of determination that person be deemed a relevant person
(1)   This section applies where, in relation to a child—
  (a)   a children's hearing determines a review of a compulsory supervision order by varying or continuing the order,
  (b)   an individual is deemed to be a relevant person by virtue of section 81, and
  (c)   it appears to the children's hearing that the individual may no longer have (nor recently have had) a significant involvement in the upbringing of the child.
[(1A)   But this section does not apply where the matter of whether the individual should continue to be deemed to be a relevant person in relation to the child—
  (a)   has been determined by a meeting of a pre-hearing panel held in relation to the children's hearing, or
  (b)   is, by virtue of section 80(3), to be determined by the children's hearing.]
(2)   The children's hearing must review whether the individual should continue to be deemed to be a relevant person in relation to the child.
(3)   If the children's hearing considers that it is appropriate to do so, the children's hearing may defer determining the review under subsection (2) until a subsequent children's hearing under this section.
(4)   Otherwise, if the children's hearing determines that the individual does not have (and has not recently had) a significant involvement in the upbringing of the child then—
  (a)   the children's hearing must direct that the individual is no longer to be deemed to be a relevant person, and
  (b)   section 81(4) ceases to apply in relation to the individual (except in relation to any appeal arising from the determination mentioned in subsection (1)(a)).

PART 14
IMPLEMENTATION OF ORDERS

Power to transfer child in cases of urgent necessity

143 Transfers in cases of urgent necessity
(1)   Subsection (2) applies where a child is residing at a particular place by virtue of a compulsory supervision order or interim compulsory supervision order containing a measure of the type mentioned in section 83(2)(a).
(2)   If it is in the interests of the child or another child in the place that the child be moved out of the place as a matter of urgent necessity then, despite the order, the chief social work officer may transfer the child to another place.

Implementation of compulsory supervision order

144 Implementation of compulsory supervision order: general duties of implementation authority
(1)   The implementation authority must give effect to a compulsory supervision order.
(2)   The implementation authority must in particular comply with any requirements imposed on it in relation to the child by the compulsory supervision order.
(3)   The duties which an implementation authority may be required to carry out under a compulsory supervision order include securing or facilitating the provision for the child of services of a kind which the implementation authority does not provide.

145 Duty where order requires child to reside in certain place

(1) Subsection (2) applies where, under a compulsory supervision order, a child is required to reside—

(a) in accommodation provided by the parents or relatives of the child, or by any person associated with them or the child, or

(b) in any other accommodation not provided by a local authority.

(2) The implementation authority must from time to time—

(a) investigate whether, while the child is resident in that accommodation, any conditions imposed under the compulsory supervision order are being complied with, and

(b) if the authority considers that conditions are not being complied with, take such steps as the authority considers reasonable.

146 Breach of duties imposed by sections 144 and 145

(1) This section applies where, on determining the review of a compulsory supervision order under section 138(3), it appears to the children's hearing that the implementation authority is in breach of a duty in relation to the child imposed on the authority under section 144 or 145.

(2) The children's hearing may direct the National Convener to give the authority notice in accordance with subsection (3) of an intended application by the National Convener to enforce the authority's duty.

(3) The notice must—

(a) set out the respects in which the authority is in breach of its duty in relation to the child, and

(b) state that if the authority does not perform that duty before the expiry of the period of 21 days beginning with the day on which the notice is given, the National Convener, on the direction of the children's hearing, is to make an application to enforce the authority's duty.

(4) The National Convener must, at the same time as giving the notice, send a copy of the notice to—

(a) the child,

(b) each relevant person in relation to the child.

(5) If a children's hearing gives a direction under subsection (2), the children's hearing must require that a further review of the compulsory supervision order take place on or as soon as is reasonably practicable after the expiry of the period of 28 days beginning on the day on which the notice is given.

(6) If, on that further review, it appears to the children's hearing carrying out the further review that the authority continues to be in breach of its duty, the children's hearing may direct the National Convener to make an application under section 147.

(7) In determining whether to direct the National Convener to make an application under section 147 to enforce the authority's duty, the children's hearing must not take into account any factor relating to the adequacy of the means available to the authority to enable it to comply with the duty.

147 Application for order

(1) The National Convener must, if directed to do so under section 146(6), apply to the relevant sheriff principal for an order to enforce an implementation authority's duty in relation to a child.

(2) The relevant sheriff principal is the sheriff principal of the sheriffdom in which the principal office of the implementation authority is situated.

(3) The National Convener may not make such an application, despite the direction given under section 146(6), unless—

(a) the National Convener has given the authority notice in relation to the duty in compliance with a direction given under section 146(2), and

(b) the authority has failed to carry out the duty within the period specified in the notice.

(4)   The application is to be made by summary application.

148   Order for enforcement
(1)   The sheriff principal may, on an application by the National Convener under section 147, make an order requiring the implementation authority that is in breach of a duty imposed by virtue of a compulsory supervision order to carry out that duty.
(2)   Such an order is final.

Compulsory supervision orders etc: further provision

149   Compulsory supervision orders etc: further provision
(1)   The Scottish Ministers may by regulations make provision about—
   (a)   the transmission of information relating to a child who is the subject of an order or warrant mentioned in subsection (2) to any person who, by virtue of the order or warrant, has or is to have control over the child,
   (b)   the provision of temporary accommodation for the child,
   (c)   the taking of the child to any place in which the child is required to reside under the order or warrant,
   (d)   the taking of the child to—
      (i)   a place of safety under section 169 or 170,
      (ii)   a place to which the child falls to be taken to under section 169(2), or
      (iii)   a person to whom the child falls to be taken to under section 170(2).
(2)   The orders and warrants are—
   (a)   a compulsory supervision order,
   (b)   an interim compulsory supervision order,
   (c)   a medical examination order,
   (d)   a warrant to secure attendance.

Movement restriction conditions: regulations etc

150   Movement restriction conditions: regulations etc
(1)   The Scottish Ministers may by regulations prescribe—
   (a)   restrictions, or
   (b)   monitoring arrangements,
that may be imposed as part of a movement restriction condition.
(2)   Regulations under subsection (1) may in particular—
   (a)   prescribe the maximum period for which a restriction may have effect,
   (b)   prescribe methods of monitoring compliance with a movement restriction condition,
   (c)   specify devices that may be used for the purpose of that monitoring,
   (d)   prescribe the person or class of person who may be designated to carry out the monitoring, and
   (e)   require that the condition be varied to designate another person if the person designated ceases to be prescribed, or fall within a class of person, prescribed under paragraph (d).
(3)   Regulations under subsection (1) are subject to the affirmative procedure.
(4)   The Scottish Ministers may—
   (a)   make arrangements (contractual or otherwise) to secure the services of such persons as they think fit to carry out monitoring, and
   (b)   make those arrangements in a way that provides differently for different areas or different forms of monitoring.
(5)   Nothing in any enactment or rule of law prevents the disclosure to a person providing a service under an arrangement made under subsection (4) of information relating to a child where the disclosure is made for the purposes only of the full and proper provision of monitoring.

Secure accommodation

151   Implementation of secure accommodation authorisation

(1)   Subsections (3) and (4) apply where a relevant order or warrant made in relation to a child includes a secure accommodation authorisation.

(2)   A relevant order or warrant is—

  (a)   a compulsory supervision order,
  (b)   an interim compulsory supervision order,
  (c)   a medical examination order,
  (d)   a warrant to secure attendance.

(3)   The chief social work officer may implement the authorisation only with the consent of the person in charge of the residential establishment containing the secure accommodation in which the child is to be placed (the 'head of unit').

(4)   The chief social work officer must remove the child from secure accommodation if—

  (a)   the chief social work officer considers it unnecessary for the child to be kept there, or
  (b)   the chief social work officer is required to do so by virtue of regulations made under subsection (6).

(5)   A secure accommodation authorisation ceases to have effect once the child is removed from secure accommodation under subsection (4).

(6)   The Scottish Ministers may by regulations make provision in relation to decisions—

  (a)   by the chief social work officer—
    (i)   whether to implement a secure accommodation authorisation,
    (ii)   whether to remove a child from secure accommodation,
  (b)   by the head of unit whether to consent under subsection (3).

(7)   Regulations under subsection (6) may in particular—

  (a)   specify—
    (i)   the time within which a decision must be made,
    (ii)   the procedure to be followed,
    (iii)   the criteria to be applied,
    (iv)   matters to be taken into account or disregarded,
    (v)   persons who must be consulted,
    (vi)   persons who must consent before a decision has effect,
  (b)   make provision about—
    (i)   notification of decisions,
    (ii)   the giving of reasons for decisions,
    (iii)   reviews of decisions,
    (iv)   the review of the order or warrant containing the secure accommodation authorisation where the head of unit does not consent.

(8)   Regulations under subsection (6) are subject to the affirmative procedure.

152   Secure accommodation: placement in other circumstances

(1)   The Scottish Ministers may by regulations make provision specifying circumstances in which a child falling within subsection (3) may be placed in secure accommodation.

(2)   Regulations under subsection (1) may in particular include provision for and in connection with—

  (a)   the procedure to be followed in deciding whether to place a child in secure accommodation,
  (b)   the notification of decisions,
  (c)   the giving of reasons for decisions,
  (d)   the review of decisions,
  (e)   the review of placements by a children's hearing.

(3)   A child falls within this subsection if—

  (a)   a relevant order or warrant is in force in relation to the child, and

(b)   the relevant order or warrant does not include a secure accommodation authorisation.

(4)   A relevant order or warrant is—

(a)   a compulsory supervision order,

(b)   an interim compulsory supervision order,

(c)   a medical examination order,

(d)   a warrant to secure attendance.

(5)   Regulations under subsection (1) are subject to the affirmative procedure.

153   Secure accommodation: regulations

(1)   The Scottish Ministers may by regulations make provision about children placed in secure accommodation by virtue of this Act.

(2)   Regulations under subsection (1) may in particular include provision—

(a)   imposing requirements on the Principal Reporter,

(b)   imposing requirements on the implementation authority in relation to a compulsory supervision order or an interim compulsory supervision order,

(c)   imposing requirements on the relevant local authority for a child in relation to a medical examination order or a warrant to secure attendance,

(d)   in connection with the protection of the welfare of the children.

(3)   Regulations under subsection (1) are subject to the affirmative procedure.

PART 15
APPEALS

Appeal against decision of children's hearing

154   Appeal to sheriff against decision of children's hearing

(1)   A person mentioned in subsection (2) may appeal to the sheriff against a relevant decision of a children's hearing in relation to a child.

(2)   The persons are—

(a)   the child,

(b)   a relevant person in relation to the child,

(c)   a safeguarder appointed in relation to the child by virtue of section 30.

(3)   A relevant decision is—

(a)   a decision to make, vary or continue a compulsory supervision order,

(b)   a decision to discharge a referral by the Principal Reporter,

(c)   a decision to terminate a compulsory supervision order,

(d)   a decision to make an interim compulsory supervision order,

(e)   a decision to make an interim variation of a compulsory supervision order,

(f)   a decision to make a medical examination order, or

(g)   a decision to grant a warrant to secure attendance.

(4)   An appeal under subsection (1) may be made jointly by two or more persons mentioned in subsection (2).

(5)   An appeal under subsection (1) must be made before the expiry of the period of 21 days beginning with the day on which the decision is made.

155   Procedure

(1)   This section applies where an appeal under section 154 is made.

(2)   The Principal Reporter must lodge with the sheriff clerk a copy of—

(a)   the decision, and the reasons for the decision, of the children's hearing,

(b)   all information provided by virtue of rules under section 177 to the children's hearing, and

(c)   the report of the children's hearing.

(3)   The appeal must not be heard in open court.

(4) The sheriff may (but need not) hear evidence before determining the appeal.

(5) The sheriff may hear evidence from—

(a)   the child,

(b)   a relevant person in relation to the child,

(c)   an author or compiler of a report or statement provided to the children's hearing that made the decision,

(d)   the Principal Reporter,

(e)   where the appeal is against a decision to make, grant, vary or continue an order or warrant including a secure accommodation authorisation in respect of the child—

(i) the person in charge of the secure accommodation specified in the secure accommodation authorisation, and

(ii) the chief social work officer, and

(f)   any other person who the sheriff considers may give material additional evidence.

(6) The sheriff may require any person to give a report to the sheriff for the purpose of assisting the sheriff in determining the appeal.

(7) Subsection (6) applies in relation to a safeguarder only if regulations under [section 34] so provide.

156 Determination of appeal

(1) If satisfied that the decision to which an appeal under section 154 relates is justified, the sheriff—

(a)   must confirm the decision, and

(b)   may take one or more of the steps mentioned in subsection (3) if satisfied that the circumstances of the child in relation to whom the decision was made have changed since the decision was made.

(2) In any other case, the sheriff—

(a)   must—

(i) where the decision is a decision to grant a warrant to secure attendance, recall the warrant,

(ii) where the decision is a decision to make an interim compulsory supervision order or a medical examination order, terminate the order,

(b)   may take one or more of the steps mentioned in subsection (3).

(3) Those steps are—

(a)   require the Principal Reporter to arrange a children's hearing for any purpose for which a hearing can be arranged under this Act,

(b)   continue, vary or terminate any order, interim variation or warrant which is in effect,

(c)   discharge the child from any further hearing or other proceedings in relation to the grounds that gave rise to the decision,

(d)   make an interim compulsory supervision order or interim variation of a compulsory supervision order, or

(e)   grant a warrant to secure attendance.

[(3A) If the sheriff continues or varies a compulsory supervision order under subsection (3)(b), the sheriff—

(a)   must, if the order contains a movement restriction condition (or is being varied so as to include such a condition), require the order to be reviewed by a children's hearing on a day or within a period specified in the order,

(b)   may, in any other case, require the order to be so reviewed.]

(4) If the sheriff discharges a child under subsection (3)(c), the sheriff must also terminate any order or warrant which is in effect in relation to the child.

(5) The fact that a sheriff makes, continues or varies an order, or grants a warrant, under subsection (1)(b) or (2)(b) does not prevent a children's hearing from continuing, varying or terminating the order or warrant.

157 Time limit for disposal of appeal against certain decisions
   (1)   This section applies where an appeal under section 154 relates to a decision of a children's hearing to—
      (a)   make a compulsory supervision order including a secure accommodation authorisation or movement restriction condition,
      (b)   make an interim compulsory supervision order,
      (c)   make an interim variation of a compulsory supervision order,
      (d)   make a medical examination order, or
      (e)   grant a warrant to secure attendance.
   (2)   The appeal must be heard and disposed of before the expiry of the period of 3 days beginning the day after the day on which the appeal is made.
   (3)   If the appeal is not disposed of within that period, the authorisation, condition, order, variation or, as the case may be, warrant ceases to have effect.

Compulsory supervision order: suspension pending appeal

158 Compulsory supervision order: suspension pending appeal
   (1)   This section applies where—
      (a)   an appeal is made under section 154 against a decision to make, vary, continue or terminate a compulsory supervision order, and
      (b)   the person making the appeal requests the Principal Reporter to arrange a children's hearing to consider whether the decision should be suspended pending the determination of the appeal.
   (2)   As soon as practicable after the request is made, the Principal Reporter must arrange a children's hearing to consider whether the decision should be suspended pending the determination of the appeal.

Frivolous and vexatious appeals

159 Frivolous and vexatious appeals
   (1)   This section applies where the sheriff—
      (a)   determines an appeal under section 154 [or 161] by confirming a decision of a children's hearing to vary or continue a compulsory supervision order, and
      (b)   is satisfied that the appeal was frivolous or vexatious.
   (2)   The sheriff may order that, during the period of 12 months beginning on the day of the order, the person who appealed must obtain leave from the sheriff before making another appeal under section 154 [or 161] against a decision of a children's hearing in relation to the compulsory supervision order.

Other appeals

160 Appeal to sheriff against relevant person determination
   (1)   A person mentioned in subsection (2) may appeal to the sheriff against—
      [(a)   a determination of a pre-hearing panel or children's hearing that an individual—
         (i)   is or is not to be deemed a relevant person in relation to a child,
         (ii)   is to continue to be deemed, or is no longer to be deemed, a relevant person in relation to a child.]
      (b)   a determination of a review under section 142(2) that an individual is to continue to be deemed, or no longer to be deemed, a relevant person in relation to a child.
   (2)   The persons are—
      (a)   the individual in question,
      (b)   the child,
      (c)   a relevant person in relation to the child,
      (d)   two or more persons mentioned in paragraphs (a) to (c) acting jointly.

(3) If satisfied that the determination to which the appeal relates is justified, the sheriff must confirm the determination.

(4) If not satisfied, the sheriff must—
  (a)   quash the determination, and
  [(b)   where the determination is of one of the following kinds, make an order deeming the individual to be a relevant person in relation to the child—
      (i)   a determination of a pre-hearing panel or children's hearing under section 81 that the individual is not to be deemed a relevant person in relation to the child,
      (ii)   a determination of a pre-hearing panel or children's hearing under section 81A that the person is no longer to be deemed a relevant person in relation to the child.]

(5) Where the sheriff makes an order under subsection (4)(b), section 81(4) applies to the individual as if a pre-hearing panel had deemed the individual to be a relevant person.

(6) An appeal under this section must be—
  (a)   made before the expiry of the period of 7 days beginning with the day on which the determination is made,
  (b)   heard and disposed of before the expiry of the period of 3 days beginning with the day on which the appeal is made.

161 Appeal to sheriff against decision affecting contact or permanence order

(1) A person mentioned in subsection (2) may appeal to the sheriff against a relevant decision of a children's hearing in relation to a child.

(2) The person is an individual (other than a relevant person in relation to the child) in relation to whom—
  (a)   a contact order is in force regulating contact between the individual and the child,
  (b)   a permanence order is in force which specifies arrangements for contact between the individual and the child, or
  (c)   the conditions specified for the purposes of section 126(2)(b) are satisfied.

(3) A relevant decision is a decision under section 126(6) relating to a compulsory supervision order.

(4) If the sheriff is satisfied that the relevant decision is justified, the sheriff must confirm the decision.

(5) If not satisfied, the sheriff must vary the compulsory supervision order by varying or removing the measure contained in the order under section 83(2)(g).

(6) An appeal under this section must be—
  (a)   made before the expiry of the period of 21 days beginning with the day on which the relevant decision is made,
  (b)   heard and disposed of before the expiry of the period of 3 days beginning with the day on which the appeal is made.

162 Appeal to sheriff against decision to implement secure accommodation authorisation

(1) This section applies where a relevant order or warrant made in relation to a child includes a secure accommodation authorisation.

(2) A relevant order or warrant is—
  (a)   a compulsory supervision order,
  (b)   an interim compulsory supervision order,
  (c)   a medical examination order,
  (d)   a warrant to secure attendance.

(3) The child or a relevant person in relation to the child may appeal to the sheriff against a relevant decision in relation to the authorisation.

(4) A relevant decision is a decision by the chief social work officer—
  (a)   to implement the authorisation,
  (b)   not to implement the authorisation,

    (c)   to remove the child from secure accommodation.

(5) An appeal under subsection (3) may be made jointly by—

    (a)   the child and one or more relevant persons in relation to the child, or

    (b)   two or more relevant persons in relation to the child.

(6) An appeal must not be held in open court.

(7) The Scottish Ministers may by regulations make further provision about appeals under subsection (3).

(8) Regulations under subsection (7) may in particular—

    (a)   specify the period within which an appeal may be made,

    (b)   make provision about the hearing of evidence during an appeal,

    (c)   make provision about the powers of the sheriff on determining an appeal,

    (d)   provide for appeals to the [Sheriff Appeal Court] and Court of Session against the determination of an appeal.

(9) Regulations under subsection (7) are subject to the affirmative procedure.

Appeals to sheriff principal and Court of Session

163 Appeals to sheriff principal and Court of Session: children's hearings etc

(1) A person mentioned in subsection (3) may appeal by stated case to the sheriff principal or the Court of Session against—

    (a)   a determination by the sheriff of—

        (i)   an application to determine whether a section 67 ground (other than the ground mentioned in section 67(2)(j) if the case was remitted to the Principal Reporter under section 49 of the Criminal Procedure (Scotland) Act 1995) is established,

        (ii)   an application under section 110(2) for review of a finding that a section 67 ground is established,

        (iii)   an appeal against a decision of a children's hearing,

        (iv)   an application under section 98 for an extension of an interim compulsory supervision order,

        (v)   an application under section 99 for a further extension of an interim compulsory supervision order,

    (b)   a decision of the sheriff under section 100 to—

        (i)   make an interim compulsory supervision order,

        (ii)   make an interim variation of a compulsory supervision order.

(2) A person mentioned in subsection (3) may, with leave of the sheriff principal, appeal by stated case to the Court of Session against the sheriff principal's decision in an appeal under subsection (1).

(3) The persons are—

    (a)   the child,

    (b)   a relevant person in relation to the child,

    (c)   a safeguarder appointed in relation to the child by virtue of section 30,

    (d)   two or more persons mentioned in paragraphs (a) to (c) acting jointly, and

    (e)   the Principal Reporter.

(4) Despite subsections (1) and (2), a safeguarder may not—

    (a)   appeal against a determination by the sheriff of a type mentioned in subsection (1)(a)(i) or (ii), or a decision of the sheriff of a type mentioned in subsection (1)(b),

    (b)   appeal to the Court of Session against the sheriff principal's decision in such an appeal.

(5) Despite subsection (1), the Principal Reporter may not appeal against a determination by the sheriff confirming a decision of a children's hearing.

(6) Subsection (7) applies in relation to—

    (a)   an appeal against a determination by the sheriff of an application under section 110(2) for review of a finding that a section 67 ground is established,

(b)   an appeal to the Court of Session against the sheriff principal's decision in such an appeal.

(7)   In subsection (3)(a) and (b)—

(a)   the references to the child are to the person in relation to whom the section 67 ground was established (even if that person is no longer a child),

(b)   the reference to a relevant person in relation to the child includes a person who was, at the time the section 67 ground was established, a relevant person in relation to the child.

(8)   An appeal under this section must be made before the expiry of the period of 28 days beginning with the day on which the determination or decision appealed against was made.

(9)   An appeal under this section may be made—

(a)   on a point of law, or

(b)   in respect of any procedural irregularity.

(10)   On deciding an appeal under subsection (1), the sheriff principal or the Court of Session must remit the case to the sheriff for disposal in accordance with such directions as the court may give.

(11)   A decision in an appeal under subsection (1) or (2) by the Court of Session is final.

(12)   In subsection (1)(a)(ii), the reference to a determination by the sheriff of an application under section 110(2) for review of a finding that a section 67 ground is established includes a reference to a determination under section 117(2)(a) that a ground is established.

164   Appeals to sheriff principal and Court of Session: relevant persons

(1)   A person mentioned in subsection (3) may appeal by stated case to the sheriff principal or the Court of Session against a decision of the sheriff in an appeal against [—

(a)   a decision of the sheriff in an appeal against a determination of a pre-hearing panel or children's hearing that an individual—

(i)   is or is not to be deemed a relevant person in relation to a child,

(ii)   is to continue to be deemed, or is no longer to be deemed, a relevant person in relation to a child,

(b)   a decision of the sheriff in an appeal against a determination of a review under section 142(2) that an individual is to continue to be deemed, or is no longer to be deemed, a relevant person in relation to a child.]

(2)   A person mentioned in subsection (3) may, with leave of the sheriff principal, appeal by stated case to the Court of Session against the sheriff principal's decision in an appeal under subsection (1).

(3)   The persons are—

(a)   the individual in question,

(b)   the child,

(c)   a relevant person in relation to the child,

(d)   two or more persons mentioned in paragraphs (a) to (c) acting jointly.

[(e)   the Principal Reporter.]

[(3A)   Despite subsection (1), the Principal Reporter may not appeal against a decision by the sheriff confirming a determination of a children's hearing.]

(4)   An appeal under this section must be made before the expiry of the period of 28 days beginning with the day on which the decision appealed against is made.

(5)   An appeal under this section may be made—

(a)   on a point of law, or

(b)   in respect of any procedural irregularity.

(6)   On deciding an appeal under subsection (1), the sheriff principal or the Court of Session must remit the case to the sheriff for disposal in accordance with such directions as the court may give.

(7)   A decision in an appeal under subsection (1) or (2) by the Court of Session is final.

165   Appeals to sheriff principal and Court of Session: contact and permanence orders

(1)   A person mentioned in subsection (3) may appeal by stated case to the sheriff principal or the Court of Session against a decision of the sheriff in an appeal under section 161.

(2)   A person mentioned in subsection (3) may, with leave of the sheriff principal, appeal by stated case to the Court of Session against the sheriff principal's decision in an appeal under subsection (1).

(3)   The person is an individual (other than a relevant person in relation to the child) in relation to whom—

    (a)   a contact order is in force regulating contact between the individual and the child,

    (b)   a permanence order is in force which specifies arrangements for contact between the individual and the child, or

    (c)   the conditions specified for the purposes of section 126(2)(b) are satisfied.

(4)   An appeal under this section must be made before the expiry of the period of 28 days beginning with the day on which the decision appealed against was made.

(5)   An appeal under this section may be made—

    (a)   on a point of law,

    (b)   in respect of any procedural irregularity.

(6)   On deciding an appeal under subsection (1), the sheriff principal or the Court of Session must remit the case to the sheriff for disposal in accordance with such directions as the court may give.

(7)   A decision in an appeal under subsection (1) or (2) by the Court of Session is final.

Requirement imposed on local authority: review and appeal

166   Review of requirement imposed on local authority

(1)   This section applies where a duty is imposed on a local authority by virtue of—

    (a)   a compulsory supervision order,

    (b)   an interim compulsory supervision order, or

    (c)   a medical examination order.

(2)   If the local authority is satisfied that it is not the relevant local authority for the child in respect of whom the duty is imposed, the local authority may apply to the sheriff for a review of the decision or determination to impose the duty on it.

(3)   The sheriff may review the decision or determination to impose the duty with or without hearing evidence.

(4)   The sheriff may hear evidence from—

    (a)   any local authority,

    (b)   the National Convener,

    (c)   the child in respect of whom the duty is imposed,

    (d)   a person representing that child,

    (e)   a relevant person in relation to that child,

    (f)   a person representing that person.

(5)   Where the duty is imposed on the local authority by a children's hearing, the sheriff may require the Principal Reporter to lodge with the sheriff clerk a copy of the decision (and reasons) of the children's hearing.

(6)   The sheriff must determine which local authority is the relevant local authority for the child.

(7)   Where the local authority that made the application under subsection (2) is

the relevant local authority for the child, the sheriff must confirm the decision of the children's hearing or the determination of the sheriff.

(8)   Where another local authority is the relevant local authority for the child, the sheriff—

(a)   must vary the order which imposed the duty so that the duty falls on that local authority, and

(b)   may make an order for that local authority to reimburse such sums as the sheriff may determine to the local authority which made the application under subsection (2) for any costs incurred in relation to the duty.

167   Appeals to sheriff principal: section 166

(1)   A local authority may appeal by stated case to the sheriff principal against—

(a)   the determination by the sheriff under section 166(6) of which local authority is the relevant local authority for a child,

(b)   the making of an order by the sheriff under section 166(8)(b).

(2)   A person mentioned in subsection (3) may appeal by stated case to the sheriff principal against the determination by the sheriff under section 166(6) of which local authority is the relevant local authority for a child.

(3)   The persons are—

(a)   the child to whom the determination relates,

(b)   a person representing that child,

(c)   a relevant person in relation to that child,

(d)   a person representing that person.

(4)   An appeal under this section must be made before the expiry of the period of 28 days beginning with the day on which the determination or, as the case may be, order was made.

(5)   An appeal under this section may be made—

(a)   on a point of law, or

(b)   in respect of any procedural irregularity.

(6)   On determining an appeal under this section, the sheriff principal must remit the case to the sheriff for disposal in accordance with such directions as the court may give.

(7)   A determination of an appeal under this section is final.

PART 16
ENFORCEMENT OF ORDERS

168   Enforcement of orders

(1)   Subsection (2) applies where a relevant order authorising the keeping of a child in a particular place (an 'authorised place') is in force in relation to a child.

(2)   An officer of law may enforce the order—

(a)   by searching for and apprehending the child,

(b)   by taking the child to the authorised place,

(c)   where—

(i)   it is not reasonably practicable to take the child immediately to the authorised place,

[. . .], and

(d)   so far as is necessary, by breaking open shut and lockfast places.

(3)   In this section, 'relevant order' means—

(a)   a child assessment order,

(b)   a child protection order,

(c)   an order under section 55,

(d)   a compulsory supervision order,

(e)   an interim compulsory supervision order,

(f)   a medical examination order.

169 Child absconding from place

(1)   This section applies where—

    (a)   a child requires to be kept in a particular place by virtue of—

        (i)   a child assessment order,

        (ii)   a child protection order,

        (iii)   an order under section 55,

        (iv)   section 56,

        (v)   section 65,

        (vi)   a compulsory supervision order,

        (vii)   an interim compulsory supervision order,

        (viii)   a medical examination order,

        (ix)   a warrant to secure attendance, or

        (x)   section 143, and

    (b)   the child absconds from that place or, at the end of a period of leave, fails to return to that place.

(2)   The child may be [. . .] taken to that place.

(3)   If a court is satisfied that there are reasonable grounds for believing that the child is within premises, the court may grant a warrant authorising an officer of law to—

    (a)   enter premises, and

    (b)   search for the child.

(4)   The court may authorise the officer of law to use reasonable force for those purposes.

(5)   Where the child is returned to the place mentioned in subsection (1), but the occupier of that place is unwilling or unable to receive the child—

    (a)   the officer of law returning the child must immediately notify the Principal Reporter of that fact, and

    (b)   the child must be kept in a place of safety until the occurrence of the relevant event.

(6)   In subsection (5), the relevant event is—

    (a)   in the case mentioned in sub-paragraph (i) of subsection (1)(a), the end of the period specified in the child assessment order,

    (b)   in the case mentioned in sub-paragraph (ii) of that subsection, whichever of the following first occurs—

        (i)   the children's hearing arranged under section 45 or 69,

        (ii)   the termination of the child protection order,

    (c)   in the case mentioned in sub-paragraph (iii) of that subsection, whichever of the following first occurs—

        (i)   the order ceasing to have effect under section 55(4) or (5),

        (ii)   the determination by the sheriff of an application for a child protection order in respect of the child,

    (d)   in the case mentioned in sub-paragraph (iv) of that subsection, whichever of the following first occurs—

        (i)   the giving of notice under subsection (5) of section 56, or

        (ii)   the end of the period mentioned in subsection (3) of that section,

    (e)   in the case mentioned in sub-paragraph (v) of that subsection, whichever of the following first occurs—

        (i)   the giving of a direction by the Principal Reporter under section 68(2) or 72(2)(a), or

        (ii)   the children's hearing arranged by virtue of section 69(2),

    (f)   in the case mentioned in sub-paragraph (vi) of that subsection, the children's hearing arranged by virtue of section 131(2)(b),

    (g)   in the cases mentioned in sub-paragraphs (vii) and (ix) of that subsection whichever of the following first occurs—

        (i)   the next children's hearing that has been arranged in relation to the child,

(ii)   the next hearing before the sheriff relating to the child that is to take place by virtue of this Act,

(h)   in the cases mentioned in sub-paragraphs (viii) and (x) of that subsection, the next children's hearing that has been arranged in relation to the child.

170   Child absconding from person

(1)   This section applies where—

(a)   a person has (or is authorised to have) control of a child by virtue of—

(i)   a child assessment order,

(ii)   a child protection order,

(iii)   an order under section 55,

(iv)   section 56,

(v)   section 65,

(vi)   a compulsory supervision order,

(vii)   an interim compulsory supervision order,

(viii)   a medical examination order,

(ix)   a warrant to secure attendance, or

(x)   section 143, and

(b)   the child absconds from that person.

(2)   The child may be [. . .] taken to that person.

(3)   If a court is satisfied that there are reasonable grounds for believing that the child is within premises, the court may grant a warrant authorising an officer of law to—

(a)   enter premises, and

(b)   search for the child.

(4)   The court may authorise the officer of law to use reasonable force for those purposes.

(5)   Where the child is returned to the person mentioned in subsection (1), but the person is unwilling or unable to receive the child—

(a)   the officer of law returning the child must immediately notify the Principal Reporter of that fact, and

(b)   the child must be kept in a place of safety until the occurrence of the relevant event.

(6)   In subsection (5), the relevant event is—

(a)   in the case mentioned in sub-paragraph (i) of subsection (1)(a), the end of the period specified in the child assessment order,

(b)   in the case mentioned in sub-paragraph (ii) of that subsection, whichever of the following first occurs—

(i)   the children's hearing arranged under section 45 or 69,

(ii)   the termination of the child protection order,

(c)   in the case mentioned in sub-paragraph (iii) of that subsection, whichever of the following first occurs—

(i)   the order ceasing to have effect under section 55(4) or (5),

(ii)   the determination by the sheriff of an application for a child protection order in respect of the child,

(d)   in the case mentioned in sub-paragraph (iv) of that subsection, whichever of the following first occurs—

(i)   the giving of notice under subsection (5) of section 56, or

(ii)   the end of the period mentioned in subsection (3) of that section,

(e)   in the case mentioned in sub-paragraph (v) of that subsection, whichever of the following first occurs—

(i)   the giving of a direction by the Principal Reporter under section 68(2) or 72(2)(a), or

(ii)   the children's hearing arranged by virtue of section 69(2),

(f)   in the case mentioned in sub-paragraph (vi) of that subsection, the children's hearing arranged by virtue of section 131(2)(b),

(g)   in the cases mentioned in sub-paragraphs (vii) and (ix) of that subsection whichever of the following first occurs—

(i)   the next children's hearing that has been arranged in relation to the child,

(ii)   the next hearing before the sheriff relating to the child that is to take place by virtue of this Act,

(h)   in the cases mentioned in sub-paragraphs (viii) and (x) of that subsection, the next children's hearing that has been arranged in relation to the child.

171   Offences related to absconding

(1)   This section applies where—

(a)   a child requires to be kept in a particular place by virtue of—

(i)   a child assessment order,

(ii)   a child protection order,

(iii)   a compulsory supervision order,

(iv)   an interim compulsory supervision order,

(v)   a medical examination order, or

(vi)   a warrant to secure attendance, or

(b)   a person has (or is authorised to have) control of a child by virtue of such an order or warrant.

(2)   A person commits an offence if the person—

(a)   knowingly assists or induces the child to abscond from the place or person,

(b)   knowingly harbours or conceals a child who has absconded from the place or person, or

(c)   knowingly prevents a child from returning to the place or person.

(3)   The person is liable on summary conviction to a fine not exceeding level 5 on the standard scale, to imprisonment for a term not exceeding 6 months or to both.

(4)   This section is subject to—

(a)   section 38(3) and (4) of the 1995 Act,

(b)   section 51(5) and (6) of the Children Act 1989, and

(c)   Article 70(5) and (6) of the Children (Northern Ireland) Order 1995.

PART 17
PROCEEDINGS UNDER PART 10: EVIDENCE

172   Use of evidence obtained from prosecutor

(1)   This section applies where an application is made to the sheriff—

(a)   to determine whether a section 67 ground is established, or

(b)   to review a grounds determination.

(2)   The Principal Reporter may request a prosecutor to give the Principal Reporter evidence held by the prosecutor in connection with the investigation of a crime or suspected crime if the Principal Reporter considers that the evidence might assist the sheriff in determining the application.

(3)   The request may relate only to evidence lawfully obtained in the course of the investigation.

(4)   The prosecutor may refuse to comply with the request if the prosecutor reasonably believes that it is necessary to retain the evidence for the purposes of any proceedings in respect of a crime (whether or not the proceedings have already commenced).

173   Cases involving sexual behaviour: evidence

(1)   This section applies where—

(a)   an application is made to the sheriff—

(i)   to determine whether a section 67 ground is established, or

(ii)   to review a grounds determination, and

(b)   the ground involves sexual behaviour engaged in by any person.

(2)   In hearing the application the sheriff must not, unless the sheriff makes an order under section 175, admit evidence, or allow questioning of a witness designed to elicit evidence, which shows or tends to show one or more of the circumstances mentioned in subsection (3) in relation to a person mentioned in subsection (4).

(3)   The circumstances are that the person—

(a)   is not of good character (whether in relation to sexual matters or otherwise),

(b)   has, at any time, engaged in sexual behaviour not forming part of the subject-matter of the ground,

(c)   has, at any time (other than shortly before, at the same time as or shortly after the acts which form part of the subject-matter of the ground), engaged in behaviour (not being sexual behaviour) that might found an inference that the person is not credible or the person's evidence is not reliable,

(d)   has, at any time, been subject to any condition or predisposition that might found the inference that the person is not credible or the person's evidence is not reliable.

(4)   The persons are—

(a)   the child,

(b)   a person giving evidence for the purposes of the hearing,

(c)   any other person evidence of whose statements is given for the purposes of the hearing.

(5)   In subsection (4)(c), 'statements' includes any representations, however made or expressed, of fact or opinion.

(6)   In this section and section 174, references to sexual behaviour engaged in include references to having undergone or been made subject to any experience of a sexual nature.

174   Cases involving sexual behaviour: taking of evidence by commissioner

(1)   Subsection (2) applies where—

(a)   a commissioner is appointed under section 19 of the Vulnerable Witnesses (Scotland) Act 2004 to take evidence for the purposes of a hearing before the sheriff—

(i)   to determine whether a section 67 ground is established, or

(ii)   to review a grounds determination, and

(b)   the ground involves sexual behaviour engaged in by any person.

(2)   The commissioner must not, unless the sheriff makes an order under section 175, take evidence which shows or tends to show one or more of the circumstances mentioned in section 173(3) in relation to a person mentioned in section 173(4).

175   Sections 173 and 174: application to sheriff for order as to evidence

(1)   On the application of a person mentioned in subsection (2), the sheriff may, if satisfied as to the matters mentioned in subsection (3) make an order—

(a)   admitting evidence of the kind mentioned in section 173(2),

(b)   allowing questioning of the kind mentioned in that section,

(c)   enabling evidence of the kind mentioned in section 174(2) to be taken.

(2)   Those persons are—

(a)   the child,

(b)   a relevant person in relation to the child,

(c)   the Principal Reporter,

(d)   a safeguarder appointed [in relation to the child by virtue of section 30].

(3)   Those matters are—

(a)   the evidence or questioning will relate only to—

(i)   a specific occurrence or specific occurrences of sexual behaviour or other behaviour demonstrating the character of the person,

(ii)   specific facts demonstrating the character of the person,

(iii)   a specific occurrence or specific occurrences of sexual behaviour or other behaviour demonstrating a condition or predisposition to which the person is or has been subject, or

(iv)   specific facts demonstrating a condition or predisposition to which the person is or has been subject,

(b)   the occurrence, occurrences or facts are relevant to establishing the ground, and

(c)   the probative value of the evidence is significant and is likely to out-weigh any risk of prejudice to the proper administration of justice arising from its being admitted or elicited.

(4)   References in this section to an occurrence or occurrences of sexual be-haviour include references to undergoing or being made subject to any experience of a sexual nature.

(5)   In this section 'proper administration of justice' includes—

(a)   appropriate protection of the person's dignity and privacy, and

(b)   ensuring the facts and circumstances of which the sheriff is made aware are relevant to an issue to be put before the sheriff and commensurate with the importance of that issue to the sheriff's decision on the question whether the ground is established.

176   [*Amends Vulnerable Witnesses (Scotland) Act 2004*]

PART 18
MISCELLANEOUS

Children's hearings: procedural rules

177 · Children's hearings: procedural rules

(1)   The Scottish Ministers may make rules about the procedure relating to chil-dren's hearings.

(2)   Rules may in particular make provision for or in connection with—

(a)   specifying matters that may be determined by pre-hearing panels,

(b)   constituting children's hearings,

(c)   arranging children's hearings,

(d)   notifying persons about children's hearings,

(e)   attendance of persons at children's hearings,

(f)   specifying circumstances in which persons may be excused from attend-ing children's hearings,

(g)   specifying circumstances in which persons may be excluded from chil-dren's hearings,

(h)   obtaining the views of the child to whom a children's hearing relates,

(i)   provision of specified documents to—

(i)   members of children's hearings,

(ii)   the child to whom a children's hearing relates,

(iii)   relevant persons in relation to the child to whom a children's hearing relates,

(iv)   any other specified persons,

(j)   withholding of specified documents from persons mentioned in para-graph (i),

(k)   prescribing the form of the statement of grounds,

(l)   the recording and transmission of information,

(m)   representation of persons at children's hearings,

(n)   payment of expenses,
(o)   appeals.
(3)   In making rules in pursuance of subsection (2)(i)(i), the Scottish Ministers must ensure that any views expressed by the child to whom a children's hearing relates are reflected in a specified document.
(4)   Rules containing provision of the type mentioned in subsection (2)(a), (e), (f), (g), (j) or (m) are subject to the affirmative procedure.
(5)   In this section—
'children's hearing' includes pre-hearing panel,
'specified' means specified in the rules.

Disclosure of information

178   Children's hearing: disclosure of information

(1)   A children's hearing need not disclose to a person any information about the child to whom the hearing relates or about the child's case if disclosure of that information to that person would be likely to cause significant harm to the child.
(2)   Subsection (1) applies despite any requirement under an enactment (including this Act and subordinate legislation made under it) or rule of law for the children's hearing—
    (a)   to give the person an explanation of what has taken place at proceedings before the hearing, or
    (b)   to provide the person with—
        (i)   information about the child or the child's case, or
        (ii)   reasons for a decision made by the hearing.

179   Sharing of information: prosecution

(1)   This section applies where—
    (a)   by virtue of this Act, the Principal Reporter, a children's hearing or the sheriff has determined, is determining or is to determine any matter relating to a child,
    (b)   criminal proceedings have been commenced against an accused,
    (c)   the proceedings have not yet been concluded, and
    (d)   the child is connected in any way with the circumstances that gave rise to the proceedings, the accused or any other person connected in any way with those circumstances.
(2)   The Principal Reporter must make available to the Crown Office and Procurator Fiscal Service any information held by the Principal Reporter relating to the prosecution which the Service requests for the purpose of—
    (a)   the prevention or detection of crime, or
    (b)   the apprehension or prosecution of offenders.

[179A   Request for information by person affected by child's offence or behaviour

(1)   This section applies—
    (a)   where the Principal Reporter is required to make a determination in relation to a child under section 66(2) and has information which suggests that—
        (i)   the child has committed an offence, or
        (ii)   the child, while under 12 years of age, has acted or behaved in a way that falls within subsection (2), or
    (b)   where, by virtue of section 71(3)(b) or 130, the Principal Reporter is required to arrange a children's hearing in relation to a child who has pled guilty to, or been found guilty of, an offence.
(2)   Action or behaviour falls within this subsection if it—
    (a)   is—
        (i)   physically violent,
        (ii)   sexually violent or sexually coercive, or

(iii)   dangerous, threatening or abusive, and

(b)   causes harm to another person.

(3)   A person mentioned in subsection (4) may request the Principal Reporter to provide the person with information about the action taken in relation to the offence or, as the case may be, the action or behaviour mentioned in subsection (1)(a)(ii).

(4)   The persons are—

(a)   any person against whom the offence mentioned in subsection (1)(a)(i) or (b) appears to have been committed,

(b)   any person who appears to have been harmed by the action or behaviour mentioned in subsection (1)(a)(ii),

(c)   where a person mentioned in paragraph (a) or (b) is a child, any relevant person in relation to that child,

(d)   any other person or class of persons the Scottish Ministers may specify by regulations (subject to any conditions specified in the regulations).

(5)   The Principal Reporter may inform any person mentioned in subsection (4)(a), (b) or (c) of the person's right to request information under subsection (3).

(6)   Subsection (7) applies where—

(a)   the Principal Reporter is required under section 68(3)(a) to provide information to a person, and

(b)   that person is entitled to request information under subsection (3).

(7)   A request made by the person for information under subsection (3) is to be treated as relating only to information which the Principal Reporter is not required to provide to the person under section 68(3)(a).]

[179B   Information to which section 179A applies

(1)   The information about the action taken in relation to the offence or, as the case may be, the behaviour mentioned in subsection (1)(a)(ii) of section 179A which may be requested under subsection (3) of that section is—

(a)   in a case mentioned in section 179A(1)(a), information as to whether or not a children's hearing required to be arranged under section 69(2) for the purpose of deciding whether a compulsory supervision order should be made in respect of the child and—

(i)   where such a hearing did not require to be arranged, the information mentioned in subsection (2)(a),

(ii)   where such a hearing did require to be arranged, the information mentioned in subsection (2)(b),

(b)   in a case mentioned in section 179A(1)(b), the information mentioned in subsection (2)(b).

(2)   The information is—

(a)   information as to—

(i)   what determination the Principal Reporter made under section 66(2), and

(ii)   any other action taken by the Principal Reporter (under section 68(5) or otherwise),

(b)   information as to—

(i)   whether a compulsory supervision order has been made in respect of the child or, as the case may be, whether a compulsory supervision order which is already in force in respect of the child has been terminated, varied or continued, or

(ii)   how the referral to the children's hearing was otherwise discharged.]

[179C   Decision by Principal Reporter following request under section 179A

(1)   The Principal Reporter may comply with a request made under section 179A(3) only if satisfied—

(a)   that the provision of the information would not be detrimental to the best interests of the child mentioned in section 179A(1) (or any other child), and

(b)   having regard to the factors mentioned in subsection (2), that it is appropriate in the circumstances of the case to provide the information.

(2)   The factors are—

(a)   the age of the child mentioned in section 179A(1),

(b)   the seriousness of the offence or, as the case may be, the action or behaviour mentioned in section 179A(1)(a)(ii),

(c)   the circumstances in which the offence or action or behaviour took place,

(d)   the effect that the offence or the action or behaviour has had on the person mentioned in section 179A(4)(a) or, as the case may be, section 179A(4)(b), and

(e)   such other factors as the Principal Reporter considers appropriate.

(3)   The Principal Reporter must not, in providing information under subsection (1), provide any more information than is necessary to inform the person who made the request of the action taken in relation to the offence or, as the case may be, the action or behaviour mentioned in section 179A(1)(a)(ii).]

180   Sharing of information: panel members

(1)   A local authority must comply with a request from the National Convener to provide to the National Convener information about the implementation of compulsory supervision orders by the authority.

(2)   The National Convener may disclose information provided by a local authority under subsection (1) to members of the Children's Panel.

Implementation of compulsory supervision orders: annual report

181   Implementation of compulsory supervision orders: annual report

(1)   The National Convener must, as soon as is reasonably practicable after the end of each financial year, prepare and submit to the Scottish Ministers a report about implementation of compulsory supervision orders during the year—

(a)   in Scotland as a whole, and

(b)   in each local authority area.

(2)   The National Convener must give a copy of the report to each member of the Children's Panel.

(3)   The Scottish Ministers must lay the report before the Scottish Parliament.

(4)   For the purposes of preparing the report, the National Convener may require each local authority to provide to the National Convener for each financial year—

(a)   information about—

(i)   the number of compulsory supervision orders for which the authority is the implementation authority,

(ii)   changes in the circumstances that led to the making of the orders,

(iii)   the ways in which the overall wellbeing of children who are subject to the orders has been affected by them, and

(b)   such other information relating to the implementation of the orders as the National Convener may require.

(5)   Information provided under subsection (4) must not identify (or enable the identification of) a particular child.

(6)   In this section, 'financial year' has the meaning given by paragraph 24(3) of schedule 1.

Publishing restrictions

182   Publishing restrictions

(1)   A person must not publish protected information if the publication of the information is intended, or is likely, to identify—

(a)   a child mentioned in the protected information, or

(b)   an address or school as being that of such a child.

(2)   A person who contravenes subsection (1) commits an offence and is liable on summary conviction to a fine not exceeding level 4 on the standard scale.

(3)   It is a defence for a person ('P') charged with a contravention of subsection (1) to show that P did not know or have reason to suspect that the publication of the protected information was likely to identify a child mentioned in the protected information, or, as the case may be, an address or school of such a child.

(4)   In relation to proceedings before a children's hearing, the Scottish Ministers may in the interests of justice—

    (a)   dispense with the prohibition in subsection (1), or

    (b)   relax it to such extent as they consider appropriate.

(5)   In relation to proceedings before the sheriff under Part 10 or 15, the sheriff may in the interests of justice—

    (a)   dispense with the prohibition in subsection (1), or

    (b)   relax it to such extent as the sheriff considers appropriate.

(6)   In relation to proceedings in an appeal to the Court of Session under this Act, the Court may in the interests of justice—

    (a)   dispense with the prohibition in subsection (1), or

    (b)   relax it to such extent as the Court considers appropriate.

(7)   The prohibition in subsection (1) does not apply in relation to the publication by or on behalf of a local authority or an adoption agency of information about a child for the purposes of making arrangements in relation to the child under this Act or the Adoption and Children (Scotland) Act 2007.

(8)   In subsection (7), 'adoption agency' has the meaning given by the Adoption and Children (Scotland) Act 2007.

(9)   In this section—

['children's hearing' includes a pre-hearing panel,]

'protected information' means—

    (a)   information in relation to—

        (i)   a children's hearing,

        (ii)   an appeal against a decision of a children's hearing,

        (iii)   proceedings before the sheriff under Part 10 or 15, or

        (iv)   an appeal from any decision of the sheriff or sheriff principal made under this Act, or

    (b)   information given to the Principal Reporter in respect of a child in reliance on, or satisfaction of, a provision of this Act or any other enactment,

'publish' includes in particular—

    (a)   to publish matter in a programme service, as defined by section 201 of the Broadcasting Act 1990, and

    (b)   to cause matter to be published.

Mutual assistance

183   Mutual assistance

(1)   A person mentioned in subsection (2) must comply with a request by another such person for assistance in the carrying out of functions conferred by virtue of this Act.

(2)   The persons are—

    (a)   CHS,

    (b)   the National Convener,

    (c)   SCRA,

    (d)   the Principal Reporter.

(3)   A person mentioned in subsection (4) must comply with a request by a local authority for assistance in the carrying out of the local authority's functions under this Act.

(4)   The persons are—

    (a)   another local authority,

(b)   a health board constituted under section 2 of the National Health Service (Scotland) Act 1978.

(5)   A request under this section must specify the assistance that is required.

(6)   Nothing in this section requires a person to comply with a request if—

(a)   it would be incompatible with any function (whether conferred by statute or otherwise) of the person to whom it is directed, or

(b)   it would unduly prejudice the carrying out by the person to whom the request is directed of the person's functions.

184   Enforcement of obligations on health board under section 183

(1)   This section applies where—

(a)   the implementation authority in relation to a compulsory supervision order has made a request for assistance from a health board under section 183(3),

(b)   the request is in connection with the implementation of the compulsory supervision order, and

(c)   the implementation authority is satisfied that the health board has unreasonably failed to comply with the request.

(2)   The implementation authority may refer the matter to the Scottish Ministers.

(3)   On receiving a reference under subsection (2), the Scottish Ministers may, if they are satisfied that the health board has unreasonably failed to comply with the request, direct the health board to comply with the request.

(4)   The health board must comply with a direction under subsection (3).

Consent of child to medical examination or treatment

186   Consent of child to medical examination or treatment

(1)   Nothing in this Act prejudices any capacity of a child enjoyed by virtue of section 2(4) of the Age of Legal Capacity (Scotland) Act 1991 (capacity of child with sufficient understanding to consent to surgical, medical or dental procedure or treatment).

(2)   In particular, where—

(a)   under an order mentioned in subsection (3) any examination or treatment is arranged for the child, and

(b)   the child has the capacity mentioned in section 2(4) of the Age of Legal Capacity (Scotland) Act 1991,

the examination or treatment may be carried out only if the child consents to it.

(3)   Those orders are—

(a)   a child assessment order,

(b)   a child protection order,

(c)   a compulsory supervision order,

(d)   an interim compulsory supervision order,

(e)   a medical examination order.

Places of safety

189   Places of safety: restrictions on use of police stations

(1)   This section applies where a person is authorised or required under this Act to keep or detain a child in a place of safety.

(2)   A child may be kept or detained in a police station only if it is not reasonably practicable to keep or detain the child in a place of safety which is not a police station.

(3)   Where a child is being kept or detained in a police station, the person must take steps to identify a place of safety which is not a police station and transfer the child to that place as soon as is reasonably practicable.

Orders made outwith Scotland

190   Effect of orders made outwith Scotland

(1)   The Scottish Ministers may by regulations make provision for a specified non-Scottish order which appears to them to correspond to a compulsory supervision order to have effect as if it were such an order.

(2)   Regulations under subsection (1)—
  (a)   may provide that a non-Scottish order is to have such effect only—
    (i)   in specified circumstances,
    (ii)   for specified purposes,
  (b)   may modify the following enactments in their application by virtue of the regulations to a non-Scottish order—
    (i)   the Social Work (Scotland) Act 1968,
    (ii)   this Act,
  (c)   are subject to affirmative procedure.

(3)   In this section—
'non-Scottish order' means an order made by a court in England and Wales or in Northern Ireland,
'specified' means specified in the regulations.

Interpretation

199   Meaning of 'child'

(1)   In this Act, 'child' means a person who is under 16 years of age (but subject to subsections (2) to (9)).

(2)   In paragraph (o) of section 67(2) and the other provisions of this Act in their application in relation to that paragraph, 'child' means a person who is of school age.

(3)   Subsection (4) applies where a person becomes 16 years of age—
  (a)   after section 66 applies in relation to the person, but
  (b)   before a relevant event.

(4)   For the purposes of the application of this Act to the person, references in this Act to a child include references to the person until a relevant event occurs.

(5)   A relevant event is—
  (a)   the making of a compulsory supervision order in relation to the person,
  (b)   the notification of the person under section 68(3) that the question of whether a compulsory supervision order should be made in respect of the person will not be referred to a children's hearing, or
  (c)   the discharge of the referral.

(6)   Subsection (7) applies if—
  (a)   a compulsory supervision order is in force in respect of a person on the person's becoming 16 years of age, or
  (b)   a compulsory supervision order is made in respect of a person on or after the person becomes 16 years of age.

(7)   For the purposes of the application of the provisions of this Act relating to that order, references in this Act to a child include references to the person until whichever of the following first occurs—
  (a)   the order is terminated, or
  (b)   the person becomes 18 years of age.

(8)   Subsection (9) applies where a case is remitted to the Principal Reporter under section 49(7)(b) of the Criminal Procedure (Scotland) Act 1995.

(9)   For the purposes of the application of this Act to the person whose case is remitted, references in this Act to a child include references to the person until whichever of the following first occurs—
  (a)   a children's hearing or the sheriff discharges the referral,
  (b)   a compulsory supervision order made in respect of the person is terminated, or
  (c)   the person becomes 18 years of age.

200 Meaning of 'relevant person'

(1) In this Act, 'relevant person', in relation to a child, means—

(a) a parent or guardian having parental responsibilities or parental rights in relation to the child under Part 1 of the 1995 Act,

(b) a person in whom parental responsibilities or parental rights are vested by virtue of section 11(2)(b) of the 1995 Act,

(c) a person having parental responsibilities or parental rights by virtue of section 11(12) of the 1995 Act,

(d) a parent having parental responsibility for the child under Part 1 of the Children Act 1989 ('the 1989 Act'),

(e) a person having parental responsibility for the child by virtue of—

(i) section 12(2) of the 1989 Act,

(ii) section 14C of the 1989 Act, or

(iii) section 25(3) of the Adoption and Children Act 2002,

(f) a person in whom parental responsibilities or parental rights are vested by virtue of a permanence order (as defined in section 80(2) of the Adoption and Children (Scotland) Act 2007),

(g) any other person specified by order made by the Scottish Ministers.

(2) For the purposes of subsection (1)(a), a parent does not have parental responsibilities or rights merely by virtue of an order under section 11(2)(d) or (e) of the 1995 Act.

(3) An order made under subsection (1)(g) is subject to the affirmative procedure.

201 Meaning of 'relevant local authority'

(1) In this Act, 'relevant local authority', in relation to a child, means—

(a) the local authority in whose area the child predominantly resides, or

(b) where the child does not predominantly reside in the area of a particular local authority, the local authority with whose area the child has the closest connection.

(2) For the purposes of subsection (1)(a), no account is to be taken of—

(a) any period of residence in a residential establishment,

(b) any other period of residence, or residence in any other place, prescribed by the Scottish Ministers by regulations.

(3) For the purposes of subsection (1)(b), no account is to be taken of—

(a) any connection with an area that relates to a period of residence in a residential establishment,

(b) any other connection prescribed by the Scottish Ministers by regulations.

202 Interpretation

(1) In this Act, unless the context otherwise requires—

'the 1995 Act' means the Children (Scotland) Act 1995,

'affirmative procedure' is to be construed in accordance with section 197,

'CHS' means Children's Hearings Scotland,

'chief social work officer' means the officer appointed under section 3 of the Social Work (Scotland) Act 1968 by—

(a) in relation to a compulsory supervision order or an interim compulsory supervision order, the implementation authority,

(b) in relation to a medical examination order or a warrant to secure attendance, the relevant local authority for the child to whom the order or warrant relates,

'child assessment order' means an order mentioned in section 35,

'child protection order' means an order mentioned in section 37,

'compulsory supervision order' has the meaning given by section 83,

'contact order' has the meaning given by section 11(2)(d) of the 1995 Act,

'crime' has the meaning given in section 307(1) of the Criminal Procedure (Scotland) Act 1995, 'functions' includes powers and duties; and 'confer', in relation to functions, includes impose,

'grounds determination' has the meaning given by section 110(1),

'grounds hearing' has the meaning given by section 90,

'implementation authority'—

(a)   in relation to a compulsory supervision order, has the meaning given by section 83(1)(b),

(b)   in relation to an interim compulsory supervision order, has the meaning given by section 86(1)(b),

'interim compulsory supervision order' has the meaning given by section 86,

'interim variation', in relation to a compulsory supervision order, has the meaning given by section 140,

'medical examination order' has the meaning given by section 87,

'movement restriction condition' has the meaning given by section 84,

'negative procedure' is to be construed in accordance with section 196,

'officer of law' has the meaning given by section 307(1) of the Criminal Procedure (Scotland) Act 1995,

'parental responsibilities' has the meaning given by section 1(3) of the 1995 Act,

'parental rights' has the meaning given by section 2(4) of the 1995 Act,

'permanence order' has the meaning given by section 80(2) of the Adoption and Children (Scotland) Act 2007,

'place of safety', in relation to a child, means—

(a)   a residential or other establishment provided by a local authority,

(b)   a community home within the meaning of section 53 of the Children Act 1989,

(c)   a police station,

(d)   a hospital or surgery, the person or body of persons responsible for the management of which is willing temporarily to receive the child,

(e)   the dwelling-house of a suitable person who is so willing, or

(f)   any other suitable place the occupier of which is so willing,

'pre-hearing panel' has the meaning given by section 79(2)(a),

'prosecutor' has the meaning given by section 307(1) of the Criminal Procedure (Scotland) Act 1995,

'residential establishment' means—

(a)   an establishment in Scotland (whether managed by a local authority, a voluntary organisation or any other person) which provides residential accommodation for children for the purposes of this Act, the 1995 Act or the Social Work (Scotland) Act 1968,

(b)   a home in England or Wales that is—

(i)   a community home within the meaning of section 53 of the Children Act 1989,

(ii)   a voluntary home within the meaning of that Act, or

(iii)   a private children's home within the meaning of that Act, or

[(c)   an establishment in Northern Ireland that is—

(i)   a private children's home within the meaning of the Children (Northern Ireland) Order 1995 (SI 1995/755),

(ii)   an authority home provided under Part VII of that Order, or

(iii)   a voluntary home provided under Part VIII of that Order,]

'safeguarder' has the meaning given by section 30(1),

'school age' has the meaning given by section 31 of the Education (Scotland) Act 1980,

'secure accommodation' means accommodation provided [for the purpose of restricting the liberty of children which—

(a)   in Scotland, is provided in a residential establishment approved in accordance with regulations made under section 78(2) of the Public Services Reform (Scotland) Act 2010 (asp 8),

(b) in England, is provided in a children's home (within the meaning of the Care Standards Act 2000 (c 14) ('the 2000 Act')) in respect of which a person is registered under Part 2 of that Act, except that before the coming into force of section 107(2) of the Health and Social Care (Community Health Standards) Act 2003 (c 43), 'secure accommodation' means accommodation in relation to England which—

    (i) is provided in a children's home (within the meaning of the 2000 Act) in respect of which a person is registered under Part 2 of that Act, and

    (ii) is approved by the Secretary of State for the purpose of restricting the liberty of children,

(c) in Wales, is provided in a children's home (within the meaning of the 2000 Act) in respect of which a person is registered under Part 2 of that Act,]

'secure accommodation authorisation' has the meaning given by section 85,

'statement of grounds' has the meaning given by section 89(3),

'subordinate legislation' means—

    (a) an order,

    (b) regulations, or

    (c) rules,

'super-affirmative procedure' is to be construed in accordance with section 198,

['supporting facts' has the meaning given by section 90(1D),]

'warrant to secure attendance' has the meaning given by section 88, and

'working day' means every day except—

    (a) Saturday and Sunday,

    (b) 25 and 26 December,

    (c) 1 and 2 January.

(2) References in this Act to a decision of a children's hearing are references to a decision of a majority of the members of a children's hearing.

[(2A) References in this Act to a determination of a pre-hearing panel are references to a determination of a majority of the members of a pre-hearing panel.]

(3) References in this Act to varying a compulsory supervision order, an interim compulsory supervision order or a medical examination order include varying the order by adding or removing measures.

General

203 Consequential amendments and repeals

(1) Schedule 5 contains minor amendments and amendments consequential on the provisions of this Act.

(2) The enactments specified in schedule 6, which include enactments that are spent, are repealed to the extent specified.

204 Ancillary provision

(1) The Scottish Ministers may by order make such supplementary, incidental or consequential provision as they consider appropriate for the purposes of, in consequence of, or for giving full effect to, any provision of this Act.

(2) An order under subsection (1) may modify any enactment (including this Act).

(3) An order under this section containing provisions which add to, replace or omit any part of the text of an Act is subject to the affirmative procedure.

205 Transitional provision etc

(1) The Scottish Ministers may by order make such provision as they consider necessary or expedient for transitory, transitional or saving purposes in connection with the coming into force of any provision of this Act.

(2) An order under subsection (1) may modify any enactment (including this Act).

206 Short title and commencement

(1) This Act may be cited as the Children's Hearings (Scotland) Act 2011.

(2) The provisions of this Act, other than sections 193 to 202, 204, 205 and this section, come into force on such day as the Scottish Ministers may by order appoint.

(3) An order under subsection (2) may contain transitional, transitory or saving provision in connection with the coming into force of this Act.

SCHEDULES

SCHEDULE 1
CHILDREN'S HEARINGS SCOTLAND

(introduced by section 3)

1 Status

(1) CHS—

   (a) is not a servant or agent of the Crown, and

   (b) does not enjoy any status, immunity or privilege of the Crown.

(2) CHS's property is not property of, or property held on behalf of, the Crown.

2 Membership

(1) The members of CHS are to be appointed by the Scottish Ministers.

(2) There are to be no fewer than five and no more than eight members.

(3) The Scottish Ministers may by order amend sub-paragraph (2) so as to substitute for the numbers of members for the time being specified there different numbers of members.

(4) A member holds and vacates office on terms and conditions determined by the Scottish Ministers.

(5) The Scottish Ministers may appoint a person to be a member only if satisfied that the person has knowledge and experience relevant to the functions of CHS and the National Convener.

(6) The Scottish Ministers may appoint a person to be a member only if satisfied that the person, after appointment, will have no financial or other interest that is likely to prejudicially affect the performance of the person's functions as a member of CHS.

(7) The Scottish Ministers may reappoint as a member a person who has ceased to be a member.

3 Persons disqualified from membership

A person is disqualified from appointment, and from holding office, as a member if the person is or becomes—

   (a) a member of the House of Commons,

   (b) a member of the Scottish Parliament, or

   (c) a member of the European Parliament.

4 Resignation of members

A member of CHS may resign office by giving notice in writing to the Scottish Ministers.

5 Removal of members

(1) The Scottish Ministers may revoke the appointment of a member of CHS if—

   (a) the member becomes insolvent,

   (b) the member is incapacitated by physical or mental illness,

(c) the member has been absent from meetings of CHS for a period longer than 3 months without the permission of CHS,

(d) the member is otherwise unfit to be a member or unable for any reason to discharge the functions of a member.

(2) For the purposes of sub-paragraph (1)(a) a member becomes insolvent when—

(a) a voluntary arrangement proposed by the member is approved,

(b) the member is adjudged bankrupt,

(c) the member's estate is sequestrated,

(d) the member's application for a debt payment programme is approved under section 2 of the Debt Arrangement and Attachment (Scotland) Act 2002, or

(e) the member grants a trust deed for creditors.

6 Remuneration, allowances etc

(1) CHS must pay to its members—

(a) such remuneration as the Scottish Ministers may determine, and

(b) such allowances in respect of expenses properly incurred by members in the performance of their functions as may be so determined.

(2) CHS must—

(a) pay to or in respect of any person who is or has been a member of CHS such pension, allowances or gratuities as the Scottish Ministers may determine, or

(b) make such payments as the Scottish Ministers may determine towards provision for the payment of a pension, allowance or gratuity to or in respect of such a person.

(3) Sub-paragraph (4) applies where—

(a) a person ceases to be a member otherwise than on the expiry of the person's term of office, and

(b) it appears to the Scottish Ministers that there are circumstances which make it right for the person to receive compensation.

(4) CHS must make a payment to the person of such amount as the Scottish Ministers may determine.

7 Chairing meetings

(1) The Scottish Ministers must appoint one of the members of CHS to chair meetings of CHS (the 'chairing member').

(2) The chairing member holds and vacates that office on terms and conditions determined by the Scottish Ministers.

(3) If a person is appointed as the chairing member for a period that extends beyond the period of the person's appointment as a member, the person's appointment as a member is taken to have been extended so that it ends on the same day as the period of appointment as chairing member ends.

(4) The chairing member may resign that office by giving notice in writing to the Scottish Ministers.

(5) If the chairing member is for any reason unable to chair a meeting of members, a majority of the members present at the meeting may elect one of those members to chair the meeting.

8 The National Convener

(1) CHS is, with the approval of the Scottish Ministers, to appoint a person as the National Convener (other than the first National Convener).

(2) CHS may, with the approval of the Scottish Ministers, reappoint a person as the National Convener.

(3) CHS must take reasonable steps to involve persons who are under 21 years of age in the process for selection of a person for appointment or reappointment under this paragraph.

(4) The period for which a person is appointed or reappointed under this paragraph is 5 years.

(5) A person appointed or reappointed under this paragraph holds and vacates office on terms and conditions determined by CHS and approved by the Scottish Ministers.

(6) The Scottish Ministers may by regulations prescribe qualifications that must be held by the National Convener.

(7) A person is disqualified from appointment, and from holding office, as the National Convener if the person is or becomes—

    (a)   a member of the House of Commons,

    (b)   a member of the Scottish Parliament, or

    (c)   a member of the European Parliament.

(8) The National Convener may appeal to the Scottish Ministers against dismissal by CHS.

(9) CHS is the respondent in an appeal under sub-paragraph (8).

(10) The Scottish Ministers may by regulations make provision about—

    (a)   the procedure to be followed in appeals under sub-paragraph (8),

    (b)   the effect of making such an appeal,

    (c)   the powers of the Scottish Ministers for disposing of such appeals (including powers to make directions about liability for expenses),

    (d)   the effect of the exercise of those powers.

9 Supplementary powers of National Convener

The National Convener may do anything that the National Convener considers appropriate for the purposes of or in connection with the functions conferred on the National Convener by virtue of this Act or any other enactment.

10 Delegation of National Convener's functions

(1) The functions of the National Convener conferred by virtue of this Act or any other enactment (other than the functions mentioned in sub-paragraph (2)) may be carried out on the National Convener's behalf by a person who is—

    (a)   authorised (whether specially or generally) by the National Convener for the purpose, or

    (b)   a person of a class of person authorised (whether specially or generally) by the National Convener for the purpose.

(2) The functions are—

    (a)   the function conferred by paragraph 24,

    (b)   functions conferred by paragraph 1(2) to (6) of schedule 2.

(3) The National Convener may not under sub-paragraph (1) authorise the Principal Reporter, SCRA or a local authority to carry out a function on behalf of the National Convener.

(4) The National Convener may not under sub-paragraph (1) authorise a person employed by SCRA or a local authority to carry out the function conferred on the National Convener by section 8.

(5) If under sub-paragraph (1) the National Convener delegates the function conferred on the National Convener by section 8, the National Convener may not delegate any other function to the same person under that sub-paragraph.

(6) Nothing in sub-paragraph (1) prevents the National Convener from carrying out any function delegated under that sub-paragraph.

(7) The Scottish Ministers may by regulations prescribe the qualifications to be held by a person to whom a function, or a function of a class, specified in the regulations is delegated.

(8) A person to whom a function is delegated under sub-paragraph (1) must comply with a direction given to the person by the National Convener about the carrying out of the function.

(9) CHS may pay to a person to whom a function is delegated under

sub-paragraph (1) such expenses and allowances as the Scottish Ministers may determine.

11 Staff

(1)   CHS may employ any staff necessary to ensure the carrying out of CHS's functions.

(2)   Staff are employed on terms and conditions determined by CHS and approved by the Scottish Ministers.

(3)   CHS may—

(a)   pay a pension, allowance or gratuity, including by way of compensation for loss of employment, to or in respect of an eligible person,

(b)   make payments towards the provision of a pension, allowance or gratuity, including by way of compensation for loss of employment, to or in respect of an eligible person,

(c)   provide and maintain schemes (whether contributory or not) for the payment of a pension, allowance or gratuity, including by way of compensation for loss of employment, to or in respect of an eligible person.

(4)   CHS may, with the approval of the Scottish Ministers, determine—

(a)   who, of the persons who are or have ceased to be employees of CHS, are to be eligible persons, and

(b)   the amount that may be paid or provided for.

(5)   Sub-paragraphs (6) and (7) apply where—

(a)   a person employed by CHS becomes a member of CHS, and

(b)   the person was (because the person was an employee of CHS) a participant in a pension scheme established and administered by CHS for the benefit of its employees.

(6)   CHS may determine that the person's service as a member of CHS is to be treated for the purposes of the scheme as service as an employee of CHS whether or not any benefits are to be payable to or in respect of the person under paragraph 6.

(7)   Any discretion which the scheme confers on CHS as to the benefits payable to or in respect of the person is to be exercised only with the approval of the Scottish Ministers.

12 Area support teams: establishment and membership

(1)   The National Convener must establish [. . .] a committee (to be known as an area support team) for each area that the National Convener designates for the purposes of this paragraph.

(2)   An area designated under sub-paragraph (1) is to consist of one or more local authority areas.

[(3)   The National Convener—

(a)   must keep the designation of areas under sub-paragraph (1) under review, and

(b)   may at any time revoke a designation or make a new one.

(3A)   In exercising the powers to make and revoke designations, the National Convener must ensure that at all times each local authority area falls within an area designated under sub-paragraph (1).

(3B)   Revocation of a designation under sub-paragraph (1) has the effect of dissolving the area support team established in consequence of the designation.

(3C)   Before deciding to make or revoke a designation under sub-paragraph (1), the National Convener must consult each affected local authority.

(3D)   In sub-paragraph (3C), "affected local authority" means—

(a)   in the case of making a designation, each local authority whose area falls within the area proposed to be designated,

(b)   in the case of revoking a designation, each constituent authority for the area support team established in consequence of the designation.

(3E)   On making or revoking a designation under sub-paragraph (1), the

National Convener must notify each local authority which was consulted under sub-paragraph (3C) in relation to the decision to make or revoke the designation.]

(4) The National Convener must appoint as members of an area support team—

(a) one person nominated by each constituent authority (if the authority chooses to make a nomination),

(b) such other persons nominated by constituent authorities as the National Convener considers appropriate,

(c) a member of the Children's Panel who lives or works in the area of the area support team, and

(d) sufficient other persons so that the number of members nominated by a local authority is no more than one third of the total number of members.

(5) An area support team may not include the Principal Reporter or a member or employee of SCRA.

(6) An area support team may establish sub-committees consisting of persons who are members of the area support team.

(7) In this paragraph and paragraphs 13 and 14 'constituent authority', in relation to an area support team (or a proposed area support team), means a local authority whose area falls within the area of the area support team.

13 Transfer of members from CPACs

(1) This paragraph applies where—

[(a)] the National Convener establishes an area support team under paragraph 12(1), and

[(b) the area of the area support team consists of or includes a new area].

(2) The National Convener must notify each relevant CPAC member of the National Convener's intention to transfer the member to the area support team.

(3) A notice under sub-paragraph (2) must state that the relevant CPAC member will become a member of the area support team unless the member notifies the National Convener within 28 days of receiving the notice that the person does not wish to become a member of the area support team.

(4) A relevant CPAC member is a person who—

(a) at the time of the establishment of the area support team, is a member of a Children's Panel Advisory Committee whose area falls wholly within the [new area concerned], and

(b) was nominated as such by the Scottish Ministers (or, as the case may be, by the Secretary of State) under paragraph 3 or 4(a) of Schedule 1 to the 1995 Act.

(5) The National Convener must appoint each relevant CPAC member as a member of the area support team unless the member notifies the National Convener in accordance with sub-paragraph (3).

(6) On appointment as a member of the area support team under sub-paragraph (5), a relevant CPAC member ceases to be a member of the Children's Panel Advisory Committee.

(7) In this paragraph—

'area', in relation to a Children's Panel Advisory Committee, means the area of the local authority (or authorities) which formed the Children's Panel Advisory Committee,

'Children's Panel Advisory Committee' includes a joint advisory committee within the meaning of paragraph 8 of Schedule 1 to the 1995 Act,

['new area' means an area which has never previously been the area (or part of the area) of an area support team].

14 Area support teams: functions

(1) An area support team is to carry out for its area the functions conferred on the National Convener by section 6.

(2)   The National Convener may delegate to an area support team to carry out for its area—

(a)   a function conferred on the National Convener by paragraph 1(1) of schedule 2,

(b)   other functions of the National Convener specified for the purpose by the National Convener.

(3)   The National Convener may not specify for the purpose of sub-paragraph (2)(b) the functions conferred on the National Convener by section 8.

(4)   Before delegating a function under sub-paragraph (2) to be carried out by an area support team the National Convener must consult each constituent authority.

(5)   A function to be carried out by an area support team by virtue of sub-paragraph (1) or (2) may not be delegated by the area support team to a person who is not a member of the area support team.

(6)   Nothing in sub-paragraph (1) or (2) prevents the National Convener from carrying out any function mentioned in those sub-paragraphs.

(7)   An area support team must comply with a direction given to it by the National Convener about—

(a)   the carrying out of the functions mentioned in sub-paragraph (1),

(b)   the carrying out of a function delegated to it under sub-paragraph (2).

(8)   Before giving a direction to an area support team as mentioned in sub-paragraph (7) the National Convener must consult each constituent authority.

[(9)   A constituent authority must provide an area support team with such administrative support as the National Convener considers appropriate.

(10)   In sub-paragraph (9), "administrative support" means staff, property or other services which the National Convener considers are required to facilitate the carrying out by an area support team of its functions.]

15   Committees

(1)   CHS may establish committees.

(2)   The members of committees may include persons who are not members of CHS.

(3)   A committee must not consist entirely of persons who are not members of CHS.

(4)   CHS must pay to a person who is not a member of CHS and who is appointed to a committee such remuneration and allowances as CHS may, with the approval of the Scottish Ministers, determine.

(5)   A committee must comply with any directions given to it by CHS.

(6)   In this paragraph, only sub-paragraph (4) applies in relation to area support teams.

16   CHS's supplementary powers

(1)   CHS may do anything that it considers appropriate for the purposes of or in connection with its functions.

(2)   CHS may in particular—

(a)   acquire and dispose of land and other property,

(b)   enter into contracts,

(c)   carry out research relating to the functions conferred on it by virtue of this Act or any other enactment,

(d)   publish, or assist in the publication of, materials relating to those functions,

(e)   promote, or assist in the promotion of, publicity relating to those functions.

17   Procedure

(1)   CHS may determine—

(a)   its own procedure (including quorum), and

(b)   the procedure (including quorum) of any of its committees.

(2)   An area support team may determine—

(a)   its own procedure (including quorum), and

(b)   the procedure (including quorum) of any of its sub-committees.

18   Delegation of CHS's functions

(1)   Any function of CHS (whether conferred by virtue of this Act or any other enactment) may be carried out on its behalf by—

(a)   a member of CHS,

(b)   a committee of CHS, or

(c)   a person employed by CHS.

(2)   Nothing in sub-paragraph (1) prevents CHS from carrying out any function delegated under that sub-paragraph.

19   Financial interests

(1)   The Scottish Ministers must from time to time satisfy themselves that the members of CHS have no financial or other interest that is likely to prejudicially affect the performance of their functions as members of CHS.

(2)   A member must comply with a requirement of the Scottish Ministers to give them any information that the Scottish Ministers consider necessary to enable them to comply with sub-paragraph (1).

20   Grants

(1)   The Scottish Ministers may make grants to CHS of amounts that they determine.

(2)   A grant is made subject to any conditions specified by the Scottish Ministers (including conditions about repayment).

21   Accounts

(1)   CHS must—

(a)   keep proper accounts and accounting records,

(b)   prepare for each financial year a statement of accounts, and

(c)   send a copy of each statement of accounts to the Scottish Ministers by such time as they may direct.

(2)   Each statement of accounts must comply with any directions given by the Scottish Ministers as to—

(a)   the information to be contained in it,

(b)   the manner in which the information is to be presented,

(c)   the methods and principles according to which the statement is to be prepared.

(3)   The Scottish Ministers must send a copy of each statement of accounts to the Auditor General for Scotland for auditing.

(4)   In this paragraph, 'financial year' means—

(a)   the period beginning on the date on which CHS is established and ending—

(i)   on 31 March next occurring, or

(ii)   if that period is of less than 6 months' duration, on 31 March next occurring after that, and

(b)   each subsequent period of a year ending on 31 March.

22   Provision of accounts and other information to Scottish Ministers

(1)   The Scottish Ministers may direct CHS to give them accounts or other information specified in the direction relating to CHS's property and activities or proposed activities.

(2)   CHS must—

(a)   give the Scottish Ministers accounts or any other information that it is directed to give under sub-paragraph (1),

(b)   give the Scottish Ministers facilities for the verification of the information given,

(c)   permit any person authorised by the Scottish Ministers to inspect and make copies of accounts and any other documents of CHS for the purposes of verifying the information given, and

(d)   give the person an explanation, reasonably required by the person, of anything that the person is entitled to inspect.

23   CHS's annual report

(1)   CHS must, as soon as is reasonably practicable after the end of each financial year, prepare and submit to the Scottish Ministers a report on the carrying out of its functions during the year.

(2)   The report must include a copy of so much of the report made to CHS by the National Convener as relates to the year.

(3)   CHS may include in the report any other information that it considers appropriate.

(4)   The Scottish Ministers must lay before the Scottish Parliament each report submitted to them.

(5)   In this paragraph, 'financial year' means—

(a)   the period beginning on the date on which CHS is established and ending—

(i)   on 31 March next occurring, or

(ii)   if that period is of less than 6 months' duration, on 31 March next occurring after that, and

(b)   each subsequent period of a year ending on 31 March.

24   National Convener's annual report

(1)   The National Convener must, as soon as is reasonably practicable after the end of each financial year, prepare and submit to CHS a report on the carrying out during the year of the functions conferred on the National Convener by virtue of this Act or any other enactment.

(2)   The National Convener may include in the report any other information that the National Convener considers appropriate.

(3)   In this paragraph, 'financial year' means—

(a)   the period beginning with the appointment of the first National Convener and ending—

(i)   on 31 March next occurring, or

(ii)   if that period is of less than 6 months' duration, on 31 March next occurring after that, and

(b)   each subsequent period of a year ending on 31 March.

25   Validity of proceedings and actions

The validity of proceedings or actions of CHS (including proceedings or actions of any of its committees) is not affected by—

(a)   any vacancy in the membership of CHS or any of its committees,

(b)   any defect in the appointment of a member of CHS or any of its committees, or

(c)   the disqualification of a person as a member of CHS after appointment.

DAMAGES (SCOTLAND) ACT 2011
(2011, asp 7)

3   Application of sections 4 to 6

Sections 4 to 6 apply where a person ('A') dies in consequence of suffering personal injuries as the result of the act or omission of another person ('B') and the act or omission—

(a)   gives rise to liability to pay damages to A (or to A's executor), or

(b)   would have given rise to such liability but for A's death.

4 Sums of damages payable to relatives

(1) B is liable under this subsection to pay—

(a) to any relative of A who is a member of A's immediate family, such sums of damages as are mentioned in paragraphs (a) and (b) of subsection (3),

(b) to any other relative of A, such sum of damages as is mentioned in paragraph (a) of that subsection.

(2) But, except as provided for in section 5, no such liability arises if the liability to pay damages to A (or to A's executor) in respect of the act or omission—

(a) is excluded or discharged, whether by antecedent agreement or otherwise, by A before A's death, or

(b) is excluded by virtue of an enactment.

(3) The sums of damages are—

(a) such sum as will compensate for any loss of support which as a result of the act or omission is sustained, or is likely to be sustained, by the relative after the date of A's death together with any reasonable expenses incurred by the relative in connection with A's funeral, and

(b) such sum, if any, as the court thinks just by way of compensation for all or any of the following—

(i) distress and anxiety endured by the relative in contemplation of the suffering of A before A's death,

(ii) grief and sorrow of the relative caused by A's death,

(iii) the loss of such non-patrimonial benefit as the relative might have been expected to derive from A's society and guidance if A had not died.

(4) The court, in making an award under paragraph (b) of subsection (3) is not required to ascribe any part of the award specifically to any of the sub-paragraphs of that paragraph.

(5) For the purpose of subsection (1)(a)—

(a) a relative of A is a member of A's immediate family if the relative falls within any of paragraphs (a) to (d) of the definition of 'relative' in section 14(1),

(b) paragraphs (a)(i) and (b) of section 14(2) are to be disregarded.

6 Relative's loss of personal services

(1) A relative entitled to damages under paragraph (a) of section 4(3) is entitled to include, as a head of damages under that paragraph, a reasonable sum in respect of the loss to the relative of A's personal services as a result of the act or omission.

(2) In subsection (1), 'personal services' has the same meaning as in section 9(1) of the Administration of Justice Act 1982 (c 53) (damages in respect of inability of injured person to render such services).

7 Assessment of compensation for loss of support

(1) Such part of an award under paragraph (a) of section 4(3) as consists of a sum in compensation for loss of support is to be assessed applying the following paragraphs—

(a) the total amount to be available to support A's relatives is an amount equivalent to 75% of A's net income,

(b) in the case of any other relative than—

(i) a person described in paragraph (a) of the definition of 'relative' in section 14(1), or

(ii) a dependent child,

the relative is not to be awarded more in compensation for loss of support than the actual amount of that loss,

(c) if—

(i) no such other relative is awarded a sum in compensation for loss of support, the total amount mentioned in paragraph (a) is to be taken to be spent by A in supporting such of A's relatives as are mentioned in sub-paragraphs (i) and (ii) of paragraph (b),

(ii) any such other relative is awarded a sum in compensation for loss of support, the total amount mentioned in paragraph (a) is, after deduction of the amount of the sum so awarded, to be taken to be spent by A in supporting such of A's relatives as are mentioned in those sub-paragraphs, and

(d) any multiplier applied by the court—

(i) is to run from the date of the interlocutor awarding damages, and

(ii) is to apply only in respect of future loss of support.

(2) But, if satisfied that it is necessary to do so for the purpose of avoiding a manifestly and materially unfair result, the court may apply a different percentage to that specified in subsection (1)(a).

(3) In subsection (1)(b)(ii), 'dependent child' means a child who as at the date of A's death—

(a) has not attained the age of 18 years, and

(b) is owed an obligation of aliment by A.

8 Further provision as regards relative's entitlement to damages

(1) Subject to subsection (3), in assessing for the purposes of section 4 or 6 the amount of any loss of support sustained by a relative of A no account is to be taken of—

(a) any patrimonial gain or advantage which has accrued or will or may accrue to the relative, by way of succession or settlement, from A or from any other person, or

(b) any insurance money, benefit, pension or gratuity which has been, or will or may be, paid as a result of A's death.

(2) In subsection (1)—

'benefit' means benefit under the Social Security Contributions and Benefits Act 1992 (c 4) or the Social Security Contributions and Benefits (Northern Ireland) Act 1992 (c 7) and any payment by a friendly society or trade union for the relief or maintenance of a member's dependants,

'insurance money' includes a return of premiums, and

'pension' includes a return of contributions and any payment of a lump sum in respect of a person's employment.

(3) Where A has been awarded a provisional award of damages under section 12(2) of the Administration of Justice Act 1982 (c 53), the making of that award does not prevent liability from arising under section 4(1); but in assessing for the purposes of section 4 or 6 the amount of any loss of support sustained by a relative the court is to take into account such part of the provisional award relating to future patrimonial loss as was intended to compensate A for a period beyond the date on which A died.

(4) In order to establish loss of support for the purposes of section 4 or 6, it is not essential for a relative to show that A was, or might have become, subject to a duty in law to provide support for, or contribute to the support of, the relative; but if any such fact is established it may be taken into account in determining whether, and if so to what extent, A would (had A not died) have been likely to provide, or contribute to, such support.

(5) Except as provided for in this Act or in any other enactment, no person is entitled by reason of relationship to damages in respect of the death of another person.

(6) In subsection (5), 'damages' includes damages by way of solatium.

14 Interpretation

(1) In this Act, unless the context otherwise requires—

'personal injuries' means—

(a) any disease, and

(b) any impairment of a person's physical or mental condition, and

'relative', in relation to a person who has died, means a person who—

(a)   immediately before the death is the deceased's spouse or civil partner or is living with the deceased as if married to, or in civil partnership with, the deceased,

(b)   is a parent or child of the deceased, accepted the deceased as a child of the person's family or was accepted by the deceased as a child of the deceased's family,

(c)   is the brother or sister of the deceased or was brought up in the same household as the deceased and accepted as a child of the family in which the deceased was a child,

(d)   is a grandparent or grandchild of the deceased, accepted the deceased as a grandchild of the person or was accepted by the deceased as a grandchild of the deceased,

(e)   is an ascendant or descendant of the deceased (other than a parent or grandparent or a child or grandchild of the deceased),

(f)   is an uncle or aunt of the deceased,

(g)   is a child or other issue of—

(i)   a brother or sister of the deceased, or

(ii)   an uncle or aunt of the deceased, or

(h)   is a former spouse or civil partner of the deceased having become so by virtue of divorce or (as the case may be) dissolution of the partnership.

(2)   In deducing a relationship for the purposes of the definition of 'relative' in subsection (1)—

(a)   any relationship—

(i)   by affinity is to be treated as a relationship by consanguinity,

(ii)   of the half blood is to be treated as a relationship of the whole blood,

(b)   a stepchild of a person is to be treated as the person's child.

(3)   In any enactment passed or made before this Act, unless the context otherwise requires, any reference to—

(a)   solatium in respect of the death of any person (however expressed), or

(b)   a loss of society award,

is to be construed as a reference to an award under paragraph (b) of section 4(3).

FORCED MARRIAGE ETC (PROTECTION AND JURISDICTION) (SCOTLAND) ACT 2011
(2011, asp 15)

PART 1
FORCED MARRIAGE PROTECTION ORDERS

Forced marriage protection orders

1   Forced marriage protection orders

(1)   The court may make an order for the purposes of protecting a person (a 'protected person')—

(a)   from being forced into a marriage or from any attempt to force the person into a marriage, or

(b)   who has been forced into a marriage.

(2)   In deciding whether to make such an order and, if so, what order to make, the court must have regard to all the circumstances including the need to secure the health, safety and well-being of the protected person.

(3)   In ascertaining the protected person's well-being, the court must, in particular, have such regard to the person's wishes and feelings (so far as they are reasonably ascertainable) as the court considers appropriate on the basis of the person's age and understanding.

(4)   For the purposes of this Part, a person ('A') is forced into a marriage if another person ('B') forces A to enter into a marriage (whether with B or another person) without A's free and full consent.

(5)   For the purposes of subsection (4), it does not matter whether the conduct of B which forces A to enter into a marriage is directed against A, B or another person.

(6)   In this Part—

'force' includes—

(a)   coerce by physical, verbal or psychological means, threatening conduct, harassment or other means,

(b)   knowingly take advantage of a person's incapacity to consent to marriage or to understand the nature of the marriage,

and related expressions are to be read accordingly,

'forced marriage protection order' means an order under subsection (1).

2   Contents of orders

(1)   A forced marriage protection order may contain such—

(a)   prohibitions, restrictions or requirements, and

(b)   other terms,

as the court considers appropriate for the purposes of the order.

(2)   The terms of such an order may, in particular, relate to—

(a)   conduct outwith (as well as, or instead of, conduct within) Scotland,

(b)   persons who force or attempt to force, or may force or attempt to force, a protected person to enter into a marriage,

(c)   persons who are, or may become, involved in other respects.

(3)   A forced marriage protection order may, among other things, require a person—

(a)   to take the protected person to a place of safety designated in the order,

(b)   to bring the protected person to a court at such time and place as the court making the order may specify,

(c)   to refrain from violent, threatening or intimidating conduct (whether against the protected person or any other person),

(d)   who is a person such as is mentioned in subsection (2)(b) or (c), to appear in court,

(e)   to disclose, if known, the whereabouts of such a person,

(f)   to refrain from taking the protected person from, or to, such place as the court may specify,

(g)   to facilitate or otherwise enable the protected person or another person to return or go to such place (whether in Scotland or another part of the United Kingdom) as the court may specify within such period as may be so specified,

(h)   to submit to the court such documents (including passports, birth certificates or other documents identifying the person and travel documents) as the court may specify,

(i)   to provide the court with such other information as it may specify.

(4)   For the purposes of subsection (2)(c), examples of involvement in other respects are—

(a)   aiding, abetting, counselling, procuring, encouraging or assisting another person to force, or to attempt to force, a person to enter into a marriage,

(b)   conspiring to force, or to attempt to force, a person to enter into a marriage.

3   Applications for orders

(1)   The court may make a forced marriage protection order on an application being made to it by—

(a)   the protected person, or

(b)   a relevant third party.

(2)   An application may be made by any other person only with the leave of the court.

(3)   In deciding whether to grant such leave, the court must have regard to all the circumstances including—

(a)   the applicant's connection with the protected person,

(b) the applicant's knowledge of the circumstances of the protected person, and

(c) the wishes and feelings of the protected person so far as they are reasonably ascertainable.

(4) But the court need only have regard to those wishes and feelings so far as it considers it appropriate, on the basis of the protected person's age and understanding, to do so.

(5) An application made to the sheriff under this section is to be made by summary application.

(6) An application made to the sheriff under this section is to be made—

(a) to the sheriff in whose sheriffdom the protected person is ordinarily resident, or

(b) where the protected person is not ordinarily resident in Scotland, to the sheriff of the sheriffdom of Lothian and Borders at Edinburgh.

(7) In this section, 'a relevant third party' means—

(a) a local authority,

(b) the Lord Advocate,

(c) a person specified, or falling within a description of persons specified, by order made by the Scottish Ministers.

4   Power to make orders without application, etc

(1) The court may make a forced marriage protection order without an application being made to it where—

(a) civil proceedings are before the court,

(b) the court considers that a forced marriage protection order should be made to protect a person (whether or not a party to the civil proceedings), and

(c) a person who would be a party to any proceedings for the forced marriage protection order (other than as the protected person) is a party to the civil proceedings.

(2) Subsection (3) applies where—

(a) criminal proceedings are before the sheriff [, the Sheriff Appeal Court] or the High Court, and

(b) the sheriff [, the Sheriff Appeal Court] or the High Court considers that a forced marriage protection order should be made to protect a person (whether or not a party to the criminal proceedings).

(3) The sheriff [, the Sheriff Appeal Court] or, as the case may be, the High Court may refer the matter to the Lord Advocate who may—

(a) apply under section 3 for a forced marriage protection order,

(b) take such other steps as the Lord Advocate considers appropriate.

Interim orders

5   Interim orders

(1) The court may, in a case where it considers that it is equitable to do so, make a forced marriage protection order in the absence of a person who is, or would be, a party to proceedings for the order (and may do so whether or not the person has been given such notice of the application for the order as would otherwise be required by rules of court).

(2) An order made by virtue of subsection (1) is an 'interim forced marriage protection order'.

(3) In deciding whether to make an interim order by virtue of subsection (1), the court must have regard to all the circumstances including any risk of significant harm to the protected person or to another person if the order is not made immediately.

(4) In this Part (unless the context otherwise requires), references to forced marriage protection orders include references to interim forced marriage protection orders.

Duration, variation, recall and extension

6 Duration of orders

A forced marriage protection order has effect—

(a)   where the order specifies a period for which it is to have effect, until the expiry of that period (unless the order is recalled under section 7 or extended under section 8),

(b)   where no such period is specified, until the order is recalled under section 7.

7 Variation and recall of orders

(1)   The court may vary or recall a forced marriage protection order on an application by—

(a)   any person who was or, in the case of an order made by virtue of section 4(1) or 5(1), would have been a party to the proceedings for the order,

(b)   the protected person (if not such a person),

(c)   any other person affected by the order, or

(d)   with the leave of the court only, any person not falling within paragraphs (a) to (c).

(2)   In deciding whether to grant leave under subsection (1)(d), the court must have regard to all the circumstances including—

(a)   the applicant's connection with the protected person,

(b)   the applicant's knowledge of the circumstances of the protected person, and

(c)   the wishes and feelings of the protected person so far as they are reasonably ascertainable.

(3)   But the court need only have regard to those wishes and feelings so far as it considers it appropriate, on the basis of the protected person's age and understanding, to do so.

(4)   In addition, the court may vary or recall a forced marriage protection order made by virtue of section 4(1) even though no application under subsection (1) of this section has been made to the court.

(5)   Section 5 applies to the variation of a forced marriage protection order as it applies to the making of an interim forced marriage protection order; and accordingly the references in that section to the making of such an interim order are to be read for the purposes of this subsection as references to varying a forced marriage protection order.

(6)   In this Part, where a forced marriage protection order specifies a period for which it is to have effect, references to varying an order do not include extending any such period.

8 Extension of orders

(1)   This section applies where a forced marriage protection order specifies a period for which it is to have effect.

(2)   Before the expiry of the period, a person mentioned in subsection (3) may apply to the court for an extension of the order.

(3)   The persons are—

(a)   any person who was or, in the case of an order made by virtue of section 4(1) or 5(1), would have been a party to the proceedings for the order,

(b)   the protected person (if not such a person),

(c)   any other person affected by the order, or

(d)   with the leave of the court only, any person not falling within paragraphs (a) to (c).

(4)   In deciding whether to grant leave under subsection (3)(d), the court must have regard to all the circumstances including—

(a)   the applicant's connection with the protected person,

(b)   the applicant's knowledge of the circumstances of the protected person, and

(c)   the wishes and feelings of the protected person so far as they are reasonably ascertainable.

(5)   But the court need only have regard to those wishes and feelings so far as it considers it appropriate, on the basis of the protected person's age and understanding, to do so.

(6)   In addition, where the order was made by virtue of section 4(1), the court may before the expiry of the period extend the order even though no application has been made to the court.

(7)   An order may be extended on more than one occasion.

(8)   Section 5 applies to the extension of a forced marriage protection order as it applies to the making of an interim forced marriage protection order; and accordingly the references in that section to the making of such an interim order are to be read for the purposes of this subsection as references to extending such an order.

Offence

9   Offence of breaching order

(1)   Any person who, knowingly and without reasonable excuse, breaches a forced marriage protection order commits an offence.

[. . .]

(4)   A person guilty of an offence under subsection (1) is liable—

(a)   on summary conviction, to imprisonment for a period not exceeding 12 months, to a fine not exceeding the statutory maximum, or to both,

(b)   on conviction on indictment, to imprisonment for a period not exceeding 2 years, to a fine, or to both.

(5)   Where a person is convicted of an offence under subsection (1) in respect of any conduct, that conduct is not punishable as a contempt of court.

Power to apply Part to civil partnerships

10   Power to apply Part to civil partnerships

(1)   The Scottish Ministers may by order make provision applying this Part (or particular provisions of it) to civil partnerships as it applies (or as the particular provisions of it apply) to marriages.

(2)   An order under subsection (1) may, for the purposes of the application mentioned in that subsection, make such modifications of enactments (including of this Act) as the Scottish Ministers consider necessary.

Supplementary

11   Guidance

(1)   The Scottish Ministers must, no later than the day on which section 1 comes into force, give guidance to such persons or descriptions of persons as Ministers consider appropriate about the effect of this Part or any provision of it.

(2)   The Scottish Ministers may give guidance to such persons or descriptions of persons as Ministers consider appropriate about matters (other than that mentioned in subsection (1)) relating to forced marriages.

(3)   A person exercising public functions to whom guidance is given under this section must have regard to it in the exercise of those functions.

(4)   The Scottish Ministers may not give guidance under this section to any court or tribunal.

12   Other protection or assistance against forced marriage

(1)   This Part does not affect any other protection or assistance available to a person who—

(a)   is being, or may be, forced into a marriage,

(b)   is being, or may be, subjected to an attempt to force the person into a marriage, or

(c)   has been forced into a marriage.

(2)   In particular, it does not affect—

(a)   the equitable jurisdiction of the High Court or the Court of Session,

(b)   any criminal liability,

(c)   any civil remedies under the Protection from Harassment Act 1997 (c 40),

(d)   any right to—

(i)   an order under the Matrimonial Homes (Family Protection) (Scotland) Act 1981 (c 59) relating to occupancy rights,

(ii)   an exclusion order under that Act,

(e)   any protection or assistance under the Children (Scotland) Act 1995 (c 36) or the Children's Hearings (Scotland) Act 2011 (asp 1),

(f) any claim in delict, or

(g)   the law of marriage.

13   *[Amends Children's Hearings (Scotland) Act 2011.]*

14 Interpretation of Part

In this Part (except where the context otherwise requires)—

'court' means the Court of Session or the sheriff [and in sections 1, 2, 4 and 5 includes the Sheriff Appeal Court],

'force' and related expressions have the meanings given by section 1(6),

'forced marriage protection order' has the meaning given by section 1(6),

'interim forced marriage protection order' has the meaning given by section 5(2),

'marriage' means any religious or civil ceremony of marriage (wherever carried out and whether or not legally binding under the law of Scotland or any other place),

'protected person' has the meaning given by section 1(1).

PART 3

GENERAL

16 Ancillary provision

(1)   The Scottish Ministers may by order make such incidental, consequential, transitional, transitory or saving provision as they consider appropriate for the purposes, or in consequence, of any provision of this Act.

(2)   An order under subsection (1) may modify any enactment (including this Act).

17 Subordinate legislation

(1)   Any power conferred by this Act on the Scottish Ministers to make orders is exercisable by statutory instrument.

(2)   Subject to subsection (3), a statutory instrument containing an order under this Act (other than one under section 19(2)) is subject to annulment in pursuance of a resolution of the Scottish Parliament.

(3)   No order under—

(a)   section 10(1),

(b)   section 16(1) containing provisions which add to, replace or omit any part of the text of any Act,

may be made unless a draft of the statutory instrument containing the order has been laid before, and approved by resolution of, the Scottish Parliament.

18 Crown application

(1)   No contravention by the Crown of—

(a)   section 9(1), or

(b) any provision made by virtue of section 10,
makes the Crown criminally liable.

(2) But the Court of Session may, on the application of any public body or office holder having responsibility for enforcing section 9(1) or any provision made by virtue of section 10, declare unlawful any act or omission of the Crown which constitutes such a contravention.

(3) Despite subsection (1), section 9(1) and any provision made by virtue of section 10 apply to persons in the public service of the Crown as they apply to other persons.

(4) Nothing in this Act affects Her Majesty in Her private capacity.

19 Short title and commencement

(1) The short title of this Act is the Forced Marriage etc (Protection and Jurisdiction) (Scotland) Act 2011.

(2) This Act (other than this section) comes into force on such day as the Scottish Ministers may by order appoint.

MARRIAGE AND CIVIL PARTNERSHIP (SCOTLAND) ACT 2014
(2014, asp 5)

PART 1
MARRIAGE

Chapter 1
Same Sex Marriage

1 – 3 *[Amend Marriage (Scotland) Act 1977.]*

4 Meaning of marriage and related expressions in enactments and documents

(1) References (however expressed) in any enactment to—
  (a) marriage (including a marriage that has ended),
  (b) a person who is (or was) married to another person, and
  (c) two people who are (or were) married to each other,
are references to marriage whether between persons of different sexes or persons of the same sex and to a party (or former party), or as the case may be the parties (or former parties), to such a marriage.

(2) Subsection (3) applies to references (however expressed) in any enactment to two people who—
  (a) are (or were) not married to each other, but
  (b) are (or were) living together as if they were husband and wife.

(3) The references include two people of the same sex who are (or were) not married to, nor in civil partnership with, each other but who are (or were) living together as if they were married to each other.

(4) References (however expressed) in any enactment to two people of the same sex who are (or were) living together as if they were in a civil partnership cease to have effect.

(5) Subsections (1) to (4)—
  (a) apply to enactments (other than private Acts) passed or made before the commencement of this section, and
  (b) do not apply in so far as the enactment, or any other enactment, provides otherwise.

(6) In so far as being (or having been) married or in a purported marriage is relevant for the operation of any rule of law, the rule of law applies equally in relation to marriage or purported marriage to a person of a different sex and marriage or purported marriage to a person of the same sex.

(7) Subsections (1) to (6) are subject to an order under subsection (8).

(8) The Scottish Ministers may by order provide for any of subsections (1) to (6)—

    (a) to have effect subject to provision made by the order, or

    (b) not to apply in cases specified in the order.

(9) An order under subsection (8)—

    (a) may make different provision for different purposes,

    (b) may include consequential, supplementary, incidental, transitional, transitory or saving provision,

    (c) may modify any enactment (including this Act),

    (d) is (except where subsection (10) applies) subject to the negative procedure.

(10) An order under subsection (8) which adds to, replaces or omits any part of the text of an Act is subject to the affirmative procedure.

(11) References (however expressed) in any document to—

    (a) marriage (including a marriage that has ended),

    (b) a person who is (or was) married to another person, and

    (c) two people who are (or were) married to each other,

are references to marriage whether between persons of different sexes or persons of the same sex and to a party (or former party), or as the case may be the parties (or former parties), to such a marriage.

(12) The following expressions in any document have the meanings given—

    (a) 'widow' includes a woman whose marriage to another woman ended with the other woman's death,

    (b) 'widower' includes a man whose marriage to another man ended with the other man's death.

(13) Subsections (11) and (12)—

    (a) apply to documents executed on or after the commencement of this section, and

    (b) do not apply in so far as the document provides otherwise.

(14) In section 26(2) of the 1977 Act (interpretation), after the definition of 'authorised registrar' insert—

"marriage' means marriage between persons of different sexes and marriage between persons of the same sex;'.

(15) In schedule 1 to the Interpretation and Legislative Reform (Scotland) Act 2010 (definitions of words and expressions), insert at the appropriate place in alphabetical order—

"marriage' means marriage between persons of different sexes and marriage between persons of the same sex (and any reference to a person being (or having been) married to another person, or to two people being (or having been) married to each other, is to be read accordingly),',

"widow' includes a woman whose marriage to another woman ended with the other woman's death,',

"widower' includes a man whose marriage to another man ended with the other man's death,'.

5 Same sex marriage: further provision

(1) For the avoidance of doubt, the rule of law which provides for a marriage to be voidable by reason of impotence has effect only in relation to a marriage between persons of different sexes.

(2) [Amends Divorce (Scotland) Act 1976.]

7 Reset: abolition of defence

(1) Any rule of law under which a wife who receives or conceals goods stolen by her husband does not commit the offence of reset ceases to apply.

(2) Subsection (1) applies only in relation to things done after the day on which this section comes into force.

Chapter 2
Marriage Between Civil Partners in Qualifying Civil Partnerships

9   Power to modify meaning of 'qualifying civil partnership'

(1)   The Scottish Ministers may by order modify the meaning of 'qualifying civil partnership' given by section 5(6) of the 1977 Act (inserted by section 8(3)(b) of this Act) so as to include civil partnerships registered outside Scotland.

(2)   An order under subsection (1)—

(a)   may make different provision for different purposes,

(b)   may include consequential, supplementary, incidental, transitional, transitory or saving provision,

(c)   may modify any enactment (including this Act),

(d)   is subject to the affirmative procedure.

(3)   Before laying a draft of an order under subsection (1) before the Scottish Parliament, the Scottish Ministers must consult the following persons on a copy of the proposed draft order—

(a)   the Registrar General of Births, Deaths and Marriages for Scotland, and

(b)   such other persons as the Scottish Ministers consider appropriate.

10   Change of qualifying civil partnership into marriage

(1)   The Scottish Ministers may by regulations make provision to establish a procedure for the parties to a qualifying civil partnership to change their civil partnership into a marriage.

(2)   Regulations under subsection (1) may in particular make provision—

(a)   about the making by the parties to a qualifying civil partnership of an application to change their civil partnership into a marriage,

(b)   about the information to be provided in support of an application,

(c)   about the provision of evidence in support of an application,

(d)   for persons who have made an application to appear before any person or appear at any place,

(e)   conferring functions on persons in relation to applications,

(f)   for fees, of such amounts as are specified in or determined in accordance with the regulations, to be payable in respect of—

(i)   the making of an application,

(ii)   the exercise of any function conferred by virtue of paragraph (e).

(3)   Functions conferred by virtue of subsection (2)(e) may include functions relating to—

(a)   the recording of information relating to qualifying civil partnerships changing into marriages,

(b)   the issuing of certified copies of any information recorded.

(4)   Before making regulations under subsection (1), the Scottish Ministers must consult the Registrar General of Births, Deaths and Marriages for Scotland.

(5)   Regulations under subsection (1)—

(a)   may make different provision for different purposes,

(b)   may include consequential, supplementary, incidental, transitional, transitory or saving provision,

(c)   may modify any enactment (including this Act),

(d)   are (except where subsection (6) applies) subject to the negative procedure.

(6)   Regulations under subsection (1) which add to, replace or omit any part of the text of an Act are subject to the affirmative procedure.

(7)   In this section 'qualifying civil partnership' has the meaning given by [section 5(6)(i)(A)] of the 1977 Act.

11   Effect of marriage between civil partners in a qualifying civil partnership

(1)   This section applies where civil partners in a qualifying civil partnership (within the meaning of section 5(6) of the 1977 Act)—

(a)   marry in accordance with that Act, or

(b)   change their civil partnership into a marriage in accordance with provision made under section 10(1).

(2)   Where this section applies—

    (a)   the qualifying civil partnership ends on the date on which—

        (i)   the marriage was solemnised, or

        (ii)   the change took effect, and

(b)   the civil partners are to be treated as having been married to each other
since the date on which the qualifying civil partnership was registered.

(3)   For the purposes of subsection (2)(b)—

    (a)   a civil partnership registered under an Order in Council made under
section 210 of the 2004 Act is to be treated as having been registered when it is
entered in the Register Book maintained under the Order,

    (b)   a civil partnership registered under an Order in Council made under
section 211 of the 2004 Act is to be treated as having been registered when the
civil partnership register is signed in accordance with the Order.

(4)   Subsection (2)(b) is subject to—

    (a)   any provision to the contrary made by or under any enactment,

    (b)   an order under subsection (5).

(5)   The Scottish Ministers may by order provide for subsection (2)(b)—

    (a)   to have effect subject to provision made by the order, or

    (b)   not to apply in cases specified in the order.

(6)   An order under subsection (5)—

    (a)   may include consequential, supplementary, incidental, transitional, tran-
sitory or saving provision,

    (b)   is subject to the negative procedure.

(7)   If a decree of aliment under section 3 of the Family Law (Scotland) Act 1985
(powers of court in action for aliment) requiring one of the civil partners to make
payments to the other is in force at the time the qualifying civil partnership ends
by virtue of subsection (2)(a) of this section, the decree continues to have effect
despite the ending of the civil partnership.

(8)   If an order under section 103(3) or (4) of the 2004 Act (regulation by court
of rights of occupancy of family home) is in force at the time the qualifying civil
partnership ends by virtue of subsection (2)(a) of this section the order has effect
from that time as if made under section 3(3) or, as the case may be, 3(4) of the
Matrimonial Homes (Family Protection) (Scotland) Act 1981 (regulation by court of
rights of occupancy of matrimonial home).

(9)   *[Amends Civil Partnership Act 2004.]*

Chapter 4
Same Sex Marriage: Protection of Freedom of Expression etc

16   Same sex marriage: protection of freedom of expression etc

(1)   For the avoidance of doubt, nothing in this Part so far as it makes provision
for the marriage of persons of the same sex and as to the persons who may solemnise such marriages affects the exercise of—

    (a)   the Convention right to freedom of thought, conscience and religion,

    (b)   the Convention right to freedom of expression, or

    (c)   any equivalent right conferred by rule of law.

(2)   'Convention right' has the same meaning as in the Human Rights Act 1998.

PART 3
MARRIAGE AND CIVIL PARTNERSHIP: OTHER PROVISION

28 Bigamy

. . .

(3) The common law offence of bigamy is abolished.

. . .

PART 4
CHANGE OF GENDER OF MARRIED PERSONS OR CIVIL PARTNERS

30 Renewed marriage or civil partnership following issue of full gender recognition certificate

(1) The Scottish Ministers may by regulations make provision about—

(a) the solemnisation of a renewed marriage between the parties to a protected Scottish marriage following the issue of a full gender recognition certificate to a party (or both parties) to the marriage,

(b) the registration of a renewed civil partnership between the parties to a protected Scottish civil partnership following the issue of full gender recognition certificates to [a party (or both parties)] to the civil partnership.

(2) Regulations under subsection (1) may in particular make provision—

(a) about the submitting by the parties to the protected Scottish marriage of notice of intention to enter into a renewed marriage,

(b) about the submitting by the parties to the protected Scottish civil partnership of notice of intention to enter into a renewed civil partnership,

(c) about the information to be provided by the parties,

(d) about the provision of evidence by the parties,

(e) for the parties to appear before any person or appear at any place,

(f) conferring functions on persons in relation to a renewed marriage or renewed civil partnership,

(g) for fees, of such amounts as are specified in or determined in accordance with the regulations, to be payable in respect of—

(i) the submitting of notice of intention to enter into a renewed marriage or renewed civil partnership,

(ii) the exercise of any function conferred by virtue of paragraph (f).

(3) Functions conferred by virtue of subsection (2)(f) may include functions relating to—

(a) the recording of information relating to a renewed marriage or renewed civil partnership,

(b) the issuing of certified copies of any information recorded,

(c) the conducting of services or ceremonies in connection with a renewed marriage or renewed civil partnership.

(4) Before making regulations under subsection (1), the Scottish Ministers must consult the Registrar General of Births, Deaths and Marriages for Scotland.

(5) Regulations under subsection (1)—

(a) may include consequential, supplementary, incidental, transitional, transitory or saving provision,

(b) may make provision applying any provision of the 1977 Act or the 2004 Act (either with or without modifications),

(c) may modify any enactment (including this Act),

(d) are (except where subsection (6) applies) subject to the negative procedure.

(6) Regulations under subsection (1) which add to, replace or omit any part of the text of an Act are subject to the affirmative procedure.

(7) In this section 'full gender recognition certificate', 'protected Scottish civil partnership' and 'protected Scottish marriage' have the meanings given by section 25 of the Gender Recognition Act 2004.

PART 6
GENERAL PROVISIONS

34 Interpretation
In this Act—
  'the 1977 Act' means the Marriage (Scotland) Act 1977,
  'the 2004 Act' means the Civil Partnership Act 2004.

35 Ancillary provision
  (1) The Scottish Ministers may by order make such supplementary, incidental, consequential, transitional, transitory or saving provision as they consider necessary or expedient for the purposes of, or in connection with, or for giving full effect to, any provision of this Act.
  (2) An order under subsection (1) may make different provision for different purposes.
  (3) An order under subsection (1) may modify any enactment (including this Act).
  (4) Subject to subsection (5), an order under subsection (1) is subject to the negative procedure.
  (5) An order under subsection (1) containing provisions which add to, replace or omit any part of the text of an Act is subject to the affirmative procedure.

36 Commencement
  (1) This section and sections 34, 35 and 37 come into force on the day after Royal Assent.
  (2) The other provisions of this Act come into force on such day as the Scottish Ministers may by order appoint.
  (3) An order under subsection (2) may include transitional, transitory or saving provision.

37 Short title
The short title of this Act is the Marriage and Civil Partnership (Scotland) Act 2014.

CHILDREN AND YOUNG PEOPLE (SCOTLAND) ACT 2014
(2014, asp 8)

PART 1
RIGHTS OF CHILDREN

1 Duties of Scottish Ministers in relation to the rights of children
  (1) The Scottish Ministers must—
    (a) keep under consideration whether there are any steps which they could take which would or might secure better or further effect in Scotland of the UNCRC requirements, and
    (b) if they consider it appropriate to do so, take any of the steps identified by that consideration.
  (2) In complying with their duty under subsection (1)(a), the Scottish Ministers must take such account as they consider appropriate of any relevant views of children of which the Scottish Ministers are aware.
  (3) The Scottish Ministers must promote public awareness and understanding (including appropriate awareness and understanding among children) of the rights of children.
  (4) As soon as practicable after the end of each 3 year period, the Scottish Ministers must lay before the Scottish Parliament a report of—
    (a) what steps they have taken in that period to secure better or further effect in Scotland of the UNCRC requirements,
    (b) what they have done in that period in pursuance of subsection (3), and
    (c) their plans until the end of the next 3 year period—

(i) to take steps to secure better or further effect in Scotland of the UNCRC requirements, and

(ii) to do things in pursuance of subsection (3).

(5) In preparing such a report the Scottish Ministers must take such steps as they consider appropriate to obtain the views of children on what their plans for the purposes of subsection (4)(c) should be.

(6) In subsection (4), '3 year period' means—

(a) the period of 3 years beginning with the day on which this section comes into force, and

(b) each subsequent period of 3 years.

(7) As soon as practicable after a report has been laid before the Scottish Parliament under subsection (4), the Scottish Ministers must publish it (in such manner as they consider appropriate).

2 Duties of public authorities in relation to the UNCRC

(1) As soon as practicable after the end of each 3 year period, an authority to which this section applies must publish (in such manner as the authority considers appropriate) a report of what steps it has taken in that period to secure better or further effect within its areas of responsibility of the UNCRC requirements.

(2) In subsection (1), '3 year period' means—

(a) the period of 3 years beginning with the day on which this section comes into force, and

(b) each subsequent period of 3 years.

(3) Two or more authorities to which this section applies may satisfy subsection (1) by publishing a report prepared by them jointly.

3 Authorities to which section 2 applies

(1) The authorities to which section 2 applies are the persons listed, or persons within a description listed, in schedule 1.

(2) The Scottish Ministers may by order modify schedule 1 by—

(a) adding a person or description of persons,

(b) removing an entry listed in it, or

(c) varying an entry listed in it.

(3) An order under subsection (2)(a) may—

(a) add a person only if the person falls within subsection (4),

(b) add a description of persons only if each of the persons within the description falls within subsection (4).

(4) A person falls within this subsection if the person—

(a) is part of the Scottish Administration,

(b) is a Scottish public authority with mixed functions or no reserved functions (within the meaning of the Scotland Act 1998), or

(c) is a publicly owned company.

(5) In subsection (4)(c), 'publicly owned company' means a company that is wholly owned by—

(a) the Scottish Ministers, or

(b) a person listed, or a person within a description listed, in schedule 1.

(6) For the purpose of subsection (5), a company is wholly owned—

(a) by the Scottish Ministers if it has no members other than—

(i) the Scottish Ministers or other companies that are wholly owned by them, or

(ii) persons acting on behalf of the Scottish Ministers or of such other companies,

(b) by a person listed, or a person within a description listed, in schedule 1 if it has no members other than—

(i) the person or other companies that are wholly owned by the person, or

(ii) persons acting on behalf of the person or of such other companies.

(7) In this section, 'company' includes any body corporate.

4   Interpretation of Part 1

(1)   In this Part—

'the rights of children' includes the rights and obligations set out in—

    (a)   the UNCRC,

    (b)   the first optional protocol to the UNCRC, and

    (c)   the second optional protocol to the UNCRC,

'the UNCRC' means the United Nations Convention on the Rights of the Child adopted and opened for signature, ratification and accession by General Assembly resolution 44/25 of 20 November 1989,

'the first optional protocol' means the Optional Protocol to the Convention on the Rights of the Child on the involvement of children in armed conflict,

'the second optional protocol' means the Optional Protocol to the Convention on the Rights of the Child on the sale of children, child prostitution and child pornography,

'the UNCRC requirements' means the rights and obligations set out in—

    (a)   Part 1 of the UNCRC,

    (b)   Articles 1 to 6(1), 6(3) and 7 of the first optional protocol, and

    (c)   Articles 1 to 10 of the second optional protocol.

(2)   A reference in subsection (1) to a UNCRC document is to be read as a reference to that document subject to—

    (a)   any amendments in force in relation to the United Kingdom at the time, and

    (b)   any reservations, objections or interpretative declarations by the United Kingdom in force at the time.

(3)   In subsection (2), 'UNCRC document'—

    (a)   means the UNCRC or any optional protocol to the UNCRC, and

    (b)   includes provision of a UNCRC document.

(4)   Where subsection (5) applies, the Scottish Ministers may by order modify subsection (1) as they consider appropriate to take account of—

    (a)   an optional protocol to the UNCRC, or

    (b)   an amendment of a document referred to in subsection (1) at the time.

(5)   This subsection applies where the protocol or amendment is one which—

    (a)   the United Kingdom has ratified, or

    (b)   the United Kingdom has signed with a view to ratification.

(6)   No modification may be made by an order under subsection (4) so as to come into force before the protocol or amendment is in force in relation to the United Kingdom.

PART 3
CHILDREN'S SERVICES PLANNING

7   Introductory

(1)   For the purposes of this Part—

'children's service' means any service provided in the area of a local authority by a person mentioned in subsection (2) which is provided wholly or mainly to, or for the benefit of—

    (a)   children generally, or

    (b)   children with needs of a particular type (such as looked after children or children with a disability or a need for additional support in learning),

'other service provider' means—

    (a)   the chief constable of the Police Service of Scotland,

    (b)   the Scottish Fire and Rescue Service,

    (c)   the Principal Reporter,

    (d)   the National Convener of Children's Hearings Scotland,

    (e)   the Scottish [Courts and Tribunals Service],

[(f)　an integration joint board under section 9 of the Public Bodies (Joint Working) (Scotland) Act 2014.]

'related service' means any service provided in the area of a local authority by a person mentioned in subsection (2) which though not a children's service is capable of having a significant effect on the wellbeing of children,

'relevant health board' means—

(a)　if the area of the local authority is the same as that of a health board, that health board,

(b)　if the area of the local authority is not the same as that of a health board, the health board within whose area the area of the local authority falls.

(2)　The persons referred to in the definitions of 'children's service' and 'related service' in subsection (1) are—

(a)　the local authority,

(b)　the relevant health board,

(c)　any other service provider,

(d)　the Scottish Ministers (but only in relation to a service provided by them in exercise of their functions under the Prisons (Scotland) Act 1989).

(3)　The Scottish Ministers may by order specify—

(a)　services which are to be considered to be included within or excluded from the definition of 'children's service' or 'related service' in subsection (1),

(b)　matters in relation to services falling within either of those definitions which are to be considered to be included within or excluded from those services.

(4)　Before making such an order, the Scottish Ministers must consult—

(a)　each health board,

(b)　each local authority, and

(c)　where the service concerned is provided by one of the other service providers, that person.

(5)　The Scottish Ministers may by order modify the definition of 'other service provider' in subsection (1) by—

(a)　adding a person or a description of persons,

(b)　removing an entry listed in it, or

(c)　varying an entry listed in it.

(6)　A function conferred by this Part on a local authority and the relevant health board is to be exercised by those persons jointly.

8　Requirement to prepare children's services plan

(1)　A local authority and the relevant health board must in respect of each 3 year period prepare a children's services plan for the area of the local authority.

(2)　In subsection (1)—

'3 year period' means—

(a)　the period of 3 years beginning with such date after the coming into force of this section as the Scottish Ministers specify by order, and

(b)　each subsequent period of 3 years,

'children's services plan' means a document setting out their plans for the provision over that period of all—

(a)　children's services, and

(b)　related services.

9　Aims of children's services plan

(1)　A children's services plan is to be prepared with a view to securing the achievement of the aims in subsection (2).

(2)　Those aims are—

(a)　that children's services in the area concerned are provided in the way which—

(i)　best safeguards, supports and promotes the wellbeing of children in the area concerned,

(ii) ensures that any action to meet needs is taken at the earliest appropriate time and that, where appropriate, action is taken to prevent needs arising,

(iii) is most integrated from the point of view of recipients, and

(iv) constitutes the best use of available resources,

(b) that related services in the area concerned are provided in the way which, so far as consistent with the objects and proper delivery of the service concerned, safeguards, supports and promotes the wellbeing of children in the area concerned.

10   Children's services plan: process

(1) In preparing a children's services plan a local authority and the relevant health board must—

(a) give each of the other service providers and the Scottish Ministers an effective opportunity (consistent with the extent to which the services they provide are to be the subject of the children's services plan) to participate in or contribute to the preparation of the plan, and

(b) consult—

(i) such organisations as appear to fall within subsection (2),

(ii) such social landlords as appear to provide housing in the area of the local authority, and

(iii) such other persons as the Scottish Ministers may by direction specify.

(2) The organisations falling within this subsection are organisations (whether or not formally constituted) which—

(a) represent the interests of persons who use or are likely to use any children's service or related service in the area of the local authority, or

(b) provide a service in the area which, if it were provided by the local authority, the relevant health board, any of the other service providers or the Scottish Ministers, would be a children's service or a related service.

(3) In subsection (1)(b)(ii), 'social landlords' has the meaning given by section 165 of the Housing (Scotland) Act 2010.

(4) A direction under subsection (1)(b)(iii) may be revised or revoked.

(5) Each of the other service providers is and the Scottish Ministers are to participate in or contribute to the preparation of the children's services plan in accordance with the opportunity given to them under subsection (1)(a).

(6) The persons to be consulted under subsection (1)(b) are to meet any reasonable request which the local authority and the relevant health board make of them—

(a) to participate in the preparation of the children's services plan for the area,

(b) to contribute to the preparation of that plan.

(7) As soon as reasonably practicable after a children's services plan has been prepared, the local authority and the relevant health board must—

(a) send a copy to—

(i) the Scottish Ministers, and

(ii) each of the other service providers, and

(b) publish it (in such manner as the local authority and the relevant health board consider appropriate).

(8) Where the Scottish Ministers or any of the other service providers disagrees with the plan in relation to any matter concerning the provision of a service by them, they must prepare and publish (in such manner as they consider appropriate)—

(a) a notice of the matters in relation to which they disagree, and

(b) a statement of their reasons for disagreeing.

11   Children's services plan: review

(1) A local authority and the relevant health board—

(a) must keep the children's services plan for the area of the local authority under review, and

(b)   may in consequence prepare a revised children's services plan.

(2)   The following provisions apply to a revised children's services plan as they apply to a children's services plan—

section 9,

section 10, and

subsection (1) of this section.

12   Implementation of children's services plan

(1)   During the period to which a children's services plan relates, the persons mentioned in subsection (2) must, so far as reasonably practicable, provide children's services and relevant services in the area of the local authority in accordance with the plan.

(2)   Those persons are—

(a)   the local authority,

(b)   the relevant health board,

(c)   the Scottish Ministers,

(d)   the other service providers.

(3)   The duty in subsection (1) to provide services in accordance with the plan—

(a)   does not apply to the extent that the person providing the service considers that to comply with it would adversely affect the wellbeing of a child,

(b)   does not apply in relation to the Scottish Ministers or the other service providers to the extent of any matter within a notice published by them under section 10(8) in relation to the plan.

13   Reporting on children's services plan

(1)   As soon as practicable after the end of each 1 year period, a local authority and the relevant health board must publish (in such manner as they consider appropriate) a report on the extent to which—

(a)   children's services and related services have in that period been provided in the area of the local authority in accordance with the children's services plan, and

(b)   that provision has achieved—

(i)   the aims listed in section 9(2),

(ii)   such outcomes in relation to the wellbeing of children in the area as the Scottish Ministers may by order prescribe.

(2)   In subsection (1), '1 year period' means—

(a)   the period of 1 year beginning with the date specified under section 8(1), and

(b)   each subsequent period of 1 year.

14   Assistance in relation to children's services planning

(1)   A person mentioned in subsection (2) must comply with any reasonable request made of them to provide a local authority and the relevant health board with information, advice or assistance for the purposes of exercising their functions under this Part.

(2)   Those persons are—

(a)   any of the other service providers or the Scottish Ministers (but only in so far as the information, advice or assistance relates to a children's service or a related service which it is a function of the person to provide),

(b)   any of the persons mentioned in section 10(1)(b).

(3)   Subsection (1) does not apply where the person considers that the provision of the information, advice or assistance concerned would—

(a)   be incompatible with any duty of the person, or

(b)   unduly prejudice the exercise of any function of the person.

15   Guidance in relation to children's services planning

(1)   A person or the persons mentioned in subsection (2) must have regard to

any guidance issued by the Scottish Ministers about the exercise of functions conferred by this Part (other than the function of complying with section 12).

(2) Those persons are—
  (a) a local authority and the relevant health board,
  (b) each of the other service providers.

(3) Before issuing or revising guidance, the Scottish Ministers must consult—
  (a) any person to which it relates, and
  (b) such other persons as they consider appropriate.

16 Directions in relation to children's services planning

(1) A person or the persons mentioned in subsection (2) must comply with any direction issued by the Scottish Ministers about the exercise of functions conferred by this Part (other than the function of complying with section 12).

(2) Those persons are—
  (a) a local authority and the relevant health board,
  (b) each of the other service providers.

(3) Before issuing, revising or revoking a direction, the Scottish Ministers must consult—
  (a) any person to which it relates, and
  (b) such other persons as they consider appropriate.

17 Children's services planning: default powers of Scottish Ministers

(1) This section applies where the Scottish Ministers consider that a local authority and the relevant health board—
  (a) are not exercising a function conferred on them by this Part (other than the function of complying with section 12), or
  (b) are in exercising such a function not complying with section 15(1).

(2) The Scottish Ministers may direct that the function—
  (a) is to be exercised in a particular way, or
  (b) is to be exercised instead by such of the persons mentioned in subsection (3) as the Scottish Ministers consider appropriate.

(3) Those persons are—
  (a) the local authority,
  (b) the relevant health board,
  (c) another local authority or health board.

(4) A direction under subsection (2)(b) may include such provision as the Scottish Ministers consider appropriate as to the making by a person who is not to be exercising the function of payment to a person who is to exercise the function by virtue of the direction.

(5) Before issuing, revising or revoking a direction under subsection (2) the Scottish Ministers must consult—
  (a) the local authority and relevant health board whose failure is to be, or is, the subject of the direction, and
  (b) such other persons as they consider appropriate.

(6) The persons to whom a direction under subsection (2) is addressed must comply with the direction.

18 Interpretation of Part 3

In this Part—
  'children's services plan' has the meaning given by section 8(2),
  'service' means any service or support—
  (a) which must be provided by the person concerned, or
  (b) which the person concerned has power to provide.

PART 9
CORPORATE PARENTING

56   Corporate parents

(1)   The persons listed, or within a description listed, in schedule 4 are 'corporate parents' for the purposes of this Part (subject to subsections (3) and (4)).

(2)   The Scottish Ministers may by order modify schedule 4 by—

(a)   adding a person or description of persons,

(b)   removing an entry listed in it, or

(c)   varying an entry listed in it.

(3)   The Scottish Ministers are not corporate parents for the purposes of sections 61 to 64.

(4)   The following persons are not corporate parents for the purposes of section 64—

(a)   the Commissioner for Children and Young People in Scotland,

(b)   a body which is a 'post-16 education body' for the purposes of the Further and Higher Education (Scotland) Act 2005.

(5)   An order under subsection (2) which adds a person, or a description of persons, to schedule 4, may modify this section so as to provide that the person is not a corporate parent, or the persons within the description are not corporate parents, for the purposes of section 64.

(6)   In this Part, references to the 'corporate parenting responsibilities' of a corporate parent are to the duties conferred on that corporate parent by section 58(1).

57   Application of Part: children and young people

(1)   This Part applies to—

(a)   every child who is looked after by a local authority, and

(b)   every young person who—

(i)   is under the age of 26, and

(ii)   was (on the person's 16th birthday or at any subsequent time) but is no longer looked after by a local authority.

(2)   This Part also applies to a young person who—

(a)   is at least the age of 16 but under the age of 26, and

(b)   is not of the description in subsection (1)(b)(ii) but is of such other description of person formerly but no longer looked after by a local authority as the Scottish Ministers may specify by order.

58   Corporate parenting responsibilities

(1)   It is the duty of every corporate parent, in so far as consistent with the proper exercise of its other functions—

(a)   to be alert to matters which, or which might, adversely affect the wellbeing of children and young people to whom this Part applies,

(b)   to assess the needs of those children and young people for services and support it provides,

(c)   to promote the interests of those children and young people,

(d)   to seek to provide those children and young people with opportunities to participate in activities designed to promote their wellbeing,

(e)   to take such action as it considers appropriate to help those children and young people—

(i)   to access opportunities it provides in pursuance of paragraph (d), and

(ii)   to make use of services, and access support, which it provides, and

(f)   to take such other action as it considers appropriate for the purposes of improving the way in which it exercises its functions in relation to those children and young people.

(2)   The Scottish Ministers may by order—

(a)   modify subsection (1) so as to confer, remove or vary a duty on corporate parents,

(b)   provide that subsection (1) is to be read, in relation to a particular corporate parent or corporate parents of a particular description, with a modification conferring, removing or varying a duty.

59   Planning by corporate parents

(1)   A corporate parent must—
(a)   prepare a plan for how it proposes to exercise its corporate parenting responsibilities, and
(b)   keep its plan under review.

(2)   Before preparing or revising a plan, a corporate parent must consult such other corporate parents, and such other persons, as it considers appropriate.

(3)   A corporate parent must publish its plan, and any revised plan, in such manner as it considers appropriate (and, in particular, plans may be published together with, or as part of, any other plan or document).

60   Collaborative working among corporate parents

(1)   Corporate parents must, in so far as reasonably practicable, collaborate with each other when exercising their corporate parenting responsibilities or any other functions under this Part where they consider that doing so would safeguard or promote the wellbeing of children or young people to whom this Part applies.

(2)   Such collaboration may include—
(a)   sharing information,
(b)   providing advice or assistance,
(c)   co-ordinating activities (and seeking to prevent unnecessary duplication),
(d)   sharing responsibility for action,
(e)   funding activities jointly,
(f)   exercising functions under this Part jointly (for example, by publishing a joint plan or joint report).

61   Reports by corporate parents

(1)   A corporate parent must report on how it has exercised—
(a)   its corporate parenting responsibilities,
(b)   its planning and collaborating functions in pursuance of sections 59 and 60, and
(c)   its other functions under this Part.

(2)   Reports may, in particular, include information about—
(a)   standards of performance,
(b)   the outcomes achieved in pursuance of this Part.

(3)   Reports are to be published in such manner as the corporate parent considers appropriate (and, in particular, reports may be published together with, or as part of, any other report or document).

62   Duty to provide information to Scottish Ministers

(1)   A corporate parent must provide the Scottish Ministers with such information as they may reasonably require about how it is—
(a)   exercising its corporate parenting responsibilities,
(b)   planning, collaborating or reporting in pursuance of sections 59, 60 or 61, or
(c)   otherwise exercising functions under this Part.

(2)   Information which is required may, in particular, include information about—
(a)   standards of performance,
(b)   the outcomes achieved in pursuance of this Part.

63   Guidance on corporate parenting

(1)   A corporate parent must have regard to any guidance about corporate parenting issued by the Scottish Ministers.

(2)   Guidance may, in particular, include advice or information about—

(a)   how corporate parents should—
    (i)   exercise their corporate parenting responsibilities,
    (ii)   promote awareness of their corporate parenting responsibilities,
    (iii)   plan, collaborate or report in pursuance of sections 59, 60 or 61, or
    (iv)   otherwise exercise functions under this Part,
(b)   outcomes which corporate parents should seek to achieve in exercising functions under this Part.
(3)   Before issuing or revising guidance, the Scottish Ministers must consult—
(a)   any corporate parent to which it relates, and
(b)   such other persons as they consider appropriate.

64   Directions to corporate parents

(1)   A corporate parent must comply with any direction issued by the Scottish Ministers about—
(a)   its corporate parenting responsibilities,
(b)   its planning, collaborating or reporting functions under sections 59, 60 or 61, or
(c)   its other functions under this Part.
(2)   Before issuing, revising or revoking a direction, the Scottish Ministers must consult—
(a)   any corporate parent to which it relates, and
(b)   such other persons as they consider appropriate.

65   Reports by Scottish Ministers

(1)   The Scottish Ministers must, as soon as practicable after the end of each 3 year period, lay before the Scottish Parliament a report on how they have exercised their corporate parenting responsibilities during that period.
(2)   In subsection (1), '3 year period' means—
(a)   the period of 3 years beginning with the day on which this section comes into force, and
(b)   each subsequent period of 3 years.

PART 12
SERVICES IN RELATION TO CHILDREN AT RISK OF BECOMING LOOKED AFTER, ETC

68   Provision of relevant services to parents and others

(1)   A local authority must make arrangements to secure that relevant services of such description as the Scottish Ministers may by order specify are made available for—
(a)   each eligible child residing in its area,
(b)   a qualifying person in relation to such a child,
(c)   each eligible pregnant woman residing in its area,
(d)   a qualifying person in relation to such a woman.
(2)   A 'relevant service' is a service comprising, or comprising any combination of—
(a)   providing information about a matter,
(b)   advising or counselling about a matter,
(c)   taking other action to facilitate the addressing of a matter by a person.
(3)   An 'eligible child' is a child who the authority considers—
(a)   to be at risk of becoming looked after, or
(b)   to fall within such other description as the Scottish Ministers may by order specify.
(4)   A 'qualifying person' in relation to an eligible child is a person—
(a)   who is related to the child,

(b)   who has any parental rights or responsibilities in relation to the child, or

(c)   with whom the child is, or has been, living.

(5)   An 'eligible pregnant woman' is a pregnant woman who the authority considers is going to give birth to a child who will be an eligible child.

(6)   A 'qualifying person' in relation to an eligible pregnant woman is a person—

(a)   who is the father of the child to whom the pregnant woman is to give birth,

(b)   who is married to, in a civil partnership with or otherwise related to the pregnant woman,

(c)   with whom the pregnant woman is living, or

(d)   who does not fall within any of paragraphs (a) to (c) but who the authority considers will, when the pregnant woman gives birth to the child, become a qualifying person in relation to the child.

(7)   The references in this section to a person who is related to another person ('the other person') includes a person who—

(a)   is married to or in a civil partnership with a person who is related to the other person,

(b)   is related to the other person by the half blood.

(8)   This section is without prejudice to section 22 of the 1995 Act.

69   Relevant services: further provision

(1)   The Scottish Ministers may by order make provision about—

(a)   when or how relevant services specified in an order under section 68(1) are to be provided,

(b)   when or how a local authority is to consider whether a child is within paragraph (a) or (b) of section 68(3),

(c)   when or how a local authority is to review whether a child continues to be within paragraph (a) or (b) of section 68(3),

(d)   such other matters about the provision of relevant services specified in an order under section 68(1) as the Scottish Ministers consider appropriate.

(2)   An order under subsection (1)(d) may include provision about—

(a)   circumstances in which relevant services specified in an order under section 68(1) may be provided subject to conditions (including conditions as to payment), and

(b)   consequences of such conditions not being met.

70   Interpretation of Part 12

The following expressions have the same meaning in this Part as they have in Part 1 of the 1995 Act—

parental responsibilities

parental rights.

PART 13

SUPPORT FOR KINSHIP CARE

71   Assistance in relation to kinship care orders

(1)   A local authority must make arrangements to secure that kinship care assistance is made available for a person residing in its area who falls within subsection (3).

(2)   'Kinship care assistance' is assistance of such description as the Scottish Ministers may by order specify.

(3)   A person falls within this subsection if the person is—

(a)   a person who is applying for, or considering applying for, a kinship care order in relation to an eligible child who has not attained the age of 16 years,

(b)   an eligible child who has not attained the age of 16 years who is the subject of a kinship care order,

(c)   a person in whose favour a kinship care order in relation to an eligible child who has not attained the age of 16 years subsists,

(d)   a child who has attained the age of 16 years, where—

(i)   immediately before doing so, the child was the subject of a kinship care order, and

(ii)   the child is an eligible child,

(e)   a person who is a guardian by virtue of an appointment under section 7 of the 1995 Act of an eligible child who has not attained the age of 16 years (but this is subject to subsection (4)),

(f)   an eligible child who has a guardian by virtue of an appointment under section 7 of the 1995 Act.

(4)   Subsection (3)(e) does not include a person who is also a parent of the child.

(5)   An 'eligible child' is a child who the local authority considers—

(a)   to be at risk of becoming looked after, or

(b)   to fall within such other description as the Scottish Ministers may by order specify.

72   Orders which are kinship care orders

(1)   In section 71, 'kinship care order' means—

(a)   an order under section 11(1) of the 1995 Act which gives to a qualifying person the right mentioned in section 2(1)(a) of that Act in relation to a child,

(b)   a residence order which has the effect that a child is to live with, or live predominantly with, a qualifying person, or

(c)   an order under section 11(1) of the 1995 Act appointing a qualifying person as a guardian of a child.

(2)   For the purposes of subsection (1), a 'qualifying person' is a person who, at the time the order is made—

(a)   is related to the child,

(b)   is a friend or acquaintance of a person related to the child, or

(c)   has such other relationship to, or connection with, the child as the Scottish Ministers may by order specify.

(3)   But a parent of a child is not a 'qualifying person' for the purposes of subsection (1).

(4)   The references in subsection (2) to a person who is related to a child include a person who is—

(a)   married to or in a civil partnership with a person who is related to the child,

(b)   related to the child by the half blood.

73   Kinship care assistance: further provision

(1)   The assistance which may be specified as kinship care assistance includes—

(a)   the provision of counselling, advice or information about any matter,

(b)   the provision of financial support (or support in kind) of any description,

(c)   the provision of any service provided by a local authority on a sub-sidised basis.

(2)   An order under section 71(1) may specify assistance by reference to assistance which a person was entitled to from, or being provided with by, a local authority immediately before becoming entitled to assistance under that section.

(3)   The Scottish Ministers may by order make provision about—

(a)   when or how kinship care assistance is to be provided,

(b)   when or how a local authority is to consider whether a child is within paragraph (a) or (b) of section 71(5),

(c)   when or how a local authority is to review whether a child continues to be within paragraph (a) or (b) of section 71(5),

(d)   such other matters about the provision of kinship care assistance as the Scottish Ministers consider appropriate.

(4)   An order under subsection (3)(d) may include provision about—

(a)   circumstances in which a local authority may provide kinship care assistance subject to conditions (including conditions as to payment for the assistance or the repayment of financial support), and

(b) consequences of such conditions not being met (including the recovery of any financial support provided).

74 Interpretation of Part 13

In this Part—

'kinship care assistance' has the meaning given by section 71(2),

'parent' has the same meaning as it has in Part 1 of the 1995 Act.

PART 18
GENERAL

97 Interpretation

(1) In this Act—

'the 1980 Act' means the Education (Scotland) Act 1980,

'the 1995 Act' means the Children (Scotland) Act 1995,

'child' means a person who has not attained the age of 18 years,

'health board' means a board constituted under section 2(1)(a) of the National Health Service (Scotland) Act 1978.

(2) References in this Act to a child being or becoming 'looked after' are to be construed in accordance with section 17(6) of the 1995 Act.

(3) The following expressions have the same meaning in this Act as they have in the 1980 Act—

education authority
grant-aided school
independent school
managers
nursery class
primary school
proprietor
public school
pupil
school age.

98 Modification of enactments

Schedule 5 (which makes minor amendments to enactments and otherwise modifies enactments for the purposes of or in consequence of this Act) has effect.

99 Subordinate legislation

(1) Any power of the Scottish Ministers to make an order under this Act includes power to make—

(a) different provision for different purposes,

(b) such supplementary, incidental, consequential, transitional, transitory or saving provision as they consider appropriate.

(2) An order made under any of the following sections is subject to the affirmative procedure—

section 3(2)
section 7(5)
section 30(1)
section 31(2)
section 37(7)
section 43(1)
section 44(2)
section 47(2)(c)(ii)
section 47(4)
section 48(2)
section 51(2)

section 56(2)
section 57(2)(b)
section 58(2)
section 68(3)(b)
section 71(5)(b)
section 96(6).

(3)   An order made under section 101 containing provisions which add to, replace or omit any part of the text of this or any other Act is subject to the affirmative procedure.

(4)   All other orders made under this Act are subject to the negative procedure.

(5)   This section does not apply to an order made under section 102(3).

100   Guidance and directions

(1)   Any power of the Scottish Ministers to issue guidance or directions under this Act may be exercised—

    (a)   to issue guidance or directions generally or for particular purposes,

    (b)   to issue different guidance or directions to different persons or otherwise for different purposes.

(2)   The Scottish Ministers must publish (in such manner as they consider appropriate) any guidance or directions issued by them under this Act.

(3)   In subsection (2)—

    (a)   the reference to guidance includes revision of guidance,

    (b)   the reference to directions includes revision and revocation of directions.

101   Ancillary provision

The Scottish Ministers may by order make—

    (a)   such supplementary, incidental or consequential provision as they consider appropriate for the purposes of, or in connection with, or for the purposes of giving full effect to, any provision made by, or by virtue of, this Act, and

    (b)   such transitional, transitory or saving provision as they consider appropriate for the purposes of, or in connection with, the coming into force of any provision of this Act.

102   Commencement

(1)   This Part (apart from sections 96, 97 and 98) comes into force on the day after Royal Assent.

(2)   Subsections (2) to (5) of section 47 also come into force on the day after Royal Assent.

(3)   The other provisions of this Act come into force on such day as the Scottish Ministers may by order appoint.

(4)   An order under this section may include transitional, transitory or saving provision.

103   Short title

The short title of this Act is the Children and Young People (Scotland) Act 2014.

SCHEDULES

SCHEDULE 4
CORPORATE PARENTS

(*introduced by section 56*)

1   The Scottish Ministers
2   A local authority
3   The National Convener of Children's Hearings Scotland
4   Children's Hearings Scotland
5   The Principal Reporter
6   The Scottish Children's Reporter Administration

7   A health board
8   A board constituted under section 2(1)(b) of the National Health Service (Scotland) Act 1978
9   Healthcare Improvement Scotland
10   The Scottish Qualifications Authority
11   Skills Development Scotland Co. Ltd (registered number SC 202659)
12   Social Care and Social Work Improvement Scotland
13   The Scottish Social Services Council
14   The Scottish Sports Council
15   The chief constable of the Police Service of Scotland
16   The Scottish Police Authority
17   The Scottish Fire and Rescue Service
18   The Scottish Legal Aid Board
19   The Commissioner for Children and Young People in Scotland
20   The Mental Welfare Commission for Scotland
21   The Scottish Housing Regulator
22   Bòrd na Gàidhlig
23   Creative Scotland
24   A body which is a 'post-16 education body' for the purposes of the Further and Higher Education (Scotland) Act 2005
[25   An integration joint board to which the functions in relation to persons under 18 years of age have been delegated in pursuance of an integration scheme prepared under section 1 or 2 of the Public Bodies (Joint Working) (Scotland) Act 2014]

CIVIL PARTNERSHIP (SCOTLAND) ACT 2020
(2020, asp 15)

3 Interim recognition of different sex relationships formed outwith Scotland

(1)   This section applies to a civil partnership between persons of different sexes—

(a)   which is formed when they register as civil partners of each other—

(i)   in England or Wales under Part 2 of the 2004 Act,

(ii)   in Northern Ireland under Part 4 of the 2004 Act,

(b)   which is formed when they register as civil partners of each other outside the United Kingdom under an Order in Council made under section 210 or 211 of the 2004 Act, or

(c)   which they are treated under Chapter 2 of Part 5 of the 2004 Act as having formed (at the time determined under that Chapter) by virtue of having registered an overseas relationship.

(2)   Two persons in a civil partnership—

(a)   mentioned in subsection (1)(a) or (c) are to be treated as being in a marriage formed under the law of the country or territory in which the civil partnership or (as the case may be) overseas relationship is registered,

(b)   mentioned in subsection (1)(b) are to be treated as having formed a marriage in the part of the United Kingdom in which the civil partnership is, by virtue of section 210(5) or (as the case may be) 211(4) of the 2004 Act, to be treated as having been registered.

(3)   Nothing in subsection (2) prevents persons in a civil partnership to which this section applies—

(a)   presenting themselves as civil partners of each other,

(b)   presenting their relationship as a civil partnership.

(4)   Subsections (2) and (2A) cease to have effect when section 4 comes into force (which is when it will become possible to register a civil partnership between persons of different sexes in Scotland).

(5)   The Scottish Ministers may by regulations—

(a)   provide for subsection (2) not to apply for purposes specified in the regulations,

(b)   make transitional or saving provision in connection with subsection (2) ceasing to have effect.

(6)   Regulations under subsection (4) are subject to the negative procedure.

(7)   In this section, 'the 2004 Act' means the Civil Partnership Act 2004.

Power to enable marriages to become civil partnerships

4   Power to enable marriages to become civil partnerships

(1)   The Scottish Ministers may by regulations make provision for, or in connection with, enabling the parties to a marriage—

(a)   to register as civil partners of each other,

(b)   to change their marriage into a civil partnership.

(2)   Regulations under subsection (1) may in particular make provision—

(a)   about the marriages to which the regulations apply,

(b)   about the ways in which marriages may be changed into civil partnerships under the regulations,

(c)   modifying the Civil Partnership Act 2004 in its application—

(i)   to registering civil partnerships and changing marriages into civil partnerships under the regulations, and

(ii)   to civil partnerships formed by registration and civil partnerships formed by marriages changing into civil partnerships under the regulations,

(d)   modifying the definition of 'qualifying civil partnership' in section 5 of the Marriage (Scotland) Act 1977,

(e)   modifying section 11(2)(b) of the Marriage and Civil Partnership (Scotland) Act 2014 in its application to qualifying civil partnerships where the parties to the civil partnership were married to each other immediately before the civil partnership was formed,

(f)   about the effect of registering civil partnerships and changing marriages into civil partnerships under the regulations,

(g)   about when the resulting civil partnership is to be treated as having been formed and when the marriage is to be treated as having ended,

(h)   for fees of such amounts as may be specified in or determined in accordance with the regulations.

(3)   Regulations which make provision under subsection (1)(b) may provide for the regulations to apply only to marriages in categories specified in the regulations.

(4)   Before making regulations under subsection (1), the Scottish Ministers must consult the Registrar General of Births, Deaths and Marriages for Scotland.

(5)   Regulations under subsection (1)—

(a)   may make different provision for different purposes,

(b)   may include incidental, supplementary, consequential, transitional, transitory or saving provision,

(c)   may modify any enactment (including this Act),

(d)   are (except where subsection (6) applies) subject to the negative procedure.

(6)   Regulations under subsection (1) which add to, replace or omit any part of the text of an Act are subject to the affirmative procedure.

Recognition of marriages converted to civil partnerships outwith Scotland

5   Recognition of marriages converted to civil partnerships outwith Scotland

(1)   The Scottish Ministers may by regulations make provision of the type

described in subsection (2) in relation to a marriage that is converted into a civil partnership in accordance with provision made under—

    (a)   section 2(5)(a) of the Civil Partnerships, Marriages and Deaths (Registration etc) Act 2019, or

    (b)   section 8(5)(a) of the Northern Ireland (Executive Formation etc) Act 2019.

  (2)   The provision mentioned in subsection (1) is—

    (a)   provision for such a marriage to be treated in the law of Scotland as if the parties had registered as civil partners of each other in England and Wales or (as the case may be) Northern Ireland,

    (b)   provision as to—

       (i)   the date on which the parties' marriage is to be treated as having ended,

       (ii) the date on which the parties are to be treated as having registered as civil partners.

  (3)   Regulations under subsection (1)—

    (a)   may make different provision for different purposes,

    (b)   may include incidental, supplementary, consequential, transitional, transitory or saving provision,

    (c)   may modify any enactment (including this Act),

    (d)   are (except where subsection (4) applies) subject to the negative procedure.

  (4)   Regulations under subsection (1) which add to, replace or omit any part of the text of an Act are subject to the affirmative procedure.

10   *[Amends the Civil Partnership Act 2004 with effect from 30 November 2021.]*

Consequential modifications

14 Consequential modifications

Schedule 2 modifies other enactments.

Final provisions

15 Ancillary provision

  (1)   The Scottish Ministers may by regulations make any incidental, supplementary, consequential, transitional, transitory or saving provision they consider appropriate for the purposes of, or in connection with, or for giving full effect to this Act or any provision made under it.

  (2)   Regulations under this section may—

    (a)   make different provision for different purposes,

    (b)   modify any enactment (including this Act).

  (3)   Regulations under this section—

    (a)   are subject to the affirmative procedure if they add to, replace or omit any part of the text of an Act, but

    (b)   otherwise are subject to the negative procedure.

16 Commencement

  (1)   The following provisions come into force on the day after Royal Assent: this section and section 15 and 17.

  (2)   The other provisions of this Act come into force on such day as the Scottish Ministers may by regulations appoint.

  (3)   Regulations under this section—

    (a)   may make different provision for different purposes,

    (b)   may include transitional, transitory or saving provision.

17 Short title

The short title of this Act is the Civil Partnership (Scotland) Act 2020.

CHILDREN (SCOTLAND) ACT 2020
(2020, asp 16)

At the date at which this volume went to press the provisions below were not in force. Consequential amendments made by provisions of this Act which are in force have been incorporated into the principal legislation.

Regard to be had to child's views

1   Proceedings under Children (Scotland) Act 1995

(1)   The Children (Scotland) Act 1995 is modified as follows.

(2)   In section 6 (views of children)—

  (a)   in subsection (1)—

    (i)   after 'shall' insert 'comply with subsections (1A) and (1D)',

    (ii)   the words after paragraph (b) are repealed,

  (b)   after subsection (1) insert—

'(1A)   The person must—

    (a)   give the child an opportunity to express the child's views in—

      (i)   the manner that the child prefers, or

      (ii)   a manner that is suitable to the child if the child has not indicated a preference or it would not be reasonable in the circumstances to accommodate the child's preference, and

    (b)   have regard to any views expressed by the child, taking into account the child's age and maturity.

(1B)   But the person is not required to comply with subsection (1A) if the person is satisfied that—

    (a)   the child is not capable of forming a view, or

    (b)   the location of the child is not known.

(1C)   In considering whether the child is capable of forming a view, the person is to start with the presumption that the child is.

(1D)   The person must, so far as is practicable, have regard to the views of any other person who has parental responsibilities or parental rights in relation to the child.'.

(3)   In section 11 (court orders relating to parental responsibilities etc.)—

  (a)   subsections (7) to (7E) are repealed,

  (b)   in subsection (8), the words ', notwithstanding subsection (7) above,' are repealed,

  (c)   subsections (9) and (10) are repealed.

(4)   After section 11 insert—

'**11ZA   Paramountcy of child's welfare, and the non-intervention presumption**

(1)   In deciding whether or not to make an order under section 11(1) and what order (if any) to make, the court must regard the welfare of the child concerned as its paramount consideration.

(2)   The court must not make an order under section 11(1) unless it considers that it would be better for the child concerned that the order be made than that none should be made at all.

(3)   When considering the child's welfare and whether it would be better for the child to make an order than not, the court must have regard to the following matters in particular—

    (a)   the need to protect the child from abuse, or the risk of abuse, which affects, or might affect, the child,

    (b)   the effect that abuse, or the risk of abuse, might have on the child,

    (c)   the ability of a person to care for, or otherwise meet the needs of, the child, where that person has carried out, or might carry out, abuse which affects, or might affect, the child,

(d) the effect that abuse, or the risk of abuse, might have on the carrying out of responsibilities in connection with the welfare of the child by a person who has (or, by virtue of an order under section 11 (1), would have) those responsibilities,

(e) whether it is, or would be, appropriate for an order to require that two or more persons co-operate with one another with regard to matters affecting the child.

(4)   In subsection (3)—

'abuse' includes—

(a) violence, harassment, threatening conduct and any other conduct giving rise, or likely to give rise, to physical or mental injury, fear, alarm or distress,

(b) abuse of a person other than the child, and

(c) domestic abuse,

'conduct' includes—

(a) speech, and

(b) presence in a particular place or area.

11ZB   Regard to be had to the child's views

(1)   In deciding whether or not to make an order under section 11(1) and what order (if any) to make, the court must—

(a) give the child concerned an opportunity to express the child's views in—

(i) the manner that the child prefers, or

(ii) a manner that is suitable to the child if the child has not indicated a preference or it would not be reasonable in the circumstances to accommodate the child's preference, and

(b) have regard to any views expressed by the child, taking into account the child's age and maturity.

(2)   But the court is not required to comply with subsection (1) if satisfied that—

(a) the child is not capable of forming a view, or

(b) the location of the child is not known.

(3)   The child is to be presumed to be capable of forming a view unless the contrary is shown.

(4)   Nothing in this section requires a child to be legally represented in any proceedings in which the child's views are sought, if the child does not wish to be.'.

(5)   In section 14 (jurisdiction and choice of law in relation to certain matters), in subsection (4), for 'subsection (7) of that section' substitute ' sections 11ZA and 11ZB '.

(6)   In section 16 (welfare of child and consideration of his views), for subsection (2) substitute—

'(2)   In the circumstances mentioned in subsection (4), the sheriff must—

(a) give the child concerned an opportunity to express the child's views in—

(i) the manner that the child prefers, or

(ii) a manner that is suitable to the child if the child has not indicated a preference or it would not be reasonable in the circumstances to accommodate the child's preference, and

(b) have regard to any views expressed by the child, taking into account the child's age and maturity.

(2A)   But the sheriff is not required to comply with subsection (2) if satisfied that—

   (a)   the child is not capable of forming a view, or

   (b)   the location of the child is not known.

(2B)   The child is to be presumed to be capable of forming a view unless the contrary is shown.'.

(7)   The italic heading preceding section 11 becomes 'Court orders relating to parental responsibilities etc'.

(8)   Before section 12, insert as an italic heading 'Exercise of court functions relating to children'.

2   Proceedings under Adoption and Children (Scotland) Act 2007

(1)   The Adoption and Children (Scotland) Act 2007 is modified as follows.

(2)   In section 14 (considerations applying to the exercise of powers)—

   (a)   in subsection (1), for '(4)' substitute '(4C)',

   (b)   subsection (4)(b) is repealed,

   (c)   after subsection (4) insert—

'(4A)   The court or adoption agency must—

   (a)   give the child an opportunity to express the child's views in—

      (i)   the manner that the child prefers, or

      (ii)   a manner that is suitable to the child if the child has not indicated a preference or it would not be reasonable in the circumstances to accommodate the child's preference, and

   (b)   have regard to any views expressed by the child, taking into account the child's age and maturity.

(4B)   But the court or adoption agency is not required to comply with subsection (4A) if satisfied that the child is not capable of forming a view.

(4C)   The child is to be presumed to be capable of forming a view unless the contrary is shown.',

   (d)   in subsection (6), for '(4)' substitute '(4C)',

   (e)   subsection (8) is repealed.

(3)   In section 84 (conditions and considerations application to making of order)—

   (a)   for subsection (5)(a) substitute—

'(a)   give the child an opportunity to express the child's views in—

      (i)   the manner that the child prefers, or

      (ii)   a manner that is suitable to the child if the child has not indicated a preference or it would not be reasonable in the circumstances to accommodate the child's preference,',

   (b)   for subsection (5)(b)(i) substitute—

'(i)   any views expressed by the child, taking into account the child's age and maturity,',

   (c)   after subsection (5) insert—

'(5A)   But the court is not required to comply with subsection (5)(a) if satisfied that the child is not capable of forming a view.

(5B)   The child is to be presumed to be capable of forming a view unless the contrary is shown.',

   (d)   subsection (6) is repealed.

3   Proceedings under Children's Hearings (Scotland) Act 2011

(1)   The Children's Hearings (Scotland) Act 2011 is modified as follows.

(2)   In section 27 (views of the child), for subsections (3) and (4) substitute—

'(3)   The children's hearing, pre-hearing panel or the sheriff must—

(a)   give the child an opportunity to express the child's views in—

(i)   the manner that the child prefers, or

(ii)   a manner that is suitable to the child if the child has not indicated a preference or it would not be reasonable in the circumstances to accommodate the child's preference, and

(b)   have regard to any views expressed by the child, taking into account the child's age and maturity.

(4)   But the children's hearing, pre-hearing panel or the sheriff is not required to comply with subsection (3) if satisfied that—

(a)   the child is not capable of forming a view, or

(b)   the location of the child is not known.

(4A)   The child is to be presumed to be capable of forming a view unless the contrary is shown.'.

Vulnerable witnesses and parties

4   Vulnerable witnesses: prohibition of personal conduct of case

(1)   The Vulnerable Witnesses (Scotland) Act 2004 is modified as follows.

(2)   In section 11 (interpretation of Part 2), in subsection (5), in the definition of 'relevant proceedings', for 'of the 2011 Act (other than section 98 or 99)' substitute 'and section 154 of the 2011 Act'.

(3)   After section 11 insert—

'11A   Deemed vulnerable witnesses: relevant proceedings

(1)   In relevant proceedings, the court is to consider a person to be a vulnerable witness if it is alleged in the statement of grounds that the person is the victim of any of the following conduct—

(a)   conduct amounting to—

(i)   an offence mentioned in schedule 1 of the Criminal Procedure (Scotland) Act 1995,

(ii)   an offence under Part 1, 4 or 5 of the Sexual Offences (Scotland) Act 2009,

(b)   domestic abuse,

(c)   being forced into a marriage or civil partnership.

(2)   For the purposes of subsection (1)—

(a)   'the statement of grounds' means the statement of grounds, within the meaning of section 89(3) of the 2011 Act, that—

(i)   gave rise to the relevant proceedings, or (as the case may be)

(ii)   gave rise to the grounds determination which, in turn, gave rise to the relevant proceedings,

(b)   the reference to being forced into a marriage is to be construed in accordance with subsections (4) to (6) of section 1 of the Forced Marriage etc. (Protection and Jurisdiction) (Scotland) Act 2011,

(c)   the reference to being forced into a civil partnership is to be construed in accordance with the provisions mentioned in paragraph (b), subject to the references in those provisions to marriage being read as references to civil partnership.

(3)   The Scottish Ministers may by regulations—

(a)   modify the list of conduct in subsection (1) by—

(i)   adding a description of conduct, or

(ii)   modifying or removing a description of conduct added to the list by regulations under this paragraph, and

(b)   make any other modifications to this section that appear to the Scottish Ministers to be necessary or expedient in consequence of provision modifying the list.

(4) Regulations under subsection (3) are subject to the affirmative procedure.

11B Deemed vulnerable witnesses: proceedings concerning order under section 11(1) of the Children (Scotland) Act 1995

(1) In proceedings to which subsection (2) applies, the court is to consider a person to whom subsection (3) or (4) applies to be a vulnerable witness.

(2) This subsection applies to proceedings, other than relevant proceedings, in which the court is considering whether to make an order under section 11(1) of the Children (Scotland) Act 1995.

(3) This subsection applies to a person if there is in force a non-harassment order, interdict or any similar order or remedy granted by a court prohibiting certain conduct towards the person by a party to the proceedings.

(4) This subsection applies to a person if—

(a) a relevant offence has been committed against the person and a party to the proceedings has been convicted of committing it, or

(b) a party to the proceedings is being prosecuted for committing a relevant offence against the person.

(5) For the purposes of subsection (4)—

(a) the following are relevant offences—

(i) an offence specified in section 288C(2) of the Criminal Procedure (Scotland) Act 1995,

(ii) an offence specified in section 288DC(1) of that Act,

(iii) an offence specified in section 288E(3) of that Act,

(iv) an offence under section 1(1) of the Prohibition of Female Genital Mutilation (Scotland) Act 2005,

(v) an offence under section 3(1) of that Act,

(vi) an offence under section 39 of the Criminal Justice and Licensing (Scotland) Act 2010,

(vii) an offence under section 122(1) of the Anti-social Behaviour, Crime and Policing Act 2014,

(viii) an offence under section 122(3) of that Act,

(ix) an offence which, in the opinion of the court, is the equivalent in the law of England and Wales, Northern Ireland or a member State of the European Union to an offence mentioned in any of the preceding sub-paragraphs,

(b) a person is to be regarded as being prosecuted for committing an offence if—

(i) a prosecutor has initiated proceedings against the person in respect of the offence, and

(ii) those proceedings have not yet been dismissed or resulted in the conviction or acquittal of the person in respect of the offence.

(6) The Scottish Ministers may by regulations—

(a) modify the list of offences in subsection (5)(a) by—

(i) adding an offence, or

(ii) removing, or modifying the description of, an offence added to the list by regulations under this paragraph, and

(b) may make any other modifications to this section that appear to the Scottish Ministers to be necessary or expedient in consequence of provision modifying the list.

(7) Regulations under subsection (6) are subject to the affirmative procedure.'.

(4) In section 12 (orders authorising the use of special measures for vulnerable witnesses), after subsection (3), insert—

'(3A)   The court may not make an order under subsection (1)(b) above in relevant proceedings if it is required by section 22C or 22D to consider the special measure described by section 22B to be the most appropriate for the purpose of taking the child witness's evidence (or one of them if the court considers other special measures to be appropriate too).'.

(5)   After section 22A insert—

'22B   Prohibition on personal conduct of case

(1)   In proceedings to which subsection (2) applies, the special measures which may be authorised by virtue of section 12 or 13 for the purpose of taking the evidence of a vulnerable witness include prohibiting the parties to the proceedings from conducting their own cases in person.

(2)   The proceedings to which this subsection applies are—

(a)   relevant proceedings, and

(b)   proceedings in which the court is considering whether to make an order under section 11(1) of the Children (Scotland) Act 1995.

(3)   The prohibition may be applied to one or more of the parties or all of them.

(4)   The prohibition does not prevent a party to whom it applies from conducting the party's own case in person until the beginning of the first hearing in the proceedings at, or for the purposes of, which a witness is to give evidence.

(5)   Where the special measure described by subsection (1) is to be used the court must—

(a)   inform the parties to whom the prohibition applies that it applies to them,

(b)   explain to those parties the effect of the prohibition, and

(c)   ascertain whether each party to whom the prohibition applies has a solicitor to conduct the party's case.

(6)   If, at any point in the proceedings, the court—

(a)   ascertains that a party to whom the prohibition applies does not have a solicitor to conduct the party's case, and

(b)   is not satisfied that the party intends to engage a solicitor to do so,

the court must appoint a solicitor to conduct the party's case.

(7)   The court may only appoint a solicitor entered on the register established in accordance with section 7 of the Children (Scotland) Act 2020.

(8)   An appointed solicitor—

(a)   is to ascertain and act upon the instructions of the party for whom the solicitor has been appointed to act, or

(b)   in the event that the party gives no instructions, or gives instructions that are inadequate or perverse, is to act in the party's best interests.

(9)   An appointed solicitor—

(a)   may not be dismissed by the party for whom the solicitor has been appointed to act,

(b)   may be relieved from the appointment by the court if the court is satisfied that the solicitor is no longer able to act upon the party's instructions or in the party's best interests.

(10)   In this section, references to a party to proceedings do not include—

(a)   the Principal Reporter,

(b)   a person appointed to act as a curator ad litem in the proceedings,

(c) a safeguarder for a child in the proceedings appointed under the 2011 Act.

(11) For the avoidance of doubt, the special measure described by this section is a measure for the purpose of taking the evidence of a vulnerable witness, notwithstanding that the measure affects the conduct of the proceedings more widely.

22C   Requirement to prohibit personal conduct of case

(1) Subsection (2) applies in relevant proceedings where—

(a) the court is considering what special measure or measures would be most appropriate for the purpose of taking a witness's evidence,

(b) because of conduct perpetrated or alleged to have been perpetrated by a party to the proceedings, the witness is deemed to be a vulnerable witness by virtue of section 11A, and

(c) that party intends to examine, or cross-examine, the witness.

(2) The court is to consider that the most appropriate special measure for the purpose of taking the witness's evidence (or one of them) is prohibiting the party referred to in subsection (1) from conducting the party's own case in person in accordance with section 22B.

(3) If the court is required—

(a) by this section to consider the special measure described by section 22B to be the most appropriate for the purpose of taking the witness's evidence, and

(b) by section 12(3) to consider another special measure to be the most appropriate for the purpose,

the court is to consider those measures together to be the most appropriate for the purpose.

22D   Presumption that personal conduct of case should be prohibited

(1) Where a court is considering what special measure or measures would be most appropriate for the purpose of taking a witness's evidence—

(a) the presumption set out in subsection (2) applies (subject to subsection (4)) in relevant proceedings, and

(b) the presumption set out in subsection (5) applies (subject to subsection (6)) in any other proceedings in which the court is considering whether to make an order under section 11(1) of the Children (Scotland) Act 1995.

(2) The presumption referred to in subsection (1)(a) is that prohibiting each party who intends to examine, or cross-examine, the witness from conducting the party's own case in person, in accordance with section 22B, is the most appropriate special measure for the purpose of taking the witness's evidence (or one of them if the court considers other special measures to be appropriate too).

(3) In subsection (2), 'party' does not include a person mentioned in section 22B(10).

(4) The presumption set out in subsection (2) is rebutted, in relation to a party, if (and only if) the court is satisfied that—

(a) applying the special measure described by section 22B to the party would, in the circumstances, give rise to a significant risk of prejudice to the fairness of the proceedings or otherwise to the interests of justice, and

(b) that risk significantly outweighs any risk of prejudice to the interests of the witness if the special measure is not applied to the party.

(5) The presumption referred to in subsection (1)(b) is that if—

(a)   the witness is deemed to be a vulnerable witness either—

(i)   by virtue of section 11B(3) because an order or remedy granted by a court prohibits certain conduct towards the witness by a party to the proceedings, or

(ii)   by virtue of section 11B(4) because a party to the proceedings committed, or is alleged to have committed, an offence against the witness, and

(b)   the party in question intends to examine, or cross-examine, the witness,

prohibiting that party from conducting the party's own case in person, in accordance with section 22B, is the most appropriate special measure for the purpose of taking the witness's evidence (or one of them if the court considers other special measures to be appropriate too).

(6)   The presumption set out in subsection (5) is rebutted if (and only if)—

(a)   the court is satisfied that—

(i)   the witness has expressed a wish to give evidence without the benefit of the special measure described by section 22B being applied to the party, and

(ii)   it is appropriate for the witness to do so, or

(b)   the court is satisfied that—

(i)   applying the special measure described by section 22B to the party would, in the circumstances, give rise to a significant risk of prejudice to the fairness of the proceedings or otherwise to the interests of justice, and

(ii)   that risk significantly outweighs any risk of prejudice to the interests of the witness if the special measure is not applied to the party.

(7)   If the court is required—

(a)   by this section to consider the special measure described by section 22B to be the most appropriate for the purpose of taking the witness's evidence, and

(b)   by section 12(3) to consider another special measure to be the most appropriate for the purpose,

the court is to consider those measures together to be the most appropriate for the purpose.'.

5   Vulnerable witnesses: requirement to consider special measures without application in certain cases

(1)   The Vulnerable Witnesses (Scotland) Act 2004 is modified as follows.

(2)   In section 12 (orders authorising the use of special measures for vulnerable witnesses), after subsection (6) insert—

'(6A)   If the witness is deemed to be a vulnerable witness by virtue of section 11B—

(a)   before the proof or other hearing at which the witness is to give evidence the court must either—

(i)   make an order under subsection (6) authorising the use of a special measure for the purpose of taking the witness's evidence, or

(ii)   make an order that the witness is to give evidence without the benefit of any special measure,

(b)   the court is to do so whether or not a vulnerable witness application is made.'.

6   Hearing to ascertain if case involves vulnerable witnesses

(1)   The Children's Hearings (Scotland) Act 2011 is modified as follows.

(2)   After Part 17 insert—

'PART 17A
PROTECTION FOR VULNERABLE WITNESSES

176A Duty to ascertain whether vulnerable witnesses to give evidence

(1) In proceedings under Part 10 or section 154, the court must fulfil the duty specified in subsection (2) at a hearing held before the first hearing in which a person is to give evidence.

(2) The duty is to ascertain whether—

(a) any of the parties have cited, or intend to cite, a person who is or may be a vulnerable witness to give evidence at any point during the proceedings, and

(b) any party who is or may be a vulnerable witness intends to give evidence at any point during the proceedings (without having been cited as a witness by one of the other parties).

(3) The hearing at which the court fulfils the duty specified in subsection (2)—

(a) is referred to in this Part as the preliminary hearing,

(b) need not be a hearing solely for the purpose of fulfilling that duty.

(4) If—

(a) the court ascertains at the preliminary hearing that—

(i) a party has cited, or intends to cite, a witness who the court is satisfied is a vulnerable witness, or

(ii) a party who the court is satisfied is a vulnerable witness intends to give evidence,

(b) no child witness notice in respect of that witness has been lodged with the court, and

(c) no vulnerable witness application in respect of that witness has been made to the court,

the court must also ascertain at the preliminary hearing the party's views as to the special measure or measures (if any) that would be most appropriate for the purpose of taking the witness's evidence.

(5) Where a party is considering for the purposes of subsection (4) which of the special measures is or are the most appropriate for the purpose of taking the evidence of a witness the party has cited, or intends to cite, section 15(2) of the Vulnerable Witnesses Act applies to the party as it would if the party were considering that matter for the purposes of a child witness notice or (as the case may be) a vulnerable witness application.

176B Power to order special measures without child witness notice

(1) This section applies where—

(a) at a preliminary hearing, the court ascertains that a party has cited, or intends to cite, a witness who the court is satisfied is a child witness, and

(b) no child witness notice in respect of that witness has been lodged with the court.

(2) At the end of the preliminary hearing, the court may make an order in relation to the witness under section 12(1) of the Vulnerable Witnesses Act.

(3) In making an order by virtue of subsection (2), the court must have regard to any views of the party mentioned in subsection (1) that were ascertained in accordance with section 176A(4).

(4) If the court makes an order by virtue of subsection (2), the party mentioned in subsection (1) is relieved of the duty under section 12(2) of the Vulnerable Witnesses Act to lodge a child witness notice in respect of the witness in question.

176C   Power to order special measures without vulnerable witness application

(1)   This section applies where—

(a)   at a preliminary hearing under section 176A, the court ascertains that a party has cited, or intends to cite, a witness who the court is satisfied—

(i)   is a vulnerable witness, but

(ii)   is not a child witness, and

(b)   no vulnerable witness application has been made to the court in respect of the witness.

(2)   The court may make an order in relation to the witness under section 12(6) of the Vulnerable Witnesses Act, despite the fact that no vulnerable witness application has been made.

(3)   In making an order by virtue of subsection (2), the court must have regard to any views of the party mentioned in subsection (1) that were ascertained in accordance with section 176A(4).

176D   Interpretation of Part

In this Part—

'child witness' has the meaning given by section 11(1)(a) of the Vulnerable Witnesses Act,

'child witness notice' has the meaning given by section 12(2) of the Vulnerable Witnesses Act,

'preliminary hearing' has the meaning given by section 176A(3),

'vulnerable witness' means a person who is a vulnerable witness for the purposes of the Vulnerable Witnesses Act (including any person deemed to be a vulnerable witness by virtue of section 11A of that Act),

'vulnerable witness application' has the meaning given by section 12(6)(a) of the Vulnerable Witnesses Act,

'the Vulnerable Witnesses Act' means the Vulnerable Witnesses (Scotland) Act 2004.'.

7   Register of solicitors for section 22B of the Vulnerable Witnesses (Scotland) Act 2004

(1)   The Scottish Ministers must—

(a)   establish, and

(b)   (subject to provision made under subsection (2)(c)) maintain,

a register of solicitors who may be appointed by a court under section 22B(6) of the Vulnerable Witnesses (Scotland) Act 2004.

(2)   The Scottish Ministers, by regulations—

(a)   must—

(i)   specify the requirements that a person must satisfy in order to be included, and remain, on the register (which may include requirements as to training and qualifications),

(ii)   set out the processes for including a person on, and removing a person from, the register (including appeal rights),

(b)   may provide for the remuneration by the Scottish Ministers of solicitors appointed under section 22B(6) of the Vulnerable Witnesses (Scotland) Act 2004, including expenses and outlays (such as counsel's fees),

(c)   may—

(i)   confer the duty of maintaining the register on a person, and

(ii)   make such modifications to other enactments as the Scottish Ministers consider appropriate for the purposes of, or in connection with, or for giving full effect to provision made by virtue of sub-paragraph (i).

(3)   Before making regulations under subsection (2), the Scottish Ministers must consult—

(a)   the Faculty of Advocates, and

    (b)   the Law Society of Scotland.

  (4)   Regulations under subsection (2)—

    (a)   are subject to the affirmative procedure if, by virtue of paragraph (c)(ii) of that subsection, they add to, replace or omit any part of the text of an Act, but

    (b)   otherwise are subject to the negative procedure.

8   Vulnerable parties

  (1)   The Children (Scotland) Act 1995 is modified as follows.

  (2)   After section 11A insert—

'11B   Vulnerable parties

    (1) In proceedings to which subsection (2) applies—

      (a) in relation to a party whom the court would be required by section 11B of the Vulnerable Witnesses (Scotland) Act 2004 to consider a vulnerable witness if the party were to give evidence in or for the purposes of the proceedings, the court must—

        (i) order the use of any special measure that the party requests,

        (ii) order the use of a special measure that the court considers appropriate and, if the party requested a different special measure, give reasons for not ordering its use, or

        (iii) give reasons for not ordering the use of any special measure,

      (b) in relation to any other party, the court may order the use of a special measure if the court considers that—

        (i) attending or participating in hearings is causing, or is likely to cause, the party distress,

        (ii) the party's distress is likely to be reduced by the use of the special measure, and

        (iii) the use of the special measure would not give rise to a significant risk of prejudice to the fairness of the proceedings or otherwise to the interests of justice.

    (2) This subsection applies to proceedings, commenced on or after section 8 of the Children (Scotland) Act 2020 comes into force, in which the court is considering, or has considered, whether to make an order under section 11(1).

    (3) An order under subsection (1) may authorise a special measure in relation to the whole of the proceedings or only a part of them.

    (4) A court may vary or revoke an order it made under subsection (1).

    (5) An order under subsection (1) or (4) may be made—

      (a) at any time, and

      (b) whether or not a party to the proceedings has applied for one.

    (6) The special measures which may be authorised by virtue of an order under subsection (1) or (4) are—

      (a) use of a live television link,

      (b) use of a screen,

      (c) use of a supporter,

      (d) any other measure prescribed by the Scottish Ministers by regulations.

    (7) Regulations under subsection (6)(d) are subject to the affirmative procedure.

    (8) In considering whether attending or participating in hearings is causing, or is likely to cause, a person distress, the court must take into account—

      (a) the nature and circumstances of any matters raised, or likely to be raised, in the proceedings,

      (b) the relationship (if any) between the person and any other party to the proceedings,

      (c) the person's age and maturity,

(d)   any behaviour towards the person on the part of—
    (i)   any other party to the proceedings,
    (ii)   members of the family or associates of any other party,
    (iii) any other person who is likely to be a party to the proceedings or a witness in the proceedings, and
(e)   such other matters as appear to the court to be relevant, including—
    (i)   the social and cultural background and ethnic origins of the person,
    (ii)   the person's sexual orientation,
    (iii) the domestic and employment circumstances of the person,
    (iv) any religious beliefs or political opinions of the person,
    (v)   any physical disability or other physical impairment which the person has.

11C   Special measures under section 11B

(1)   If a court orders the use of a live television link, the court must make such arrangements as seem to it appropriate to enable the vulnerable party to watch and hear the proceedings by means of such a link.

(2)   If a court orders the use of a screen, a screen must be used to conceal the vulnerable party from the sight of the other parties to the proceedings.

(3)   If a court—
(a)   orders the use of—
    (i)   a live television link, or
    (ii)   a screen, and
(b)   considers it necessary or appropriate for the other parties to be able, during the proceedings, to—
    (i)   hear the vulnerable party,
    (ii)   watch the vulnerable party, or
    (iii) both,
the court must make such arrangements as seem to it appropriate to enable the other parties to do so.

(4)   Where—
(a)   a court has ordered the use of a live television link or a screen in proceedings in a sheriff court, but
(b)   the court lacks accommodation or equipment necessary to enable the measure to be used,
the sheriff may by order transfer all or any part of the proceedings to any sheriff court in the same sheriffdom which has such accommodation or equipment available.

(5)   If a court orders the use of a supporter, another person ('the supporter') nominated by or on behalf of the vulnerable party may be present alongside the vulnerable party for the purpose of providing support during the proceedings.

(6)   The supporter—
(a)   must not prompt or otherwise seek to influence the vulnerable party in the course of a hearing,
(b)   may not act as the supporter, within the meaning of subsection (5), while the vulnerable party is giving evidence,
(c)   may not act as the supporter, if the supporter is to give evidence in the proceedings, at any time before giving evidence.

(7)   Subsection (6)(b) does not preclude the same person from being both—
(a)   a supporter within the meaning of subsection (5), and
(b)   a supporter within the meaning of section 22 of the Vulnerable Witnesses (Scotland) Act 2004.

(8) In this section—
(a) references to a measure being ordered are to its being ordered under section 11B,
(b) 'vulnerable party' means the party for whose benefit the court ordered the use of the measure in question.'.

Register for child welfare reporters

9 [*Amends the Children (Scotland) Act 1995, with effect from 25 October 2021.*]

Contact

10 Regulation of provision of contact services
(1) The Children (Scotland) Act 1995 is modified as follows.
(2) In section 11 (court orders relating to parental responsibilities etc)—
(a) in subsection (2)(d), at end insert '(see subsection (14))',
(b) after subsection (13) insert—

'(14) Where the court makes a contact order which requires any contact to take place within Scotland at a contact centre, the court may only require that contact to take place through a regulated contact service as defined in section 101C.'.

(3) [*Amends the Children (Scotland) Act 1995, with effect from 25 October 2021.*]

11 Referrals by solicitors to contact services
(1) The Children (Scotland) Act 1995 is modified as follows.
(2) After section 101C (which is inserted by section 10(3) of this Act) insert—

'101D Contact services: referrals by solicitors
(1) A solicitor must not—
(a) refer a person to a contact service that is not a regulated contact service, or
(b) allow another person to do so on the solicitor's behalf.
(2) If a solicitor fails to comply with subsection (1), that failure may be treated as professional misconduct or unsatisfactory professional conduct.
(3) In this section, 'contact service' and 'regulated contact service' have the meanings given in section 101C(5).'.

12 Arrangements for contact services
(1) The Children (Scotland) Act 1995 is modified as follows.
(2) After section 101D (which is inserted by section 11(2) of this Act) insert—

'101E Contact services: arrangements by Scottish Ministers
The Scottish Ministers may enter into an arrangement with a person for the provision of services to facilitate contact between children and other individuals.'.

13 [*Amends the Children (Scotland) Act 1995, s 17 with effect from 26 July 2021.*]

14 [*Amends the Children's Hearings (Scotland) Act 2011, s 29A with effect from 26 July 2021.*]

Further provision about orders under section 11(1) of the Children (Scotland) Act 1995

15 [*Amends the Children (Scotland) Act 1995, s 11 with effect from 17 January 2021.*]

16 Factors to be considered before making order
(1) The Children (Scotland) Act 1995 is amended as follows.
(2) In section 11ZA (paramountcy of child's welfare, and the non-intervention

presumption) (which is inserted by section 1(4) of this Act), in subsection (3) after paragraph (e) insert—

> '(f)   the effect that the order the court is deciding whether or not to make might have on—
>> (i)   the involvement of the child's parents in bringing the child up, and
>> (ii)   the child's important relationships with other people.'.

17   Curators ad litem

(1)   The Children (Scotland) Act 1995 is modified as follows.

(2)   After section 11C (which is inserted by section 8(2) of this Act) insert—

> **'11D   Appointment of curator ad litem**
>
> (1)   Where a court is considering making an order under section 11(1), the court—
>> (a)   may only appoint a person to act as curator ad litem to a child if the court is satisfied that it is necessary to do so to protect the child's interests,
>> (b)   may only appoint a person who is included on the register maintained in accordance with section 101B,
>> (c)   is to give reasons for the appointment.
>
> (2)   Where, in the course of considering making an order under section 11(1), a court has appointed a curator ad litem, the court must—
>> (a)   decide whether to continue the appointment every 6 months, and
>> (b)   if it decides to continue the appointment, give reasons for the decision.
>
> (3)   Subsection (2) does not apply in relation to a curator ad litem appointed before section 17 of the Children (Scotland) Act 2020 comes into force.'.

(3)   [*Amends the Children (Scotland) Act 1995, with effect from 25 October 2021.*]

18   Duty to consider child's best interests when allowing access to information

(1)   The Children (Scotland) Act 1995 is modified as follows.

(2)   After section 11D (which is inserted by section 17(2) of this Act) insert—

> **'11E   Duty to consider child's best interests when allowing access to information**
>
> (1)   Where the court—
>> (a)   is considering making an order under section 11(1), and
>> (b)   has to decide whether a person should have access to anything in which private information about a child is recorded,
>
> in making that decision it must comply with subsections (2) and (3) in relation to that child.
>
> (2)   The court must regard the best interests of the child as a primary consideration.
>
> (3)   The court must—
>> (a)   give the child an opportunity to express the child's views in—
>>> (i)   the manner that the child prefers, or
>>> (ii)   a manner that is suitable to the child if the child has not indicated a preference or it would not be reasonable in the circumstances to accommodate the child's preference, and
>> (b)   have regard to any views expressed by the child, taking into account the child's age and maturity.
>
> (4)   But the court is not required to comply with subsection (3) if satisfied that—

(a)   the child is not capable of forming a view, or

(b)   the location of the child is not known.

(5)   The child is to be presumed to be capable of forming a view unless the contrary is shown.

(6)   In this section, 'private information' means information in which the child could have a reasonable expectation of privacy.'.

19   Local authority reporters

(1)   The Matrimonial Proceedings (Children) Act 1958 is modified as follows.

(2)   In section 11 (reports as to arrangements for future care and upbringing of children), after subsection (1A) insert—

'(1B)   Where—

(a)   the court is considering whether to make an order under section 11(1) of the Children (Scotland) Act 1995, and

(b)   a local authority is appointed under subsection (1) to investigate and report to the court,

the person that the local authority assigns to perform that task on its behalf must be a child welfare reporter.

(1C)   In subsection (1B), 'a child welfare reporter' means a person included on the register maintained in accordance with section 101A of the Children (Scotland) Act 1995.'.

20   Explanation of decisions to the child

(1)   The Children (Scotland) Act 1995 is modified as follows.

(2)   After section 11E (which is inserted by section 18(2) of this Act) insert—

'**11F   Explanation of court decisions to the child**

(1)   This section applies when—

(a)   the court decides whether or not to make an order under section 11(1),

(b)   the court decides to vary or discharge an order made under section 11(1),

(c)   the court—

(i)   decides to decline to vary or discharge an order made under section 11(1), and

(ii)   considers it appropriate to explain that decision to the child concerned.

(2)   The court must ensure that the decision is explained to the child concerned in a way that the child can understand.

(3)   But the court is not required to comply with subsection (2) if satisfied that—

(a)   the child would not be capable of understanding an explanation however given,

(b)   it is not in the best interests of the child to give an explanation, or

(c)   the location of the child is not known.

(4)   The court may fulfil its duty under subsection (2) by—

(a)   giving the explanation to the child itself, or

(b)   arranging for it to be given by a child welfare reporter (see section 101A).

(5)   In this section, references to a decision include an interim decision.

(6)   The Scottish Ministers may by regulations modify subsection (4)(b) to—

(a)   add a description of a person,

(b)   vary a description of a person,

(c)   remove a description of a person.

(7)   Regulations under subsection (6) are subject to the affirmative procedure.'.

21   Duty to ensure availability of child advocacy services

(1)   The Children (Scotland) Act 1995 is modified as follows.

(2)   After section 100 insert—

'100A   Duty to ensure availability of child advocacy services

(1)   The Scottish Ministers must make such provision as they consider necessary and sufficient to ensure that all children concerned in relevant proceedings have access to appropriate child advocacy services.

(2)   In this section—

'child advocacy services' means services of support and representation provided for the purposes of assisting a child in relation to the child's involvement in relevant proceedings,

'relevant proceedings' means proceedings in which the court is considering making an order under section 11(1).'.

22   Failure to obey order

(1)   The Children (Scotland) Act 1995 is modified as follows.

(2)   After section 11F (which is inserted by section 20(2) of this Act) insert—

'11G   Duty to investigate failure to obey order under section 11

(1)   This section applies where a court is considering whether to—

(a)   find a person in contempt of court for failing to obey an order under section 11, or

(b)   vary or discharge an order under section 11 on the basis (solely or partly) that a person has failed to obey it.

(2)   If it is satisfied that the person has failed to obey the order, the court must—

(a)   seek to establish the reasons for that failure, and

(b)   in so doing—

(i)   give the child concerned an opportunity to express the child's views in—

(A)   the manner that the child prefers, or

(B)   a manner that is suitable to the child if the child has not indicated a preference or it would not be reasonable in the circumstances to accommodate the child's preference, and

(ii)   have regard to any views expressed by the child, taking into account the child's age and maturity.

(3)   But the court is not required to comply with subsection (2)(b) if satisfied that—

(a)   the child is not capable of forming a view, or

(b)   the location of the child is not known.

(4)   The child is to be presumed to be capable of forming a view unless the contrary is shown.

(5)   The court may appoint a child welfare reporter to investigate and report to the court on the person's failure (or alleged failure) to obey the order (see section 101A).

(6)   References in this section to an order include an interim order.

(7)   The Scottish Ministers may by regulations modify subsection (5) to—

(a)   add a description of person,

(b)   vary a description of person,

(c)   remove a description of person.

(8)   Regulations under subsection (7) are subject to the affirmative procedure.'.

Alternative dispute resolution

23 Funding for alternative dispute resolution

(1) The Scottish Ministers must—

(a) set up a scheme to make assistance available so that individuals can meet the costs of alternative dispute resolution procedures in relation to a dispute of the kind described in subsection (2), or

(b) arrange for assistance to be made available from the Scottish Legal Aid Fund so that individuals can meet those costs.

(2) The kind of dispute referred to in subsection (1) is a dispute that—

(a) is about any of the matters mentioned in section 11(1) of the Children (Scotland) Act 1995, and

(b) either—

(i) has resulted in an order being sought under that section, or

(ii) is likely to do so if it is not resolved through an alternative dispute resolution procedure.

(3) Entitlement to the assistance that is to be made available by virtue of subsection (1) may be made to depend on an individual satisfying any eligibility conditions that the Scottish Ministers consider appropriate.

(4) But any eligibility conditions relating to an individual's financial circumstances may not render an individual ineligible for assistance if the individual's circumstances are such that the individual could not be refused civil legal aid under section 15 of the Legal Aid (Scotland) Act 1986.

(5) Any scheme set up, or arrangement made, in accordance with subsection (1), must be framed so that assistance under it is only available to meet the costs of alternative dispute resolution procedures that ensure regard is had to children's views to at least the same extent as a court would be required to have regard to them by section 11ZB of the Children (Scotland) Act 1995.

(6) Having fulfilled their duty under subsection (1), the Scottish Ministers must lay before the Scottish Parliament a statement explaining how they have done so.

(7) If, at the end of a period described by subsection (8), the Scottish Ministers have not fulfilled their duty under subsection (1), they must lay before the Scottish Parliament a statement explaining why not and stating when they expect to fulfil it.

(8) For the purposes of subsection (7)—

(a) the first period begins on Royal Assent,

(b) after that, a new period begins with the last day of the previous period,

(c) each period ends with the day falling 6 months after it began,

(d) if the previous period ended on the 29th, 30th or 31st of a month and the month falling 6 months later has no such day, the period ends on the last day of that month.

(9) The Scottish Ministers may by regulations make any provision that they consider necessary or appropriate for the purpose of fulfilling their duty under subsection (1).

(10) Regulations under subsection (9) may—

(a) make different provision for different purposes or areas,

(b) modify any enactment.

(11) Regulations under subsection (9) are subject to the affirmative procedure.

24 Pilot scheme for mandatory alternative dispute resolution meetings

(1) The Scottish Ministers must arrange a pilot scheme under which a court, in proceedings to which the scheme applies, may only make an order under section 11(1) of the Children (Scotland) Act 1995—

(a) where the parties to the proceedings have attended a meeting at which the options available to resolve the dispute giving rise to the proceedings are explained, or

(b) if the terms of the scheme allow, where the court has decided on cause shown that it would not be appropriate to require the parties to attend such a meeting.

(2) The terms of the pilot scheme are to be determined by the Scottish Ministers, but the scheme—

(a) must be time limited, and

(b) must not apply to proceedings in which there is a proven or alleged history of abuse between some or all of the parties.

(3) Having fulfilled their duty under subsection (1), the Scottish Ministers must lay before the Scottish Parliament a statement—

(a) describing the pilot scheme,

(b) if the application of the scheme is subject to exceptions (other than an exception required by subsection (2)(b)), an explanation of why the Scottish Ministers consider those exceptions to be appropriate, and

(c) how the Scottish Ministers intend to evaluate—

(i) the scheme's outcomes for—

(A) the children in respect of whom the making of an order under section 11(1) of the Children (Scotland) Act 1995 was considered in proceedings to which the scheme applies,

(B) the parties to proceedings to which the scheme applies, and

(ii) where the scheme has led to a dispute being resolved without an order under section 11(1) of the Children (Scotland) Act 1995 being made, whether regard was had to the child's views in the resolution of the dispute to at least the same extent as a court would have had regard to the child's views when making such an order.

(4) If, at the end of a period described by subsection (5), the Scottish Ministers have not fulfilled their duty under subsection (1), they must lay before the Scottish Parliament a statement explaining why not and stating when they expect to fulfil it.

(5) For the purposes of subsection (4)—

(a) the first period begins on Royal Assent,

(b) after that, a new period begins with the last day of the previous period,

(c) each period ends with the day falling 6 months after it began,

(d) if the previous period ended on the 29th, 30th or 31st of a month and the month falling 6 months later has no such day, the period ends on the last day of that month.

(6) The Scottish Ministers may by regulations make any provision that they consider necessary or appropriate for the purpose of fulfilling their duty under subsection (1).

(7) Regulations under subsection (6) may—

(a) make different provision for different purposes or areas,

(b) modify any enactment.

(8) Regulations under subsection (6) are subject to the affirmative procedure.

(9) As soon as practicable after the pilot scheme ends, the Scottish Ministers must lay before the Scottish Parliament a report setting out—

(a) their findings about—

(i) the scheme's outcomes for the persons mentioned in subsection (3)(c)(i),

(ii) whether, in cases where the scheme has led to a dispute being resolved without an order under section 11(1) of the Children (Scotland) Act 1995 being made, regard was had to children's views in the resolution of those disputes to at least the same extent as a court would have had regard to their views when making such an order, and

(b) what (if anything) they intend to do in light of those findings.

Children's hearings

25, 26 [*Amend the Children's Hearings (Scotland) Act 2011 with effect from 26 July 2021.*]

27 Appeals to Sheriff Appeal Court and Court of Session

(1) The Children's Hearings (Scotland) Act 2011 is modified as follows.

(2) The italic heading preceding section 163 becomes 'Appeals to Sheriff Appeal Court and Court of Session'.

(3) In section 163 (appeals to sheriff principal and Court of Session: children's hearings etc)—

(a) in subsection (1), for 'sheriff principal or the Court of Session' substitute 'Sheriff Appeal Court',

(b) for subsection (2) substitute—

'(2) A person mentioned in subsection (3) may appeal to the Court of Session against a Sheriff Appeal Court's decision in an appeal under subsection (1) only—

(a) with the permission of the Sheriff Appeal Court, or

(b) if that Court has refused permission, with the permission of the Court of Session.

(2A) The Sheriff Appeal Court or the Court of Session may grant permission under subsection (2) only if the Court considers that—

(a) the appeal would raise an important point of principle or practice, or

(b) there is some other compelling reason for the Court of Session to hear the appeal.

(2B) The Sheriff Appeal Court's decision in an appeal under subsection (1) may not be appealed against under section 113 of the Courts Reform (Scotland) Act 2014.',

(c) in subsection (4)(b), for 'sheriff principal's' substitute 'Sheriff Appeal Court's',

(d) in subsection (6)(b), for 'sheriff principal's' substitute 'Sheriff Appeal Court's',

(e) in subsection (10), for 'sheriff principal or the Court of Session' substitute 'Sheriff Appeal Court',

(f) in subsection (11) the words '(1) or' are repealed,

(g) the section's title becomes '**Appeals to Sheriff Appeal Court and Court of Session: children's hearings etc**'.

(4) In section 164 (appeals to sheriff principal and Court of Session: relevant persons)—

(a) in subsection (1), for 'sheriff principal or the Court of Session' substitute 'Sheriff Appeal Court',

(b) for subsection (2) substitute—

'(2) A person mentioned in subsection (3) may appeal to the Court of Session against a Sheriff Appeal Court's decision in an appeal under subsection (1) only—

(a) with the permission of the Sheriff Appeal Court, or

(b) if that Court has refused permission, with the permission of the Court of Session.

(2A) The Sheriff Appeal Court or the Court of Session may grant permission under subsection (2) only if the Court considers that—

(a) the appeal would raise an important point of principle or practice, or

(b) there is some other compelling reason for the Court of Session to hear the appeal.

(2B)   The Sheriff Appeal Court's decision in an appeal under subsection (1) may not be appealed against under section 113 of the Courts Reform (Scotland) Act 2014.',

(c)   in subsection (6), for 'sheriff principal or the Court of Session' substitute 'Sheriff Appeal Court',

(d)   in subsection (7), the words '(1) or' are repealed,

(e)   the section's title becomes '**Appeals to Sheriff Appeal Court and Court of Session: relevant persons**'.

(5)   In section 165 (appeals to sheriff principal and Court of Session: contact and permanence orders)—

(a)   in subsection (1), for 'sheriff principal or the Court of Session' substitute 'Sheriff Appeal Court',

(b)   for subsection (2) substitute—

'(2)   A person mentioned in subsection (3) may appeal to the Court of Session against a Sheriff Appeal Court's decision in an appeal under subsection (1) only—

(a)   with the permission of the Sheriff Appeal Court, or

(b)   if that Court has refused permission, with the permission of the Court of Session.

(2A)   The Sheriff Appeal Court or the Court of Session may grant permission under subsection (2) only if the Court considers that—

(a)   the appeal would raise an important point of principle or practice, or

(b)   there is some other compelling reason for the Court of Session to hear the appeal.

(2B)   The Sheriff Appeal Court's decision in an appeal under subsection (1) may not be appealed against under section 113 of the Courts Reform (Scotland) Act 2014.',

(c)   in subsection (6), for 'sheriff principal or the Court of Session' substitute 'Sheriff Appeal Court',

(d)   in subsection (7), the words '(1) or' are repealed,

(e)   the section's title becomes '**Appeals to Sheriff Appeal Court and Court of Session: contact and permanence orders**'.

(6)   In section 167 (appeals to sheriff principal: section 166)—

(a)   in subsection (1), for 'sheriff principal' substitute 'Sheriff Appeal Court',

(b)   in subsection (2), for 'sheriff principal' substitute 'Sheriff Appeal Court',

(c)   in subsection (6), for 'sheriff principal' substitute 'Sheriff Appeal Court',

(d)   the section's title becomes '**Appeals to Sheriff Appeal Court: section 166**'.

(7)   In section 182 (publishing restrictions), in subsection (9), in paragraph (a) (iv) of the definition of 'protected information', for 'sheriff principal' substitute 'Sheriff Appeal Court'.

Miscellaneous provisions

28   Conferral of parental responsibilities and parental rights: births registered outwith UK

(1)   The Children (Scotland) Act 1995 is modified as follows.

(2)   After section 4A insert—

'**4B   Conferral of parental responsibilities and parental rights where birth is registered outwith the United Kingdom**

(1)   The Scottish Ministers may by regulations make provision for the conferral of parental responsibilities and parental rights on the following persons—

(a)   a father who has not acquired those responsibilities and rights under section 3(1)(b), 4 or 11, or

(b)   a second female parent who has not acquired those responsibilities and rights under section 3(1)(c) or (d), 4A or 11.

(2)   Regulations under subsection (1) may only make provision for the conferral of parental responsibilities and parental rights on a person in a case where—

(a)   the child's birth is registered outwith the United Kingdom,

(b)   the person acquired parental duties, rights or responsibilities in relation to the child through a process specified in the regulations, and

(c)   the mother of the child has consented to that person acquiring those duties, rights or responsibilities.

(3)   Regulations under subsection (1) are subject to the negative procedure.'.

29   Extension to sheriff of enforcement powers under Family Law Act 1986

(1)   The Family Law Act 1986 is modified by subsections (2) and (3).

(2)   After section 29 insert—

'29A   Enforcement: special Scottish rule

(1)   For the purposes of its enforcement, a Part 1 order that is registered in the Court of Session under section 27 is to be regarded as also registered under that section in every sheriff court.

(2)   A sheriff may entertain an application for the enforcement of a Part 1 order if the sheriff would have jurisdiction under Chapter 3 of this Part to make a Part 1 order in respect of the child concerned.

(3)   In reading Chapter 3 of this Part for the purposes of subsection (2)—

(a)   sections 11 and 13 are to be ignored, and

(b)   any reference to the date of the application is to be read as a reference to the date of the application for the enforcement of the Part 1 order.'.

(3)   In section 31(2) (dismissal of enforcement proceedings), after 'Court of Session' insert 'or sheriff court',

(4)   The Courts Reform (Scotland) Act 2014 is modified by subsection (5).

(5)   In section 43(3)(c) (jurisdiction over persons etc.), after 'Part 1' insert 'and section 29A'.

30   Delay in proceedings likely to prejudice child's welfare

(1)   The Children (Scotland) Act 1995 is modified by subsections (2) and (3).

(2)   In section 11ZA (paramountcy of child's welfare, and the non-intervention presumption) (which is inserted by section 1(4) of this Act), after subsection (2) insert—

'(2A)   When considering the child's welfare, the court is to have regard to any risk of prejudice to the child's welfare that delay in proceedings would pose.'.

(3)   In section 16 (welfare of child and consideration of his views), after subsection (1) insert—

'(1A)   When considering the child's welfare, the court is to have regard to any risk of prejudice to the child's welfare that delay in proceedings would pose.'.

(4)   The Adoption and Children (Scotland) Act 2007 is modified by subsection (5).

(5)   In section 14 (considerations applying to the exercise of powers), after subsection (3) insert—

'(3A)   When considering the child's welfare, the court is to have regard to any risk of prejudice to the child's welfare that delay in proceedings would pose.'.

(6)   The Children's Hearings (Scotland) Act 2011 is modified by subsection (7).

(7)   In section 25 (welfare of the child), after subsection (2) insert—

'(3)   The children's hearing, pre-hearing panel or court is to have regard to any risk of prejudice to the child's welfare that delay in proceedings would pose.'.

Final provisions

31   Review of children's ability to participate

(1)   The Scottish Ministers must review the ability of children to effectively participate in the making of decisions in relation to which one of the following enactments requires that the child be given an opportunity to express a view and that regard be had to any view expressed—

(a)   sections 11ZB(1), 11E(3), 11G(2)(b) and 16(2) of the Children (Scotland) Act 1995,

(b)   sections 14(4A) and 84(5) of the Adoption and Children (Scotland) Act 2007,

(c)   section 27(3) of the Children's Hearings (Scotland) Act 2011.

(2)   The review must, in particular, consider the resources required to ensure effective participation by children in the making of the decisions.

(3)   The review must be completed no later than 5 years after the date of Royal Assent.

(4)   As soon as practicable after completing the review, the Scottish Ministers must—

(a)   make a report of the review publicly available, and

(b)   lay a copy of the report before the Scottish Parliament.

(5)   The report must set out—

(a)   the steps, if any, that the Scottish Ministers propose to take in light of the review,

(b)   a proposed timetable for taking the steps, and

(c)   if any of the steps are not to be taken in the parliamentary session during which the copy of the report is laid before the Parliament, an explanation of why the Ministers do not propose to take those steps before that session ends.

(6)   In subsection (5)(c), 'parliamentary session' has the meaning given in section 19(1) of the Interests of Members of the Scottish Parliament Act 2006.

32   Power to replace descriptions with actual dates

(1)   The Scottish Ministers may by regulations amend—

(a)   section 11B(2) of the Children (Scotland) Act 1995 ('the 1995 Act'), and

(b)   section 11D(3) of the 1995 Act,

so that, instead of referring to the day on which the relevant amending section comes into force, they specify the date on which the relevant amending section actually came into force.

(2)   The relevant amending section—

(a)   in relation to section 11B(2) of the 1995 Act is section 8 of this Act,

(b)   in relation to section 11D(3) of the 1995 Act is section 17 of this Act.

33   Ancillary provision

(1)   The Scottish Ministers may by regulations make any incidental, supplementary, consequential, transitional, transitory or saving provision they consider appropriate for the purposes of, or in connection with, or for giving full effect to this Act or any provision made under it.

(2)   Regulations under this section may—

    (a)   make different provision for different purposes,

    (b)   modify any enactment (including this Act).

  (3) Regulations under this section—

    (a)   are subject to the affirmative procedure if they add to, replace or omit any part of the text of an Act, but

    (b)   otherwise are subject to the negative procedure.

34 Commencement

  (1) The following provisions come into force on the day after Royal Assent: this section and sections 32, 33 and 35.

  (2) The other provisions of this Act come into force on such day as the Scottish Ministers may by regulations appoint.

  (3) Regulations under this section—

    (a)   may make different provision for different purposes,

    (b)   may include transitional, transitory or saving provision.

35 Short title

The short title of this Act is the Children (Scotland) Act 2020.

PART II

INTERNATIONAL CONVENTIONS

EUROPEAN CONVENTION FOR THE PROTECTION OF HUMAN RIGHTS AND FUNDAMENTAL FREEDOMS (1950)

Article 6

1. In the determination of his civil rights and obligations or of any criminal charge against him, everyone is entitled to a fair and public hearing within a reasonable time by an independent and impartial tribunal established by law. Judgment shall be pronounced publicly but the press and public may be excluded from all or part of the trial in the interests of morals, public order or national security in a democratic society, where the interests of juveniles or the protection of the private life of the parties so require, or to the extent strictly necessary in the opinion of the court in special circumstances where publicity would prejudice the interests of justice.

2. Everyone charged with a criminal offence shall be presumed innocent until proved guilty according to law.

3. Everyone charged with a criminal offence has the following minimum rights:

(a) to be informed promptly, in a language which he understands and in detail, of the nature and cause of the accusation against him;

(b) to have adequate time and facilities for the preparation of his defence;

(c) to defend himself in person or through legal assistance of his own choosing or, if he has not sufficient means to pay for legal assistance, to be given it free when the interests of justice so require;

(d) to examine or have examined witnesses against him and to obtain the attendance and examination of witnesses on his behalf under the same conditions as witnesses against him;

(e) to have the free assistance of an interpreter if he cannot understand or speak the language used in court.

Article 8

1. Everyone has the right to respect for his private and family life, his home and his correspondence.

2. There shall be no interference by a public authority with the exercise of this right except such as is in accordance with the law and is necessary in a democratic society in the interests of national security, public safety or the economic well-being of the country, for the prevention of disorder or crime, for the protection of health or morals, or for the protection of the rights and freedoms of others.

Article 12

Men and women of marriageable age have the right to marry and to found a family, according to the national laws governing the exercise of this right.

Article 14

The enjoyment of the rights and freedoms set forth in this Convention shall be secured without discrimination on any ground such as sex, race, colour, language, religion, political or other opinion, national or social origin, association with a national minority, property, birth or other status.

UNITED NATIONS CONVENTION ON THE RIGHTS OF THE CHILD
(1989)

Article 1
For the purposes of the present Convention, a child means every human being below the age of eighteen years unless, under the law applicable to the child, majority is attained earlier.

Article 2
1. States Parties shall respect and ensure the rights set forth in the present Convention to each child within their jurisdiction without discrimination of any kind, irrespective of the child's or his or her parent's or legal guardian's race, colour, sex, language, religion, political or other opinion, national, ethnic or social origin, property, disability, birth or other status.

2. States Parties shall take all appropriate measures to ensure that the child is protected against all forms of discrimination or punishment on the basis of the status, activities, expressed opinions, or beliefs of the child's parents, legal guardians, or family members.

Article 3
1. In all actions concerning children, whether undertaken by public or private social welfare institutions, courts of law, administrative authorities or legislative bodies, the best interests of the child shall be a primary consideration.

2. States Parties undertake to ensure the child such protection and care as is necessary for his or her well-being, taking into account the rights and duties of his or her parents, legal guardians, or other individuals legally responsible for him or her, and to this end, shall take all appropriate legislative and administrative measures.

3. States Parties shall ensure that the institutions, services and facilities responsible for the care or protection of children shall conform with the standards established by competent authorities, particularly in the areas of safety, health, in the number and suitability of their staff, as well as competent supervision.

Article 5
States Parties shall respect the responsibilities, rights and duties of parents or, where applicable, the members of the extended family or community as provided for by local custom, legal guardians or other persons legally responsible for the child, to provide, in a manner consistent with the evolving capacities of the child, appropriate direction and guidance in the exercise by the child of the rights recognized in the present Convention.

Article 6
1. States Parties recognise that every child has the inherent right to life.

2. States Parties shall ensure to the maximum extent possible the survival and development of the child.

Article 7
1. The child shall be registered immediately after birth and shall have the right from birth to a name, the right to acquire a nationality and, as far as possible, the right to know and be cared for by his or her parents.

2. States Parties shall ensure the implementation of these rights in accordance with their national law and their obligations under the relevant international instruments in this field, in particular where the child would otherwise be stateless.

Article 9
1. States Parties shall ensure that a child shall not be separated from his or her parents against their will, except when competent authorities subject to judicial review determine, in accordance with applicable law and procedures, that such

separation is necessary for the best interests of the child. Such determination may be necessary in a particular case such as one involving abuse or neglect of the child by the parents, or one where the parents are living separately and a decision must be made as to the child's place of residence.

2. In any proceedings pursuant to paragraph 1 of the present article, all interested parties shall be given the opportunity to participate in the proceedings and make their views known.

3. States Parties shall respect the right of the child who is separated from one or both parents to maintain personal relations and direct contact with both parents on a regular basis, except if it is contrary to the child's best interests.

4. Where such separation results from any action initiated by a State Party, such as the detention, imprisonment, exile, deportation or death (including death arising from any cause while the person is in the custody of the State) of one or both parents or of the child, that State Party shall, upon request, provide the parents, the child or, if appropriate, another member of the family with the essential information concerning the whereabouts of the absent member(s) of the family unless the provision of the information would be detrimental to the well-being of the child. States Parties shall further ensure that the submission of such a request shall of itself entail no adverse consequences for the person(s) concerned.

Article 10

1. In accordance with the obligation of States Parties under article 9, paragraph 1, applications by a child or his or her parents to enter or leave a State Party for the purposes of family reunification shall be dealt with by States Parties in a positive, humane and expeditious manner. States Parties shall further ensure that the submission of such a request shall entail no adverse consequences for the applicants and for the members of their family.

2. A child whose parents reside in different States shall have the right to maintain on a regular basis, save in exceptional circumstances, personal relations and direct contacts with both parents. Towards that end and in accordance with the obligation of States Parties under article 9, paragraph 1, States Parties shall respect the right of the child and his or her parents to leave any country, including their own, and to enter their own country. The right to leave any country shall be subject only to such restrictions as are prescribed by law and which are necessary to protect the national security, public order (*ordre public*), public health or morals or the rights and freedoms of others and are consistent with the other rights recognised in the present Convention.

Article 12

1. States Parties shall assure to the child who is capable of forming his or her own views the right to express those views freely in all matters affecting the child, the views of the child being given due weight in accordance with the age and maturity of the child.

2. For this purpose, the child shall in particular be provided the opportunity to be heard in any judicial and administrative proceedings affecting the child, either directly, or through a representative or an appropriate body, in a manner consistent with the procedural rules of national law.

Article 18

1. States Parties shall use their best efforts to ensure recognition of the principle that both parents have common responsibilities for the upbringing and development of the child. Parents or, as the case may be, legal guardians, have the primary responsibility for the upbringing and development of the child. The best interests of the child will be their basic concern.

2. For the purpose of guaranteeing and promoting the rights set forth in the present Convention, States Parties shall render appropriate assistance to parents and legal guardians in the performance of their child-rearing responsibilities and

shall ensure the development of institutions, facilities and services for the care of children.

3. States Parties shall take all appropriate measures to ensure that children of working parents have the right to benefit from child-care services and facilities for which they are eligible.

Article 22

1. States Parties shall take appropriate measures to ensure that a child who is seeking refugee status or who is considered a refugee in accordance with applicable international or domestic law and procedures shall, whether unaccompanied or accompanied by his or her parents or by any other person, receive appropriate protection and humanitarian assistance in the enjoyment of applicable rights set forth in the present convention and in other international human rights or humanitarian instruments to which the said States are Parties.

2. For this purpose, States Parties shall provide, as they consider appropriate, co-operation in any efforts by the United Nations and other competent inter-governmental organisations or non-governmental organisations co-operating with the United Nations to protect and assist such a child and to trace the parents or other members of the family of any refugee child in order to obtain information necessary for reunification with his or her family. In cases where no parents or other members of the family can be found, the child shall be accorded the same protection as any other child permanently or temporarily deprived of his or her family environment for any reason, as set forth in the present Convention.

Article 40

1. States Parties recognise the right of every child alleged as, accused of, or recognised as having infringed the penal law to be treated in a manner consistent with the promotion of the child's sense of dignity and worth, which reinforces the child's respect for the human rights and fundamental freedoms of others and which takes into account the child's age and the desirability of promoting the child's reintegration and the child's assuming a constructive role in society.

2. To this end, and having regard to the relevant provisions of international instruments, States Parties shall, in particular, ensure that:

(a) No child shall be alleged as, be accused of, or recognised as having infringed the penal law by reason of acts or omissions that were not prohibited by national or international law at the time they were committed;

(b) Every child alleged as or accused of having infringed the penal law has at least the following guarantees:

(i) To be presumed innocent until proven guilty according to law;

(ii) To be informed promptly and directly of the charges against him or her, and, if appropriate, through his or her parents or legal guardians, and to have legal or other appropriate assistance in the preparation and presentation of his or her defence;

(iii) To have the matter determined without delay by a competent, independent and impartial authority or judicial body in a fair hearing according to law, in the presence of legal or other appropriate assistance and, unless it is considered not to be in the best interest of the child, in particular, taking into account his or her age or situation, his or her parents or legal guardians;

(iv) Not to be compelled to give testimony or to confess guilt; to examine or have examined adverse witnesses and to obtain the participation and examination of witnesses on his or her behalf under conditions of equality;

(v) If considered to have infringed the penal law, to have this decision and any measures imposed in consequence thereof reviewed by a higher competent, independent and impartial authority or judicial body according to law;

(vi) To have the free assistance of an interpreter if the child cannot understand or speak the language used;

(vii) To have his or her privacy fully respected at all stages of the proceedings.

3. States Parties shall seek to promote the establishment of laws, procedures, authorities and institutions specifically applicable to children alleged as, accused of, or recognised as having infringed the penal law, and, in particular:

(a) The establishment of a minimum age below which children shall be presumed not to have the capacity to infringe the penal law;

(b) Whenever appropriate and desirable, measures for dealing with such children without resorting to judicial proceedings, providing that human rights and legal safeguards are fully respected.

4. A variety of dispositions, such as care, guidance and supervision orders; counselling; probation; foster care; education and vocational training programmes and other alternatives to institutional care shall be available to ensure that children are dealt with in a manner appropriate to their well-being and proportionate both to their circumstances and the offence.

PART III

RULES OF COURT

ACT OF SEDERUNT (CHILD CARE AND MAINTENANCE RULES) 1997
(SI 1997/291)

For provisions applying to applications lodged before the specified dates for each Chapter or Part of these Rules, see the website of Scottish Courts at www.scotcourts.gov.uk.

CHAPTER 1
PRELIMINARY

Chapter 1 as reproduced here applies to applications lodged on or after 24 June 2013.

1.1 Citation and commencement

(1) This Act of Sederunt may be cited as the Act of Sederunt (Child Care and Maintenance Rules) 1997 and shall come into force on 1st April 1997.

(2) This Act of Sederunt shall be inserted in the Books of Sederunt.

1.2 Interpretation

(1) In this Act of Sederunt, unless the context otherwise requires—

'Ordinary Cause Rules' means the First Schedule to the Sheriff Courts (Scotland) Act 1907;

['Principal Reporter' is the person referred to in section 14 of the Children's Hearings (Scotland) Act 2011 or any person carrying out the functions of the Principal Reporter by virtue of paragraph 10(1) of schedule 3 to that Act;]

'sheriff clerk' includes sheriff clerk depute.

(2) Unless the context otherwise requires, any reference in this Act of Sederunt to a specified Chapter, Part or rule shall be construed as a reference to the Chapter, Part or rule bearing that number in this Act of Sederunt, and a reference to a specified paragraph, sub-paragraph or head shall be construed as a reference to the paragraph, sub-paragraph or head so numbered or lettered in the provision in which that reference occurs.

(3) Any reference in this Act of Sederunt to a numbered Form shall be construed as a reference to the Form so numbered in Schedule 1 to this Act of Sederunt and includes a form substantially to the same effect with such variation as circumstances may require.

1.3 Affidavits

An affidavit required in terms of any provision of this Act of Sederunt may be emitted—

(a) in the United Kingdom, before a notary public or any other competent authority;

(b) outwith the United Kingdom, before a British diplomatic or consular officer, or any person authorised to administer an oath or affirmation under the law of the place where the oath or affirmation is made.

1.4 Revocations and transitional provisions

(1) Subject to paragraphs (2) and (3), the Acts of Sederunt mentioned in column (1) of Schedule 2 to this Act of Sederunt are revoked to the extent specified in column (3) of that Schedule.

(2)   Nothing in paragraph (1) or in Chapter 2 shall affect any cause which has been commenced before 1st April 1997 and to which that Chapter would otherwise apply, and such a cause shall proceed according to the law and practice in force immediately before that date.

(3)   Nothing in paragraph (1) shall affect any cause to which paragraph 8(1) of Schedule 3 to the Children (Scotland) Act 1995 applies, and such a cause shall proceed according to the law and practice in force immediately before 1st April 1997.

[1.5   Vulnerable witnesses

(1)   This rule shall apply to proceedings under these rules, except those proceedings to which the rules in Part XI of Chapter 3 apply.

(2)   At any hearing on an application under these rules, the sheriff shall ascertain whether there is or is likely to be a vulnerable witness who is to give evidence at or for the purposes of any proof or hearing, consider any child witness notice or vulnerable witness application that has been lodged where no order has been made under section 12(1) or (6) of the Vulnerable Witnesses (Scotland) Act 2004 and consider whether any order under section 12(1) of that Act requires to be made.

(3)   Except where the sheriff otherwise directs, where a vulnerable witness is to give evidence at or for the purposes of any proof or hearing in an application under these rules, any application in relation to the vulnerable witness or special measure that may be ordered shall be dealt with in accordance with the rules within Chapter 45 of the Ordinary Cause Rules.

(4)   In this rule, 'vulnerable witness' means a witness within the meaning of section 11(1) of the Vulnerable Witnesses (Scotland) Act 2004.]

1.6   Lodging audio or audio-visual recordings of children

(1)   In this rule 'child' is a person under the age of 16 on the date of commencement of the proceedings and 'children' shall be construed accordingly.

(2)   Except where the sheriff otherwise directs, where a party seeks to lodge an audio or audio-visual recording of a child as a production in an application under this Act of Sederunt, this shall be done in accordance with and regulated by Chapter 50 of the Ordinary Cause Rules.

(3)   A party who has lodged a recording of a child shall—

(a)   within 28 days after the final determination of the application, where no subsequent appeal has been [made], or

(b)   within 28 days after the disposal of any appeal [made in relation to] the final determination of the application,

uplift the recording from process.

(4)   Where a recording has not been uplifted as required by paragraph (3), the sheriff clerk shall intimate to—

(a)   the solicitor who lodged the recording, or

(b)   where no solicitor is acting, the party or such other party as seems appropriate,

that if he or she fails to uplift the recording within 28 days after the date of such intimation, it will be disposed of in such a manner as the sheriff directs.

CHAPTER 2
ADOPTION OF CHILDREN

PART I
General

Part I of Chapter 2 relates to applications lodged on or after 6 April 2010.

2.1   Interpretation

In this Chapter, unless the context otherwise requires—
    'the Act' means the Adoption (Scotland) Act 1978;

'the 1995 Act' means the Children (Scotland) Act 1995;

'Her Majesty's Forces' means the regular forces as defined in section 374 of the Armed Forces Act 2006; and

'Registrar General' means the Registrar General of Births, Deaths and Marriages for Scotland.

2.2 Expenses

The sheriff may make such an order with regard to the expenses, including the expenses of a reporting officer and a curator *ad litem* or any other person who attended a hearing, of an application under this Chapter as he thinks fit and may modify such expenses or direct them to be taxed on such scale as he may determine.

PARTS II TO V

Parts II to V of Chapter 2 are revoked by SSI 2009/284 with effect from 28 September 2009. Paragraph 4 of SSI 2009/284 makes savings and transitional provision in relation to applications made prior to that date. For applications lodged before 28 September 2009, or on or after 28 September 2009 and before 6 April 2010, see the website of Scottish Courts.

PART VI
Human Fertilisation and Embryology

Part VI of Chapter 2 relates to applications lodged on or after 6 April 2010: SSI 2010/137, para 2(2).

2.45 Interpretation

In this Part—

'2007 Act' means the Adoption and Children (Scotland) Act 2007;

'2008 Act' means the Human Fertilisation and Embryology Act 2008;

'parental order' means an order under section 54 [or 54A(5)] of the 2008 Act; and

'the Regulations' means the Human Fertilisation and Embryology (Parental Orders) Regulations 2010.

2.46 Form of application and productions

(1) An application for a parental order is to be made by petition in Form 22.

(2) The following documents must be lodged in process along with the petition—

(a) an extract or a certified copy of the entry in the Register of Births relating to the child who is the subject of the application;

(b) extracts or certified copies of any entries in the Register of Births relating to the birth of each of the petitioners;

(c) in the case of an application under section 54(2)(a) of the 2008 Act, an extract or a certified copy of the entry in the Register of Marriages relating to the marriage of the petitioners;

(d) in the case of an application under section 54(2)(b) of the 2008 Act, an extract or a certified copy of the entry in the Register of Civil Partnerships relating to the civil partnership of the petitioners; and

(e) any other document founded on by the petitioners in support of the terms of the petition.

2.47 Confidentiality

(1) Unless the sheriff otherwise directs, all documents lodged in process (including the reports by the curator *ad litem* and reporting officer) are to be available only to the sheriff, the curator *ad litem*, the reporting officer and the parties; and such documents must be treated as confidential by all persons involved in, or party to, the proceedings and by the sheriff clerk.

(2)   The reporting officer and the curator *ad litem*—
(a)   must treat all information obtained in the exercise of their duties as confidential; and
(b)   must not disclose any such information to any person unless disclosure of such information is necessary for the purpose of their duties.
(3)   This rule is subject to rule 2.53.

2.48   Orders for evidence

(1)   The sheriff may, before determining the cause, order—
(a)   production of further documents (including affidavits); or
(b)   parole evidence.
(2)   A party may apply by motion for the evidence of a person to be received in evidence by affidavit; and the sheriff may make such order as the sheriff thinks fit.

2.49   Protection of identity of petitioners

(1)   Where persons who propose to apply for a parental order wish to prevent their identities being disclosed to any person whose agreement to the parental order is required, they may, before presenting the petition, apply by letter to the sheriff clerk for a serial number to be assigned to them for all purposes connected with the petition.
(2)   On receipt of an application under paragraph (1), the sheriff clerk must—
(a)   assign a serial number to the applicants; and
(b)   enter a note of the number opposite the name of the applicants in a register of serial numbers kept by the sheriff clerk.
(3)   The contents of the register of serial numbers and the names of the persons to whom each number relates must be treated as confidential by the sheriff clerk and must not be disclosed to any person other than the sheriff.
(4)   Where a serial number has been assigned under paragraph (2)(a), any form of agreement to a parental order under section 54(6) [or 54A(5)] of the 2008 Act—
(a)   must refer to the petitioners by means of the serial number assigned to them;
(b)   must not contain the names and designation of the petitioners; and
(c)   must specify the year in which and the court by which the serial number was assigned.

2.50   Appointment of a curator *ad litem* and reporting officer

(1)   The sheriff must on the lodging of a petition under rule 2.46, appoint a curator *ad litem* and reporting officer.
(2)   The same person may be appointed as curator *ad litem* and reporting officer in the same petition, if the sheriff considers that doing so is appropriate in the circumstances.
(3)   The sheriff may appoint a person who is not a member of a panel established under regulations made by virtue of section 101(1) of the 1995 Act to be curator *ad litem* or a reporting officer.
(4)   The sheriff may, on cause shown, appoint a reporting officer prior to the lodging of such a petition.
(5)   An application for an appointment under paragraph (4) is to be made by letter addressed to the sheriff clerk specifying the reasons for the appointment, and shall not require to be intimated to any other person.
(6)   The sheriff clerk must intimate the appointment of a curator *ad litem* and reporting officer under paragraph (1) or (4) to the petitioner and to the person or persons appointed.
(7)   Where the curator *ad litem* is not also the reporting officer, the sheriff may order the reporting officer to make available to the curator *ad litem* any report or information in relation to the child.

2.51 Duties of reporting officer and curator *ad litem*

(1) The other duties of a reporting officer appointed under [rule 2.50] prescribed for the purposes of section 108(1)(b) of the 2007 Act as modified and applied in relation to applications for parental orders by regulation 4 of, and Schedule 3, to the Regulations (rules: appointment of curators *ad litem* and reporting officers) are—

(a) to ascertain the whereabouts of all persons whose agreement to the making of a parental order in respect of the child is required;

(b) to ascertain whether there is any person other than those mentioned in the petition upon whom notice of the petition should be served;

(c) in the case of each person who is not a petitioner and whose agreement to the making of a parental order is required under section 54(6) [or 54A(5)] of the 2008 Act—

(i) to ascertain whether that person understands the effect of the parental order;

(ii) to ascertain whether alternatives to a parental order have been discussed with that person;

(iii) to confirm that that person understands that he or she may withdraw his or her agreement at any time before an order is made;

(iv) to ascertain whether that person suffers or appears to suffer from a mental disorder within the meaning of section 328 of the Mental Health (Care and Treatment) (Scotland) Act 2003; and

(d) to ascertain whether the conditions in subsections (2) to [(8A) of section 54 or subsections (2) to (8) of section 54A] of the 2008 Act have been satisfied;

(e) to draw to the attention of the court any matter which may be of assistance; and

(f) to report in writing on the matters mentioned in subparagraphs (a) to (e) to the sheriff within 4 weeks from the date of the interlocutor appointing the reporting officer, or within such other period as the sheriff in his or her discretion may allow.

(2) A curator *ad litem* appointed under rule 2.50(1) must—

(a) have regard to safeguarding the interests of the child as his or her paramount duty;

(b) enquire, so far as he or she considers necessary, into the facts and circumstances stated in the petition;

(c) establish that the petitioners understand the nature and effect of a parental order and in particular that the making of the order will render them responsible for the maintenance and upbringing of the child;

(d) ascertain whether any money or other benefit which is prohibited by section 54(8) [or 54A(7)] of the 2008 Act (prohibition on gift or receipt of money or other benefit) has been received or agreed upon;

(e) ascertain whether it may be in the interests of the welfare of the child that the sheriff should make the parental order subject to particular terms and conditions or require the petitioners to make special provision for the child and, if so, what provision;

(f) ascertain whether it would be better for the child that the court should make the order than it should not make the order;

(g) establish whether the proposed parental order is likely to safeguard and promote the welfare of the child throughout the child's life; and

(h) ascertain from the child whether he or she wishes to express a view and, where a child indicates his or her wish to express a view, ascertain that view.

(3) Subject to paragraph (4), the curator *ad litem* must report in writing on the matters mentioned in paragraph (2) to the sheriff within 4 weeks from the date of the interlocutor appointing the curator, or within such other period as the sheriff in his or her discretion may allow.

(4) Subject to any order made by the sheriff under rule 2.53(1), the views of

the child ascertained in terms of paragraph (2)(h) may, if the curator *ad litem* considers appropriate, be conveyed to the sheriff orally.

(5)   The reporting officer must, on completion of his or her report in terms of paragraph (1), in addition send to the sheriff clerk—

(a)   a copy of his or her report for each party; and

(b)   any agreement for the purposes of section 54(6) [or 54A(5)] of the 2008 Act.

(6)   The curator *ad litem* must, on completion of his or her report in terms of paragraph (3), in addition send a copy of it for each party to the sheriff clerk.

2.52   Agreement

(1)   The agreement of a person required by section 54(6) [or 54A(5)] of the 2008 Act is to be in Form 23.

(2)   The form of agreement mentioned in paragraph (1) must be witnessed—

(a)   where it is executed in Scotland, by the reporting officer appointed under [rule 2.50];

(b)   where it is executed outwith Scotland but within the United Kingdom, by a justice of the peace or commissioner for oaths;

(c)   where it is executed outwith the United Kingdom—

(i)   if the person who executes the agreement is serving in Her Majesty's Forces, by an officer holding a commission in any of those forces; or

(ii)   in any other case, by a British diplomatic or consular official or any person authorised to administer an oath or affirmation under the law of the place where the agreement is executed.

2.53   Procedure where child wishes to express a view

(1)   Where a child to whom section 54(11) [or 54A(11)] of the 2008 Act applies indicates his or her wish to express a view, the sheriff, without prejudice to rule 2.51(2)(h)—

(a)   may order such procedural steps to be taken as the sheriff considers appropriate to ascertain the views of that child; and

(b)   must not make an order under this Part unless an opportunity has been given for the views of that child to be obtained or heard.

(2)   Where the views of a child, whether obtained under this rule or under rule 2.51(2)(h) have been recorded in writing, the sheriff may direct that such a written record is to—

(a)   be sealed in an envelope marked 'Views of the child – confidential';

(b)   be available to a sheriff only;

(c)   not be opened by any person other than a sheriff; and

(d)   not form a borrowable part of the process.

2.54   Hearing

(1)   On receipt of the reports referred to in rule 2.51, the sheriff must fix a hearing.

(2)   The sheriff may—

(a)   order any person whose agreement is required to attend the hearing;

(b)   order intimation of the date of the hearing to any person not mentioned in paragraph (3)(a), (b) or (c); and

(c)   order the reporting officer or curator *ad litem* to perform additional duties to assist him or her in determining the petition.

(3)   The petitioners or, where a serial number has been assigned under rule 2.49, the sheriff clerk, must intimate the date of the hearing in Form 24 by registered post or recorded delivery letter to—

(a)   every person whose whereabouts are known to them and whose agreement is required;

(b)   the reporting officer appointed under [rule 2.50];

(c)   the curator *ad litem* appointed under rule 2.50(1); and

(d) any person on whom intimation has been ordered under paragraph (2)(b).

(4) At the hearing—

(a) the petitioners, the reporting officer and the curator *ad litem* must, if required by the sheriff, appear and may be represented;

(b) any other person required by the sheriff to attend the hearing must appear and may be represented; and

(c) any other person to whom intimation was made under paragraph (3)(a) or (d) may appear or be represented.

2.55 Applications under sections 22 and 24 of the 2007 Act

(1) An application under section 22(3) (restrictions on removal: application for parental order pending), section 24(1) (return of child removed in breach of certain provisions) or section 24(2) (order directing person not to remove child) of the 2007 Act all as modified and applied in relation to applications for parental orders by regulation 4 of, and Schedule 3 to, the Regulations, is to be made by minute in the process of the petition for a parental order to which it relates.

(2) A minute under paragraph (1) must include an appropriate crave and statement of facts.

(3) On receipt of a minute under paragraph (1), the sheriff must—

(a) order a diet of hearing to be fixed; and

(b) ordain the minuter, or where a serial number has been assigned under rule 2.49, the sheriff clerk, to send a notice of such hearing in Form 25 together with a copy of the minute, by recorded delivery letter to the curator *ad litem* in the original petition, to any person who may have care and possession of the child and to such other persons as the sheriff considers appropriate.

2.56 Amendment of parental order

(1) An application under paragraph 7 of Schedule 1 to the 2007 Act, as modified and applied in relation to parental orders by regulation 4 of, and Schedule 3 to, the Regulations (amendment of orders and rectification of registers) is to be made by petition to the court which made the parental order.

(2) The sheriff may order the petitioners to intimate the petition to such persons as the sheriff considers appropriate.

2.57 Communication to the Registrar General

The communication to the Registrar General of a parental order required to be made by the sheriff clerk under paragraph 4(1) of Schedule 1 to the 2007 Act, as modified and applied in relation to parental orders by regulation 4 of, and Schedule 3 to, the Regulations (registration of parental orders), is to be made by sending a certified copy of the order to the Registrar General either by recorded delivery post in an envelope marked 'Confidential', or by personal delivery by the sheriff clerk in a sealed enveloped marked 'Confidential'.

2.58 Extract of order

An extract of a parental order must not be issued except by order of the court on an application to it—

(a) where there is a petition for the parental order depending before the court, by motion in that process; or

(b) where there is no such petition depending before the court, by petition.

2.59 Final procedure

(1) After the granting of a parental order the court process must, immediately upon the communication under rule 2.57 being made or, in the event of an extract of the order being issued under rule 2.58, immediately upon such issue, be sealed by the sheriff clerk in an envelope marked 'Confidential'.

(2) The envelope referred to in paragraph (1) is not to be unsealed by the sheriff clerk or by any other person having control of the records of that or any court,

and the process is not to be made accessible to any person for one hundred years after the date of the granting of the order except—

(a)   to the person who is the subject of the parental order after he or she has reached the age of 16 years; and

(b)   to a person on the granting of an application made by him or her to the sheriff setting forth the reason for which access to the process is required.

[2.60   Appeals
An appeal to the Sheriff Appeal Court against an order of the sheriff under this Part is to be made in accordance with Chapter 6 of the Act of Sederunt (Sheriff Appeal Court Rules) 2015.]

CHAPTER 3
[CHILDREN'S HEARINGS: APPLICATIONS TO THE SHERIFF]

Except where otherwise indicated, Chapter 3 as reproduced here applies to applications lodged on or after 24 June 2013.

PART I
Interpretation

3.1   Interpretation
(1)   In this Chapter, unless the context otherwise requires—

['1995 Act' means the Children (Scotland) Act 1995 and (except where the context otherwise requires) references to terms defined in that Act have the same meaning here as given there;]

['2011 Act' means the Children's Hearings (Scotland) Act 2011 and (except where the context otherwise requires) references to terms defined in that Act have the same meaning here as given there;]

['CPSA 1995' means the Criminal Procedure (Scotland) Act 1995 and (except where the context otherwise requires) references to terms defined in that Act have the same meaning here as given there;]

['relevant person' means—

(aa) a person referred to in section 200(1) of the 2011 Act or

[(bb) a person deemed a relevant person by virtue of section 81(3), 160(4)(b) or 164(6) of the 2011 Act];]

'service' includes citation, intimation or the giving of notice as required in terms of this Chapter.

[(2)   In this Chapter any reference, however expressed, to disputed grounds shall be construed as a reference to a statement of grounds which forms the subject of an application under section 93(2)(a) or 94(2)(a) of the 2011 Act.

(3)   Except as otherwise provided, this Chapter applies to applications to the sheriff (including reviews and appeals) under [the 1995 Act, the 2011 Act or section 44A of the CPSA 1995].

(4)   All hearings in respect of applications to the sheriff must be held in private.]

PART II
General Rules

Procedure in Respect of Children

[3.2   Application of rules 3.3 to 3.5A
(1)   Rules 3.3 to 3.5 apply where a sheriff is coming to a decision about a matter relating to a child within the meaning of section 27 of the 2011 Act.

(2)   Rule 3.5A applies in the circumstances referred to in paragraph (1) and in respect of applications under Part V of this Chapter.

[(3)　Rules 3.3, 3.3A, 3.5 and 3.5A apply in respect of appeals to the sheriff under section 44A of the CPSA 1995.]]

[3.3　Power to dispense with service on child
Where the sheriff is satisfied, so far as practicable and taking account of the age and maturity of the child, that it would be inappropriate to order service on the child, the sheriff may dispense with service on the child.]

[3.3A　Child to attend hearing
　[(1)　This rule applies where an application is made to the sheriff under—
　　(a)　the 2011 Act, other than where section 103 or 112 of the 2011 Act applies; or
　　(b)　section 44A of the CPSA 1995.]
　(2)　A child must attend all hearings, unless the sheriff otherwise directs.
　(3)　A child may attend a hearing even if the child is excused from doing so.
　(4)　If the child is not excused from attending the hearing but does not attend the sheriff may grant a warrant to secure attendance in relation to the child.
　(5)　Paragraph (6) applies if—
　　(a)　the hearing of the application is to be continued to another day; and
　　(b)　the sheriff is satisfied that there is reason to believe that the child will not attend on that day.
　(6)　The sheriff may grant a warrant to secure attendance in relation to the child.]

3.4　Service on child
　(1)　Subject to rule 3.3 and to paragraph (2), after the issue of the first order or warrant to cite, as the case may be, the applicant shall forthwith serve a copy of the application and first order or warrant to cite on the child, together with a notice or citation in—
　　(a)　Form 26 in respect of an application for a child assessment order under Part III of this Chapter;
　　(b)　Form 27 in respect of an application to vary or [terminate] a child protection order in terms of rule 3.33;
　　(c)　Form 28 in respect of an application for an exclusion order in terms of rules 3.34 to 3.39;
　　(d)　Form 29 in respect of an application to vary or recall an exclusion order in terms of rule 3.40;
　　[. . .]
　　[(f)　subject to subparagraph (g), in Form 31 in respect of an application under section 93(2)(a) or 94(2)(a) of the 2011 Act;
　　(g)　Form 31A in respect of an application under section 94(2)(a) of the 2011 Act where a procedural hearing has been fixed; and
　　(h)　Form 31B in respect of an application under section 110(2) of the 2011 Act.]
　(2)　The sheriff may, on application by the applicant or of his own motion, order that a specified part of the application is not served on the child.

3.5　[Procedure for obtaining a child's view]
　[(1)　Subject to section 27(3) of the 2011 Act and regulation 11A(5) and (6) of the Secure Accommodation (Scotland) Regulations 2013, the sheriff—
　　(a)　may order such steps to be taken as he considers appropriate to ascertain the views of that child; and
　　(b)　shall not come to a decision about a matter relating to a child within the meaning of section 27 of the 2011 Act or in respect of an appeal under section 44A of the CPSA 1995 unless an opportunity has been given for the views of that child to be obtained or heard.]
　(2)　Subject to any order made by the sheriff under paragraph (1)(a) and to any

other method as the sheriff in his discretion may permit, the views of the child may be conveyed—

(a)   by the child orally or in writing;

(b)   by an advocate or solicitor acting on behalf of the child;

(c)   by any safeguarder [. . .];

[(ca) by any curator *ad litem;*]

(d)   by any other person (either orally or in writing), provided that the sheriff is satisfied that that person is a suitable representative and is duly authorised to represent the child.

(3)   Where the views of the child are conveyed orally to the sheriff, the sheriff shall record those views in writing.

(4)   The sheriff may direct that any written views given by a child, or any written record of those views, shall—

(a)   be sealed in an envelope marked 'Views of the child - confidential';

(b)   be kept in the court process without being recorded in the inventory of process;

(c)   be available to a sheriff only;

(d)   not be opened by any person other than a sheriff, and

(e)   not form a borrowable part of the process.

[3.5A   Confidentiality

(1)   Unless the sheriff otherwise directs, all documents lodged in process are to be available only to the sheriff, the reporter, the safeguarder, the curator *ad litem* and the parties; and such documents must be treated as confidential by all persons involved in, or party to, the proceedings and by the sheriff clerk.

(2)   The safeguarder and the curator *ad litem* must—

(a)   treat all information obtained in the exercise of their duties as confidential; and

(b)   not disclose any such information to any person unless disclosure of such information is necessary for the purpose of their duties.

(3)   This rule is subject to rule 3.5.]

Safeguarders

3.6   Application

Rules 3.7 [to 3.9] apply, as regards a safeguarder, to all applications and proceedings to which this Chapter applies except for an application under section 37 of the 2011 Act for a child protection order.

3.7   Appointment of safeguarder

(1) [Where a safeguarder has not been appointed for the child, the sheriff]—

(a)   shall, as soon as reasonably practicable after the lodging of an application or the commencing of any proceedings, consider whether it is necessary to appoint a safeguarder in the application or proceedings; and

(b)   may at that stage, or at any later stage of the application or proceedings, appoint a safeguarder.

[(2)   Where a sheriff appoints a safeguarder, the appointment and the reasons for it must be recorded in an interlocutor.]

3.8   Rights, powers and duties of safeguarder on appointment

A safeguarder appointed in an application shall—

(a)   have the powers and duties at common law of a curator *ad litem* in respect of the child;

(b)   be entitled to receive from the Principal Reporter copies of the application, all of the productions in the proceedings and any papers which were before the children's hearing;

(c)   subject to rule 3.5(1)(a), determine whether the child wishes to express his views in relation to the application and, if so, where the child so wishes transmit his views to the sheriff;

(d)   make such enquiries so far as relevant to the application as he considers appropriate; and

(e)   without delay, and in any event before the hearing on the application, intimate in writing to the sheriff clerk whether or not he intends to become a party to the proceedings.

[(f)   whether or not a party, be entitled to receive from the sheriff clerk all interlocutors subsequent to his or her appointment.]

3.9   [Representation of safeguarder]

(1)   A safeguarder may appear personally in the proceedings or instruct an advocate or solicitor to appear on his behalf.

(2)   Where an advocate or a solicitor is appointed to act as a safeguarder, he shall not act also as advocate or solicitor for the child in the proceedings.

[. . .]

Fixing of First Hearing

3.11   Assigning of diet for hearing

Except where otherwise provided in these Rules, after the lodging of any application the sheriff clerk shall forthwith assign a diet for the hearing of the application and shall issue a first order or a warrant to cite in Form 32[, Form 32A] or Form 33, as the case may be.

Service, Citation and Notice

3.12   Service and notice to persons named in application

(1)   Subject to the provisions of rule 3.4 (service on child), after the issue of the first order or warrant to cite, as the case may be, the applicant shall forthwith give notice of the application by serving a copy of the application and the first order or warrant to cite together with a notice or citation, as the case may be, on the persons named in the application or, as the case may be, a person who should receive notice of the application (subject to paragraph (2)) in—

(a)   Form 34 in respect of an application for a child assessment order under Part III of this Chapter;

(b)   Form 35 in respect of an application to vary or [terminate] a child protection order in terms of rule 3.33;

(c)   Form 36 in respect of an application for an exclusion order in terms of rules 3.34 to 3.39;

(d)   Form 37 in respect of an application to vary or recall an exclusion order in terms of rule 3.40;

[. . .]

[(f)   subject to subparagraph (g), in Form 39 in respect of an application under section 93(2)(a) or 94(2)(a) of the 2011 Act made under Part VII of this Chapter; or

(g)   in Form 39A where a procedural hearing has been fixed in respect of an application under section 94(2)(a) of the 2011 Act made under Part VII of this Chapter.]

(2)   Notice of the application shall be given in the case of a safeguarder [or curator *ad litem*] by serving a copy of the application and the first order or warrant to cite together with notice in Form 40.

3.13   Period of notice

(1)   Subject to paragraph (2), citation or notice authorised or required by this Chapter shall be made not later than forty-eight hours, or in the case of postal

citation seventy-two hours, before the date of the diet to which the citation or notice relates.

(2) Paragraph (1) shall not apply in relation to citation or notice of the following applications or proceedings—

[(a) an appeal referred to in section 157(1), 160(1), 161(1) or 162(3) of the 2011 Act;]

[(aa) an appeal under section 44A of the CPSA 1995;]

(b) a hearing in respect of an exclusion order where an interim order has been granted in terms of rule 3.36;

[(c) a hearing on an application to vary or terminate a child protection order;]

(d) an application for a child assessment order,

in which cases the period of notice and the method of giving notice shall be as directed by the sheriff.

3.14 Citation of witnesses, parties and persons having an interest

(1) The following shall be warrants for citation of witnesses, parties and havers:—

(a) the warrant for the [hearing on evidence] in an application;

(b) an interlocutor fixing a diet for the continued hearing of an application; and

(c) an interlocutor assigning a diet for a hearing of an appeal or application.

(2) In an application or an appeal, witnesses or havers may be cited in Form 41.

(3) The certificate of execution of citation of witnesses and havers shall be in Form 42.

3.15 Modes of service

(1) Service authorised or required by this Chapter shall be made by any mode specified in paragraphs (2) and (3).

(2) It shall be deemed legal service to or on any person if such service is—

(a) delivered to him personally;

(b) left for him at his dwelling-house or place of business with some person resident or employed therein;

(c) where it cannot be delivered to him personally and he has no known dwelling-house or place of business, left for him at any other place at which he may at the time be resident;

(d) where he is the master of, or a seaman or other person employed in, a vessel, left with a person on board or connected with the vessel;

(e) sent by first class recorded delivery post, or the nearest equivalent which the available postal service permits, to his dwelling-house or place of business, or if he has no known dwelling-house or place of business to any other place in which he may at the time be resident;

(f) where the person has the facility to receive facsimile or other electronic transmission, by such facsimile or other electronic transmission; or

(g) where the person has a numbered box at a document exchange, given by leaving at the document exchange.

(3) Where service requires to be made and there is not sufficient time to employ any of the methods specified in paragraph (2), service shall be effected orally or in such other manner as the sheriff directs.

3.16 Persons who may effect service

(1) Subject to paragraphs (2) and (3), service shall be effected—

(a) in the case of any of the modes specified in rule 3.15(2), by a sheriff officer;

(b) in the case of any of the modes specified in rule 3.15(2)(e) [to (g)], by a solicitor, the sheriff clerk, the Principal Reporter or an officer of the local authority; or

(c)   in the case of any mode specified by the sheriff in terms of rule 3.15(3), by such person as the sheriff directs.

(2)   In relation to the citation of witnesses, parties and havers in terms of rule 3.14 or service of any application, 'officer of the local authority' in paragraph (1)(b) includes any officer of a local authority authorised to conduct proceedings under these Rules in terms of rule 3.21 (representation).

[(3)   Where required by the sheriff, the sheriff clerk shall cite the Principal Reporter, the authors or compilers of any reports or statements and any other person whom the sheriff may wish to examine under section 155(5) of the 2011 Act (procedure in appeal to sheriff against decision of children's hearing)].

3.17   Production of certificates of execution of service

(1)   The production before the sheriff of—

(a)   a certificate of execution of service in Form 43; and

(b)   additionally in the case of postal service, a receipt of the registered or recorded delivery letter,

shall be sufficient evidence that service was duly made.

(2)   It shall be sufficient to lodge the execution of service at the hearing, unless the sheriff otherwise directs or on cause shown.

3.18   Power to dispense with service

Subject to rule 3.3, the sheriff may, on cause shown, dispense with service on any person named.

Miscellaneous

3.19   Expenses

No expenses shall be awarded in any proceedings to which this Chapter applies.

3.20   Record of proceedings

Proceedings under this Chapter shall be conducted summarily.

3.21   Representation

(1)   In any proceedings any party may be represented by an advocate or a solicitor or, subject to paragraphs (2) and (3), other representative authorised by the party.

(2)   Such other representative must throughout the proceedings satisfy the sheriff that he is a suitable person to represent the party and that he is authorised to do so.

(3)   Such other representative may in representing a party do all such things for the preparation and conduct of the proceedings as may be done by an individual on his own behalf.

[3.22   Applications for evidence by live link

(1)   On cause shown, a party may apply in the form prescribed in paragraph (3) for authority for the whole or part of—

(a)   the evidence of a witness or party; or

(b)   a submission,

to be made through a live link.

(2)   In paragraph (1)—

'witness' means a person who has been or may be cited to appear before the sheriff as a witness (including a witness who is outwith Scotland), except in circumstances where such witness is a vulnerable witness within the meaning of section 11(1) of the Vulnerable Witnesses (Scotland) Act 2004;

'submission' means any oral submission which would otherwise be made to the court by the party or such party's representative in person including an oral submission in support of an application;

'live link' means a live television link or such other arrangement as may be specified in the application by which the witness, party or representative, as the case may be, is able to be seen and heard in the proceedings or heard in the proceedings and is able to see and hear or hear the proceedings while at a place which is outside the courtroom.

(3)   An application under paragraph (1) shall be made—

    (a)   in Form 44A in the case of a witness or party;

    (b)   in Form 44B in the case of a submission.

(4)   The application shall be lodged with the sheriff clerk prior to the hearing at which the witness is to give evidence or the submission is to be made (except on special cause shown).

(5)   The sheriff shall—

    (a)   order intimation of the application to be made to the other party or parties to the proceedings in such form as he or she prescribes; and

    (b)   hear the application as soon as reasonably practicable.]

3.23   Orders and transfer of cases

(1)   The sheriff who hears an application under rule 3.22 shall, after hearing the parties and allowing such further procedure as the sheriff thinks fit, make an order granting or refusing the application.

(2)   Where the sheriff grants the application, he may—

    (a)   transfer the case to be heard in whole; or

    (b)   hear the case himself or such part of it as he shall determine,

in another sheriff court in the same sheriffdom.

3.24   Exclusion of certain enactments

The enactments specified in column (1) of Schedule 3 to this Act of Sederunt (being enactments relating to matters with respect to which this Chapter is made) shall not, to the extent specified in column (3) of that Schedule, apply to an application or appeal.

PART III

Child Assessment Orders

3.25   Interpretation

In this Part, 'application' means an application for a child assessment order in terms of [section 35(1) of the 2011 Act].

3.26   Form of application

An application shall be made in Form 45.

3.27   Orders

(1)   After hearing parties and allowing such further procedure as he thinks fit, the sheriff shall make an order granting or refusing the application.

(2)   Where an order is made granting the application, that order shall be made in Form 46 and shall contain the information specified therein.

(3)   Where the sheriff, in terms of [section 36(3) of the 2011 Act], has decided to make a child protection order pursuant to an application, rules 3.31 to 3.33 shall apply.

3.28   Intimation

The local authority shall intimate the grant or refusal of an application to such persons, if any, as the sheriff directs.

PART IV

Child Protection Orders

3.29   Interpretation

In this Part, 'application' means, except in rule 3.33, an application for a child protection order in terms of [section 37 of the 2011 Act].

3.30 Form of application
An application made by a local authority shall be in Form 47 and an application made by any other person shall be in Form 48.

3.31 Determination of application
(1) On receipt of an application, the sheriff, having considered the grounds of the application and the supporting evidence, shall forthwith grant or refuse it.

(2) Where an order is granted, it shall be in Form 49 and it shall contain any directions made under [section 40, 41 or 42 of the 2011 Act].

3.32 Intimation of making of order
Where an order is granted, the applicant shall forthwith serve a copy of the order on—

    (a) the child, along with a notice in Form 50;

    [(b) the persons referred to in section 43(1)(a), (c), (d) and (e) of the 2011 Act, along with a notice in Form 51; and

    (c) such other persons as the sheriff may direct and in such manner as he or she may direct.]

3.33 [Application to vary or terminate a child protection order]
(1) An application under [section 48 of the 2011 Act] for the variation or [termination] of a child protection order [. . .] shall be made in Form 52.

(2) A person applying under section 48 of the 2011 Act for the variation or termination of a child protection order shall require to lodge with his application a copy of that order.

(3) Without prejudice to rule 3.5, any person on whom service is made [under section 49 of the 2011 Act] may appear or be represented at the hearing of the application.

(4) [. . .] The sheriff, after hearing parties and allowing such further procedure as he thinks fit, shall grant or refuse the application.

(5) Where an order is made granting the application for variation, that order shall be in Form 53.

(6) Where the sheriff so directs, intimation of the granting or refusing of an application shall be given by the applicant to such person as the sheriff shall direct.

PART V

Exclusion Orders

3.34 Interpretation
In this Part, 'application' means, except in rule 3.40, an application by a local authority for an exclusion order in terms of sections 76 to 80 of [the 1995 Act]; and 'ancillary order' and 'interim order' shall be construed accordingly.

3.35 Form of application
An application shall be made in Form 54.

3.36 Hearing following interim order
Where an interim order is granted under subsection (4) of section 76 of [the 1995 Act], the hearing under subsection (5) of that section shall take place not later than 3 working days after the granting of the interim order.

3.37 Orders
(1) After hearing parties and allowing such further procedure as he thinks fit, the sheriff shall make an order granting or refusing the application.

(2) Where the sheriff grants an order in terms of paragraph (1), it shall be in Form 55 and shall be served forthwith by the local authority on—

    (a) the named person;

    (b) the appropriate person;

(c)   the relevant child; and
(d)   the Principal Reporter.

3.38   Certificates of delivery of documents to chief constable

(1)   After the local authority have complied with section 78(4) of the 1995 Act, they shall forthwith lodge in process a certificate of delivery in Form 56.

(2)   After a person has complied with section 78(5) of [the 1995 Act], he shall lodge in process a certificate of delivery in Form 56.

[3.39   Power to make child protection order in an application for an exclusion order

Where the sheriff, in terms of section 76(8) of the 1995 Act, has decided to make a child protection order under Part 5 of [the 2011 Act] pursuant to an application, rules 3.31 to 3.33 shall apply.]

3.40   Variation or recall of an exclusion order

(1)   Any application for the variation or recall of an exclusion order and any warrant, interdict, order or direction granted or made under section 77 of [the 1995 Act] shall be in Form 57.

(2)   After hearing parties and allowing such further procedure as he thinks fit, the sheriff shall make an order granting or refusing the application.

(3)   Where an order is made granting the application for variation, that order shall be in Form 58.

(4)   Intimation of the granting or refusing of an application shall be given by the applicant to such persons as the sheriff shall direct.

PART VI repealed by SSI 2013/172

PART VII
[Procedure in Applications Under Section 93(2)(a) or 94(2)(a) of the 2011 Act]

3.44   Interpretation

In this Part, 'application' means an application under [section 93(2)(a) or 94(2)(a) of the 2011 Act].

3.45 Lodging of application, etc

[(1)   Within a period of 7 days beginning with the date on which the Principal Reporter was directed in terms of section 93(2)(a) or 94(2)(a) of the 2011 Act to make an application to the sheriff, the Principal Reporter shall lodge an application in Form 60 with the sheriff clerk of the sheriff court district in which the child is habitually resident.]

[(1A) Paragraph (1) is subject to the terms of section 102(2) of the 2011 Act.

(1B)   The sheriff may, on cause shown, remit any application to another sheriff court.

(1C)   Not later than 28 days after the day on which the application is lodged the sheriff clerk shall fix a hearing on evidence as required under section 101(2) of the 2011 Act.]

(2)   Where a safeguarder has been appointed by [. . .] the children's hearing, the Principal Reporter shall intimate such appointment to the sheriff clerk and shall lodge along with the application any report made by the safeguarder.

[(3)   Paragraphs (4) to (7) apply where an application under paragraph (1) is made by virtue of section 94(2)(a) of the 2011 Act.

(4)   The sheriff may fix a procedural hearing to determine whether or not the section 67 grounds in the statement of grounds are accepted by each relevant person.

(5)   Such procedural hearing must take place before the expiry of the period of 7 days beginning with the day on which the application is lodged.

(6)   The sheriff shall appoint service and intimation of the procedural hearing as the sheriff thinks fit.

(7)   Subject to paragraph (9)(a) and (b), subsequent to the procedural hearing the sheriff may discharge the hearing on evidence and determine the application.

(8)   Where paragraph (7) applies the sheriff shall make such orders for intimation as the sheriff thinks fit.

(9) Where—

(a)   a relevant person does not accept the section 67 grounds in the statement of grounds at the procedural hearing;

(b)   section 106(2)(a) or (b) of the 2011 Act applies; or

(c)   the sheriff has not fixed a procedural hearing;

a hearing on evidence must take place in accordance with rule 3.47.]

3.46   [Withdrawal of application]

(1)   At any stage of the proceedings before the application is determined the Principal Reporter may [withdraw] the application, either in whole or in part, by lodging a minute to that effect or by motion at the hearing.

(2)   The Principal Reporter shall intimate such [withdrawal] to—

(a)   the child, except where service on the child has been dispensed with in terms of rule 3.3;

(b)   any relevant person whose whereabouts are known to the Principal Reporter; and

(c)   any safeguarder [and curator *ad litem*].

(3)   In the event of withdrawal in whole in terms of paragraph (1), the sheriff shall dismiss the application and discharge the referral.

[3.46A   Expeditious determination of application

Prior to or at a hearing on evidence under rule 3.47 (or any adjournment or continuation thereof under rule 3.49), the sheriff may order parties to take such steps as the sheriff deems necessary to secure the expeditious determination of the application, including but not limited to—

(a)   instructing a single expert;

(b)   using affidavits;

(c)   restricting the issues for proof;

(d)   restricting witnesses;

(e)   applying for evidence to be taken by live link in accordance with rule 3.22.]

3.47   [Hearing on evidence]

[(A1) If, at a hearing on evidence (or any adjournment or continuation thereof under rule 3.49), the section 67 grounds (or as they may be amended) are no longer in dispute, the sheriff may determine the application without hearing evidence.]

(1)   In the case of [every section 67 ground] the sheriff shall, in relation to any [ground] which is in dispute, hear evidence tendered by or on behalf of the Principal Reporter, including evidence given pursuant to an application granted under rule 3.23.

(2)   At the close of the evidence led by the Principal Reporter in a case where it is disputed that the [ground set out in section 67(2)(j) of the 2011 Act applies], the sheriff shall consider whether sufficient evidence has been led to establish that [ground] and shall give all the parties an opportunity to be heard on the question of sufficiency of evidence.

(3)   Where the sheriff is not satisfied that sufficient evidence has been led as mentioned in paragraph (2), he shall make a [determination] to that effect.

[(4)   Paragraph (4A) applies where—

(a)   paragraph (2) applies and the sheriff is satisfied that sufficient evidence has been led;

(b)   any other section 67 ground is in dispute.]

[(4A) The child, the relevant person and any safeguarder may give evidence and may, with the approval of the sheriff, call witnesses with regard to the ground in question.]

[(5)   Where the sheriff excuses the child from attending all or part of the hearing in accordance with section 103(3) of the 2011 Act, the following persons shall be permitted to remain during the absence of the child—

(a)   any safeguarder appointed in relation to the child;

(b)   any curator *ad litem* appointed in relation to the child;

(c)   any relevant person;

(d)   the child's representative.]

(6)   Subject to paragraph (7), the sheriff may exclude any person, including the relevant person, while any child is giving evidence if the sheriff is satisfied that this is necessary in the interests of the child and that—

(a)   he must do so in order to obtain the evidence of the child; or

(b)   the presence of the person or persons in question is causing, or is likely to cause, significant distress to the child.

(7)   Where the relevant person is not legally represented at the hearing and has been excluded under paragraph (6), the sheriff shall inform that relevant person of the substance of any evidence given by the child and shall give that relevant person an opportunity to respond by leading evidence or otherwise.

(8)   Where evidence [. . .] has been heard in part and a safeguarder thereafter becomes a party to proceedings, the sheriff may order the evidence to be reheard in whole or in part.

3.48   Amendment of the statement of grounds

The sheriff may at any time, on the application of any party or of his own motion, allow amendment of any statement of grounds.

3.49   Adjournment for inquiry, etc

[. . .] The sheriff on the motion of any party or on his own motion may continue the hearing [fixed under [rule 3.45(1C)]] in order to allow time for further inquiry into any application, in consequence of the amendment of any statement under rule 3.48, or for any other necessary cause, for such reasonable time as he may in the circumstances consider necessary.

3.50   Power of sheriff in making findings as to offences

Where in a [statement of grounds] it is alleged that an offence has been committed by or against any child, the sheriff may [determine] that any other offence established by the facts has been committed.

3.51   Decision of sheriff

(1)   Subject to rule 3.47(3), the sheriff shall give his decision orally at the conclusion of the hearing.

(2)   The sheriff clerk shall forthwith send a copy of the interlocutor containing that decision to—

(a)   the child, except where service on the child has been dispensed with in terms of rule 3.3;

(b)   any relevant person whose whereabouts are known;

(c)   any safeguarder [and curator *ad litem*];

(d)   the Principal Reporter; and

[(e)   such other persons as the sheriff may direct].

(3)   The sheriff may, when giving his decision in terms of paragraph (1) or within 7 days thereafter, issue a note of the reasons for his decision and the sheriff clerk shall forthwith send a copy of such a note to the persons referred to in paragraph (2).

3.52   Signature of warrants

[(1)   Subject to paragraph (3) a warrant granted under the 2011 Act may be signed by the sheriff or the sheriff clerk.

(2)   A warrant signed by the sheriff clerk shall be treated for all purposes as if it had been signed by the sheriff.

(3)   A warrant to secure attendance must be signed by the sheriff.]

PART VIII
[Procedure in Appeals to the Sheriff Against Decisions of Children's Hearings]

3.53   Form of appeal

[(1)   This Part applies to appeals to the sheriff under sections 154(1), 160(1), 161(1) and 162(3) of the 2011 Act.]

[(1A) An appeal to the sheriff under the sections of the 2011 Act prescribed in paragraph (1B) must be—

(a)   made in the form prescribed in paragraph (1B);

(b)   accompanied by a copy of the decision complained of and any document relevant to it that was before the children's hearing; and

(c)   lodged with the sheriff clerk of the sheriff court district in which the child is habitually resident or, on cause shown, such other court as the sheriff may direct.

(1B)   The prescribed sections and form of appeal are—

(a)   in the case of an appeal under section 154(1) (appeal to sheriff against decision of children's hearing), in Form 61;

(b)   in the case of an appeal under section 160(1) (appeal to sheriff against relevant person determination), in Form 62;

(c)   in the case of an appeal under section 161(1) (appeal to sheriff against decision affecting contact or permanence order), in Form 63;

(d)   in the case of an appeal under section 162(3) (appeal to sheriff against decision to implement secure accommodation authorisation), in Form 63A.]

(2)   Subject to paragraph (3), the appeal shall be signed by the appellant or his representative [. . .].

(3)   An appeal by a child may be signed on his behalf by any safeguarder.

[(4)   Where leave to appeal is required by virtue of section 159(2) of the 2011 Act, such application for leave shall be—

(a)   made by letter addressed to the sheriff clerk setting out the grounds on which the application is made;

(b)   accompanied by a copy of the decision referred to in section 159(2) of the 2011 Act;

(c)   lodged with the sheriff clerk with the relevant form of appeal.

(5)   On receipt of such application the sheriff clerk shall forthwith fix a hearing and intimate the application and the date of the hearing to the other parties to the proceedings.

(6)   Where leave to appeal is granted, the appeal will proceed in accordance with rule 3.54.]

3.54   Appointment and intimation of first diet

(1)   On the lodging of the appeal, the sheriff clerk shall forthwith assign a date for the hearing and shall at the same time intimate to the appellant or his representative and, together with a copy of the appeal, to—

(a)   the Principal Reporter;

(b)   subject to the provisions of paragraph (4), the child (if not the appellant);

(c)   [any relevant person] (if not the appellant);

(d)   [. . .] any safeguarder;

(e)   any other person the sheriff [considers necessary, including those referred to in section 155(5)(c) and (e) of the 2011 Act];

[(f)   in the case of appeals under section 162(3), the chief social work officer of the relevant local authority for the child.]

(2)   The sheriff clerk shall endorse on the appeal a certificate of execution of intimation under paragraph (1).

(3)   Intimation to a child in terms of paragraph (1)(b) shall be in Form 64.

(4)   The sheriff may dispense with intimation to a child in terms of paragraph (1)(b) where he considers that such dispensation is appropriate.

(5)   The date assigned for the hearing under paragraph (1) shall be [within the time limits prescribed in, or by virtue of, the 2011 Act and in any event], no later than 28 days after the lodging of the appeal.

3.55   Answers

[(1)   Subject to paragraph (1A), if any person on whom service of the appeal has been made wishes to lodge answers to the appeal, he or she must do so not later than 7 days before the diet fixed for the hearing of the appeal.]

[(1A) Paragraph (1) does not apply to those appeals referred to in section 157(1), 160(1), 161(1) or 162(3) of the 2011 Act.]

(2)   Any person who has lodged answers shall forthwith intimate a copy thereof to any other person on whom service has been made under rule 3.54(1).

3.56   Procedure at hearing of appeal

(1)   Before proceeding [. . .] to examine the Principal Reporter and the authors or compilers of any reports or statements, the sheriff shall hear the appellant or his representative and any party to the appeal.

(2)   On receipt of [any further report required by the sheriff under or by virtue of the 2011 Act], the sheriff shall direct the Principal Reporter to send a copy of the report to every party to the appeal.

(3)   At any appeal the sheriff may hear evidence—

(a)   where a ground of the appeal is an alleged irregularity in the conduct of a hearing, as to that irregularity;

(b)   in any other circumstances where he considers it appropriate to do so.

(4)   Where the nature of the appeal or of any evidence is such that the sheriff is satisfied that it is in the interests of the child that he should not be present at any stage of the appeal, the sheriff may exclude the child from the hearing during that stage and, in that event, any safeguarder appointed and [any relevant person] or representative of the child shall be permitted to remain during the absence of the child.

(5)   Subject to paragraph (6), the sheriff may exclude [any relevant person], or that person and any representative of his, or any such representative from any part or parts of the hearing for so long as he considers it is necessary in the interests of any child, where he is satisfied that—

(a)   he must do so in order to obtain the views of the child in relation or

(b)   the presence of the person or persons in question is causing, or is likely to cause, significant distress to the child.

(6)   Where [any relevant person] has been excluded under paragraph (5) the sheriff shall, after that exclusion has ended, explain to him the substance of what has taken place in his absence and shall give him an opportunity to respond to any evidence given by the child by leading evidence or otherwise.

(7)   Where an appeal has been heard in part and a safeguarder thereafter becomes a party to the appeal, the sheriff may order the hearing of the appeal to commence of new.

3.57   Adjournment or continuation of appeals

[(1)]   The sheriff may, on the motion of any party or on his own motion, adjourn [or continue] the hearing of the appeal for such reasonable time and for such purpose as may in the circumstances be appropriate.

[(2) In the event of such adjournment or continuation the sheriff may make such order as the sheriff deems necessary to secure the expeditious determination of the appeal.]

3.58   Decision of sheriff in appeals

(1)   The sheriff shall give his decision orally either at the conclusion of the

appeal or on such day as he shall appoint, [subject to the provisions of, or by virtue of, the 2011 Act].

(2) The sheriff may issue a note of the reasons for his decision, and shall require to do so where he [takes any of the steps referred to in section 156(2) or (3) of the 2011 Act];

(3) Any note in terms of paragraph (2) shall be issued at the time the sheriff gives his decision or within 7 days thereafter.

(4) The sheriff clerk shall forthwith send a copy of the interlocutor containing the decision of the sheriff, and where appropriate of the note referred to in paragraph (2), to the Principal Reporter, to the appellant (and to the child or [any relevant person], if not the appellant) and[, any safeguarder and such other persons as the sheriff may direct] and shall also return to the Principal Reporter any documents lodged [with the sheriff clerk].

[(5) Where section 159 of the 2011 Act applies the sheriff clerk shall send a copy of the interlocutor containing the decision of the sheriff to the Scottish Legal Aid Board.]

[PART VIIIA
Applications for Review by Local Authority

3.58A Review applications by local authority

(1) This Part of Chapter 3 applies to applications to the sheriff for a review under section 166(2) of the 2011 Act.

(2) An application shall be made in Form 64A and must contain—

    (a) the name and address of the local authority;

    (b) the name of the child in respect of whom the duty was imposed and the child's representative (if any);

    (c) the name and address of any relevant person in relation to the child and such person's representative (if any);

    (d) the name and address of any safeguarder;

    (e) the name and address of any curator *ad litem*;

    (f) the name and address of any other party to the application;

    (g) the name and address of any other local authority with an interest;

    (h) the date and determination made and the place of the sheriff court which made the determination, or alternatively the date and decision made by the children's hearing;

    (i) the grounds for the making of the application;

    (j) any reports, affidavits and productions upon which the applicant intends to rely.

3.58B Hearing on application

(1) After lodging the application in terms of rule 3.58A, the sheriff clerk shall assign a date for hearing the application and shall issue a warrant to cite in Form 64B, which shall require any party to lodge answers if so advised within such time as the sheriff shall appoint.

(2) Subject to the provisions of rule 3.3 (power to dispense with service on child), after the issue of the warrant to cite, the applicant shall forthwith give notice of the application by serving a copy and the warrant on the persons referred to in rule 3.58A.

(3) At the hearing the sheriff may determine the application or allow such further procedure as the sheriff thinks fit.

(4) The provisions of rule 3.51 shall apply to any order made under this Part.]

[PART VIIIB
Procedure in Appeals to the Sheriff Under Section 44A of the CPSA 1995

Part VIIIB came into force on 1 February 2016 (SSI 2015/424).

3.58C   Form of appeal

(1)   An appeal to the sheriff under section 44A of the CPSA 1995 must be—

    (a)   made in Form 64C;

    (b)   accompanied by a copy of the decision complained of and any document relevant to it that was taken into account by the local authority when making that decision;

    (c)   lodged with the sheriff clerk of the sheriff court district in which the child is habitually resident or, on cause shown, such other court as the sheriff may direct.

(2)   The appeal must be signed by the appellant or the appellant's representative.

3.58D Appointment and intimation of appeal hearing

(1)   On the lodging of an appeal, the sheriff clerk must—

    (a)   assign a date for the hearing;

    (b)   intimate the date of the hearing to the appellant or the appellant's representative;

    (c)   intimate the date of the hearing, together with a copy of the appeal, to the persons specified in paragraph (2).

(2)   Those persons are—

    (a)   the child, unless the child is the appellant;

    (b)   the chief social work officer of the appropriate local authority;

    (c)   any relevant person, other than a relevant person who is the appellant;

    (d)   any other person that the sheriff considers necessary.

(3)   The sheriff clerk must endorse a certificate of execution on the appeal.

(4)   Where an appeal is intimated to a child, that intimation must be in Form 64D.

(5)   The sheriff may dispense with intimation to a child if the sheriff considers it appropriate to do so.

3.58E   Procedure at hearing of appeal

(1)   At any appeal the sheriff may hear evidence where he or she considers it appropriate to do so.

(2)   The sheriff must hear the appellant or the appellant's representative and any party to the appeal before examining—

    (a)   the chief social work officer;

    (b)   the authors or compilers of any reports or statements;

    (c)   the Principal Reporter.

(3)   Where the nature of the appeal or of any evidence is such that the sheriff is satisfied that it is in the interests of the child not to be present at any stage of the appeal, the sheriff may exclude the child from the hearing during that stage.

(4)   Where the sheriff excludes a child, any relevant person or representative of the child will be permitted to remain during the child's absence.

(5)   Where the sheriff is satisfied that—

    (a)   it is necessary in order to obtain the views of the child in relation to the hearing; or

    (b)   the presence of the person or persons in question is causing, or is likely to cause, significant distress to the child,

the sheriff may exclude the persons mentioned in paragraph (6) from the hearing for so long as the sheriff considers it necessary in the interests of the child.

(6)   Those persons are—

    (a)   a relevant person;

(b)   any representative of a relevant person.

(7)   After the exclusion of any person under paragraph (5), the sheriff must—

(a)   explain the substance of what has taken place in that person's absence;

(b)   give that person an opportunity to respond to any evidence given by the child by leading evidence or otherwise.

3.58F   Adjournment or continuation of appeals

(1)   The sheriff may adjourn or continue the hearing of the appeal on the motion of any party or on the sheriff's own motion.

(2)   Where the sheriff adjourns or continues a hearing, the sheriff may make any order that is necessary to secure the expeditious determination of the appeal.

3.58G   Decision of sheriff in appeals

(1)   The sheriff must give his or her decision orally, either at the conclusion of the appeal or on such day as the sheriff may appoint.

(2)   The sheriff may issue a note of the reasons for his or her decision.

(3)   Any note in terms of paragraph (2) must be issued at the time the sheriff's decision is given or within 7 days after the date of the decision.

(4)   The sheriff clerk must immediately send to the persons mentioned in paragraph (5)—

(a)   a copy of the interlocutor containing the sheriff's decision;

(b)   where a note of reasons has been issued, a copy of that note.

(5)   Those persons are—

(a)   the appellant;

(b)   the child, unless the child is the appellant;

(c)   any relevant person, other than a relevant person who is the appellant;

(d)   any other person that the sheriff may direct.

(6)   The sheriff clerk must return to the Principal Reporter any documents that the Principal Reporter may have lodged with the sheriff clerk.]

PART IX
[Procedure in Appeals by Stated Case Under Part 15 of the 2011 Act]

[3.59   Appeals: applications for stated case

[(A1)   This Part applies to appeals by stated case under section 163(1), 164(1), 165(1) and 167(1) of the 2011 Act.]

[(1)   An application to the sheriff to state a case for the purposes of an appeal applies [. . .] shall specify the point of law upon which the appeal is to proceed or the procedural irregularity, as the case may be.]

(2)   The appellant shall, at the same time as lodging [the application for a stated case], intimate the lodging of an appeal from the decision of the sheriff to—

(a)   the Principal Reporter;

(b)   the child (if not the appellant), except where service on the child has been dispensed with in terms of rule 3.3;

(c)   any relevant person (if not the appellant);

(d)   any safeguarder;

(e)   any other party to proceedings.

(3)   The sheriff shall, within 21 days of the lodging of [the application for a stated case], issue a draft stated case—

(a)   containing findings in fact and law or, where appropriate, a narrative of the proceedings before him;

(b)   containing appropriate questions of law or setting out the procedural irregularity concerned; and

(c)   containing a note stating the reasons for his decisions in law,

and the sheriff clerk shall send a copy of the draft stated case to the appellant and to parties referred to in paragraph (2).

(4)   Within 7 days of the issue of the draft stated case—

(a)   the appellant or a party referred to in paragraph (2) may lodge with the sheriff clerk a note of any adjustments which he seeks to make;

(b)   the appellant or such a party may state any point of law or procedural irregularity which he wishes to raise in the appeal; and

(c)   the note of adjustment and, where appropriate, point of law or procedural irregularity shall be intimated to the appellant and the other such parties.

(5)   The sheriff may, on the motion of the appellant or a party referred to in paragraph (2) or of his own accord, and shall where he proposes to reject any proposed adjustment, allow a hearing on adjustments and may provide for such further procedure under this rule prior to the hearing of the appeal as he thinks fit.

(6)   The sheriff shall, within 14 days after—

(a)   the latest date on which a note of adjustments has been or may be lodged; or

(b)   where there has been a hearing on adjustments, that hearing,

and after considering such note and any representations made to him at the hearing, state and sign the case.

(7)   The stated case signed by the sheriff shall include—

(a)   questions of law, framed by him, arising from the points of law stated by the parties and such other questions of law as he may consider appropriate;

(b)   any adjustments, proposed under paragraph (4), which are rejected by him;

(c)   a note of the procedural irregularity averred by the parties and any questions of law or other issue which he considers arise therefrom,

as the case may be.

[. . .]

(10)   The sheriff may, on an application by any party or of his own motion, reduce any of the periods mentioned in paragraph (3), (4) or (6) to such period or periods as he considers reasonable.

(11)   Where the sheriff is temporarily absent from duty for any reason, the sheriff principal may extend any period specified in paragraph (3) or (6) for such period or periods as he considers reasonable.]

3.60   Lodging reports and information in appeals

Where, in an appeal—

(a)   it appears to the sheriff that any report or [information] lodged under section 155(2) of the 2011 Act is relevant to any issue which is likely to arise in the stated case; and

(b)   the report or [information] has been returned to the Principal Reporter,

the sheriff may require the Principal Reporter to lodge the report or information with the sheriff clerk.

[. . .]

PART X
[Applications for Review of Grounds Determination]

[3.62   Application

(1)   An application under section 110 of the 2011 Act for a review of a grounds determination made in terms of section 108 of the 2011 Act (determination that grounds for referral established) shall contain—

(a)   the name and address of the applicant and his or her representative (if any);

(b)   the name and address (if known) of the person who is the subject of the grounds determination (even if that person is no longer a child), if not the applicant;

(c)   the name and address of the safeguarder (if any);

(d)   the name and address of the curator *ad litem* (if any);

(e)   the name and address of any person who is, or was at the time the grounds determination was made, a relevant person in relation to the child, if not the applicant;

(f)   the date and grounds determination made and the place of the sheriff court which made the grounds determination;

(g)   the grounds for the making of the application;

(h)   specification of the nature of evidence in terms of section 111(3) of the 2011 Act not considered by the sheriff who made the grounds determination;

(i)   the explanation for the failure to lead such evidence on the original application; and

(j)   any reports, affidavits and productions upon which the applicant intends to rely.

(2)   Where the applicant does not wish to disclose the address or whereabouts of the child or any other person to persons receiving notice of the application, the applicant shall set out his or her reasons for this.]

3.63   Hearing on application

[(1)   Where an application has been lodged in terms of rule 3.62, the sheriff clerk shall—

(a)   assign a diet for hearing the application;

(b)   issue a warrant to cite in Form 65 requiring the Principal Reporter to lodge answers if so advised within such time as the sheriff shall appoint.]

(2)   Subject to the provisions of rule 3.4 (service on child), after the issue of the warrant to cite, the applicant shall forthwith give notice of the application by serving a copy and the warrant on the persons named in rule 3.62 [and such other persons as the sheriff directs].

[(3)   After hearing parties and having considered the terms of section 111(3) of the 2011 Act and allowing such further procedure as the sheriff thinks fit to secure the expeditious determination of the application, the sheriff shall make an order as appropriate.

(4)   The provisions of rule 3.51 shall apply to any order made under paragraph (3).]

[PART XA
Orders Under the Children's Hearings (Scotland) Act 2011

3.64A   Interim compulsory supervision order

(1)   Where a sheriff makes an interim compulsory supervision order under section 100, 109 or 156(3)(d) of the 2011 Act, such order shall be in Form 65A and, subject to rule 3.3, shall be intimated forthwith to the child by the Principal Reporter in Form 65B.

(2)   An application for the extension or extension and variation of an interim compulsory supervision order shall be made to the sheriff in Form 65C.

(3)   An application for the further extension or further extension and variation of an interim compulsory supervision order shall be made to the sheriff in Form 65D.

(4)   Subject to rule 3.3, an application under paragraph (2) or (3) must be intimated forthwith by the applicant to the child and each relevant person and such other persons as the sheriff determines and in such manner as the sheriff determines.

(5)   Where the sheriff grants an application under paragraph (2) or (3), the interlocutor shall state the terms of such extension or extension and variation and subject to rule 3.3, shall be intimated forthwith to the child by the Principal Reporter in Form 65B.

(6)   Subject to paragraphs (1) and (5), where the sheriff—

(a)   makes an interim compulsory supervision order under paragraph (1); or

(b)   grants an application under paragraph (2) or (3),

the Principal Reporter shall intimate the order forthwith to the implementation authority and to such other persons as the sheriff determines in Form 65E.

3.64B Compulsory supervision order

Where a sheriff varies or continues a compulsory supervision order, the interlocutor shall state the terms of such variation or continuation and shall be intimated forthwith by the sheriff clerk to the parties and the relevant implementation authority.

3.64C Medical examination order

Where a sheriff varies or continues a medical examination order, the interlocutor shall state the terms of such variation or continuation and shall be intimated forthwith by the sheriff clerk to the parties and the relevant local authority or establishment.]

[PART XI
Vulnerable Witnesses (Scotland) Act 2004

3.65 Interpretation

In this Part—

'the Act of 2004' means the Vulnerable Witnesses (Scotland) Act 2004;
[. . .]
'child witness notice' has the meaning given in section 12(2) of the Act of 2004;
'review application' means an application for review of arrangements for vulnerable witnesses pursuant to section 13 of the Act of 2004;
['vulnerable witness application' has the meaning given in section 12(6)(a) of the Act of 2004].

[3.66 Extent of application of this Part

This Part of Chapter 3 shall apply to proceedings where—

(a) an application is made to the sheriff under section 93(2)(a), 94(2)(a) or 110 of the 2011 Act;

(b) an appeal is made to the sheriff under Part 15 of the 2011 Act; or

(c) an appeal is made under section 44A of the CPSA 1995.]

Child Witness Notice

3.67 A child witness notice lodged in accordance with section 12(2) of the Act of 2004 shall be in Form 75.

3.68

(1) The party lodging a child witness notice shall intimate a copy of the child witness notice to all other parties to the proceedings and to any safeguarder [. . .] and complete a certificate of intimation.

(2) A certificate of intimation referred to in this rule shall be in Form 76 and shall be lodged together with the child witness notice.

3.69

(1) On receipt of a child witness notice, a sheriff may—

(a) make an order under section 12(1) of the Act of 2004 without holding a hearing;

(b) require of any of the parties further information before making any further order;

(c) fix a date for a hearing of the child witness notice and grant warrant to cite witnesses and havers.

(2) The sheriff may, subject to any statutory time limits, make an order altering the date of the proof or other hearing at which the child is to give evidence and make such provision for intimation of such alteration to all parties concerned as he deems appropriate.

(3)   An order fixing a hearing for a child witness notice shall be intimated by the sheriff clerk—

(a)   on the day the order is made; and

(b)   in such manner as may be prescribed by the sheriff,

to all parties to the proceedings and such other persons as are named in the order where such parties or persons are not present at the time the order is made.

[Vulnerable Witness Application
3.69A

A vulnerable witness application made in accordance with section 12(6)(a) of the Act of 2004 shall be in Form 76A.

3.69B

(1)   The party making a vulnerable witness application shall intimate a copy of the vulnerable witness application to all other parties to the proceedings and to any safeguarder [. . .] and complete a certificate of intimation.

(2)   A certificate of intimation referred to in this rule shall be in Form 76B and shall be lodged together with the vulnerable witness application.

3.69C

(1)   On receipt of a vulnerable witness application a sheriff may–

(a)   make an order under section 12(6) of the Act of 2004 without holding a hearing;

(b)   require of any of the parties further information before making any further order; or

(c)   fix a date for a hearing of the vulnerable witness application and grant warrant to cite witnesses and havers.

(2)   The sheriff may, subject to any statutory time limits, make an order altering the date of the proof or other hearing at which the vulnerable witness is to give evidence and make such provision for intimation of such alteration to all parties concerned as he deems appropriate.

(3)   An order fixing a hearing for a vulnerable witness application shall be intimated by the sheriff clerk–

(a)   on the day the order is made; and

(b)   in such manner as may be prescribed by the sheriff,

to all parties to the proceedings and such other persons as are named in the order where such parties or persons are not present at the time the order is made.]

Review of arrangements for vulnerable witnesses
3.70

(1)   A review application shall be in Form 77.

(2)   Where the review application is made during the sheriff's hearing of the case, the sheriff may dispense with the requirements of paragraph (1).

3.71

(1)   Where a review application is in Form 77, the applicant shall intimate a copy of the review application to all other parties to the proceedings and to any safeguarder [. . .] and complete a certificate of intimation.

(2)   A certificate of intimation referred to in this rule shall be in Form 78 and shall be lodged together with the review application.

3.72

(1)   On receipt of a review application, a sheriff may—

(a)   if he is satisfied that he may properly do so, make an order under section 13(2) of the Act of 2004 without holding a hearing or, if he is not so satisfied, make such an order after giving the parties an opportunity to be heard;

(b)   require of any of the parties further information before making any further order;

(c)   fix a date for a hearing of the review application and grant warrant to cite witnesses and havers.

(2)   The sheriff may, subject to any statutory time limits, make an order altering the date of the proof or other hearing at which the [witness] is to give evidence and make such provision for intimation of such alteration to all parties concerned as he deems appropriate.

(3)   An order fixing a hearing for a review application shall be intimated by the sheriff clerk—

(a)   on the day the order is made; and

(b)   in such manner as may be prescribed by the sheriff,

to all parties to the proceedings and such other persons as are named in the order where such parties or persons are not present at the time the order is made.

3.73   Determination of special measures

When making an order under section 12(1)[, 12(6)] or 13(2) of the Act of 2004 a sheriff may, in light thereof, make such further orders as he deems appropriate in all the circumstances.

3.74   Intimation of an order under section 12(1), 12(6) or 13(2)

An order under section 12(1)[, 12(6)] or 13(2) of the Act of 2004 shall be intimated by the sheriff clerk—

(a)   on the day the order is made; and

(b)   in such manner as may be prescribed by the sheriff,

to all parties to the proceedings and such other persons as are named in the order where such parties or persons are not present at the time the order is made.

3.75   Lodging audio and audio-visual recordings and documents

(1)   Where evidence is taken on commission pursuant to an order made under section 12(1)[, 12(6)] or 13(2) of the Act of 2004 the commissioner shall lodge any audio or audio-visual recording of the commission and relevant documents with the sheriff clerk.

(2)   On any audio or audio-visual recording and any documents being lodged the sheriff clerk shall—

(a)   note—

(i)   the documents lodged;

(ii)   by whom they were lodged; and

(iii)   the date on which they were lodged, and

(b)   intimate what he has noted to all parties concerned.

3.76   Custody of audio and audio-visual recordings and documents

(1)   The audio and audio-visual recordings and documents and documents referred to in rule 3.75 shall, subject to paragraph (2), be kept in the custody of the sheriff clerk.

(2)   Where the audio and audio-visual recordings and documents of the evidence of a witness is in the custody of the sheriff clerk under this rule and where intimation has been given to that effect under rule 3.75(2), the name and address of that witness and the record of his evidence shall be treated as being in the knowledge of the parties; and no party shall be required, notwithstanding any enactment to the contrary—

(a)   to include the name of that witness in any list of witnesses; or

(b)   to include the record of his evidence in any list of productions.

[PART XIA
Cases Involving Sexual Behaviour

3.76A   Interpretation and application of this Part

(1)   This Part of Chapter 3 applies to proceedings where—

(a)   an application is made to the sheriff under section 93(2)(a), 94(2)(a) or 110 of the 2011 Act or an appeal is made under Part 15 of the 2011 Act; and

(b)   the section 67 ground involves sexual behaviour engaged in by any person.

(2)   In the case of relevant appeals the provisions of sections 173 to 175 of the 2011 Act shall be deemed to apply as they apply to applications.

(3)   The evidence referred to in section 173(2) of the 2011 Act may be in writing or take the form of an audio or audio-visual recording.

(4)   In this Part an 'admission application' means an application to the sheriff for an order as to evidence pursuant to section 175(1) of the 2011 Act.

3.77   Application for admission of restricted evidence

(1)   An admission application shall be in Form 79.

(2)   Where an admission application is made during the sheriff's hearing of the case, the sheriff may dispense with the requirements of paragraph (1).

3.78

(1)   Where an admission application [is made under rule 3.77], the applicant shall intimate a copy of the admission application to all other parties to the proceedings and to any safeguarder [. . .] and complete a certificate of intimation.

(2)   A certificate of intimation referred to in this rule shall be in Form 80 and shall be lodged together with the admission application.

3.79

(1)   On receipt of an admission application, a sheriff may—

[(a)   grant the admission application in whole or in part;]

(b)   require of any of the parties further information before making any further order;

(c)   fix a date for a hearing of the admission application and grant warrant to cite witnesses and havers.

(2)   The sheriff may, subject to any statutory time limits, make an order altering the date of the proof or other hearing to which the admission application relates and make such provision for intimation of such alteration to all parties concerned as he deems appropriate.

(3)   An order fixing a hearing for an admission application shall be intimated by the sheriff clerk—

(a)   on the day the order is made; and

(b)   in such manner as may be prescribed by the sheriff,

to all parties to the proceedings and such other persons as are named in the order where such parties or persons are not present at the time the order is made.

3.80

(1)   When making an order pursuant to rule 3.79(1)(a) a sheriff may, in light thereof, make such further orders as he deems appropriate in all the circumstances.

3.81

(1)   An order made pursuant to rule 3.79(1)(a) shall be intimated by the sheriff clerk—

(a)   on the day the order is made; and

(b)   in such manner as may be prescribed by the sheriff,

to all parties to the proceedings and such other persons as are named in the order where such parties or persons are not present at the time the order is made.]

[3.81A   Lodging restricted evidence

(1)   Where the sheriff makes an order under section 175(1)(a) or (c) of the 2011 Act, the applicant shall lodge any relevant recording and documents with the sheriff clerk.

(2)   On the recording and documents being lodged the sheriff clerk shall—
  (a)   note—
    (i)   the evidence lodged;
    (ii)   by whom they were lodged;
    (iii) the date on which they were lodged; and
  (b)   intimate what he or she has noted to all parties concerned.

(3)   The recording and documents referred to in paragraph (1) shall, subject to paragraph (4), be kept in the custody of the sheriff clerk.

(4)   Where the recording of the evidence of a witness is in the custody of the sheriff clerk under this rule and where intimation has been given to that effect under paragraph (2), the name and address of that witness and the record of his or her evidence shall be treated as being in the knowledge of the parties; and no party shall be required, notwithstanding any enactment to the contrary—
  (a)   to include the name of that witness in any list of witnesses; or
  (b)   to include the record of his or her evidence in any list of productions.]

CHAPTER 4
REGISTRATION OF CHILD CUSTODY ORDERS

4.1   Interpretation

In this Chapter, unless the context otherwise requires—

'the Act' means the Family Law Act 1986;

'appropriate court' means the High Court in England and Wales or the High Court in Northern Ireland or, in relation to a specified dependent territory, the corresponding court of that territory, as the case may be;

'appropriate register' means the sheriff court book in which there is registered the action in which the Part I order was made;

'corresponding court', in relation to a specified dependent territory, means the corresponding court specified in relation to that territory in Schedule 3 to the Family Law Act 1986 (Dependent Territories) Order 1991;

'Part I order' has the meaning assigned to it by sections 1, 32, 42(5) and 42(6) of the Act;

'proper officer' means the Secretary of the Principal Registry of the Family Division of the High Court in England and Wales or the Master (Care and Protection) of the High Court in Northern Ireland or, in relation to a specified dependent territory, the corresponding officer of the appropriate court in that territory, as the case may be; and

'specified dependent territory' means a territory specified in column 1 of Schedule 1 to the Family Law Act 1986 (Dependent Territories) Order 1991.

4.2   Applications for registration of Part I order in another court

(1)   An application under section 27 of the Act (registration) to register a Part I order made by a sheriff court in an appropriate court shall be made by letter to the sheriff clerk of the court in which the order was made.

(2)   An application under paragraph (1) of this rule shall be accompanied by—
  (a)   a copy of the letter of application;
  (b)   an affidavit by the applicant;
  (c)   a copy of that affidavit;
  (d)   a certified copy of the interlocutor making the Part I order and any variation thereto which is still in force; and
  (e)   any other document relevant to the application together with a copy of it.

(3)   The affidavit required under this rule shall set out—
  (a)   the name and address of the applicant and his right under the Part I order;
  (b)   the name and date of birth of the child in respect of whom the Part I order was made, the present whereabouts or suspected whereabouts of the child and the name of any person with whom he is alleged to be;

(c)   the name and address of any other person who has an interest in the Part I order;

(d)   the appropriate court in which it is sought to register the Part I order;

(e)   whether the Part I order is in force;

(f)   whether the Part I order is already registered and, if so, where it is registered; and

(g)   details of any order known to the applicant which affects the child and is in force in the jurisdiction in which the Part I order is to be registered.

4.3   Transmission of application for registration

(1)   Unless it appears to the court that the Part I order is no longer in force, the sheriff clerk shall send the documents mentioned in section 27(3) of the Act to the proper officer of the court in which the Part I order is to be registered.

(2)   For the purposes of section 27(3) of the Act the prescribed particulars of any variation of a Part I order which is in force shall be a certified copy of the interlocutor making any such variation.

(3)   On sending an application under paragraph (1) of this rule, the sheriff clerk shall record the date and particulars of the application and the Part I order in the appropriate register.

(4)   On receiving notification from the appropriate court that the Part I order has been registered in that court under section 27(4) of the Act, the sheriff clerk shall record the date of registration in the appropriate register.

4.4   Notification of refusal of application

Where the court refuses to send an application under rule 4.2 to the appropriate court on the ground that the Part I order is no longer in force, the sheriff clerk shall notify the applicant in writing of the court's decision.

4.5   Retention of application and related documents

The sheriff clerk shall retain the letter of application under rule 4.2 together with any documents which accompanied it and which are not transmitted to the appropriate court under section 27(3) of the Act.

4.6   Cancellation or variation of registered Part I order

(1)   Where the court revokes, recalls or varies a Part I order which it has made and which has been registered under section 27(4) of the Act, the sheriff clerk shall—

(a)   send a certified copy of the appropriate interlocutor to the proper officer of the court in which the Part I order is registered;

(b)   record the transmission of the certified copy in the appropriate register; and

(c)   record the revocation, recall or variation in the appropriate register.

(2)   On receiving notification from the court in which the Part I order is registered that the revocation, recall or variation has been recorded, the sheriff clerk shall record that fact in the appropriate register.

CHAPTER 5

MAINTENANCE ORDERS

Chapter 5 applies to applications lodged on or after 1 August 2014.

PART I

General

5.1   Interpretation

In this Chapter, unless the context otherwise requires—

'the 1950 Act' means the Maintenance Orders Act 1950;

'the 1958 Act' means the Maintenance Orders Act 1958;

'the 1972 Act' means the Maintenance Orders (Reciprocal Enforcement) Act 1972;

'the 1982 Act' means the Civil Jurisdiction and Judgments Act 1982;

['2011 Regulations' means the Civil Jurisdiction and Judgments (Maintenance) Regulations 2011;]

['2012 Regulations' means the International Recovery of Maintenance (Hague Convention 2007) (Scotland) Regulations 2012;]

'clerk of court' means the clerk to the magistrates' court in England or Northern Ireland and, in relation to a county court in England or Northern Ireland, means the registrar of that court;

'clerk of the magistrates' court' means the clerk to the magistrates' court in England or Northern Ireland as the case may be;

['Contracting State' means a State bound by the Convention other than an EU Member State;]

['the Convention' means the Convention on the International Recovery of Child Support and other forms of Family Maintenance done at The Hague on 23rd November 2007;]

['Convention Maintenance Decision' means a decision, or part of a decision, to which Chapter V of the Convention applies by virtue of Article 19(1) made by—

(a) a court in a Contracting State; or

(b) a sheriff;

'Court in a Hague Convention Country' includes any judicial or administrative authority in a Hague Convention Country;

[. . .]

['Hague Convention Country' means a country or territory specified in Schedule 1 to the Reciprocal Enforcement of Maintenance Orders (Hague Convention Countries) Order 1993;]

['Maintenance Decision' has the meaning given to 'decision' by Article 2(1) of the Maintenance Regulation;]

['Maintenance Regulation' means Council Regulation (EC) No 4/2009 of 18th December 2008 including as applied in relation to Denmark by virtue of the Agreement made on 19th October 2005 between the European Community and the Kingdom of Denmark;]

['Maintenance Regulation State' in the application of any provision in relation to the Maintenance Regulation, refers to any of the Member States;]

'order' includes decree;

'reciprocating country' has the meaning assigned to it by section 1 of the 1972 Act;

'the Registrar', in relation to the High Court in England, means the Senior Registrar of the principal Registry of the Family Division of the High Court in England.

5.2 Application

(1) Part II of this Chapter shall have effect in relation to the registration in other parts of the United Kingdom of orders granted by the sheriff to which the 1950 and 1958 Acts apply and such orders are referred to in this Chapter as 'outgoing orders under the 1950 Act'.

(2) Part III of this Chapter shall have effect in relation to the registration outwith the United Kingdom of orders to which the 1972 Act, or the 1972 Act as amended by any order in Council made under Part III of the 1972 Act, applies and such orders are referred to as 'outgoing orders under the 1972 Act'.

(3) Part IV of this Chapter shall have effect in relation to the registration in the sheriff court of orders made by courts in other parts of the United Kingdom to which the 1950 Act applies and such orders are referred to in this Chapter as 'incoming orders under the 1950 Act'.

(4) Part V of this Chapter shall have effect in relation to the registration in the sheriff court of orders made by courts outwith the United Kingdom to which the

1972 Act, or the 1972 Act as amended by any Order in Council made under Part III of the 1972 Act, applies and such orders are referred to in this Chapter as 'incoming orders under the 1972 Act'.

(5)   Part VI of this Chapter shall have effect in relation to the registration in the sheriff court of orders made by courts outwith the United Kingdom to which the 1982 Act applies and such orders are referred to in this Chapter as 'incoming orders under the 1982 Act'.

[(6) Part VII of this Chapter shall have effect in relation to a Maintenance Decision.

(7) Part VIII of this Chapter shall have effect only in relation to—

(a)   a Maintenance Decision made by a court in Denmark; and

(b)   a Maintenance Decision to which sections 2 and 3 of Chapter IV of the Maintenance Regulation apply by virtue of Article 75(2)(a) or (b) of that Regulation.]

[(8) Part IX of this Chapter shall have effect in relation to a Convention Maintenance Decision.]

5.3   Prescribed officer

(1)   The sheriff clerk shall be—

(a)   the prescribed officer for the purposes of the 1950, 1958 and 1972 Acts, the 1972 Act as amended by any Order in Council, [the 1982 Act and the 2011 Regulations]; and

(b)   the proper officer for the purposes of Schedules 6 and 7 to the 1982 Act (enforcement of UK judgments).

(2)   Unless otherwise provided, all communications which the prescribed officer is required to send to—

(a)   an addressee in the United Kingdom shall be sent by first class recorded delivery post; and

(b)   an addressee outwith the United Kingdom shall be sent registered letter or the nearest equivalent which the available postal service permits.

5.4   Maintenance Orders Register

(1)   The sheriff clerk shall maintain a Register called 'the Maintenance Orders Register' for the purpose of the 1950, 1958 and 1972 Acts, the 1972 Act as amended by any Order in Council, [the 1982 Act, the Maintenance Regulation and the 2012 Regulations], Part I of which shall relate to outgoing orders and Part II to incoming orders.

(2)   The sheriff clerk shall make appropriate entries in the Maintenance Orders Register in respect of any action taken by him or notified to him in accordance with [the relevant provisions], and shall keep in such manner as he considers appropriate any documents sent to him in connection with any such action.

(3)   Every entry registering a maintenance order shall specify [the relevant provision including] and where appropriate any Order in Council under which the maintenance order in question is registered.

(4)   When a registered maintenance order is varied, revoked or cancelled, the sheriff clerk shall make an appropriate entry against the entry for the original order.

5.5   Inspection

(1)   The sheriff clerk shall, on an application by—

(a)   any person entitled to, or liable to make, payments under an order in respect of which any entry has been made in the Maintenance Orders Register; or

(b)   a solicitor acting on behalf of any such person,

permit that person or his solicitor, as the case may be, to inspect any such entry and any document in his possession relating to that entry and to take copies of any such entry or document.

(2) On an application by or on behalf of any other person, the sheriff clerk may, on being satisfied of that person's interest, grant that person or his solicitor permission to inspect or take copies of any such entry or document.

PART II
Outgoing Orders Under the 1950 Act

5.6 Commencement of proceedings

(1) Every writ by which proceedings are begun in a sheriff court having jurisdiction under or by virtue of Part I of the 1950 Act against a person residing in another part of the United Kingdom, and all parts of process (other than productions) lodged in any proceedings taken in a sheriff court under or by virtue of the 1950 Act or the 1958 Act, shall be headed 'Maintenance Orders Act 1950' or as the case may be 'Maintenance Orders Act 1958'.

(2) The warrant of citation granted upon any writ which by virtue of those Acts is to be served upon a person residing in another part of the United Kingdom shall proceed upon a period of notice of 21 days, and such warrant of citation may be signed by the sheriff clerk.

(3) In connection with the service under section 15 of the 1950 Act (service of process) of a writ from a sheriff court the expressions 'initial writ', 'writ' and 'summons' in the said section and in the forms contained in the Second Schedule to that Act shall include the warrant of citation relative thereto.

5.7 Application for registration

(1) An application for registration in a magistrates' court in England or Northern Ireland of an order granted by a sheriff court to which the 1950 Act applies shall be made by lodging with the sheriff clerk—

(a) a letter of application;

(b) an affidavit by the applicant;

(c) a copy of that affidavit; and

(d) a certified copy of the order.

(2) An affidavit under this rule shall include—

(a) the name and address of the person liable to make payments under the order;

(b) details of any arrears due under the order and the date to which they are calculated;

(c) the reason for the application; and

(d) a statement that the order is not already registered under the 1950 Act.

5.8 Transmission

On the grant of an application under rule 5.7, the sheriff clerk shall send to the clerk of the magistrates' court—

(a) the affidavit of the applicant;

(b) the certified copy of the order; and

(c) a letter requesting registration of the order.

5.9 Application to adduce evidence

(1) An application to a sheriff court under section 22(5) of the 1950 Act to adduce evidence in connection with an order granted by that court and registered in a court in England or Northern Ireland shall be made by initial writ.

(2) Any evidence adduced in pursuance of such an application shall be recorded in such manner as the sheriff shall direct and the record of evidence certified by the sheriff shall be the transcript or summary of the evidence adduced, and shall be signed by the deponent, together with any documentary productions referred to therein.

(3) Where the sheriff clerk of a court in which an order was granted receives a transcript or summary of evidence connected with that order adduced, under

section 22(5) of the 1950 Act, in the court where the order was registered, he shall lodge such transcript or summary in the process containing that order.

5.10   Re-registration in the High Court

(1)   When an order has been registered in the magistrates' court, an application to the sheriff court for the re-registration of that order in the High Court in England under the 1958 Act shall be made by lodging with the sheriff clerk—

    (a)   a letter of application;

    (b)   an affidavit by the applicant;

    (c)   a certified copy of that affidavit; and

    (d)   a certified copy of the order.

(2)   An affidavit under this rule shall include—

    (a)   the name and address of the person liable to make payments under the order;

    (b)   details of any arrears due under the order and the date to which they are calculated;

    (c)   the reason for the application;

    (d)   the date and place of the original registration;

    (e)   where the order has been re-registered, the date and place of the last re-registration and whether or not that has been cancelled, or where any of these facts is not known a statement to that effect; and

    (f)   a declaration that no process remains in force for the enforcement of the registered order.

5.11   Transmission for re-registration

If an application under rule 5.10 is granted, the sheriff clerk shall send to the Registrar—

    (a)   the affidavit of the applicant; and

    (b)   a letter stating that the application has been granted and requesting him to take steps to have the order registered in the High Court.

5.12   Discharge and variation

Where an interlocutor is pronounced in the sheriff court varying or discharging an order registered under the 1950 Act or the 1958 Act, the sheriff clerk shall send to the clerk of the magistrates' court and, as the case may be, to the Registrar—

    (a)   a certified copy of the interlocutor; and

    (b)   a letter requesting the clerk of the magistrates' court and, as the case may be, the Registrar to take the appropriate action under those Acts, in accordance with the interlocutor, and to notify him of the result.

5.13   Cancellation of registration

(1)   An application under section 24(2) of the 1950 Act (cancellation of registration) in connection with an order granted by a sheriff court and registered in a court in England or Northern Ireland shall be made by lodging with the sheriff clerk an affidavit by the person liable to make payments under the order stating the facts on which the application is founded.

(2)   Where it appears to the sheriff clerk that the applicant has ceased to reside in England or Northern Ireland, as the case may be, the sheriff clerk shall send notice to that effect to the clerk of the magistrates' court and the Registrar, as the case may be, of any court in which the order is registered.

PART III
Outgoing Orders Under the 1972 Act

5.14   Application for transmission of order for enforcement in a reciprocating country

(1)   An application for the transmission of a maintenance order for enforcement in a reciprocating country shall be made by letter addressed to the sheriff clerk.

(2)   There shall be lodged with any such application—
   (a)   a certified copy of the relevant order;
   (b)   a statement signed by the applicant or his solicitor of any arrears outstanding in respect of the order;
   (c)   a statement signed by the applicant or his solicitor giving such information as to the whereabouts of the payer as he possesses;
   (d)   a statement signed by the applicant or his solicitor giving such information as the applicant possesses for facilitating the identification of the payer;
   (e)   where available, a photograph of the payer.

[. . .]

5.16   Application for transmission of order to Hague Convention Country

(1)   An application for the transmission of a maintenance order to a Court in a Hague Convention Country for registration and enforcement shall be made by letter addressed to the sheriff clerk.

(2)   There shall be lodged with any such application—
   (a)   a certified copy of the relevant order;
   (b)   a statement signed by the applicant or his solicitor of any arrears outstanding in respect of that order;
   (c)   a statement signed by the applicant or his solicitor giving such information as to the whereabouts of the payer as he possesses;
   (d)   a statement signed by the applicant or his solicitor giving such information as the applicant possesses for facilitating the identification of the payer;
   (e)   where available, a photograph of the payer;
   (f)   a statement signed by the applicant or his solicitor which establishes that notice of the order was sent to the payer;
   (g)   if the payee received legal aid in the proceedings, a statement to that effect; and
   (h)   if the payer did not appear in the proceedings in which the maintenance order was made, the original or a certified true copy of a document which establishes that notice of the institution of the proceedings was served on the payer.

[5.16A   Application for transmission of order for enforcement [. . .] in the USA

(1)   An application for the transmission of a maintenance order to the United States of America for enforcement shall be made by letter addressed to the sheriff clerk.

(2)   There shall be lodged with any such application—
   (a)   three certified copies of the maintenance order;
   (b)   a certificate of arrears signed by the applicant or his solicitor;
   (c)   a sworn statement signed by the payee—
      (i)   giving the address of the payee;
      (ii)   giving such information as is known as to the whereabouts of the payer; and
      (iii)   giving a description, so far as is known, of the nature and location of any assets of the payer available for execution; and
   (d)   a statement signed by the applicant giving such information as the applicant possesses for facilitating the identification of the payer including a photograph if available.]

5.17   Service on defender in Hague Convention Country

For the purposes of section 4(4) of the 1972 Act as applied in respect of a defender in a Hague Convention Country, service on such a defender shall be effected in accordance with the Ordinary Cause Rules.

[5.17A   Service of notice of proceedings on payer residing in USA

Where service of a document is executed in accordance with section 5(4)(a) of the 1972 Act as applied to the United States of America, the Scottish Ministers shall obtain and lodge with the sheriff clerk a certificate by a person who is conversant with the law of the United States of America and who practises or who has practised law in that country or is a duly accredited representative of the Government of the United States of America, stating that the method of service employed is in accordance with the law of the place where service was executed.]

5.18　Provisional order made with a view to transmission to a reciprocating country
A certificate signed by the sheriff clerk in terms of section 3(5)(c) of the 1972 Act (certificate of grounds), as read with section 4(6) thereof, shall also be signed by the sheriff.

5.19　Evidence adduced prior to confirmation of provisional order
(1)　Where under section 5(9) of the 1972 Act it appears to the sheriff that a provisional order ought not to have been made, the sheriff clerk shall send by first class recorded delivery a notice on Form 66 to the person on whose application the order was made.

(2)　Where such a person wishes to make representations, he shall lodge with the sheriff clerk within 21 days of the date of posting of the notice a minute narrating the representations and the further evidence which he intends to adduce.

(3)　On the expiry of the period of 21 days, the cause shall be enrolled before the sheriff who shall appoint a diet for the hearing of further evidence or make such other order as may be appropriate.

5.20　Provisions in relation to intimation and entering appearance
(1)　Where the 1972 Act provides that on intimation to a payee of the receipt by the Court of a provisional order the payee is to enter appearance within a prescribed period, intimation shall be given in Form 67 and the period shall be—
(a)　21 days from the date of posting where the payee is resident in Europe; and
(b)　42 days from the date of posting where the payee is resident outside Europe.

(2)　To enter appearance in terms of section 5(6) of the 1972 Act, the payee shall lodge an application—
(a)　stating that he opposes confirmation of the order; and
(b)　setting forth averments in answer to the case upon which the provisional order was made, supported by the appropriate pleas-in-law.

(3)　Where the payee enters appearance in terms of section 5(6) of the 1972 Act, the sheriff shall appoint a diet for the hearing of evidence or make such other order as may be appropriate to enable the court to proceed in accordance with the procedure and practice in ordinary civil proceedings in the sheriff court as if the application for the variation or revocation of the maintenance order had been made to it.

5.21　Authentication of documents*
Where the 1972 Act provides that a document is to be authenticated in a prescribed manner, it shall be authenticated by a certificate signed by the sheriff clerk declaring that the document is authentic.

---

* For authentication of documents, see now SSI 2016/306.

5.22　Application under section 4 or 5 of the 1972 Act
An application for a provisional order under section 4 of the 1972 Act or an application under section 5 of that Act for variation or revocation of a maintenance order shall [proceed as an ordinary cause in accordance with the terms of Chapter 33 (family actions) or 33A (civil partnership actions), as the case may be, of the Ordinary Cause Rules].

[5.22A　Representations or evidence by payer residing in the USA
(1)　Where notices are provided in accordance with section 5(4) of the 1972 Act as applied to the United States of America, the sheriff clerk shall notify the

recipients of the notices that if the payer wishes the court in Scotland to take into account any representations made by him or any evidence adduced by him or on his behalf, then such representations or evidence must be lodged with the sheriff clerk not later than 21 days before the date fixed for the hearing.

(2) Where such representations are lodged, or such evidence is lodged, the sheriff clerk shall serve a copy of the representations or evidence—

    (a) where the payee is represented by a solicitor, on that solicitor, by—

        (i) personal delivery;

        (ii) facsimile transmission;

        (iii) first class ordinary post; or

        (iv) delivery to a document exchange; and

    (b) where the payee is not represented by a solicitor, on the payee, by any of the methods of service provided for in Chapter 5 of the Ordinary Cause Rules (citation, service and intimation).]

[5.22B Application by payer residing in the USA for variation or revocation of order

(1) Where an application is made in accordance with section 5(6) of the 1972 Act as applied to the United States of America, the sheriff clerk shall give notice of institution of the proceedings, including notice of the substance of the application, in accordance with subparagraph (2) or (3).

(2) Where the payee is represented by a solicitor, the document referred to in subparagraph (1) shall be served on that solicitor by—

    (a) personal delivery;

    (b) facsimile transmission;

    (c) first class ordinary post; or

    (d) delivery to a document exchange.

(3) Where the payee is not represented by a solicitor, the document referred to in subparagraph (1) shall be served on the payee by any of the methods of service provided for in Chapter 5 of the Ordinary Cause Rules (citation, service and intimation).]

5.23 Evidence

(1) Where any request to take evidence is made by or on behalf of a court in terms of section 14 of the 1972 Act, or section 14 of the 1972 Act as amended by any Order in Council made under Part III of that Act, or by the Secretary of State in terms of section 38 thereof, such evidence shall be taken before a sheriff of the sheriffdom in which the witness resides and shall be—

    (a) recorded by tape recording or other mechanical means approved by the court; or

    (b) taken down by a shorthand writer, or where the sheriff so directs, by the sheriff,

and the extended notes of evidence certified by the sheriff shall be the notes of the evidence taken.

(2) Where a provisional order is made under section 4 or 5 of the 1972 Act and evidence has been taken by a shorthand writer, the applicant or his solicitor shall provide the sheriff clerk with a copy of the extended notes of evidence.

[5.23A Taking of evidence at request of a court in the USA

Where evidence is taken by a sheriff under section 14(1) of the 1972 Act as applied to the United States of America, rules 29.7 (citation of witnesses), 29.9 (second diligence against a witness) and 29.10 (failure of witness to attend) of the Ordinary Cause Rules shall apply in respect of the matters set out in those rules.]

[5.23B Requests for the taking of evidence by a court in the USA

An application made to a sheriff for the purposes of section 14(5) of the 1972 Act as applied to the United States of America shall follow as nearly as may be the procedure set out in rule 28.14 of the Ordinary Cause Rules (letters of request), subject to any modifications necessitated by that provision of the 1972 Act as so applied.]

[5.23C Communication with courts in the USA
In so far as applicable to outgoing orders under the 1972 Act to the United States of America, for the purposes of the provisions in Part I of the 1972 Act, the sheriff may communicate with a court or courts in the United States of America in such circumstances and in such manner as he thinks fit.]

[5.23D Disapplication of provisions where payer resides or has assets in the USA
In any case in which the payer under a maintenance order made by a court in Scotland is residing or has assets in the United States of America, none of the provisions in this Part shall apply except this rule and rules 5.16A, 5.17A, 5.21, 5.22, 5.22A, 5.22B, 5.23, 5.23A, 5.23B and 5.23C.]

PART IV
Incoming Orders Under the 1950 Act

5.24 Registration
(1) On receiving a certified copy of a maintenance order made by a court in England or Northern Ireland, the sheriff clerk shall—
  (a) retain any certificate or affidavit sent with the certified copy of the order as to the amount of any arrears due under the order;
  (b) endorse on the certified copy order a declaration in Form 68 and retain such certified copy order and declaration; and
  (c) notify the clerk of the court which made the order that it has been registered.
(2) The sheriff clerk may issue an extract of the order with the declaration thereon, and such extract shall have the same force and effect as, and may be enforced in all respects as if it was, an extract decree of the sheriff court in which the certified copy is registered.

5.25 Variation of rate of payment
An application to a sheriff court under section 22(1) of the 1950 Act for variation of the rate of payment under a maintenance order made by a court in England or Northern Ireland and registered in that sheriff court shall be made by initial writ.

5.26 Application to adduce evidence
(1) An application to a sheriff court under section 22(5) of the 1950 Act to adduce evidence in connection with a maintenance order made by a court in England or Northern Ireland and registered in that sheriff court shall be made by initial writ.
(2) Any evidence adduced in pursuance of such an application shall be recorded in such manner as the sheriff shall direct and the record of evidence certified by the sheriff shall be the transcript or summary of the evidence adduced.
(3) Where the sheriff clerk of a court in which an order is registered receives a transcript or summary of evidence connected with that order adduced under section 22(5) of the 1950 Act in the court where that order was made, he shall lodge such transcript or summary in the process of any proceedings for variation of the order before the sheriff court.

5.27 Discharge and variation
(1) Where a maintenance order made by a court in England or Northern Ireland and registered under the 1950 Act in a sheriff court is varied by that sheriff court, the sheriff clerk shall give notice of the variation to the clerk of the court by which the order was made by sending him a certified copy of the interlocutor varying the order.
(2) Where a maintenance order made by a court in England or Northern

Ireland and registered in a sheriff court is discharged or varied by any court other than that sheriff court, the sheriff clerk shall on receipt of a certified copy of the order discharging or varying the registered order notify the clerk of the appropriate court that the discharge or variation has been entered in the Maintenance Orders Register.

(3)   Paragraphs (1)(a) and (b) and (2) of rule 5.24 shall apply to an order varying a registered order as they apply to the registered order.

5.28   Cancellation of registration

(1)   An application under section 24(1) of the 1950 Act for the cancellation of the registration of a maintenance order made by a court in England or Northern Ireland and registered in a sheriff court shall be made by lodging with the sheriff clerk—

(a)   an application for that purpose which shall state the date of the registration of the order; and

(b)   a copy of the order the registration of which is sought to be cancelled.

(2)   Where under section 24(1) or (2) of the 1950 Act the sheriff clerk cancels the registration of a maintenance order, he shall—

(a)   notify the clerk of the court by which the order was made; and

(b)   notify the person liable to make payments under the order.

PART V
Incoming Orders Under the 1972 Act

5.29   Provisions in relation to intimation and entering appearance

(1)   Where the 1972 Act provides that on intimation to a payer of the receipt by the court of a provisional order the payer is to enter appearance within a prescribed period, intimation shall be given in Form 67 and the period shall be—

(a)   21 days from the date of posting where the payer is resident in Europe; and

(b)   42 days from the date of posting where the payer is resident outside Europe.

(2)   To enter appearance in terms of section 7(4) or 9(7) of the 1972 Act, the payer shall lodge an application

(a)   stating that he opposes confirmation of the order; and

(b)   setting forth averments in answer to the case upon which the provisional order was made, supported by appropriate pleas-in-law.

(3)   Where the payer enters appearance in terms of section 7(4) of the 1972 Act, the sheriff shall appoint a diet for the hearing of evidence or make such other order as may be appropriate to enable the court to proceed in accordance with the procedure and practice in ordinary civil proceedings in the sheriff court as if an application for a maintenance order against the payer had been made to it.

(4)   Where the payer enters appearance in terms of section 9(7) of the 1972 Act, the sheriff shall appoint a diet for the hearing of evidence or make such other order as may be appropriate to enable the court to proceed in accordance with the procedure and practice in ordinary civil proceedings in the sheriff court as if an application for the variation of the maintenance order had been made to it.

5.30   Authentication of documents*

Where the 1972 Act provides that a document is to be authenticated in a prescribed manner, it shall be authenticated by a certificate signed by the sheriff clerk declaring that the document is authentic.

For authentication of documents, see now SSI 2016/306.

5.31 Application under sections 9 and 20 of the 1972 Act

(1) An application under section 9 of the 1972 Act (variation and revocation of maintenance orders) for variation or revocation of a maintenance order shall be brought as an ordinary cause.

(2) An application under section 20 of the 1972 Act (restriction on enforcement of arrears) for leave to enforce the payment of any arrears due under a maintenance order registered in Scotland shall be made by lodging a minute in the process.

5.32 Information to be provided where payer has ceased to reside in Scotland

(1) Where the registration of an order is cancelled in the circumstances set out in section 10(2) of the 1972 Act, the payee or his solicitor shall provide the sheriff clerk so far as is possible with information to enable the sheriff clerk to prepare the certificate and statement referred to in section 10(7) of the 1972 Act.

(2) Where the sheriff clerk is required in terms of section 32(1) of the 1972 Act (transfer of orders) to send to the Secretary of State the related documents specified in section 32(8) of that Act, the payee or his solicitor shall provide the sheriff clerk so far as possible with information to enable the sheriff clerk to prepare the certificate and statement to be included among those documents.

5.33 Evidence

Where a provisional order is made under section 9 of the 1972 Act and evidence has been taken by a shorthand writer, the applicant or his solicitor shall provide the sheriff clerk with a copy of the extended notes of evidence.

[. . .]

5.36 Intimation of registration of, or refusal to register, an order made in a Hague Convention Country

(1) Intimation of the registration of a maintenance order in terms of section 6 of the 1972 Act as applied to an order made in a Hague Convention Country shall be given by the sheriff clerk—

(a) to the payer, by sending an intimation in Form 72; and

(b) to the payee, by sending a notice in Form 70.

(2) Notice of a refusal to register a maintenance order on any of the grounds set out in section 6(5), (6) or (7) of the 1972 Act as applied to an order made in a Hague Convention Country shall be given by the sheriff clerk to the payee, by sending a notice in Form 71.

5.37 Application to set aside registration of, or to set aside decision not to register, an order made in a Hague Convention Country

Application to the court under section 6(9) or (12) of the 1972 Act as applied to an order made in a Hague Convention Country shall be made by summary application setting out the grounds of the application.

[5.37A Taking of evidence at the request of a court in the USA

Where evidence is taken under section 38(2) of the 1972 Act in consequence of a request made by a court in the United States of America under section 38(1) of that Act, rules 29.7 (citation of witnesses), 29.9 (second diligence against a witness) and 29.10 (failure of witness to attend) of the Ordinary Cause Rules shall apply in respect of the matters set out in those rules.]

[5.37B Communication with courts in the USA

In so far as applicable to incoming orders under the 1972 Act from the United States of America, for the purposes of the provisions in Part I of the 1972 Act, the sheriff may communicate with a court or courts in the United States of America in such circumstances and in such manner as he thinks fit.]

[5.37C Disapplication of provisions in respect of orders made by courts in the USA
In any case in which a maintenance order is made by a court in the United States of America which falls to be dealt with under sections 6 to 11 of the 1972 Act as those provisions are applied to the United States of America, none of the provisions in this Part shall apply except this rule and rules 5.30, 5.32, 5.37A and 5.37B.]

PART VI
Incoming Orders Under the 1982 Act

5.38 Applications under [section 5A] of the 1982 Act
(1) [Applications] under [section 5A] of the 1982 Act shall be in writing addressed to [the Scottish Ministers], signed by the applicant, or a solicitor or professional person qualified to act in such matters in the Contracting State of origin on his behalf, and shall specify—
(a) an address within Scotland for service on the applicant;
(b) the usual and last known address of the person against whom judgement was granted;
(c) the place where the applicant seeks to enforce the judgement;
(d) whether at the date of the application the judgement has been satisfied in whole or in part;
(e) whether interest is recoverable under the judgement in accordance with the law of the country in which it was granted and, if so, the rate of interest and the date from which interest became due; and
(f) whether the time for bringing an appeal against the judgement has expired without an appeal having been brought or whether an appeal has been brought against the judgement and is pending or has been finally disposed of.
(2) An application under paragraph (1) shall be accompanied by—
(a) a copy of the judgement authenticated by the court which made the order;
(b) documents which establish that, according to the law of the country in which the judgement has been given, the judgement is enforceable and has been served;
(c) in the case of a judgement given in default, documents which establish that the party in default was served with the documents instituting the proceedings;
(d) where appropriate, a document showing that the applicant is in receipt of legal aid in the country in which the judgement was given; and
(e) where the judgement or any of the documents specified in sub-paragraphs (b) to (d) are in a language other than English, a translation into English certified by a person qualified to do so in one of the Contracting States.
(3) Where the applicant does not produce a document required under paragraph (2)(c) or (d), the sheriff clerk may—
(a) fix a time within which the document is to be produced;
(b) accept an equivalent document; or
(c) dispense with production of the document.

5.39 Address of applicant's solicitor for service
Where the sheriff clerk is informed by a solicitor practising in Scotland that he is acting on behalf of the applicant, the business address of the solicitor shall thereafter be treated as the address for service on the applicant.

5.40 Notice of determination of application
Immediately after determination of an application for the recognition or enforcement of an order, the sheriff clerk shall serve, in accordance with the Ordinary Cause Rules so far as not inconsistent with the terms of this Chapter, a

notice in Form 73 on the applicant and on the person against whom enforcement is sought.

5.41 Appeal by party against whom enforcement is authorised

(1) Where enforcement of a maintenance order is authorised to any extent, the party against whom enforcement is authorised may appeal by way of summary application to the sheriff against the decision of the sheriff clerk—

(a) within one month from the date of service of the notice under rule 5.40; or

(b) if the person against whom enforcement is sought is domiciled in a Contracting State other than the United Kingdom, within two months from the date of service of such notice.

(2) The determination of the sheriff of such a summary application shall be subject to a final appeal on a point of law to the Inner House of the Court of Session in accordance with the Ordinary Cause Rules.

5.42 Appeal by applicant

(1) Where the application for enforcement of a maintenance order is refused, the applicant may appeal by way of summary application to the sheriff within one month from the date of service of the notice under rule 5.40.

(2) The determination of the sheriff of such a summary application shall be subject to a final appeal on a point of law to the Inner House of the Court of Session in accordance with the Ordinary Cause Rules.

5.43 Enforcement of registered order

The applicant may obtain an extract of a registered order and proceed to arrest in execution, to intimate the order (for the purposes of section 54(1) of the Debtors (Scotland) Act 1987), to inhibit and to charge and poind thereon, but may not proceed to an action of furthcoming in respect of an arrestment, serve a current maintenance arrestment schedule, make application for a conjoined arrestment order, proceed to adjudication in respect of inhibition or sale in respect of a poinding until the time for appeal against the determination of the sheriff under rules 5.41 or 5.42 has elapsed and any appeal has been disposed of.

[PART VII
Maintenance Decisions Under the Maintenance Regulation

5.44 Application for transmission of a Maintenance Decision to another Maintenance Regulation State

(1) This rule applies to applications under Article 40 of the Maintenance Regulation to enforce a Maintenance Decision of a sheriff in another Maintenance Regulation State.

(2) On receipt of an application in the form of a letter, the sheriff clerk will provide the applicant with a certified copy of the Maintenance Decision and a completed extract from the decision in the form of Annex I or II to the Maintenance Regulation as the case may be.

(3) The letter must be addressed to the sheriff clerk and must include—

(a) the name and National Insurance number (if known) of the parties to the proceedings;

(b) the date, or approximate date, of the proceedings in which the Maintenance Decision was made and the nature of those proceedings;

(c) the Maintenance Regulation State in which the application for recognition or enforcement has been made or is to be made; and

(d) the postal address of the applicant.

5.45 Enforcement of a Maintenance Decision made by a court in a Maintenance Regulation State other than Denmark

The 'enforcing court' under paragraph 4(2) of Schedule 1 to the 2011 Regulations, means the sheriff court having jurisdiction in the matter in accordance with Schedule 8 to the 1982 Act.]

PART VIII
Recognition and Enforcement of Maintenance Decisions made by Courts in Denmark etc

5.46 Recognition and enforcement of a Maintenance Decision made in Denmark etc

The 'registering court' under paragraph 6(2) of Schedule 1 to the 2011 Regulations, means the sheriff court having jurisdiction in the matter in accordance with Schedule 8 to the 1982 Act.

5.47 Recognition and enforcement of a Maintenance Decision made in Denmark etc

(1)   Intimation of the registration of a Maintenance Decision in accordance with Article 31 of the Maintenance Regulation shall be given by the sheriff clerk—

    (a)   to the payer, by sending an intimation in Form 73A; and

    (b)   to the payee, by sending a notice in Form 73B.

(2)   Notice of a refusal to register a Maintenance Decision shall be given by the sheriff clerk to the payee, by sending a notice in Form 73C.

5.48 Application to set aside registration of, or to set aside decision not to register, a Maintenance Decision made in Denmark etc

An application under Article 32 of the Maintenance Regulation shall be by summary application setting out the grounds of the application.

5.49 Sist of proceedings

An application under Article 35 of the Maintenance Regulation shall be made by motion.

PART IX
Recognition and Enforcement of Convention Maintenance Decisions

5.50 Application for transmission of Convention Maintenance Decision to a Contracting State

(1)   This rule applies to an application under Article 10(1) of the Convention to enforce a Convention Maintenance Decision of a sheriff in another Contracting State.

(2)   On receipt of an application in the form of a letter, the sheriff clerk must provide the applicant with a certified copy of the Convention Maintenance Decision.

(3)   The letter must be addressed to the sheriff clerk and must include—

    (a)   the name and National Insurance number (if known) of the parties to the proceedings;

    (b)   the date, or approximate date, of the proceedings in which the Convention Maintenance Decision was made and the nature of those proceedings;

    (c)   the Contracting State in which the application for recognition or enforcement has been made or is to be made; and

    (d)   the postal address of the applicant.

5.51 Intimation of registration of, or refusal to register, a Convention Maintenance Decision

(1)   Intimation of the registration of a Convention Maintenance Decision in accordance with Article 23 of the Convention shall be given by the sheriff clerk—

    (a)   to the payer, by sending an intimation in Form 73D; and

    (b)   to the payee, by sending a notice in Form 73E.

(2)   Notice of a refusal to register a Convention Maintenance Decision shall be given by the sheriff clerk to the payee, by sending a notice in Form 73F.

CHAPTER 6
APPLICATIONS UNDER THE SOCIAL SECURITY ADMINISTRATION ACT 1992

6.1 Interpretation
In this Chapter 'the Act' means the Social Security Administration Act 1992 and, unless the context otherwise requires, expressions used in this Chapter which are also used in that Act shall have the meaning assigned to them by the Act.

6.2 Applications under section 106 of the Act
(1)   An application to the sheriff under section 106(1) of the Act (recovery of expenditure on benefit from person liable for maintenance) shall be by summary application.
(2)   Where, in such an application, a sum is craved which represents or includes a personal allowance element, that element shall be identified in the application.

6.3 Transfer of rights under section 107 of the Act
(1)   The sheriff clerk, on receiving notice from the Secretary of State of a transfer of rights to an order by virtue of section 107(3) or (8) of the Act, shall endorse on the interlocutor sheet a certificate in Form 74.
(2)   Where, following a transfer by virtue of section 107(3) or (8) of the Act, the dependent parent or the Secretary of State requests an extract of the order originally granted, the sheriff clerk shall issue an extract with a certified copy of the latest certificate referred to in paragraph (1) endorsed on it.

6.4 Notice to Secretary of State under section 108(5) of the Act
The notice required to be given to the Secretary of State by the sheriff clerk under section 108(5) of the Act (notice of application to vary etc a maintenance order), as read with regulation 3 of the Income Support (Liable Relatives) Regulations 1990), shall—
(a)   be in writing;
(b)   specify any date assigned for the hearing of the application;
(c)   be accompanied by a copy of the application; and
(d)   be sent by recorded delivery post.

6.5 Notice to Secretary of State of making of maintenance order
Where an order granted by the sheriff in favour of the Secretary of State under section 106(2) of the Act has been transferred to the dependent parent in accordance with section 107(3) of that Act and a maintenance order is subsequently granted by the sheriff in favour of the dependent relative, the sheriff clerk shall forthwith notify the Secretary of State in writing and by recorded delivery post of the granting of the maintenance order.

SCHEDULE

For the Schedule of Forms, see the website of Scottish Courts.

ACT OF SEDERUNT (SHERIFF COURT RULES AMENDMENT) (ADOPTION AND CHILDREN (SCOTLAND) ACT 2007) 2009 (SSI 2009/284)

SCHEDULE
SHERIFF COURT ADOPTION RULES

Unless otherwise indicated these Rules as reproduced here apply to adoption applications lodged on or after 24 June 2013. They are shown as amended by SSIs 2012/271; 2013/139; 2013/172; 2015/5; 2015/419 and 2016/194.

CHAPTER 1
GENERAL

1 Citation and interpretation

(1) These Rules may be cited as the Sheriff Court Adoption Rules 2009.

(2) In these Rules—

'the 1995 Act' means the Children (Scotland) Act 1995;

'the 2002 Act' means the Adoption and Children Act 2002;

'the 2007 Act' means the Adoption and Children (Scotland) Act 2007;

['the 2011 Act' means the Children's Hearings (Scotland) Act 2011 and (except where the context otherwise requires) references to terms defined in that Act have the same meaning here as given there;]

'the 2009 Regulations' means the Adoptions with a Foreign Element (Scotland) Regulations 2009;

'adoption agency' means—

(a) a local authority;

(b) a registered adoption service within the meaning of section 2(3) of the 2007 Act;

(c) an adoption agency within the meaning of section 2(1) of the 2002 Act (adoption agencies in England and Wales); or

(d) an adoption agency within the meaning of article 3 of the Adoption (Northern Ireland) Order 1987;

'Her Majesty's Forces' means the regular forces as defined in section 374 of the Armed Forces Act 2006;

'Ordinary Cause Rules' means the first Schedule to the Sheriff Courts (Scotland) Act 1907;

['Principal Reporter' is the person referred to in section 14 of the Children's Hearings (Scotland) Act 2011 or any person carrying out the functions of the Principal Reporter by virtue of paragraph 10(1) of schedule 3 to that Act;]

['referral' means where a sheriff, in relevant proceedings, makes a referral to the Principal Reporter under section 62(2) of the 2011 Act;]

'Registrar General' means the Registrar General of Births, Deaths and Marriages for Scotland.

['relevant person' means—

(a) a person referred to in section 200(1) of the 2011 Act or

(b) a person deemed a relevant person by virtue of section 81(3) or 160(4)(b) of the 2011 Act;

'relevant proceedings' means those proceedings referred to in section 62(5)(k) and (l) of the 2011 Act;

'section 62 statement' has the meaning given in section 62(4) of the 2011 Act.]

(3) Any reference to a specified Chapter or rule shall be construed as a reference to the Chapter or rule bearing that number in these Rules, and a reference to a specified paragraph or subparagraph shall be construed as a reference to the paragraph or subparagraph so numbered or lettered in the provision in which that reference occurs.

(4)   A form referred to by number means the form so numbered in the Appendix to these Rules or a form substantially to the same effect with such variation as circumstances may require.

2   Expenses

The sheriff may—

(a)   make such order as he thinks fit with regard to the expenses of an application under these Rules, including the expenses of a reporting officer and a curator ad litem or any other person who attended a hearing; and

(b)   modify such expenses or direct them to be taxed on such scale as he may determine.

[3   Referrals to Principal Reporter

(1)   Where a referral is made, there shall be attached to the interlocutor a section 62 statement, which shall be intimated forthwith by the sheriff clerk to the Principal Reporter.

(2)   Where a referral is made and the Principal Reporter considers that it is necessary for a compulsory supervision order to be made in respect of the child and arranges a children's hearing under section 69(2) of the 2011 Act, the Principal Reporter shall intimate to the court which issued the section 62 statement the matters referred to in paragraph (3).

(3)   The matters referred to in paragraph (2) are—

(a)   the decision to arrange such a hearing;

(b)   where no appeal is made against the decision of that children's hearing prior to the period for appeal expiring, the outcome of the children's hearing; and

(c)   where such an appeal has been made, that an appeal has been made and, once determined, the outcome of that appeal.

(4)   Where a referral has been made and the Principal Reporter determines that—

(a)   none of the section 67 grounds apply in relation to the child; or

(b)   it is not necessary for a compulsory supervision order to be made in respect of the child

the Principal Reporter shall intimate that decision to the court which issued the section 62 statement.]

4   Power of sheriff to make orders etc

(1)   The sheriff may make such order as he thinks fit for the expeditious progress of an application under the 2007 Act, including an application for a Convention adoption order, in so far as it is not inconsistent with the provisions of these Rules.

(2)   The sheriff may relieve a party from the consequences of failure to comply with a provision in these Rules which is shown to be due to mistake, oversight or other excusable cause, on such conditions as he thinks fit.

(3)   Where the sheriff relieves a party from the consequences of a failure to comply with a provision in these Rules under paragraph (2), he may make such order as he thinks fit to enable the cause to proceed as if the failure to comply with the provision had not occurred.

5   Vulnerable witnesses

(1)   At any hearing on an application under these Rules, the sheriff shall ascertain whether there is likely to be a vulnerable witness who is to give evidence at or for the purposes of any proof or hearing, consider any child witness notice or vulnerable witness application that has been lodged where no order has been made under section 12(1) or (6) of the Vulnerable Witnesses (Scotland) Act 2004 and consider whether any order under section 12(1) of that Act requires to be made.

(2)   Except where the sheriff otherwise directs, where a vulnerable witness is to give evidence at or for the purposes of any proof or hearing in an application

under these Rules, any application in relation to the vulnerable witness or special measure that may be ordered shall be dealt with in accordance with the rules within Chapter 45 of the Ordinary Cause Rules.

(3)   In this rule 'vulnerable witness' means a witness within the meaning of section 11(1) of the Vulnerable Witnesses (Scotland) Act 2004.

[5A   Lodging audio or audio-visual recordings of children

(1)   In this rule 'child' is a person under the age of 16 on the date of commencement of the proceedings and 'children' shall be construed accordingly.

(2)   Except where the sheriff otherwise directs, where a party seeks to lodge an audio or audio-visual recording of a child as a production in an application under these Rules, this must be done in accordance with and regulated by Chapter 50 of the Ordinary Cause Rules.

(3)   A party who has lodged a recording of a child shall—

(a)   within 14 days after the final determination of the application, where no subsequent appeal has been [made], or

(b)   within 14 days after the disposal of any appeal [made in relation to] the final determination of the application,

uplift the recording from process.

(4)   Where a recording has not been uplifted as required by paragraph (3), the sheriff clerk shall intimate to—

(a)   the solicitor who lodged the recording, or

(b)   where no solicitor is acting, the party or such other party as seems appropriate,

that if he or she fails to uplift the recording within 28 days after the date of such intimation, it will be disposed of in such a manner as the sheriff directs.]

NOTE: Sub-paragraph (3) as amended applies to appeals against the decision of the sheriff made on or after 1 January 2016: SSI 2015/419.

6   Service of documents

Rules 5.2(4) to (6), 5.3 to 5.6 and 5.10 of the Ordinary Cause Rules are to apply, with any necessary modifications, to the service or intimation of any document under these Rules as they apply to the service or intimation of any document under the Ordinary Cause Rules.

[7   Appeals

An appeal to the Sheriff Appeal Court against an order of the sheriff under these Rules is to be made in accordance with Chapter 6 of the Act of Sederunt (Sheriff Appeal Court Rules) 2015.]

NOTE: Rule 7 as substituted applies to appeals against decisions of the sheriff made on or after 1 January 2016: SSI 2015/419.

CHAPTER 2

ADOPTION ORDERS

8   Application for adoption order

(1)   An application for an adoption order under section 29 (adoption by certain couples) or 30 (adoption by one person) of the 2007 Act is to be made by petition in Form 1.

(2)   An application for an order vesting parental responsibilities and parental rights relating to a child under section 59(1) of the 2007 Act (preliminary order where child to be adopted abroad) is to be made by petition in Form 2.

(3)   The following documents must be lodged in process along with a petition under paragraph (1) or (2):—

(a) an extract of the entry in the Register of Births relating to the child who is the subject of the application;

(b) in the case of an application under section 29 of the 2007 Act by a relevant couple who are married to each other, an extract or a certified copy of the entry in the Register of Marriages relating to their marriage;

(c) in the case of an application under section 29 of the 2007 Act by a relevant couple who are civil partners of each other, an extract or a certified copy of the entry in the Register of Civil Partnerships relating to their civil partnership;

(d) any report by the local authority required by section 19(2) (investigation by local authority on receipt of notice of intention to apply for adoption order) of the 2007 Act, if available;

(e) any report by an adoption agency required by section 17 (report on the suitability of the applicants and other matters) of the 2007 Act, if available;

(f) where appropriate, an extract of the order freeing the child for adoption; where appropriate, an extract of the permanence order made in respect of the child under section 80 of the 2007 Act;

(g) where appropriate, the consent under section 19(1) (placing children with parental consent: England and Wales) of the 2002 Act of each parent or guardian to the child being placed for adoption, in the form prescribed under section 52(7) of that Act, if available;

(h) where appropriate, the consent under section 20(1) (advance consent to adoption: England and Wales) of the 2002 Act of each parent or guardian to the making of a future adoption order, in the form prescribed under section 52(7) of that Act, if available;

(j) any notice given under section 20(4) (notice that information about application for adoption order not required: England and Wales) of the 2002 Act by a parent or guardian of the child to an adoption agency, if available;

(k) a certified copy of any placement order made under section 21(1) (placement orders: England and Wales) of the 2002 Act, if available; and

(l) any other document founded upon by the petitioner in support of the terms of the petition.

(4) A report by a local authority under section 19(2) or an adoption agency under section 17 of the 2007 Act must be in numbered paragraphs and include the following matters:—

(a) information about how the needs of the child came to the notice of the authority or agency;

(b) the family circumstances of the child;

(c) where the child was placed for adoption by an adoption agency, a description of the physical and mental health of the child (including any special needs) and his emotional, behavioural and educational development;

(d) an account of the discussion with the parents or guardians of the child and, if appropriate, with the child about their wishes and the alternatives to adoption;

(e) the position of other relatives or persons likely to be involved;

(f) an account of any search for a parent or guardian who cannot be found;

(g) information about the mutual suitability of the petitioner and the child for the relationship created by adoption and the ability of the petitioner to bring up the child including an assessment of the personality of the petitioner and, where appropriate, that of the child;

(h) particulars of all members of the household of the petitioner and their relationship to the petitioner;

(i) a description of the accommodation in the home of the petitioner;

(j) in a petition by only one member of a relevant couple within the meaning of section 29(3) of the 2007 Act, why the other member of that couple has not joined in the application;

(k) whether the petitioner understands the nature and effect of an adoption

order and in particular that the order, if made, will make the petitioner responsible for the maintenance and upbringing of the child;

(l) whether the means and standing of the petitioner are such as to enable
him to maintain and bring up the child suitably;

(m) whether the child has any right or interest in property and, if so, what
right or interest;

(n) whether any payment or other reward in consideration of the adoption,
other than an approved adoption allowance, has been received or agreed upon;

(o) what insurance has been offered on the life of the child;

(p) the religious persuasion, racial origin and cultural and linguistic background of the child and of the petitioner;

(q) consideration arising from the difference in age between the petitioner
and the child if this is more or less than the normal difference in age between
parents and children;

(r) whether adoption is likely to safeguard and promote the welfare of the
child throughout his life;

[(s) whether the child is subject to a compulsory supervision order and, if so,
what steps have been taken to comply with sections 131 and 141 of the 2011
Act;]

(t) where paragraph (5) applies, the information mentioned in paragraph (6);

(u) whether there has been a contravention of section 75 of the 2007 Act in
relation to the child;

(v) whether there has been a failure to comply with section 76(2) of the 2007
Act in relation to the child;

(w) any other matters relevant to the operation of section 14 of the 2007 Act
in relation to the application;

(x) where appropriate, information about whether—

(i) in an application under section 29(1) of the 2007 Act, the petitioners
are a relevant couple within the meaning of section 29(3)(c) or (d) of the 2007
Act; or

(ii) in an application under section 30(1) of the 2007 Act, the petitioner is a
member of a relevant couple within the meaning of section 29(3)(c) or (d) of
the 2007 Act;

(y) in the case of a petition under paragraph (2) to which regulation 50 of
the 2009 Regulations applies, the details referred to in paragraph (7);

(z) any other information which may be of assistance to the court.

(5) This paragraph applies where—

(a) the child was placed for adoption under section 19(1) (placement with
parental consent: England and Wales) of the 2002 Act;

(b) the child was placed for adoption under a placement order made under
section 21(1) (placement orders: England and Wales) of the 2002 Act; or

(c) each parent or guardian has consented under section 20(1) (advance consent to adoption: England and Wales) of the 2002 Act to the making of a future
adoption order.

(6) The information referred to in paragraph (4)(t) is any available information
about whether—

(a) any placement order has been revoked;

(b) any of the consents referred to in section 31(8) or (9) of the 2007 Act have
at any time been withdrawn;

(c) a parent or guardian of the child wishes to seek leave to oppose the petition; and

(d) there has been any change of circumstances since the consent of the
parent or guardian was given or, as the case may be, the order under section 21
(1) (placement orders: England and Wales) of the 2002 Act was made.

(7) The details mentioned in paragraph (4)(y) are—

(a) details of any reviews carried out under regulation 10 of the Adoption Agencies (Scotland) Regulations 2009; and

(b) details of any visits carried out under regulation 25(1)(a) of those Regulations.

(8) If a report mentioned in paragraph (3)(d) or (e) is unavailable to be lodged along with the petition, the sheriff shall pronounce an interlocutor requiring the adoption agency or local authority concerned to prepare and lodge such a report within 2 weeks from the date of the interlocutor, or within such other period as the sheriff in his discretion may allow.

(9) If any of the of the documents required to be lodged in process under paragraph (3)(f), (g), (h), (i), (j) or (k) is unavailable to be lodged by reason of its being in the possession of an adoption agency, the sheriff shall pronounce an interlocutor requiring the agency to lodge the document within 4 weeks from the date of the interlocutor, or within such other period as the sheriff in his discretion may allow.

(10) A petition under this rule must include a crave for warrant for intimation to the persons mentioned in rule 14(1)(b) to (d) as appropriate.

9 Additional requirements where child to be adopted abroad

(1) The additional requirements in this Rule apply to a petitioner in an application for an order under section 59 of the 2007 Act.

(2) In the case of an application to which regulation 7 of the 2009 Regulations applies, the petitioner must lodge in process along with the petition—

(a) the confirmation required under regulation 7(3)(a)(i) of the 2009 Regulations;

(b) the documents mentioned in regulation 8 of the 2009 Regulations;

(c) copies of the confirmations to the adoption agency referred to in regulation 7(3)(b)(i), (iii) and (iv) of the 2009 Regulations;

(d) a copy of the report mentioned in regulation 7(3)(b)(ii) of the 2009 Regulations;

(e) a copy of the confirmation to the adoption agency referred to in regulation 7(3)(c) or (d), as the case may be, of the 2009 Regulations.

(3) In the case of an application to which regulation 50 of the 2009 Regulations applies, the petitioner must lodge along with the petition the reports, confirmations and other documents referred to in regulation 50(3)(a) to (d), (f) and (g) of those Regulations or, where appropriate, copies thereof.

(4) Where appropriate, the petitioner must also lodge in process a translation into English of any document referred to in paragraph (2) or (3) together with the certificate referred to in paragraph (5).

(5) The certificate mentioned in paragraph (4) is a certificate by the translator—

(a) certifying that the translation is in conformity with the original document; and

(b) giving the full name, address and qualifications of the translator.

(6) The petitioner must adduce evidence of the law of adoption in the country or territory in which it is intended to adopt to the child.

(7) The evidence of the law of adoption required under paragraph (6) may be in the form of an affidavit by a person who is conversant with that law and who—

(a) practises or has practised law in that country or territory; or

(b) is a duly accredited representative of the government of that country or territory in the United Kingdom.

10 Protection of identity of petitioner

(1) When any person who proposes to apply under rule 8 wishes to prevent his identity being disclosed to any person whose consent to the order is required, he may before presenting the petition apply by letter to the sheriff clerk for a serial number to be assigned to him for all purposes connected with the petition.

(2) On receipt of an application under paragraph (1), the sheriff clerk must—

(a) assign a serial number to the applicant; and

(b)   enter a note of the number opposite the name of the applicant in a register of serial numbers.

(3)   The contents of the register of serial numbers and the names of the persons to whom each number relates shall be treated as confidential by the sheriff clerk and are to not be disclosed to any person other than the sheriff.

(4)   Where a serial number has been assigned to an applicant under paragraph (2) any form of consent to an adoption order or order under section 59 of the 2007 Act—

(a)   must refer to the applicant by means of the serial number assigned to him;

(b)   must not contain the name and designation of the applicant; and

(c)   must specify the year in which and the court by which the serial number was assigned.

[(5)   Where a serial number has been assigned the applicant must provide the sheriff clerk with an appropriate service copy petition as required under rule 14(1).]

11   Appointment of a curator ad litem and reporting officer

(1)   The sheriff must on the lodging of a petition under rule 8 appoint a curator ad litem and reporting officer.

(2)   But, subject to paragraph (3), the sheriff must not appoint a reporting officer where one or more of the following applies—

(a)   an order freeing the child for adoption has been made;

(b)   a permanence order with provision granting authority for the child to be adopted has been granted under section 80 of the 2007 Act;

(c)   the petition is founded on one or other or both of section 31(8) (advance consent to adopt) or (9) (placement of child: England and Wales) of the 2007 Act.

(3)   Notwithstanding paragraph (2), a reporting officer must be appointed—

(a)   in any case in which the petition is founded on the condition in section 31(2) of the 2007 Act, whether or not it is also founded on section 31(8) or (9) of that Act; or

(b)   where the child who is the subject of the application is aged 12 or over, for the purpose of witnessing that child's consent, if it is to be executed in Scotland.

(4)   The same person may be appointed as curator ad litem and reporting officer in the same petition if the sheriff considers that doing so is appropriate in the circumstances.

(5)   The sheriff may appoint a person who is not a member of a panel established under regulations made by virtue of section 101 of the 1995 Act to be curator ad litem or a reporting officer.

(6)   The sheriff may, on cause shown, appoint a reporting officer prior to the lodging of such a petition.

(7)   An application for an appointment under paragraph (6) is to be made by letter addressed to the sheriff clerk specifying the reasons for the appointment, and shall not require to be intimated to any other person.

(8)   The sheriff clerk must intimate the appointment of a curator ad litem and reporting officer under paragraph (1) or (6) to the petitioner and to the person or persons appointed.

12   Duties of reporting officer and curator ad litem

(1)   The other duties of a reporting officer appointed under rule 11, other than under rule 11(3)(b), prescribed for the purposes of section 108(1)(b) of the 2007 Act are—

(a)   to ascertain the whereabouts of all persons whose consent to the making of an adoption order or order under section 59 of the 2007 Act in respect of the child is required;

(b)   to ascertain whether there is any person other than those mentioned in the petition upon whom notice of the petition should be served;

(c) in the case of each person who is not a petitioner and whose consent to the making of an adoption order or order under section 59 of the 2007 Act is required or may be dispensed with—

(i) to ascertain whether that person understands the effect of the adoption order or order under section 59 of the 2007 Act;

(ii) to ascertain whether alternatives to adoption have been discussed with that person;

[(iia) to ascertain whether that person consents to the making of an adoption order or order under section 59 of the 2007 Act;]

(iii) to confirm that that person understands that he may withdraw his consent at any time before an order is made;

(iv) to ascertain whether that person suffers or appears to suffer from a mental disorder within the meaning of section 328 of the Mental Health (Care and Treatment) (Scotland) Act 2003;

(d) to report in writing on the matters mentioned in subparagraphs (a) to (c) to the sheriff within 4 weeks from the date of the interlocutor appointing the reporting officer, or within such other period as the sheriff in his discretion may allow.

(2) References in paragraph (1) to 'consent' are to consent within the meaning of section 31(2)(a) or 32(1) of the 2007 Act, as the case may be.

(3) A curator ad litem appointed under rule 11 must—

(a) have regard to safeguarding the interests of the child as his paramount duty;

(b) inquire, so far as he considers necessary, into the facts and circumstances stated in the petition and in the report mentioned in rule 8(4);

(c) obtain particulars of accommodation in the home of the petitioner and the condition of the home;

(d) obtain particulars of all members of the household of the petitioner and their relationship to the petitioner;

(e) in the case of a petition by only one member of a relevant couple within the meaning of section 29(3) of the 2007 Act, ascertain the reason of the other member of the couple for not joining in the application;

(f) ascertain whether the means and status of the petitioner are sufficient to enable him to maintain and bring up the child suitably;

(g) ascertain what rights or interest in property the child has;

(h) establish that the petitioner understands the nature and effect of an adoption order and in particular that the making of the order will render him responsible for the maintenance and upbringing of the child;

(i) where appropriate, ascertain when the mother of the child ceased to have the care and possession of the child and to whom care and possession was then transferred;

(j) ascertain whether any payment or other reward in consideration of the adoption has been given or agreed upon;

(k) ascertain whether the child is subject to a [compulsory supervision order];

(l) ascertain whether the life of the child has been insured and if so for what sum;

(m) ascertain whether it may be in the interests of the welfare of the child that the sheriff should make the adoption order or order under section 59 of the 2007 Act subject to particular terms and conditions or require the petitioner to make special provision for the child and, if so, what provision;

(n) where the petitioner is not ordinarily resident in the United Kingdom, establish whether a report has been obtained on the home and living conditions of the petitioner from a suitable agency in the country in which he is ordinarily resident;

(o) establish the reasons of the petitioner for wishing to adopt the child;

(p)   establish the religious persuasion, racial origin and cultural and linguistic background of the child and of the petitioner;

(q)   assess the considerations which might arise where the difference in ages as between the petitioner and the child is greater or less than the normal difference in age between parents and their children;

(r)   consider such other matters, including the personality of the petitioner and, where appropriate, that of the child, which might affect the suitability of the petitioner and the child for the relationship created by adoption and affect the ability of the petitioner to bring up the child;

(s)   ascertain whether it would be better for the child that the court should make the order than it should not make the order;

(t)   establish whether the adoption is likely to safeguard and promote the welfare of the child throughout his life;

(u)   ascertain from the child whether he wishes to express a view and, where a child indicates his wish to express a view, ascertain that view.

(4)   Subject to paragraph (5) the curator ad litem must report in writing on the matters mentioned in paragraph (3) to the sheriff within 4 weeks from the date of the interlocutor appointing the curator, or within such other period as the sheriff in his discretion may allow.

(5)   Subject to any order made by the sheriff under rule 17(1)(a), the views of the child ascertained in terms of paragraph (3)(u) may, if the curator ad litem considers appropriate, be conveyed to the sheriff orally.

13   Consents

(1)   The consent of a parent or guardian required by section 31(2)(a) of the 2007 Act is to be in Form 3.

(2)   The consent of a child required by section 32(1) of the 2007 Act is to be in Form 4.

(3)   A form of consent mentioned in paragraph (1) or (2) must be witnessed—

(a)   where it is executed in Scotland, by the reporting officer appointed under rule 11;

(b)   where it is executed outwith Scotland but within the United Kingdom, by a justice of the peace or commissioner for oaths;

(c)   where it is executed outwith the United Kingdom—

(i)   if the person who executes the consent is serving in Her Majesty's forces, by an officer holding a commission in any of those forces; or

(ii)   in any other case, by a British diplomatic or consular official or any person authorised to administer an oath or affirmation under the law of the place where the consent is executed.

14   Intimation of application

(1)   On the lodging of a petition under rule 8—

(a)   the sheriff clerk must fix a date for a preliminary hearing [which must take place (except on cause shown)] not less than 6 and not more than 8 weeks after the date of lodging the petition;

(b)   in the case of a petition under rule 8(1), the petitioner or, where a serial number has been assigned under rule 10, the sheriff clerk, must send [a service copy of the petition in Form 1A] along with a notice of intimation in Form 5 to—

(i)   every person who can be found and whose consent to the making of the order is required to be given or dispensed with under the 2007 Act;

(ii)   if no such person can be found, a relative of the child within the meaning of section 119(1) of the 2007 Act, unless the address of such a relative is not known to the petitioner and cannot reasonably be ascertained;

(iii)   every person who has consented to the making of the order under section 20 of the 2002 Act (and has not withdrawn the consent) unless the person has given a notice under subsection (4)(a) of that section which has effect; and

(iv) every person who, if leave were given under section 31(12) of the 2007
Act, would be entitled to oppose the making of the order;

(c)   in the case of a petition under rule 8(2) the petitioner or, where a serial
number has been assigned under rule 10, the sheriff clerk must send [a service
copy of the petition in Form 2A] along with a notice of intimation in Form 5 to
every person who can be found and whose consent to the making of the order
would be required if the application were for an adoption order (other than a
Convention adoption order);

(d)   in the case of a petition under rule 8(1) the petitioner or, where a serial
number has been assigned under rule 10, the sheriff clerk must send [a service
copy of the petition in Form 1A] along with a notice of intimation in Form 6 to
the father of the child if he does not have, and has never had, parental responsibilities or parental rights in relation to the child and if he can be found;

(e)   the sheriff clerk must intimate the date of the preliminary hearing to the
curator ad litem and to any reporting officer appointed by the sheriff under rule 11;

(f)   the sheriff may order the petitioner or, where a serial number has been
assigned under rule 10, the sheriff clerk to intimate the application to such other
person and in such terms as he considers appropriate.

(2)   A notice of intimation under paragraph (1)(b) or (c) must state—

(a)   that an application for adoption has been made;

(b)   the date on which, and place where, the preliminary hearing will be
held;

(c)   the fact that the person is entitled to be heard on the application;

(d)   the fact that, unless the person wishes, or the court requires, the person
need not attend the hearing.

(3)   A notice of intimation under paragraph (1)(d) must state the matters mentioned in paragraph (2)(a) and (b).

(4)   The sheriff clerk or petitioner on making intimation shall complete a certificate of intimation in Form 7.

15   Orders for intimation

In any application for an adoption order or for an order under section 59 of the
2007 Act, the sheriff may at any time order intimation to be made in such terms as
he considers appropriate on any person who in his opinion ought to be given
notice of the application.

16   Form of response

(1)   Any person who has received intimation of an application by virtue of rule
14 or 15 and who intends to oppose that application shall lodge a form of response
in Form 8 not later than 21 days after the date of intimation of the application or
such other period as the sheriff may direct.

[(2)   A form of response under paragraph (1)—

(a)   must contain a brief statement of the respondent's reasons for opposing
the application but shall be without prejudice to any answers lodged under rule
18(1)(b)(ix);

(b)   must be intimated by the respondent to the petitioner at the time of lodging.]

[16A   Opposed applications

Within 14 days of a form of response being lodged, the petitioner shall lodge and
intimate to all other parties a brief statement in numbered paragraphs setting out
the facts upon which the petitioner intends to rely including averments in relation
to—

(a)   considerations under section 14 of the 2007 Act;

(b)   terms and conditions under section 28(3) of the 2007 Act;

(c)   consent under section 31 of the 2007 Act.]

17 Procedure where child wishes to express a view

(1) Where a child has indicated his wish to express his views the sheriff, without prejudice to rule 12(3)(u)—

(a) may order such procedural steps to be taken as he considers appropriate to ascertain the views of that child; and

(b) must not make an order under this Chapter unless an opportunity has been given for the views of that child to be obtained or heard.

(2) Where the views of a child, whether obtained under this rule or under rule 12(3)(u) have been recorded in writing, the sheriff may direct that such a written record is to—

(a) be sealed in a envelope marked 'Views of the child – confidential';

(b) be available to a sheriff only;

(c) not be opened by any person other than a sheriff; and

(d) not form a borrowable part of the process.

18 Preliminary hearing

(1) At the preliminary hearing the sheriff must—

(a) if no form of response has been lodged under rule 16, dispose of the case or make such other order as he considers appropriate;

[(b) if a form of response has been lodged—

(i) ascertain the nature of the issues in dispute, including any questions of admissibility of evidence or any legal issues;

(ii) ascertain the names of all witnesses, including expert witnesses, parties intend to call and whose evidence they intend to rely on at proof;

(iii) consider the scope for use of affidavits and other documents in place of oral evidence;

(iv) consider whether sanction is sought for the employment of counsel;

(v) consider the reasonable estimate of time needed by each party for examination-in-chief, cross-examination and submissions;

(vi) order the lodging of joint minutes of agreement, affidavits, expert reports and any other documents within such period as the sheriff considers appropriate;

(vii) fix a diet of proof not less than 12 and not more than 16 weeks after the date of the preliminary hearing or any continuation thereof unless, on cause shown, a longer period is appropriate;

(viii) fix a pre-proof hearing not less than 6 and not more than 8 weeks before the diet of proof;

(ix) order answers to the statement referred to in rule 16A to be lodged within 14 days of the date of the preliminary hearing or any continuation thereof or such other period as the sheriff considers appropriate; and

(x) ascertain from the parties what, if any, expert evidence is required and consider the scope for joint instruction of a single expert.]

[(2) The sheriff may, if satisfied that there is sufficient reason for doing so for the expeditious resolution of the cause, continue the preliminary hearing for such period or periods as he or she thinks fit.]

(3) At the preliminary hearing the sheriff may—

(a) if he is not satisfied that the facts stated in the petition are supported by the documents lodged with it or by the reports of the curator ad litem and reporting officer order the production of further documents; and

(b) make such other order as he considers appropriate for the expeditious progress of the case.

[(4) The answers lodged under paragraph (1)(b)(ix) must be in numbered paragraphs and respond to the statement referred to in rule 16A.]

[18A List of witnesses etc

Not later than 7 days prior to the pre-proof hearing the parties shall lodge in process and intimate to all other parties—

(a) a list of the witnesses, including expert witnesses, they intend to call and whose evidence they intend to rely on at proof;

(b) all documents upon which they intend to rely at proof;

(c) a notice of agreed facts;

(d) a notice of disputed issues.]

19 Pre-proof hearing

(1) The parties must provide the sheriff with sufficient information to enable him to conduct the hearing as provided for in this rule.

[(2) At the pre-proof hearing the sheriff must consider—

(a) the extent to which the parties have complied with any orders made by the sheriff under rule 18;

(b) the extent to which further information or orders are required in respect of matters referred to in rule 18;

(c) the state of preparation of the parties;

(d) the availability of witnesses;

(e) the nature of productions.]

[(2A) At the pre-proof hearing the sheriff must ascertain, so far as is reasonably practicable, whether the case is likely to proceed to proof on the date fixed for that purpose, whether the appropriate number of days have been allowed and if further days may be required.]

(3) At the pre-proof hearing the sheriff may—

(a) discharge the proof and fix a new date for such proof;

(b) adjourn the pre-proof hearing;

[...]

(d) make such other order as he thinks fit to secure the expeditious progress of the case [including restricting the issues for proof and, on the motion of either party, on cause shown, or of the sheriff's own motion, excluding specified documents, reports and/or witnesses from proof].

[20 Proof

(1) A proof shall be taken on the allocated days and parties shall adhere to the estimates provided under rule 18(1) (b)(v) or 19(2)(b), but the sheriff may adjourn the diet from time to time.

(2) Except where the sheriff otherwise directs, at the proof no witnesses other than those named on a witness list may be called to give evidence.]

21 Confidentiality

(1) Unless the sheriff otherwise directs, all documents lodged in process including the reports by the curator ad litem and reporting officer are to be available only to the sheriff, the curator ad litem, the reporting officer and the parties; and such documents must be treated as confidential by any persons involved in, or a party to, the proceedings and by the sheriff clerk.

(2) The reporting officer and the curator ad litem—

(a) must treat all information obtained in the exercise of their duties as confidential; and

(b) must not disclose any such information to any person unless disclosure of such information is necessary for the purpose of their duties.

(3) This rule is subject to rule 17.

22 Pronouncement of decision

(1) At the conclusion of the proof the sheriff may—

(a) pronounce a decision; or

(b) reserve judgment.

(2) If the sheriff pronounces his decision at the end of the proof, he—

(a) must state briefly the grounds of his decision, including the reasons for his decision on any questions of fact or law or of admissibility of evidence; and

(b)   may, and if requested to do so by one of the parties must, append to the interlocutor a note setting out those matters and his findings in fact and law.

(3)   If the sheriff pronounces his decision after reserving judgment, he must give to the sheriff clerk within 4 weeks of the conclusion of the proof—

(a)   an interlocutor giving effect to his decision and incorporating findings in fact and law; and

(b)   a note setting out the matters mentioned in paragraph (2)(a).

(4)   The sheriff clerk must forthwith send copies of the documents mentioned in paragraph (2) or (3) to each of the parties.

(5)   The sheriff principal may extend the period mentioned in paragraph (3) for such further period as he considers reasonable.

(6)   Where the sheriff reserves his decision—

(a)   the date of the interlocutor of the sheriff shall be the date on which it is received by the sheriff clerk; and

(b)   the sheriff clerk shall enter that date in the interlocutor.

(7)   If the question of expenses has been reserved the sheriff must deal with that issue within 21 days of the date of the interlocutor disposing of the merits of the application.

(8)   In any case in which a serial number has been assigned to the petitioner under rule 10 or where the sheriff so directs, any document issued under this rule shall not disclose the identity of the petitioner.

23   Communication to the Registrar General

The communication to the Registrar General of an adoption order required to be made by the sheriff clerk under paragraph 4(1) of Schedule 1 to the 2007 Act is to be made by sending a certified copy of the order to the Registrar General either by recorded delivery post in an envelope marked 'Confidential', or by personal delivery by the sheriff clerk in a sealed envelope marked 'Confidential'.

24   Adoption orders

(1)   An adoption order granted by the sheriff must specify the name and address of the adoption agency, if any, which has taken part in the arrangements for placing the child in the care of the petitioner.

(2)   No extract of an adoption order is to be issued except with the authority of the sheriff who made the order or, in that sheriff's absence, the sheriff principal.

(3)   The authority required by paragraph (2) is to be obtained by lodging a petition setting forth the reasons for which the extract is required.

25   Final procedure

(1)   After the granting of an adoption order or order under section 59 of the 2007 Act, the court process must, immediately upon the communication under rule 23 being made or, in the event of an extract of the order being issued under rule 24, immediately upon such issue, be sealed by the sheriff clerk in an envelope marked 'Confidential'.

(2)   The envelope referred to in paragraph (1) is not to be unsealed by the sheriff clerk or by any other person having control of the records of that or any court, and the process is not to be made accessible to any person for one hundred years after the date of the granting of the order except—

(a)   to an adopted child who has attained the age of 16 and to whose adoption the process refers;

(b)   to the sheriff clerk, on an application being made to him by an adoption agency, and with the consent of the adopted person for the purpose only of ascertaining the name of the agency, if any, responsible for the placement of that person and informing the applicant of that name;

(c)   to a person on the granting of an application made by him to the sheriff setting forth the reason for which access to the process is required;

(d)   to a court, public authority or administrative board (whether in the

United Kingdom or not) having power to authorise an adoption, on petition by it to the court which granted the original order requesting that information be made available from the process for the purpose of discharging its duties in considering an application for adoption and specifying the precise reason for which access to the process is required;

(e)   to a person who is authorised by the Scottish Ministers to obtain information for the purposes of such research as is intended to improve the working of adoption law and practice.

(3)   The sheriff clerk must—

(a)   where the court also makes an order under section 36(2) (revocation of supervision requirement) of the 2007 Act, intimate that order to the Principal Reporter; and

(b)   where appropriate, intimate the making of an adoption order or order under section 59 of the 2007 Act to the court by which—

(i)   an order freeing the child for adoption was made; or

(ii)   a permanence order with provision granting authority for the child to be adopted was made.

26   Amendment of an adoption order

(1)   An application under paragraph 7 of Schedule 1 to the 2007 Act (amendment of orders and rectification of registers) is to be made by petition to the court which made the adoption order.

(2)   The sheriff may order the petitioner to intimate the petition to such persons as the sheriff considers appropriate.

27   Applications under sections 20 to 24

(1)   An application under section 20(2) (restrictions on removal: child placed for adoption with consent), section 21(3) (restrictions on removal: notice of intention to adopt given), 22(3) (restrictions on removal: application for adoption order pending), 23(3) (restrictions on removal of child looked after by local authority), 24(1) (return of child removed in breach of certain provisions) or 24(2) (order directing person not to remove child) of the 2007 Act shall be made—

(a)   if there is pending in respect of the child an application for an adoption order, by minute in the process of that application; or

(b)   in any other case, by petition.

(2)   A minute or petition under paragraph (1) shall set out the relevant facts and the crave which the minuter or petitioner, as the case may be, wishes to make.

(3)   On receipt of a minute under paragraph (1)(a) the sheriff shall—

(a)   order a diet of hearing to be fixed; and

(b)   ordain the minuter to send a notice of such hearing in Form 9 together with a copy of the minute, by recorded delivery letter to the petitioner in the original petition, to the curator ad litem in the original petition, to any person who may have care and possession of the child and to such other persons as the sheriff considers appropriate.

(4)   On receipt of a petition under paragraph (1)(b) the sheriff shall—

(a)   order a diet of hearing to be fixed; and

(b)   ordain the petitioner to send a notice of such hearing in Form 9 together with a copy of the petition, by recorded delivery letter to any person who may have care and possession of the child and to such other persons as the sheriff considers appropriate.

(5)   The sheriff may, on the motion of a party and on cause shown, remit any petition lodged under paragraph (1)(b) to another sheriff court.

(6)   On the making of an order under paragraph (5) the sheriff—

(a)   must state his reasons for doing so in the interlocutor;

(b)   may make such other order as he thinks fit.

(7)   The court to which a petition is transferred under paragraph (5) shall accept the petition.

(8)   A petition transferred under paragraph (5) shall proceed in all respects as if it had been brought in the court to which it is transferred.

CHAPTER 3
CONVENTION ADOPTION ORDERS

28   Interpretation
In this Chapter, unless the context otherwise requires—
'the Convention' means the Convention on Protection of Children and Co-operation in respect of Intercountry Adoption, concluded at The Hague on 29th May 1993;
'Convention adoption order' means an adoption which, by virtue of regulation 53(2) of the 2009 Regulations, is made as a Convention adoption order;
'Convention country' means any country or territory in which the Convention is in force; and
'Central Authority' means the Scottish Executive.

29   Process and form of application
(1)   An application for a Convention adoption order is to be made by petition in Form 10.
(2)   The following documents must be lodged in process along with a petition under paragraph (1):—
(a)   a certificate, register extract, or other proof of date of birth relating to the child who is the subject of the application, issued or authenticated by the applicable Convention country authority;
(b)   in the case of a joint petition by a married couple, a certificate, register extract or other proof of their marriage, issued or authenticated by the applicable Convention country authority;
(c)   in the case of a joint petition by a couple who are civil partners of each other, a certificate, register extract or other proof of their civil partnership, issued or authenticated by the applicable Convention country authority;
(d)   any report by the local authority required by section 19(2) (investigation by local authority on receipt of notice of intention to apply for adoption order) of the 2007 Act, if available;
(e)   any report by an adoption agency required by section 17 (report on the suitability of the applicants and other matters) of the 2007 Act, if available;
(f)   where appropriate, an extract of the order freeing the child for adoption;
(g)   where appropriate, an extract of the permanence order made in respect of the child under section 80 of the 2007 Act;
(h)   in the case of a petition to which the provisions of Chapter 1 of Part 3 of the 2009 Regulations apply—
(i)   copies of the Article 16 Information and the Agreement under Article 17(c) of the Convention referred to in regulation 34(c) of those Regulations; and
(ii)   the confirmation referred to in regulation 34(d) of those Regulations;
(i)   in the case of a petition to which the provisions of Chapter 2 of Part 3 of the 2009 Regulations apply—
(i)   copies of the Article 16 Report and the Agreement under Article 17(c) of the Convention referred to in regulation 51(c) of those Regulations; and
(ii)   the confirmation referred to in regulation 51(d) of those Regulations;
(j)   any other document founded on by the petitioner in support of the petition;
(k)   where appropriate, a translation into English of any document referred to in subparagraphs (a) to (j), together with the certificate referred to in paragraph (3).
(3)   The certificate mentioned in paragraph (2)(k) is a certificate by the translator—

(a)   certifying that the translation is in conformity with the original document; and

(b)   giving the full name, address and qualifications of the translator.

(4)   A report by a local authority under section 19(2), or an adoption agency under section 17 of the 2007 Act must be in numbered paragraphs and include the following matters:—

(a)   a description of the petitioner's background, including his family history, medical history, his social environment, his reasons for wishing to adopt, his eligibility and suitability to adopt, and in particular his suitability for a Convention adoption order;

(b)   a description of the child's background, including his family history, his medical history and that of his family, his social environment, his physical and mental health (including any special needs), and his emotional, behavioural and educational development;

(c)   information about the mutual suitability of the petitioner and the child for the relationship created by adoption, and the ability of the petitioner to bring up the child, including an assessment of the personalities of the petitioner and of the child;

(d)   particulars of all the members of the household of the petitioner, and their relationship to the petitioner;

(e)   a description of the accommodation in the home of the petitioner;

(f)   in a petition by only one member of a relevant couple within the meaning of section 29(3) of the 2007 Act, why the other member of that couple has not joined in the application;

(g)   whether the petitioner understands the nature and effect of an adoption order and in particular that the order, if made, will make the petitioner responsible for the maintenance and upbringing of the child;

(h)   whether the means and standing of the petitioner are such as to enable him to maintain and bring up the child suitably;

(i)   whether the child has any right or interest in property and, if so, what right or interest;

(j)   whether any payment or other reward in consideration of the proposed adoption, other than an approved adoption allowance has been received or agreed;

(k)   what insurance has been offered on the life of the child;

(l)   the religious persuasion, racial origin, and cultural and linguistic background of the child and of the petitioner;

(m)   considerations arising from the difference in age between the petitioner and the child if this is more or less than the normal difference between parents and children;

(n)   whether adoption is likely to safeguard and promote the welfare of the child throughout his life;

[(o)   whether the child is subject to a compulsory supervision order and, if so, what steps have been taken to comply with sections 131 and 141 of the 2011 Act;]

(p)   whether there has been a contravention of section 75 of the 2007 Act in relation to the child;

(q)   whether there has been a failure to comply with section 76(2) of the 2007 Act in relation to the child;

(r)   any other matters relevant to the operation of section 14 of the 2007 Act in relation to the application;

(s)   where appropriate, information about whether—

(i)   in an application under section 29(1) of the 2007 Act, the petitioners are a relevant couple within the meaning of section 29(3)(c) or (d) of the 2007 Act;

(ii)   in an application under section 30(1) of the 2007 Act, the petitioner is a member of a relevant couple within the meaning of section 29(3)(c) or (d) of the 2007 Act;

(t)   in the case of a petition to which the provisions of Chapter 1 of Part 3 of the 2009 Regulations apply, the confirmation, the date and the details referred to respectively in regulation 33(a), (b) and (c) of those Regulations;

(u)   any other information which may be of assistance to the court.

(5)   If no report mentioned in paragraph (2)(d) or (e) is available to be lodged with the petition, the sheriff shall pronounce an interlocutor requiring the local authority or adoption agency to prepare and lodge such a report in court within 2 weeks from the date of the interlocutor, or within such other period as the sheriff in his discretion may allow.

30 Application of Chapter 2 to Convention adoption orders

Rules 11 to 27 (other than paragraphs (1), (2) and (3)(n) of rule 12) of Chapter 2 are to apply to an application under this Chapter, so far as they are not inconsistent with this Chapter, except that—

(a)   rule 11 (appointment of curator ad litem and reporting officer) is to be read as if—

(i)   in paragraph (1), for 'rule 8' there were substituted 'rule 29';

(ii)   in paragraph (1) the words 'and reporting officer' were omitted; and

(iii)   for paragraphs (2) and (3) there were substituted—

'(2)   Subject to paragraph (3), the sheriff must not appoint a reporting officer;

(3)   But a reporting officer must be appointed where the child who is the subject of the application is aged 12 or over, for the purpose of witnessing that child's consent where that consent is to be executed in Scotland.';

(b)   rule 14 (intimation of application) is to be read as if—

(i)   in paragraph (1), for 'rule 8' there were substituted 'rule 29';

(ii)   for paragraph (1)(b) there were substituted—

'(b)   the petitioner must send a copy of the petition along with a notice of intimation in Form 5 to—

(i)   the curator ad litem and the reporting officer;

(ii)   any person or body who has care or possession of the child; and

(iii)   any local authority or adoption agency that has prepared a report under section 17 or 19(2) of the 2007 Act.'; and

(iii)   paragraph (1)(c) and (d) were omitted; and

(c)   rule 23 (communication to the Registrar General) is to be read as if for it there were substituted—

'**Communications to the Registrar General and the Central Authority**

23—(1) The making of a Convention adoption order is to be intimated in accordance with this rule to the Registrar General and the Central Authority by the sheriff clerk.

(2)   A certified copy of the order making a Convention adoption order must be sent to the Registrar General and the Central Authority either by recorded delivery post in an envelope marked 'Confidential', or by personal delivery by the sheriff clerk in a sealed envelope marked 'Confidential.'.

CHAPTER 4

PERMANENCE ORDERS

31 Application for permanence order

(1)   An application for a permanence order under section 80 of the 2007 Act is to be made by petition in Form 11.

(2)   The following documents must be lodged in process along with a petition under paragraph (1):—

(a)   an extract of the entry in the Register of Births relating to the child who is the subject of the application;

(b)   a report by the petitioner in numbered paragraphs, if available, which deals with the following matters:—

(i)   how the needs of the child came to the notice of the petitioner;

(ii)   any relevant family circumstances of the child;

(iii)   a description of the physical and mental health of the child (including any special needs) and his emotional, behavioural and educational development;

(iv)   an account of the discussion by the petitioner with the parents or guardians of the child and, if appropriate, with the child about their wishes and the alternatives to a permanence order;

(v)   where appropriate, whether the father of the child has been given notice and provided with the prescribed information under section 105(2) of the 2007 Act;

(vi)   the knowledge of the petitioner of the position of other relatives or persons likely to be involved;

(vii)   an account of the search by the petitioner for any parent or guardian who cannot be found;

(viii)   the arrangements of the petitioner to care for the child after the making of a permanence order (including the arrangements for contact between the child and any other person);

(ix)   the child's religious persuasion, racial origin and cultural and linguistic background;

(x)   the likely effect on the child of the making of a permanence order;

(xi)   whether there is a person who has the right mentioned in section 2(1)(a) of the 1995 Act to have the child living with the person or otherwise to regulate the child's residence and, where there is such a person, evidence that the child's residence with the person is or is likely to be seriously detrimental to the welfare of the child;

(xii)   whether the child is or has been married or a civil partner;

(xiii)   in the case of a petition containing a request that the order include provision granting authority for the child to be adopted, the matters mentioned in paragraph (3);

(xiv)   in the case of a petition in respect of a child who is aged 12 or over, whether the child consents to the making of the order or is incapable of doing so;

(xv)   whether the child is subject to a [compulsory supervision order];

(xvi)   any other information which may be of assistance to the court having regard, in particular, to sections 83 (if appropriate) and 84 of the 2007 Act;

(c)   any other document founded upon by the petitioner in support of the terms of the petition.

(3)   The matters referred to in paragraph (2)(xiii) are—

(a)   whether the child has been, or is likely to be, placed for adoption;

(b)   whether each parent or guardian of the child understands what the effect of making an adoption order would be and consents to the making of such an order in relation to the child, or the grounds on which such consent should be dispensed with.

(4)   If the report mentioned in paragraph (2)(b) is unavailable to be lodged with the petition, the sheriff shall pronounce an interlocutor requiring the petitioner to prepare and lodge such a report within 2 weeks of the date of the interlocutor, or within such other period as the sheriff in his discretion may allow.

32   Appointment of curator ad litem and reporting officer

(1)   The sheriff must, on the lodging of a petition under rule 31 appoint a curator ad litem and reporting officer.

(2)   But, subject to paragraph (3) the sheriff is not to appoint a reporting officer where the petition does not request that the order include provision granting authority for the child to be adopted.

(3)   Notwithstanding paragraph (2), a reporting officer must be appointed where the child who is the subject of the application is aged 12 or over for the purpose of witnessing that child's consent where that consent is to be executed in Scotland.

(4)   The same person may be appointed as curator ad litem and reporting officer in the same petition, if the sheriff considers that doing so is appropriate in the circumstances.

(5)   The sheriff may appoint a person who is not a member of a panel established under regulations made by virtue of section 101 of the 1995 Act to be curator ad litem or a reporting officer.

(6)   The sheriff may, on cause shown, appoint a reporting officer prior to the lodging of a petition.

(7)   An application for an appointment under paragraph (6) is to be made by letter addressed to the sheriff clerk specifying the reasons for the appointment, and shall not require to be intimated to any other person.

(8)   The sheriff clerk must intimate the appointment of a curator ad litem and reporting officer under paragraph (1) or (6) to the person or persons appointed.

33   Intimation of application

(1)   On the lodging of a petition under rule 31—

(a)   the sheriff clerk must fix a date for a preliminary hearing[, which must take place (except on cause shown)] not less than 6 and not more than 8 weeks after the date of lodging the petition;

(b)   where the petition does not contain a request that the order include provision granting authority for the child to be adopted, the petitioner must send [a service copy of the petition in Form 11A] along with a notice of intimation in Form 12 to—

(i)   any person who has parental responsibilities or parental rights in relation to the child;

(ii)   any person who claims to have an interest;

(c)   where the petition contains such a request—

(i)   the petitioner must send [a service copy of the petition in Form 11A] along with a notice of intimation in Form 12 to the persons mentioned in paragraph (2); and

(ii)   the petitioner must send a service copy of the petition in Form 11A along with a notice of intimation in Form 13 to the father of the child if he does not have, and never has had, parental responsibilities and parental rights in relation to the child;

(d)   the sheriff clerk must intimate the date of the preliminary hearing to the curator ad litem and to any reporting officer appointed under rule 32;

(e)   the sheriff may order the petitioner to intimate the application to such other person [and in such terms] as he considers appropriate.

(2)   The persons referred to in paragraph (1)(c)(i) are—

(a)   every person who can be found and whose consent to the making of the order is required to be given or dispensed with under the 2007 Act;

(b)   if no such person can be found, a relative of the child within the meaning of section 119(1) of the 2007 Act unless the address of such a relative is not known to the petitioner and cannot reasonably be ascertained.

(3)   A notice of intimation under paragraph (1)(c)(i) must include the following matters:—

(a)   that an application for a permanence order containing a request that the order include provision granting authority for the child to be adopted has been made;

(b)   the date on which and place where the preliminary hearing will be held;

(c)   the fact that the person is entitled to be heard on the application;

(d)   the fact that, unless the person wishes, or the court requires, the person need not attend the hearing.

(4)   A notice of intimation under paragraph (1)(c)(ii) must include the matters mentioned in paragraphs (3)(a) and (b).

(5)   The sheriff clerk or petitioner on making intimation shall complete a certificate of intimation in Form 14.

34 Form of response

[(1)]   Any person who has received intimation of an application for a permanence order under rule 33 and who intends to oppose that application must lodge a form of response in Form 15 not later than 21 days after the date of intimation of the application.

[(2)   A form of response lodged under paragraph (1) must be intimated by the respondent to the petitioner at the time of lodging.]

[34A Opposed applications

Within 14 days of a form of response being lodged, the petitioner shall lodge and intimate to all other parties a brief statement in numbered paragraphs setting out the facts upon which the petitioner intends to rely including averments in relation to—

(a)   considerations under section 14 of the 2007 Act;

(b)   ancillary provisions under section 82 of the 2007 Act;

(c)   conditions under section 83 of the 2007 Act;

(d)   conditions and considerations under section 84 of the 2007 Act.]

35 Preliminary hearing

(1)   At the preliminary hearing the sheriff must—

(a)   if no form of response has been lodged under rule 34, dispose of the case or make such other order as he considers appropriate;

[(b) if a form of response has been lodged—

(i)   ascertain the nature of the issues in dispute, including any questions of admissibility of evidence or any legal issues;

(ii) ascertain the names of all witnesses, including expert witnesses, parties intend to call and whose evidence they intend to rely on at proof;

(iii) consider the scope for use of affidavits and other documents in place of oral evidence;

(iv) consider whether sanction is sought for the employment of counsel;

(v) consider the reasonable estimate of time needed by each party for examination-in-chief, cross-examination and submissions;

(vi) order the lodging of joint minutes of agreement, affidavits, expert reports and any other documents within such period as the sheriff considers appropriate;

(vii) fix a diet of proof not less than 12 and not more than 16 weeks after the date of the preliminary hearing or any continuation thereof unless, on cause shown, a longer period is appropriate;

(viii) fix a pre-proof hearing not less than 6 and not more than 8 weeks before the diet of proof;

(ix) order answers to the statement referred to in rule 34A to be lodged within 14 days of the date of the preliminary hearing or any continuation thereof or such other period as the sheriff considers appropriate; and

(x) ascertain from the parties what, if any, expert evidence is required and consider the scope for joint instruction of a single expert.]

[(2)   The sheriff may, if satisfied that there is sufficient reason for doing so for the expeditious resolution of the cause, continue the preliminary hearing for such period or periods as he or she thinks fit.]

(3)   At the preliminary hearing the sheriff may—

(a)   if he is not satisfied that the facts stated in the petition are supported by the documents lodged with it or by the reports of the curator ad litem and reporting officer, order the production of further documents; and

(b)   make such other order as he considers appropriate for the expeditious progress of the case.

[(4)   The answers lodged under paragraph (1)(b)(ix) must be in numbered paragraphs and respond to the statement referred to in rule 34A.]

[35A   List of witnesses etc

Not later than 7 days prior to the pre-proof hearing the parties shall lodge in process and intimate to all other parties—

(a)   a list of the witnesses, including expert witnesses, they intend to call and whose evidence they intend to rely on at proof;

(b)   all documents upon which they intend to rely at proof;

(c)   a notice of agreed facts;

(d)   a notice of disputed issues.]

36   Pre-proof hearing

(1)   It is the duty of the parties to provide the sheriff with sufficient information to enable him to conduct the hearing as provided for in this rule.

[(2)   At the pre-proof hearing the sheriff must consider—

(a)   the extent to which the parties have complied with any orders made by the sheriff under rule 35;

(b)   the extent to which further information or orders are required in respect of matters referred to in rule 35;

(c)   the state of preparation of the parties;

(d)   the availability of witnesses;

(e)   the nature of productions.]

[(2A)   At the pre-proof hearing the sheriff must ascertain, so far as is reasonably practicable, whether the case is likely to proceed to proof on the date fixed for that purpose, whether the appropriate number of days have been allowed and if further days may be required.]

(3)   At the pre-proof hearing the sheriff may—

(a)   discharge the proof and fix a new date for such proof;

(b)   adjourn the pre-proof hearing;

[...]

(d)   make such other order as he considers appropriate to secure the expeditious progress of the case [including restricting the issues for proof and, on the motion of either party, on cause shown, or of the sheriff's own motion, excluding specified documents, reports and/or witnesses from proof].

[37   Proof

(1)   A proof shall be taken on the allocated days and parties shall adhere to the estimates provided under rule 35(1)(b)(v) or 36(2)(b), but the sheriff may adjourn the diet from time to time.

(2)   Except where the sheriff otherwise directs, at the proof no witnesses other than those named on a witness list may be called to give evidence.]

38   Pronouncement of decision

(1)   At the conclusion of the proof the sheriff may—

(a)   pronounce a decision; or

(b)   reserve judgment.

(2)   If the sheriff pronounces his decision at the end of the proof, he—

(a)   must state briefly the grounds of his decision, including the reasons for his decision on any questions of law or of admissibility of evidence; and

(b)   may, and if requested to do so by one of the parties must, append to the interlocutor a note setting out those matters and his findings in fact and law.

(3) If the sheriff pronounces his decision after reserving judgment, he must give to the sheriff clerk within 4 weeks of the conclusion of the proof—

(a) an interlocutor giving effect to his decision and incorporating findings in fact and law; and

(b) a note setting out the matters mentioned in paragraph (2)(a).

(4) The sheriff clerk must forthwith send copies of the documents mentioned in paragraph (2) or (3) to each of the parties.

(5) The sheriff principal may extend the period mentioned in paragraph (3) for such further period as he considers reasonable.

(6) Where the sheriff reserves judgment—

(a) the date of the interlocutor of the sheriff shall be the date on which it is received by the sheriff clerk; and

(b) the sheriff clerk shall enter that date in the interlocutor.

(7) If the question of expenses has been reserved the sheriff must deal with that issue within 21 days of the date of the interlocutor disposing of the merits of the application.

(8) In any case in which a serial number has been assigned in respect of the child's address under rule 43, or where the sheriff so directs, any document issued under this rule shall not disclose the child's address.

39 Final procedure

[(1) This rule applies where a permanence order is granted.]

[(1A) The sheriff clerk must issue an extract of the order to the petitioner after—

(a) the expiry of the period within which an appeal may be made, if no appeal is made; or

(b) the appeal has been finally disposed of.

(1B) Where the court has also made an order under section 89(2) of the 2007 Act (revocation of compulsory supervision order on making of permanence order), the sheriff clerk must intimate the making of that order to the Principal Reporter.]

(2) Where the permanence order includes provision granting authority for the child to be adopted the sheriff clerk must, after complying with [paragraphs (1A) and (1B)] seal the process in an envelope marked 'Confidential'.

(3) The envelope referred to in paragraph (2) must not be unsealed by the sheriff clerk or any other person having control of the records of that or any court, and the process shall not be made accessible to any person for one hundred years after the date of the granting of the order except—

(a) to the person to whom the permanence order relates once he has attained the age of 16 years;

(b) to the sheriff clerk, on an application made to him by an adoption agency, with the consent of the person to whom the process relates, for the purpose only of ascertaining the name of the agency, if any, responsible for the placement of that person and informing the applicant of that name;

(c) to a person, on an application made by him to the sheriff setting forth the reasons for which access to the process is required;

(d) to a court, public authority or administrative board (whether in the United Kingdom or not) having power to authorise an adoption, on petition by it to the court which granted the original order requesting that information be made available from the process for the purpose of discharging its duties in considering an application for adoption and specifying the precise reasons for which access to the process is required; or

(e) to a person who is authorised by the Scottish Ministers to obtain information from the process for the purpose of such research as is intended to improve the working of adoption law and practice.

40 Variation of ancillary provisions in order

(1) An application under section 92(2) (application for variation of ancillary

provisions) of the 2007 Act is to be made by minute in Form 16 in the process of the original application.

(2) A minute under paragraph (1) must contain—

    (a) the name and address of the applicant;

    (b) the applicant's relationship to and interest in the child;

    (c) the name and address of the local authority on whose application the permanence order was granted;

    (d) details of the original application;

    (e) details of any other person affected by the order;

    (f) the grounds on which variation is sought;

    (g) details of whether the child is subject to a [compulsory supervision order];

details of the order sought by the applicant.

(3) On the lodging of a minute under paragraph (1) the sheriff must order the applicant to intimate the minute to the petitioner in the original application, where it is not the applicant, to any other person affected by the order and to such other persons as the sheriff considers appropriate.

(4) A person to whom intimation is given under paragraph (3) may, within 14 days after the date on which intimation is made, lodge answers to the minute.

(5) The sheriff must, on the lodging of a minute under paragraph (1), appoint a curator ad litem.

(6) Where answers have been lodged under paragraph (4) the sheriff must order a hearing to be fixed.

(7) Where no answers have been lodged under paragraph (4) the sheriff may order a hearing to be fixed.

(8) Where the sheriff orders a hearing to be fixed under paragraph (6) or (7) he may also order a pre-proof hearing to be fixed not less than 2 and not more than 6 weeks before the hearing.

(9) Rule 36 is to apply, with any necessary modifications, to any pre-proof hearing fixed under paragraph (8).

(10) The sheriff shall order the applicant to intimate any hearing fixed under paragraph (6), (7) or (8) to the petitioner in the original application, where it is not the applicant, to any other person affected by the order and to such other persons as the sheriff considers appropriate.

(11) A hearing fixed under this rule is to be taken continuously so far as possible but the sheriff may adjourn the diet from time to time.

41 Amendment of order to grant authority for child to be adopted

(1) An application under section 93(2) (amendment of order to include provision granting authority for child to be adopted) of the 2007 Act is to be made by minute in Form 17 in the process of the original application.

(2) A minute under paragraph (1) must contain—

    (a) the name and address of the applicant;

    (b) details of the original application;

    (c) details of the following matters—

      (i) whether the child has been, or is likely to be, placed for adoption;

      (ii) whether each parent or guardian of the child understands what the effect of making an adoption order would be and consents to the making of such an order in relation to the child, or the grounds on which such consent should be dispensed with;

      (iii) the child's religious persuasion, racial origin and cultural and linguistic background;

      (iv) whether the child is subject to a [compulsory supervision order];

      (v) the likely effect on the child of the making of the order.

(3) On the lodging of a minute under paragraph (1)—

(a) the sheriff clerk must fix a date for a preliminary hearing not less than 6 and not more than 8 weeks after the date of lodging the application;

(b) the applicant must send a copy of the minute along with a notice of intimation in Form 18 to every person who can be found and whose consent to the making of the order is required to be given or dispensed with under the 2007 Act;

(c) the applicant must send a copy of the minute along with a notice of intimation in Form 19 to the father of the child if he does not have, and never has had, parental responsibilities in relation to the child;

(d) the sheriff may order the applicant to intimate the minute to such other persons as he considers appropriate;

(e) the sheriff must appoint a curator ad litem and reporting officer and the same person may be appointed as curator ad litem and reporting officer if the sheriff considers that doing so is appropriate in the circumstances.

(4) A notice of intimation under paragraph (3)(b) must state the following matters:—

(a) that an application has been made;

(b) the date on which, and place where, the preliminary hearing will be heard;

(c) the fact that the person is entitled to be heard on the application;

(d) the fact that, unless the person wishes, or the court requires, the person need not attend the hearing.

(5) A notice of intimation under paragraph (3)(c) must state the matters mentioned in paragraph (4)(a) and (b).

(6) The minuter on making intimation shall complete a certificate of intimation in Form 14.

(7) Rules 34 to 39 are to apply, with any necessary modifications, to an application under this rule as they apply to an application under rule 31.

42 Revocation

(1) An application under section 98(1) of the 2007 Act for revocation of a permanence order shall—

(a) be made by minute in Form 20 in the process of the original application; and

(b) specify detailed proposals for the future welfare of the child.

(2) A minute under paragraph (1) must contain—

(a) the name and address of the applicant;

(b) the applicant's relationship to and interest in the child;

(c) the name and address of the local authority on whose application the permanence order was granted;

(d) details of the original application;

(e) details of any other person affected by the order;

(f) the grounds on which revocation is sought;

(g) details of whether the child is subject to a [compulsory supervision order];

(h) details of the order sought by the applicant.

(3) On the lodging of a minute under paragraph (1), the sheriff must order the applicant to intimate the minute to the petitioner in the original application, where it is not the applicant, to any other person affected by the order and to such other persons as he considers appropriate.

(4) Any person to whom intimation has been given under paragraph (3) may, within 14 days after the date on which intimation is made, lodge answers to the minute.

(5) The sheriff must, on the lodging of a minute under paragraph (1), appoint a curator ad litem.

(6) Where answers have been lodged under paragraph (4), the sheriff—

(a)   must order a hearing to be fixed; and

(b)   may order the relevant local authority to submit a report to him.

(7)   Where no answers have been lodged under paragraph (4) the sheriff may—

(a)   order the relevant local authority to submit a report to him;

(b)   order a hearing to be fixed;

(c)   order both such a report and such a hearing.

(8)   Where the sheriff orders a hearing to be fixed under paragraph (6) or (7) he may also order a pre-proof hearing to be fixed not less than 2 and not more than 6 weeks before the hearing.

(9)   Rule 36 is to apply, with any necessary modifications, to any pre-proof hearing fixed under paragraph (8).

(10)   The sheriff shall order the applicant to intimate any hearing fixed under paragraph (6), (7) or (8) to the petitioner in the original application, where it is not the applicant, to any other person affected by the order and to such other persons as the sheriff considers appropriate.

(11)   A hearing fixed under this rule is to be taken continuously so far as possible but the sheriff may adjourn the diet from time to time.

(12)   An order made in respect of an application under paragraph (1) may specify the person—

(a)   on whom parental responsibilities are imposed in consequence of the making of the order; and

(b)   to whom parental rights are given in consequence of the making of the order.

43   Protection of address of child

(1)   Where an applicant under this Chapter wishes to prevent the address of the child being disclosed to any person whose consent to the making of an order is required, the applicant may apply to the sheriff clerk for a serial number to be assigned for that purpose.

(2)   On receipt of an application under paragraph (1) the sheriff clerk must—

(a)   assign a serial number in respect of the child's address; and

(b)   enter a note of the number opposite the child's address in a register of serial numbers.

(3)   The contents of the register of serial numbers and the addresses of the children to whom each number relates shall be treated as confidential by the sheriff clerk and are not to be disclosed to any person other than the sheriff.

(4)   Where a serial number has been assigned under paragraph (2), any form of consent to a permanence order—

(a)   must refer to the child's address by means of the serial number assigned to it; and

(b)   must specify the year in which and the court by which the serial number was assigned.

44   Duties of reporting officer and curator ad litem

(1)   The other duties of a reporting officer appointed under this Chapter, other than under rule 32(3), which are prescribed for the purposes of section 108(1)(b) of the 2007 Act are—

(a)   to ascertain the whereabouts of all persons whose consent to the making of an adoption order in respect of the child is required;

(b)   to ascertain whether there is any person other than those mentioned in the petition or minute, as the case may be, upon whom notice of the application should be served;

(c)   in the case of each person whose consent to the making of an adoption order is required or may be dispensed with, to—

(i)   ascertain whether that person understands what the effect of making an adoption order would be;

(ii) ascertain whether alternatives to adoption have been discussed with that person;

[(iia) ascertain whether that person consents to the making of an adoption order;]

(iii) confirm that that person understands that he may withdraw his consent at any time before an order is made;

(d) to confirm that each parent or guardian of the child who can be found is aware that he may apply to the court for—

(i) variation of the ancillary provisions in the permanence order under section 92 of the 2007 Act; and

(ii) revocation of a permanence order under section 98 of the 2007 Act, and of the appropriate procedure for these applications.

(e) to report in writing on the matters mentioned in subparagraphs (a) to (d) to the sheriff within 4 weeks from date of interlocutor appointing the reporting officer, or within such other period as the sheriff in his discretion may allow.

(2) References in paragraph (1) to consent are to consent within the meaning of section 83(1)(c), 84(1) or 93(3) of the 2007 Act as the case may be.

(3) A curator ad litem appointed under this Chapter must—

(a) have regard to safeguarding the interests of the child as his paramount duty;

(b) inquire, so far as he considers necessary into the facts and circumstances stated in the petition or minute, as the case may be, and in any report lodged under rule 31(2)(b);

(c) where appropriate, establish the child's religious persuasion, racial origin and cultural and linguistic background;

(d) where appropriate, establish whether the order is likely to safeguard and promote the welfare of the child throughout childhood;

(e) ascertain whether the child is subject to a [compulsory supervision order];

(f) ascertain from the child whether he wishes to express a view and, where the child indicates his wish to express a view, ascertain that view;

(g) ascertain the likely effect on the child of the making of the order;

(h) where appropriate, ascertain whether it would be better for the child that the order be made than that it should not be made;

(i) where appropriate, ascertain whether it would be better for the child if the court were to grant authority for the child to be adopted than if it were not to grant such authority;

(j) where appropriate, ascertain whether the child has been, or is likely to be, placed for adoption.

(4) Subject to paragraph (5) the curator ad litem must report in writing on the matters mentioned in paragraph (3) to the sheriff within 4 weeks from the date of the interlocutor appointing the curator, or within such other period as the sheriff in his discretion may allow.

(5) Subject to any order made by the sheriff under rule 46(1)(a) the views of the child ascertained in terms of paragraph (3)(f) may, if the curator ad litem considers appropriate, be conveyed to the sheriff orally.

45 Consents

(1) The consent of a parent or guardian required by section 83(1)(c) or 93(3) of the 2007 Act is to be in Form 21.

(2) The consent of the child required under section 84(1) of the 2007 Act is to be in Form 22.

(3) A form of consent mentioned in paragraph (1) or (2) must be witnessed—

(a) where it is executed in Scotland, by the reporting officer appointed under this Chapter;

(b)　where it is executed outwith Scotland but within the United Kingdom, by a justice of the peace or commissioner for oaths; or

(c)　where it is executed outwith the United Kingdom—

(i)　if the person who executes the form is serving in Her Majesty's forces, by an officer holding a commission in any of those forces; or

(ii)　in any other case, by a British diplomatic or consular official or any person authorised to administer an oath or affirmation under the law of the place where the consent is executed.

46　Procedure where child wishes to express a view

(1)　Where a child has indicated his wish to express his views the sheriff, without prejudice to rule 44(3)(f)—

(a)　may order such procedural steps to be taken as he considers appropriate to ascertain the views of that child; and

(b)　must not make an order under this Chapter unless an opportunity has been given for the views of that child to be obtained or heard.

(2)　Where the views of a child, whether obtained under this rule or under rule 44, have been recorded in writing, the sheriff may direct that such a written record is to—

(a)　be sealed in a envelope marked 'Views of the child – confidential';

(b)　be available to a sheriff only;

(c)　not be opened by any person other than a sheriff; and

(d)　not form a borrowable part of the process.

47　Confidentiality

(1)　Unless the sheriff otherwise directs, all documents lodged in process including the reports by the curator ad litem and reporting officer shall be available only to the sheriff, the curator ad litem, the reporting officer and the parties; and such documents must be treated as confidential by any persons involved in, or a party to, the proceedings and by the sheriff clerk.

(2)　The reporting officer and the curator ad litem—

(a)　must treat all information obtained in the exercise of their duties as confidential; and

(b)　must not disclose any such information to any person unless disclosure of such information is necessary for the purpose of their duties.

(3)　This rule is subject to rule 46 [and rule 51].

48　Procedure where leave of court required

(1)　Where leave of the court is required under section 94(4) or 98(2)(b) of the 2007 Act before an application for variation or revocation of a permanence order may be made, the applicant must lodge along with the minute a written application in the form of a letter addressed to the sheriff clerk stating—

(a)　the grounds on which leave is sought; and

(b)　whether or not the applicant has applied for legal aid.

(2)　Where the applicant has applied for legal aid he must also lodge along with the minute written confirmation from the Scottish Legal Aid Board that it has determined, under regulation 7(2)(b) of the Civil Legal Aid (Scotland) Regulations 2002 that notification of the application should be dispensed with or postponed pending the making by the sheriff of an order for intimation under paragraph (4)(b).

(3)　Subject to paragraph (4)(b), an application under paragraph (1) shall not be served or intimated to any party.

(4)　The sheriff shall consider an application under paragraph (1) without hearing the applicant and may—

(a)　refuse the application and pronounce an interlocutor accordingly; or

(b)　if he is minded to grant the application order the applicant—

(i)　to intimate the application to such persons as the sheriff considers appropriate; and

(ii) to lodge a certificate of intimation in, as near as may be, Form 7.

(5) If any person who receives intimation of an application under paragraph (4)(b) wishes to be heard he shall notify the sheriff clerk in writing within 14 days of receipt of intimation of the application.

(6) On receipt of the notification under paragraph (5) the sheriff clerk shall fix a hearing and intimate the date of the hearing to the parties.

49 Transfer of process

(1) Where an application under rule 40, 41 or 42 is made in a sheriff court other than the sheriff court in which the process relating to the permanence order is held—

(a) the minute of application must contain averments as to the sheriff court in which the process relating to the permanence order is held;

(b) the sheriff clerk with whom the application is lodged must notify the sheriff clerk of the sheriff court in which the process relating to the permanence order is held; and

(c) the sheriff clerk of the sheriff court in which the process relating to the permanence order is held must, not later than 4 working days after receipt of such notification transfer that process to the sheriff clerk of the sheriff court in which the application is made.

(2) For the purposes of paragraph (1), the sheriff court in which the process relating to the order is held is the sheriff court in which the permanence order was granted or, where the process has been transferred under that paragraph, the last sheriff court to which the process has been transferred.

(3) A failure of the sheriff clerk to comply with paragraph (1) does not invalidate the application.

50 Intimation to Principal Reporter

Where an application under this Chapter is made in respect of a child whose case has been referred to a children's hearing or who is subject to a [compulsory supervision order], the sheriff clerk shall intimate the fact that the application has been made to the Principal Reporter.

51 Report of children's hearing

[(1) This rule applies where the sheriff is given a report from a children's hearing under section 95(2) of the 2007 Act.]

[(1A) The sheriff clerk shall lodge in the process of the application—

(a) the report, and

(b) where paragraph (1C) applies, the documents referred to in that paragraph.

(1B) Subject to paragraph (1D), the sheriff clerk shall send a copy of the report together with a notice in Form 23 to—

(a) the parties to the application;

(b) any relevant person in relation to the child; and

(c) such other person as the sheriff considers appropriate.

(1C) This paragraph, and paragraphs (1D) and (1E) apply where, pursuant to rule 77(7) of the Children's Hearings (Scotland) Act 2011 (Rules of Procedure in Children's Hearings) Rules 2013, the sheriff is given, in addition to the report referred to in paragraph (1)—

(a) a redacted report, and

(b) details of the children's hearing's determination of a non-disclosure request.

(1D) The sheriff shall, having regard to the details referred to in paragraph (1C)(b), determine in respect of each person referred to in paragraph (1B) whether that person is to be sent a copy of the redacted report in place of a copy of the report, and paragraph (1B) shall apply accordingly.

(1E) Unless the sheriff otherwise directs, the report lodged in the process shall not be available to any person to whom a copy of the redacted report has been sent pursuant to paragraph (1D).]

(2)   Any person who receives notice under paragraph [(1B)] and who wishes to oppose the proposals of the children's hearing must lodge a form of response in Form 24 within 7 days of the date notice was given.

(3)   Thereafter the sheriff shall consider the report and any form of response lodged under paragraph (2) and decide whether to refer the child's case to the Principal Reporter as mentioned in section 96(3) of the 2007 Act.

(4)   Where the sheriff decides to refer the child's case to the Principal Reporter as mentioned in section 96(3) of the 2007 Act, he shall pronounce an order to this effect which shall narrate in terms that he is referring the child's case to the Principal Reporter as mentioned in that provision.

(5)   Where the sheriff decides not to refer the child's case to the Principal Reporter, he may nevertheless make such other order he considers appropriate for the expeditious progress of the case.

(6)   In order to assist him to decide what to do under paragraph (3), the sheriff may order the holding of a hearing.

(7)   If the sheriff so decides, he shall fix a date for the hearing which shall be not more than 7 days after the date of the order.

(8)   The sheriff clerk shall intimate any hearing under paragraph (6) to—

(a)   the parties to the application;

(b)   any person who lodged a form of response under paragraph (2);

(c)   any relevant person in relation to the child within the meaning given by section 93(2) of the 1995 Act; and

(d)   such other person as the sheriff considers appropriate.

(9)   The sheriff may allow a continuation of a hearing under paragraph (6) on two occasions only, each for a period not exceeding 14 days.

(10)   After the sheriff has made his decision under paragraph (3), the sheriff clerk shall send a notice in Form 25 to the Principal Reporter.

52   Interim orders

(1)   An application for an interim order under section 97 of the 2007 Act is to be made by motion.

(2)   Chapter 15 of the Ordinary Cause Rules shall apply, with any necessary modifications, to a motion under this rule as it applies to a motion under the Ordinary Cause Rules.

SCHEDULE

For the Schedule of Forms, see the website of Scottish Courts.

CHILDREN'S HEARINGS (SCOTLAND) ACT 2011 (RULES OF PROCEDURE IN CHILDREN'S HEARINGS) 2013 (SSI 2013/194)

These Rules are reproduced as amended by SSIs 2015/21; 2017/452 and 2021/68.

PART 1

Introductory and General

1 Citation, commencement and application

(1) These Rules may be cited as the Children's Hearings (Scotland) Act 2011 (Rules of Procedure in Children's Hearings) Rules 2013 and come into force on the same day as section 177 (children's hearings: procedural rules) of the Act.*

(2) These Rules shall only apply to proceedings commenced on or after the day on which they come into force.

Section 177 came into force on 24 June 2013: SSI 2013/195, art 2.

---

2 Interpretation

(1) In these Rules—

'the Act' means the Children's Hearings (Scotland) Act 2011;

'chairing member' means the member of the Children's Panel selected to chair a pre-hearing panel or children's hearing, as the case may be;

'a contact direction' has the same meaning as in section 126(1) (review of contact direction) of the Act;

'National Convener' means the National Convener of Children's Hearings Scotland;

'member of the pre-hearing panel' and 'member of the children's hearing' means a member of the Children's Panel selected under section 6 (selection of members of children's hearing) of the Act, in relation to that hearing or pre-hearing, and 'member' is to be construed accordingly;

'relevant person' means a relevant person in relation to a child and includes a person deemed to be a relevant person under section 81 (determination of claim that person be deemed a relevant person) or section 160(4)(b) (appeal to sheriff against relevant person determination) of the Act;

'Reporter' means the Principal Reporter or any person carrying out a function on behalf of the Principal Reporter by virtue of paragraph 10(1) (delegation of Principal Reporter's functions) of schedule 3 to the Act;

'section 62 statement' has the same meaning as in section 62(4) (provision of information by court) of the Act.

(2) For the purposes of rule 1(2) of these Rules, proceedings are commenced on the date when any of the following occurs—

(a) a children's hearing is arranged by the Reporter under section 69(2) of the Act;

(b) an application is made under Part 5 of the Act; or

(c) an appeal is made under Part 15 of the Act.

[2A Individuals to be afforded opportunity to participate

(1) This rule applies only in respect of children's hearings held, or to be held, by virtue of—

(a) section 69(2) of the Act (determination under section 66: referral to children's hearing),

(b) Parts 9 to 11 of the Act (children's hearing; proceedings before sheriff; subsequent children's hearings), or

(c) Part 13 of the Act (review of compulsory supervision order).

(2) An individual is to be afforded an opportunity to participate in relation to a

children's hearing if the Reporter is satisfied, or a pre-hearing panel or children's hearing has determined—

(a)   that the criteria in paragraph (3) are met by the individual in relation to the children's hearing, or

(b)   in the case of a children's hearing arranged (wholly or partly) in consequence of a request being made under section 132A of the Act (right of person not afforded opportunity to participate to require review), that subsection (2) of that section applies to the individual.

(3)   The criteria referred to in paragraph (2) are—

(a)   the individual is living or has lived with the child,

(b)   the individual and the child have an ongoing relationship with the character of a relationship between siblings (whether or not they have a parent in common),

(c)   the children's hearing is likely to make a decision significantly affecting contact or the possibility of contact between the individual and the child, and

(d)   the individual is capable of forming a view on the matter of contact between the individual and the child.

(4)   In considering whether the criteria in paragraph (3) are met, regard is to be had to the views of the child and any relevant person.

(5)   These Rules give an individual who is to be afforded an opportunity to participate the rights mentioned in section 79(5ZA) of the Act (referral of certain matters for pre-hearing determination).]

PART 2

Selection of Children's Hearings and Pre-hearing Panel Members and Duties of Members

3   Selection of members of children's hearing and pre-hearing panel – supplementary

(1)   Where a children's hearing is held in relation to a child, by virtue of the Act or any other enactment, the children's hearing may request that the National Convener select, where practicable, one of the members of that children's hearing to be a member of the next children's hearing to be arranged in relation to that child.

(2)   In selecting members of a pre-hearing panel in terms of section 79(2)(a) (referral of certain matters for pre-hearing determination) of the Act the National Convener must ensure that the pre-hearing panel—

(a)   includes both male and female members of the Children's Panel; and

(b)   so far as practicable, consists only of members of the Children's Panel who live or work in the area of the local authority which is the relevant local authority for the child to whom the pre-hearing panel relates.

4   Selection of chairing member for pre-hearing panels and children's hearings

(1)   Paragraph (2) applies where a pre-hearing panel or children's hearing has been arranged by virtue of the Act or any other enactment and the National Convener or relevant area support team has not selected a chairing member for that pre-hearing panel or children's hearing.

(2)   Immediately before beginning the pre-hearing panel or children's hearing, as the case may be, the members of that pre-hearing panel or children's hearing must determine which of their number is to chair the pre-hearing panel or children's hearing, as the case may be.

(3)   A member may only be selected to chair a children's hearing if that member has successfully completed the relevant training provided by or on behalf of the National Convener relating to chairing a children's hearing.

5   Duties of members of the pre-hearing panel or children's hearing relating to documents and information

(1)   Any documents which are given to a member of the pre-hearing panel or

children's hearing by the Reporter under, or by virtue of, the Act or these Rules must be kept securely in that member's custody and returned to the Reporter at the conclusion of the pre-hearing panel or children's hearing to which those documents relate.

(2)   The member must not cause or permit any information which they have obtained by virtue of their involvement in a pre-hearing panel or children's hearing to be disclosed, except as permitted by the Act or these Rules.

6   Duties of chairing member of a pre-hearing panel or children's hearing

(1)   The chairing member of the children's hearing or pre-hearing panel must—
(a)   take reasonable steps to ensure that the child and each relevant person are able to—
(i)   understand the proceedings; and
(ii)   participate in those proceedings;
(b)   where, during the proceedings, the child wishes to express a view, make reasonable arrangements to enable the child to express those views in the manner preferred by the child;
(c)   ensure that a record is made of—
(i)   the decisions or determinations made by the children's hearing or pre-hearing panel, as the case may be; and
(ii)   the reasons for those decisions or determinations; and
(d)   sign and date the record of the decisions or determinations.

(2)   Any requirement on the chairing member to inform those attending a children's hearing of the substance of any report, document or information or to explain any matter is subject to any decision of the children's hearing to withhold information under section 178 (children's hearing: disclosure of information) of the Act or by virtue of a non-disclosure request made in accordance with Part 19 of these Rules.

7   Procedure at children's hearings and pre-hearing panels where not otherwise specified

(1)   The procedure at any children's hearing or pre-hearing panel required to be held by virtue of the Act or any other enactment, unless that procedure is provided for under the Act or these Rules, is to be determined by the chairing member.

(2)   The children's hearing or pre-hearing panel, if it considers it appropriate to do so, may adjourn the children's hearing or pre-hearing panel, as the case may be—
(a)   on the initiative of the children's hearing or pre-hearing panel; or
(b)   on the request of any person attending the hearing.

(3)   Where a children's hearing or pre-hearing panel has been adjourned it must re-convene on the same day as the adjournment was made.

PART 3
Duties and Roles of Persons Attending or Preparing Documents for Children's Hearings and Pre-hearing Panels

8   Requirement to include child's views in documents

Where any document is to be given to members of the children's hearing or pre-hearing panel under, or by virtue of, the Act, or these Rules, the document must contain any views expressed by the child which have been given to the person who has prepared that document.

9   Duties of safeguarder in respect of information and documents

(1)   Any documents which are given to a safeguarder by the Reporter under, or by virtue of, the Act or any other enactment must be kept securely in the safeguarder's custody and returned to the Reporter on the termination of the safeguarder's appointment.

(2)   The safeguarder must not cause or permit any information which they have obtained by virtue of their appointment as a safeguarder under the Act to be disclosed, except as permitted by virtue of the Act or any other enactment.

10   Attendance at children's hearings by member of the Administrative Justice and Tribunals Council or the Scottish Committee of that Council or a member of an Area Support Team

(1)   Any documents which are given to members of the children's hearing or pre-hearing panel must be given by the Reporter to any of the following persons attending the children's hearing or pre-hearing panel where that person so requests—

(a)   a member of the Administrative Justice and Tribunals Council or the Scottish Committee of that Council (acting in that person's capacity as such);

(b)   a member of an area support team (acting in that person's capacity as such).

(2)   Where documents are given to a person under paragraph (1) those documents must be kept securely in that person's custody and returned to the Reporter at the conclusion of the children's hearing or pre-hearing panel to which they relate.

(3)   The person to whom the documents are given under paragraph (1) must not cause or permit any information which they have obtained by virtue of their attendance at a pre-hearing panel or children's hearing to be disclosed, except as permitted by the Act or these Rules.

11   [Role of representatives]

(1)   Where [a person mentioned in paragraph (3) (referred] to in this rule as 'the accompanied person') is accompanied at a children's hearing or pre-hearing panel by a representative that representative may assist the accompanied person to discuss any issues arising for discussion before the children's hearing or pre-hearing panel.

(2)   The right of the accompanied person to be represented at the children's hearing or pre-hearing panel is without prejudice to any right of the accompanied person to legal representation by a solicitor or counsel.

[(3)   The persons referred to in paragraph (1) are—

(a)   the child,

(b)   any relevant person,

(c)   any person who wants to be deemed to be a relevant person,

(d)   any person who is or wants to be afforded an opportunity to participate in relation to the children's hearing by virtue of rule 2A.]

PART 4
General Duties of the Reporter

12   Record keeping by the Reporter of investigation and determination

(1)   This rule applies where section 66(1) (investigation and determination by Principal Reporter) of the Act applies.

(2)   The Reporter must keep a record of—

(a)   the name and address (if available) of any person providing the notice, information, statement or evidence;

(b)   the details of any investigation carried out by the Reporter under section 66 of the Act;

(c)   the determination made by the Reporter under section 66(2) of the Act; and

(d)   the details of any action taken by the Reporter under sections 68(2), 68(5) (determination under section 66: no referral to children's hearing) or 72(2) (child in place of safety: Principal Reporter's powers) of the Act.

(3)   Where the Reporter is required to arrange a children's hearing under

section 69(2) (determination under section 66: referral to children's hearing) of the Act the Reporter must notify—

(a)   where the information was provided under section 60 (local authority's duty to provide information to Principal Reporter) of the Act, the local authority which provided the information;

(b)   where the information was provided under section 61 (constable's duty to provide information to Principal Reporter) of the Act or [section 53(2) of the Criminal Justice (Scotland) Act 2016 (duty to inform Principal Reporter if child not being prosecuted)], the chief constable of the Police Service of Scotland.

13   Record keeping duties of the Reporter in relation to children's hearings

(1)   The Reporter must keep a record of the proceedings at each children's hearing and pre-hearing panel held by virtue of the Act or any other enactment.

(2)   The record to be kept by the Reporter must include the information mentioned in paragraph (3) and such other information about the proceedings as the Reporter considers appropriate.

(3)   That information is—

(a)   the particulars of the place and date of the children's hearing or pre-hearing panel;

(b)   the full name and address, date of birth and sex of the child in relation to whom the children's hearing or pre-hearing panel is held;

(c)   the full name and address of each relevant person;

(d)   which of the persons mentioned in sub-paragraphs (b) and (c) attended the children's hearing or pre-hearing panel;

(e)   the full name and address of any representative attending the children's hearing or pre-hearing panel;

(f)   the full name and address of any safeguarder attending the children's hearing or pre-hearing panel;

(g)   the details of any other person attending the children's hearing or pre-hearing panel;

(h)   the details of any decision or determination made by the children's hearing or pre-hearing panel or any other course of action taken by the children's hearing or pre-hearing panel;

(i)   where the children's hearing to which the record relates is a grounds hearing—

(i)   the details of any section 67 ground which is accepted, or not accepted, or is not understood and by whom;

(ii)   the detail of any direction given by the grounds hearing under section 93(2)(a) (grounds not accepted: application to sheriff or discharge) or 94(2)(a) (child or relevant person unable to understand grounds) of the Act to the Reporter to make an application to the sheriff.

14   The statement of grounds

Where the statement of grounds prepared by the Reporter under section 89 (Principal Reporter's duty to prepare statement of grounds) of the Act includes a ground mentioned in section 67(2)(j) (the child has committed an offence) the facts relating to that ground must have the same degree of specification as is required by section 138(4) (complaints) of, and Schedule 3 (indictments and complaints) to, the Criminal Procedure (Scotland) Act 1995 in a charge in a complaint, and the statement of grounds must also specify the nature of the offence in question.

15   Duties of Reporters where information to be withheld from a person

(1)   Where information is to be withheld from a person under the Act or these Rules the Reporter must ensure that the relevant information is removed from the report or other document or information to be given under the Act, or these Rules, to the person from whom that information is to be withheld.

(2)   Where information is withheld under the Act or these Rules the Reporter

must inform the persons to whom the report or other document or information has been given under the Act, or these Rules, of the identity of the person from whom the information is being withheld, and what information is being withheld from that person.

16 Withholding of specified documents and information by the Reporter
(1) This rule applies where a children's hearing or pre-hearing panel is to be held or has been held in relation to a child by virtue of the Act or these Rules and the Reporter is arranging the hearing, notifying persons of the hearing or issuing information or documents for the hearing or is taking any action required as a consequence of the hearing.
(2) Where the Reporter is carrying out the functions referred to in paragraph (1) and considers that disclosing the whereabouts of the child to whom the children's hearing or pre-hearing panel relates, or of any relevant person, would be likely to cause significant harm to the child or any relevant person the Reporter may withhold that information.
(3) Where the address of the child or relevant person is withheld under paragraph (2) the Reporter will give the address of the child or relevant person as that of the Reporter.

17 Duties of the Reporter where a child is detained under a warrant to secure the attendance of the child
(1) This rule applies where the children's hearing has granted a warrant to secure the attendance of the child at a children's hearing under section 123 (general power to grant warrant to secure attendance) of the Act and the child is being kept in a place of safety under that warrant.
(2) The Reporter must, wherever practicable, arrange the children's hearing to take place on the first working day after the child was first detained in pursuance of the warrant.

18 Notification and provision of information to a young child
(1) This rule applies where, under the Act or these Rules, the Reporter must—
    (a) notify a child of the date, time and place of a children's hearing or pre-hearing panel to be held in relation to that child; or
    (b) provide a child with any information, confirmation, report or other document in relation to a children's hearing or pre-hearing panel.
(2) The Reporter need not so notify the child or provide the information, confirmation, report or other document where, taking account of the child's age and maturity, the child would not be capable of understanding the notification, information, confirmation, report or other document.

[PART 5
Attendance

Authorisation to attend

19 Attendance by individual afforded opportunity to participate at children's hearing
(1) An individual who is to be afforded an opportunity to participate in relation to a children's hearing by virtue of rule 2A is authorised to attend the hearing for a period (or periods) beginning and ending in accordance with paragraph (2).
(2) A period—
    (a) begins at such time as the chairing member considers appropriate, and
    (b) ends when the chairing member decides that the individual's attendance is no longer necessary for the proper consideration of how a decision of the hearing may affect contact or the possibility of contact between the individual and the child.

**20	Attendance by representative of individual afforded opportunity to participate at children's hearing**

(1)	An individual who is authorised to attend a children's hearing by virtue of rule 19 may appoint another person to be the individual's representative.

(2)	The individual's representative is authorised to attend the children's hearing as a person accompanying the individual (see rule 11).

**20A	Attendance by custody officer, etc at pre-hearing panel or children's hearing**

An individual is authorised to attend a pre-hearing panel or children's hearing if—

(a)	another person is in the individual's lawful custody, and

(b)	that other person is attending the panel or hearing.

Attendance by electronic means

**20B	Request to attend pre-hearing panel or hearing by electronic means**

(1)	The Scottish Children's Reporter Administration must take all reasonable steps to enable an individual to attend a pre-hearing panel or children's hearing by electronic means if the conditions in paragraph (2) are met.

(2)	The conditions referred to in paragraph (1) are—

(a)	the individual—

(i)	has a right to attend the pre-hearing panel or children's hearing under section 78(1) of the Act (rights of certain persons to attend children's hearing), or

(ii)	is otherwise entitled to attend by virtue of section 78(2) of the Act,

(b)	the individual has made a request to the Reporter to be allowed to attend the panel or hearing by electronic means, and

(c)	the Reporter is satisfied that either—

(i)	the individual has a good reason for not physically attending the panel or hearing, or

(ii)	the individual would be better able to effectively participate in the panel or hearing by attending by electronic means rather than by physically attending it.

(3)	In this rule—

'children's hearing' includes part of a children's hearing,

'electronic means' includes telephone and video link.

**20C	Requirement that person attend children's hearing only by electronic means**

(1)	Where a pre-hearing panel has determined in accordance with paragraph (2) or (4) that a person, or category of persons, should be allowed to attend a children's hearing only by electronic means—

(a)	the person, or persons, may attend the hearing by electronic means only, and

(b)	the Scottish Children's Reporter Administration must take all reasonable steps to enable the person, or persons, to attend the hearing by electronic means.

(2)	A pre-hearing panel may determine that a person mentioned in paragraph (3) should be allowed to attend a children's hearing only by electronic means if satisfied that the person's physical presence at the hearing, or any part of it, is likely to—

(a)	prevent the hearing from obtaining the views of the child or a relevant person, or

(b)	cause significant distress to the child or a relevant person.

(3)	The persons referred to in paragraph (2) are—

(a)	a relevant person,

(b)	a person representing a relevant person,

(c)	a person who is to authorised to attend the hearing by virtue of rule 19,

(d)   a person representing a person who is authorised to attend the hearing by virtue of rule 19,

(e)   a particular representative of a newspaper or news agency.

(4)   A pre-hearing panel may determine that all representatives of newspapers and news agencies should be allowed to attend a children's hearing only by electronic means if satisfied that the physical presence at the hearing, or any part of it, of any person in that category of persons is likely to—

(a)   prevent the hearing from obtaining the views of the child or a relevant person, or

(b)   cause significant to distress to the child or a relevant person.

(5)   In this rule, 'electronic means' is to be construed in accordance with rule 20B.

Exclusion

20D   Exclusion from children's hearing or pre-hearing panel

(1)   The chairing member may exclude from a pre-hearing panel or children's hearing, for as long as is necessary—

(a)   any person whose conduct at the panel or hearing is—

(i)   violent or abusive, or

(ii)   otherwise so disruptive that, unless the person is excluded, the chairing member would consider it necessary to end or adjourn the panel or hearing,

(b)   any person mentioned in paragraph (3) if, in the chairing member's opinion, the person's presence—

(i)   is preventing, or likely to prevent, the panel or hearing from obtaining the views of a relevant person, or

(ii)   is causing, or likely to cause, significant distress to a relevant person attending the hearing.

(2)   After the exclusion has ended, the chairing member must explain to the person what has taken place in the person's absence.

(3)   The persons referred to in paragraph (1) are—

(a)   a relevant person,

(b)   a person representing a relevant person,

(c)   a representative of a newspaper or news agency.]

PART 6
Arranging Children's Hearings – General

21   Application of Part

This part does not apply where rule 29 or 36 applies.

22   Notification of children's hearings – general

(1)   Where a children's hearing is to be held in relation to a child by virtue of section 69(2) (determination under section 66: referral to children's hearing) or Parts 9 to 11 (children's hearing; proceedings before sheriff; subsequent children's hearings) or 13 (review of compulsory supervision order) of the Act the Reporter must notify the persons mentioned in paragraph (2) of the date, time and place of the children's hearing, as soon as practicable and no later than 7 days before the intended date of the children's hearing.

(2)   Those persons are—

(a)   the child;

(b)   each relevant person;

[(ba) any individual who is to be afforded an opportunity to participate in relation to the children's hearing by virtue of rule 2A;]

(c)   any [other individual] who appears to the Reporter to have or recently have had significant involvement in the upbringing of the child;

   (d)   any appointed safeguarder;

   (e)   the chief social work officer of the relevant local authority for the child;

   (f)   the National Convener.

23 Other information to be given with notification of a children's hearing to the child and each relevant person

The Reporter must when issuing the notice under rule 22(1) to the child and each relevant person also give to the child and each relevant person—

   (a)   information on the availability to the child and relevant person of legal advice;

   (b)   confirmation of the child's duty to attend the children's hearing under section 73 (child's duty to attend children's hearing) of the Act;

   (c)   confirmation of the relevant person's duty to attend the children's hearing under section 74 (relevant person's duty to attend children's hearing) of the Act;

   (d)   confirmation of the right of the child and each relevant person to request a pre-hearing panel or children's hearing to determine whether—

      (i)   a particular individual should be deemed to be a relevant person;

      (ii)   the child or relevant person should be excused from all or part of the children's hearing;

      (iii)   it is likely that the children's hearing will consider making a compulsory supervision order including a secure accommodation authorisation in relation to the child;

   (e)   information on the means by which the child [and each relevant person] may express views to the children's hearing;

   (f)   confirmation of the right of the child and each relevant person to give any report or other document for the consideration of the children's hearing or pre-hearing panel.

[23A Other information to be given with notification of a children's hearing to individuals with an opportunity to participate

The Reporter must when issuing the notice under rule 22(1) to an individual who is to be afforded an opportunity to participate in relation to the children's hearing by virtue of rule 2A also give to the individual—

   (a)   confirmation of the individual's right to attend the hearing in accordance with rule 19,

   (b)   information on the means by which the individual may express views to the hearing,

   (c)   confirmation of the individual's right to give any report or other document for the consideration of the hearing or pre-hearing panel.]

24 Other information to be given with notification of a children's hearing to certain other persons

(1) Where rule 22 applies, when issuing the notification required under that rule the Reporter must also give to any individual other than a relevant person who appears to the Reporter to have or recently have had significant involvement in the upbringing of the child the information mentioned in paragraph (2).

(2) That information is confirmation of the right of the individual to require a pre-hearing panel or a children's hearing to determine whether the individual should be deemed to be a relevant person.

25 Information to be sent to the members of the children's hearing

Wherever practicable 7 days before, and no later than 3 days before, the intended date of the children's hearing the Reporter must give to the three members of the children's hearing notification of the date, time and place of the hearing.

26 Provision of information prior to children's hearing

(1) Where the child or any relevant person wish to give to a children's hearing

to be held by virtue of section 69(2) (determination under section 66: referral to children's hearing) or Parts 9 to 11 (children's hearing; proceedings before sheriff; subsequent children's hearings), or 13 (review of compulsory supervision order) of the Act any report or other document for the consideration of the children's hearing the child or relevant person, as the case may be, must give a copy of the report or other document to the Reporter, so far as practicable, no later than 4 days before the intended date of the hearing.

(2)   Wherever practicable the Reporter must give a copy of any report or other document given under paragraph (1) to the persons mentioned in paragraph (4) (except where that person gave the report or other document to the Reporter) no later than 3 days before the intended date of the hearing.

(3)   Where the Reporter obtains any information (including any views of the child given orally to the Reporter) or document which is material to the children's hearing and has not previously been given to the persons mentioned in paragraph (4) the Reporter must give that information or a copy of the document to those persons as soon as possible before the beginning of the children's hearing.

(4)   Those persons are—
   (a)   the child;
   (b)   each relevant person;
   (c)   any appointed safeguarder;
   (d)   the three members of the children's hearing.

[(5)   Where an individual is to be afforded an opportunity to participate in relation to a children's hearing by virtue of rule 2A, the Reporter must—
   (a)   as soon as practicable before the hearing begins, give the individual a copy of any contact direction that regulates contact between the individual and the child, and
   (b)   give the individual any information (including information contained in a document) that—
      (i)   the Reporter is required by these Rules to give to a relevant person, and
      (ii)   is about—
         (aa)   the individual,
         (bb)   contact between the child and the individual, or
         (cc)   how contact or the possibility of contact between the child and the individual may be affected by a decision of the children's hearing.

(6)   But paragraph (5)(b) does not require the Reporter to give an individual the statement of grounds prepared by the Reporter under section 89 of the Act (Principal Reporter's duty to prepare statement of grounds).

(7)   Where the Reporter is required by these Rules to give a copy of a report or other document to the members of a children's hearing before the hearing begins, the Reporter must also give a copy of the report or other document to—
   (a)   the chief social work officer of the relevant local authority for the child, or
   (b)   if the child is subject to a compulsory supervision order or an interim compulsory supervision order, the chief social work officer of the implementation authority.

(8)   Paragraph (7) does not require the Reporter to give the chief social work officer of an authority a copy of a report or other document prepared, or given to the Reporter, by the authority.]

PART 7
Specific Provision for Arranging Grounds Hearings

27   Additional information to be given to the child and each relevant person in relation to a grounds hearing

(1)   Where the Reporter is required to arrange a grounds hearing, when

notifying the date, time and place of the intended children's hearing under rule 22 the Reporter must give to the persons mentioned in paragraph (2) the information mentioned in paragraph (3).

(2) Those persons are—
(a) the child;
(b) each relevant person; and
(c) any appointed safeguarder (except the information mentioned in paragraph (3)(b)).

(3) That information is—
(a) a copy of the statement of grounds prepared under section 89 (Principal Reporter's duty to prepare statement of grounds) of the Act in relation to the child;
(b) information relating to the retention of the child's DNA and other records kept in connection with the acceptance by the child and relevant person, or the establishment by the sheriff, of an offence specified in an order made by the Scottish Ministers under section 113A(6)(ba) (criminal record certificates) of the Police Act 1997;
(c) a copy of any relevant requirement made by a sheriff under section 156 (3)(a) (determination of appeal) of the Act.

(4) Where the Reporter is required to arrange a grounds hearing, no later than 3 days before the intended date of the hearing the Reporter must also give to the persons mentioned in paragraph (5) the information mentioned in paragraph (6).

(5) Those persons are—
(a) the child;
(b) each relevant person; and
(c) any appointed safeguarder (except the information mentioned in paragraph (6)(a)).

(6) That information is—
(a) a copy of any available report or interim report prepared by a safeguarder under section 33(1)(a) (functions of safeguarder) of the Act;
(b) a copy of any report or information provided by the local authority to the Reporter under section 66(4) (investigation and determination by Principal Reporter) or 69(4) (determination under section 66: referral to children's hearing) of the Act;
(c) a copy of any views of the child given to the Reporter by the child or any other person;
(d) a copy of any other report or other document material to the children's hearing's consideration.

(7) This rule does not apply where rule 29 applies.

28 Information to be given to the members of the grounds hearing

(1) Wherever practicable 7 days before, and no later than 3 days before, the intended date of the grounds hearing the Reporter must give to the three members of the children's hearing a copy of the statement of grounds.

(2) No later than 3 days before the intended date of the grounds hearing the Reporter must give to the three members of the children's hearing—
(a) a copy of any relevant requirement made by a sheriff under section 156 (3)(a) (determination of appeal) of the Act;
(b) a copy of any available report or interim report prepared by a safeguarder under section 33(1)(a) (functions of safeguarder) of the Act;
(c) a copy of any report or information provided by the local authority to the Reporter under section 66(4) (investigation and determination by Principal Reporter) or 69(4) (determination under section 66: referral to children's hearing) of the Act;

(d)   a copy of any views of the child given to the Reporter by the child or any other person;

(e)   a copy of any other report or other document material to the children's hearing's consideration.

(3)   This rule does not apply where rule 29 applies.

29   Provision of information for a grounds hearing where section 69(3) (determination under section 66: referral to children's hearing) of the Act applies or following the making of a child protection order under section 38 (consideration by sheriff: application by local authority only) or 39 (consideration by sheriff: application by local authority or other person) of the Act

(1)   This rule applies where—

(a)   section 69(3) of the Act applies; or

(b)   following receipt of a notice under section 43 (notice of child protection order) of the Act of the making of a child protection order the Reporter is required to arrange a children's hearing under section 69(2) of the Act which is to be held no later than—

(i)   where the order contains an authorisation of the type mentioned in section 37(2)(b) (child protection orders) of the Act, the end of the period of 8 working days beginning on the day [after the day on which] the child was removed to a place of safety; or

(ii)   where the order does not contain such an authorisation, the end of the period of 8 working days beginning on the day [after the day on which] the order was made.

(2)   As soon as practicable before the beginning of the grounds hearing, the Reporter must notify the persons mentioned in paragraph (3) of the date, time and place of the hearing.

(3)   Those persons are—

(a)   the child;

(b)   each relevant person;

(c)   any appointed safeguarder;

[(ca) any individual who is to be afforded an opportunity to participate in relation to the children's hearing by virtue of rule 2A;]

(d)   any [other individual] who appears to the Reporter to have or recently have had significant involvement in the upbringing of the child;

(e)   the three members of the children's hearing;

(f)   the National Convener.

(4)   As soon as practicable before the beginning of the hearing, the Reporter must give to the persons mentioned in paragraph (3)(a) to (c) such of the information mentioned in paragraph (5) as is available.

(5)   That information is the information mentioned in rules 23, 26, 27 and where applicable rule 30.

[(5A)   As soon as practicable before the beginning of the hearing, the Reporter must give to the persons mentioned in paragraph (3)(ca)—

(a)   the information mentioned in rule 23A, and

(b)   any information (including information contained in a document) that—

(i)   the Reporter is required by these Rules to give to a relevant person, and

(ii)   is about—

(aa)   the individual,

(bb)   contact between the child and the individual, or

(cc)   how contact or the possibility of contact between the child and the individual may be affected by a decision of the children's hearing.

(5B)   But paragraph (5A)(b) does not require the Reporter to give an individual the statement of grounds prepared by the Reporter under section 89 of the Act (Principal Reporter's duty to prepare statement of grounds).]

(6) As soon as practicable before the beginning of the hearing, the Reporter must give to the persons mentioned in paragraph (3)(e) the information mentioned in paragraph (7) as is available.

(7) That information is—

(a) the information mentioned in rules 26, 28 and where applicable rule 30;

(b) a copy of any relevant child protection order made in relation to the child under section 38 or 39 of the Act.

(8) As soon as practicable before the beginning of the hearing, the Reporter must give to the persons mentioned in paragraph (3)(d) the information mentioned in rule 24.

[(9) Where the Reporter is required by these Rules to give a copy of a report or other document to the members of a children's hearing before the hearing begins, the Reporter must also give a copy of the report or other document to—

(a) the chief social work officer of the relevant local authority for the child, or

(b) if the child is subject to a compulsory supervision order or an interim compulsory supervision order, the chief social work officer of the implementation authority.

(10) Paragraph (9) does not require the Reporter to give the chief social work officer of an authority a copy of a report or other document prepared, or given to the Reporter, by the authority.]

30 Arranging a grounds hearing where a compulsory supervision order is already in force in relation to the child

(1) This rule applies where a grounds hearing is to be arranged and a compulsory supervision order is already in force in relation to the child to whom the hearing relates.

(2) No later than 3 days before the intended date of the children's hearing the Reporter must in addition to the information to be given under this Part give to the persons mentioned in paragraph (3) the information mentioned in paragraph (4).

(3) Those persons are—

(a) the child;

(b) each relevant person;

(c) any appointed safeguarder;

(d) the three members of the children's hearing.

(4) That information is—

(a) copies of all decisions and reasons for those decisions made by all pre-hearing panels and children's hearings arranged in relation to the child;

(b) a copy of any notice by the implementation authority under section 131 (duty of implementation authority to require review) of the Act.

(5) This rule does not apply where rule 29 applies.

PART 8
Specific Provision for Arranging a Children's Hearing to be held under Section 119 (children's hearing following deferral or proceedings under Part 10) of the Act

31 Provision of information to the child, relevant persons and any appointed safeguarder for a children's hearing to which section 119 (children's hearing following deferral or proceedings under Part 10) of the Act applies

(1) Where the Reporter is required to arrange a children's hearing to which section 119 of the Act applies, as soon as practicable, and at least 3 days before the intended date of the children's hearing, the Reporter must give to the following persons the information mentioned in paragraph (2)—

(a) the child;

(b) each relevant person;

(c) any appointed safeguarder (except the information mentioned in paragraph (2)(a)).

(2) That information is—

(a) any available report or interim report prepared by the safeguarder under section 33(1)(a) or (c) (functions of safeguarder) of the Act or these Rules;

(b) any report prepared by the local authority;

(c) a copy of any relevant direction by a sheriff under section 108 (determination: ground established), 115 (recall: power to refer other grounds) or 117 (new section 67 ground established: sheriff to refer to children's hearing) of the Act;

(d) a copy of any relevant remit by a court under section 49 (reference or remit to children's hearing) of the Criminal Procedure (Scotland) Act 1995;

(e) a copy of any relevant statement by a sheriff under section 12(1B) (sheriff's power to refer case to children's hearing) of the Antisocial Behaviour etc (Scotland) Act 2004;

(f) a copy of any relevant requirement made by a sheriff under section 156 (3)(a) (determination of appeal) of the Act;

(g) copies of all decisions and reasons for those decisions made by all pre-hearing panels and children's hearings arranged in relation to the child;

(h) any other report, document or information relevant to the matter to be considered by the children's hearing.

(3) This rule does not apply where rule 33 applies.

32 Information to be given to the members of the children's hearing to which section 119 (children's hearing following deferral or proceedings under Part 10) of the Act applies

Where rule 31 applies, wherever practicable 7 days before, and no later than 3 days before, the intended date of the children's hearing the Reporter must give to the three members of the children's hearing—

(a) a copy of the statement of grounds;

(b) any available report or interim report prepared by the appointed safeguarder under section 33(1)(a) or (c) (functions of safeguarder) of the Act or these Rules;

(c) any report prepared by the local authority;

(d) a copy of any relevant direction by a sheriff under section 108 (determination: ground established), 115 (recall: power to refer other grounds) or 117 (new section 67 ground established: sheriff to refer to children's hearing) of the Act;

(e) a copy of any relevant remit by a court under section 49 (reference or remit to children's hearing) of the Criminal Procedure (Scotland) Act 1995;

(f) a copy of any relevant statement by a sheriff under section 12(1B) (sheriff's power to refer case to children's hearing) of the Antisocial Behaviour etc (Scotland) Act 2004;

(g) a copy of any relevant requirement made by a sheriff under section 156 (3)(a) (determination of appeal) of the Act;

(h) copies of all decisions and reasons for those decisions made by all pre-hearing panels and children's hearings arranged in relation to the child;

(i) a copy of any decision of a pre-hearing panel or children's hearing held in relation to the child and the reasons for that decision;

(j) any other report, document or information relevant to the matter to be considered by the children's hearing;

(k) a copy of any relevant child protection order made in relation to the child under section 38 (consideration by sheriff: application by local authority only) or 39 (consideration by sheriff: application by local authority or other person) of the Act.

(2) This rule does not apply where rule 33 applies.

33 Provision of information for children's hearing to which section 119 (children's hearing following deferral or proceedings under Part 10) of the Act applies where section 109(7) (determination: power to make interim compulsory supervision order etc), 115(5) (recall: power to refer other grounds) or 117(5) (new section 67 ground established: sheriff to refer to children's hearing) of the Act also applies.

(1) This rule applies where section 109(7), 115(5) or 117(5) F4 of the Act applies.

(2) As soon as practicable before the beginning of the children's hearing, the Reporter must notify the persons mentioned in paragraph (3) of the date, time and place of the hearing.

(3) Those persons are—

  (a) the child;

  (b) each relevant person;

  (c) any appointed safeguarder;

  (d) any individual other than a relevant person who appears to the Reporter to have or recently have had significant involvement in the upbringing of the child;

  (e) the three members of the children's hearing.

(4) As soon as practicable before the beginning of the hearing, the Reporter must give to the persons mentioned in paragraph (3)(a) to (c) such of the information mentioned in rules 23, 26 and 31 as is available.

(5) As soon as practicable before the beginning of the hearing, the Reporter must give to the persons mentioned in paragraph (3)(e) such of the information mentioned in rules 26 and 32 as is available.

(6) As soon as practicable before the beginning of the hearing, the Reporter must give to the persons mentioned in paragraph (3)(d) the information mentioned in rule 24.

PART 9

Specific Provision for Arranging a Children's Hearing to which Section 137 (duty to arrange children's hearing) of the Act applies

34 Provision of information to the child and relevant persons for a children's hearing to which section 137 (duty to arrange children's hearing) of the Act applies

(1) Where the Reporter is required to arrange a children's hearing by virtue of section 137(2) of the Act, as soon as practicable and no later than 7 days before the intended date of the children's hearing the Reporter must also give to the persons mentioned in paragraph (2) the information mentioned in paragraph (3).

(2) Those persons are—

  (a) the child;

  (b) each relevant person;

  (c) any appointed safeguarder.

(3) That information is—

  (a) a copy of the compulsory supervision order to be reviewed;

  (b) copies of all decisions and reasons for those decisions made by all pre-hearing panels and children's hearings arranged in relation to the child;

  (c) a copy of any relevant remit by a court under section 49 (reference or remit to children's hearing) of the Criminal Procedure (Scotland) Act 1995;

  (d) a copy of any relevant requirement by a sheriff under section 12(1A) (sheriff's power to refer case to children's hearing) of the Antisocial Behaviour etc (Scotland) Act 2004;

  (e) a copy of any relevant requirement made by a sheriff under section 156 (3)(a) (determination of appeal) of the Act;

  (f) a copy of any notice by the implementation authority under section 131 (duty of implementation authority to require review) of the Act.

(4)   No later than 3 days before the intended date of the hearing the Reporter must also give to the persons mentioned in paragraph (5) the information mentioned in paragraph (6).

(5)   Those persons are—
   (a)   the child;
   (b)   each relevant person;
   (c)   any appointed safeguarder.

(6)   That information is—
   (a)   a copy of any available report or interim report prepared by an appointed safeguarder under section 33(1)(a) or (c) (functions of safeguarder) of the Act;
   (b)   a copy of any report or other information provided by the local authority under section 137(4) or (5) (duty to arrange children's hearing) of the Act;
   (c)   a copy of any views of the child given to the Reporter by the child or any other person;
   (d)   a copy of any other report or other document material to the children's hearing's consideration.

(7)   This rule does not apply where rule 36 applies.

35   Information to be given to the members of the children's hearing to which section 137 (duty to arrange children's hearing) of the Act applies

(1)   Where rule 34 applies no later than 3 days before the intended date of the children's hearing to which section 137 of the Act applies, the Reporter must give to the three members of that children's hearing—
   (a)   a copy of the compulsory supervision order to be reviewed;
   (b)   copies of all decisions and reasons for those decisions made by all pre-hearing panels and children's hearings arranged in relation to the child;
   (c)   a copy of any relevant remit by a court under section 49 (reference or remit to children's hearing) of the Criminal Procedure (Scotland) Act 1995;
   (d)   a copy of any relevant requirement by a sheriff under section 12(1A) (sheriff's power to refer case to children's hearing) of the Antisocial Behaviour etc (Scotland) Act 2004;
   (e)   a copy of any relevant requirement made by a sheriff under section 156 (3)(a) (determination of appeal) of the Act;
   (f)   a copy of any notice by the implementation authority under section 131 (duty of implementation authority to require review) of the Act;
   (g)   a copy of any available report or interim report prepared by a safeguarder under section 33(1)(a) or (c) (functions of safeguarder) of the Act;
   (h)   a copy of any report or other information provided by the local authority under section 137(4) or (5) (duty to arrange children's hearing) of the Act;
   (i)   a copy of any views of the child given to the Reporter by the child or any other person;
   (j)   a copy of any other report or other document material to the children's hearing's consideration.

(2)   This rule does not apply where rule 36 applies.

36   Provision of information for a review hearing where section 136 (duty to initiate review where child transferred) of the Act applies

(1)   This rule applies where section 136 of the Act applies.

(2)   As soon as practicable before the beginning of the children's hearing, the Reporter must notify the persons mentioned in paragraph (3) of the date, time and place of the hearing.

(3)   Those persons are—
   (a)   the child;
   (b)   each relevant person;
   (c)   any appointed safeguarder;

[(ca) any individual who is to be afforded an opportunity to participate in relation to the children's hearing by virtue of rule 2A;]

(d) any [other individual] who appears to the Reporter to have or recently have had significant involvement in the upbringing of the child;

(e) the three members of the children's hearing;

(f) the National Convener.

(4) As soon as practicable before the beginning of the hearing, the Reporter must give to the persons mentioned in paragraph (3)(a) to (c) such of the information mentioned in rules 23, 26 and 34 as is available.

[(4A) As soon as practicable before the beginning of the hearing, the Reporter must give to the persons mentioned in paragraph (3)(ca)—

(a) the information mentioned in rule 23A, and

(b) any information (including information contained in a document) that—

(i) the Reporter is required by these Rules to give to a relevant person, and

(ii) is about—

(aa) the individual,

(bb) contact between the child and the individual, or

(cc) how contact or the possibility of contact between the child and the individual may be affected by a decision of the children's hearing.

(4B) But paragraph (4A)(b) does not require the Reporter to give an individual the statement of grounds prepared by the Reporter under section 89 of the Act (Principal Reporter's duty to prepare statement of grounds).]

(5) As soon as practicable before the beginning of the hearing, the Reporter must give to the persons mentioned in paragraph (3)(e) such of the information mentioned in rules 26 and 35 as is available.

(6) As soon as practicable before the beginning of the hearing, the Reporter must give to the persons mentioned in paragraph (3)(d) the information mentioned in rule 24.

[(7) Where the Reporter is required by these Rules to give a copy of a report or other document to the members of a children's hearing before the hearing begins, the Reporter must also give a copy of the report or other document to—

(a) the chief social work officer of the relevant local authority for the child, or

(b) if the child is subject to a compulsory supervision order or an interim compulsory supervision order, the chief social work officer of the implementation authority.

(8) Paragraph (7) does not require the Reporter to give the chief social work officer of an authority a copy of a report or other document prepared, or given to the Reporter, by the authority.]

PART 10

Arranging a Grounds Hearing where Grounds Hearing or Review Hearing has Deferred or Application made to the Sheriff

37 Papers to be sent when new grounds presented after grounds hearing deferred or application made to the sheriff

(1) This rule applies where—

(a) a grounds hearing deferred making a decision on whether to make a compulsory supervision order until a subsequent children's hearing under section 91(2) (grounds accepted: powers of grounds hearing) of the Act or directed the Reporter under section 93(2)(a) (grounds not accepted: application to sheriff or discharge) or 94(2)(a) (child or relevant person unable to understand grounds) of the Act to make an application to the sheriff; or

(b) a children's hearing to which section 119 (children's hearing following deferral or proceedings under Part 10) of the Act applies is to be arranged by the Reporter;

and in either case the Reporter is required by virtue of section 69(2) (determination under section 66: referral to children's hearing) of the Act to arrange a further grounds hearing in relation to that child.

(2) In addition to complying with Part 7 of these Rules the Reporter must also comply, so far as practicable, with Part 8.

38 Papers to be sent when new grounds presented after review hearing deferred

(1) This rule applies where—

(a) the Reporter is required by virtue of section 137(2) (duty to arrange children's hearing) of the Act to arrange a children's hearing in relation to the child; and

(b) the Reporter is required by virtue of section 69(2) (determination under section 66: referral to children's hearing) of the Act to arrange a grounds hearing in relation to that child.

(2) In addition to complying with Part 7 of these Rules the Reporter must also comply, so far as practicable, with Part 9.

PART 11

Arranging Other Children's Hearings

39 Arranging a children's hearing under section 45 (review by children's hearing where child in place of safety) or 46 (review by children's hearing where order prevents removal of child) of the Act – 2nd working day hearing

(1) This rule applies where section 45(2) or 46(2) of the Act applies.

(2) As soon as practicable before the beginning of the children's hearing, the Reporter must notify the persons mentioned in paragraph (3) of the date, time and place of the children's hearing.

(3) Those persons are—

(a) the child;

(b) each relevant person;

(c) any individual other than a relevant person who appears to the Reporter to have or recently have had significant involvement in the upbringing of the child;

(d) the person who applied for the child protection order or child assessment order, as the case may be;

(e) the person specified in the child protection order under section 37(2)(a) (child protection orders) of the Act;

(f) any other person prescribed by rules of court for the purposes of section 48 (application for variation or termination) or 49 (notice of application for variation or termination) of the Act;

(g) the three members of the children's hearing;

(h) any appointed safeguarder;

(i) the chief social work officer of the relevant local authority for the child;

(j) the National Convener.

(4) As soon as practicable before the beginning of the hearing, the Reporter must give to the persons mentioned in paragraph (3)(a) to (i) such of the information mentioned in paragraph (5) as is available.

(5) That information is—

(a) a copy of the child protection order;

(b) a copy of the application for the child protection order, or child assessment order, as the case may be;

(c) a copy of any report or other document which is relevant to the children's hearing's consideration.

40 Arranging a children's hearing under section 50 (children's hearing to provide advice to sheriff in relation to application) of the Act

(1) Where a hearing is to be arranged under section 50 of the Act, as soon as practicable after determining to arrange the hearing the Reporter must notify the persons mentioned in paragraph (2) of the date, time and place of the children's hearing.

(2) Those persons are—

(a) the child;

(b) each relevant person;

(c) any individual other than a relevant person who appears to the Reporter to have or recently have had significant involvement in the upbringing of the child;

(d) the person who applied for the child protection order, or child assessment order, as the case may be;

(e) the person who applied for the child protection order to be varied or terminated;

(f) the person specified in the child protection order under section 37(2)(a) (child protection orders) of the Act;

(g) any other person, to whom the applicant for variation or termination of a child protection order is required to give notice of the making of the application, prescribed by rules of court for the purposes of section 48 (application for variation or termination) or 49 (notice of application for variation or termination) of the Act;

(h) the three members of the children's hearing;

(i) any appointed safeguarder;

(j) the chief social work officer of the relevant local authority for the child;

(k) the National Convener.

(3) As soon as practicable before the beginning of the hearing, the Reporter must give to the persons mentioned in paragraph (2)(a) to (j) such of the information mentioned in paragraph (4) as is available.

(4) That information is—

(a) a copy of the child protection order;

(b) a copy of the application for the child protection order or child assessment order, as the case may be;

(c) a copy of the application under section 48 of the Act for the variation or termination of the child protection order;

(d) any other relevant document or information.

41 Provision of information for a children's hearing under section 96(2) (children's hearing to consider need for further interim compulsory supervision order)

(1) This rule applies where a children's hearing under section 96(2) of the Act is to be arranged by the Reporter.

(2) Wherever practicable when issuing notice under rule 22 and in all cases no later than 7 days before the intended date of the children's hearing, the Reporter must give to the persons mentioned in paragraph (3) the information mentioned in paragraph (4).

(3) Those persons are—

(a) the child;

(b) each relevant person;

(c) any appointed safeguarder;

(d) the three members of the children's hearing;

(4) That information is—

(a) copies of all decisions and reasons for those decisions made by all pre-hearing panels and children's hearings arranged in relation to the child;

(b)   a copy of any interim compulsory supervision order made in relation to the child;

(c)   any relevant document or other information for the consideration of the children's hearing.

42   Arranging a children's hearing under section 126 (review of contact direction) of the Act

(1)   Where section 126 of the Act applies, the Reporter must, as soon as practicable and no later than 3 days after the children's hearing mentioned in section 126 (1)(a) of the Act, inform those persons mentioned in paragraph (2) of the place, date and time of any children's hearing to be held under section 126(2)(a) or (b) of the Act and the right of those mentioned in paragraph (2)(a) to (g) to attend that hearing.

(2)   Those persons are—

(a)   the child;

(b)   each relevant person;

(c)   any person other than a relevant person who appears to the Reporter to have or recently have had significant involvement in the upbringing of the child;

(d)   any person who has a contact order regulating contact between the individual and the child;

(e)   any person having a right of contact with the child under a permanence order;

(f)   any person who requested a children's hearing be held under section 126 (2)(b) of the Act;

(g)   any appointed safeguarder;

(h)   the three members of the children's hearing;

(i)   the chief social work officer of the implementation authority or relevant local authority for the child as the case may be;

(j)   the National Convener.

(3)   Wherever possible when informing the persons mentioned in paragraph 2 (a) to (h) and in all cases no later than 3 days prior to the intended date of the children's hearing under section 126 of the Act, the Reporter must give to those persons—

(a)   a copy of the contact direction in the relevant order made by the children's hearing mentioned in section 126(1) of the Act and the reasons for that contact direction;

(b)   any document or part of any document which is relevant to the children's hearing to be held under section 126 of the Act.

(4)   In this rule 'relevant order' means—

(a)   a compulsory supervision order;

(b)   an interim compulsory supervision order;

(c)   a medical examination order.

43   Arranging a children's hearing under section 142 (review of determination that person be deemed a relevant person)

(1)   This rule applies where a children's hearing under section 142(3) of the Act deferred determining the review under section 142(2) of the Act until a subsequent children's hearing.

(2)   Wherever practicable when issuing notice under rule 22 and in all cases as soon as practicable before the beginning of the children's hearing to be held by virtue of section 142 of the Act, the Reporter must give to the persons mentioned in paragraph (3) any relevant document or other information for the consideration of the children's hearing.

(3)   Those persons are—

(a)   the child;

(b)   any relevant person;

(c)   any appointed safeguarder;

(d)   the three members of the children's hearing.

44   Arranging a children's hearing for the purposes of section 49 (reference or remit to children's hearing) of the Criminal Procedure (Scotland) Act 1995

(1)   Where a children's hearing is required to provide a report under section 49 (1)(b), (3) or (6) of the Criminal Procedure (Scotland) Act 1995, as soon as practicable and no later than 7 days before the intended date of the hearing the Reporter must notify the persons mentioned in paragraph (2) of the date, time and place of the hearing.

(2)   Those persons are—
(a)   the child;
(b)   each relevant person;
(c)   any appointed safeguarder;
(d)   the three members of the children's hearing;
(e)   the chief social work officer of the relevant local authority for the child;
(f)   the National Convener.

(3)   As soon as practicable and no later than 3 days before the intended date of the hearing, the Reporter must give to the persons mentioned in paragraph (2)(a) to (c) such of the information mentioned in paragraph (4) as is available.

(4)   That information is—
(a)   a copy of any relevant remit by a court under section 49 of the Criminal Procedure (Scotland) Act 1995;
(b)   copies of all decisions and reasons for those decisions made by all pre-hearing panels and children's hearings arranged in relation to the child;
(c)   confirmation of the child's duty to attend the children's hearing under section 73 (child's duty to attend children's hearing) of the Act;
(d)   confirmation of the relevant person's duty to attend the children's hearing under section 74 (relevant person's duty to attend children's hearing) of the Act;
(e)   information on the means by which the child may express views to the children's hearing;
(f)   confirmation of the right of the child and each relevant person to give any report or other document for the consideration of the children's hearing.

(5)   As soon as practicable and no later than 3 days before the intended date of the hearing, the Reporter must give to the persons mentioned in paragraph (2)(d) such of the information mentioned in paragraph (4)(a) and (b) as is available.

PART 12
Pre-hearing Panels and Determination of Matters which may be Referred to Pre-hearing Panels

[44A   Specification of matters that may be determined by pre-hearing panel
Whether a person should be allowed to attend a children's hearing only by electronic means (see rule 20C) is specified for the purpose of these Rules as a matter that may be determined by pre-hearing panels.]

45   Arranging pre-hearing panel – determination of relevant person status

(1)   Where a pre-hearing panel is to be arranged by virtue of section 79(2)(a) or (b) (referral of certain matters for pre-hearing determination) of the Act (whether or not it is also to determine any matter mentioned in section [79(2)(ba) or (bb), (3) or (5A)]), wherever practicable at least 5 days before the intended date of the pre-hearing panel the Reporter must give notice of the pre-hearing panel to the persons mentioned in paragraph (2).

(2)   Those persons are—
(a)   the child;
(b)   each relevant person;

(c) any individual requesting a determination that they be deemed a relevant person under section 79(2)(a) of the Act;

(d) any individual other than a relevant person who appears to the Reporter to have or recently have had significant involvement in the upbringing of the child;

(e) any appointed safeguarder;

(f) the three members of the pre-hearing panel;

(g) the National Convener.

(3) The notice must inform—

(a) the persons mentioned in paragraph (2) of the date, time and place of the pre-hearing panel;

(b) the persons mentioned in paragraph (2)(a) to (e) that they—

(i) have the right to attend the pre-hearing panel;

(ii) [subject to paragraph (3A)(b),] may make representations (orally or in writing) to the pre-hearing panel relating to whether the individual mentioned in paragraph (2)(c) or (d) should be deemed to be a relevant person;

(iii) may give any report or other document relevant to that matter for the consideration of the pre-hearing panel;

(iv) have the right to request that the Reporter takes all reasonable steps to enable the child, each relevant person, or the individual in question, as the case may be, to attend the pre-hearing panel by way of telephone, through video link or by using any other method of communication; and

(c) the individual mentioned in paragraph (2)(c) or (d) that the individual, if deemed a relevant person under section 81(3) (determination of claim that person be deemed a relevant person) of the Act after that determination has been made, may request the pre-hearing panel to determine any matter mentioned in section 79(3) of the Act.

[(3ZA) Where the pre-hearing panel will also determine in respect of an individual a matter referred under section 79(2)(ba) or (bb) of the Act, the notice must—

(a) state that fact and the name of the person,

(b) inform the individual mentioned in paragraph (2)(c) or (d) that the individual will not be entitled to take part in any discussion on the matter referred under section 79(2)(ba) or (bb) of the Act unless the individual is deemed to be a relevant person,

(c) inform any individual whose status as a relevant person has been referred under section 79(5A) of the Act that the individual will not be entitled to take part in any discussion on the matter referred under section 79(2)(ba) or (bb) of the Act unless the individual continues to be deemed to be a relevant person,

(d) inform the persons mentioned in paragraph (2)(a), (b) or (e), subject to sub-paragraph (c), that they may—

(i) make representations (orally or in writing) to the pre-hearing panel in relation to the matter referred under section 79(2)(ba) or (bb) of the Act, and

(ii) give any report or other document relevant to that matter for the consideration of the pre-hearing panel.]

[(3A) Where the pre-hearing panel will also determine a matter referred under section 79(5A)(a) or (b) (power to determine that deeming of person as relevant person to end) of the Act, the notice must—

(a) state that fact and the name of the individual whose status as a relevant person has been referred under section 79(5A) of the Act;

(b) inform the individual mentioned in sub-paragraph (a) that, notwithstanding paragraph (3)(b)(ii) above, the individual will not be entitled to take part in any discussion on matters referred under section 79(2)(a) or (b) of the Act unless they continue to be deemed to be a relevant person; and

(c) inform the persons mentioned in paragraph (2)(a), (b) or (e) that they may—

(i) make representations (orally or in writing) to the pre-hearing panel in relation to the matter referred under section 79(5A) of the Act; and

(ii) give any report or other document relevant to that matter for the consideration of the pre-hearing panel.]

(4) Where the pre-hearing panel will also determine any other matter referred under section 79(2)(c) of the Act the notice must state that fact and—

(a) inform the individual mentioned in paragraph (2)(c) or (d) that the individual will not be entitled to take part in any discussion on that matter unless they are deemed to be a relevant person;

[(aa) inform any individual whose status as a relevant person has been referred under section 79(5A) of the Act that the individual will not be entitled to take part in any discussion on the matter referred under section 79 (2)(c) unless they continue to be deemed to be a relevant person; and]

(b) inform the persons mentioned in [paragraph] (2)(a), (b) or (e) [, subject to sub-paragraph (aa),] that they may—

(i) make representations (orally or in writing) to the pre-hearing panel in relation to any matter to be determined by the panel; and

(ii) give any report or other document relevant to those matters for the consideration of the pre-hearing panel.

[(5) Paragraph (6) applies where an individual is both—

(a) a person in respect of whom a matter has been referred to the pre-hearing panel under section 79(2)(ba) or (bb) of the Act, and

(b) a person mentioned in paragraph (2)(c) or (d).

(6) The notice—

(a) is not to inform the individual referred to in paragraph (5) of the things that it would otherwise be required to by virtue of paragraph (3ZA), and

(b) is instead to inform the individual that the individual may—

(i) make representations (orally or in writing) to the pre-hearing panel relating to the matter in respect of the individual that has been referred under section 79(2)(ba) or (bb) of the Act, and

(ii) give any report or other document relevant to that matter for the consideration of the pre-hearing panel.

(7) Paragraph (8) applies where an individual is both—

(a) a person in respect of whom a matter has been referred to the pre-hearing panel under section 79(2)(ba) or (bb) of the Act, and

(b) a person whose status as a relevant person has been referred to the pre-hearing panel under section 79(5A) of the Act.

(8) The notice—

(a) is not to inform the individual referred to in paragraph (7) of the things that it would otherwise be required to by virtue of paragraph (3ZA), and

(b) is instead to inform the individual that—

(i) the individual may make representations (orally or in writing) to the pre-hearing panel relating to the matter in respect of the individual that has been referred under section 79(2)(ba) or (bb) of the Act,

(ii) the individual may give any report or other document relevant to that matter for the consideration of the pre-hearing panel,

(iii) if a matter has been referred under section 79(2)(ba) or (bb) of the Act in respect of another person too, the individual will not be entitled to take part in any discussion on that matter unless the individual continues to be deemed to be a relevant person.]

[45A Arranging pre-hearing panels to determinate opportunity to participate – notice to persons other than person seeking opportunity

(1) Where a pre-hearing panel is to be arranged by virtue of section 79(2)(ba) or (bb), but not by virtue of section 79(2)(a), (b) or (5A), of the Act (whether or not it is also to determine any matter mentioned in section 79(3) of the Act), wherever practicable at least 5 days before the intended date of the pre-hearing panel the

Reporter must give notice of the pre-hearing panel to the persons mentioned in paragraph (2).

(2)   Those persons are—

    (a)   the child,

    (b)   each relevant person,

    (c)   any appointed safeguarder,

    (d)   the members of the pre-hearing panel,

    (e)   the National Convener.

(3)   The notice must inform—

    (a)   the persons mentioned in paragraph (2) of the date, time and place of the pre-hearing panel,

    (b)   the persons mentioned in paragraph (2)(a) to (d)—

        (i)   that the pre-hearing panel is to determine in respect of an individual a matter referred under section 79(2)(ba) or (bb) of the Act,

        (ii)   of the name of the individual,

    (c)   the persons mentioned in paragraph (2)(a) to (c) that they—

        (i)   have the right to attend the pre-hearing panel,

        (ii)   may make representations (orally or in writing) to the pre-hearing panel relating to the matter referred under section 79(2)(ba) or (bb) of the Act,

        (iii)   may give any report or document relevant to that matter for the consideration of the pre-hearing panel,

        (iv)   have the right to request that the Reporter takes all reasonable steps to enable the individual in question to attend the pre-hearing panel by way of telephone, through video link or by using any other method of communication.

(4)   Where the pre-hearing panel will also determine a matter referred under section 79(2)(c) of the Act, the notice must—

    (a)   state that fact,

    (b)   inform the persons mentioned in paragraph (2)(a) to (c) that they may—

        (i)   make representations (orally or in writing) to the pre-hearing panel in relation to any matter to be determined by the panel, and

        (ii)   give any report or other document relevant to those matters for the consideration of the panel.]

[45B   Arranging pre-hearing panels to determine opportunity to participate – notice to person seeking opportunity

(1)   Where a pre-hearing panel is to be arranged to determine in respect of an individual a matter referred under section 79(2)(ba) or (bb) of the Act (whether or not the panel is to be arranged for another purpose too), the Reporter must give the individual notice of the pre-hearing panel.

(2)   The notice must inform the individual that the individual—

    (a)   has the right to attend the pre-hearing panel,

    (b)   may make representations (orally or in writing) to the pre-hearing panel relating to the matter in respect of the individual that has been referred under section 79(2)(ba) or (bb) of the Act,

    (c)   may give any report or document relevant to that matter for the consideration of the pre-hearing panel,

    (d)   has the right to request that the Reporter takes all reasonable steps to enable the individual to attend the pre-hearing panel by way of telephone, through video link or by using any other method of communication.

(3)   Notice of a pre-hearing panel is not to be given to an individual under this rule if the individual is to be given notice of the pre-hearing panel—

    (a)   under rule 45, on account of being a person mentioned in paragraph (2)(b) to (d) of that rule, or

    (b)   under rule 45A or 46A, on account of being a relevant person.]

46   Arranging pre-hearing panels to determine matter in section 79(3) (referral of certain matters for pre-hearing determination) of the Act

(1)   Where a pre-hearing panel is to be arranged by virtue only of section 79(2)(c) of the Act wherever practicable at least 5 days before the intended date of the pre-hearing panel the Reporter must give notice of the pre-hearing panel to the persons mentioned in paragraph (2).

(2)   Those persons are—

   (a)   the child;

   (b)   each relevant person;

   (c)   any appointed safeguarder;

   (d)   the three members of the pre-hearing panel;

   (e)   the National Convener.

(3)   The notice must inform—

   (a)   the persons mentioned in paragraph (2) of the date, time and place of the pre-hearing panel;

   (b)   the persons mentioned in paragraph (2)(a) to (d) of the matters to be determined by the pre-hearing panel; and

   (c)   the persons mentioned in paragraph (2)(a) to (c) that they—

      (i)   have the right to attend the pre-hearing panel;

      (ii)   may make representations (orally or in writing) to the pre-hearing panel;

      (iii)   may give any report or other document for the consideration of the pre-hearing panel;

      (iv)   have the right to request that the Reporter takes all reasonable steps to enable the child and each relevant person to attend the pre-hearing panel by way of telephone, through video link or by using any other method of communication.

[46A   Arranging pre-hearing panels to determine whether deeming of relevant person to end

(1)   Where a pre-hearing panel is to be arranged by virtue of section 79(5A), but not by virtue of section 79(2)(a) or (b), of the Act (whether or not it is also to determine any matter mentioned in section [79(2)(ba) or (bb) or (3)), wherever practicable at least 5 days before the intended date of the pre-hearing panel the Reporter must give notice of the pre-hearing panel to the persons mentioned in paragraph (2).

(2)   Those persons are—

   (a)   the child;

   (b)   each relevant person;

   (c)   any appointed safeguarder;

   (d)   the three members of the pre-hearing panel;

   (e)   the National Convener.

(3)   The notice must inform—

   (a)   the persons mentioned in paragraph (2) of the date, time and place of the pre-hearing panel;

   (b)   the persons mentioned in paragraph (2)(a) to (d) that the pre-hearing panel is to determine whether an individual deemed to be a relevant person by virtue of section 81 of the Act should continue to be deemed to be a relevant person in relation to the child and the name of that individual; and

   (c)   the persons mentioned in paragraph (2)(a) to (c) that they—

      (i)   have the right to attend the pre-hearing panel;

      (ii)   may make representations (orally or in writing) to the pre-hearing panel relating to whether the individual whose status as a relevant person has been referred under section 79(5A) should continue to be deemed to be a relevant person;

      (iii)   may give any report or other document relevant to that matter for the consideration of the pre-hearing panel;

(iv) have the right to request that the Reporter takes all reasonable steps to enable the child and each relevant person to attend the pre-hearing panel by way of telephone, through video link or by using any other method of communication.

(4) Where [the pre-hearing panel] will also determine any matter referred under section 79(2)(c) the notice must state that fact and—

(a) inform the individual whose status as a relevant person has been referred under section 79(5A) that the individual will not be entitled to take part in any discussion on the matter referred under section 79(2)(c) unless that individual continues to be deemed a relevant person; and

(b) inform the persons mentioned in paragraph (2)(a) to (c) that, subject to sub-paragraph (a), they may—

(i) make representations (orally or in writing) to the pre-hearing panel in relation to any matter to be determined by the panel; and

(ii) give any report or other document relevant to those matters for the consideration of the pre-hearing panel.]

[(5) Where the pre-hearing panel will also determine in respect of a person a matter referred under section 79(2)(ba) or (bb) of the Act, the notice must—

(a) state that fact and the name of the person,

(b) inform the individual whose status as a relevant person has been referred under section 79(5A) of the Act that the individual will not be entitled to take part in any discussion on the matter referred under section 79(2)(ba) or (bb) of the Act unless the individual continues to be deemed a relevant person,

(c) inform the persons mentioned in paragraph (2)(a) to (c) that, subject to sub-paragraph (b), they may—

(i) make representations (orally or in writing) to the pre-hearing panel in relation to the matter referred under section 79(2)(ba) or (bb) of the Act, and

(ii) give any report or other document relevant to that matter for the consideration of the pre-hearing panel.

(6) Paragraph (7) applies where an individual is both—

(a) a person in respect of whom a matter has been referred to the pre-hearing panel under section 79(2)(ba) or (bb) of the Act, and

(b) a person whose status as a relevant person has been referred to the pre-hearing panel under section 79(5A) of the Act.

(7) The notice—

(a) is not to inform the individual referred to in paragraph (6) of the thing that it would otherwise be required to by virtue of paragraph (5)(b), and

(b) is instead to inform the individual that—

(i) the individual may make representations (orally or in writing) to the pre-hearing panel relating to the matter in respect of the individual that has been referred under section 79(2)(ba) or (bb) of the Act,

(ii) the individual may give any report or other document relevant to that matter for the consideration of the pre-hearing panel,

(iii) if a matter has been referred to the pre-hearing panel under section 79(2)(ba) or (bb) of the Act in respect of another person too, notwithstanding paragraph (5)(c)(i), the individual will not be entitled to take part in any discussion on that matter unless the individual continues to be deemed a relevant person.]

47 Provision of information to pre-hearing panel

(1) Where any person [with a right to make representation], wishes to make written representations or give any report or other document for the consideration of the pre-hearing panel, as soon as possible and wherever practicable no later than 4 days before the intended date of the pre-hearing panel, that person must give those representations, report or other document to the Reporter.

(2) Subject to the provisions of paragraphs (6) and (7), where the Reporter

receives any representations, report or other document under paragraph (1), wherever practicable no later than 3 days before the intended date for the pre-hearing panel the Reporter must give a copy of that information to the persons mentioned in rule 45(2)(a) to (f) [, 46(2)(a) to (d) or 46A(2)(a) to (d)], as the case may be, (unless that person gave the information in question to the Reporter).

(3) Where any person [with a right to make representation] is unable to attend the pre-hearing panel and wishes to make oral representations for the consideration of the pre-hearing panel that person may make those representations to the Reporter.

(4) The Reporter must make a record of any representations given under paragraph (3) and give a copy of that record to those persons mentioned in rule 45(2)(a) to (f) [, 46(2)(a) to (d) or 46A(2)(a) to (d)], as the case may be, as soon as possible before the beginning of the pre-hearing panel.

(5) As soon as possible before the beginning of the pre-hearing panel the Reporter must also give the persons mentioned in rule 45(2)(a) to (f) [, 46(2)(a) to (d) or 46A(2)(a) to (d)], as the case may be, any other document, or part of a document, that is relevant to the issues to be determined by the pre-hearing panel and is in the possession of the Reporter.

(6) Where the matter referred to a pre-hearing panel concerns the question of whether a particular person should be deemed to be a relevant person [or continue to be deemed to be a relevant person], the obligation under paragraph (2) shall only apply to such material as the Reporter considers relevant to the question of whether that person should be deemed to be a relevant person [or continue to be deemed to be a relevant person].

[(6A) Where a matter in respect of an individual has been referred to the pre-hearing panel under section 79(2)(ba) or (bb) of the Act, and the individual is not a person referred to in paragraph (8)(a), the Reporter must give to the individual any information (including information contained in a document) that—

(a)   the Reporter is required by this rule to give to a relevant person, and

(b)   is relevant to the matter that has been referred in respect of the individual.]

(7) The provisions of Part 19 of these Rules apply to any representations, report or other document received by the Reporter under paragraph (1) as they apply to any document relating to a children's hearing.

[(8) In this rule, references to a person with a right to make representations refer—

(a)   to the persons mentioned in paragraph (2) of whichever of rules 45, 45A, 46 or 46A applies to the pre-hearing panel, apart from—

(i)   the members of the pre-hearing panel, and

(ii)   the National Convener, and

(b)   to any individual in respect of whom a matter has been referred to the pre-hearing panel under section 79(2)(ba) or (bb) of the Act.]

[47A   Procedure at pre-hearing panel – general

(1) At the beginning of a pre-hearing panel, the chairing member must explain the purpose of the pre-hearing panel.

(2) In relation to each matter that is to be determined by a pre-hearing panel, the chairing member must invite each of the following individuals who is in attendance to make representations—

(a)   the child,

(b)   any relevant person.

(3) Where a pre-hearing panel is determining whether to deem an individual who is in attendance to be a relevant person, the chairing member must invite the individual to make representations in relation to that matter.

(4) Where a pre-hearing panel is determining whether an individual should be afforded an opportunity to participate in relation to a children's hearing by virtue

of rule 2A, the chairing member must invite the individual who is in attendance to make representations in relation to that matter.

(5)   The chairing member of a pre-hearing panel may invite any person who is in attendance to make representations in relation to any matter that is to be determined by the panel if the panel considers it appropriate to do so.

(6)   A person invited by the chairing member to make representations to a pre-hearing panel may—

   (a)   do so orally or in writing,
   (b)   submit any document to the panel that the person wishes.

(7)   Each member of a pre-hearing panel must state, in relation to each matter that the panel is to determine—

   (a)   the member's determination on the matter, and
   (b)   the reasons for it.

(8)   Once the members of a pre-hearing panel have stated their individual determinations on each matter in accordance with paragraph (7), the chairing member must confirm—

   (a)   the panel's determination on each matter, and
   (b)   the reasons for each determination.

(9)   Where a pre-hearing panel has made a determination about whether an individual should be, or should continue to be, deemed to be a relevant person, the chairing member must inform the following persons of their right to appeal that determination under section 160 of the Act—

   (a)   the individual in question,
   (b)   the child,
   (c)   each relevant person.]

48   Procedure at pre-hearing panel determination of whether to deem an individual to be a relevant person

[…]

(2)   The pre-hearing panel, despite a referral not having been made under section 79(2) (referral of certain matters for pre-hearing determination) of the Act, must consider whether to deem an individual, who is present at the pre-hearing panel, to be a relevant person on the request of—

   (a)   the child;
   (b)   any relevant person;
   (c)   the individual in question.

(3)   Where the pre-hearing panel is to consider whether to deem an individual to be a relevant person under paragraph (2) the provisions of the Act (other than section [80 (determination of matter referred to under section 79)) and these Rules apply as if the matter had been referred under section 79 of the Act.

[…]

[48A   Procedure at pre-hearing panel – determination of whether individual to be afforded opportunity to participate

(1)   This rule applies only in relation to a pre-hearing panel that is arranged in connection with a children's hearing that is to be held by virtue of an enactment mentioned in rule 2A(1).

(2)   The pre-hearing panel, despite a referral not having been made under section 79(2) of the Act (referral of certain matters for pre-hearing determination), must determine whether an individual, who is present at the pre-hearing panel, meets the criteria in rule 2A(3) to be afforded an opportunity to participate in relation to the children's hearing on the request of—

   (a)   the child,
   (b)   any relevant person,
   (c)   the individual in question.

(3)   Where the pre-hearing panel is to make a determination by virtue of paragraph (2), the provisions of the Act (other than section 80 (determination of matter

referred under section 79)) and these Rules apply as if the matter had been referred under section 79(2)(ba) of the Act.]

[Rules 49 and 49A omitted by SSI 2021/68 from 26 July 2021.]

50 Notice of pre-hearing panel determination
(1) As soon as practicable after the pre-hearing panel the Reporter must give notice of any determination of the pre-hearing panel and the reasons for that determination to the persons mentioned in paragraph (2) as regards—
  (a) whether any individual should or should not be deemed to be a relevant person;
  [(b) whether an individual should continue to be deemed to be a relevant person in relation to the child; and
  (c) any other matter referred to the pre-hearing panel.]
(2) Those persons are—
  (a) the child;
  (b) each relevant person;
  (c) any appointed safeguarder;
  (d) the chief social work officer of the relevant local authority for the child.
(3) Where a pre-hearing panel determined that an individual is not to be deemed a relevant person, as soon as practicable after the pre-hearing panel the Reporter must give notice of that determination to the individual in question and the reasons for that determination.
[(3A) Where the pre-hearing panel determined that an individual is no longer to be deemed a relevant person, as soon as practicable after the pre-hearing panel the Reporter must give notice of that determination to the individual in question and the reasons for that determination.]
(4) When issuing the notice under paragraph (1) [, (3) or (3A)] the Reporter must also give notice of any relevant right of appeal of the recipient of the notice under section 160 (appeal to sheriff against relevant person determination) of the Act.
[(4A) When a pre-hearing panel has determined whether an individual is to be afforded an opportunity to participate in relation to a children's hearing by virtue of rule 2A, as soon as practicable after the pre-hearing panel, the Reporter must give notice of that determination to the individual and the reasons for that determination.]
(5) Where the pre-hearing panel has determined that a child or relevant person is to be excused from attending all or part of the children's hearing, the Reporter must inform the child and relevant person as the case may be, that—
  (a) the child or relevant person has been excused;
  (b) the child or relevant person has the right to attend the hearing; and
  (c) they have the right to request that the Reporter make arrangements to enable the child, or the relevant person, as the case may be, to attend the children's hearing or part of the children's hearing by way of telephone, video link or any other method of communication.
(6) Where the pre-hearing panel has determined that it is likely that a children's hearing will consider making a compulsory supervision order or an interim compulsory supervision order including a secure accommodation authorisation in relation to the child, the Reporter must, as soon as possible after that determination, notify the Scottish Legal Aid Board of that fact and the name and address of the child.
(7) Where the pre-hearing panel has determined that—
  (a) for the purpose of enabling a child or any relevant person to participate effectively in the proceedings before the children's hearing it may be necessary that the child or relevant person be represented by a solicitor or counsel; and
  (b) it is unlikely that the child or relevant person will arrange to be represented by a solicitor or counsel,

the Reporter must, as soon as possible after that determination, notify the Scottish Legal Aid Board of that determination and the reasons for it and the name and address of the child or relevant person.

**51	Provision of information to persons deemed to be relevant persons**
Where the pre-hearing panel deems a person to be a relevant person under section 81(3) (determination of claim that person be deemed a relevant person) of the Act, as soon as practicable after that determination, the Reporter must give to that person all information given under these Rules which is to be given to each relevant person.

**52	Notification of matter to be determined under section 79 (referral of certain matters for pre-hearing determination) where not practicable to arrange a pre-hearing panel before the date fixed for the children's hearing**
(1)	Where section 80(3) (determination of matter referred under section 79) of the Act applies, as soon as practicable, the Reporter must give notice to the persons mentioned in paragraph (2) that the matter to be referred to a pre-hearing panel under section 79(2) [or 79(5A)] of the Act will be referred to the children's hearing.
(2)	Those persons are—
    (a)	the child;
    (b)	each relevant person;
    (c)	any individual requesting a determination that they be deemed a relevant person;
    (d)	any individual other than a relevant person who appears to the Reporter to have or recently have had significant involvement in the upbringing of the child;
    (e)	any appointed safeguarder;
    (f)	the three members of the children's hearing.
(3)	The notice under paragraph (1) must inform—
    (a)	the persons mentioned in paragraph (2)(a) to (e)—
        (i)	of the date, time and place of the children's hearing;
        (ii)	of the matters to be determined by the children's hearing by virtue of section 80(3) of the Act;
        (iii)	that they have the right to attend that part of the children's hearing;
        (iv)	that they have the right to request that the Reporter takes all reasonable steps to enable the child, relevant person, or the person mentioned in paragraph (2)(c) or (d), as the case may be, to attend the children's hearing by way of telephone, through video link or by using any other method of communication;
        (v)	that they may make representations (orally or in writing) to the children's hearing relating to any matter referred under section 79 of the Act, except where paragraph (4) [(5) or (6)] applies;
        (vi)	that they may give any report or other document relevant to that matter for the consideration of the children's hearing; and
    (b)	the individual mentioned in paragraph (2)(c) or (d), that the individual, where deemed to be a relevant person under section 81(3) (determination of claim that person be deemed a relevant person) of the Act, may request the children's hearing to determine any matter mentioned in section 79(3) of the Act.
[(4)	Where the children's hearing will determine a matter referred under section 79(5A) of the Act the notice must inform the individual whose status as a relevant person has been referred under that section that the individual will not be entitled to take part in any discussion on any matter also referred under section 79(2) unless the individual continues to be deemed to be a relevant person.
(5)	Where the children's hearing will determine any matter referred under section 79(2)(c) of the Act the notice must inform the individual mentioned in paragraph (2)(c) or (d) that the individual will not be entitled to take part in any

discussion on that matter unless they are deemed to be a relevant person or they continue to be deemed to be a relevant person.]

[(6)   In the circumstance described by paragraph (7), the notice—

(a)   is not to inform the individual referred to in that paragraph of the thing that it would otherwise be required to by virtue of paragraph (4) or (as the case may be) (5),

(b)   is instead to inform the individual that, unless the individual is deemed or continues to be deemed a relevant person, the individual will not be entitled to take part in any discussion on any matter that has been referred under section 79(2) of the Act other than a matter that has been referred in respect of the individual.

(7)   The circumstance referred to in paragraph (6) is that the children's hearing will determine in respect of the same individual—

(a)   a matter that has been referred under section 79(2)(ba) or (bb) of the Act, and

(b)   a matter that has been referred under section 79(2)(a), (b) or (5A) of the Act.]

[52A   Notification of matter to be determined under section 79 person seeking opportunity to participate

(1)   Where—

(a)   section 80(3) of the Act (determination of matter under section 79) applies,

(b)   the matter being referred to the children's hearing (or one of them) is a matter mentioned in section 79(2)(ba) or (bb) of the Act, and

(c)   the individual in respect of whom the matter has been referred is not a person to whom notice must be given under rule 52,

the Reporter must give notice of the hearing to the individual.

(2)   The notice must inform the individual—

(a)   of the date, time and place of the hearing,

(b)   that the individual—

(i)   has the right to attend that part of the children's hearing,

(ii)   has the right to request that the Reporter takes all reasonable steps to enable the individual to attend the children's hearing by way of telephone, through video link or by using any other method of communication,

(iii)   may make representations (orally or in writing) to the hearing relating to the matter in respect of the individual that has been referred under section 79(2)(ba) or (bb) of the Act,

(iv)   may give any report or other document relevant to that matter for the consideration of the hearing.]

53   Provision of information relating to matter referred under section 79 (referral of certain matters for pre-hearing determination) of the Act to the children's hearing

(1)   Where any person mentioned in rule 52(2)(a) to (e) wishes to make written representations or give any report or other document for the consideration of the children's hearing, as soon as practicable, and wherever practicable no later than 4 days before the date fixed for the children's hearing that person must give those representations, report or other document to the Reporter.

(2)   Where the Reporter receives any representations, reports or other document under paragraph (1), as soon as practicable before the beginning of the children's hearing, the Reporter must give a copy of that information to the persons mentioned in rule 52(2) (unless that person gave the information in question to the Reporter).

(3)   Where any person mentioned in rule 52(2)(a) to (e) is unable to attend the children's hearing and wishes to make oral representations for the consideration of the children's hearing that person may make those representations to the Reporter.

(4) The Reporter must make a record of any representations given under paragraph (3) and give a copy of that record to those persons mentioned in rule 52(2) as soon as practicable before the beginning of the children's hearing.

(5) As soon as practicable before the beginning of the children's hearing the Reporter must also give the persons mentioned in rule 52(2) any other document or part of a document that is relevant to the issues under section 79 of the Act to be determined by the children's hearing and is in the possession of the Reporter.

[(6) Where the children's hearing will determine in respect of an individual a matter which has been referred under section 79(2)(ba) or (bb) of the Act, and the individual is not a person mentioned in rule 52(2), the Reporter must give to the individual any information (including information contained in a document) that—

(a)　the Reporter is required by this rule to give to a relevant person, and

(b)　is either—

(i)　relevant to the matter under section 79(2)(ba) or (bb) of the Act that has been referred in respect of the individual, or

(ii)　is otherwise about—

(aa)　the individual,

(bb)　contact between the child and the individual, or

(cc)　how contact or the possibility of contact between the child and the individual may be affected by a decision of the children's hearing.

(7) But paragraph (6) does not require the Reporter to give an individual the statement of grounds prepared by the Reporter under section 89 of the Act (Principal Reporter's duty to prepare statement of grounds).]

54 Children's hearing determining a matter referred under section 79 (referral of certain matters for pre-hearing determination) of the Act

Where by virtue of section 80(3) (determination of matter referred under section 79) of the Act the children's hearing is to determine a matter referred under section 79 of the Act—

(a)　rules [47A (other than paragraph (1)) to 48A] apply; and

(b)　references in those rules to the pre-hearing panel are to be read as references to the children's hearing.

55 Children's hearings' power to determine whether a person should be deemed to be a relevant person where no referral made under section 79 (referral of certain matters for pre-hearing determination) of the Act

(1) A children's hearing held in relation to a child by virtue of section 69(2) (determination under section 66: referral to children's hearing) or Part 9 to 11 (children's hearing; proceedings before sheriff; subsequent children's hearings) or 13 (review of compulsory supervision order) of the Act, despite a referral not having been made under section 79 of the Act, must consider whether to deem an individual who is present at the hearing to be a relevant person on the request of—

(a)　the child;

(b)　any relevant person;

(c)　the individual in question.

(2) Where the children's hearing is to consider whether to deem an individual to be a relevant person under paragraph (1) the provisions of the Act (other than section 80 (determination of matter referred under section 79) and these Rules apply as if the matter had been referred under section 79 of the Act.

[55A Children's hearings' power to determine whether person to be afforded opportunity to participate where no referral made under section 79 of the Act

(1) A children's hearing held in relation to a child by virtue of an enactment mentioned in paragraph (1) of rule 2A must determine whether an individual who is present at the hearing meets the criteria in paragraph (3) of that rule to be afforded an opportunity to participate in relation to the hearing on the request of—

(a)   the child,
(b)   any relevant person,
(c)   the individual in question.

(2)   Where the children's hearing is to make a determination under paragraph (1), the provisions of the Act (other than section 80) and these Rules apply as if the matter had been referred under section 79(2)(ba) of the Act.]

PART 13
Appointment of Safeguarder and Safeguarders' Reports

56   Appointment of safeguarder by pre-hearing panel or children's hearing

(1)   Where the pre-hearing panel appoint a safeguarder for the child the Reporter must—

(a)   inform the safeguarder of the date, time and place (if known) of the next children's hearing to be held in relation to the child; and

(b)   give to the safeguarder the information mentioned in paragraph (3), as soon as practicable before the intended date of the hearing.

(2)   Where the children's hearing appoint a safeguarder for the child the Reporter must—

(a)   inform the safeguarder of the date, time and place (if known) of the next children's hearing to be held in relation to the child, or the hearing to take place under Part 10 (proceedings before sheriff) of the Act, as the case may be; and

(b)   give to the safeguarder the information mentioned in paragraph (3) as soon as practicable and no later than 7 days before the intended date of the hearing.

(3)   That information is—

(a)   any information given to the three members of the children's hearing under these Rules;

(b)   a copy of the pre-hearing panel's or the children's hearing's decision and the reasons for that decision; and

(c)   the reasons for the decision by the pre-hearing panel or the children's hearing to appoint a safeguarder.

(4)   Where the safeguarder is required to prepare a report under section 33(1)(a) (functions of safeguarder) of the Act, within 35 days of being appointed the safeguarder must prepare and give a report or interim report to the Reporter.

(5)   Where an interim report is given to the Reporter under paragraph (4) the safeguarder must also give to the Reporter—

(a)   a statement explaining the reasons for the production of an interim report;

(b)   details of further investigations or information to be sought by the safeguarder; and

(c)   an estimate of how much more time the safeguarder requires to complete the report.

57   Duty of Reporter on receipt of report from safeguarder

(1)   Where the Reporter receives from a safeguarder any report or interim report prepared under section 33(1)(a) or (c) (functions of safeguarder) of the Act, as soon as practicable after receiving that report or interim report the Reporter must arrange a children's hearing to decide whether to make a compulsory supervision order or to review the compulsory supervision order in effect in relation to the child, as the case may be.

(2)   Where the Reporter arranges a children's hearing under paragraph (1) and the children's hearing is to make a decision on whether to make a compulsory supervision order the provisions of section 119 (children's hearing following deferral or proceedings under Part 10) of the Act apply to that hearing as if it was arranged by virtue of section 119(2) of the Act.

(3)   Where the Reporter arranges a children's hearing under paragraph (1) and

the children's hearing is to review the compulsory supervision order in effect in relation to the child section 137 (duty to arrange children's hearing) of the Act applies to that hearing as if it was arranged by virtue of section 137(2) of the Act.

PART 14
Procedure at Children's Hearings – General

58　Children's hearings procedure – general
(1)　At the beginning of a children's hearing the chairing member must—
(a)　introduce the members of the children's hearing and explain the purpose of the hearing;
(b)　ask whether the child, each relevant person and any appointed safeguarder has received all relevant information and documents sent under these Rules;
(c)　confirm whether the child, each relevant person and any appointed safeguarder has had the opportunity to review the information and documents sent under these Rules and whether these have been understood by the child and each relevant person.
(2)　Where, in response to the chairing member's query under section 121 (confirmation that child given opportunity to express views before hearing) of the Act, the child confirms that the documents provided to the child do not accurately reflect the child's views the chairing member must endeavour to clarify the child's views on the relevant matter.

PART 15
Procedure at Grounds Hearing and Children's Hearings to which Section 119
(children's hearing following deferral or proceedings under Part 10) or 137 (duty
to arrange children's hearing) of the Act applies

59　Procedure at a grounds hearing – grounds put to the child and relevant person
[...]
(4)　The children's hearing may, where it considers it appropriate to do so, amend the statement of grounds by [...] amending the facts narrated in the statement of grounds.
(5)　Where paragraph (4) applies the children's hearing may not amend the section 67 ground specified in the statement of grounds.
(6)　Where paragraph (4) applies the children's hearing must be satisfied that any amendments to the facts narrated in the statement of grounds do not call into question the acceptance of a section 67 ground by the child or any relevant person.

60　Procedure where section 91(1) (grounds accepted: powers of grounds hearing), 119(1) (children's hearing following deferral or proceedings under Part 10), or 138(1) (powers of children's hearing on review) of the Act applies
(1)　This rule applies where section 91(1), 119(1) or 138(1) of the Act apply.
(2)　The chairing member—
(a)　must inform those present at the hearing of the substance of any relevant report or other relevant document;
(b)　must take all reasonable steps to obtain the views of the child, each relevant person and any appointed safeguarder in relation to—
(i)　any relevant report, document or matter being considered by the hearing; and
(ii)　what, if any, measures would be in the best interests of the child;
(c)　may invite any other person present at the hearing, as the children's hearing considers appropriate, to express their views on, or provide any other information relevant to, any matter or action being considered by the hearing.
(3)　Where the children's hearing has been given an interim report and

statement prepared by the safeguarder under these Rules the hearing must consider that interim report and statement.

(4) After considering the interim report and statement the children's hearing may set a further date up to a maximum of 35 days for the provision of the report from the safeguarder and defer making a decision on whether to make a compulsory supervision order until a subsequent children's hearing.

61 Procedure when proceedings under section 91(2) (grounds accepted: powers of grounds hearing), 119(2) (children's hearing following deferral or proceedings under Part 10) or 138(2) (powers of children's hearing on review) of the Act

(1) Where the children's hearing proceeds under section 91(2), 119(2) or 138(2) of the Act, without prejudice to the powers of the children's hearing in section 92 (powers of grounds hearing on deferral), 120 (powers of children's hearing on deferral under section 119) or 139 (powers of children's hearing on deferral under section 138) of the Act, the children's hearing may—

(a) appoint a safeguarder if one has not already been appointed;

(b) require the Reporter to obtain any report from any person which the children's hearing considers would be relevant to any matter to be determined by the hearing;

(c) set a date for the subsequent children's hearing to be held under section 119 or 139 of the Act, as the case may be;

(d) determine that—

(i) for the purpose of enabling a child or any relevant person to participate effectively in the proceedings before the children's hearing it may be necessary that the child or relevant person be represented by a solicitor or counsel; and

(ii) it is unlikely that the child or relevant person will arrange to be represented by a solicitor or counsel;

(e) require the Reporter, as soon as possible after the determination in subparagraph (d), to notify the Scottish Legal Aid Board of that determination, the reasons for that determination and the name and address of the child or relevant person;

(f) require the Reporter to make arrangements for an interpreter for the child or any relevant person or take any other step with a view to securing participation of the child or any relevant person in the hearing;

(g) give any other direction on any other matter as is necessary to enable the hearing to make a decision on whether to make a compulsory supervision order and if so the measures to be included in that order.

(2) Each member of the children's hearing must—

(a) state their decision on the exercise of the power conferred by section 91(2), 119(2) or 138(2) of the Act, as the case may be, and the reason for that decision;

(b) state their decision on the exercise of the power conferred by section 92(2) or (3), 120(3), (5) or (6), 123 (general power to grant warrant to secure attendance) or 139(3) (powers of children's hearing on deferral under section 138) of the Act as the case may be, and the reasons for that decision;

(c) where the decision is to make an interim compulsory supervision order, interim variation of a compulsory supervision order, medical examination order or to grant a warrant to secure attendance, state the member's decision in relation to any measure to be contained in the order or warrant and the reasons for the inclusion of the proposed measure; and

(d) where any other decision is made to exercise any other power, give any direction or impose any requirement, state their decision on that matter and reasons for that decision.

(3) The chairing member must—

(i) confirm and explain the decision of the children's hearing;

(ii)   state the reasons for that decision; and

(iii)   subject to sections 73 (child's duty to attend children's hearing), 74 (relevant person's duty to attend children's hearing), 75 (power to proceed in absence of relevant person) and 79 (referral of certain matters for pre-hearing determination) of the Act, inform the child, each relevant person and any safeguarder appointed of the right to appeal the children's hearing's decision to make an interim compulsory supervision order, interim variation of a compulsory supervision order, medical examination order or to grant a warrant to secure the attendance under section 154 (appeal to sheriff against decision of children's hearing) of the Act within 21 days of that decision.

62   Procedure where section 91(3) (grounds accepted: powers of grounds hearing), 119(3) (children's hearing following deferral or proceedings under Part 10) or 138(3) (powers of children's hearing on review) of the Act applies

(1)   This rule applies where the children's hearing is required to proceed under section 91(3), 119(3) or 138(3) of the Act.

(2)   Each member of the children's hearing must—

(a)   state their decision on whether to make a compulsory supervision order or to terminate, vary or continue the compulsory supervision order, as the case may be, and the reason for that decision; and

(b)   where the decision is to make a compulsory supervision order, continue or vary the compulsory supervision order, state the member's decision in relation to any measure to be contained in the order and the reasons for the inclusion of the proposed measure.

(3)   The chairing member must—

(a)   confirm and explain the decision of the children's hearing;

(b)   state the reasons for that decision;

(c)   subject to sections 73 (child's duty attend children's hearing), 74 (relevant person's duty to attend children's hearing), 75 (power to proceed in absence of relevant person) and 79 (referral of certain matters for pre-hearing determination) of the Act, inform the child, each relevant person and any safeguarder appointed of the right to appeal the children's hearing's decision to make a compulsory supervision order, or discharge the referral or terminate, vary or continue the compulsory supervision order under section 154 (appeal to sheriff against decision of children's hearing) of the Act within 21 days of that decision; and

(d)   where the decision of the children's hearing is to make a compulsory supervision order, or terminate, vary or continue the compulsory supervision order, subject to sections 73, 74, 75 and 79 of the Act, inform the child, each relevant person and any appointed safeguarder of the right to seek a suspension of the children's hearing's decision under section 158 (compulsory supervision order: suspension pending appeal) of the Act.

63   Grounds hearing procedures where section 93 (grounds not accepted: application to sheriff or discharge) or 94 (child or relevant person unable to understand grounds) of the Act applies

(1)   This rule applies where section 93 or 94 of the Act applies.

(2)   Each member of the children's hearing must—

(a)   state their decision on whether to proceed under section 93(2)(a) or (b), or 94(2)(a) or (b) of the Act as the case may be, and the reason for that decision;

(b)   state any decision on the exercise of the power conferred by section 93(5) or 123 (general power to grant warrant to secure attendance) of the Act and the reasons for that decision;

(c)   where the decision is to make an interim compulsory supervision order or grant a warrant to secure attendance state the member's decision in relation to any measure to be contained in the order or warrant and the reasons for the inclusion of the proposed measure.

(3)   The chairing member must—
    (i)   confirm and explain the decision of the children's hearing;
    (ii)   state the reasons for that decision; and
    (iii)   subject to sections 73 (child's duty to attend children's hearing), 74 (relevant person's duty to attend children's hearing), 75 (power to proceed in absence of relevant person) and 79 (referral of certain matters for pre-hearing determination) of the Act, inform the child, each relevant person and any safeguarder appointed of the right to appeal the children's hearing's decision to discharge the referral, make an interim compulsory supervision order, or grant a warrant to secure attendance under section 154 (appeal to sheriff against decision of children's hearing) of the Act within 21 days of that decision.

64   Procedure where section 95 (child fails to attend grounds hearing) of the Act applies
(1)   Where section 95(1) of the Act applies each member of the children's hearing must state their decision on whether to require the Reporter under section 95(2) of the Act to arrange another grounds hearing and their reasons for that decision.
(2)   The chairing member must—
    (a)   confirm and explain the decision of the children's hearing; and
    (b)   state the reasons for that decision;
(3)   Where the children's hearing do not require the Reporter to arrange another grounds hearing under section 95(2) of the Act the children's hearing must discharge the referral.
(4)   Where paragraph (3) applies, subject to sections 73 (child's duty to attend children's hearing), 74 (relevant person's duty to attend children's hearing), 75 (power to proceed in absence of relevant person) and 79 (referral of certain matters for pre-hearing determination) of the Act, the chairing member must inform each relevant person and any appointed safeguarder of the right to appeal the children's hearing's decision to discharge the referral under section 154 (appeal to sheriff against decision of children's hearing) of the Act within 21 days of that decision.
[(5)   Where the children's hearing requires the Reporter to arrange another grounds hearing under section 95(2) of the Act, each member of the children's hearing must—
    (a)   state their decision on the exercise of the power conferred by section 95(4) of the Act and the reason for that decision; and
    (b)   where the decision is to make an interim compulsory supervision order, state their decision in relation to any measure to be contained in the order and the reasons for the inclusion of the proposed measure.
(6)   Where paragraph (5) applies, the chairing member must—
    (a)   confirm and explain the decision of the children's hearing;
    (b)   state the reasons for that decision; and
    (c)   subject to sections 74 (relevant person's duty to attend children's hearing), 75 (power to proceed in absence of relevant person) and 79 (referral of certain matters for pre-hearing determination) of the Act, inform each relevant person and any safeguarder appointed of the right to appeal the children's hearing's decision to make an interim compulsory supervision order under section 154 (appeal to sheriff against decision of children's hearing) within 21 days of that decision.]

65   Procedure where report required under section 141 (preparation of report in circumstances relating to permanence order or adoption) of the Act
(1)   Where a children's hearing is required to produce a report under section 141 of the Act, subject to sections 73 (child's duty to attend children's hearing), 74 (relevant person's duty to attend children's hearing), 75 (power to proceed in

absence of relevant person) and 79 (referral of certain matters for pre-hearing determination) of the Act, the chairing member must—

(a)   explain to the child and each relevant person the purpose of the report to be prepared;

(b)   inform the child and each relevant person of the substance of any document or information which is material to the advice to be contained in the report to be prepared by the children's hearing.

(2)   Before preparing the report the children's hearing must subject to sections 73, 74, 75 and 79 of the Act—

(a)   discuss the case with the child and each relevant person and any safeguarder appointed;

(b)   seek the views of the child, each relevant person and the safeguarder on the arrangements which would be in the best interests of the child; and

(c)   confirm the advice to be contained in the report.

(3)   The chairing member must—

(a)   make, or cause to be made, a report of the advice;

(b)   sign and date the report; and

(c)   give the report to the Reporter at the conclusion of the hearing.

(4)   The Reporter must give a copy of the report within 5 days of receiving it under paragraph (3) to—

(a)   the child;

(b)   each relevant person;

(c)   any appointed safeguarder;

(d)   the court which requires to come to a decision about an application of the type mentioned in section 131(2)(c) or (e) (duty of implementation authority to require review) of the Act;

(e)   the chief social work officer of the implementation authority;

(f)   the couple making the application under section 29 (adoption by certain couples) of the Adoption and Children (Scotland) Act 2007 or the person making the application under section 30 (adoption by one person) of that Act, as the case may be.

66   Procedure where there is a review of determination that person be deemed a relevant person

(1)   Where the children's hearing is reviewing whether an individual should continue to be deemed to be a relevant person under section 142(2) (review of determination that person be deemed a relevant person) of the Act the chairing member must inform those present of the purpose of the review.

(2)   The chairing member—

(a)   must invite the child, each relevant person and any appointed safeguarder to express their views in relation to whether the individual should continue to be deemed to be a relevant person;

(b)   may invite any other person present at the hearing, as the children's hearing considers appropriate, to express their views on that matter.

(3)   Where the children's hearing exercises the power under section 142(3) of the Act—

(a)   each member of the children's hearing must state their decision and the reasons for that decision;

(b)   the chairing member must confirm and explain the decision of the children's hearing on the exercise of that power and the reasons for it;

(c)   the chairing member must confirm that the individual will continue to be deemed to be a relevant person.

(4)   Where the children's hearing determine the review under section 142(2) of the Act—

(a)   each member of the children's hearing must state their determination on the matter and the reasons for that determination;

(b) the chairing member must—
    (i) confirm and explain the determination of the children's hearing;
    (ii) state the reasons for the determination; and
    (iii) subject to sections 73 (child's duty to attend children's hearing), 74 (relevant person's duty to attend children's hearing), 75 (power to proceed in absence of relevant person) and 79 (referral of certain matters for pre-hearing determination) of the Act, inform the child, each relevant person, the individual in relation to whom the determination was made and any safeguarder appointed of the right to appeal the children's hearing's decision under section 160 (appeal to sheriff against relevant person determination) of the Act within 7 days of that determination;

(5) As soon as practicable and no later than 2 working days from the day of the children's hearing the Reporter must give to the persons mentioned in paragraph (6) the information mentioned in paragraph (7).

(6) Those persons are—
    (a) the child;
    (b) each relevant person;
    (c) the individual in relation to whom the determination was made.

(7) That information is—
    (a) a copy of the determination of the children's hearing in relation to whether the individual should continue to be deemed to be a relevant person and the reasons for that determination; and
    (b) details of the rights of the child, each relevant person and the individual in relation to whom the determination was made, to appeal that decision under section 160 of the Act.

67 Breach of duties imposed by sections 144 (implementation of compulsory supervision order: general duties of implementation authority) or 145 (duty where order requires child to reside in certain place) of the Act

(1) Where the children's hearing direct the National Convener under section 146(2) (breach of duties imposed by sections 144 and 145) of the Act the chairing member—
    (a) must include in the record of the decision of the children's hearing details of the ways in which the implementation authority is in breach of its duty in relation to the child; and
    (b) may prepare a report for the National Convener providing such additional information on that matter as the children's hearing considers appropriate.

(2) As soon as practicable after the children's hearing the Reporter must give to the National Convener—
    (a) a copy of the children's hearing's decision; and
    (b) any report prepared under paragraph (1)(b).

(3) Where it appears to the children's hearing at the further review of the compulsory supervision order to be held by virtue of section 146(5) of the Act that the implementation authority continues to be in breach of its duty and the children's hearing under section 146(6) of the Act directs the National Convener to make an application under section 147 (application for order) of the Act the chairing member—
    (a) must include in the record of the decision of the children's hearing details of the ways in which the implementation authority continues to be in breach of its duty in relation to the child; and
    (b) may prepare a further report for the National Convener providing such additional information on that matter as the children's hearing considers appropriate.

(4) As soon as practicable after the children's hearing the Reporter must give to the National Convener—

(a)   a copy of the children's hearing's decision; and
(b)   any report prepared under paragraph (3)(b).

PART 16
Procedure where Part 10 of these Rules applies

68   Procedure where rule 37 applies
(1)   This rule applies where rule 37 applies.
(2)   In relation to the further grounds hearing referred to in rule 37, section 91 (grounds accepted: powers of grounds hearing) of the Act applies as if for subsections (2) and (3) there were substituted—

'(2)   The grounds hearing is to be treated as if it were a hearing to which section 119 of the Act applies.'.

(3)   Where the further grounds hearing proceeds under section 93(2)(a) (grounds not accepted: application to sheriff or discharge) or 94(2)(a) (child or relevant person unable to understand grounds) of the Act, sections 93 (grounds not accepted: application to sheriff or discharge) and 96 (children's hearing to consider need for further interim compulsory supervision order) of the Act apply as if they were modified as follows—
(a)   in section 93 of the Act—
(i)   after subsection (4) there were inserted—

'(4A)   Subsection (5) applies if immediately before the grounds hearing an interim compulsory supervision order was not in force in relation to the child.'; and
(ii)   after subsection (5) there were inserted—

'(5A)   Subsection (5B) applies if immediately before the grounds hearing an interim compulsory supervision order was in force in relation to the child.
(5B)   If the children's hearing is satisfied that the nature of the child's circumstances is such that for the protection, guidance, treatment or control of the child it is necessary that a further interim compulsory supervision order be made, the children's hearing may make a further interim compulsory supervision order in relation to the child.'.

(iii)   in subsection (6) after 'subsection (5)' there were inserted ' or (5B) ';
(b)   in section 96 of the Act in subsection (1)(a) for 'a grounds hearing' there were substituted ' or 93(5B) a grounds hearing '.
(4)   Where the further grounds hearing proceeds under section 93(2)(b) or 94(2)(b) of the Act the children's hearing may proceed, where appropriate, as if the hearing was a hearing to which section 119 (children's hearing following deferral or proceedings under Part 10) applies in relation to any section 67 ground previously accepted or determined by the sheriff to be established under section 108 (determination: ground established) or 117 (new section 67 ground established: sheriff to refer to children's hearing) of the Act.
(5)   In paragraph (4) 'accepted' has the same meaning as in section 93(7) (grounds not accepted: application to sheriff or discharge) of the Act.

69   Procedure where rule 38 applies
(1)   This rule applies where rule 38 applies.
(2)   Where the further grounds hearing proceeds under section 93(2)(a) (grounds not accepted: application to sheriff or discharge) or 94(2)(a) (child or relevant person unable to understand grounds) of the Act the grounds hearing may continue the compulsory supervision order until the subsequent children's hearing.
(3)   Where the further grounds hearing proceeds under section 93(2)(b) or 94(2)(b) of the Act the children's hearing may proceed, where appropriate, to review

the compulsory supervision order under section 138 (powers of children's hearing on review) of the Act.

PART 17
Procedure at Other Children's Hearings

70 Procedure at a children's hearing held under section 45 (review by children's hearing where child in place of safety) or 46 (review by children's hearing where order prevents removal of child) of the Act

(1) This rule applies where a children's hearing is held by virtue of section 45 or 46 of the Act.

(2) The chairing member—

(a) must inform those present at the hearing of the substance of any relevant report or other relevant document;

(b) must take all reasonable steps to obtain the views of the child, each relevant person and any appointed safeguarder in relation to—

(i) any report, document or matter being considered by the hearing; and

(ii) what, if any, measures would be in the best interests of the child;

(c) may invite any other person present at the hearing, as the children's hearing considers appropriate, to express their views on, or provide any other information relevant to, any matter or action being considered by the hearing.

(3) Each member of the children's hearing must—

(a) state their decision on whether the conditions for making the child protection order are met and the reasons for that decision; and

(b) where the decision is that the conditions are met state the member's decision in relation to whether the order should be varied and if so the authorisation or requirement to be included in the varied order and the reasons for the inclusion of the proposed authorisation or requirement.

(4) The chairing member must—

(a) confirm and explain the decision of the children's hearing;

(b) state the reasons for that decision; and

(c) where the children's hearing decide to continue the child protection order, subject to sections 73 (child's duty to attend children's hearing), 74 (relevant person's duty to attend children's hearing), 75 (power to proceed in absence of relevant person) and 79 (referral of certain matters for pre-hearing determination) of the Act, inform the child, each relevant person and the other persons in section 48(1) (application for variation or termination) of the Act of the right to make an application to the sheriff under section 48(1) to vary the order or under section 48(2) of the Act to terminate the order, as the case may be.

71 Procedure where Reporter receives notice under section 49 (notice of application for variation or termination) of the Act after arranging hearing under section 45 or 46 (review by children's hearing where child in place of safety or order prevents removal of child) of the Act

(1) Where the Reporter receives notice under section 49 of the Act of an application to vary or terminate the child protection order, after issuing the notice under rule 39 but before that hearing begins, the Reporter must, as soon as practicable before the beginning of the children's hearing, notify the persons mentioned in paragraph (2)—

(a) that the Reporter has received notice under section 49 of the Act; and

(b) that the hearing will proceed as if it was arranged by virtue of section 50 (children's hearing to provide advice to sheriff in relation to application) of the Act.

(2) Those persons are—

(a) the child in respect of whom the child protection order is made;

(b) each relevant person;

(c)   any individual other than a relevant person who appears to the Reporter to have or recently have had significant involvement in the upbringing of the child;

(d)   the person who applied for the child protection order or child assessment order, as the case may be;

(e)   the person who applied for the child protection order to be varied or terminated;

(f)   the person specified in the child protection order under section 37(2)(a) (child protection orders) of the Act;

(g)   any other person to whom the applicant for variation or termination of the child protection order is required to give notice of the making of the application under rules of court;

(h)   the three members of the children's hearing;

(i)   any appointed safeguarder;

(j)   the chief social work officer of the relevant local authority for the child;

(k)   the National Convener.

72   Procedure where hearing held by virtue of section 50 (children's hearing to provide advice to sheriff in relation to application) of the Act

(1)   This rule applies where a children's hearing is held by virtue of section 50 of the Act.

(2)   The chairing member—

(a)   must inform those present at the hearing of the substance of any relevant report or other relevant document;

(b)   must take all reasonable steps to obtain the views of the child, each relevant person and any appointed safeguarder in relation to—

(i)   any report, document or matter being considered by the hearing; and

(ii)   what, if any, advice would be in the best interests of the child;

(c)   may invite any other person present at the hearing as the children's hearing considers appropriate, to express their views on, or provide any other information relevant to, any matter or advice being considered by the hearing; and

(d)   must confirm to the child, each relevant person, the person who applied for the child protection order, the person who applied for the order to be varied or terminated, and any appointed safeguarder the advice to be given to the sheriff to assist the sheriff in the determination of the application under section 48 (application for variation or termination) of the Act.

(3)   The chairing member must—

(a)   make, or cause to be made, a report of the advice;

(b)   sign and date the report; and

(c)   give the report to the Reporter at the conclusion of the hearing.

(4)   As soon as possible following receipt of the report the Reporter must give a copy of the report to—

(a)   the child in respect of whom the child protection order is made;

(b)   each relevant person;

(c)   any appointed safeguarder;

(d)   the sheriff who is to determine the application under section 48 of the Act;

(e)   the person who applied for the child protection order, or child assessment order, as the case may be;

(f)   the person who applied for the child protection order to be varied or terminated;

(g)   the person specified in the child protection order under section 37(2)(a) (child protection orders) of the Act;

(h)   any person other than a relevant person who appears to the Reporter to have or recently have had significant involvement in the upbringing of the child;

(i)   any other person to whom the applicant for variation or termination of the child protection order is required to give notice of the making of the application under rules of court;

    (j)   the chief social work officer of the relevant local authority for the child.

73 Procedure at a children's hearing arranged under section 96(2) (children's hearing to consider need for further interim compulsory supervision order) of the Act

(1) This rule applies where a children's hearing is held by virtue of section 96 (2) of the Act.

(2) The chairing member—

    (a)   must inform those present of the substance of any relevant report or other relevant document;

    (b)   must take all reasonable steps to obtain the views of the child, each relevant person and any appointed safeguarder in relation to—

        (i)   any report, document or matter being considered by the hearing; and

        (ii) what, if any, measures would be in the best interests of the child; and

    (c)   may invite any other person present at the hearing, as the children's hearing considers appropriate, to express their views on, or provide any other information relevant to, any matter or action being considered by the hearing.

(3) Each member of the children's hearing must—

    (a)   state their decision on any exercise of the power conferred by section 96 (3) of the Act and the reason for that decision;

    (b)   where the decision is to make a further interim compulsory supervision order state the member's decision and the reasons in relation to any measure to be included in the order.

(4) The chairing member must—

    (a)   confirm the decision of the children's hearing;

    (b)   state the reasons for that decision; and

    (c)   subject to sections 73 (child's duty to attend children's hearing), 74 (relevant person's duty to attend children's hearing), 75 (power to proceed in absence of relevant person) and 79 (referral of certain matters for pre-hearing determination) of the Act, inform the child, each relevant person and any appointed safeguarder of the right to appeal the children's hearing's decision to make an interim compulsory supervision order, under section 154 (appeal to sheriff against decision of children's hearing) of the Act within 21 days of that decision.

74 Procedure at a children's hearing held under section 126 (review of contact direction) of the Act

(1) This rule applies where a children's hearing is held by virtue of section 126 of the Act.

(2) Where an individual claims that the conditions specified for the purposes of section 126(2)(b) of the Act are satisfied in relation to the individual, the children's hearing must consider that claim before reviewing the contact direction.

(3) Each member of the children's hearing must state whether the member considers that the conditions specified for the purposes of section 126(2)(b) of the Act are satisfied in relation to the individual and the reasons for reaching that view.

(4) The chairing member must confirm whether the children's hearing considers that the conditions specified for the purposes of section 126(2)(b) of the Act are satisfied in relation to the individual and the reason for reaching that view.

(5) After considering, where applicable, whether the conditions specified for the purposes of section 126(2)(b) are satisfied the children's hearing must, where proceeding to review a contact direction, seek views on the contact direction from—

    (a)   the child;

    (b)   each relevant person;

    (c)   any appointed safeguarder;

(d) any individual satisfying the conditions specified in an order under section 126(2)(b) of the Act;

(e) any individual who has a contact order regulating contact between the individual and the child;

(f) any individual who has a permanence order which specifies arrangements for contact between the individual and the child.

(6) Each member of the children's hearings must state their decision in relation to the contact direction and their reasons for that decision.

(7) The chairing member must—

(a) confirm and explain the decision of the children's hearing in relation to the contact direction;

(b) state the reasons for that decision; and

(c) inform any individual of any applicable right of appeal of the children's hearing's decision under section 126(6) of the Act which that individual has under section 161 (appeal to sheriff against decision affecting contact or permanence order) of the Act.

75 Procedure where advice required under section 49 (reference or remit to children's hearing) of the Criminal Procedure (Scotland) Act 1995

(1) This rule applies where a children's hearing is held following a request to the Reporter under section 49(1)(b), (3) or (6) of the Criminal Procedure (Scotland) Act 1995.

(2) The chairing member—

(a) must inform those present at the hearing of the substance of any relevant report or other relevant document;

(b) must take all reasonable steps to obtain the views of the child, each relevant person and any appointed safeguarder in relation to—

(i) any report, document or matter being considered by the hearing; and

(ii) what, if any, advice or measures would be in the best interests of the child;

(c) may invite any other person present at the hearing, as the children's hearing considers appropriate, to express their views on, or provide any other information relevant to, any matter or advice being considered by the hearing; and

(d) must confirm to the child, each relevant person, and any appointed safeguarder the advice to be given to the court.

(3) The chairing member must—

(a) make, or cause to be made, a report of the advice;

(b) sign and date the report; and

(c) give the report to the Reporter at the conclusion of the hearing.

(4) As soon as possible following receipt of the report the Reporter must give a copy of the report to—

(a) the child;

(b) each relevant person;

(c) any appointed safeguarder;

(d) the court which made the request for advice under section 49 of the Criminal Procedure (Scotland) Act 1995;

(e) the chief social work officer of the relevant local authority for the child.

76 Procedure where application to suspend the decision of the children's hearing made under section 158 (compulsory supervision order: suspension pending appeal) of the Act

(1) Where the Reporter is required under section 158(2) of the Act to arrange a children's hearing, as soon as practicable the Reporter must give notice of the date, time and place of the children's hearing at which the application for the suspension of the children's hearing's decision will be considered, to the persons mentioned in paragraph (2).

(2)   Those persons are—
(a)   the child;
(b)   any relevant person;
(c)   any appointed safeguarder;
(d)   the three members of the children's hearing;
(e)   the chief social work officer of the implementation authority for the child;
(f)   the National Convener.

(3)   If the person who applied for the suspension of the children's hearing's decision under section 158 of the Act is required by section 73(2) (child's duty to attend children's hearing) or 74(2) (relevant person's duty to attend children's hearing) of the Act to attend the hearing and fails to do so the children's hearing may, if it considers it appropriate, take no further action in relation to the application.

(4)   Before making any decision on the application under section 158 of the Act the children's hearing must invite the child, any relevant person and any appointed safeguarder present at the hearing to make such representations as they wish to make.

(5)   Each member of the children's hearing must state their decision on the suspension of the children's hearing's decision under section 158 of the Act, and the reasons for that decision.

(6)   The chairing member must confirm the decision of the children's hearing and the reasons for that decision.

77   Procedure at a children's hearing where a report is required under section 95(2) of the Adoption and Children (Scotland) Act 2007 (duty of children's hearing to prepare report for court)

(1)   This rule applies where a children's hearing is required to prepare a report by virtue of section 95(2) of the Adoption and Children (Scotland) Act 2007 (permanence orders – duty of children's hearing to prepare report for court).

(2)   The chairing member must explain to the child, any relevant person and any appointed safeguarder the purpose of the report to be prepared.

(3)   The report must be prepared when the children's hearing have considered the case of the child and determined whether to make a compulsory supervision order or to vary, or vary and continue, the compulsory supervision order, as the case may be.

(4)   Before preparing the report the chairing member must explain to the child, any relevant person and any appointed safeguarder—
(a)   that the hearing has determined to make a compulsory supervision order or to vary, or vary and continue, the compulsory supervision order, as the case may be;
(b)   the reasons for reaching that determination; and
(c)   that the hearing is unable to make a decision to make a compulsory supervision order or to vary, or vary and continue, the compulsory supervision order, pending the decision of the sheriff on the permanence order application or to remit the case under section 96 (application: effect on compulsory supervision order) of the Adoption and Children (Scotland) Act 2007.

(5)   The chairing member must—
(a)   make, or cause to be made, a report of the advice;
(b)   sign and date the report; and
(c)   give the report to the Reporter.

(6)   [Subject to paragraph (7),] the Reporter must, within 5 days of the hearing, give the report to—
(a)   the court which requires to come to a decision on the permanence order application;
(b)   the child;

(c)   any relevant person;

(d)   any appointed safeguarder;

(e)   the chief social work officer of the implementation authority for the child.

[(7)   Where a non-disclosure request made under Part 19 of these Rules has been determined by the children's hearing in relation to information contained in the report and in consequence of that determination the Reporter has, by virtue of rule 15, ensured the removal of that information from the report to be given to a specified person, the Reporter must, within 5 days of the hearing, give to the court mentioned in paragraph (6)(a)—

(a)   the report;

(b)   the redacted report; and

(c)   the details of the determination of the children's hearing of the non-disclosure request made under Part 19 of these Rules and which the Reporter must keep a record of in accordance with rule 13.

(8)   In paragraph (7)—

'non-disclosure request' has the meaning given by rule 84(1);

'redacted report' means the report which has had information removed from it by virtue of rule 15, to give effect to a determination of the children's hearing of a non-disclosure request made under Part 19 of these Rules; and

'specified person' is to be construed in accordance with rule 84(1).]

PART 18

General Issues for Children's Hearings

78   Procedure where a warrant to secure attendance may be granted under section 123 (general power to grant warrant to secure attendance) of the Act

(1)   This rule applies where the children's hearing, on the application of the Reporter, is under section 123 of the Act considering granting a warrant to secure the attendance of the child at a children's hearing or a hearing to take place under Part 10 (proceedings before sheriff) of the Act.

(2)   The children's hearing must seek the views of the child, each relevant person, and any appointed safeguarder, if present at the hearing.

(3)   Where a warrant to secure the attendance of the child is granted, the Reporter must as soon as practicable give to the child, each relevant person and any appointed safeguarder—

(a)   a copy of the warrant; and

(b)   details of the rights of the child, each relevant person and the safeguarder to appeal the grant of the warrant under section 154 (appeal to sheriff against decision of children's hearing) of the Act.

79   Procedure where advice sought by children's hearing from National Convener under section 8 (provision of advice to children's hearing) of the Act

(1)   This rule applies where a children's hearing seeks advice under section 8 of the Act from the National Convener.

(2)   Where a children's hearing defers making a decision or determination on any matter until a subsequent children's hearing and seeks advice from the National Convener under section 8 of the Act the chairing member must—

(a)   prepare a request for advice setting out the nature of the advice to be provided and such other details as the children's hearing considers appropriate;

(b)   include in the record of the children's hearing decision details of the request for advice and reasons for that request;

(c)   give that request for advice to the Reporter; and

(d)   direct the Reporter to forward to the National Convener the request for advice and a copy of the children's hearing decision and the reasons for that decision.

(3)   Where the children's hearing has directed the Reporter to forward a request

for advice to the National Convener the Reporter must, as soon as practicable and within 5 days of receiving the request prepared under paragraph (2), forward it to the National Convener.

(4) The National Convener must respond to any request for advice forwarded under paragraph (3) within 14 days of receiving the request.

(5) The children's hearing must give the advice received from the National Convener under paragraph (4) to all those present at the hearing.

80 Requirements where compulsory supervision order to be made
The children's hearing may not make a compulsory supervision order requiring a child to reside at a place where the child would be under the charge or control of a person who is not a relevant person or vary any compulsory supervision order so that it includes such a requirement unless the children's hearing has—

(a) received and considered a report or information provided by the local authority or implementation authority under section 66(4) (investigation and determination by Principal Reporter), 69(4) (determination under section 66: referral to children's hearing), 137(4) or (5) (duty to arrange children's hearing) of the Act, as the case may be, which provides the local authority's or implementation authority's recommendations on—

(i) the needs of the child;

(ii) the suitability to meet those needs of the place or places in which the child is to reside by virtue of the compulsory supervision order;

(iii) the suitability to meet those needs of the person who is to have charge or control over the child; and

(b) the local authority or implementation authority as the case may be have confirmed that in compiling the report they have carried out the procedures and gathered the information described in regulations 3 and 4 of the Looked After Children (Scotland) Regulations 2009.

81 Requirements where section 126 (review of contact direction) of the Act applies
(1) This rule applies where—

(a) section 69(2) or (3) of the Act applies;

(b) Parts 9 to 11 or 13 of the Act apply;

(c) following receipt of a notice under section 43 of the Act of the making of a child protection order the Reporter is required to arrange a children's hearing under section 69(2) of the Act which is to be held no later than—

(i) where the order contains an authorisation of the type mentioned in section 37(2)(b) of the Act, the end of the period of 8 working days beginning on the day the child was removed to a place of safety; or

(ii) where the order does not contain such an authorisation, the end of the period of 8 working days beginning on the day the order was made.

(2) Where this rule applies and a children's hearing is to be held in relation to a child the Reporter must notify the persons mentioned in paragraph (3) that a children's hearing is to be held in relation to a child, on the date to be specified in the notification, and, when issuing that notification, also give those persons the information mentioned in paragraphs (4) and (5).

(3) Those persons are—

(a) any individual other than a relevant person who appears to the Reporter to have or recently have had significant involvement in the upbringing of the child;

(b) any individual who has a contact order regulating contact between the individual and the child;

(c) any individual who has a permanence order which specifies arrangements for contact between the individual and the child.

(4) That information is confirmation that, where a children's hearing—

(a) makes, continues or varies a compulsory supervision order; or

(b)   makes an interim compulsory supervision order, interim variation of a compulsory supervision order or a medical examination order which is to have effect for more than 5 working days,

and the order contains (or is varied so as to contain) a contact direction, the Reporter must arrange a children's hearing under section 126 of the Act for the purposes of reviewing the contact direction if—

(i)   a contact order or permanence order mentioned in section 126(3) of the Act is in force; or

(ii) the Reporter is requested to arrange a hearing by an individual who claims to have or recently have had significant involvement in the upbringing of the child.

(5)   That information is confirmation that, where a children's hearing is arranged under section 126 of the Act, they will have the right to attend.

82   Requirements where section 127 (referral where failure to provide education for excluded pupil) of the Act applies

(1)   Where the children's hearing requires the National Convener under section 127(2) of the Act to make a referral to the Scottish Ministers, the chairing member—

(a)   must include in the record of the decision of the children's hearing details of the ways in which the education authority is in breach of its duty under section 14(3) (education for children unable to attend school etc) of the Education (Scotland) Act 1980 in relation to the child; and

(b)   may make, or cause to be made, a report for the National Convener providing such additional information on that matter as the children's hearing considers appropriate.

(2)   As soon as practicable after the children's hearing the Reporter must give to the National Convener—

(a)   a copy of the children's hearing's decision and the reasons for the decision; and

(b)   any report made under paragraph (1)(b).

83   Requirements where section 128 (duty to consider applying for parenting order) of the Act applies

Where the children's hearing requires the Reporter under section 128(2) of the Act to consider whether to apply under section 102(3) (applications) of the Antisocial Behaviour etc (Scotland) Act 2004 for a parenting order in respect of a parent of the child, the chairing member—

(a)   must include in the record of the decision of the children's hearing details of the reasons why the children's hearing considers that it might be appropriate for a parenting order to be made in respect of that parent of the child; and

(b)   may make, or cause to be made a report for the Reporter providing such additional information on that matter as the children's hearing considers appropriate.

PART 19
Procedure at a Pre-hearing Panel or a Children's Hearing where a Non-disclosure Request is made

84   Non-disclosure requests

(1)   In this Part a 'non-disclosure request' is a request made by any person that any document or part of a document or information contained in a document relating to a pre-hearing panel or to a children's hearing should be withheld from a specified person falling within the categories specified in section 177(2)(i)(ii) to (iv) of the Act on the grounds that disclosure of that document or part of the document or any information contained in it would be likely to cause significant harm to the child to whom the hearing relates.

(2) The following documents may not be the subject of a non-disclosure request—

(a) the statement of grounds;

(b) a copy of any relevant remit by a court under section 49 of the Criminal Procedure (Scotland) Act 1995;

(c) a copy of any relevant requirement by a sheriff under section 12(1A) or statement under section 12(1B) of the Antisocial Behaviour etc (Scotland) Act 2004;

(d) any order or warrant to which the child is subject under the Act or these Rules.

(3) A non-disclosure request must—

(a) specify the document or part of the document or information for which non-disclosure is requested and give reasons in each instance for non-disclosure; and

(b) specify the persons to whom the document or part of the document or information is not to be disclosed and give reasons in each instance for non-disclosure.

(4) In this Part reference to 'children's hearing' includes pre-hearing panel, where the non-disclosure request relates to documents or information to be considered at a pre-hearing panel.

85 Determination of a non-disclosure request

(1) The Reporter must refer any non-disclosure request received from any person to a children's hearing for determination.

(2) The Reporter may submit a non-disclosure request to a children's hearing for determination at the Reporter's own initiative.

86 Procedure following receipt of a non-disclosure request made prior to a children's hearing

(1) A children's hearing must, except in the case of a grounds hearing, consider any non-disclosure request made prior to that hearing at the beginning of the children's hearing.

(2) Where a non-disclosure request has been made prior to a grounds hearing, the non–disclosure request may be determined by the grounds hearing before making a decision on whether to make a compulsory supervision order.

(3) Where the children's hearing requires to consider a request in accordance with paragraph (1) or paragraph (2) it may exclude from the children's hearing the person to whom the documents are requested not to be disclosed where it considers that the presence of that person would prevent proper consideration of the non-disclosure request.

(4) The children's hearing must consider and determine the non-disclosure request.

(5) The person excluded under paragraph (3) must be invited to return to the children's hearing and advised of the children's hearing's determination under paragraph (4).

(6) Where the non-disclosure request is rejected under paragraph (4) the children's hearing must ensure that the document or part of the document or information is given to the excluded person at such time, and in such manner, as it considers appropriate having regard to the best interests of the child to whom the hearing relates.

87 Procedure following receipt of a non-disclosure request made during a children's hearing

(1) A non-disclosure request may be made during a children's hearing by the child, any relevant person, any appointed safeguarder, the Reporter or the author of any document that is the subject of the non-disclosure request.

(2) Where such a request is made the children's hearing may exclude from the

children's hearing the person to whom the documents are requested not to be disclosed where it considers that the presence of that person would prevent proper consideration of the non-disclosure request.

(3)   The children's hearing must consider and determine the non-disclosure request.

(4)   The person excluded under paragraph (2) must be invited to return to the children's hearing and advised of the children's hearing's determination under paragraph (3).

(5)   Where the non-disclosure request is rejected under paragraph (3) the children's hearing must ensure that the document or part of the document or information is given to the excluded person at such time, and in such manner, as it considers appropriate having regard to the best interests of the child to whom the hearing relates.

PART 20
Notifying Decisions

88   Notifying decision of a children's hearing to the child, relevant person and appointed safeguarder

(1)   Where by virtue of the Act or any other enactment a children's hearing has been held in relation to a child the Reporter must give to the persons mentioned in paragraph (2) the information mentioned in paragraph (3) within 5 days of the children's hearing.

(2)   Those persons are—
   (a)   the child;
   (b)   each relevant person;
   (c)   any appointed safeguarder.

(3)   That information is—
   (a)   the decision of the children's hearing;
   (b)   the reasons for that decision;
   (c)   a copy of any compulsory supervision order, interim compulsory supervision order, medical examination order made, or warrant to secure attendance granted;
   (d)   a notice of any right to appeal the children's hearing's decision under section 154 (appeal to sheriff against decision of children's hearing) or 160 (appeal to sheriff against relevant person determination) of the Act;
   (e)   where the child or any relevant person is subject to an order under section 159 (frivolous and vexatious appeals) of the Act, confirmation of the need for that person to seek leave from the sheriff to appeal the decision;
   (f)   details of any right to seek a suspension of the children's hearing's decision to make, vary, continue or terminate a compulsory supervision order under section 158 (compulsory supervision order: suspension pending appeal) of the Act;
   (g)   details of the child's and each relevant person's right to seek a review of a compulsory supervision order under, or by virtue of, section 132 (right of child or relevant person to require review) of the Act.

(4)   This rule does not apply where rules 66(7), 91, 92, 93 or 96 apply.

[88A   Notifying decision of a children's hearing to an individual afforded an opportunity to participate

Where a children's hearing makes a direction which regulates contact between the child and an individual afforded an opportunity to participate in relation to the hearing by virtue of rule 2A, the Reporter must give to the individual—
   (a)   a copy of the direction, and
   (b)   the reasons for the direction.]

89   Information to be given to the implementation authority and others
(1)   Where rule 88 applies within 5 days of the children's hearing the Reporter must give to the persons mentioned in paragraph (2) the information mentioned in rule 88(3)(a) to (c).
(2)   Those persons are—
   (a)   the chief social work officer of the implementation authority where the decision was to make a compulsory supervision order or interim compulsory supervision order and in any other case the chief social work officer of the relevant local authority for the child;
   (b)   any person who under the compulsory supervision order, interim compulsory supervision order, medical examination order or warrant to secure attendance is responsible for providing any service, support, or accommodation in respect of the child.
(3)   Where by virtue of any compulsory supervision order, interim compulsory supervision order or medical examination order the person with whom the child is required to reside is a person other than the implementation authority or a relevant person paragraph (4) applies.
(4)   The Reporter must give the information mentioned in rule 88(3)(a) to (c)—
   (a)   where a social work officer from the implementation authority or relevant local authority for the child, as the case may be, attended the children's hearing resulting in the order in question, and it is reasonably practicable to do so, to that social work officer immediately following the children's hearing;
   (b)   in any other case, to the chief social work officer of the implementation authority, or relevant local authority for the child, as the case may be, no later than the end of the working day following the conclusion of the children's hearing.

90   Information to be given to the chief constable and use of that information
(1)   Where rule 88 applies and the grounds hearing has proceeded under section 91(3) (grounds accepted: powers of grounds hearing) of the Act or, where rule 68 applies, section 119(3) (children's hearing following deferral or proceedings under Part 10) of the Act, the Reporter must notify the children's hearing's decision to the chief constable of the Police Service of Scotland under section 61 (constable's duty to provide information to Principal Reporter) of the Act or section 43 (5) (arrangements where children arrested) of the Criminal Procedure (Scotland) Act 1995.
(2)   Where rule 88 applies and the decision of the children's hearing is to make a compulsory supervision order in respect of a person aged 16 years or older, as soon as reasonably practicable, the Reporter must notify the chief constable of the area in which the person resides.
(3)   When a child subject to a compulsory supervision order reaches the age of 16 years, the Reporter must, as soon as reasonably practicable, notify the chief constable of the area in which the child resides.
(4)   Where section 199(3) and (4) (meaning of 'child') of the Act applies to a person, the Reporter must, as soon as reasonably practicable, notify the chief constable of the area in which the person resides of—
   (a)   the application of section 199(3) and (4) of the Act to that person; and
   (b)   when a relevant event in section 199(5) of the Act has taken place in relation to that person.
(5)   When a person under paragraph (2), (3) or (4) is no longer subject to a compulsory supervision order, the Reporter must, as soon as reasonably practicable, notify the chief constable of the area in which that person resides.
(6)   Information disclosed to the chief constable under paragraph (1), (2), (3), (4) or (5) may be used by the chief constable and police forces only for the purpose of—
   (a)   enabling or assisting them to perform their functions under or by virtue

of this Act, the Police Act 1997, or the Protection of Vulnerable Groups (Scotland) Act 2007;

    (b) the prevention or detection of crime;

    (c) the apprehension or prosecution of offenders; or

    (d) the protection of children.

91 Notifying decision of section 45 or 46 (review of children's hearing where child in place of safety or order prevents removal of child) hearing

(1) The Reporter must as soon as practicable after the hearing held by virtue of section 45 or 46 of the Act give to the persons mentioned in paragraph (2) the information mentioned in paragraph (3).

(2) Those persons are—

    (a) the child in respect of whom the child protection order is made;

    (b) each relevant person;

    (c) any individual other than a relevant person who appears to the Reporter to have or recently have had significant involvement in the upbringing of the child;

    (d) the person who applied for the child protection order or child assessment order, as the case may be;

    (e) the person specified in the child protection order under section 37(2)(a) (child protection orders) of the Act;

    (f) any other person prescribed by rules of court for the purposes of section 48 (application for variation or termination) or 49 (notice of application for variation or termination) of the Act;

    (g) any appointed safeguarder.

(3) That information is—

    (a) the decision of the children's hearing;

    (b) the reasons for that decision;

    (c) where the children's hearing's decision was to continue the child protection order, the right of those persons in paragraph (2) to make an application to the sheriff under section 48(1) of the Act to vary the order or under section 48(2) of the Act to terminate the order.

(4) The Reporter must give to the persons mentioned in paragraph (5) the information mentioned in paragraph (3)(a) and (b).

(5) Those persons are—

    (a) the chief social work officer of the relevant local authority for the child;

    (b) any person who under the child protection order is responsible for providing any service, support, or accommodation in respect of the child.

92 Notifying decision of section 126 (review of contact direction) hearing

(1) Within 5 days of the children's hearing held under section 126 of the Act the Reporter must give to the persons mentioned in paragraph (2) the information mentioned in paragraph (3).

(2) Those persons are—

    (a) the child;

    (b) each relevant person;

    (c) any appointed safeguarder;

    (d) any individual who has a contact order regulating contact between the individual and the child;

    (e) any individual who has a permanence order which specifies arrangement for contact between the individual and the child;

    (f) any person who requested a children's hearing be held under section 126 (2)(b) of the Act.

(3) That information is—

    (a) details of the decision of the children's hearing;

    (b) the reasons for that decision;

    (c) notice of any right to appeal the children's hearing's decision under section 161 (appeal to sheriff against decision affecting contact or permanence order) of the Act;

(d) where the person is subject to an order under section 159 (frivolous and vexatious appeals) of the Act, confirmation of the need for that person to seek leave from the sheriff to appeal the decision.

(4) The Reporter must give to the persons mentioned in paragraph (5) the information mentioned in paragraph (3)(a) and (b).

(5) Those persons are—

(a) the implementation authority where the decision was to make a compulsory supervision order or interim compulsory supervision order and in any other case the relevant local authority for the child;

(b) any person who under the compulsory supervision order, interim compulsory supervision order, medical examination order or warrant to secure attendance is responsible for providing any service, support or accommodation in respect of the child.

93   Notifying decision of section 158 (compulsory supervision order: suspension pending appeal) hearing

(1) Where a children's hearing has been held by virtue of section 158 of the Act the Reporter must give to the persons mentioned in paragraph (2) the information mentioned in paragraph (3) within 5 days of the children's hearing.

(2) Those persons are—

(a) the child;

(b) each relevant person;

(c) any appointed safeguarder.

(3) That information is—

(a) the decision of the children's hearing;

(b) the reasons for that decision.

PART 21
Specific Provision for Children's Hearings Arranged under the Children's Hearings (Scotland) Act 2011 (Implementation of Secure Accommodation Authorisation) (Scotland) Regulations 2013

94   Provision of information for review of secure accommodation authorisation

(1) This rule applies where a children's hearing is to be arranged by virtue of regulation 9 of the Children's Hearings (Scotland) Act 2011 (Implementation of Secure Accommodation Authorisation) (Scotland) Regulations 2013 ('the 2013 Regulations').

(2) As soon as practicable before the beginning of the children's hearing, the Reporter must notify the persons mentioned in paragraph (3) of the date, time and place of the hearing.

(3) Those persons are—

(a) the child;

(b) each relevant person;

(c) the chief social work officer who made the decision under regulation 4 or 7 of the 2013 Regulations;

(d) the head of unit who made the decision under regulation 6 of the 2013 Regulations;

(e) any appointed safeguarder;

(f) any individual other than a relevant person who appears to the Reporter to have or recently have had a significant involvement in the upbringing of the child;

(g) the three members of the children's hearing; and

(h) the National Convener.

(4) The Reporter must, when issuing the notice under paragraph (2), provide those persons mentioned in paragraph (3)(a) to (g) with a copy of—

(a)   all decisions and reasons for those decisions made by all pre-hearing panels and children's hearings arranged in relation to the child;

(b)   the decision of the chief social work officer made under regulation 5 of the 2013 Regulations; and

(c)   the decision of the head of unit made under regulation 6 of the 2013 Regulations.

95   Procedure where children's hearing to review secure accommodation authorisation

(1)   This rule applies where a children's hearing is to be held by virtue of regulation 9 of the Children's Hearings (Scotland) Act 2011 (Implementation of Secure Accommodation Authorisation) (Scotland) Regulations 2013 ('the 2013 Regulations').

(2)   The children's hearing must provide the following persons with the opportunity to make representations if they are present at the hearing:—

(a)   the child;

(b)   each relevant person;

(c)   any appointed safeguarder;

(d)   the chief social work officer who made the decision under regulation 4 or 7 of the 2013 Regulations; and

(e)   the head of unit who made the decision under regulation 6 of the 2013 Regulations.

(3)   Each member of the children's hearing must state their decision in relation to the secure accommodation authorisation and the reasons for that decision.

(4)   The chairing member must—

(a)   confirm and explain the decision of the children's hearing in relation to the secure accommodation authorisation;

(b)   state the reasons for that decision; and

(c)   inform the child, each relevant person and any safeguarder appointed of any applicable right to appeal the children's hearing's decision under section 154 (appeal to sheriff against decision of children's hearing) of the Act within 21 days of that decision.

96   Notifying decision of review of secure accommodation authorisation

(1)   Within 5 days of the children's hearing held under regulation 9 of the Children's Hearings (Scotland) Act 2011 (Implementation of Secure Accommodation Authorisation) (Scotland) Regulations 2013 ('the 2013 Regulations') the Reporter must give to the persons mentioned in paragraph (2) the information mentioned in paragraph (3).

(2)   Those persons are—

(a)   the child;

(b)   each relevant person;

(c)   any appointed safeguarder;

(d)   the chief social work officer who made the decision under regulation 4 or 7 of the 2013 Regulations;

(e)   the head of unit who made the decision under regulation 6 of the 2013 Regulations.

(3)   The information is—

(a)   the decision of the children's hearing;

(b)   the reasons for that decision;

(c)   notice of any right to appeal the children's hearing's decision under section 154 (appeal to sheriff against decision of children's hearing) of the Act.

PART 22

Miscellaneous

97 Travelling and subsistence expenses

(1) The persons mentioned in paragraph (2) may make a claim, to the relevant local authority for the child, in respect of that person's attendance at a pre-hearing panel or children's hearing.

(2) Those persons are—

(a) the child;

(b) any relevant person;

[(ba) any person who is to be afforded an opportunity to participate in relation to the children's hearing by virtue of rule 2A;]

(c) any person representing [a person mentioned in sub-paragraph (a), (b) or (ba)];

(d) any interpreter acting on behalf of [a person mentioned in sub-paragraph (a), (b) or (ba)];

[(da) any individual who claimed to qualify to be afforded an opportunity to participate in relation to the children's hearing by virtue of rule 2A;]

(e) any individual who claimed to have or recently have had significant involvement in the upbringing of the child;

(f) any individual who has a contact order regulating contact between the individual and the child;

(g) any individual who has a permanence order which specifies arrangements for contact between the individual and the child.

(3) Where a claim is made to the relevant local authority for the child under paragraph (1) the local authority must pay to the claimant travelling expenses and such other expenses and subsistence as have, in the opinion of the local authority, been reasonably incurred by the claimant.

(4) This rule does not apply to a solicitor or counsel representing [a person mentioned in paragraph (2)(a), (b) or (ba)] at a pre-hearing panel or children's hearing.

98 Authentication of documents

(1) Any order, warrant to secure the attendance of a child, notice, report, record or other writing required to be made, granted, given or kept by the children's hearing or pre-hearing panel or chairing member of that hearing under or by virtue of these Rules is sufficiently authenticated if it is signed by the chairing member of the relevant children's hearing or pre-hearing panel.

(2) Any document or notice authorised or required by these Rules to be kept or given by the Reporter is sufficiently authenticated if it is signed by the Reporter.

(3) Any copy of a document to be given to any person by the Reporter may be certified a true copy by the Reporter.

[(4) For the purposes of this rule—

'signed' includes signed by means of an electronic signature,

'electronic signature' is to be construed in accordance with section 7(2) of the Electronic Communications Act 2000(5), but includes a version of an electronic signature which is reproduced on a paper document.]

99 Written communications

Section 193 (formal communications) of the Act applies to these Rules and any type of communication made or given under these Rules is also a formal communication and section 193(2) to (4) applies to them.

100 Service of notification and documents

Any notice or other document authorised or required under these Rules to be given by the Reporter to any person may be given by the Reporter or by any police constable.